"This volume is far more than a 'how-to' manual of procedures: It includes discussions of the conceptual foundations of the science of verbal behavior, its relation to other disciplines, professional challenges, and deep analyses, not only of the elementary verbal operant classes, but of multiple control, the behavior of the listener, and emergent relations. Moreover, the extraordinary cast of participating authors includes the foremost experts in the field."

David C. Palmer, PhD, *Western New England University*

"This book provides an excellent overview of recent scientific research in verbal behavior with a focus on its clinical application. I cannot think of a better resource that embodies the scientist-practitioner model, and I believe both researchers and practitioners would benefit from reading it."

Mirela Cengher, PhD, BCBA-D, *University of Maryland, Baltimore County*

Promoting Language for Learners with Autism Spectrum Disorder

Promoting Language for Learners with Autism Spectrum Disorder: A Verbal Behavior Guide for Practitioners introduces the core principles of verbal behavior and provides practical, evidence-based strategies for teaching language skills to children with autism in applied settings.

The book opens with a section that orients the reader to a functional approach to language, best practices for assessing verbal repertoires, and common models for arranging language-training environments. The second section focuses on teaching critical verbal operants and derived language skills. The final section addresses professional matters relevant to practitioners, including the importance of basic and translational research in verbal behavior, considerations related to diversity, and best practices for interdisciplinary collaboration.

Grounded in the science of behavior analysis and aligned with Skinner's (1957) analysis of verbal behavior, this book equips professionals with tools to assess language, design effective teaching environments, and build essential repertoires like manding, tacting, and conversation skills. Intended for professionals and students alike, this text is broad enough to support graduate-level instruction and specific enough to serve as a valuable reference for practicing clinicians.

Jason C. Vladescu, PhD, BCBA-D, is a professor and the founding chair of the ABA Program at SUNY Downstate, Editor-in-Chief of *Behavior Analysis in Practice*, and co-founder of The Capstone Center.

April N. Kisamore, PhD, BCBA-D, is an associate professor and director of the ABA Programs at Hunter College. She co-founded The Capstone Center and publishes on verbal behavior, skill acquisition, and parent training.

Promoting Language for Learners with Autism Spectrum Disorder

A Verbal Behavior Guide for Practitioners

Edited by Jason C. Vladescu and April N. Kisamore

Routledge
Taylor & Francis Group

NEW YORK AND LONDON

Designed cover image: Getty Images

First published 2026
by Routledge
605 Third Avenue, New York, NY 10158

and by Routledge
4 Park Square, Milton Park, Abingdon, Oxon, OX14 4RN

Routledge is an imprint of the Taylor & Francis Group, an informa business

© 2026 selection and editorial matter, Jason C. Vladescu and April N. Kisamore; individual chapters, the contributors

The right of Jason C. Vladescu and April N. Kisamore to be identified as the authors of the editorial material, and of the authors for their individual chapters, has been asserted in accordance with sections 77 and 78 of the Copyright, Designs and Patents Act 1988.

For Product Safety Concerns and Information please contact our EU representative GPSR@taylorandfrancis.com. Taylor & Francis Verlag GmbH, Kaufingerstraße 24, 80331 München, Germany.

Trademark notice: Product or corporate names may be trademarks or registered trademarks, and are used only for identification and explanation without intent to infringe.

ISBN: 9781032560632 (hbk)
ISBN: 9781032560625 (pbk)
ISBN: 9781003433668 (ebk)

DOI: 10.4324/9781003433668

Typeset in Times New Roman
by Deanta Global Publishing Services, Chennai, India

Access the Support Material: www.routledge.com/9781032560625

Jason C. Vladescu dedication:
"To the well-placed 'I think we can do better,' reminding us that, with the right words, better is always possible."

April N. Kisamore dedication:
"To all the Verbal Behavior researchers and clinicians who came before; thank you for the excellent examples. I hope this work does you proud."

Contents

Foreword

When B. F. Skinner's (1957) book *Verbal Behavior* was published, it was met with little fanfare. Behaviorists at the time were focused on developing the experimental analysis of behavior with rats and pigeons, and the applied field had yet to emerge. Few behaviorists were interested in the book, and it was ignored in the literature. Linguists, philosophers, and psychologists were heavily influenced by Chomsky's (1959) negative review of *Verbal Behavior* and most rejected the work. For example, Neisser (1967) wrote "Chomsky's 32-page review of *Verbal Behavior* is far more than effective refutation of the behavioristic approach to language" (p. 246). MacCorquodale's (1969) excellent "retrospective appreciation" of *Verbal Behavior* and his rebuttal to Chomsky (MacCorquodale, 1970) attempted to rescue Skinner's analysis from obscurity, but they did not have much of an impact on that trend, or on verbal behavior research and applications.

Twenty-five years after Skinner's book was published, there was still very little basic or applied verbal behavior research in the literature (McPherson et al., 1984; Sundberg & Partington, 1982). There were only a few thematic lines of research on verbal behavior, and applications to language intervention for children with autism spectrum disorder (ASD) or other intellectual disabilities were just beginning. Papers on verbal behavior were scarce in the *Journal of Applied Behavior Analysis* and the *Journal of the Experimental Analysis of Behavior*, as well as in journals related to speech pathology and linguistics. *Verbal Behavior* went out of print in the late 1970s after its first run in 1957 of only 3,000 copies. The initial publisher, Appleton-Century-Crofts, sold the rights to Prentice-Hall, where it went out of print again.[1] Yet, in 1978 Skinner wrote "*Verbal behavior...* will, I believe, prove to be...my most important work" (p. 122).

Skinner's optimism about his book may have been related to several developments that were occurring during the late 1970s in behavior analysis and in the verbal behavior specialty area. The establishment of the Midwestern Association for Behavior Analysis (MABA, now the Association for Behavior Analysis International) and its annual convention provided a verbal community for those interested in verbal behavior. Several members of this community established the Verbal Behavior Special Interest Group (VB-SIG) and held their first meeting at the 1977 MABA convention. The meeting was chaired by W. Scott Wood and Jack Michael, and with Skinner in attendance, an action agenda was created that focused on developing several aspects of Skinner's analysis of verbal behavior (Sundberg, 1997). More verbal behavior research and applications began to occur, and in 1985, the journal *The Analysis of Verbal Behavior* was established by the VB-SIG. Verbal behavior courses were offered in more behavioral programs, and finally, the systematic development of Skinner's analysis of verbal behavior was underway in earnest.

Now, almost 50 years after that first VB-SIG meeting, the current book, *Promoting Language for Learners with Autism Spectrum Disorder: A Guide for Applied Behavior Analysis Practitioners* edited by Jason Vladescu and April Kisamore, demonstrates that Skinner's most important work has not fallen into obscurity, but quite the opposite. This book showcases the extensive body of empirical research and applications of Skinner's analysis of verbal behavior that now exists in the literature. The editors have assembled some of the most prolific verbal behavior researchers in the field today, most of whom have specialized in teaching language to children with ASD. The collective content from these authors supplies the reader with detailed language assessment and intervention procedures for each of Skinner's elementary verbal operants (e.g., mand, echoic, tact, and intraverbal) as well as procedures for teaching listener repertoires, selecting a response form, and for establishing several types of generative learning. This book would also be an excellent modern textbook for a course on verbal behavior and its applications to language assessment and intervention.

The order and content of the chapters in this book generally follow the order and content of the chapters in *Verbal Behavior*. As in Skinner's book, each of the earlier chapters contributes to the foundation of the later chapters. The current book is divided into three sections: Introduction, Teaching, and Professionalism. The Introduction contains three chapters. In Chapter 1, the author presents the foundational elements of Skinner's functional analysis of verbal behavior. This chapter will provide the lens through which all other chapters are viewed. The author begins with a brief history of Skinner's work in the book and a discussion of the radical behavioral philosophy underlying Skinner's functional analysis. This is followed by a presentation of Skinner's distinction between the speaker and the listener and an overview of each of the elementary verbal operants and listener repertoires.

A language intervention program for a child with ASD should begin with an assessment of the child's existing linguistic skills. No two children are alike, and an assessment can guide the practitioner and the child's family in choosing meaningful and measurable goals and objectives. The authors of Chapter 2 describe four language assessment tools that are based on *Verbal Behavior*. An overview of the administration instructions for each tool is provided, along with case studies that demonstrate how an assessment can guide an intervention program. Information is presented on the reliability and validity of each assessment, and which tool might be the most effective for a specific child. Chapter 3 describes two common approaches for arranging educational environments for teaching verbal behavior to children with autism: analog and naturalist arrangements. Discrete trial training developed by Lovaas (1981) is presented as an example of analog training, and incidental teaching developed by Hart and Risley (1975) exemplifies naturalistic teaching. The author provides a brief history and the strengths and limitations of these models, as well as other models, and suggests that both types of teaching arrangements should be included in an intervention program when clinically indicated.

The "Teaching" section of the book contains eight chapters covering elementary verbal operants, listener skills, generative learning, multiple control, and augmentative and alternative communication (AAC). These chapters describe how Skinner's analysis of verbal behavior can provide an individualized curriculum guide and specific teaching procedures to meet the unique needs of a learner. Chapters 4–8 cover the elementary verbal operants (i.e., mand, echoic, tact, and intraverbal) and listener skills. Each chapter begins with a user-friendly introduction to the domain (e.g., mand), then provides detailed information on assessment, curriculum design, teaching procedures, tactics for promoting generalization and maintenance, supporting research, and strategies for troubleshooting. Readers will find that this collection of five chapters, along with the Introduction content, provides them with a basic understanding of Skinner's functional analysis of verbal behavior and how to apply it to language assessment and intervention for early learners.

Beginning around 2 years of age, a neurotypical child's language skills begin to grow rapidly in vocabulary size and linguistic complexity. It has been proposed that this burst in language acquisition is due to an effect identified as generative learning (Wittrock, 1974). Chapter 9 describes the relevant environmental variables that produce four types of generative learning: bidirectional naming, the emergence of intraverbals, recombinative generalization, and problem-solving. The authors present an introduction to each type of generative learning, its conceptual and empirical foundations, the prerequisite and component skills required, developments in research, and information on assessment and intervention procedures for children with autism.

Chapter 10 contains an extensive treatment of Skinner's analysis of multiple control. This chapter is essential for teaching language to more advanced learners given that multiple control is the behavioral process through which more complex verbal behavior such as bidirectional naming, joint control, stimulus equivalence, and relational framing are acquired and function. The authors present a clear explanation of convergent and divergent multiple control, along with a discussion of the most current basic and applied research. In addition, this chapter contains methods for assessing and teaching several types of multiply controlled generative learning that children with autism may have difficulty acquiring.

Many individuals with ASD have limited speaking abilities, and as a result, their speech is insufficient to meet their communication needs. For these individuals, there are several options available for an augmentative and alternative communication (AAC) system. Chapter 11 provides an overview of AAC and a review of several of the most common types (e.g., sign language, Picture Exchange Communication System (PECS) speech-generating devices). In addition, the authors offer direction for assessment and for designing and implementing AAC interventions. A theme throughout this chapter is the value of collaboration between the fields of applied behavior analysis and speech-language pathology (also see Chapter 14). The authors suggest that the combined information from each profession can enhance AAC interventions.

The final section of the book is titled "Professionalism" and contains three chapters that address issues related to practitioners. Chapter 12 describes the importance of practitioners contacting and consuming basic and translational verbal behavior research for guiding language intervention programs for children with autism. This research can provide empirical support for conceptual distinctions, such as the functional independence of the mand and tact, which, in turn, can inform intervention programs. The author of Chapter 12 provides the reader with a historical overview of basic and translational verbal behavior research along with several prominent research projects. The author recommends that familiarity with this literature may help achieve a deeper understanding of problems encountered in practice.

A common scenario faced by educators and practitioners involves the needs of children with ASD who are exposed to a language other than English in their homes. This population has been identified as *culturally and linguistically diverse* (CLD) learners. Chapter 13 describes the complexities involved with CLD learners and the process of making difficult decisions, such as what language to focus on in ABA and school programs. The authors provide an overview of the CLD research on language assessment and intervention, behaviors that interfere with learning, skill acquisition, and learner preference. Chapter 14 stresses the importance and value of interdisciplinary collaboration between ABA providers and other professionals working with individuals with autism. The authors identify six key professions (Board Certified Behavior Analyst (BCBA)s), Psychologists, School Psychologists, Special Education Teachers, Speech-language Pathologist (SLP)s, and Occupational Therapist (OT)s) that frequently provide concurrent services to individuals diagnosed with ASD. The authors summarize the scopes of practice, training, and competence for each profession, as well as offer insightful examples of collaboration.

This book is a valuable resource for practitioners who are faced with the challenges of teaching language and communication skills to a child with ASD. The authors make use of recent developments in verbal behavior and ASD research to guide readers through the process of language assessment and intervention for a child at any language level. Skinner's analysis of verbal behavior has much to offer ASD treatment, and Vladescu and Kisamore's book makes that obvious. On a personal note, it is quite satisfying for me to see how far the research and applications of Skinner's (1957) *Verbal Behavior* have come in the past 50 years. This body of work has improved the lives of many children with ASD around the world. The scope, power, and utility of Skinner's analysis of verbal behavior are on display in the current book, and as a result, it provides support for Skinner's belief that *Verbal Behavior* would prove to be his most important work.

Mark L. Sundberg

April 6, 2025

Note

1 *Verbal Behavior* is now published by the B. F. Skinner Foundation (bfskinner.org).

References

Chomsky, N. (1959). Review of Skinner's Verbal Behavior. Language, (35), 26–58.

Hart, B., & Risley, T. R. (1975). Incidental teaching of language in the preschool. *Journal of Applied Behavior Analysis, 8*(4), 411–420. https://doi.org/10.1901/jaba.1975.8-411

Lovaas, O. I. (1981). *Teaching developmentally disabled children: The me book.* University Park Press.

MacCorquodale, K. (1969). B. F. Skinner's *Verbal behavior*: A retrospective appreciation. *Journal of the Experimental Analysis of Behavior, 12*(5), 831–841. https://doi.org/10.1901/jeab.1969.12-831

MacCorquodale, K. (1970). On Chomsky's review of Skinner's Verbal behavior. *Journal of the Experimental Analysis of Behavior, 13,* 83–99. https://doi.org/10.1901/jeab.1970.13-83

McPherson, A., Bonem, M., Green, G., & Osborne, J. G. (1984). A citation analysis of the influence on research of Skinner's *Verbal Behavior. The Behavior Analyst, 7*(2), 157–167. https://doi.org/10.1007/BF03391898

Neisser, U. (1967). *Cognitive psychology.* Appleton-Century-Crofts.

Skinner, B. F. (1957). *Verbal behavior.* Appleton-Century-Crofts.

Skinner, B. F. (1978). *Reflections on behaviorism and society.* Prentice-Hall.

Sundberg, M. L. (1997). Editorial. *The Analysis of Verbal Behavior, 14,* 1–4.

Sundberg, M. L., & Partington, J. W. (1982). Skinner's book *Verbal behavior*: A reference list. *The Analysis of Verbal Behavior, 1,* 9–13. https://doi.org/10.1007/BF03392793

Wittrock, M. C. (1974). Learning as a generative process. *Educational Psychologist, 11*(2), 87–95. https://doi.org/10.1080/00461527409529129

Preface

We open this volume by reiterating one of the most influential ideas of the 20th century: that language is a set of learned behaviors shaped and maintained by their consequences. This simple but powerful idea underscores everything in this book. For children diagnosed with autism spectrum disorder (ASD), learning meaningful language opens doors to friendship, self-advocacy, and academic success—yet it also presents notable challenges. This book explores how professionals can integrate the current advances in behavior analysis to help children with ASD find their voices, expand their language repertoires, and ultimately thrive.

Of little surprise to those who have found their way here, this text stands on the shoulders of B. F. Skinner's groundbreaking work, *Verbal Behavior*. Skinner introduced a functional view of language that has inspired thousands of clinical applications. However, since *Verbal Behavior* was first published in 1957, behavior analysis has evolved considerably: new lines of research have emerged, technology has advanced, and practitioners increasingly serve culturally and linguistically diverse populations. Despite this evolution, we often encounter modern professionals who struggle to find updated, practical guidance that speaks to the day-to-day challenges of supporting the language development of the individuals they serve.

This book addresses this void by offering a clear, accessible framework for promoting language repertoires. We have organized the text into three sections. First, we revisit the foundational concepts and best practices in assessing and arranging learning environments. Next, we delve into the primary verbal operants and consider a host of related repertoires and necessary outcomes, like listener behavior, generative language, and complex stimulus control. Finally, we discuss professional issues relevant to modern practitioners: the importance of basic and translational research, cultural and linguistic diversity, and teaming with professionals across multiple disciplines.

Throughout the chapters, you will find a balance of conceptual analysis, real-world examples, and actionable recommendations. Each of our contributors brings expertise from research and practice and has labored to improve outcomes for individuals with ASD. As your eyes dance across these pages, we hope they spark a contemporary understanding to equip you with a roadmap that can be readily applied.

We invite you to use this resource as a launching pad—one that ignites new practices, raises new clinical questions to be solved, and ultimately drives meaningful change in the lives of the learners you serve. As you engage with, adapt, refine, and further develop the presented content, we encourage you to share your journey, successes, and challenges. Only by expanding and enhancing our collective understanding can we transform our shared vision for promoting the language of children with ASD from mere aspiration to actionable steps, thereby ensuring that every learner acquires the powerful tool of language and the countless opportunities that come with it. Let us make the influential work that began with Skinner a reality for every child needing a stronger voice.

Jason C. Vladescu
April N. Kisamore

Contributors

Judah B. Axe, PhD, BCBA-D, LABA, is a Professor at Simmons University. His research includes verbal behavior, problem-solving, matrix training, and antecedent interventions.

Beth Bellone, MS, CCC-SLP, BCBA, directs Speech & Language Services at NECC and teaches at Worcester State. Her work centers on AAC and behavior analysis.

Vincent J. Carbone, EdD, BCBA-D, is founder/director of Carbone Clinics in NY, MA, London, and Dubai. His work focuses on verbal behavior, joint control, and motivating operations.

Chuelsia Carvalho, MS, BCBA, is a PhD student at Simmons University researching verbal behavior, culturally responsive interventions, and staff training.

Serena Cates, MS, BCBA, is a PhD student at Simmons University researching verbal behavior, trauma-informed care, and staff training.

Catia Cividini-Motta, PhD, BCBA-D, is an Assistant Professor and Associate Director of ABA Programs at the University of South Florida. Her work includes verbal and challenging behavior.

Sarah B. Costa, MSEd, BCBA, LBA, LABA, is a PhD student at Simmons and Director of Clinical Excellence at Bierman Autism Centers. She studies behavioral skills training and precision teaching.

Andresa De Souza, PhD, BCBA-D, is an Associate Professor and Director of ABA at the University of Missouri–St. Louis. Her research includes verbal behavior and international dissemination.

Samantha S. De Vasconcelos, MS, BCBA, LABA, is a behavior analyst providing home and center-based ABA services for children with autism.

Barbara E. Esch, PhD, BCBA-D, CCC-SLP, is a consultant and author of the Early Echoic Skills Assessment and Program Planner, publishing on verbal behavior acquisition and rehabilitation.

Maya J. Fallon, PhD, LBA, BCBA-D, directs Early and Advanced Learner Programs at the Center for Pediatric Behavioral Health. Her research focuses on social skill development in autism.

Gloria Leyla Fanning, MS, BCBA, LABA, is the Chair of the Center for Autism Research and Education Student Subcommittee at UMass Lowell and is active in the Verbal Behavior SIG.

Sarah E. Frampton, PhD, BCBA-D, is an Assistant Professor at the University of Nebraska, Omaha, researching verbal behavior, generative learning, and autism interventions.

Mary E. Halbur, PhD, BCBA-D, LBA, is an Assistant Professor at the University of Nebraska Medical Center's Munroe-Meyer Institute.

Adrienne M. Jennings, PhD, BCBA-D, LBA, is an Assistant Professor at Daemen University and co-founder of the AI Consortium for ABA.

Tamara S. Kasper, MS, CCC-SLP, BCBA, is an international consultant and co-founder of Bridgify, focusing on engagement, communication, and speech production.

Paula Braga Kenyon, PhD, BCBA-D, is an Adjunct Professor at Northeastern and has held executive and consulting roles in the United States and Brazil.

Shawn Kenyon, EdD, BCBA, is an Adjunct Professor at Northeastern and a consultant for public and private schools in the United States and Brazil.

Tiffany Kodak, PhD, BCBA-D, is a Professor at Marquette and Director of the Center for Language Acquisition and Social Skills Intervention. She researches skill acquisition and verbal behavior.

Danielle LaFrance, PhD, BCBA-D, is a Clinical Consultant at ABA Technologies, co-founder of Verbale, and publishes on verbal behavior and collaboration.

Sarah A. Lechago, PhD, BCBA-D, LBA, is an Associate Professor at the University of Houston–Clear Lake and directs the Verbal Behavior Clinic.

Caio F. Miguel, PhD, BCBA-D, is a Professor at CSU Sacramento, Doctoral Advisor at Endicott College, former editor of *The Analysis of Verbal Behavior,* and co-founder of Verbale.

Haven S. Niland, PhD, BCBA-D, LBA, is an Assistant Professor at Texas Tech and the Burkhart Center. Her research includes skill acquisition, supervision technology, and verbal behavior.

Todd M. Owen, PhD, BCBA-D, LBA, is an Assistant Professor at the Munroe-Meyer Institute, University of Nebraska Medical Center.

Anna Ingeborg Petursdottir, PhD, is an Associate Professor in the behavior analysis program at the University of Nevada, Reno.

Lilith M. Reuter-Yuill, PhD, CCC-SLP, BCBA-D, co-founded Bridgify and specializes in AAC, verbal behavior, and interprofessional collaboration.

Nicole M. Rodriguez, PhD, BCBA-D, LBA, is a Professor and Director of ABA Doctoral and Early Intervention Programs at the Munroe-Meyer Institute.

Rocío Rosales, PhD, BCBA-D, LABA, is an Associate Professor and Program Coordinator at UMass Lowell.

David Roth, MA, BCBA, is a consultant in autism support classrooms and an editorial contributor to the B.F. Skinner Foundation's publications.

Henry D. Schlinger, Jr., PhD, BCBA-D, is a Professor at CSU Los Angeles and coordinator of the ABA Certificate Program.

M. Alice Shillingsburg, PhD, BCBA-D, is a Professor and Yale Family Endowed Chair at the Munroe-Meyer Institute, specializing in autism interventions.

Tina M. Sidener, PhD, BCBA-D, is a Professor and Clinical Supervisor at Caldwell University, publishing on play, skill acquisition, and verbal behavior.

Lina M. Slim, PhD, BCBA-D, CCC-SLP, is an adjunct faculty and international consultant focused on autism, culturally responsive care, and interprofessional collaboration.

Mark L. Sundberg, PhD, BCBA-D, is the co-author of the ABLLS, author of the VB-MAPP, and founder/former editor of *The Analysis of Verbal Behavior*.

Bruce A. Tinor, EdD, BCBA, LBS, is a special education administrator in Pennsylvania and founder of Tinor Educational Consultation LLC.

Section 1

Introduction

Chapter 1

Verbal Behavior

A Functional Approach to Language

Henry D. Schlinger, Jr

One of the defining characteristics of individuals diagnosed with autism spectrum disorder (ASD) is deficits in social communication and interaction (American Psychiatric Association, 2013). The phrase "social communication and interaction" encompasses a wide range of behaviors, most of which involve language. Typically, humans communicate and interact with one another verbally. Thus, one of the main tasks facing applied behavior analytic (ABA) practitioners when working with individuals diagnosed with ASD is teaching appropriate language skills. Other professionals who are often called on to help with language skills include speech-language pathologists (SLPs) (see also Chapter 14 in this volume). But while SLPs can help with the diagnoses and treatment of articulation, swallowing, and some language disorders, only ABA practitioners can functionally analyze language behaviors (see Schlinger, 2017b). Once they do this, they can create treatment programs that draw upon the basic principles of behavior analysis to teach effective and productive verbal behavior to their autistic clients (see LaFrance & Miguel, 2014). Treatment programs usually begin with an assessment of an individual's verbal repertoire, typically using the *Verbal Behavior Milestones Assessment and Placement Program* (*VB-MAPP*; Sundberg, 2008) and the *Early Echoic Skills Assessment and Program Planner* (*EESAPP*; Esch, 2023) (see also Chapters 2 and 5 in this volume). Both the *VB-MAPP* and the *EESAPP* are based on Skinner's (1957) functional analysis of verbal behavior. And most ABA treatment programs are based, at least in part, on the analysis of verbal behavior first suggested by Skinner (1957) and expanded upon in the decades since by many other behavior analysts (e.g., Barbera, 2007; Greer & Ross, 2004, 2008; Sundberg & Michael, 2001). The purpose of this chapter is to provide an overview of Skinner's *Verbal Behavior* so that practitioners interested in effectively applying that analysis to assessing and teaching verbal behavior might better understand its theoretical and philosophical foundations as well as its many practical implications and applications.

DOI: 10.4324/9781003433668-2

A Brief History of Skinner's Verbal Behavior

No Black Scorpion

At the end of his magnum opus, *Verbal Behavior*, Skinner (1957) offered two personal epilogues. In the second one, "No Black Scorpion," he recounted an incident that led him to begin writing the book. It was 1934 and he was at a dinner at the Harvard Society of Fellows seated next to the well-known British mathematician and philosopher Alfred North Whitehead. As Skinner tells it, he was excitedly talking up behaviorism. Apparently, Whitehead agreed that behaviorism would be a useful approach to understanding behavior, but he drew the line at language. That should not have surprised Skinner because, beginning at least formally with René Descartes, philosophers had for hundreds of years proclaimed human language to be a unique human quality and separate from other human functions. This is what is usually meant by dualism, mind-body dualism, or Cartesian (from Descartes) dualism. Descartes believed that human language, unlike the actions of the body, including reflexes, was a product of a rational mind that was separate from the mechanistic body. Cartesian dualism persists to the present day not only among most laypeople but also among some psychologists, linguists, and philosophers. When Skinner claimed that behaviorism (what we would today call behavior analysis) could explain human language, Whitehead challenged Skinner by saying, "Let me see you … account for my behaviour as I sit here saying, 'No black scorpion is falling upon this table.'" Of course, as Skinner wrote, no one would ask any other natural scientist to explain any momentary event on the spot. Although Skinner did not take the bait, as he said, "The next morning I drew up the outline of the present study" (1957, p. 457). So, in 1934, Skinner began working on what would eventually be published in 1957 as *Verbal Behavior* (*VB*). Interestingly, Skinner began *VB* before he published his first book, *The Behavior of Organisms* (Skinner, 1938), in which he detailed the results of his experiments with rats, which he began in the early 1930s, and which became the experimental foundation of behavior analysis, subsequently called the Experimental Analysis of Behavior.

"The Operational Analysis of Psychological Terms"

In the 23 years during which Skinner worked on his book, he published other books and articles where he offered some clues as to what he was writing in *VB*. The most notable example was an article titled "The Operational Analysis of Psychological Terms" (Skinner, 1945). This article was the first publication of the basic premise of *VB*; namely, that verbal behavior, just like non-verbal behavior, could be understood and explained as operant behavior. As such, the basic unit of operant analysis—the four-term contingency—could be used to functionally analyze verbal behavior. In behavior analysis, a four-term contingency refers to a response, a motivating operation (MO), a discriminative stimulus (S^D), and a consequence (e.g., reinforcement). When analyzing language, behavior analysts look at an individual's responses, that is, what they say (or write, sign, etc.). Skinner (1945) used the word "operational" (analysis) in the title of his article, but he really meant "functional" (analysis) (Schlinger, 2013). He made essentially two points in his article. The first was that we should deal "with terms, concepts, constructs, and so on, quite frankly in the form in which they are observed—namely, as verbal responses" (Skinner, 1945, p. 271)—the dependent variables in a behavior analysis. In a behavioral approach, words, whether heard by a listener or read by a reader, are simply the products of the behaviors of speaking or writing. His second point was that psychological terms had no meaning separate from the variables that evoked them in a given speaker. He wrote, "Meanings, contents, and references are to be found among the determiners, not the properties, of a response" (p. 271). In other words, the independent variables are not vague, abstract meanings but the circumstances (i.e., MOs and S^Ds) that evoke the verbal responses. This was and still is a revolutionary approach to the study of language, both outside of and within behavior analysis.

In addition to the two points mentioned above, Skinner's (1945) article also revealed that by 1945, he had mostly worked out his concept of the tact, in particular, how abstract tacts (see the section 'Chapter 5: The Tact' below) can be taught. Skinner then described how tacts can come under the control of private events, thus providing a behavioral view of subjectivity. In so doing, Skinner introduced the concept of radical behaviorism and distinguished it from what he called "methodological behaviorism." For Skinner, methodological behaviorism either rejects the notion of private events outright or accepts them but rules them out of a psychological analysis because they cannot be observed. Radical behaviorism, on the other hand, not only accepts that private events exist but treats them just like public events (stimuli and behavior) and ascribes to them the same functions (i.e., causes) as public events.

As if all of that were not enough to warrant considering Skinner's (1945) article revolutionary, at the end of the article, and based on his analysis of how the verbal community teaches individuals to tact private events, he provided a brief but concise analysis of what it means to be conscious (see also Schlinger, 2008a, 2009). All very heady stuff in 1945 and even today.

Science and Human Behavior

By the time Skinner published his book *Science and Human Behavior* (1953), he had more fully worked out his analysis of abstract tacts and how the verbal community brings verbal responses under the control of private events. In the chapter "Private Events in a Natural Science," in a section titled "Verbal Responses to Private Events," Skinner described the tact—without using that term—in greater detail than he had in the 1945 article, including an extensive exposition of verbal responses to private events and how the verbal community teaches individuals to respond to their own public and private behaviors.

Verbal Behavior

Verbal Behavior was finally published in 1957 to mostly favorable reviews (Knapp, 1992). However, as most behavior analysts know, there was one review that garnered substantial attention. It was written by a young linguist named Noam Chomsky. Cognitive psychologists latched onto Chomsky's review and his rational theory of language and cited it as one of the main driving forces behind the so-called cognitive revolution (e.g., Hunt, 1982; Miller, 2003; Pléh, 2019; but see Roediger, 2004). The review was said to have demolished not only the analysis in Skinner's book but behaviorism writ large (but see Schlinger, 2008b). Unfortunately, even by his own admission, Skinner should have replied to Chomsky's review, but he found its tone distasteful (see Skinner, 1972). It was not until 1970 that the American psychologist Kenneth MacCorquodale replied to Chomsky's review. Unfortunately, even though MacCorquodale submitted his reply to the journal *Language*, the same journal in which Chomsky's review appeared, it was not even reviewed. MacCorquodale's (1970) rebuttal was eventually published in the *Journal of the Experimental Analysis of Behavior*, where it was read only, or mostly, by behavior analysts.[1]

Even though Chomsky still considers his review of *VB* to be accurate and correct (see Virués-Ortega, 2006), over the last few decades, at least in the behavioral community, *VB* has seen an upsurge in popularity (e.g., Schlinger, 2008b) and in basic and applied research (e.g., Oah & Dickinson, 1989; Petursdottir, 2018; Petursdottir & Devine, 2017; Sautter & LeBlanc, 2006). Meanwhile, Chomsky's theory of generative grammar has gone the way of so many other rational theories lacking experimental support. Even some of Chomsky's former students have criticized his theories (e.g., Bickerton, 2008; Lakoff, 1995; Postal, 1995). And more modern cognitive theories of language, called usage-based theories, have abandoned innate generative theories such as Chomsky's altogether (Schlinger, 2023). So, it seems that Chomsky won the battle at the time, but Skinner won the war, at least within the behavioral community.

Verbal Behavior

Skinner divided *VB* into five parts. In Part I: A Program, Skinner introduced a functional analysis of verbal behavior in which he contrasted a functional account with the traditional one and then discussed general problems, including those associated with considering verbal behavior as a dependent variable, as well as the independent variables in an operant analysis (e.g., conditioning and extinction, motivation, and stimulus control). In Part II: Controlling Variables, Skinner devoted individual chapters to the mand, tact, verbal behavior under the control of verbal stimuli, including the echoic, textual, and intraverbal, and the audience. Part III: Multiple Variables was devoted primarily to multiple causation. In Part IV, The Manipulation of Verbal Behavior, Skinner introduced the autoclitic and discussed different types as they contribute to grammar and syntax. Lastly, in Part V: The Production of Verbal Behavior, Skinner put it all together in his treatment of self-editing, self-strengthening of verbal behavior, logical and scientific verbal behavior, and, finally, thinking. In the present chapter, I will only address Parts I and II. Before doing so, however, I consider two caveats.

Two Caveats

The Definition of Verbal Behavior

The first caveat deals with Skinner's definition of verbal behavior. Skinner introduced *VB* by distinguishing between behavior that acts directly on the world "through mechanical action," for example, reaching for and grabbing a glass of water, and behavior that only affects the (non-social) environment indirectly "from which the ultimate consequences of behavior emerge" (p. 1), for example, when someone asks for a glass a water. In both instances, the ultimate consequence is the same—the person gets the glass of water. According to Skinner, in the latter case, "the glass of water reaches the speaker only as a result of a complex series of events including the behavior of the listener" (p. 1). Thus, Skinner defined verbal behavior as "behavior reinforced through the mediation of other persons" (p. 2). In the above latter example, the water only gets to the speaker through the mediation of the behavior of the listener. Later in the book, Skinner refined the definition such that when reinforcing the behavior of the speaker, "the 'listener' must be responding in ways which have been conditioned precisely...to reinforce the behavior of the speaker" (p. 225).[2] In other words, listeners must be trained by the verbal community to reinforce speakers' verbal behavior. The process begins when parents of language-learning children teach their children to reinforce the verbal behavior of others, for example, by doing what they ask or by simply paying attention. By adding "this further provision," Skinner attempted to restrict the definition to "a field of inquiry having certain unitary properties" (p. 224), which he called not language, but verbal behavior.

Much has been made of Skinner's definition of verbal behavior within the past few decades. This debate was initiated by proponents of relational frame theory (RFT) who claimed that Skinner's definition was flawed and indistinguishable from non-verbal behavior (Hayes, 1994; Hayes et al., 2001). They called for a new definition in light of research on so-called derived relations. Others have defended Skinner's definition, noting that verbal (operant) behavior as Skinner defined and analyzed it is, in fact, functionally no different than non-verbal operant behavior (e.g., Normand, 2009; Palmer, 2008). Some scholars were not so sure that we need a new definition, at least not yet (Leigland, 1997).

Regardless of the debate, it must be pointed out that Skinner's definition of verbal behavior occupies fewer than three pages in his 470-page book and only occurs in two places. We can, thus, conclude that the definition was not that important to the analysis presented in the book. Moreover, if we want to critique Skinner's definition, we might point out that it literally applies only to the mand (see below) because it is only with the mand that the listener mediates reinforcement for the speaker. For all the other verbal operants, the listener directly reinforces the speaker's verbal behavior. Nonetheless, we can categorically say that "Skinner's unique contribution to the study of language as verbal behavior was that it is not fundamentally different from other operant behavior" (Schlinger, 2008c, p. 147) and that the criticisms are really "much ado about nothing" (Normand, 2009).

The Listener and Listening

The second caveat deals with Skinner's treatment of the speaker and listener. Skinner's *VB* was mostly about the speaker, but it would be incorrect to say that he neglected the behavior of the listener. As Schlinger (2008c) wrote, "if sheer number of words is any indication of the importance Skinner placed on the listener, the word listener occurs 793 times compared to 893 instances of the word speaker" (p. 147). In fact, as mentioned previously, Skinner's definition of the verbal behavior of the speaker included the behavior of the listener who "must be responding in ways which have been conditioned precisely…to reinforce the behavior of the speaker" (p. 225). At the beginning of *VB*, Skinner seemed to minimize the actions of the listener. For example, he wrote, "an adequate account of verbal behavior need cover only as much of the behavior of the listener as is needed to explain the behavior of the speaker" (p. 2). Just a few pages later, however, he suggested that the behavior of the listener was more complex and needed to be considered more fully.

> Still another set of problems arises from the fact, often pointed out, that a speaker is normally also a listener. He reacts to his own behavior in several important ways. Part of what he says is under the control of other parts of his verbal behavior. We refer to this interaction when we say that the speaker qualifies, orders, or elaborates his behavior at the moment it is produced. The mere emission of responses is an incomplete characterization when behavior is composed. As another consequence of the fact that the speaker is also a listener, some of the behavior of listening resembles the behavior of speaking, particularly when the listener "understands" what is said.
>
> (Skinner, 1957, pp. 10–11)

This brief paragraph is remarkable, in part, because it reveals Skinner's confidence that an analysis of the speaker as listener can potentially solve such intractable problems as what it means to understand language. More simply, this paragraph suggests that the behaviors of listening and speaking may be insepa-rable, especially when we say that the listener listens, pays attention to, or under-stands the speaker. At the end of Chapter 2, in a footnote, Skinner wrote, "We shall see later that in many important instances the listener is also behaving at the same time as a speaker" (p. 34). Here, Skinner is referring to listening. Thus, any analysis of speaking also applies to listening because listening and speaking involve the very same behaviors. As Schlinger (2008c) wrote, "distinguishing between speaking and listening may be specious" (p. 149).

The above discussion has implications for what we mean when we speak of "listener behavior." Typically, when behavior analysts speak of listener behav-ior, they are referring to non-verbal responses to a verbal stimulus. For example, if a parent asks a child, "Where's the book?" or tells the child, "Bring me the book," and the child looks at or points to or brings the book to the parent, their behavior is described as listener behavior. However, literally, "listener behav-ior" should refer to any behavior by the listener that is evoked by stimuli pro-duced by a speaker's verbal behavior. An important type of such behavior is verbal in the form of echoics, tacts, or intraverbals. Sometimes all the above types of listener behaviors occur in one instance, as for example, when a parent asks a child to, "Find the book," and the child immediately begins looking for the book but simultaneously echoes (and then possibly self-echoes), "book" or "find the book," or engages in intraverbals such as, "Now where did I see that book?" Thus, when referring to listener behavior, it may be important to define and identify all behaviors in the listener that are evoked by stimuli produced by a speaker's verbal behavior (see Chapter 8 in this volume for a more extensive discussion of listener behavior).

Part I: A Program

Part I of *VB* includes two chapters. Chapter 1 is titled "A Functional Analysis of Verbal Behavior." In the first part of that chapter, in addition to introduc-ing the first version of his definition of verbal behavior, Skinner (a) argued for the term *verbal behavior* (as opposed to *language* or *speech*), (b) described the role of the listener in the total verbal episode, that is, "the combined behav-ior of two or more individuals" and nothing more (p. 2), and (c) described the goals of the analysis of verbal behavior as prediction, control, and understanding (which might be better ordered as control, prediction, and understanding) (see Schlinger, 2018, p. 165).

Skinner then contrasted his functional approach and its emphasis on behavior and its environmental causes with a traditional linguistic formulation and its emphasis on semantics and such concepts as ideas and meanings. To wit, Skinner introduced what he termed *explanatory fictions* (aka circular explanations), in which the evidence for some explanation is no different from the behaviors to be explained. For example, one usage-based theorist claims that children as listeners recognize the goals and intentions of mature speakers and then learn to use the same grammatical structures to achieve their own ends as speakers, and that children go beyond the individual utterances they hear and generalize to more abstract grammatical constructions (Tomasello, 2009). However, as Schlinger (2023) noted, *recognizing* and *generalizing* are not actions but are invented after the fact to explain the very behaviors used to infer them in the first place—talking—and are, thus, circular explanations. As Skinner wrote, "It is the function of an explanatory fiction to allay curiosity and to bring inquiry to an end" (p. 6). Skinner also pointed out that one unfortunate consequence of the traditional view of language is that speech is viewed as having "an independent existence apart from the behavior of the speaker" (p. 7). In this view, words are viewed as tools used to express ideas and meanings and are seen as having an existence independent of the behavior of the speaker. This view is apparent when we ask a child to "use your words." Behavior analysts reject these notions of speech, ideas, and meanings and consider them to be explanatory fictions when used to explain behavior. As Skinner wrote, "What is lacking" in the traditional approach "is a satisfactory causal or functional treatment" (p. 5). Skinner offered such an alternative functional approach in his "new formulation" where he listed five tasks: (a) to describe the topography of verbal behavior, (b) to explain verbal behavior by identifying the variables of which it is a function (i.e., the MOs and S^Ds), (c) to account for the dynamic characteristics of verbal behavior, (d) to consider the behavior of the listener, and (e) to consider that verbal behavior is multiply caused. (Notice, again, his inclusion of consideration of the listener's behavior.)

Skinner concluded Chapter 1 with the following: "the conditions appealed to in the analysis be, so far as possible, accessible and manipulable. The formulation is inherently practical and suggests immediate technological applications at almost every step" (p. 12). Thus, although the book is theoretical in the typical sense of theory in science, that is, the extrapolation of principles discovered in the experimental laboratory to the real, messier world, Skinner informed the reader that the analysis has numerous practical implications. The technological applications he mentions have been incorporated by applied behavior analysts for decades to teach verbal behavior; hence, the present book.

In Chapter 2, "General Problems," Skinner mentioned that verbal behavior does not specify any particular "form, mode, or medium." In other words, verbal behavior does not have to be vocal (see Chapter 13 in this volume). However, there is no question that for the majority of humans, the mode is speech. Skinner then described some different ways that vocal behavior as a dependent variable may be recorded, including as audible speech and the phonetic alphabet. He made an important distinction that he initially made in his classic article, "The Generic Nature of Stimuli and Responses" (Skinner, 1935) between a single instance of a response and a class of responses, all of which produce the same effect on the environment, which he termed an *operant*. Skinner then moved on to a discussion of a unit of (verbal) behavior "composed of a response of identifiable form functionally related to one or more independent variables" (p. 20), which he contrasted with traditional units of language, which are not functional units (e.g., words, sentences). This chapter is also where he introduced the concept of a *verbal repertoire* in which:

> responses of various forms appear in his behavior from time to time in relation to identifiable conditions. A repertoire, as a collection of verbal operants, describes the potential behavior of a speaker. To ask where a verbal operant is when a response is not in the course of being emitted is like asking where one's knee-jerk is when the physician is not tapping the patellar tendon.
>
> (p. 21)

The last sentence of the quotation addressed the issue of words as having an independent existence, which is why, traditionally, we refer to people "having" or "acquiring words." When Skinner talked about the potential behavior of the speaker, he was referring to an important concept in the analysis of (verbal) behavior: probability of response. Skinner wrote on the next page, "Our basic datum (to be predicted and controlled) is not the occurrence of a given response as such, but the probability that it will occur at a given time" (p. 22). This is the dependent variable in an operant analysis. The independent variables are well known to all behavior analysts: reinforcement, extinction, stimulus control, and motivation.

Skinner concluded Chapter 2 with a brief discussion of the listener. It is in this section that Skinner's ambivalence about the listener becomes apparent. On the one hand, Skinner tried to distance himself from linguists and psycholinguists who were "primarily concerned with the listener—with what words mean to those who hear them, and with what kinds of sentences are judged grammatical or ungrammatical" (Skinner, 1977, p. 379). On the other hand, Skinner recognized the importance of the listener as more than just one who reinforces the behavior of the speaker. He concluded the chapter by writing:

> Our interest in the listener is not, however, merely an interest in what happens to the verbal stimuli created by the speaker. In a complete account of a verbal episode we need to show that the behavior of the listener does in fact provide the conditions we have assumed in explaining the behavior of the speaker. We need separate but interlocking accounts of the behaviors of both speaker and listener if our explanation of verbal behavior is to be complete. In explaining the behavior of the speaker we assume a listener who

will reinforce his behavior in certain ways. In accounting for the behavior of the listener we assume a speaker whose behavior bears a certain relation to environmental conditions. The interchanges between them must explain all the conditions thus assumed. The account of the whole episode is then complete.

(p. 34)

When speakers also behave as listeners and listeners behave as speakers, as they do once a sufficient verbal repertoire is present, then there may be no need to distinguish between them.

Part II: Controlling Variables

Most ABA practitioners have heard of or taught mands, tacts, echoics, and intra-verbals to children with language deficits. But what are mands, tacts, echoics, and intraverbals really? Part II of *VB* is devoted to describing and explicating the variables that control (i.e., evoke) verbal behavior. As the analysis in the book is based solely on the four-term contingency—the basic operant unit of analysis—Part II lays the foundation for the rest of the book by providing a taxonomy of what some have termed the *elementary verbal operants* based on the antecedent variables (i.e., MOs and S^{D}s) that evoke them. Skinner identified five elementary verbal relations (operants) based on their controlling variables.

Chapter 3: Mand

The first elementary verbal operant described by Skinner is the mand. Skinner defined the mand as "a verbal operant in which the response is reinforced by a characteristic consequence and is therefore under the functional control of relevant conditions of deprivation or aversive stimulation" (pp. 35–36). However, functionally speaking, the mand is a response of a given form that is evoked by an establishing operation (EO).[3] So, put simply, if the responses, "Water please" or "Give me water," are evoked by water deprivation and have been reinforced in the past by getting water, then they are considered to be mands. Skinner made it clear that the mand is not based on form alone, although he notes that in a given verbal community, certain response forms, for example, "Give me..." "Be quiet," "Stop..." are probably mands. Traditionally, mands may be viewed as requests or demands. But these terms do not identify functional relations. Moreover, many mands cannot be classified as any of these traditional terms.

Skinner also pointed out that the mand benefits the speaker. That raises the question of why a listener would ever reinforce a mand; in other words, what does the listener get out of it? The answer is that in a total speech episode in which a speaker mands something from a listener, the speaker reinforces the listener's compliance with generalized reinforcement in the form of a "Thank you" (which functionally could be interpreted as "do it again"). Most of us are taught from a young age to thank people for things they do for us. But sometimes listeners revolt because mands can create aversive conditions for a listener depending on the way they are expressed. So, for example, "Give me the phone" might create an EO for the listener to either give the phone, escape from the (de)mand, or revolt. Thus, according to Skinner, sometimes mands are softened or concealed. In such instances, mands take the forms of other verbal operants but are still evoked by an EO. So, rather than (de)manding, "Water!" a speaker might say, "I'm really thirsty." The form of this response looks like a tact but functions as a mand if it gets water for the speaker. Remember, however, that it is only a mand if it is evoked by an EO (e.g., water deprivation) and reinforced by getting water. You can test this with a speaker by saying something like, "I'm sorry to hear that you're thirsty," or "Thank you for sharing that with me." If the response was indeed a tact, then you should hear no more from the speaker, but if it was a mand, then the speaker should say something like, "No, I mean can you please get me some water?" The latter form is what Skinner calls a softened mand as it appears to only mand for the verbal response from the listener, "Yes, I can."

Because mands are defined functionally, the form of the response can vary widely. For example, simple sounds, such as a grunt, a whine, or a cry, can be mands if such response forms are evoked by EOs and reinforced by what Skinner calls a "characteristic consequence," such as getting food or being picked up. On the other hand, non-vocal responses can be mands as, for example, when pointing by a non-vocal child is evoked by an EO and reinforced by getting whatever object they point to. On the other hand, mands can have more complex forms, such as when someone asks, "Would you please go and get me a tall glass of cold water?"

It is important to point out that even though mands are evoked by EOs and reinforced by characteristic consequences—what the speaker mands for—mands are multiply controlled, not only by the EO, but by the listener as an S^D and by other contextual variables, including, sometimes, the object being manded for. An EO never occurs in a vacuum and mands are reinforced by listeners, or what Skinner calls the *audience*. Thus, the form of the mand is controlled partly by the EO—if it is food deprivation, then the speaker will mand for some kind of food—and partly by the audience (i.e., listener). So, for example, if a particular listener has always reinforced concealed mands, then the speaker will utter a concealed mand. If a particular listener has reinforced more forceful mands, the speaker's mand will be more forceful. Or, if the listener is hard of hearing, the speaker will mand louder. Also, if a specific type of food is present, that may exert some stimulus control over the form of the response as when a child asks for cookies that she can see.

Recall that for Skinner, the basic datum to be considered in the analysis of (verbal) behavior is the probability of a given response under a given set of circumstances. The given set of circumstances includes relevant MOs and S^{D}s. For example, in Chapter 4 of *VB*, Skinner described different levels of probability of manding "candy" by a child when there is a strong EO. The lowest level of probability of response (and reinforcement) is when there is no listener present. If a listener appears, the probability of manding "candy" increases. The probability is even greater if the listener has given the child candy in the past for manding. And the probability is greatest when the child can see that the listener has candy. This latter instance is an example of multiple control over the response "candy," by the EO, the presence of a listener (as an audience), and the sight of the candy, all of which combine to produce a strong response.[4] Skinner obviously wrote a lot more about mands, but I have tried to describe the basics that would be important to teach someone to mand (see Chapter 4 in this volume for a more extensive discussion of mands and techniques for teaching them).

There are several ways to teach someone to mand (e.g., Brodhead et al., 2016; Howlett et al., 2011; Lechago et al., 2010; Shafer, 1995; Sundberg et al., 2001), but they all have at least two things in common: establishing or altering an EO and providing the characteristic consequence. In some cases, it might be advisable to use unconditioned reinforcers, such as food or water, but a more ethical approach may be to use a procedure called the behavior chain interruption strategy (BCIS) (Goetz et al., 1985; see Carnett et al., 2017 for a review). In a BCIS, a well-established behavior chain is interrupted until the individual mands for the next step in the chain. So, for example, suppose a child who is learning to mand likes to draw. Using a BCIS, the practitioner would block one of the steps, such as getting access to the crayon, and require the child to mand for it. The assumption is that blocking access to the crayon increases the EO (which we can call crayon deprivation).

Chapter 4: Verbal Behavior under the Control of Verbal Stimuli

As mentioned previously, the mand is the only verbal operant whose primary controlling variable is the EO. In all the other verbal operants, the form of the response is evoked primarily by an S^D. In Chapter 4 of *VB*, Skinner described several types of verbal relations in which the S^D is a verbal stimulus. As he noted, he was only concerned with the evocative effects of verbal stimuli on verbal responses, or the probability of a given response under a given circumstance.

Echoic Behavior. The first verbal relation Skinner discussed was echoic behavior, which he called the simplest case. I would argue, however, that it is far from simple, at least in terms of its implications for more complex verbal behavior. Because of that, one could argue that the echoic is the most important of all the verbal operants (but see Sundberg, 2015), even though Skinner only devoted about ten pages to it.

Skinner defined all the verbal operants evoked by verbal stimuli in terms of two characteristics: formal similarity and point-to-point correspondence between the evoking stimulus and the product of the response. With echoic behavior, there is formal similarity between the auditory stimulus and the product of the echoic response, which is also an auditory stimulus; in other words, both the echoic stimulus and the echoic response product are in the same sense mode. In simpler terms, what the listeners hear themselves say matches what they hear the speaker say; in other words, both stimuli are auditory. This feature of formal similarity has important implications for the reinforcement of the echoic (see below). Moreover, the echoic stimulus and the echoic response product also have point-to-point correspondence in that the beginning, middle, and end of the stimulus match the beginning, middle, and end of the response product.

In contrast to the mand, which is reinforced by the consequence specified by the mand, echoic behavior, as with all verbal behavior whose form is determined primarily by S^Ds, is reinforced by generalized conditioned reinforcement, usually in the form of attention. Skinner called it *educational reinforcement*, which he defined elsewhere in *VB* as "reinforcement supplied primarily because it establishes and maintains a particular form of behavior in the speaker" (p. 84). In other words, parents and teachers use generalized conditioned reinforcers (e.g., attention and praise) to teach new behaviors, including echoic behavior.

But, there are other reinforcers for echoic behavior that may precede the use of educational reinforcers by parents. I am talking about automatic reinforcement (Vaughan & Michael, 1982). Skinner referenced automatic reinforcement several times in *VB*, and one can distill a definition as the reinforcement of a response by the (stimulus) product of the response. If a child hears their parent say a word and the child echoes it, just hearing themselves sound like their parent may be enough to reinforce that response (see also Palmer, 1996). As Skinner pointed out, automatic reinforcement can also strengthen vocal forms that are not verbal, as, for example, when a child's behavior of duplicating "the sounds of airplanes, streetcars, automobiles, vacuum cleaners, birds, dogs, cats" is automatically reinforced (p. 164). The origins of the automatic reinforcement of a child's behavior are unclear. Some suggest that the stimulus produced by a response must have been paired at some time with another reinforcing stimulus (e.g., Sundberg et al., 1996). However, there is another possibility. As Schlinger (1995) suggested,

> First, from birth, or even before … the infant constantly hears the phonological sounds of the language community. These sounds are heard when the infant is feeding, being held and caressed, and being played with, and also at times when the infant is not interacting with others. The effect of the constant correlation of these sounds with other stimulus events establishes the sounds as conditioned reinforcers. The second step is the shaping of the infant's own sound-making into the phonological sounds of the language

community that he or she has been hearing for months. The only difference between this shaping and that which involves more direct tangible reinforcers is that the reinforcers in this case are automatic. In the present example, when the infant makes sounds that resemble those that he or she has heard from the language community and that also function as reinforcement, it follows that the closer the sound match, the stronger the reinforcing effect. As Vaughan and Michael (1982) point out, this type of reinforcement also explains how children learn to speak with the accent or dialect of their parents, not to mention the actual sounds of the parents' voices.

(pp. 159–160; see also Skinner, 1957, p. 58)

How does echoic behavior work? The answer is that when we echo, we essentially transfer the echoic stimulus produced by the speaker's verbal behavior into our own response (Palmer, 2007). This seemingly simple conversion of a stimulus into a response has profound implications for language learning, listening, remembering, and relational responding referred to as derived. Before discussing these implications, it is important to clarify one thing. When we speak of echoics, we do not always mean that the listener hears a word or phrase and then echoes it. It is more likely that when we are said to listen (see Schlinger, 2008c), we are speaking along with the speaker; in other words, echoing what the speaker says as the speaker says it. This is a difficult claim to prove as we listen (talk along with the speaker) sub-audibly. If the listener were to speak along with the speaker out loud, it would be a veritable tower of babble, and the speaker's verbal behaviors would be much less effective. Skinner (1957) was aware of this when he wrote, "The speaker and listener do not, of course, emit the responses simultaneously. The time required for the echoic response may be of the order of a fraction of a second" (p. 270).

But why would listeners (the verbal community) teach echoic behavior in the first place? Skinner answered by saying that:

An echoic repertoire is established in the child through "educational" reinforcement because it is useful to parents, teachers, and others. It makes possible a short-circuiting of the process of progressive approximation since it can be used to evoke new units of response upon which other types of reinforcement may then be made contingent.

(p. 56)

Thus, instead of shaping each verbal response form (i.e., word), which would be impossible, we can simply teach an echoic repertoire, which allows one-trial learning (Palmer, 2005). So-called one-trial learning can be explained by the basic principles of operant learning (see Schlinger, 2008d), but it requires an echoic repertoire. The upshot is that with an echoic repertoire, one can learn a seemingly infinite number of words (response forms). We may call this the generative feature of the echoic. This feature alone is why practitioners working with autistic individuals who do not have an echoic repertoire should consider trying to establish one (see Chapter 5 in this volume). The generative feature of the echoic also leads to a discussion of the importance of the echoic. I mentioned that the echoic may be the most important verbal operant. The reason I made that hyperbolic statement is that the echoic seems essential for (a) learning all other speech forms, (b) the behavior we call listening or paying attention (see Schlinger, 2008c), (c) what we speak of as remembering, and (d) what some speak of as emergent or derived relations.

As already mentioned, an echoic repertoire allows listeners to listen, which means that they talk (i.e., echo) along with the speaker (Schlinger, 2008c). An echoic repertoire also permits us to remember what someone else said. For example, if I meet someone new and she says, "Hi, my name is Sarah," and I echo, "Sarah," either overtly or covertly, I have taken the first step to remembering her name later. I have converted the echoic stimulus produced by her response, "Sarah," into my own response, "Sarah." That, of course, does not mean I will be able to say, "Sarah" when I see her again or if someone asks me who I met (i.e., remember her name). Thus, an echoic response is necessary, but not sufficient because I would have to engage in some other conditioning of my own verbal behavior, probably by engaging in some intraverbals (see below) or problem-solving (see Palmer, 1991). The reinforcement for the echoic can be social, if when I echo, "Sarah" out loud, she says something like, "Right, it is Sarah." But there is also automatic reinforcement from me hearing that what I said sounds like what Sarah said. Remember that the product of the echoic response has formal similarity with the echoic stimulus—they are in the same sense mode: auditory. Thus, the closer the match between the two, the greater the probability of automatic reinforcement (Palmer, 1996). In order for the conditioning of my own behavior—"Sarah"—to occur, I would have to talk to myself a little more, for example, by saying something like, "Sarah, that's a nice name; it reminds me of my mother, whose name was Sarah." If I engage in this sort of intraverbal, either in the presence of Sarah or, for example, while visually imagining her (also behavior), then I am more likely to be able to say her name when I see her or if someone asks me who I met earlier that day. In other words, my behavior of saying, "Sarah" has been conditioned (see Schlinger, 2008d; Skinner, 1957, pp. 358–365).

Finally, an echoic repertoire seems necessary when auditory stimuli are involved in verbal relations in humans (Horne & Lowe, 1996; Schlinger & Blakely, 2024) called *emergent* or *derived*. In a simple matching-to-sample procedure in which a child is taught to select a picture of a car when they hear, "car," if they echo, "car" at the same time reinforcement occurs for the correct match, then the response, "car" is reinforced in the presence of the picture so that the picture can now evoke the response, "car" as a tact, or what some refer to as *symmetry*. Similarly, if the child hears, "car" and selecting the printed word CAR is reinforced, then the printed word CAR will now evoke saying, "car" as a textual response, also an instance of symmetry. Thus, saying "car" to the picture or to the word did not emerge and was not derived but rather directly, though not explicitly, trained. This kind of analysis has profound implications for theories of derived relations because if there are no truly derived relations, then theories of derived relations may not be necessary (Schlinger & Blakely, 2024).

It should be clear that the echoic is critically important for a wide range of important verbal phenomena. It should then come as no surprise that the echoic is also a very practical verbal operant in that it can be used to teach other verbal operants. And even though Skinner was neither an applied behavior analyst nor a practitioner, his understanding of the basic principles led him to suggest several ways that verbal operants could be taught. Skinner pointed out that the echoic could be used to prompt other verbal operants, in particular, the tact. For example, he suggested that if we want to teach a child to say, "alligator" in the presence of one, we should evoke the response, "alligator" as an echoic in the presence of the alligator and reinforce it. Thus, the presence (or picture) of an alligator should thereafter evoke "alligator" as a tact. Of course, in listeners with sophisticated verbal repertoires, just saying, "this is an alligator" (Skinner, 1957, p. 360] called this *ostensive definition*) in the presence of one, is sufficient to establish the tact. This appears to be yet another instance of a derived relation, as the tact did not appear to be directly trained. However, if the listener echoed, "alligator" either out loud or covertly and that response was reinforced automatically by the match with the auditory stimulus from the speaker, or if the speaker reinforced the audible echoic in the presence of the alligator, then the tact *was* directly trained, and in only one trial; and, thus, not derived.

ABA practitioners have devised numerous ways to teach echoic behavior (e.g., Cividini-Motta et al., 2017; Drash et al., 1999) as well as to use echoic prompts to teach other verbal operants (e.g., Valentino & Shillingsburg, 2012). In conclusion, although Skinner only devoted about ten pages to the echoic, he mentioned it 323 times in the book, thus suggesting that it is indeed an extremely important verbal operant (see Chapter 5 in this volume for a more extensive discussion of echoics and techniques for teaching them to children for whom the echoic is either absent or defective as in echolalia).

Textual Behavior. Whereas in echoic behavior, the S^D is an auditory stimulus, in *textual behavior*, the S^D is a textual stimulus, otherwise known as a printed word. So, for example, seeing the visual stimulus CAT evokes saying, "cat." In textual behavior, there is no formal similarity as the S^D (the printed word) is a visual stimulus and the response product (hearing oneself say "cat") is an auditory stimulus. There is, however, point-to-point correspondence between the S^D and the response product. It is important to note that textual behavior is necessary for what we term *reading* but not sufficient. As Skinner wrote,

We are concerned here only with his vocal behavior as it is controlled by the written or printed stimulus. Since the term "reading" usually refers to many processes at the same time, the narrower term "textual behavior" will be used here.

(pp. 65–66)

First, Skinner should have referred to a *visual stimulus*, not *written* or *printed*, as those terms refer to responses. More importantly, he distinguished between purely textual behavior and the behaviors we refer to as reading. You have probably had the experience where your eyes look at or scan words as you "read," but you are thinking (i.e., talking to yourself) or imagining about something else completely. The result is that even though you engaged in textual behavior, you cannot say what it is you "read" because there are other behaviors that we engage in when we read, most likely intraverbals (and imagining) evoked by the textual stimuli. In other words, seeing the printed words causes us to talk to ourselves about (and visualize) what we are seeing.

Textual behavior, unlike echoic behavior, is reinforced originally by educational reinforcement from parents and teachers. Automatic reinforcement does play a significant role in textual behavior, however, but only after such behavior has been acquired through generalized conditioned reinforcement. Skinner (1957) pointed out an important distinction between echoic and textual behavior with respect to automatic reinforcement: correctly echoing automatically reinforces the form of the echoic; the automatic reinforcement from reading an interesting text, however, only reinforces continued reading; "it does not differentially reinforce correct forms at the phonetic level" (p. 69). Skinner made an important point about the automatic reinforcement of textual behavior that is relevant to teaching reading. As you may know, there is some debate among educators about how to best teach reading (e.g., Castles et al., 2018; Jeynes, 2008; Watkins, 1997). Without getting into the weeds of that debate, suffice it to say that teaching phonetic reading has one big advantage with respect to textual behavior, namely, if a child is taught to decode a word, and they do so out loud, then once they hear themselves pronounce it correctly, that behavior is automatically reinforced because it matches how they heard others say the word (i.e., parity). As Skinner (1957) put it, "the beginning reader … must hear himself pronounce the word—perhaps several times—before reacting to it with behavior with which he has already acquired as a listener" (p. 66) because we learn to talk about things before we learn to read words.

Intraverbal Behavior. In contrast to verbal operants that show point-to-point correspondence between the stimulus and the response product, intraverbal response products show no point-to-point correspondence with the S^Ds that evoke them. Formal similarity is not an issue as the verbal response can either be spoken, written, or signed, although they are most often spoken. Simple examples include the answer "four" to the question "What is two plus two?" or the answer "Sacramento" to the question "What is the capital of California?" Much of our everyday conversational verbal behavior is also intraverbal. However, because it is not always a specific response to a specific question, rather than calling it intraverbal behavior, it is probably more appropriate to refer to the type of control as *intraverbal control* (Palmer, 2016). However, this locution leaves a hole in talking about the kind of behavior. So, when I refer to *intraverbal behavior*, I mostly mean behavior under intraverbal control as Palmer (2016) suggested.

Like the section on the echoic, the section on the intraverbal is very short—about eight pages. However, the brevity of the section belies the importance of intraverbal behavior because intraverbals, or behavior under intraverbal control, comprise most of our verbal behavior, including our conversations and self-talk. Palmer (2016) distinguished between a broad and a narrow definition of intraverbals. Under the narrow view, "an intraverbal is a verbal response directly under control of a prior verbal stimulus as the result of a history of reinforcement for emitting that response in the presence of that stimulus" (Palmer, 2016, p. 97). Thus, the response "four" is directly under the control of the question, "What is two plus two?" This is mostly how Skinner defined the intraverbal, and it squarely identifies the controlling variables of the response and the corresponding history of generalized conditioned (i.e., educational) reinforcement. But under the broad view, "an intraverbal response is any verbal response, of a different form, to a prior verbal stimulus" (p. 97). When we say that behavior is under intraverbal control, whether we know it or not, we are referring to multiple variables that determine the resulting form of responding (i.e., divergent multiple control, Michael et al., 2011). Identifying those sources of control is a herculean task, especially when trying to carry out a functional analysis of intraverbal behavior while teaching such forms to individuals with language deficits (see Eikeseth & Smith, 2013; Sundberg & Sundberg, 2011; also see Michael et al., 2011, and Chapter 10 in this volume for a more extensive discussion of multiple control and techniques for establishing it). Intraverbal behavior, like other verbal operants, is commonly lacking in some autistic learners. To that end, much has been written about how to teach intraverbal behavior (e.g., Goldsmith et al., 2007; Partington & Bailey, 1993) (see also Chapter 7 in this volume for a more extensive discussion of intraverbal behavior).

Chapter 5: The Tact

Before describing the tact in Chapter 5, the longest chapter by far in *VB*, Skinner alluded to the tact numerous times in the preceding chapters, thus revealing its importance to Skinner. Up to this point, Skinner described verbal operants controlled either by EOs (the mand) or by verbal S^Ds (echoic, textual, intraverbal). In Chapter 5, Skinner addressed the tact, a verbal operant that is controlled (i.e., evoked) by a non-verbal S^D, or as Skinner (1957) stated, "nothing less than the whole of the physical environment—the world of things and events which a speaker is said to 'talk about'" (p. 81). Of course, the audience, or listener, is also a non-verbal S^D that exerts evocative control over a speaker's verbal behavior. But that type of control does not usually determine the specific form of response, as do echoics, textuals, tacts but rather a general strengthening (i.e., evoking) of verbal behavior. This is because listeners (i.e., the audience) reinforce a wide variety of forms of verbal operant. Skinner defined the tact as a verbal operant whose response form is evoked "by a particular object or event or property of an object or event" (p. 82). This definition specifies that the controlling stimulus can either be an object (e.g., a car), a picture of an object (e.g., a photo or drawing of a car), or a property of objects in general (i.e., their color, shape, size, etc.).

Because Skinner addressed so much in the chapter on the tact, I can only provide a cursory overview here. Before I describe what most interests me in the chapter and how it might be useful for practitioners, let me just list some of the issues he discussed. After comparing the tact ("the most important of verbal operants," p. 83) with the other verbal operants, Skinner discussed (a) different ways that tacts can be extended (i.e., generalized) (generic, metaphorical, metonymical, and solecistic extension), (b) how tacts are used in what he called "nomination" (i.e., proper and common names), (c) abstraction, (d) reference, (e) verbal behavior (i.e., tacts) under the control of private stimuli, and (f) verbal behavior (i.e., tacts) under the control of other aspects of the speaker's own (present, past, and future) behavior.

I want to briefly discuss two of those topics as they pertain to frequent errors that autistic learners are reported to make. First, abstraction. A synonym for *to abstract* is to *separate*. In Skinner's use of the term *abstraction*, a stimulus property belonging to a collection of objects or pictures of objects is separated from all the other stimulus properties of those objects. Color is a good example. There are many objects that we would call *red*, for example, apples, fire engines, stop signs, and chili peppers. These objects share very few, if any, other features except for one: redness. One might also talk about the concept of *red*. Sometimes we talk about whether a child "has learned the concept of red." Whether we call it *abstraction* or *concept formation*, the question for an operant analysis of verbal behavior is: How do we learn to respond by saying "red" to all those different objects, even though they share few if any other features? Of course, the answer is quite simple if you understand operant learning and discrimination training. In fact, as Skinner (1957) noted, abstraction can be taught to pigeons. For example, if we show a variety of objects to a pigeon that differ in all respects except that some have red in them and some do not, we can reinforce key pecking by the pigeon only when red is present and not reinforce (i.e., extinguish) pecking when no red is present. As a result, if we now show the pigeon new objects, some of which contain red and some of which do not, the response of key pecking will only occur (i.e., be evoked) for the objects with red. In other words, the color red has been abstracted—pulled out—by the discrimination training (not by the pigeon). With a child, we carry out the same discrimination training, except the response is saying, "red." We could say that the concept of red has been taught in that the pigeon or child discriminates between red objects and non-red objects, that is, they respond differentially to red. For present purposes, the pigeon and child now tact "red." Skinner made an important point about abstraction: "Abstraction is a peculiarly verbal process because a non-verbal environment cannot provide the necessary restricted contingency" (p. 109). What he meant was that there are no contingencies in nature that will produce abstraction. Using our example above, there is no reason in the natural world for any organism to respond only to the redness of things. This also applies to the roundness, largeness, brightness, etc., of things. Only a verbal community can provide the discrimination training to create abstract tacts.

The second topic in the tact chapter that I want to address is Skinner's discussion, mentioned previously, of how the verbal community teaches its members to tact private events. This issue has profound implications and is the basis of Skinner's distinction between radical behaviorism (which assumes that private events exist, but only as more stimuli and behaviors) and what he called methodological behaviorism (which either assumes that private events do not exist or, if they do, they cannot be considered in a science of behavior because they cannot be observed). A radical behaviorist position is important for practitioners because much of our behavior, especially our verbal behavior, is private and is involved in problem-solving, remembering, etc. Also, there are stimuli that, though they are private, have the same function as public stimuli, that is, as S^Ds and conditional stimuli. The question is: How does a verbal community that teaches us to tact public events also teach us to tact events to which it has no direct access? The key term is "direct" because the verbal community does have indirect access to our private events. Consider how we learn to say, "ouch," or otherwise to tact that we are in pain. Our verbal community cannot "feel" our pain in the same way it can see the same color red that we see. According to Skinner, the verbal community uses public accompaniments, which include responses that are collateral to the pain. Suppose, for example, parents see their child limping with a cut or scrape on their leg and maybe crying. They ask, "Does it hurt?" while pointing to the cut or scrape. The child has not yet learned to tact the pain, and they echo, "hurt," so the parents say something like, "Yes, it hurts," and maybe pay a lot of attention to them and give them a special treat. (You will recognize this as using an echoic prompt to teach a tact.) The result is that the child learns to say "hurt" when they feel the stimulation from pain receptors, or, possibly, when they find themself limping or crying. As Skinner pointed out, these ways of establishing tacts (or intraverbals) to private stimuli do not guarantee precise control over the verbal responses by the stimuli because the verbal community does not have direct access to the private events and cannot be sure that the tact is indeed under the control of the painful stimulus and not some other undefined stimulus. Practitioners attempting to teach tacts of private stimuli are at the same disadvantage and must rely on the same indirect evidence.

I have only really scratched the surface of the chapter on the tact. Skinner leaves few stones unturned in the chapter, so practitioners interested in teaching tacts and the nuances associated with them would do well to plow through the chapter, preferably with the help of a study guide (see Blakely, 2021). (See Chapter 6 in this volume for a more extensive discussion of the tact and strategies for teaching tacts.)

Duplic and Codic Behavior

Before offering some concluding comments, I would like to briefly discuss a suggested modification of Skinner's taxonomy of verbal operants. Michael (1982) recommended what he called a "terminological refinement" to make Skinner's taxonomy more exhaustive. Michael was motivated by the commitment to auditory and visual stimuli with the terms echoic and textual, respectively. Moreover, two other relations Skinner mentioned—taking dictation and copying a text—appear in a separate section in the chapter on control by verbal stimuli, which he titled Transcription. In taking dictation, the stimulus is auditory, and the response product of writing is visual (seeing the written word), whereas in copying a text, both the stimulus and response product are visual. Michael's terminological refinement did away with echoic and textual as categories and replaced them with *duplic* and *codic*. In both duplic and codic behavior, the response form is controlled (i.e., evoked) by a verbal stimulus. The difference is that in duplic behavior, the response product has formal similarity with the verbal S^D, and in codic, there is no formal similarity between the two. This change allowed Michael to classify both echoic behavior and copying a text as duplic (from "to duplicate") and to classify both textual behavior and taking dictation as codic (from "to code") behavior. The resulting taxonomy of five elementary verbal operants is then: mand, tact, intraverbal, duplic, and codic.

Remaining Chapters in Part II

The three remaining chapters in Part II are "Chapter 6: Special Conditions Affecting Stimulus Control," "Chapter 7: The Audience," and "Chapter 8: The Verbal Operant as a Unit of Analysis." A brief word about each is in order. In Chapter 6, Skinner discussed how what he called "special measures" of both generalized and non-generalized reinforcement can distort the stimulus control of the tact and intraverbal. So, for example, as the description of the size of the fish one caught includes increasingly bigger and bigger fish, the more the speaker's (intra)verbal behavior about the fish's size garners generalized reinforcement from listeners. After all, one will not get much attention for talking about catching a small fish.[5] Another example of distorted stimulus control over the intraverbal is the little boy who cried wolf. Of course, as Skinner noted, "the social system composed of speaker and listener rapidly deteriorates" (p. 153) because the villagers stop reinforcing the little boy's lies about the wolf; the story does not end well when a real wolf appears. An example of special measures of non-generalized reinforcement is when a speaker tacts, "I'm hungry," and a listener gives her food. The food reinforcement converts the original tact, "I'm hungry," into a response that is part tact and part mand. Recall that Skinner called such mands "concealed" because they have the form of a tact. Of course, in any given instance, one would have to analyze all the controlling variables and, if possible, the proportion of control they exert over the response. Skinner also inserted an interesting tidbit in Chapter 6 regarding what we mean behaviorally when we talk about the listener's belief in what the speaker says. Skinner wrote, "Our belief in what someone tells us is similarly a function of, or identical with, our tendency to act upon the verbal stimuli which he provides" (p. 160). Thus, we can say that the villagers initially believed the little boy when he cried wolf because they ran out to protect the boy and the village from the wolf. However, they ceased to believe the little boy after finding no wolf, such that when there really was a wolf, the villagers did not run outside to protect the boy. It is important for practitioners to understand these special measures of generalized and non-generalized reinforcement so that they can prevent too much distortion of stimulus control over the verbal behavior of their clients.

I have already mentioned Skinner's use of the term *audience* to refer to the discriminative effects on the speaker's verbal behavior by the presence of a listener. Skinner discussed different kinds of audiences that control (i.e., evoke) subdivisions of verbal behavior in Chapter 7. For example, the largest subdivisions of verbal behavior—the languages we speak (e.g., French, Swahili, Spanish)—are controlled by audiences that reinforce speaking those languages. But there are also smaller subdivisions of verbal behavior controlled by more specific audiences, such as the audience of behavior analysts who reinforce and, therefore, become discriminative for speaking using behavior-analytic terminology. Of course, the smallest subdivision of verbal behavior controlled by an audience is our own self-talk, which is automatically reinforced and, therefore, comes under the control of ourselves as listeners. In other words, we act as our own listeners. Skinner concluded the chapter on the audience with a theoretical gem of analysis: If we define the audience as an S^D for verbal behavior, then other stimuli, such as a location (e.g., a particular classroom where verbal behavior has been reinforced), may also exert discriminative control over a speaker's verbal behavior. Thus, when students enter a classroom where they have taken a class on behavior analysis, the probability of talking about behavior analysis increases. And most mind-blowing of all, our own verbal behavior comes to exert stimulus control over subsequent verbal responses. Skinner wrote, "Since responses seldom occur singly, early parts of a segment of [verbal] behavior generate stimuli at the time of emission of later parts" (p. 182). In other words, what we say at one point will exert stimulus control over what we say at later points. These analyses follow in a straightforward manner from a basic understanding of operant learning.

Finally, Skinner devoted Chapter 8 to a discussion of "The Verbal Operant as a Unit of Analysis." When behavior analysts talk about the operant as a unit of analysis, they mean

> the smallest functional relation that displays order. In behavior analysis, the most fundamental unit is a functional relation between three events: a motivational variable or EO, a class of behavior, and a consequence, for example, a reinforcer. This functional relation is called a contingency, where "contingency" refers to the functional relation between the three events.
>
> (Schlinger, 1995, pp. 33–34)

Adding an S^D expands the contingency or relation to four events, sometimes called a four-term contingency. In the second half of Chapter 8, Skinner described the behavioral processes relevant to understanding verbal behavior (e.g., conditioning, extinction, motivation, and emotion [the latter two of which would nowadays be considered as MOs]) and included a section on variables that cause verbal behavior to stop. He concluded the chapter with his refined definition of verbal behavior, which I addressed previously.

However, at the beginning of the chapter, Skinner discussed issues important to the ABA practitioner regarding the same word (i.e., response form) in different verbal operants. For example, the response "water" can be a mand (evoked by the EO of water deprivation and a listener, of course, who reinforces the form with water), a tact (evoked by the sight of a glass of water and a listener who reinforces the form with attention), a textual response (evoked by seeing the printed word WATER and a listener who reinforces the form with attention), an echoic (evoked by hearing someone say, "water" and a listener who reinforces the form with attention), or an intraverbal (evoked by the question, "What is in a swimming pool?" and a listener who reinforces the form with attention). Traditionally, one would say that the word "water" has one meaning: water. Skinner's functional approach, however, identifies the meaning of the response form according to the controlling variable (i.e., EO or S^D) and, thus, does away with the concept of meaning altogether. This implication is good for practitioners because it enables them to focus on what is needed to teach these similar response forms under all the possible evoking circumstances, as well as to analyze and correct learner errors.

It is in the section on the same response form evoked by different variables that Skinner addressed a particularly important point for practitioners, namely, whether teaching one verbal operant (e.g., a tact) automatically transfers to another verbal operant (e.g., a mand). For example, if we teach a child to tact, "cup," would they then automatically be able to mand for a cup? A traditional account of language that claims we learn words and can then use them for differ-ent purposes would suggest that such transfer occurs. Behaviorally, this would be called functional interdependence of verbal operants (see Fryling, 2017). However, this may not always be the case. So, the question is whether and under what circumstances there is functional independence as opposed to functional interdependence. Some research has shown the functional independence of ver-bal operants (e.g., Lamarre & Holland, 1985); other research has been equivo-cal (e.g., Gamba et al., 2015). For present purposes, the question is: What are the necessary and sufficient prerequisite skills for functional interdependence of verbal operants? Skinner suggested a possible mechanism. Suppose a child with a sufficient repertoire sees a snow cone and mands, "What is that?" When told, "This is a snow cone," the child echoes, "snow cone" in the presence of the snow cone, then says, "Buy me a snow cone" and gets the snow cone. Of course, as a result of this interaction, the child can also tact, "snow cone" in the presence of one. The child may never have said, "Buy me a snow cone," and subsequently contacted reinforcement, but they have contacted reinforcement for saying, "Buy me ___." The response "snow cone" as the variable part of the frame "Buy me__" was acquired as a result of echoing the speaker (see also Petursdottir et al., 2005), receiving either automatic or social reinforcement from the speaker for a correct echoic, and then getting the snow cone. Thus, the tact and the mand are acquired within the same learning trial. It would therefore be incorrect to say that the tact or the mand "emerged" because both were directly, although not explicitly, reinforced. Skinner also noted that "the events which reinforce a mand often resemble the discriminative stimuli which control a tact" and "that the presence of the reinforcing object is an optimal condition for reinforcement" (p. 189) of the mand. Thus, the snow cone, which reinforces the mand, "Buy me a snow cone," is the same one that is the S^D for tacting, "snow cone," and the child is more likely to get the snow cone when one is present.

Skinner's functional analysis of language (verbal behavior) suggests that practitioners need to be thoughtful and organized about the way they plan and organize verbal behavior assessment and teaching trials to ensure that they are evaluating and teaching verbal behavior under the appropriate conditions. Doing this contributes to more naturalistic verbal behavior and to the maintenance and generalization of verbal behavior as well.

Conclusion

In this chapter, I have only barely scratched the surface of Skinner's magnum opus, *VB*. But I have tried to cover the theoretical foundations of the more extensive and detailed analysis, which he presented in the remainder of the book and on which others have expanded in the years since it was published. I have also tried to suggest the practical implications for practitioners when pos-sible. To repeat what Skinner wrote at the end of Chapter 1, "The formulation is inherently practical and suggests immediate technological applications at almost every step" (p. 12). This is because the analysis, complicated as it is at times, is based only on stimuli and responses in the four-term contingency, which are, for the most part, observable. This feature is also what makes Skinner's analysis both elegant and parsimonious. Approaches based on Skinner's analysis in *VB* have shown remarkable success in teaching learners with ASD and related disorders, and there is much empirical support for the approach. Carr and Firth (2005) called for more empirical support for what we may term the "verbal behavior approach." And even though such support has grown since then, more is surely needed. The present book goes a long way toward summarizing the current state of that approach broadly defined.

Skinner made numerous significant contributions to the analysis of behavior, including his discoveries of (a) rate of response as a sensitive dependent variable, (b) reinforcement, (c) extinction, (d) stimulus control, (e) schedules of reinforcement, (f) shaping, and (g) chaining, among other important concepts and procedures. So, it might be surprising to learn that he believed his most important contribution was his analysis of verbal behavior presented in *VB* (Skinner, 1977). The book has generated its share of controversy both within and outside the field of behavior analysis (see Schlinger, 2008b, 2010). But it has also spawned a great deal of further research, theorizing, and practical applications. I expect it will continue to do so, as evidenced by the current book.

Notes

1 For those interested in more of the Chomsky-Skinner debate, see Czubaroff (1988), Gudmundsson (2018), Palmer (1986, 2000, 2006), Richelle et al. (1976), Schlinger (2017a), Stemmer (1990), and Virués-Ortega (2006)

2 We should change "other persons" in Skinner's definition to "others" because non-verbal organisms can also function as listeners, as when, for example, you teach your cat to give you her paw by saying "Give me your paw." By giving you her paw, she is reinforcing your verbal behavior (mand), which you had to condition her precisely to do.

3 An EO is a type of motivating operation (MO), which evokes a response because similar responses have been reinforced when that EO has been present. For example, if a parent has given a child some type of food when the child cries because she is hungry (i.e., reinforced the crying), the next time she is hungry for that type of food, we would predict she would cry; that is, the hunger will evoke crying. See Chapter 4 in this volume for a more thorough description of MOs with respect to mands.

4 This type of multiple control, where two or more variables combine to evoke a single response, has been called convergent (vs. divergent) multiple control in which one variable controls two or more responses (Michael et al., 2011). See Chapter 10 in this volume for an extended discussion of multiple control.

5 One does not necessarily have to catch a big fish to attract a lot of generalized conditioned reinforcement. When my son was five, he did get a lot of attention for telling the story of how he caught a piranha in the Rio Negro in the Brazilian Amazon jungle, even though it was a small fish!

References

American Psychiatric Association. (2013). *Diagnostic and statistical manual of mental disorders* (5th ed.). https://doi.org/10.1176/appi.books.9780890425596

Barbera, M. L. (2007). *The verbal behavior approach: How to teach children with autism and related disorders*. Jessica Kingsley Publishers.

Bickerton, D. (2008). Syntax for non-syntacticians: A primer. In D. Bickerton & E. Szathmáry (Eds.), *Biological foundations and origins of syntax*. The MIT Press.

Blakely, E. (2021). *Verbal behavior: Extended edition: Study guide*. B. F. Skinner Foundation.

Brodhead, M. T., Higbee, T. S., Gerencser, K. R., & Akers, J. S. (2016). The use of a discrimination-training procedure to teach mand variability to children with autism. *Journal of Applied Behavior Analysis*, *49*(1), 34–48.

Carnett, A., Waddington, H., Hansen, S., Bravo, A., Sigafoos, J., & Lang, R. (2017). Teaching mands to children with autism spectrum disorder using behavior chain interruption strategies: A systematic review. *Advances in Neurodevelopmental Disorders*, *1*, 203–220.

Carr, J. E., & Firth, A. M. (2005). The verbal behavior approach to early and intensive behavioral intervention for autism: A call for additional empirical support. *Journal of Early and Intensive Behavior Intervention*, *2*(1), 18–27.

Castles, A., Rastle, K., & Nation, K. (2018). Ending the reading wars: Reading acquisition from novice to expert. *Psychological Science in the Public Interest*, *19*(1), 5–51. https://doi.org/10.1177/1529100618772271

Cividini-Motta, C., Scharrer, N., & Ahearn, W. H. (2017). An assessment of three procedures to teach echoic responding. *The Analysis of Verbal Behavior*, *33*, 41–63.

Czubaroff, J. (1988). Criticism and response in the Skinner controversies. *Journal of the Experimental Analysis of Behavior*, *49*(2), 321–329.

Drash, P. W., High, R. L., & Tudor, R. M. (1999). Using mand training to establish an echoic repertoire in young children with autism. *The Analysis of Verbal Behavior*, *16*, 29–44.

Eikeseth, S., & Smith, D. P. (2013). An analysis of verbal stimulus control in intraverbal behavior: Implications for practice and applied research. *The Analysis of Verbal Behavior*, *29*, 125–135.

Esch, B. E. (2023). *Early echoic skills assessment and program planner, Guide and Protocol*. Different Roads to Learning.

Fryling, M. J. (2017). The functional independence of Skinner's verbal operants: Conceptual and applied implications. *Behavioral Interventions*, *32*(1), 70–78.

Gamba, J., Goyos, C., & Petursdottir, A. I. (2015). The functional independence of mands and tacts: Has it been demonstrated empirically?. *The Analysis of Verbal Behavior*, *31*, 10–38.

Goetz, L., Gee, K., & Sailor, W. (1985). Using a behavior chain interruption strategy to teach communication skills to students with severe disabilities. *Journal of the Association for Persons with Severe Handicaps*, *10*(1), 21–30.

Goldsmith, T. R., LeBlanc, L. A., & Sautter, R. A. (2007). Teaching intraverbal behavior to children with autism. *Research in Autism Spectrum Disorders*, *1*(1), 1–13.

Greer, R. D., & Ross, D. E. (2004). Verbal behavior analysis: A program of research in the induction and expansion of complex verbal behavior. *Journal of Early and Intensive Behavior Intervention, 1*(2), 141–165.

Greer, R. D., & Ross, D. E. (2008). *Verbal behavior analysis: Inducing and expanding new verbal capabilities in children with language delays.* Pearson.

Gudmundsson, K. (2018). The Skinner-Chomsky debate. *Behavior and Philosophy, 46,* 1–24.

Hayes, S. C. (1994). Relational frame theory: A functional approach to verbal events. In S. C. Hayes, L. J. Hayes, M. Sato, & K. Ono (Eds.), *Behavior analysis of language and cognition* (pp. 9–30). Context Press.

Hayes, S. C., Blackledge, J. T., & Barnes-Holmes, D. (2001). Language and cognition: Constructing an alternative approach within the behavioral tradition. In S. C. Hayes, D. Barnes-Holmes, & B. Roche (Eds.), *Relational frame theory: A post-Skinnerian account of human language and cognition* (pp. 3–20). Kluwer Academic/Plenum.

Horne, P. J., & Lowe, C. F. (1996). On the origins of naming and other symbolic behavior. *Journal of the Experimental Analysis of Behavior, 65*(1), 185–241. https://doi.org/10.1901/jeab.1996.65-185

Howlett, M. A., Sidener, T. M., Progar, P. R., & Sidener, D. W. (2011). Manipulation of motivating operations and use of a script-fading procedure to teach mands for location to children with language delays. *Journal of Applied Behavior Analysis, 44*(4), 943–947.

Hunt, M. (1982). *The universe within: A new science explores the human mind.* Touchstone.

Jeynes, W. H. (2008). A meta-analysis of the relationship between phonics instruction and minority elementary school student academic achievement. *Education and Urban Society, 40*(2), 151–166. https://doi.org/10.1177/0013124507304128

Knapp, T. J. (1992). *Verbal behavior*: The other reviews. *The Analysis of Verbal Behavior, 10,* 87–95.

LaFrance, D. L., & Miguel, C. F. (2014). Teaching verbal behavior to children with autism spectrum disorders. In J. Tarbox, D. R. Dixon, P. Sturmey, & J. L. Matson (Eds.), *Handbook of early intervention for autism spectrum disorders: Research, policy, and practice* (pp. 315–340). Springer.

Lakoff, G. (1995). In conversation with John Goldsmith. In G. J. Huck & J. A. Goldsmith (Eds.), *Ideology and linguistic theory* (pp. 107–119). Routledge.

Lamarre, J., & Holland, J. G. (1985). The functional independence of mands and tacts. *Journal of the Experimental Analysis of Behavior, 43*(1), 5–19.

Lechago, S. A., Carr, J. E., Grow, L. L., Love, J. R., & Almason, S. M. (2010). Mands for information generalize across establishing operations. *Journal of Applied Behavior Analysis, 43*(3), 381–395.

Leigland, S. (1997). Is a new definition of verbal behavior necessary in light of derived relational responding? *The Behavior Analyst, 20,* 3–9.

MacCorquodale, K. (1970). On Chomsky's review of Skinner's Verbal behavior. *Journal of the Experimental Analysis of Behavior, 13*(1), 83–99.

Michael, J. (1982). Skinner's elementary verbal relations: Some new categories. *The Analysis of Verbal Behavior, 1,* 1–3

Michael, J., Palmer, D. C., & Sundberg, M. L. (2011). The multiple control of verbal behavior. *The Analysis of Verbal Behavior, 27*, 3–22.

Miller, G. A. (2003). The cognitive revolution: A historical perspective. *Trends in Cognitive Sciences, 7*(3), 141–144.

Normand, M. P. (2009). Much ado about nothing? Some comments on BF Skinner's definition of verbal behavior. *The Behavior Analyst, 32*, 185–190.

Oah, S. Z., & Dickinson, A. M. (1989). A review of empirical studies of verbal behavior. *The Analysis of Verbal Behavior, 7*, 53–68.

Palmer, D. C. (1986). Chomsky's nativism: A critical review. In P. N. Chase & L. J. Parrott (Eds.), *Psychological aspects of language* (pp. 44–60). Thomas.

Palmer, D. C. (1991). A behavioral interpretation of memory. In L. J. Hayes & P. N. Chase (Eds.), *Dialogues on verbal behavior* (pp. 261–279). Context Press.

Palmer, D. C. (1996). Achieving parity: The role of automatic reinforcement. *Journal of the Experimental Analysis of Behavior, 65*(1), 289–290.

Palmer, D. C. (2000). Chomsky's nativism reconsidered. *The Analysis of Verbal Behavior, 17*, 51–56.

Palmer, D. C. (2005). Ernst Moerk and the puzzle of zero-trial learning. *The Analysis of Verbal Behavior, 21*(1), 9–12.

Palmer, D. C. (2006). On Chomsky's appraisal of Skinner's Verbal behavior: A half century of misunderstanding. *The Behavior Analyst, 29*, 253–267.

Palmer, D. C. (2007). Verbal behavior: What is the function of structure? *European Journal of Behavior Analysis, 8*, 161–175.

Palmer, D. C. (2008). On Skinner's definition of verbal behavior. *International Journal of Psychology and Psychological Therapy, 8*, 295–307.

Palmer, D. C. (2016). On intraverbal control and the definition of the intraverbal. *The Analysis of Verbal Behavior, 32*, 96–106.

Partington, J. W., & Bailey, J. S. (1993). Teaching intraverbal behavior to preschool children. *The Analysis of Verbal Behavior, 11*, 9–18.

Partington, J. W. (2006). The assessment of basic language and learning skills-revised. Pleasant Hill, CA: Behavior Analysts.

Petursdottir, A. I. (2018). The current status of the experimental analysis of verbal behavior. *Behavior Analysis: Research and Practice, 18*(2), 151–168.

Petursdottir, A. I., Carr, J. E., & Michael, J. (2005). Emergence of mands and tacts of novel objects among preschool children. *The Analysis of Verbal Behavior, 21*, 59–74.

Petursdottir, A. I., & Devine, B. (2017). The impact of verbal behavior on the scholarly literature from 2005 to 2016. *The Analysis of Verbal Behavior, 33*, 212–228.

Pléh, C. (2019). The inspirational role of Chomsky in the cognitive turn of psychology. *Acta Linguistica Academica. An International Journal of Linguistics (Until 2016 Acta Linguistica Hungarica), 66*(3), 397–428.

Postal, P. M. (1995). In conversation with John Goldsmith. In G. J. Huck & J. A. Goldsmith (Eds.), *Ideology and linguistic theory* (pp. 107–119). Routledge.

Richelle, M., Foster, W. S., & Rondal, J. A. (1976). Formal analysis and functional analysis of verbal behavior: Notes on the debate between Chomsky and Skinner. *Behaviorism, 4*(2), 209–221.

Roediger, R. (2004, March). What happened to behaviorism? *APS Observer.*

Sautter, R. A., & LeBlanc, L. A. (2006). Empirical applications of Skinner's analysis of verbal behavior with humans. *The Analysis of Verbal Behavior, 22*, 35–48.

Schlinger, H. D. (1995). *A behavior-analytic view of child development*. Plenum.

Schlinger, H. D. (2008a). Consciousness is nothing but a word. *Skeptic, 13*, 58–63.

Schlinger, H. D. (2008b). The long goodbye: Why B. F. Skinner's *Verbal Behavior* is alive and well on the 50th anniversary of its publication. *The Psychological Record, 58*, 329–337.

Schlinger, H. D. (2008c). Listening is behaving verbally. *The Behavior Analyst, 31*, 145–161.

Schlinger, H. D. (2008d). Conditioning the behavior of the listener. *International Journal of Psychology and Psychotherapy, 8*, 309–322.

Schlinger, H. D. (2009). Some clarifications on the role of inner speech in consciousness. *Consciousness and Cognition, 18*, 530–531.

Schlinger, H. D. (2010). The impact of Skinner's Verbal behavior: A response to Dymond and Alonso-Alvarez. *The Psychological Record, 60*, 361–368.

Schlinger, H. D. (2013). A functional analysis of psychological terms redux. *The Behavior Analyst, 36*(2), 255–266. https://doi.org/10.1007/BF03392312.

Schlinger, H. D. (2017a). Reflections on *Verbal Behavior* at 60. *The Analysis of Verbal Behavior, 33*(2), 179–190.

Schlinger, H. D. (2017b). The importance of analysis in applied behavior analysis. *Behavior Analysis: Research and Practice, 17*(4), 334–346. https://doi.org/10.1037/bar0000080

Schlinger, H. D. (2018). The heterodoxy of behavior analysis. *Archives of Scientific Psychology, 6*, 159–168. https://doi.org/10.1037/arc0000051

Schlinger, H. D. (2023). Contrasting accounts of early speech perception and production. *Perspectives on Behavior Science, 46*(3–4), 561–583. https://doi.org/10.1007/s40614-023-00371-4

Schlinger, H. D., & Blakely, E. (2024). A mediational theory of equivalence relations and transformation of function. *Journal of the Experimental Analysis of Behavior*, 1–17. https://doi.org/10.1002/jeab.4204

Shafer, E. (1995). A review of interventions to teach a mand repertoire. *The Analysis of Verbal Behavior, 12*, 53–66.

Skinner, B. F. (1935). The generic nature of the concepts of stimulus and response. *The Journal of General Psychology, 12*(1), 40–65.

Skinner, B. F. (1938). *The behavior of organisms: An experimental analysis*. Appleton-Century and Macmillan.

Skinner, B. F. (1945). The operational analysis of psychological terms. *Psychological Review, 52*(5), 270–277.

Skinner, B. F. (1953). *Science and human behavior*. Macmillan.

Skinner, B. F. (1957). *Verbal behavior*. Appleton-Century-Crofts.

Skinner, B. F. (1972). A lecture on "having a poem". In B. F. Skinner (Ed.), *Cumulative record: A selection of papers* (pp. 345–355). Appleton-Century-Crofts

Skinner, B. F. (1977). The experimental analysis of operant behavior. *Annals of the New York Academy of Sciences, 291*(1), 374–385.

Stemmer, N. (1990). Skinner's verbal behavior, Chomsky's review, and mentalism. *Journal of the Experimental Analysis of Behavior, 54*(3), 307–315.

Sundberg, M. L. (2008). *Verbal behavior milestones assessment and placement program: The VB-MAPP*. AVB Press.

Sundberg, M. L. (2015). The most important verbal operant. *VB News, 14*(2), 3–5.

Sundberg, M. L., Loeb, M., Hale, L., Eigenheer, P., Behavior Analysts, Inc., & STARS School. (2001). Contriving establishing operations to teach mands for information. *The Analysis of Verbal Behavior, 18*(1), 15–29.

Sundberg, M. L., & Michael, J. (2001). The benefits of Skinner's analysis of verbal behavior for children with autism. *Behavior Modification, 25*(5), 698–724.

Sundberg, M. L., Michael, J., Partington, J. W., & Sundberg, C. A. (1996). The role of automatic reinforcement in early language acquisition. *The Analysis of Verbal Behavior, 13*, 21–37.

Sundberg, M. L., & Sundberg, C. A. (2011). Intraverbal behavior and verbal conditional discriminations in typically developing children and children with autism. *The Analysis of Verbal Behavior, 27*, 23–44.

Tomasello, M. (2009). The usage-based theory of language acquisition. In E. L. Bavin (Ed.), *The Cambridge handbook of child language* (pp. 69–87). Cambridge University Press. https://doi.org/10.1017/CBO9780511576164.005

Valentino, A. L., Shillingsburg, M. A., & Call, N. A. (2012). Comparing the effects of echoic prompts and echoic prompts plus modeled prompts on intraverbal behavior. *Journal of Applied Behavior Analysis, 45*(2), 431–435.

Vaughan, M. E., & Michael, J. L. (1982). Automatic reinforcement: An important but ignored concept. *Behaviorism, 10*(2), 217–227.

Virués-Ortega, J. (2006). The case against B. F. Skinner 45 years later: An encounter with N. Chomsky. *The Behavior Analyst, 29*, 243–251.

Watkins, C. L. (1997). *Project follow through*. Cambridge Center for Behavioral Studies.

Chapter 2

Assessment of Verbal Behavior Repertoires

Judah B. Axe, Serena Cates, Chuelsia Carvalho, Sarah B. Costa, and Bruce A. Tinor

The major goal of intervention derived from applied behavior analysis (ABA) is to improve the social-communication skills of individuals with autism spectrum disorder (ASD) and related developmental disabilities to provide them with the potential to meaningfully interact with others and lead fulfilling lives (Leaf et al., 2021; Schwartz & Kelly, 2021). Skinner's (1957) analysis of verbal behavior (see Chapter 1 in this volume) has augmented this goal by offering functional definitions and classifications of common communication skills, as well as many unique instructional procedures (DeSouza et al., 2017; LaFrance & Miguel, 2014; Sundberg & Michael, 2001). However, before delving into instruction, one must assess the extent of a learner's verbal repertoire (Gould et al., 2011). A verbal behavior assessment should target the range of verbal skills such as mands, tacts, intraverbals, reading, writing, and socialization. A verbal behavior assessment allows a behavior analyst to (a) identify the learner's strengths and (b) identify gaps in their verbal behavior repertoire. Once these strengths and gaps are identified, the behavior analyst can set learning goals. It is at that point that teaching may begin. Follow-up assessments are conducted to measure progress.

Before 2000, the Vineland Adaptive Behavior Scales (VABS; Sparrow et al., 2016) was the assessment most commonly used by practitioners who were implementing behavior-analytic interventions with individuals with ASD (Luiselli et al., 2001). The VABS is a norm-referenced rating scale completed by parents or teachers with technical adequacy data to support its use. It assesses adaptive behavior for individuals from birth to 90 years old across four domains: communication, daily living, socialization, and motor skills. Relevant to the analysis of verbal behavior, items in the receptive communication subdomain range from "Points to at least three major body parts when asked" to "Listens to an information talk for at least 30 minutes." Items in the expressive communication subdomain include: "Repeats or tries to repeat common words immediately upon hearing them," "Uses regular past tense verbs," "Says own telephone number when asked," and "Presents oral reports at least 10 minutes long." These examples illustrate the lack of distinction between echoics (see Chapter 5 in this volume), linguistics/autoclitics, and intraverbals (see Chapter 7 in this volume).

DOI: 10.4324/9781003433668-3

Written communication is an additional subdomain, and the socialization domain contains three subdomains: interpersonal relationships, play and leisure time, and coping skills. In addition to the lack of distinction among the operants, the other major limitation of the VABS, with respect to ABA, is the reliance on verbal report rather than direct observation.

In addition to the VABS, there are a plethora of commercially available standardized language assessments. However, when Esch et al. (2010) examined 28 of these assessments, they found only two targeted mands, though this was through parent/caregiver report. In addition, the language assessments reviewed focused on the form of language, and none examined language from a functional perspective. Further, the authors noted that none of the language assessments included in the review included observing or manipulating motivating operations (MOs) to evaluate the mand repertoire. Similar limitations exist with diagnostic assessments for ASD, such as the Autism Diagnostic Observation Schedule (ADOS; Harris et al., 2014; Lord et al., 2008).

The first assessment based on Skinner's (1957) analysis of verbal behavior, the Assessment of Basic Language and Learning Skills (ABLLS; Partington & Sundberg, 1998), was published in 1998. This was the first assessment to explicitly distinguish among the verbal operants in an effort to assess skill sets related to each. The ABLLS was later revised and updated as the ABLLS-Revised (ABLLS-R; Partington, 2006). Thereafter, the Verbal Behavior Milestones Assessment and Placement Program (VB-MAPP; Sundberg, 2008, 2014) was published.

These Skinnerian-based language assessments have become the go-to for behavior-analytic practitioners. In a survey of 1,428 ABA practitioners, Padilla (2020) found that 76% reported using the VB-MAPP, 45% reported using the ABLLS-R, 34% reported using the VABS, 14% reported using the Promoting the Emergence of Advanced Knowledge (PEAK) Relational Training System (Dixon, 2014), and 5% reported using the Essential for Living (EFL; McGreevy et al., 2012). Given these data, as well as the need for ABA practitioners to effectively and efficiently administer verbal behavior assessments to gather information that should be used to inform teaching goals, the purpose of this chapter is to provide a complete description of the VB-MAPP with two case studies, descriptions of additional verbal behavior assessments with case studies, and conclusions and recommendations for future directions.

Verbal Behavior Milestones Assessment and Placement Program (VB-MAPP)

Description of the VB-MAPP

The VB-MAPP is a criterion-referenced assessment, defined as an assessment method to "determine an individual's performance by comparing it to a predetermined criterion or standard for the purpose of making decisions or classifications (e.g., skill level, mastery, proficiency, certification)" (Padilla & Akers, 2021, p. 4055). The VB-MAPP aims to establish a baseline level of performance, use the results to develop intervention goals, and monitor progress.

The VB-MAPP is sequenced based on the developmental milestones that neurotypical children reach and spans neurotypical development from 0–4 years old. This means the assessment is appropriate for young children in that age range. However, it is also relevant for individuals of any age—children, adolescents, and adults—as long as their language skills fall within the typically developing 0–4-year-old level. It is important to note that these age ranges are derived from informal observations of children rather than from rigorous testing subjected to psychometric scrutiny. When assessing older individuals, the materials and examples should be altered to make them more age-appropriate. Milestones, rather than all verbal behavior skills, are used to assess an individual's repertoire relatively quickly. The sequencing of milestones based on neurotypical development implies that the goal of the VB-MAPP is to assess an individual's skills with respect to approximated milestones in neurotypical language development. This sequencing further implies that language interventions are designed for individuals to approach the verbal behavior repertoires of neurotypical children.

The VB-MAPP is comprised of five parts: Milestones Assessment, Barriers Assessment, Transition Assessment, Task Analysis and Skills Tracking Chart, and Curriculum Placement and Individualized Education Plan (IEP) Goals. The Milestones Assessment is broken into three age levels: Level 1 (approximately 0–18 months), Level 2 (approximately 18–30 months), and Level 3 (approximately 30–48 months). There are 16 categories in the Milestones Assessment, ranging from simple vocal play to listener skills, mands, learning in a group, and performing math and reading skills (Table 2.1). In general, each category contains five milestones at each Level (1–3). An example of a Level 1 Mand Milestone is "Emits 4 different mands without prompts (except *What do you want?*)—the desired item may be present." An example of a Level 2 Tact Milestone is "Tacts 50 two-component verb-noun or noun-verb combinations." An example of a Level 3 Intraverbal Milestone is "Describes 25 different events, videos, stories, etc. with 8+ words (e.g., *Tell me what happened...The big monster scared everybody and they all ran into the house*)."

In the Milestones Assessment, the Echoic category is scored using the Early Echoic Skills Assessment (EESA; Esch, 2014). There are five types of echoic skills on the EESA: simple and reduplicated syllables, two-syllable combinations, three-syllable combinations, prosody (emphasis), and prosody (pitch, loudness, and duration). (Readers are also referred to Chapter 5 in this volume for details regarding the expansion of the EESA to the Early Echoic Skills Assessment and Program Planner [Esch, 2023].) The Barriers Assessment

Table 2.1 Milestones and Targets in the Barriers and Transitions Assessments of the VB-MAPP

	Milestones Assessment	Barriers Assessment	Transition Assessment
1	Mand	Negative Behaviors	Milestones Assessment Score
2	Tact	Instructional Control (Escape and Avoidance of Instructions)	Barriers Assessment Score
3	Listener Responding	Absent, Weak, or Defective (AWD) Mand Repertoire	Negative Behaviors, Instructional Control
4	Visual-Perceptual Skills Matching-to-Sample	AWD Tact Repertoire	Classroom Routines, Group Skills
5	Independent Play	AWD Motor Imitation	Social Behavior, Social Play
6	Social Behavior, Social Play	AWD Echoic Repertoire	Independent on Academic Tasks
7	Motor Imitation	AWD Visual-Perceptual Skills and Matching-to-Sample	Generalization across Time, Settings, People
8	Echoic	AWD Listener Repertoires	Range of Items as Reinforcers
9	Spontaneous Vocal Behavior	AWD Intraverbal Repertoire	Rate of Acquiring New Skills
10	Listener Responding by Feature, Function, Class	AWD Social Skills	Retention of New Skills
11	Intraverbal	Prompt Dependent	Learning from the Natural Environment
12	Classroom Routines, Group Skills	Scrolling Responses	Transfers between Verbal Operants w/o Training
13	Linguistic Structure	Defective Scanning Skills	Adaptability to Change
14	Reading	Failure to Make Conditional Discriminations	Spontaneous Behaviors
15	Writing	Failure to Generalize	Self-Directed Play, Leisure Skills
16	Math	Weak or Atypical Motivating Operations (MOs)	General Self-Help Skills
17		Response Requirement Weakens the MO	Toileting Skills
18		Reinforcement Dependent	Eating Skills
19		Self-Stimulation	
20		Articulation Problems	
21		Obsessive-Compulsive Behavior	
22		Hyperactive Behavior	
23		Failure to Make Eye Contact or Attend to People	
24		Sensory Defensiveness	

contains 24 items that examine barriers to effective learning, such as interfering behaviors, problems with skill generalization, and limited motivation. The Transition Assessment contains 18 items regarding skills needed for success in an inclusive educational environment. Some of these skills are social skills, the ability to retain new information, and toileting skills. The Task Analysis and Skills Tracking Chart is used to select teaching goals. It lists 900 skills across 13 skill areas sequenced around the Milestones.

In terms of scoring the Milestones Assessment, a child receives 1 point if they emit the entire milestone, ½ point if they emit around half of the milestone (e.g., 25 tacts in the example above), and 0 points if they do not display the repertoire of the milestone. For the Barriers Assessment, the child is scored on a scale from 0–4 depending on the severity of the barrier (0 = "no problem;" 4 = "severe problem"). The Transition Assessment is scored on a scale from 1–5 depending on the degree of skill/repertoire with each item (1 = low level of the skill; 5 = extensive repertoire with respect to the skill). Finally, each of the 900 skills in the Task Analysis might be filled in if the child can exhibit the skill. For the Milestones, Barriers, and Transition Assessment, there is space for four administrations of the assessments; a child may be reassessed every 6–12 months. Scores for each administration can be filled in with different colors for easy viewing of progress over time.

Administering the VB-MAPP

"The VB-MAPP brings together the procedures and teaching methodology of ABA and Skinner's analysis of verbal behavior in an effort to provide a behaviorally based language assessment program for all children with language delays" (Sundberg, 2014, p. 1). To administer the VB-MAPP, the assessor should have four key repertoires. First, the assessor should be well-versed in the concepts, principles, and intervention strategies frequently used in ABA, including reinforcement, motivating operations, shaping, and chaining. Second, the assessor should have knowledge of Skinner's analysis of verbal behavior, including functional definitions of language, mands, tacts, intraverbals, echoics, and other aspects of verbal behavior. Esch et al. (2010) thoroughly explained approaching assessment using a functional analysis of language. Third, the assessor should have a background in linguistics, such as prefixes, suffixes, affixes, and prosody. Finally, the assessor should have a background in augmentative and alternative communication (AAC; see also Chapter 11 in this volume) as the VB-MAPP references sign language and the Picture Exchange Communication System (PECS; Bondy & Frost, 1994). For example, the first Mand Milestone is "Emits 2 words, signs, or PECS…"

Administering the VB-MAPP is different from administering many norm-referenced assessments. For context, norm-referenced tests are standardized tests in that each administration is completed in a specified fashion. The reason is that norm-referenced tests are used to compare a test taker's performance to some norm group (e.g., same-aged peers)—this requires the test to be administered the same way across all individuals. In contrast, criterion-referenced tests, like the VB-MAPP, do not provide a means for comparison to some norm group, only to some criterion. Therefore, there is no set way to administer the VB-MAPP. To illustrate this, when the VB-MAPP is administered in schools, multiple members of a child's educational team may conduct the Milestones, Barriers, and Transition assessments. For example, the behavior analyst might evaluate most skills, particularly Mands, Matching-to-sample, and Negative Behaviors. The teacher may complete the sections on Classroom Routines and Group Skills, Reading, Math, Instructional Control, and Works Independently on Academic Tasks. The speech/language pathologist may complete the Tacts, Listener Responding, Echoics, Linguistic Structure, and Articulation Problems sections. Finally, the occupational therapist may focus on Writing, Sensory Defensiveness, Self-Help Skills, and Eating Skills.

Another way the VB-MAPP is administered differently from norm-referenced tests is that the assessor does not need to administer the items in order, and not all items are directly tested. Some items may be scored by examining other related, reliable, valid, and recent assessments, as well as data recordings of a child's repertoires. A familiar person's report about a skill area, with some verification, may be a starting point for scoring certain skills. For example, if a parent reports that their child mands for around 20 items per day, the assessor may have the parent write the child's mands down and briefly observe some of them. The assessor may then give a score of 1 for all five Mand skills in Level 1. If an educational team reports that a child almost never makes eye contact, the assessor might briefly observe and then mark a score of 4 on that Barrier item.

Assessors can use the concept of a "floor," in which all items that come earlier in the assessment domain than a correctly scored item may be scored as correct. Assessors may also use the concept of a "ceiling." That is, if a child scores a 0 on three consecutive milestones, the assessor may score the rest of the milestones as 0. However, it is important to consider higher-level milestones and perhaps test some, as many children with ASD perform skills out of sequence. For example, a child might have mastered "Politely mands to stop an undesirable activity" (Level 3) before mastering "Spontaneously emits 15 different mands" (Level 2).

When looking at the 170 milestones and directly testing many of those milestones, the VB-MAPP can seem overwhelming and take many days, or even weeks, to administer. However, the VB-MAPP was designed to be administered quickly and efficiently. Although research is lacking research validating administration and scoring methodologies are lacking, the VB-MAPP recommends a set of guidelines. The behavior analyst might first meet with the parents and educational team and fill in as much information as possible, especially below the "floor" and above the "ceiling." Many skills in the VB-MAPP are scored by observing the child in a natural environment, including mands, vocal behavior, play, social skills, group skills, negative behaviors, self-stimulation, eye contact, learning from the natural environment, adaptability to change, and eating skills. Of course, many skills near the child's "operant level," or where they are functioning, need to be directly tested. The milestones contain codes indicating if they should be directly tested, tested through observation, tested through either direct testing or observation, or "timed observation." Examples of milestones with timed observations are "Shows variation in play..." (30 minutes) and "Spontaneously mands to peers with a WH question 5 times" (60 minutes).

The VB-MAPP manual contains several additional tips for direct testing. The assessor should provide positive reinforcement during testing by administering a reinforcer survey or preference assessment, conducting pre-session pairing with reinforcement to build rapport and trust, delivering reinforcement for reasonable attempts at responding, and providing reinforcement contingent on correct responses. The latter is not a concern, as individuals with significant language delays often require many sessions to gain new language skills. In keeping with a basic principle of verbal behavior, the assessor should accept approximations of responses as long as they are functional (i.e., "function over form;" Sundberg, 2020). For example, if a child says "kee-kee" when they see a cookie and not when they see other items, that utterance should be considered correct for tacting or manding for a cookie.

Assessors should note children's errors and approximations, as analyzing errors often suggests teaching objectives (Esch et al., 2010). For example, Tact Milestone 11 (Level 3) is

> Tacts the color, shape, and function of 5 objects (15 trials) when each object and question is presented in a mixed order (e.g., *What color is the refrigerator? What shape is the valentine? What do you do with the ball?*) (This is part tact and part intraverbal).

If a child answers those example questions with "food," "love," and "throw," the third one is correct, but the first two suggest the child's responses are only under control of the final word and not the other words in the question. This represents a failure to emit verbal conditional discriminations (a barrier; Axe, 2008) and may be remedied by requiring echoics to ensure that all relevant words control the child's response (e.g., *color* AND *refrigerator, shape* AND *valentine*; Kisamore et al., 2016; Meleshkevich et al., 2021).

Additional testing guidelines outlined in the VB-MAPP manual include continuously interspersing opportunities to mand for reinforcers among other types of trials. Therefore, assessors need to carefully observe the child's behavior, which might reveal the presence of MOs or shifts in MOs. Assessors should use age-appropriate materials, not prompt responses, request a skill two to three times to ensure the child cannot emit it, provide breaks, and make testing fun! Supplementary materials, other resources, and updates are provided on the VB-MAPP website (avbpress.com), and materials for the VB-MAPP and similar assessments (described below) are available through Different Roads to Learning (https://difflearn.com/).

Following are two case studies on administering the VB-MAPP with children with ASD: Luca, who demonstrated zero milestones, and Jasmine, who scored in the middle of Level 3. It is important to note that given the limited repertoires of a child like Luca, there is little to report regarding the VB-MAPP. On the other hand, Jasmine's case contains richer reporting on the levels of her skills and the areas where she has gaps.

Case Study 1: VB-MAPP

Luca is a sweet 5-year-old boy with a rare genetic disorder that severely limits his communication and adaptive skills. He lives with his parents and attends a substantially separate classroom for children with a range of developmental disabilities in a public school. He receives speech, occupational, and physical therapies. Luca scored a 0 on the Milestones Assessment because he had no mands, tacts, imitation, echoics, matching, or other skills. He scored high (74) on the Barriers Assessment, with all items scored as a "severe problem" except negative behaviors, escape/avoid instructional demands, scrolling, self-stimulation, obsessive-compulsive behavior, hyperactive behavior, and sensory defensiveness. On the Transition Assessment, Luca scored relatively low (22) with all 1s (most limited demonstration of the skill) except negative behaviors and adaptability to change.

A score of 0 on the Milestones Assessment suggests Luca might be missing skills that developmentally precede the first milestones. Therefore, the Task Analysis was extremely helpful in generating teaching objectives for Luca because it contains skills at lower levels than the first milestones. See Table 2.2 for sample objectives generated for Luca. A significant outcome for Luca was that his team contrived MOs for his favorite food—pickles—by holding them in view and out of reach (Frampton et al., 2024) and taught him to mand by exchanging an icon to receive a piece of pickle.

Case Study 2: VB-MAPP

Jasmine is a bright, happy 4-year-old girl who enjoys looking at books, doing puzzles, watching videos, and playing with her cat. She lives with her parents and attends an early childhood school 5 days per week. When she was 3 years old, she was diagnosed with Pervasive Developmental Disorder-Not Otherwise Specified. She receives occupational therapy two hours per week, and although she presents delays in social skills, she plays well with her peers and interacts socially with adults. The assessor interviewed Jasmine's mom, observed her in her preschool, and directly tested many skills.

On the Milestones Assessment, Jasmine had a total score of 138.5. She performed all Level 1 and Level 2 skills, and some Level 3 skills, placing her language and learning skills in Level 3 (approximately 30–48 months). One of Jasmine's strengths was tacting, as she tacted at the highest levels on the VB-MAPP, including tacting with complete sentences with four or more words and having a tacting repertoire of over 1000 words. A gap in Jasmine's tacting repertoire was tacting using prepositions and pronouns. Another strength was math, as Jasmine's mother reported that Jasmine could count to 29, count out 1–5 objects from a larger set, and match a numeral to a quantity and vice versa. One gap in math was tacting using comparative words, such as long, short, full, and empty. Two other areas of strength for Jasmine were independent play and reading. Jasmine independently played with arts and crafts activities and other toys and activities for 10 minutes or more without adult prompts. A gap in this area was sustained independent engagement with pre-academic activities, such as matching worksheets and tracing letters and numbers. With reading, Jasmine read all letters of the alphabet and her name. She did not match a printed word to a corresponding picture and vice versa.

Table 2.2 Sample Goals for Luca from the Task Analysis of the VB-MAPP

Goals for Luca	
Mand 1-a	Makes eye contact as a mand for attention or other reinforcers
Mand 1-d	Points or gestures toward a reinforcer in order to obtain it 2 times
Mand 1-M	Emits 2 mands using PECS with prompts
LR 2-M	Responds to hearing his own name 5 times (e.g., looks at the speaker)
LR 3-f	Discriminates between 2 objects when they are presented at eye level
VPS 1-M	Visually tracks a moving object for 2 seconds
VPS 2-b	Uses index finger to poke things or for other uses 5 times
VPS 4-M	Places 3 items in a container, stacks 3 blocks, or places 3 rings on a peg for 2 of these or similar activities
VPS 5-d	Attempts to scribble with any writing instrument
VPS 5-M	Matches 5 identical objects (1/2 of milestone)
Play 1-c	Transfers items from one hand to another
Play 1-d	Looks at a toy when it is picked up by an adult
Imitation 1-M	Imitates 2 gross motor movements when prompted with, "Do this"
Imitation 2-a	Imitates 2 actions with an object (e.g., pounding with a toy hammer, rolling at a ball)
Echoic 1-M	Vocally imitates simple 1- and 2-syllable sounds (e.g., ah, baba, oo)

Jasmine performed moderately in listener responding and visual performance. She emitted many listener responses but struggled with prepositions and pronouns. She had difficulty following 3-step directions. She emitted many Listener responding by feature, function, class (LRFFC) skills, though she struggled with more complex questions (e.g., "Which fruit grows on trees?"). Jasmine matched many items in varying combinations and completed puzzles, but she did not sort objects based on their categories (e.g., clothes, animals, furniture).

Four areas of relative difficulty related to Jasmine's social skills were mands, social skills, intraverbals, and performing in a group. Jasmine manded fluently, spontaneously, and with complex language structures, but she did not emit social mands, such as asking peers, "What's your name?" and "What do you want to play?" Jasmine also did not mand using adjectives, prepositions, or adverbs. Regarding social skills, she engaged with peers in pretend play for at least 5 minutes without adult prompts, but she did not socially initiate or respond to peers. Jasmine had many strong intraverbal skills but did not answer questions after being read a short passage or describe previous events with at least eight words. In a group, Jasmine responded to whole-group instructions but did not work independently for 5 minutes on academic tasks or learn two new behaviors in a 15-minute group activity. In terms of writing, Jasmine imitated at least five writing actions and traced some shapes, though she did not copy letters or numbers or spell her name without copying. With linguistic structure, Jasmine used plurals and possessive forms and exhibited difficulty with tenses and pronouns.

On the Barriers Assessment, Jasmine scored 14.5. Out of 24 barriers, 13 were not a concern for her. Four barriers scored as "moderate problem" were behavior problems (dropping, screaming, and intentionally bumping her head), problems with instructional control (not immediately complying with adult requests), delays in social skills (limited verbal interactions with peers), and delays in eye contact. Seven barriers were rated as "occasional problem": intraverbal, scanning visual stimuli, verbal discriminations, motivational problems with demands, dependence on external reinforcers, obsessive-compulsive behavior, and sensory defectiveness. On the Transition Assessment, Jasmine scored a total of 75. She scored a 5 (full demonstration of the skill) for skill generalization and retaining new skills, learning new skills quickly, learning from the natural environment, self-directed leisure time, and eating. She scored a 4 on spontaneous behavior and self-help skills and a 3 on negative behavior, group skills, range of reinforcers, adaptability to change, and toileting.

Based on these Milestones, Barriers, and Transition Assessment results, the assessor recommended several teaching goals from the Task Analysis for Jasmine (see Table 2.3).

Other Verbal Behavior Assessments

The VB-MAPP is the most widely used verbal behavior assessment, though there are others, including the ABLLS-R, EFL, and PEAK. As described in this section, the ABLLS-R might be useful if an educational team wants information on a wider array of skills than what is covered in the VB-MAPP. The EFL may be more appropriate for adolescents and adults with severely limited verbal repertoires, and the PEAK is useful for learners ready to learn more complex verbal relations.

Assessment of Basic Language and Learning Skills–Revised (ABLLS-R)

Like the VB-MAPP, the ABLLS-R is appropriate for individuals of any age, but the skills span those of neurotypical children who are approximately 0–6 years old. The assessment includes 544 skills across 25 domains spanning language, social interaction, self-help, academic, and motor skills. In each domain, the skills gradually increase in complexity. For example, the receptive language domain (57 skills) begins with simple discriminations, such as responding to their name, and ends with behaviors requiring multi-step conditional discriminations, such as selecting pictures representing social interactions involving teasing, arguing, and practicing.

Each skill in the ABLLS-R is scored between 0–2 points or 0–4 points, and the criteria for scoring are specified and designed to be simple for professionals and parents to use. For example, the ninth skill in "vocal imitation" is imitating words with consonant-vowel repetitions, such as "mamama" and "bye bye." The child receives 0 points if they do not exhibit the skill, 1 point if they imitate at least three phonemes (e.g., "mom"), and 2 points if they imitate at least six phonemes (e.g., "mamama"). Another skill in this domain—imitating words with consonant blends (e.g., "street," "reach")—is scored between 0–4 points: 1 point for imitating two words, 2 points for imitating five words, 3 points for imitating 15 words, and 4 points for imitating almost any word with consonant blends found in different positions within the word. Testing and scoring the ABLLS-R is similar to testing and scoring the VB-MAPP. Once all sections are scored in the protocol binder, scores are charted in an easy-to-read chart. When a child scores 2 on a skill, two boxes are shaded next to the listed skill. Like the VB-MAPP, the ABLLS-R has space for four administrations, with boxes filled in using a different color each time, allowing progress tracking over time.

Case Study: ABLLS-R

Cashton is an energetic 5-year-old boy diagnosed with ASD. Results of the ABLLS-R indicated that he used one-word vocal approximations and was sometimes understood by an unfamiliar listener. He labeled preferred items and used

Table 2.3 Sample Goals for Jasmine from the Task Analysis of the VB-MAPP

Goals for Jasmine

Mand 11-a	Mands to peers and asks peers questions (e.g., "What's your name? Where do I go?") 5 times in a 60-minute observation
Mand 12-e	Asks peers to participate in an activity (e.g., "Come play," "Help dig")
Tact 12-c	Tacts the class and function of 10 items (e.g., show the child a cookie and say, "A cookie is a type of..." and then, "What do you do with this?")
Tact 12-3	Tacts people with 2 different pronouns (e.g., "Who has the hat on?" "...you do")
LR 13-b	Identifies 10 items based on a subject, adjective, and noun (e.g., "Show me the girl's red hair")
LR 13-c	Performs 10 actions based on a subject, proposition, and noun (e.g., "Put the horse in the barn")
Play 15-b	Spontaneously assists in daily activities (e.g., setting the table, planting seeds in the garden, sorting socks)
Play 15-d	Plays computer or video games and properly operates the equipment
Social 11-d	Asks peers WH questions 2 times (e.g., "Where's the shovel?" "What's your name?")
Social 12-a	Spontaneously imitates a peer's behavior in a pretend play activity 2 times
LRFFC 12-c	Selects an item from an array of 10 given a function (e.g., "color on it") and a class (e.g., "art supplies") for 25 items
LRFFC 12-d	Selects an item from an array of 10, given a feature (e.g., "wheels," "wings) and a class (e.g., "animals," "vehicles") for 25 items (e.g., "Where's a vehicle with wheels?" "Where's a vehicle with wings?")
IV 12-a	Provides at least 3 members of 10 classes (e.g., "What do you see on a playground?")
IV 12-c	Provides 10 categories when given several members (e.g., "a horse, cow, and pig are all...")
Group 12-a	Raises a hand to take a turn in a group setting (e.g., "Who wants to pick a song?")
Group 12-c	Emits some irregular past-tense verbs appropriately (e.g., "dug," "ran," "built")

vocal approximations to mand for those items when not in view. For example, he said "pad pad" when he wanted to use his iPad® and "joo" when he wanted juice. If Cashton did not receive a reinforcer due to an unintelligible mand, he took the adult's hand and led them to the desired item while pointing or reaching toward it. When Cashton did not want an item that was presented, he took the item and tossed it to the floor. When he could not do something, such as open a container or reach an item on a high shelf, Cashton did not ask for help and engaged in challenging behaviors, including crying and dropping. When given a choice between two preferred items, Cashton reached for both and tossed one on the floor.

Cashton enjoyed listening to music and often filled in words or attempted to sing along with songs, though unintelligibly. He approached peers and showed interest in toys, though he often did not interact with his peers or play with the toys as intended. Cashton engaged in parallel play for up to 10 minutes and remained safe next to other children. He sat next to his peers in a group setting for about 1 minute but did not attend to a teacher giving instructions. Cashton waited his turn with frequent verbal and gestural prompts without becoming agitated. He struggled to work on tasks independently and needed frequent reminders to stay on task. Cashton did not show an understanding of concepts such as more and less. He tacted and behaved as a listener toward the letters of the alphabet but did not trace all the letters or read simple words. See Table 2.4 for a list of goals generated for Cashton based on the results of the ABLLS-R.

Essential for Living (EFL)

The EFL assesses individuals with moderate-to-severe intellectual and developmental disabilities (McGreevy et al., 2012). The main book is *A Communication, Behavior, and Functional Skills Curriculum, Assessment, and Professional Practitioner's Handbook*. It contains over 3,000 skills in the domains of communication, self-help, social, health, safety, and tolerance, as well as barriers to learning, such as interfering behaviors. The EFL is useful for individuals with significantly impacted communication, delayed self-help repertoires, and high rates of interfering behaviors, and it includes items specifically for individuals with visual or hearing impairments. The EFL can also be a resource when selecting an AAC system for learners who have not yet developed a functional communication repertoire.

Table 2.4 Sample Goals for Cashton Based on the Results of the ABLLS-R

Goals for Cashton

1. Cashton will expressively identify at least 20 preferred items.
2. Cashton will echo 10 different 2-word requests (i.e., "want iPad").
3. After indicating he doesn't want an item, Cashton will indicate "no" verbally or by shaking his head across 3 contexts.
4. Cashton will ask for "help" without engaging in crying or dropping across 5 contexts.
5. Cashton will fill in the last part of 10 common songs or phrases.
6. Cashton will request a preferred item from a peer across 3 peers.
7. Cashton will take at least 3 turns with a peer across 3 different games with no more than gestural prompts.
8. Cashton will sit next to a peer during a group activity for at least 5 minutes.
9. Cashton will make a choice when presented with the option of 2 items across 10 preferred items.
10. Cashton will respond to 2 instructions within the context given in a group setting of at least 3 peers.

Before administering the EFL, it is important to identify the learner's current level of functioning with the Essential Eight Skills see Table 2.5. Using the Quick Assessment caregiver interview, the assessor asks caregivers to rate the learner's skills in each domain (e.g., communication, self-help) on a Likert scale ranging from 1 (significantly limited) to 4 (reliable skill demonstration). For example, see Table 2.5 for the scale for the "Naming and Describing Domain (the tendency to name and describe items, activities, people, places, locations, and items with features that are part of routine events)." If caregivers and clinicians disagree on any ratings, the assessor uses the lower of the two scores.

The next step in the EFL is considering the learner's current Methods of Speaking, whether it is Saying Words or using Alternative Methods of Speaking (AMS), such as using signs, pointing, or a speech-generating device (SGD). This information is used to assign a Vocal Profile. Learners with Vocal Profile 1 have strong manding, tacting, echoic, and intraverbal repertoires. Learners with Vocal Profile 3 may only be understood by familiar listeners due to atypical speech patterns, such as scripting, pronunciation errors, and syntax errors. Finally, a learner with Vocal Profile 6 has very limited verbal sounds and might display whining, grunting, or babbling.

Learners with Vocal Profiles 4–6 are assigned an AMS. The EFL suggests 46 alternative methods of speaking! First, the assessor considers the learner's hearing, vision, ambulatory skills, fine motor coordination, imitation skills, matching skills, and the magnitude of interfering behaviors. Based on the results, the

Table 2.5 Components from the Essentials for Living (EFL)

Essential Eight Skills	Scale for the Naming and Describing Domain
1. Manding (requesting)	1. Does not exhibit any names or descriptions
2. Waiting following a request	2. Names some items and activities that are part of 1–3 routine events
3. Accepting removals	3. Names many items, activities, familiar people, and places that are part of 5–6 routine events
4. Completing required and previously acquired tasks	4. Names/describes many items, activities, people, locations, and items with features that are part of 7 or more routine events
5. Accepting "no"	
6. Following directions related to health and safety	
7. Completing daily living skills related to health and safety	
8. Tolerating stimuli and routines related to health and safety	

EFL recommends AMSs, such as teaching the learner to physically guide listeners; forming a repertoire of standard, adapted, and idiosyncratic signs; teaching the learner to gesture yes/no when given closed-ended choices; targeting distinguishable noises that familiar listeners understand; introducing a picture exchange system of communication; and introducing an SGD.

Following the Quick Assessment, selection of a Vocal Profile, and selection of an AMS, as necessary, the assessor uses direct observation to test specific skills. The skills in the EFL are broken down into four stages: Must Have Skills (e.g., indicating interest in items and activities), Should Have Skills (e.g., making choices), Good to Have Skills (e.g., requesting using three words), and Nice to Have Skills (e.g., indicating the presence of feelings). Parent report may be needed for infrequently utilized skills, such as tolerating rides in taxis and drilling at the dentist.

Case Study: EFL

Aki is an 18-year-old female diagnosed with ASD and intellectual disability. She communicates by reaching toward objects, physically guiding listeners, and signing "more." Aki engages in self-injurious behavior, whining, tantrums, and both vocal and motor stereotypy. The assessor conducted a record review and discovered that she displayed significant delays across all domains of the VB-MAPP, scoring mostly in Level 1. Aki's therapists previously taught her American Sign Language (ASL) and PECS, though she did not acquire them. Her stakeholders wanted to identify a functional repertoire of communication and self-help skills for her. With the EFL, Aki was assigned Vocal Profile 6. The assessor learned from Aki's behavior analyst that she is ambulatory, engages in severe problem behavior, and has limited fine motor coordination, motor imitation skills, and matching skills. See Table 2.6 for the recommended AMSs for Aki. Aki's behavior analyst decided to move forward with AMS #45 and AMS #3. Given Aki's lack of imitation skills, the behavior analyst started with behaviors with which Aki can be physically prompted (with assent). See Table 2.6 for the goals identified for Aki.

Promoting the Emergence of Advanced Knowledge (PEAK) Relational Training System

The PEAK is a four-module assessment and curriculum guide focused on the types of verbal behaviors targeted in the VB-MAPP, as well as skills based on stimulus equivalence and Relational Frame Theory (RFT; Dixon, 2014). Each module contains 184 programs that gradually increase in complexity. The Direct Teaching Module contains the same types of skills as the Milestones Assessment of the VB-MAPP (e.g., mands, tacts, intraverbals). The Generalization Module

Table 2.6 Recommended AMSs and Sample Goals for Aki Based on the Results of the EFL

Recommended AMSs for Aki	Goals for Aki
AMS #3: Forming a repertoire of standard, adapted, and idiosyncratic signs	1. Aki will indicate interest in items and activities identified in R1 (determining learner interested through the caregiver report)
AMS #8: Making distinguishable noises or sounds that are understood and discriminated only by a familiar audience	2. Aki will tolerate touch, physical guidance, or physical prompts
AMS #46: Touching a photograph or printed words using a speech-generating device that contains only one message	3. Aki requests highly preferred snack foods or drinks (identified in R1) using AMS #45 (reaching or pointing)
AMS #42: Listening to "do you want _____" and activating a switch to indicate "yes" or one of two switches to indicate "yes" and "no"	4. Aki requests highly preferred non-food items or activities that can be made frequently and immediately available (identified in R1) using AMS #45 (reaching or pointing)
AMS #45: Reaching, pointing, gesturing, or gazing toward items or familiar locations for items	5. Aki requests highly preferred snack foods or drinks (identified in R1) using AMS #3 (adaptive and idiosyncratic signs)
AMS #34: Visually scanning and selecting items presented two at a time	6. Aki requests highly preferred non-food items or activities that can be made frequently and immediately available (identified in R1) using AMS #3 (adaptive/ idiosyncratic signs)
	7. Aki will hold and maintain contact with the hand of an instructor, care provider, or parent when directed
	8. Aki will turn toward others when her name is called and make two consecutive listener responses

takes skills from the Direct Teaching Module, as well as more advanced concepts, such as symbolism, metaphors, and memory skills, and expands on them with the goal of generalization across settings, people, and materials. The Equivalence Module focuses on relating concepts according to the theory of stimulus equivalence, such as relating spoken words, printed words, and pictures, when only some of the relations are taught. Finally, the Transformation Module focuses on relating concepts according to RFT, such as sameness, oppositeness, hierarchy, and perspective-taking. For example, if a learner is taught that an apple is a fruit and a fruit is a food, they might respond that an apple is a food without direct teaching.

The PEAK is a standardized, criterion-referenced assessment (Dixon et al., 2017) with some norm referencing (Dixon et al., 2014; though it is not a norm-referenced assessment). It is recommended for students ages 18 months through adolescence. It is appropriate for learners with extremely limited verbal skills and those with skills above those of a neurotypical 4-year-old, that is, above the highest level of the VB-MAPP. Additionally, the PEAK may be suitable for learners who demonstrate acquisition but limited generalization of language skills. Finally, when caregivers express concerns that their child uses "black and white thinking" or their child's language feels "robotic," a clinician might consider using the PEAK system.

The PEAK begins with directly observing social interactions, communication, and restricted or repetitive behavior, including "makes odd requests using gestures, pointing, or guiding the assessor's hand," "displays repetitive or contextually inappropriate vocalizations," and "uses an odd volume, pitch, or tone while speaking." The assessor ranks the frequency of each behavior based on it occurring never (0), sometimes (1), or frequently (2), as well as the intensity of the behavior based on it having no (0), minimal (1), or high (2) intensity. These scores are averaged to arrive at the Autism Symptomology score, coupled with scores based on challenging behavior, to derive the level of intervention.

The next step is administering the PEAK and scoring each skill as demonstrated (1) or not demonstrated (0). Skills are assessed using "flipbooks" that contain instructions and visual stimuli. There is also a student workbook for drawing and writing tasks. Each module comprises 184 skills. The Transformation module is divided into two sections—receptive and expressive language—each containing six domains with 16 skills. The sample of skills tested by the PEAK is used to determine the learner's factor profile (or skill repertoire), which is translated into an estimated age-referenced score. The Assessment Factor Scoring Grid weighs the demonstrated skills across domains. For example, if a learner demonstrates 16/16 skills on the Discrete Training Verbal Comprehension Factor, they are given a full weighted score of 100 points and an estimated age equivalence of 9–10 years. Demonstrating 14/16 is considered just below the estimated age equivalence of 3–4 years. When a student does not score the full factor score, an assessor may supplement their score by testing that factor's remaining skills (e.g., 100 verbal comprehension skills).

Case Study: PEAK

Amir is a 6-year-old boy diagnosed with ASD who vocally communicates in complete sentences and demonstrates nearly age-typical play skills. Amir's caregivers are concerned about his social-emotional development. He does not tact his feelings or display age-typical empathy responses. For example, when his sister cries, he does not hug her or ask, "What's wrong?" Amir also displays rigid language, such as listing each student in his class when his parents ask him who he played with at school. Finally, he cries and whines when his routine is interrupted. Amir's behavior analyst administered the PEAK to better understand his relational repertoires and identify new goals. He scored relatively low on social interactions, including a 2 on the frequency and 1 on the intensity of "shows less interest in the assessor than objects in the room." In terms of communication, Amir frequently, but with low intensity, "engages in rote or scripted responses and has limited flexibility in phrases or sentences." He also sometimes "repeats what the assessor says, or part of what the assessor says." In the restricted or repetitive behavior domain, Amir sometimes, and with minimal intensity, "interrupts the assessment process and fixates on odd or very specific subject matters."

Amir scored at least 15/16 across all the factors of the Direct Training module. In the Generalization module, he scored 14/16 in Foundational Learning and Basic Social Skills; 11/16 in Basic Verbal Comprehension Memory and Advanced Math Skills; 5/16 in Advanced Verbal Comprehension, Basic Problem Solving, and Advanced Math Skills; and 0/16 in Verbal Reasoning, Advanced Problem Solving, and Advanced Reading and Writing Skills. This placed Amir just below age equivalence for a 5–6-year-old. See Table 2.7 for Amir's goals based on the PEAK.

Discussion

In summary, there are four major assessments—VB-MAPP, ABLLS-R, EFL, and PEAK—used to describe verbal behavior repertoires and identify teaching goals for individuals with ASD and language delays. It is important to consider research on these assessments, cultural considerations when administering these

Table 2.7 Sample Goals for Amir Based on the Results of the PEAK

Goals for Amir

1. Amir will determine if information is credible based on who presented it. For example, when shown a picture of a little boy and presented with the discriminative stimulus "this boy tells you how to fly an airplane, should you believe him?" Amir will answer, "no, kids don't know how to fly airplanes."
2. Amir will complete rhyming intraverbal phrases.
3. Amir will engage in metaphorical tacting. For example, when shown a picture of a raincloud and asked, "how does this feel?", Amir will answer, "sad."
4. Amir will receptively identify items based on uncommon names. For example, when asked to go find the "channel changer," he will pick up the TV remote.
5. Amir will nickname items based on their feature, function, or class. For example, when asked to nickname a stuffed animal dog, he will say "Barky."
6. Amir will engage in intermediate intraverbals about his day.
7. Amir will respond appropriately to the emotional state of others.
8. Given a short story, Amir will identify which sentence does not belong.

assessments (see also Chapter 13 in this volume for additional content on cultural considerations), and future directions.

Research on Verbal Behavior Assessments

The quality of an assessment rests on the volume and rigor of research documenting its validity and reliability. An assessment has validity if the types of results align with the stated purposes of the assessment. One type of relevant validity may be evaluated by comparing one individual's results from an assessment with their results from a different, established assessment that has the same purpose (e.g., assess language skills; i.e., convergent validity). Two ways to evaluate reliability are having one administrator assess a child twice and having two administrators assess a child once. The extent of reliability is the extent to which the two scores in either case are the same. When assessments have research documenting their validity and reliability, administrators have confidence in obtaining true and meaningful results, and the larger research and practice communities (i.e., non-behavior analysts) find them acceptable.

Padilla et al. (2023) examined the extent of validity and reliability research supporting assessments used in ABA programs. Although the VB-MAPP is the most widely used verbal behavior assessment (Padilla, 2020) and frequently used in research on verbal behavior, Padilla et al. (2023) found only two studies documenting its reliability. In contrast, they found 11 studies documenting the reliability (e.g., Dixon et al., 2016) and validity (e.g., Belisle et al., 2022) of the PEAK. It is important to point out that 9 of those 11 studies included the developer of the PEAK as an author, and other independent researchers should corroborate the findings. The ABLLS-R has one study on reliability (Partington et al., 2018) and one study on validity (Usry et al., 2018), and there do not appear to be studies on the validity or reliability of the EFL.

One type of validity—content validity—is a common measure of the quality of an assessment and highlights the extent to which the assessment measures relevant skills that align with the purpose of the assessment. Padilla and Akers (2021) evaluated the content validity of the VB-MAPP in terms of how well items were defined, how well skill areas were represented, how relevant the skill areas were, how age-appropriate the items were, and how good the measurement system was for each item. They recruited 13 subject matter experts (SMEs) certified as Board Certified Behavior Analysts (BCBA®s) and BCBA-Ds from around the United States. The SMEs examined all items in the Milestones Assessment, EESA, and Barriers Assessment and scored items against 3-point Likert scales (e.g., "Not Necessary," "Useful, but Not Essential," and "Essential;" "Not Appropriate," "Somewhat Appropriate," and "Very Appropriate;" and "Inadequate," "Somewhat Adequate," and "Adequate"). Padilla and Akers concluded: "In general, the VB-MAPP has moderate to strong evidence supporting its domain relevance, age appropriateness, method of measurement appropriateness, and domain representation" (p. 4065). The few areas with weak content validity were echoics' classroom routines and group skills; visual-perceptual skills and matching-to-sample (VPS/MTS); independent play; social behavior and social play; and writing.

In a study on the inter-rater reliability of the VB-MAPP, Montallana et al. (2019) had 24 assessors (23 were BCBAs; 9 reported having formal VB-MAPP training) conduct the VB-MAPP with 32 children. Evaluations of "good," "moderate," and "poor" reliability were based on high, moderate, and low values of intraclass correlation coefficients. The researchers found that the total Milestones score had good inter-rater reliability. Individual milestones had moderate or good reliability, except for Group Skills, which had poor reliability. In addition, the total Barriers score had moderate reliability; however, only three individual barrier scores had moderate reliability (Defective Echoic, Reinforcer Dependent, and Defective Listener), while the rest had poor reliability.

A final study on the VB-MAPP was on training people to administer it. Barnes et al. (2014) found that when two school psychologists implemented the VB-MAPP after reading the manual, they implemented it with a range of 40%–72% fidelity. However, after reading the manual and receiving behavioral skills training, the participants implemented the VB-MAPP with a range of 78%–98% fidelity. This study stresses how important it is for assessors to receive extensive training on the VB-MAPP. Given that BCBAs, and not school psychologists, typically administer the VB-MAPP, as well as the need for replication in research, this study should be replicated with BCBAs.

Cultural Considerations

It is fairly well known that cultural bias is inherent in psychological and norm-referenced testing (Reynolds & Suzuki, 2013). Potential sources of bias are inadequate standardization across populations, content (e.g., pictures and prompts in test-specific booklets) related only to the majority population, and a focus on only the English language. Bias in assessments leads to differentially categorizing individuals from different cultural and racial groups, which further perpetuates discrimination and racist practices. Within several assessments for ASD (e.g., the ADOS), standardization did not include children from diverse backgrounds (Harris et al., 2014).

Cultural considerations with the types of criterion-referenced assessments described in this chapter are critical, but they might differ from norm-referenced assessments in two respects. First, because there is no norm group with criterion-referenced assessments, considerations about that group's makeup are irrelevant. Second, there are no required prompts or materials as part of the assessments described in this chapter (except for parts of the PEAK), deeming the cultural representativeness of the assessments less critical. A reason for this is the focus on a functional analysis of language, which applies to all humans across the globe. Individuals around the world emit mands, tacts, intraverbals, and echoics. In this vein, the assessments described in this chapter may be administered across cultural and linguistic groups, as well as across geographical locations. Notably, the VB-MAPP is available in at least 12 languages: Arabic, Castilian Spanish, English, French, Italian, Korean, Lithuanian, Mandarin, Polish, Russian, Mexican Spanish, and Turkish. Finally, assessors working with English Language Learners (ELLs) should determine the need for interpreters and consider that children often use different languages at home and school (Dennison et al., 2019).

In contrast to the basic principles of behavior and verbal behavior, the content of the antecedent stimuli and responses in criterion-referenced assessment is of most concern with respect to cultural, linguistic, and geographical diversity. In considering the content of antecedent stimuli and responses in the VB-MAPP, examples in the VB-MAPP booklet may be considered Eurocentric and not understood in all cultures, such as "shaking a maraca" (Motor Imitation Milestone), "matches a Ford truck to a Toyota truck" (Visual-Perceptual Skills and Matching-to-Sample Milestone), and "Mr. Potatohead" (Independent Play Milestone). Additionally, as stated above, commercially available materials often used to administer these assessments are available through Different Roads to Learning (https://difflearn.com/) and the VB-MAPP website (avbpress.com), and these are likely Eurocentric. Therefore, it is incumbent on behavior analysts to use prompts and materials that align with each client's culture(s), as well as to examine and address other ways in which administering these assessments may be culturally biased. For example, when assessing Black children, assessors should modify materials by altering the people depicted in icons, making other materials and stimuli culturally relevant, and welcoming speech patterns that vary from Standard English (Čolić et al., 2022).

To this end, Beaulieu et al. (2019) suggested that behavior analysts need to revise ABA-based assessments to include questions "about potentially important cultural variables, including religion, family structure and hierarchy, important family events or celebrations, and preferred modes and style of communication" (p. 566). Further, graduate training programs should teach trainees to conduct assessments while incorporating cultural and linguistic differences (Conners et al., 2019). In general, behavior analysts must continue working toward cultural humility (Wright, 2019), increasing self-awareness of one's culture to reduce bias (Beaulieu & Jimenez-Gomez, 2022), and conducting cultural analyses of assessment practices (Fong et al., 2017).

Future Directions

There are many future directions for the assessment of verbal behavior. As mentioned above, the necessary repertoires of individuals administering verbal behavior assessments are vast, including knowledge of ABA, verbal behavior, linguistics, and AAC. This is a "blessing" (a thorough evaluation of a child's verbal behavior repertoire) and a "curse" (many educators and psychologists do not possess these repertoires). Future research is needed to expand the numbers and locations of people who have sufficient repertoires. Padilla's (2020) survey results from 1,428 ABA practitioners showed that 71% reported receiving training on administering verbal behavior assessments from their supervisor; 39% were self-taught, 29% received online training, and 28% received training during a graduate course. It is reasonable to assume that course- or supervisor-taught learning is superior to self-taught learning in that professors and supervisors can ensure mastery over critical conceptual and procedural factors.

As discussed above, more research is needed on the psychometric properties of verbal behavior assessments, particularly the VB-MAPP (Padilla, 2020). In addition, given that 30%–40% of children with ASD are minimally verbal (i.e., have a limited number of single words in their repertoire; Anderson et al., 2007; Thurm et al., 2015), many of those children use SGDs (Chavers et al., 2021; Crowe et al., 2021; Lorah & Griffen, 2022). However, SGDs are not addressed in the VB-MAPP or the other verbal behavior assessments. Although the selection-based responding with an SGD may be functionally equivalent to responding with PECS (Petursdottir & Ingvarsson, 2023), assessment guidelines for students who use SGDs are needed. Finally, to fully demonstrate the applicability of verbal behavior assessments, researchers should examine their use with other populations, such as older adults with dementia and aphasia (Gross et al., 2013).

Summary and Conclusions

Behavior analysts often focus on increasing the social-communication skills of individuals with ASD and related disabilities. However, before teaching such skills, the behavior analyst must conduct an assessment(s) to identify strengths and gaps in a client's verbal repertoire. Prior to 2000, the VABS and other assessments were common, but they relied on verbal report and a formal, as opposed to functional, analysis of language. Once the ABLLS, which was based on Skinner's (1957) analysis of verbal behavior, was published in 1998, behavior analysts could use direct observation to assess and analyze the array of verbal operants, including mands, tacts, listener responses, and intraverbals.

The ABLLS, a criterion-referenced assessment, was revised as the ABLLS-R and then the VB-MAPP. Two other verbal behavior assessments are the PEAK and the EFL. According to a survey by Padilla(2020), the vast majority (76%) of behavior analysts use the VB-MAPP. The VB-MAPP is structured around developmental milestones and assesses verbal skills, as well as barriers to effective learning and measures of readiness for transitioning from substantially separate learning environments to general education classrooms. Unlike norm-referenced assessments, there is no set way to administer the VB-MAPP and no set of required materials. Assessors use a combination of record review, direct testing, and classroom observations. Given this approach and the focus on Skinner's analysis of verbal behavior, assessors must have expertise in that analysis and the basic principles of behavior analysis, as well as familiarity with linguistics and AAC. Finally, the Task Analysis of the VB-MAPP is used to select teaching objectives based on the assessment.

The other verbal behavior assessments have many similarities to the VB-MAPP: the ABLLS-R assesses a broader array of skills; the EFL was designed for adolescents and adults with severely limited verbal repertoires; and the PEAK addresses skills that surpass those found in the VB-MAPP. Although there is some research on the validity and reliability of these assessments—mostly with PEAK—more such research is needed. Additionally, although these assessments are based on a functional analysis of language, which is ubiquitous culturally and globally, assessors must ensure that the prompts and materials used in the assessments are culturally relevant to the clients. Finally, future research is needed on incorporating SGDs into these assessments and methods of training people to conduct them. Fortunately, behavior analysts have a variety of tools for assessing verbal behavior and designing effective teaching programs.

References

Anderson, D. K., Lord, C., Risi, S., DiLavore, P. S., Shulman, C., Thurm, A., Welch, K., & Pickles, A. (2007). Patterns of growth in verbal abilities among children with autism spectrum disorder. *Journal of Consulting and Clinical Psychology, 75*(4), 594–604. https://doi.org/10.1037/0022-006X.75.4.594

Axe, J. B. (2008). Conditional discrimination in the intraverbal relation: A review and recommendations for future research. *The Analysis of Verbal Behavior, 24*, 159–174. https://doi.org/10.1007/BF03393064

Barnes, C. S., Mellor, J. R., & Rehfeldt, R. A. (2014). Implementing the Verbal Behavior Milestones Assessment and Placement Program (VB-MAPP): Teaching assessment techniques. *The Analysis of Verbal Behavior, 30*(1), 36–47. https://doi.org/10.1007/s40616-013-0004-5

Beaulieu, L., Addington, J., & Almeida, D. (2019). Behavior analysts' training and practices regarding cultural diversity: The case for culturally competent care. *Behavior Analysis in Practice, 12*(3), 557–575. https://doi.org/10.1007/s40617-018-00313-6

Beaulieu, L., & Jimenez, G. C. (2022). Cultural responsiveness in applied behavior analysis: Self-assessment. *Journal of Applied Behavior Analysis, 55*(2), 337–356. https://doi.org/10.1002/jaba.907

Belisle, J., Dixon, M. R., Munoz, B. E., & Fricke-Steuber, K. (2022). The convergent validity of the PEAK-E-PA and two common assessments of language development: The ABLLS-R and the TOLD 1:4. *Journal of Behavioral Education, 31*(4), 699–717. https://doi.org/10.1007/s10864-020-09426-x

Bondy, A., & Frost, L. (1994). The picture exchange communication system. *Focus on Autism and Other Developmental Disabilities, 9*(3), 1–19. https://doi.org/10.1177/108835769400900301

Chavers, T. N., Morris, M., Schlosser, R. W., & Koul, R. (2021). Effects of a systematic augmentative and alternative communication intervention using a speech-generating device on multistep requesting and generic small talk for children with severe autism spectrum disorder. *American Journal of Speech-Language Pathology, 30*(6), 2476–2491. https://doi.org/10.1044/2021_AJSLP-20-00319

Čolić, M., Araiba, S., Lovelace, T. S., & Dababnah, S. (2022). Black caregivers' perspectives on racism in ASD services: Toward culturally responsive ABA practice. *Behavior Analysis in Practice, 15*(4), 1032–1041. https://doi.org/10.1007/s40617-021-00577-5

Conners, B., Johnson, A., Duarte, J., Murriky, R., & Marks, K. (2019). Future directions of training and fieldwork in diversity issues in applied behavior analysis. *Behavior Analysis in Practice, 12*(4), 767–776. https://doi.org/10.1007/s40617-019-00349-2

Crowe, B., Machalicek, W., Wei, Q., Drew, C., & Ganz, J. (2021). Augmentative and alternative communication for children with intellectual and developmental disability: A mega-review of the literature. *Journal of Developmental and Physical Disabilities, 34,* 1–42. https://doi.org/10.1007/s10882-021-09790-0

Dennison, A., Lund, E. M., Brodhead, M. T., Mejia, L., Armenta, A., & Leal, J. (2019). Delivering home-supported applied behavior analysis therapies to culturally and linguistically diverse families. *Behavior Analysis in Practice, 12*(4), 887–898. https://doi.org/10.1007/s40617-019-00374-1

DeSouza, A. A., Akers, J. S., & Fisher, W. W. (2017). Empirical application of Skinner's verbal behavior to interventions for children with autism: A review. *The Analysis of Verbal Behavior, 33*(2), 229–259. https://doi.org/10.1007/s40616-017-0093-7

Dixon, M. R. (2014). *The PEAK relational training system.* Shawnee Scientific Press.

Dixon, M. R., Belisle, J., McKeel, A., Whiting, S., Speelman, R., Daar, J. H., & Rowsey, K. (2017). An internal and critical review of the PEAK relational training system for children with autism and related intellectual disabilities: 2014–2017. *The Behavior Analyst, 40*(2), 493–521. https://doi.org/10.1007/s40614-017-0119-4

Dixon, M. R., Belisle, J., Whiting, S. W., & Rowsey, K. E. (2014). Normative sample of the PEAK relational training system: Direct training module and subsequent comparisons to individuals with autism. *Research in Autism Spectrum Disorders, 8*(11), 1597–1606. https://doi.org/10.1016/j.rasd.2014.07.020

Dixon, M. R., Stanley, C. R., Belisle, J., & Rowsey, K. E. (2016). The test-retest and interrater reliability of the promoting the emergence of advanced knowledge-direct training assessment for use with individuals with autism and related disabilities. *Behavior Analysis: Research and Practice, 16*(1), 34–40. https://doi.org/10.1037/bar0000027

Esch, B. E. (2014). Early echoic skills assessment (EESA). In M. L. Sundberg (Ed.), *VB-MAPP: Verbal behavior milestones assessment and placement program: A language and social skills assessment program for children with autism or other developmental disabilities* (2nd ed., pp. 42–48). AVB Press.

Esch, B. E. (2023). *Early echoic skills assessment and program planner.* Different Roads.

Esch, B. E., LaLonde, K. B., & Esch, J. W. (2010). Speech and language assessment: A verbal behavior analysis. *The Journal of Speech and Language Pathology–Applied Behavior Analysis, 5*(2), 166–191. https://doi.org/10.1037/h0100270

Fong, E. H., Ficklin, S., & Lee, H. Y. (2017). Increasing cultural understanding and diversity in applied behavior analysis. *Behavior Analysis: Research and Practice, 17*(2), 103–113. https://doi.org/10.1037/bar0000076

Frampton, S. E., Davis, C. R., Meleshkevich, O., & Axe, J. B. (2024). A clinical tutorial on methods to capture and contrive establishing operations to teach mands. *Behavior Analysis in Practice, 17*(4), 1270–1282. https://doi.org/10.1007/s40617-024-00985-3

Gould, E., Dixon, D. R., Najdowski, A. C., Smith, M. N., & Tarbox, J. (2011). A review of assessments for determining the content of early intensive behavioral intervention programs for autism spectrum disorders. *Research in Autism Spectrum Disorders, 5*(3), 990–1002. https://doi.org/10.1016/j.rasd.2011.01.012

Gross, A. C., Fuqua, R. W., & Merritt, T. A. (2013). Evaluation of verbal behavior in older adults. *The Analysis of Verbal Behavior, 29,* 85–99. https://doi.org/10.1007/BF03393126

Harris, B., Barton, E. E., & Albert, C. (2014). Evaluating autism diagnostic and screening tools for cultural and linguistic responsiveness. *Journal of Autism and Developmental Disorders, 44*(6), 1275–1287. https://doi.org/10.1007/s10803-013-1991-8

Kisamore, A. N., Karsten, A. M., & Mann, C. C. (2016). Teaching multiply controlled intraverbals to children and adolescents with autism spectrum disorders. *Journal of Applied Behavior Analysis, 49*(4), 826–847. https://doi.org/10.1002/jaba.344

LaFrance, D. L., & Miguel, C. F. (2014). Teaching verbal behavior to children with autism spectrum disorders. In J. Tarbox, D. R. Dixon, P. Sturmey, & J. L. Matson (Eds.), *Handbook of early intervention for autism spectrum disorders: Research, policy, and practice* (pp. 403–436). Springer Science + Business Media. https://doi.org/10.1007/978-1-4939-0401-3_16

Leaf, J. B., Cihon, J. H., Ferguson, J. L., Milne, C. M., Leaf, R., & McEachin, J. (2021). Advances in our understanding of behavioral intervention: 1980 to 2020 for individuals diagnosed with autism spectrum disorder. *Journal of Autism and Developmental Disorders, 51*(12), 4395–4410. https://doi.org/10.1007/s10803-020-04481-9

Lorah, E. R., & Griffen, B. (2022). Teaching children with autism traveling skills for using a speech-generating device for manding. *Journal of Developmental and Physical Disabilities, 34*(3), 509–522. https://doi.org/10.1007/s10882-022-09863-8

Lord, C., Rutter, M., DiLavore, P., & Risi, S. (2008). *Autism diagnostic observation schedule.* Western Psychological Services.

Luiselli, J. K., Campbell, S., Cannon, B., DiPietro, E., Ellis, J. T., Taras, M., & Lifter, K. (2001). Assessment instruments used in the education and treatment of persons with autism: Brief report of a survey of national service centers. *Research in Developmental Disabilities, 22*(5), 389–398. https://doi.org/10.1016/S0891-4222(01)00079-8

McGreevy, P., Fry, T., & Cornwall, C. (2012). *Essential for living.* McGreevy.

Meleshkevich, O., Axe, J. B., & degli Espinosa, F. (2021). Effects of time delay and requiring echoics on answering questions about visual stimuli. *Journal of Applied Behavior Analysis, 54*(2), 725–743. https://doi.org/10.1002/jaba.790

Montallana, K. L., Gard, B. M., Lotfizadeh, A. D., & Poling, A. (2019). Inter-rater agreement for the milestones and barriers assessments of the Verbal Behavior Milestones Assessment and Placement Program (VB-MAPP). *Journal of Autism and Developmental Disorders, 49*(5), 2015–2023. https://doi.org/10.1007/s10803-019-03879-4

Padilla, K. L. (2020). Global assessment use and practices in applied behavior analysis: Surveying the field. *Research in Autism Spectrum Disorders, 79,* 101676. https://doi.org/10.1016/j.rasd.2020.101676

Padilla, K. L., & Akers, J. S. (2021). Content validity evidence for the Verbal Behavior Milestones Assessment and Placement Program (VB-MAPP). *Journal of Autism and Developmental Disorders, 51*(11), 4054–4066. https://doi.org/10.1007/s10803-020-04864-y

Padilla, K. L., Weston, R., Morgan, G. B., Lively, P., & O'Guinn, N. (2023). Validity and reliability evidence for assessments based in applied behavior analysis: A systematic review. *Behavior Modification, 46*(6), 857–887. https://doi.org/10.1177/01454455221098151

Partington, J. W., Bailey, A., & Partington, S. W. (2018). A pilot study examining the test–retest and internal consistency reliability of the ABLLS-R. *Journal of Psychoeducational Assessment, 36*(4), 405–410. https://doi.org/10.1177/0734282916678348

Partington, J. W., & Sundberg, M. L. (1998). *The assessment of basic language and learning skills*. Behavior Analysts, Inc.

Petursdottir, A. I., & Ingvarsson, E. T. (2023). Revisiting topography-based and selection-based verbal behavior. *The Analysis of Verbal Behavior*. https://doi.org/10.1007/s40616-023-00182-3

Reynolds, C. R., & Suzuki, L. A. (2013). Bias in psychological assessment: An empirical review and recommendations. In J. R. Graham, J. A. Naglieri, & I. B. Weiner (Eds.), *Handbook of psychology: Assessment psychology* (Vol. 10, 2nd ed., pp. 82–113). John Wiley & Sons, Inc.

Schwartz, I. S., & Kelly, E. M. (2021). Quality of life for people with disabilities: Why applied behavior analysts should consider this a primary dependent variable. *Research and Practice for Persons with Severe Disabilities, 46*(3), 159–172. https://doi.org/10.1177/15407969211033629

Skinner, B. F. (1957). *Verbal behavior*. Appleton-Century-Crofts.

Sparrow, S. S., Cicchetti, D. V., & Saulnier, C. A. (2016). *Vineland adaptive behavior scales* (3rd ed.). Pearson.

Sundberg, M. L. (2008). Verbal behavior milestones assessment and placement program: The VB-MAPP. Concord. CA: AVB Press.

Sundberg, M. L. (2014). The verbal behavior milestones assessment and placement program: The VB-MAPP (2nd ed.). AVB Press.

Sundberg, M. L. (2020). Verbal behavior. In J. O. Cooper, T. E. Heron, & W. L. Heward (Eds.), *Applied behavior analysis* (3rd ed., pp. 412–449). Pearson.

Sundberg, M. L., & Michael, J. (2001). The benefits of Skinner's analysis of verbal behavior for children with autism. *Behavior Modification, 25*(5), 698–724. https://doi.org/10.1177/0145445501255003

Thurm, A., Manwaring, S. S., Swineford, L., & Farmer, C. (2015). Longitudinal study of symptom severity and language in minimally verbal children with autism. *Journal of Child Psychology and Psychiatry, 56*(1), 97–104. https://doi.org/10.1111/jcpp.12285

Usry, J., Partington, S. W., & Partington, J. W. (2018). Using expert panels to examine the content validity and inter-rater reliability of the ABLLS-R. *Journal of Developmental and Physical Disabilities, 30*(1), 27–38. https://doi.org/10.1007/s10882-017-9574-9

Wright, P. I. (2019). Cultural humility in the practice of applied behavior analysis. *Behavior Analysis in Practice, 12*(4), 805–809. https://doi.org/10.1007/s40617-019-00343-8

Chapter 3

Analog and Naturalistic Arrangements for Teaching Language to Individuals with Autism Spectrum Disorder

Tina M. Sidener

History of Trial-Based Teaching

The formal beginning of language training with individuals with autism spectrum disorder (ASD) is often considered the work conducted and published by Ivar Lovaas in the 1960s. However, Lovaas traced his work to early behavior analysts such as Allyon, Baer, Bijou, Goldiamond, Risley, and Wolf (Ozerk et al., 2016; Smith & Eikeseth, 2011), later crediting his colleagues with helping him "contribute to bridging the gap between behavioral psychology and clinical application" (Lovaas, 1993, p. 618). While an assistant professor at the Child Development Institute at the University of Washington in the late 1950s, Lovaas conducted research with Bijou, who was applying Skinner's principles of behavior to neurotypical children and individuals with neurodevelopmental disorders (Ozerk et al., 2016). He observed Risley conducting trial-based teaching with children with intellectual disability using a preparation based on the Wisconsin General Test Apparatus. He was inspired by how this tabletop device allowed for control, clear observation, stimulus presentation, and consequence delivery. Lovaas was also influenced by the innovative research published by these behavior analysts, which reported the effectiveness of interventions based on reinforcement and stimulus control with individuals with neurodevelopmental disorders. This groundbreaking work demonstrated that children with ASD could learn new behavior via the arrangement of antecedents and consequences, challenging the current belief and practice of lifetime institutional placements (Ghezzi, 2007). For example, Wolf et al. (1964) described one of the first published demonstrations of ABA with a child with ASD. Although "Dicky" learned to wear his glasses via a shaping procedure, trial-based teaching with echoic prompts was effective for teaching him a tact repertoire.

Discrete Trial Teaching

Lovaas continued the work he had observed at the Child Development Institute when he began teaching at UCLA in 1961 (Ozerk et al., 2016). For example,

DOI: 10.4324/9781003433668-4

Lovaas et al. (1966) described using a combination of shaping and trial-based instruction to teach an initial echoic repertoire to two boys with ASD:

> Early in training the child was rewarded only if he emitted a sound within a certain time after an adult had emitted a sound. Next he was rewarded only if the sound he emitted within the prescribed interval resembled the adult's sound. Toward the end of training, he was rewarded only if his vocalization very closely matched the adult's vocalization—that is, if it was, in effect, imitative. Thus verbal imitation was taught through the development of a series of increasingly fine discriminations.
>
> (p. 705)

In the late 1960s, Lovaas established the UCLA Young Autism Project (YAP), a home-based, comprehensive program for teaching skills to children with ASD (Lovaas, 1993). The primary approach for teaching in this program (especially in a child's first year of intervention) came to be called discrete trial teaching (DTT). The important findings from an evaluation of a later version of this program were reported in the seminal study by Lovaas (1987). Children with ASD in the intensive DTT group made significant gains across domains of verbal behavior, academics, daily living, pre-vocational, play, and social interaction, and 47% of participants in this group no longer met the criteria for an autism diagnosis, obtained IQ scores within the normal range, and functioned independently in typical education classrooms. Publication of this study led to the widespread endorsement of early intensive behavioral intervention for children with ASD, and DTT subsequently became one of the most important, powerful, and well-researched teaching approaches for children with ASD (Lovaas & Smith, 2003; Tarbox & Najdowski, 2008).

DTT has been described as "a specific type of one-to-one, teacher-child-directed instruction that individualizes, simplifies, and structures teaching in a specific way to maximize learning" (Klintwall & Eikeseth, 2014; p. 125); it "involves breaking down complex skills into subskills and teaching them through repeated practice" (Tarbox & Najdowski, 2008, p. 181). It is important to note that DTT as a teaching paradigm differs from a *discrete trial*, a unit of instruction consisting of five parts (see Table 3.1). Each trial is "discrete" because it has a clear beginning and end (Smith, 2001). In contrast, DTT is a teaching paradigm that may include a variety of additional procedures such as repeated practice and individualization of EOs, settings, stimuli, antecedents, prompts/prompt-fading, error correction, consequences, and mastery criteria to maximize learning (Frank-Crawford et al., 2024; Geiger et al., 2012).

One reason DTT may be so strikingly effective with children with ASD is that it addresses key features of the disorder related to stimulus control and the reinforcing value of social stimuli. Researchers have speculated that limited salience of social stimuli (e.g., eye contact) in infants with ASD may impede the

Table 3.1 Parts of a Discrete Trial

Part	Description	Example
Presentation of antecedent stimulus	Instructor presents verbal and/or non-verbal stimuli; Becomes discriminative stimulus after repeated practice	Instructor says, "Who's this?" and shows a picture of Sonic the Hedgehog
Prompt	Instructor provides guidance with or after antecedent stimulus	Instructor says, "say, Sonic"
Learner response	Learner engages in independent, prompted, or no response	Learner says, "Sonic"
Consequence	Instructor provides consequence—may differ for independent, prompted, incorrect responses	Instructor smiles and says, "Exactly right, that's Sonic!" and delivers a token
Intertrial interval	Time between consequence delivered and next antecedent stimulus	Instructor waits 5 s before beginning the next trial

development of those stimuli as conditioned stimuli, conditioned reinforcers, and discriminative stimuli and subsequently increase the value of stimulation from stereotypy (Ahearn et al., 2015; Eikeseth, 2016; Gale et al., 2019; Klin et al., 2015; Spradlin & Brady, 1999). Together, these differences in children with ASD appear to have exponentially impacting effects on the capacity to learn from the natural environment as neurotypical children do (Ahearn et al., 2015). DTT may address this challenge by providing repeated, consistent relations between stimuli, responses, and consequences; delivering preferred items as reinforcers without delay; pairing social stimuli with preferred items across many trials; reinforcing eye contact; and arranging teaching in a way that prevents restricted stimulus control (Spradlin & Brady, 1999). Behavior analysts have noted several other advantages of DTT, including that the instructor can individualize and maximize learning, as needed, by reducing distractions, increasing the salience of relevant stimuli, and tailoring antecedents and consequences to a specific learner; a high rate of trials may be conducted because the instructor controls teaching opportunities; the structured nature of DTT makes data collection and instructor training relatively simple; target responses are easy to identify; preferred items are easy to deliver; curriculum is straightforward; progress is observable; and many types of skills, including all verbal operants, can be targeted (Sundberg & Partington, 1998; Tarbox & Najdowski, 2008).

Limitations of DTT

Many of the criticisms of DTT have been related to learners not displaying skills as desired in the natural or "speaking" environment (Carnett et al., 2022; Geiger et al., 2012; LeBlanc et al., 2006). These limitations may be broadly categorized as limitations in natural antecedent and consequence control. The first criticism, limited natural antecedent control, is related primarily to issues with generalized responding, which Lovaas observed in an early version of his program: "Gains tended to be situation-specific; despite improving with therapists in clinical settings, children's behavior often remained unchanged with caregivers in everyday settings such as home or school" (Lovaas & Smith, 2003, p. 327). This led to Lovaas including intensive caregiver training in the home as a central component of YAP; however, some criticized DTT as using a "train and hope" approach rather than programming for generalized outcomes, as recommended by Stokes and Baer (1977). Teaching with instructional stimuli, antecedents, instructors, and/or setting characteristics that do not vary and/or are markedly different from those that occur in the natural environment can result in a high degree of stimulus control over responding rather than generalized responding. This type of tight stimulus control might result from consistently employing the following procedures: training in one setting with no distractions; contriving the position of the stimuli/learner/instructor; using staff instructors only (rather than family and community members); using contrived and few exemplars of objects, pictures, and videos as instructional stimuli; and using contrived and few exemplars of the form, prosody, and pacing of instructions (Delprato, 2001; Green, 2001; LeBlanc et al., 2006; Sundberg & Partington, 1998). See Table 3.2 for examples of contrived and natural antecedents for different learner responses. Control by natural antecedents may be particularly relevant when teaching verbal behavior to children with ASD because of the different natural antecedent control of the verbal operants: mand (EO), tact (non-verbal stimulus), and echoic and intraverbal (verbal stimulus). Although neurotypical children learn these operants without specific training, some require specific teaching arrangements to learn these responses under natural antecedent control (Sundberg & Michael, 2001).

Table 3.2 Examples of Natural and Contrived Antecedents for Different Learner Responses

Learner Response	Natural Antecedent	Contrived Antecedent
Puts in a puzzle piece	EO to play with/complete puzzle	Instructor says, "Put in"
Points to car and says, "car"	EO for attention, sight of car, L present	Instructor says, "What's that?"
Says, "3"	EO for social interaction, someone says, "How old are you?"	Instructor holds up card with a 3 on it
Mands, "cookie"	EO for cookie, L present	Instructor says, "say, cookie"

Note: EO = establishing operation; L = listener.

The second criticism, limited control by natural consequences, could result from responding coming under the control of a different type, magnitude, or schedule of reinforcement than occurs in the natural environment. Procedures producing a lack of control by natural consequences can be the result of using only contrived, immediate, powerful consequences on a continuous schedule of reinforcement (Carnett et al., 2022; Delprato, 2001; Ghezzi, 2007; Sundberg & Michael, 2001; Sundberg & Partington, 1998). See Table 3.3 for examples of contrived and natural consequences for different learner responses. Lack of control by natural consequences is particularly relevant when teaching verbal behavior to children with ASD because of the different natural reinforcer control for different types of mands (for items, information of different types, help, social interaction, escape from something aversive) and the other verbal operants (attention, approval, social interaction). When teaching is not arranged to produce natural consequence control, some children with ASD learn verbal behavior that has a different function than might appear based on its topography. Consider the example of a child with ASD for whom social interactions do not function as reinforcers; their instructor decides to teach conversation skills using tokens (for backup preferred activities) because these consequences function as reinforcers. Although the child's engaging in conversation may appear (to a brief observer) to be maintained by social interaction, it instead has a tangible function.

Although some DTT programs have employed only procedures producing tight stimulus control as described above, it is important to note that these are not inherent features of DTT as a teaching paradigm (Weiss, 2005). However,

Table 3.3 Examples of Natural and Contrived Consequences for Different Learner Responses

Learner Response	Natural Consequence	Contrived Consequence
Puts in a puzzle piece	Automatic reinforcement: Sees/feels puzzle piece click in; sees puzzle closer to being completed; sees more of picture	Praise/attention and token: Instructor says, "You found the piece!" and gives token
Points to car and says, "car"	Praise/attention: L says, "That IS a car! That's mommy's car!"	Tangible: L gives preferred toy
Answers "3" when asked, "how old are you?"	Praise/attention and continued social interaction: L says, "That's right! You're really growing up! Show me 3…"	Escape from demands/ social interaction
Mands, "cookie"	Item manded: L gives a cookie	Praise/attention: L says, "Great job saying, "cookie!"

Note: L = listener.

understanding the sources and rationales for these criticisms is important because they have led to the development of novel teaching strategies. One reason that DTT might be described as only using contrived procedures that produce tight stimulus control is that, although YAP changed over time, students who worked in his program may not have had the opportunity to observe those changes. As Lovaas's students Leaf and McEachin (2016) described, "In reality, there is no single Lovaas model because the work done at UCLA was dynamic, creative, and ever-changing. We were constantly evolving. When I started in 1973, it was completely different than when I left in 1984" (p. 12). Aspects of YAP that some students may have experienced as limitations may have later changed; however, without observing those changes, they may have gone on to characterize and implement DTT in outdated ways. Another reason there may be variability in how DTT is described is the impact of DTT being adopted by other behavior analysts outside of YAP over time. Although these behavior analysts working outside of YAP implemented DTT, they may not have included all aspects of YAP, such as the specific sequencing of programs or intensive parent training. In addition, over time, behavior analysts outside of YAP conducted research demonstrating optimal methods for increasing effectiveness, efficiency, and generalization of DTT procedures that were not necessarily included in YAP (Geiger et al., 2012; Green, 2001; Weiss, 2005). A final issue that may have contributed to variable descriptions of DTT is how it has been implemented throughout the country since the 1980s. As Lovaas's promising new program was disseminated, it offered hope to many families with children with ASD. The demand then (as now) for behavioral intervention was urgently felt and far exceeded the availability of skilled, well-trained instructors and supervisors. Instructors working in homes outside of YAP were sometimes trained quickly, provided with infrequent supervision, and relied on their problem-solving. For example, Lovaas's (1981) guide, *The ME Book*, was phased out of YAP early on, and they "stopped using it before it was even published. Ivar saw the book as a book of basic recipes that required adaptation, innovation and analysis" (Leaf & McEachin, 2016, p. 25). However, instructors who were not part of YAP at the time sometimes strictly adhered to it without other guiding sources (Leaf & McEachin, 2016).

History of Naturalistic Teaching

Limitations in the effects of DTT on children with ASD resulted in some clinicians and researchers developing new ways of teaching, which together may be referred to as different iterations of *naturalistic teaching* (NT). Beginning in the 1970s and 1980s, many behavior analysts who developed NT procedures were influenced by the work of Stokes and Baer (1977) and others who emphasized the importance of programming for and producing generalized responding (LeBlanc et al., 2006). They used three broad strategies to address limitations in control by natural antecedents and consequences: training diversely, using natural consequences, and incorporating mediators (Allen & Cowan, 2008; Stokes & Osnes, 1989). NT procedures were developed by various behavior analysts working independently rather than beginning with one program (as with DTT). Overall, NT procedures have been demonstrated to be effective in teaching various skills and producing generalized responding in children with ASD, particularly in the development of early verbal behavior, social interactions, and play skills (Allen & Cowan, 2008). They are widely recommended by multiple sources, such as the Division for Early Childhood of the Council for Exceptional Children and the National Research Council (Lane et al., 2016). Most NT procedures share common features of the instructor waiting for the learner to initiate for access to an item (or activity), preventing access to that item, delivering the item contingent upon responding (i.e., using natural consequences), conducting sessions in the natural environment (i.e., incorporating mediators), and with a variety of stimuli in the natural environment (training diversely, incorporating mediators). Instructors may be a variety of paid staff, family members, or community members (i.e., training diversely, incorporating mediators). Other beneficial aspects of NT noted by authors have included ease of implementation, high social validity, reduced need for specific procedures to program for generalization, reduced problem behavior, reduced need for aversive control, and ease of mixing opportunities for teaching different verbal operants under multiple control (Delprato, 2001; LeBlanc et al., 2006; Sundberg & Partington, 1998).

Naturalistic Teaching Approaches

The first well-known NT procedure was incidental teaching, developed by Betty Hart and Todd Risley at the University of Kansas in the 1960s. In their seminal study, Hart and Risley (1968) advocated for a new approach to language instruction because "… 'knowing'—the ability to respond correctly when asked—is not considered sufficient; the criterion for 'skill' is usage, spontaneous emission as functional language in everyday situations" (p. 109). They used incidental teaching to teach colors to preschool children with "families with extremely low incomes" by prompting them to say the color and item when requesting preferred items. Publication of these important findings led to many behavior analysts using incidental teaching, especially with children with ASD. Rather than being "by the way" teaching as might be inferred by its name, incidental teaching as a teaching strategy is a specific sequence of steps in which an instructor (a) arranges preferred item(s) in view of the learner, (b) waits for the learner to engage in an initiation (i.e., behavior that indicates an EO for the item; may be approach, reach, vocalization, sign, picture, depending on the learner), (c) prevents the learner from accessing the reinforcing properties of the item (and may prompt a target response), and (d) allows the learner to access the reinforcing properties of the item contingent upon criterion responding (Fenske et al., 2001). Variations of this procedure have been shown to produce acquisition and generalization when teaching a variety of responses, including preposition tacts (e.g., McGee et al., 1985), requests for toys and food (e.g., Farmer-Dougan, 1994; McGee et al., 1986, 1992), reading sight words on tokens before exchanging them (e.g., Fabry et al., 1984), pointing to items required to make lunch (e.g., McGee et al., 1983), and sign language (e.g., Schepis et al., 1982).

Incidental teaching has been used in two primary ways. In the first way, an instructor may observe a learner initiate something and *capture* the EO to teach something new or assess responding under novel conditions (Shafer, 1994). For example, at recess time, an instructor might prevent the door from opening when a learner tries to open it to go outside to play (i.e., capturing the EO) and open the door contingent upon the mand "open." A second way incidental teaching is conducted is similar to what Charlop-Christy and Carpenter (2000) called multiple incidental teaching sessions (MITS). This variation of incidental teaching provides more teaching opportunities to a learner. An instructor might plan to conduct incidental teaching sessions at specific times and places, target specific responses, and *contrive* EOs for items by arranging preferred items within view but out of reach or having broken or missing components in an interrupted chain (Shafer, 1994; Hall & Sundberg, 1987). For example, an instructor might select the target "book" to teach a learner in their incidental teaching program because books are highly preferred. The instructor could place the books on a high shelf where the learner can see but not reach them (i.e., contriving the EO) and provide them contingent upon the mand "book."

It should be noted that, although the target behavior in most incidental teaching studies (e.g., Farmer-Dougan, 1994; McGee et al., 1992), as well as in clinical applications, is requests for items, incidental teaching is different from mand training in that the goal is not always to teach a mand. For example, incidental teaching has been used to teach listener behavior (e.g., McGee et al., 1983), preposition tacts (e.g., McGee et al., 1985), and reading sight words (e.g., Fabry et al., 1984). Overall, incidental teaching aims "to get elaborated language by waiting for another person to initiate conversation about a topic and then responding in ways that ask for more language from that person" (Hart & Risley, 1982, p. 5). Both mand training and incidental teaching may involve capturing or contriving EOs; however, a variety of operants may be taught during incidental teaching. For example, an instructor might wait for a learner's initiation for a toy frog (preferred item), ask the learner, "What letter does 'frog' start with?" and deliver the frog contingent upon the learner saying "f." The instructor uses the EO for an item as an opportunity to teach a response *related* in some way to the item but not necessarily a mand. During another opportunity, when the learner initiates for the frog, the instructor might instead say, "Show me how a frog moves," and deliver the frog contingent upon the learner hopping. The response taught does not necessarily become a mand because various questions/ responses result in the toy frog across trials.

A second widely used NT procedure is the natural language paradigm (NLP), developed by Koegel et al. (1987). The steps of NLP include the instructor (a) presenting two to three toys, (b) preventing access to the toy, (c) modeling play with the toy before modeling a contextual vocalization, (d) giving the learner access to the toy contingent upon them saying something contextual, and (e) continuing to model actions and vocalizations as they play together (Gillett & LeBlanc, 2007). Although NLP shares features with incidental teaching (i.e., the instructor arranges items in view of the learner, waits for the learner to initiate for an item, prevents access to the item, models responses, delivers the item selected contingent upon behavior), there are several differences, including that in NLP the items are typically toys, the instructor models both play actions and contextual vocalizations, and attempts (rather than specific identified responses) are reinforced. Variations of this procedure have been shown to produce increases in and generalization of vocalizations with children with ASD (e.g., Camarata, 1996; Gillett & LeBlanc, 2007; Koegel et al., 1987; Koegel, Camarata et al., 1998; Koegel, Koegel et al., 1998; Laski et al., 1988) and even with older adults with neurocognitive disorder (e.g., LeBlanc et al., 2007). NLP later became the first step of a multicomponent naturalistic program for children with ASD called pivotal response training (PRT; Koegel et al., 2003).

A third widely used NT procedure is natural environment training (NET), developed by Sundberg and Partington (1998). NET is a "contrived and planned exercise and includes data collection—it just happens in the child's natural environment, not in the therapy room" (Barbera & Rasmussen, 2007, p. 133). The instructor waits for the learner to initiate interaction with something in the natural environment; items present may be contrived or naturally occurring, and the instructor prevents and then allows the learner to access reinforcing properties of the item contingent upon responding (Weiss, 2001). A unique feature of NET is the common use of activities rather than just items, allowing for extended interaction and practice with various verbal operants during a session, often building on targets taught during DTT sessions. As Sundberg and Partington described,

> If a child shows interest in a play set, it may be quite easy to teach the mand "train," as well as tacts for items related to the train, such as track, light, caboose, engine, wheels, etc., and intraverbals such as "It's a choo choo..."
>
> (p. 207)

Although NET was initially conceptualized as being based on NLP procedures, there are at least two important differences. First, NET primarily involves teaching verbal operants, as identified by Skinner (1957). Second, NET is combined with (rather than instead of) DTT (Barbera & Rasmussen, 2007; Sundberg & Partington, 1998; Weiss, 2005).

Limitations of Naturalistic Teaching

One of the main criticisms of NT procedures is that it may be difficult for instructors to conduct sufficient training opportunities in the natural environment to change a learner's behavior (Geiger et al., 2012; Sundberg & Partington, 1998). In addition, conducting sessions in the natural environment necessarily means that distractions (e.g., people talking, pets jumping up, visually stimulating decorations) will occur, and stimuli and antecedents will vary. Unlike DTT, NT procedures do not provide the consistent, individualized changes to distractions, stimuli, antecedents, and consequences that facilitate acquisition for some learners, especially those who display stimulus overselectivity (i.e., restricted stimulus control; Carnett et al., 2022). Using only natural consequences may not result in acquisition for some learners. For example, if social interactions do not reinforce a learner's behavior, teaching tacts and intraverbals with natural reinforcement (i.e., social interaction) will likely be ineffective. Other criticisms of NT procedures have included difficulty training instructors, cumbersome procedures, challenging data collection, and inadequate rigor of studies evaluating NT (Lane et al., 2016; Sundberg & Partington, 1998). Finally, although NT procedures are arranged so that the setting, instructors, stimuli, antecedents, and consequences commonly resemble the natural environment, these variables may sometimes be contrived. For example, the stimuli or instructor may be positioned to facilitate attending and/or salience, and praise/tickles may be used as consequences when the target response would not result in that type of reinforcement in the natural environment (e.g., Jobin, 2020; Jones et al., 2006; Koegel et al., 1992). As Green (2001) described,

> It should be noted that although incidental teaching and NLP procedures are often characterized as child-initiated because learning opportunities begin when the child shows interest in a preferred item, it is often necessary (and desirable) for interventionists to prompt a response. At that point the instruction becomes adult-directed. Adults also arrange antecedents and control access to reinforcers in typical incidental teaching and NLP interactions. Therefore the difference between these naturalistic procedures and discrete-trial procedures for teaching communication skills to learners with autism is not as substantial as some have suggested.
>
> (p. 83)

Which One Is Better?

A relatively small number of studies have compared the effects of DTT and NT on children with ASD. Unfortunately, it is difficult to draw conclusions from this body of literature due to two primary limitations (Geiger et al., 2012). First, many of these studies varied not only the teaching procedure but also the dependent variable that was taught. In the NT condition, the dependent variable is typically a mand (or is multiply controlled). In the DTT condition, the dependent variable is often a different operant such as a tact (e.g., Koegel et al., 1987), imitation (e.g., Koegel et al., 1992; Sigafoos et al., 2006), or receptive labeling (e.g., Sigafoos et al., 2006). Second, as noted by Geiger et al. (2012), the DTT procedures evaluated in these studies often do not reflect best practices such as conducting stimulus preference assessments to identify preferred items (e.g., McGee et al., 1985; Williams et al., 1981) or employing multiple exemplar training (e.g., Jobin, 2020).

Some authors have suggested that optimal outcomes for children with ASD will result from a careful combination of DTT and NT because they target different challenges experienced by individuals with ASD (Allen & Cowan, 2008; Weiss, 2005). For example, some authors have noted that DTT might be selected to teach skills requiring repeated practice, a high degree of stimulus control, and skills that are not automatically reinforcing, such as tacting, imitation, and listener skills; whereas, NT might be selected to teach skills that require generalization, such as initiations, manding, and conversation (Weiss, 2005). Sundberg and Michael (2001) recommended selecting DTT or NT based on the verbal operant being taught (p. 719):

> DTT is often contrasted with NET in the behavioral literature, with studies attempting to show that one approach is more beneficial than the other (e.g., Elliott et al., 1991; Koegel et al., 1992). However, a verbal behavior analysis suggests that the two focus on different verbal operants. Both teach receptive and expressive language, but NET is primarily based on mand training by using the child's current EOs and delivering specific reinforcement, whereas DTT is primarily based on tact and receptive training with nonverbal and verbal stimuli and delivering nonspecific reinforcement. From a verbal behavior perspective, a more complete language repertoire would be acquired from a combination of DTT and NET procedures.
>
> (M. L. Sundberg & Partington, 1999, p. 719)

Some behavior analysts have employed DTT and NT in different combinations throughout their intervention programs. For example, Lovaas and Smith (2003) described the intervention stages of a relatively recent version of the UCLA YAP program: Stage 1—DTT (reinforce direction-following, extinguish escape-maintained problem behavior); Stage 2—DTT (direction-following, matching, imitation, receptive object identification, toy play, dressing); Stage 3—DTT and incidental teaching combined (echoics, tacts, receptive, play); Stage 4—DTT, incidental teaching (tacts, play), dyads with typical peers; Stage 5—DTT, incidental teaching, small group instruction (intraverbals, perspective-taking, observational learning, working independently). Sundberg and Partington (1998) emphasized that teaching should always include DTT and NET, but in different amounts, depending on the skills taught. They recommended the following intervention phases: Phase 1—NET > DTT (mands, pairing instructor with rein-forcers, establishing compliance and stimulus control); Phase 2—NET = DTT (mands, tacts, receptive, imitation, echoics, intraverbals); Phase 3—DTT > NET (academics); Phase 4—NET > DTT (learning from group instruction, peers, without high level of structure); Phase 5—DTT > NET (academics, learning in structured classroom). Unfortunately, there is no research base to guide clini-cians on the optimal sequencing of programs or teaching strategies.

Another way that behavior analysts have combined DTT and NT is to mod-ify a procedure to teach a specific skill. For example, MITS (described above) "was designed to combine aspects of the discrete trial method that are said to increase the speed of acquisition with features of incidental teaching and the mand-model that enhance generalization" (Charlop-Christy & Carpenter, 2000, p. 99). Another example of this type of combination is called embedded instruc-tion, which involves

> incorporating structured learning opportunities into naturally occurring activities...One way to arrange embedded instruction is to identify play-based activities based on a learner's established preferences (e.g., Thomas the Tank Engine) and the type of skill that needs to be taught (e.g., receptive discriminations). The reinforcers could be directly embedded in the play-based activity such that if the learner responds correctly to the instructional trial, the reinforcer is advancement in a game (e.g., moving forward on a game board) or access to additional pieces of a desired play structure within the game or activity, respectively.
>
> (Geiger et al., 2012, p. 50)

DeBiase et al. (2022) noted that an advantage of embedded instruction is that the learner is not required to leave the activity to return to instruction. Geiger et al. (2012) compared the effects of DTT and embedded instruction on the receptive picture identification of two preschoolers with ASD. DTT comprised the contrived positioning of picture cards, instructions, and preferred items as consequences for picture selection. Embedded instruction comprised contrived positioning of game stimuli, instructions, and preferred items as consequences. One participant played Jump To It for embedded instruction, in which he jumped to the correct picture and then remained standing on it until the next trial (i.e., a possible natu-ral automatic reinforcer). A second participant played with Thomas the Train for embedded instruction, in which the array of pictures was presented on a piece of train track; correct picture selection resulted in access to that piece of track, all previously earned pieces, and time to play (i.e., possible automatic reinforcer). Results showed that DTT and embedded instruction were similarly effective and efficient for both participants. One participant displayed similar affect and prefer-ence for both conditions; one participant displayed more positive affect and prefer-ence for embedded instruction. Haq and Aranki (2019) replicated these findings with a school-age child with ASD. In a replication and extension with adults with ASD, DeBiase et al. found that participants preferred, had more positive affect, and learned more quickly with embedded instruction but required longer sessions. Geiger et al. suggested several variables to consider when developing an embedded instruction program, including time and money available, necessary prerequisite skills, preferred items and skills that can be incorporated, and relative efficiency and learner preference for embedded instruction.

Recommendations: An Analog-Naturalistic Teaching Continuum

When selecting procedures for teaching a skill to a learner, a behavior analyst considers several variables to bring about effective, efficient, socially valid, generalized, and durable results while balancing resources of time, expertise, staff availability, materials, and finances. The teaching arrangement can be made more or less like the natural or "speaking" environment, depending on the characteristics and preferences of the learner, goals of teaching, resources available, and values of the learner's family and community. Rather than viewing approaches for teaching language as a dichotomy, LeBlanc et al. (2006) proposed conceptualizing them as a continuum that reflects correspondence between the training context and the eventual desired performance context, with early DTT having little correspondence and NT having high correspondence.

Figure 3.1 shows a continuum of language instruction based on correspondence with the natural environment across four major areas: settings, instructors, teaching stimuli, and putative reinforcers. The left side represents low correspondence ("pure" analog or contrived teaching), and the right side represents high correspondence ("pure" naturalistic teaching); in practice, it is unlikely that there are behavioral intervention programs at either end of this continuum across all variables. Instead, programs are more likely to employ procedures that fall at

Low correspondence with natural environment	High correspondence with natural environment
Contrived teaching setting; No distractions	Natural settings; distractions are variable, naturally occurring
Instructors are 1:1 clinicians; individualized, contrived positioning	Instructors are family, friends, teachers; ratio is variable, naturally occurring
Teaching stimuli are individualized, contrived: selection, arrangement, positioning, modality, topography, pacing	Teaching stimuli are variable, naturally occurring
Consequences are individualized, contrived items, activities. interactions	Consequences are variable, naturally occurring

Figure 3.1 Language instruction continuum based on correspondence with the natural environment.

different places on the continuum, varying across learners and skills. Although "DTT" has been used to describe teaching toward the left side of this continuum, continued use of this term may lead to confusion because of a long history of misconceptions, its inaccurate equivalence with ABA and/or the UCLA YAP program, and because NT (and most procedures resulting in operant learning) also involves teaching with discrete trials. Some authors (e.g., Allen & Cowan, 2008; Koegel et al., 2003; Sundberg & Partington, 1998) have used "analog" or "contrived" as an alternative because these terms function as opposites to "naturalistic" and accurately reflect the use of contrived teaching procedures.

It may be beneficial to begin developing a teaching procedure by considering procedures on the right side of the continuum, the learner's natural environment, because performance in that context is the ultimate goal. Teaching procedures can be made more contrived in different areas for different skills as needed. Increasing contrivance is perhaps best done thoughtfully with clear rationales, which may include a goal of increasing effectiveness, efficiency, social validity, and/or due to the availability of resources in time, expertise, staff, materials, and finances. Any modifications made to the training situation/procedures that make them different from what happens in the learner's "speaking" environment are perhaps best viewed as similar to prompts—that is, to be removed as soon as possible. For some learners, removing contrived aspects of language instruction may be achieved more quickly if frequent probes are conducted to assess performance under natural environment conditions. For other learners, modifications may remain in place longer and be removed more slowly as the behavior analyst addresses issues such as overselectivity (Carnett et al., 2022). In addition, for some learners, optimal procedures might include a high level of modifications in some variables or for some skills, and not others.

The first three areas (i.e., setting, instructors, teaching stimuli) are primarily related to stimulus control and generalization. Specific procedures may be used for facilitating generalization (e.g., Stokes & Osnes, 1989), such as training diversely, incorporating mediators, and matrix training. Regarding setting, it may be impractical or ineffective to teach in the natural environment. For example, when developing a program for teaching a learner to say a prayer at their place of worship, if teaching cannot be conducted in that setting, a behavior analyst might identify critical features of the setting that can be brought into the training setting (i.e., training mediators) or teach in a variety of settings (i.e., multiple exemplar training) to facilitate generalization. A behavior analyst may alter visual, auditory, or other types of sensory stimulation (e.g., pictures on walls, sounds, an open door, people/pets walking through the room) in the teaching environment to increase control by relevant stimuli. Distractions may be systematically programmed and changed over time to help the learner reach the goal. Considerations for contriving this variable include the type/frequency of distractions that occur in the teaching environment, how distractions impact acquisition of the target skill, and the type/frequency of distractions in the natural environment in which the skill is needed. Similarly, it may be impractical or not optimal for family, friends, and teachers to function as instructors. Instead, some or all instructors may be paid staff who may differ from individuals in a learner's natural environment in various ways, such as their training, time to focus solely on the learner, and physical characteristics due to variables such as gender, age, or skin color. Instructors may position themselves in relation to the learner (e.g., close proximity, eye level) to increase attending or so that prompts and error correction can be quickly and easily implemented. To program for generalization, a behavior analyst might arrange for instructors to teach across the learner's programs (i.e., multiple exemplar training) and train the most important people in the learner's life (i.e., incorporating mediators). Contrived positioning may be systematically programmed and changed over time toward the goal of variable, naturally occurring positioning of instructors.

Also related to stimulus control, a behavior analyst may individualize and contrive the stimuli used for teaching in various ways to facilitate acquisition and prevent faulty stimulus control. Contrived objects or pictures may be used, allowing an instructor to teach multiple exemplars that may not readily occur in the natural environment. Videos may be individualized to increase the salience of specific aspects of a model (e.g., Charlop-Christy et al., 2000). Verbal stimuli may be altered in terms of length, volume, form, prosody, and/or pacing; audio or textual models may be used to prompt verbal behavior if a second instructor is unavailable or because they may be faded more quickly than in vivo models for that learner (e.g., Patil et al., 2021). Teaching stimuli may be selected so they are maximally discriminable to a learner to address issues related to stimulus salience and/or disparity; for example, the targets "cat," "juice," and "boat" might be selected rather than "cat," "cap," and "cab" to facilitate differential listener responding for an early learner (Halbur et al., 2021). Teaching trials may be sequenced in specific orders, and the positioning of stimuli may be contrived to prevent faulty stimulus control (e.g., Grow & LeBlanc, 2013). Research has also demonstrated the effectiveness of including additional antecedent components to a trial, including the instructor teaching the learner to engage in an observing response (e.g., Petursdottir & Aguilar, 2016) or differential observing response (e.g., Walpole et al., 2007) or presenting sample and comparison stimuli in a specific sequence (e.g., Bergmann et al., 2021). For example, in the natural environment, a child might learn to point to pictures in a book of animals by reading the book with their parent. The parents' instruction to point to an animal might vary across readings (e.g., "Where's the pig?" "Find the piggy"), and the pacing of the book might be leisurely and include completing the entire book. When the child correctly points to the animal, the parent might praise; when the child incorrectly points or doesn't respond, the parent might point to the animal. A child with ASD might have difficulty learning to correctly point to animals in this natural situation for several reasons. Some difficulties related to issues with teaching stimuli may include the child not attending to the correct pictures (or relevant features of the pictures); the parent's instructions or prompts being too variable; because the pictures are in the same place and the same order every reading, responding may come under the control of variables other than the verbal antecedent; and the natural pacing and duration of reading might result in lower levels of attention. Initially, to teach this child this type of skill, it might be necessary to have them engage in an observing response, use a different type of consistent prompt that evokes the correct response, systematically fade prompts, randomize the position and sequence of the pictures, and read just a few pages at a faster pace.

The last area listed in Figure 3.1 refers to putative reinforcers. As with stimulus control, it may be beneficial to begin developing a teaching procedure by considering procedures on the right side of the continuum and discovering what type, magnitude, quality, schedule, and delay will naturally occur for that learner for the target response in the natural environment. The type of reinforcer is of particular importance for children with ASD because most verbal behavior (e.g., mands for information, bids for joint attention, intraverbals) is maintained by some type of social interaction. For some people with ASD, social stimuli may be less effective as reinforcers than non-social stimuli (e.g., Butler & Graff, 2021; Morris & Vollmer, 2021). For example, in the scenario described above with the animal book, a natural consequence that would be effective in teaching a neurotypical child to correctly point to animals in the book might be the parent praising (e.g., "Yep, there's the piggy!"). It may not, however, be effective in teaching the same skill to a child with ASD. Researchers have attempted to address this issue in several ways. When the natural reinforcer for a target response does not function as such, behavior analysts may teach using contrived preferred items as reinforcers. Research indicates that best practice includes instructors ensuring that an EO for the item being used as a reinforcer is in effect when using contrived preferred items. This may be accomplished by preventing access to those items for specific periods to increase the EO and/or conducting a preference assessment before presenting the antecedent or immediately after the learner responds. It should be noted that although using contrived preferred items often allows for rapid acquisition, if the consequences delivered in the natural environment for the newly acquired behaviors do not function as reinforcers, the new behaviors will not maintain. Removing the contrived preferred items will result in extinction of the new behavior if it no longer contacts reinforcement. Unfortunately, we do not yet have a research-based technology for establishing and maintaining conditioned reinforcement effects with children with ASD (Dozier et al., 2012; Sainsbury et al., 2024). However, there is a related line of research showing effective "pairing" procedures for increasing learner approaches/closeness to instructors and in-seat behavior (e.g., Kelly et al., 2015; Morris & Vollmer, 2022; Shillingsburg et al., 2014; Shillingsburg et al., 2019).

Some studies have used idiosyncratic forms of social reinforcement or a larger magnitude/quality of social interaction than would occur in the natural environment. For example, to teach joint attention skills to children with ASD, Jones et al. (2006) noted,

> Because the consequences inherent in the social interaction described are typically not reinforcing for children with autism, we added specific idiosyncratic forms of social attention, such as a loud "Wow!," a big smile, or a brief tickle, identified by parents and teachers as preferred by each child.
>
> (p. 793)

Although this type of reinforcement is still contrived (i.e., different type, quality, or magnitude of social interaction), it may be preferred over using more disparate contrived consequences (e.g., preferred tangible items). A behavior analyst may conduct a systematic assessment to identify how a learner responds to general and idiosyncratic forms of social interactions (e.g., Morris & Vollmer, 2022).

Other modifications that might be made to increase acquisition are to alter the quality, schedule, or delay to the consequence, or to provide instructive feedback to the learner (e.g., Johnson et al., 2017; Nottingham et al., 2020). Instructors may individualize consequences in other ways to maximize learning. For example, if loud sounds are aversive to a learner, the instructor might praise quietly; to prevent satiation, the instructor might give the learner smaller pieces of cookie than would be given in the natural environment when a learner mands for a cookie, use a token system, or rotate items used as reinforcers. Especially during teaching a new skill, instructors may deliver preferred items/activities on a denser reinforcement schedule than in the natural environment. For example, a continuous schedule of reinforcement might be used for acquisition even though the target response is not maintained by continuous reinforcement in their natural environment.

Conclusions

Many behavior analysts have contributed to developing effective analog and naturalistic procedures for teaching individuals with ASD. The science of behavior analysis has progressed substantially, providing us with a rich conceptual knowledge of learning and research demonstrating ways to improve how we impact the lives of learners. These innovations have allowed the expansion of separate teaching models into a continuum of options for arranging language training. Rather than choosing a type of teaching model, instructors may select from the full spectrum of research-based procedures that range from closely corresponding to the natural environment to being highly contrived, to provide the most effective, efficient, socially valid, generalized, and durable outcomes for their clients. As scientist-practitioners, behavior analysts continue to expand this continuum of options as research informs us on how to best reach this goal.

References

Ahearn, W., H., Parry-Cruwys, D., Toran, T., & MacDonald, J. (2015). Stimulus salience in autism: A social learning disorder. In F. D. Digennaro Reed & D. D. Reed (Eds.), *Autism service delivery: Bridging the gap between science and practice* (pp. 75–111). Springer. https://doi.org/10.1007/978-1-4939-2656-5

Allen, K. D., & Cowan, R. J. (2008). Naturalistic teaching procedures. In J. K. Luiselli, D. C. Russo, W. P. Christian, & S. M. Wilczynski (Eds.), *Effective practices for children with autism: Educational and behavior support interventions that work* (pp. 240–270). Oxford University Press. https://doi.org/10.1093/med:psych/9780195317046.003.0011

Barbera, M. L., & Rasmussen, T. (2007). *The verbal behavior approach: How to teach children with autism and related disorders.* Jessica Kingsley.

Bergmann, S., Turner, M., Kodak, T., Grow, L. L., Meyerhofer, C., Niland, H. S., & Edmonds, K. (2021). Replicating stimulus-presentation orders in discrimination training. *Journal of Applied Behavior Analysis, 54*(2), 793–812. https://doi.org/10.1002/jaba.797

Butler, C., & Graff, R. B. (2021). Stability of preference and reinforcing efficacy of edible, leisure, and social attention stimuli. *Journal of Applied Behavior Analysis, 54*(2), 684–699. https://doi.org/10.1002/jaba.807

Camarata, S. M. (1996). On the importance of integrating naturalistic language, social intervention, and speech-intelligibility training. In L. Koegel, R. Koegel, & G. Dunlap (Eds.), *Positive behavioral support: Including people with difficult behavior in the community* (pp. 333–351). Brookes.

Carnett, A., Sigafoos, J., & Neely, L. (2022). Programming for generalization and maintenance. In J. L. Matson & P. Sturmey (Eds.), *Handbook of autism and pervasive developmental disorder, Autism and child psychopathology series* (pp. 801–820). Springer Nature Switzerland. https://doi.org/10.1007/978-3-030-88538-0_34

Charlop-Christy, M. H., & Carpenter, M. H. (2000). Modified incidental teaching sessions: A procedure for parents to increase spontaneous speech in their children with autism. *Journal of Positive Behavior Interventions, 2*(2), 98–112. https://doi.org/10.1177/109830070000200203

Charlop-Christy, M. H., Le, L., & Freeman, K. A. (2000). A comparison of video modeling with in vivo modeling for teaching children with autism. *Journal of Autism and Developmental Disorders, 30*(6), 537–552.

Delprato, D. J. (2001). Comparisons of discrete-trial and normalized behavioral language intervention for young children with autism. *Journal of Autism and Developmental Disorders, 31*(3), 315–325.

Dozier, C. L., Iwata, B. A., Thomason-Sassi, J., Worsdell, A. S., & Wilson, D. M. (2012). A comparison of two pairing procedures to establish praise as a reinforcer. *Journal of Applied Behavior Analysis, 45*(4), 721–735. https://doi.org/10.1901/jaba.2012.45-721

Eikeseth, S. (2016). Psychopathology as a result of selection by consequences exemplified by autism spectrum disorders (ASD). *Norsk Tidsskrift for Atferdsanalyse, 43*(1), 35–38.

Elliott, R. O., Jr., Hall, K., & Soper, H. V. (1991). Analog language teaching versus natural language teaching: Generalization and retention of language learning for adults with autism and mental retardation. *Journal of Autism and Developmental Disorders, 21,* 433–447.

Fabry, B. D., Mayhew, G. L., & Hanson, A. (1984). Incidental teaching of mental retarded students within a token system. *American Journal of Mental Deficiency, 89*(1), 29–36.

Farmer-Dougan, V. (1994). Increasing requests by adults with developmental disabilities using incidental teaching by peers. *Journal of Applied Behavior Analysis, 27*(3), 533–544. https://doi.org/10.1901/jaba.1994.27-533

Fenske, E. C., Krantz, P. J., & McClannahan, L. E. (2001). Incidental teaching: A not-discrete-trial teaching procedure. In C. Maurice, G. Green, & R. M. Foxx (Eds.), *Making a difference: Behavioral intervention for autism* (pp. 75–81). Pro-ed.

Frank-Crawford, M. A., Borrero, J. C., Fisher, A., Talhelm, P., & Fernandez, N. (2024). Discrete-trial teaching: A scoping review. *Behavioral Interventions.* Advance online publication. https://doi.org/10.1002/bin.2012

Gale, C. M., Eikeseth, S., & Klintwall, L. (2019). Children with autism show atypical preference for non-social stimuli. *Scientific Reports, 9*(1), 1–10.

Geiger, K. B., Carr, J. E., LeBlanc, J. E., Hanney, N. M., & Pollock, A. S. (2012). Teaching receptive discriminations to children with autism: A comparison of traditional and embedded discrete trial teaching. *Behavior Analysis in Practice, 5*(2), 49–59. https://doi.org/10.1007/bf03391823

Ghezzi, P. M. (2007). Discrete trials teaching. *Psychology in the Schools, 44*(7), 667–679. https://doi.org/10.1002/pits.20256

Gillett, J. N., & LeBlanc, L. A. (2007). Parent-implemented natural language paradigm to increase language and play in children with autism. *Research in Autism Spectrum Disorders, 1*(3), 247–255. https://doi.org/10.1016/j.rasd.2006.09.003.

Green, G. (2001). Behavior analytic instruction for learners with autism: Advances in stimulus control technology. *Focus on Autism and Other Developmental Disabilities, 16*(2), 72–85. https://doi.org/10.1177/108835760101600203

Grow L., & LeBlanc L. A. (2013). Teaching receptive language skills: Recommendations for instructors. *Behavior Analysis in Practice, 6*(1), 56–75. https://doi.org/10.1007/BF03391791.

Halbur, M. E., Caldwell, R. K., & Kodak, T. (2021). Stimulus control research and practice: Considerations of stimulus disparity and salience for discrimination training. *Behavior Analysis in Practice, 14*(1), 272–282. https://doi.org/10.1007/s40617-020-00509-9

Hall, G., & Sundberg, M. L. (1987). Teaching mands by manipulating conditioned establishing operations. *The Analysis of Verbal Behavior, 5,* 41–53. https://doi.org/10.1007/BF03392819

Haq, S. S., & Aranki, J. (2019). Comparison of traditional and embedded DTT on problem behavior and responding to instructional targets. *Behavior Analysis in Practice, 12,* 396–400. https://doi.org/10.1007/s40617-018-00324-3

Hart, B. M., & Risley, T. R. (1968). Establishing use of descriptive adjectives in the spontaneous speech of disadvantaged preschool children. *Journal of Applied Behavior Analysis, 1*(2), 109–120. https://doi.org/10.1901/jaba.1968.1-109

Hart, B., & Risley, T. R. (1982). *How to use incidental teaching for elaborating language.* H & H Enterprises.

Jobin, A. (2020). Varied treatment response in young children with autism: A relative comparison of structured and naturalistic behavioral approaches. *Autism*, *24*(2), 338–351. https://doi.org/10.1177/1362361319859726

Johnson, K. A., Vladescu, J. C., Kodak, T., & Sidener, T. M. (2017). An assessment of differential reinforcement procedures for learners with autism spectrum disorder. *Journal of Applied Behavior Analysis*, *50*(2), 290–303. https://doi.org/10.1002/jaba .372

Jones, E. A., Carr, E. G., & Feeley, K. M. (2006). Multiple effects of joint attention intervention for children with autism. *Behavior Modification*, *30*(6), 782–834. https:// doi.org/10.1177/0145445506289392

Kelly, A. N., Axe, J. B., Allen, R. F., & Maguire, R. W. (2015). Effects of presession pairing on the challenging behavior and academic responding of children with autism. *Behavioral Interventions*, *30*, 135–156. https://doi.org 10.1002/bin.1408

Klin, A., Shultz, S., & Jones, W. (2015). Social visual engagement in infants and toddlers with autism: Early developmental transitions and a model of pathogenesis. *Neuroscience & Biobehavioral Reviews*, *50*, 189–203. https://doi.org/10.1016/j .neubiorev.2014.10.006

Klintwall, L., & Eikeseth, S. (2014). Early and intensive behavioral intervention in autism. In V. B. Patel, V. R. Preedy, & C. R. Martin (Eds.), *Comprehensive guide to autism* (pp. 117–137). Springer. https://doi.org/10.1007/978-1-4614-4788-7_129

Koegel, L. K., Koegel, R. L., & Carter, C. (1998). Pivotal responses and the natural language teaching paradigm. *Seminars in Speech and Language*, *19*, 355–371. https:// doi.org/10.1055/s-2008-1064054

Koegel, R. L., Camarata, Koegel, L. K., Ben-Tall, A., & Smith, A. E. (1998). Increasing speech intelligibility in children with autism. *Journal of Autism and Developmental Disorders*, *28*, 241–250.

Koegel, R. L., Koegel, L. K., & Brookman, L. I. (2003). Empirically supported pivotal response interventions for children with autism. In A. E. Kazdin & J. R. Weisz (Eds.), *Evidence-based psychotherapies for children and adolescents* (pp. 341–357). The Guilford Press.

Koegel, R. L., Koegel, L. K., & Surratt, A. (1992). Language intervention and disruptive behavior in preschool children with autism. *Journal of Autism and Developmental Disorders*, *22*(2), 141–153. https://doi.org/10.1007/bf01058147

Koegel, R. L., O'Dell, M. C., & Koegel, L. K. (1987). A natural language paradigm for teaching non-verbal autistic children. *Journal of Autism and Developmental Disorders*, *17*, 187–199. https://doi.org/10.1007/bf01495055

Lane, J. D., Lieberman-Betz, R., & Gast, D. L. (2016). An analysis of naturalistic interventions for increasing spontaneous expressive language in children with autism spectrum disorder. *The Journal of Special Education*, *50*(1), 49–61. https://doi.org/10 .1177/0022466915614837

Laski, K. E., Charlop, M. H., & Schreibman, L. (1988). Training parents to use the natural language paradigm to increase their autistic children's speech. *Journal of Applied Behavior Analysis*, *21*(4), 391–400. https://doi.org/10.1901/jaba.1988.21-391

Leaf, R., & McEachin, R. (2016). The Lovaas model: Love it or hate it, but first understand it. In R. G. Romanczyk & R. Leaf (Eds.), *Comprehensive models of autism spectrum disorder treatment* (pp. 7–43). Springer International Publishing. https://doi.org/10 .1007/978-3-319-40904-7_2

LeBlanc, L. A., Esch, J., Sidener, T. M., & Firth, A. K. (2006). Behavioral language interventions for children with autism: Comparing applied verbal behavior and naturalistic teaching approaches. *The Analysis of Verbal Behavior, 22,* 49–60. https:// doi.org/10.1007/bf03393026

LeBlanc, L. A., Geiger, K. B., Sautter R. A., & Sidener T. M. (2007). Using the natural language paradigm (NLP) to increase vocalizations of older adults with cognitive impairments. *Research in Developmental Disabilities, 28*(4), 437–444. https://doi.org /10.1016/j.ridd.2006.06.004.

Lovaas, O. I. (1987). Behavioral treatment and normal educational and intellectual functioning in young autistic children. *Journal of Consulting and Clinical Psychology, 55*(1), 3–9. https://doi.org/10.1037/0022-006X.55.1.3

Lovaas, O. I. (1991). *Teaching developmentally disabled children: The me book.* University Park Press.

Lovaas, O. I. (1993). The development of a treatment-research project for developmentally disabled and autistic children. *Journal of Applied Behavior Analysis, 26*(4), 617–630. https://doi.org/10.1901/jaba.1993.26-617

Lovaas, O. I., Berberich, J. P., Perloff, B. F., & Schaffer, B. (1966). Acquisition of imitative speech by schizophrenic children. *Science, 151*(3711), 705–707. https://doi .org/10.1126/science.151.3711.705

Lovaas, O. I., & Smith, T. (2003). Early and intensive behavioral intervention in autism. In A. E. Kazdin & J. R. Weisz (Eds.), *Evidence-based psychotherapies for children and adolescents* (pp. 325–338). The Guilford Press.

McGee, G. G., Almeida, M. C., Sulzer-Azaroff, B., & Fedman, R. S. (1992). Promoting reciprocal interactions via peer incidental teaching. *Journal of Applied Behavior Analysis, 25*(1), 117–126. https://doi.org/10.1901/jaba.1992.25-117

McGee, G. G., Krantz, P. J., Mason, D., & McClannahan, L. E. (1983). A modified incidental-teaching procedure for autistic youth: Acquisition and generalization of receptive object labels. *Journal of Applied Behavior Analysis, 16*(3), 329–338. https:// doi.org/10.1901/jaba.1983.16-329

McGee, G. G., Krantz, P. J., & McClannahan, L. E. (1985). The facilitative effects of incidental teaching on preposition use by autistic children. *Journal of Applied Behavior Analysis, 18*(1), 17–31. https://doi.org/10.1901/jaba.1985.18-17

McGee, G. G., Krantz, P. J., & McClannahan, L. E. (1986). An extension of incidental teaching procedures to reading instruction for autistic children. *Journal of Applied Behavior Analysis, 19*(2), 147–157. https://doi.org/10.1901/jaba.1986.19-47

Morris, S. L., & Vollmer, T. R. (2021). Evaluating the function of social interaction for children with autism. *Journal of Applied Behavior Analysis, 54*(4), 1456–1467. https://doi.org/10.1002/jaba.850

Morris, S. L., & Vollmer, T. R. (2022). Increasing social time allocation and concomitant effects on mands, item engagement, and rigid or repetitive behavior. *Journal of Applied Behavior Analysis, 55*(3), 814–851. https://doi.org/10.1002/jaba.919

Nottingham, C. L., Vladescu, J. C., DeBar, R. M., Deshais, M., & DeQuinzio, J. (2020). The influence of instructive feedback presentation schedule: A replication with children with autism spectrum disorder. *Journal of Applied Behavior Analysis*, *53*(4), 2287–2302. https://doi.org/10.1002/jaba.706

Ozerk, K., Vea, G. D., Eikeseth, S., & Ozerk, M. (2016). Ole Ivar Lovaas - His life, merits and legacy. *International Electronic Journal of Elementary Education*, *9*(2), 243–262.

Patil, P., Sidener, T. M., Pane, H., Reeve, S. A., & Nirgudkar, A. (2021). Teaching children with autism spectrum disorder to mand "why?". *The Analysis Verbal Behavior*, *37*, 1–16. https://doi.org/10.1007/s40616-020-00138-x

Petursdottir, A. I., & Aguilar, G. (2016). Order of stimulus presentation influences children's acquisition in receptive identification tasks. *Journal of Applied Behavior Analysis*, *49*(1), 58–68. https://doi.org/10.1002/jaba.264

Sainsbury, E. L., Sidener, T. M., Taylor-Santa, C., Reeve, K. F., & Sidener, D. W. (2024). Evaluation of a discrimination training procedure for establishing praise as a reinforcer. *Journal of Applied Behavior Analysis*, *57*(3), 776–783. https://doi.org/10.1002/jaba .1071

Schepis, M. M., Reid, D. H., Fitzgerald, J. R., Faw, G. D, Van Den Pol, R. A., & Welty, P. A. (1982). A program for increasing manual signing by autistic and profoundly retarded youth within the daily environment. *Journal of Applied Behavior Analysis*, *15*(3), 363–379. https://doi.org/10.1901/jaba.1982.15-363

Shafer, E. (1994). A review of interventions to teach a mand repertoire. *The Analysis of Verbal Behavior*, *12*, 53–66. https://doi.org/10.1007/BF0339287

Shillingsburg, M. A., Bowen, C. N., & Shapiro, S. K. (2014). Increasing social approach and decreasing social avoidance in children with autism spectrum disorder during discrete trial training. *Research in Autism Spectrum Disorders*, *8*, 1443–1453. http:// dx.doi.org/10.1016/j.rasd.2014.07.013

Shillingsburg, M. A., Hansen, B., & Wright, M. (2019). Rapport building and instructional fading prior to discrete trial instruction: Moving from child-led play to intensive teaching. *Behavior Modification*, *43*(2) 288–306. https://doi.org/10.1177 /0145445517751436

Sigafoos, J., O'Reilly, M., Hui Ma, C., Edrisinha, C., Cannella, H., & Lancioni, G. E. (2006). Effects of embedded instruction versus discrete-trial training on self-injury, correct responding, and mood in a child with autism. *Journal of Intellectual & Developmental Disability*, *31*, 196–203. https://doi.org/10.1080/13668250600999160

Skinner, B. F. (1957). *Verbal behavior*. Appleton-Century-Crofts.

Smith, T. (2001). Discrete trial training in the treatment of autism. *Focus on Autism and Other Developmental Disabilities*, *16*(2), 86–92. https://doi.org/10.1177 /108835760101600204

Smith, T., & Eikeseth, S. (2011). O. Ivar Lovaas: Pioneer of applied behavior analysis and intervention for children with autism. *Journal of Autism and Developmental Disorders*, *41*, 375–378. https://doi.org/10.1007/s10803-010-1162-0

Spradlin, J. E., & Brady, N. C. (1999). Early childhood autism and stimulus control. In P. M. Ghezzi, W. L. Williams, & J. E. Carr (Eds.), *Autism: Behavior analytic perspectives* (pp. 49–65). Context Press.

Stokes, T. F., & Baer, D. M. (1977). An implicit technology of generalization. *Journal of Applied Behavior Analysis*, *10*(2), 349–367. https://doi.org/10.1901/jaba.1977.10-349

Stokes, T. F., & Osnes, P. G. (1989). An operant pursuit of generalization. *Behavior Therapy*, *20*(3), 337–355. https://doi.org/10.1016/s0005-7894(89)80054-1

Sundberg, M. L., & Michael, J. (2001). The benefits of Skinner's analysis of verbal behavior for children with autism. *Behavior Modification, 25*(5), 698–724. https://doi.org/10.1177/0145445501255003

Sundberg, M. L., & Partington, J. W. (1998). *Teaching language to children with autism and other developmental disabilities.* Behavior Analysts, Inc.

Tarbox, R. S. F., & Najdowski, A. C. (2008). Discrete trial training as a teaching paradigm. In J. K. Luiselli, D. C. Russo, W. P. Christina, & S. M. Wilczynski (Eds.), *Effective practices for children with autism* (pp. 181–194). Oxford University Press. https://doi.org/10.1093/med:psych/9780195317046.003.0009

Walpole, C. W., Roscoe, E. M., & Dube, W. V. (2007). Use of a differential observing response to expand restricted stimulus control. *Journal of Applied Behavior Analysis, 40*(4), 707–712. https://doi.org/10.1901/jaba.2007.707–712

Weiss, M. (2001). Expanding ABA interventions in intensive programs for children with autism: The inclusion of natural environment training and fluency based instruction. *The Behavior Analyst Today, 2*(3), 182–186. https://doi.org/10.1037/h0099946

Weiss, M. (2005). Comprehensive ABA programs: Integrating and evaluating the implementation of varied instructional approaches. *The Behavior Analyst Today, 6*(4), 249–256. https://doi.org/10.1037/h0100077

Williams, J. A., Koegel, R. L., & Egel, A. L. (1981). Response-reinforcer relationships and improved learning in autistic children. *Journal of Applied Behavior Analysis, 14*(1), 53–60. https://doi.org/10.1901/jaba.1981.14-53

Wolf, M., Risley, T., & Mees, H. (1964). Application of operant conditioning procedures to the behaviour problems of an autistic child. *Behaviour Research and Therapy, 1*(2–4), 305–312. https://doi.org/10.1016/0005-7967(63)90045-7

Section 2

Teaching

Chapter 4

Strategies for Assessing and Teaching the Mand

Sarah A. Lechago and Mary E. Halbur

Defining the Mand

The mand, derived from "command" and "demand," is a verbal operant under the primary influence of the prevailing motivating operation(s) (MOs; MOs refer to motivation, which we will discuss in greater detail later in the chapter) and is reinforced by a characteristic consequence (Michael, 1982; Skinner, 1957). Manding benefits the speaker by providing the listener with information about the speaker's current condition. This enables the speaker to exercise control over the environment and have their needs met. Manding can lead to the acquisition of new behavior and reductions in problem behavior. Some would suggest that the mand is the first operant an infant acquires, as evidenced by the varied cries and sounds evoked by different MOs (e.g., hunger, physical discomfort, distress; Sagi, 1981). For example, a wet, uncomfortable diaper might influence a cry that consistently produces the removal of the diaper, and food deprivation might influence a different-sounding cry that results in the presentation of food. Mands are emitted early and are an essential part of socialization and development.

Starting early in a child's life, it is common for caregivers and teachers to differentially reinforce attempts at vocal[1] utterances and approximations of words. For example, a child might reach for a ball (suggesting an MO for the reinforcer of stimulation and play), to which the caregiver might say, "ball" as they give the ball to the child, to which the child might attempt to imitate by making the "b" sound, resulting in gaining access to the ball. This reinforces the emission of the "b" sound, and if the "b" sound reliably produces access to the ball under similar conditions, it will come to function as a mand. Over time, this vocal utterance will be shaped to the form "ba" and, finally, "ball." As a child's oral-motor skills develop and their environmental interactions expand, they will imitate multiple words with greater ease and emit numerous mands and mand frames for items, activities, and people. Mand frames are mands with an extended mean length utterance that can consist of a subject, verb, and object. Mand frames can be short and simple, "Want chocolate," or long and more advanced, "Yes, I would like the chocolate, please." As children learn to exert greater control over

DOI: 10.4324/9781003433668-6

their body and environment, they will learn to emit negatively reinforced mands (mands reinforced by the removal of or delay to something). This is when we start to observe the characteristic and ubiquitous "no" common to children 2–3 years old. The word "no" often produces the removal of unwanted or aversive items, foods, people, or demands. Negatively reinforced mands become more sophisticated with expanded frames and greater specificity over time. For example, if a caregiver turns on a movie their child does not want to watch, they might say, "I don't want this movie," resulting in the caregiver turning off the movie. Eventually, as their manding repertoire becomes increasingly advanced, children learn to mand for information (Who? What? When? Where? Why? How?). This suggests that over time, information is conditioned as a reinforcer. This occurs through numerous pairings between information and other reinforcers. For example, interacting with grandma may function as a reinforcer, making information about her location important and also function as a reinforcer, influencing the mand for information, "Where is grandma?" Manding for information is essential for success across a variety of contexts. Some examples include manding for clarification on an assignment (education), manding for the location of the Human Resources office (vocational), and manding for information about someone's status (social—"How is your father feeling?"). Importantly, manding for information is also essential to problem-solving as we frequently engage in mands for information and function as our own listener ("Where was the last place I had my keys?").

The mand directly benefits the speaker. Therefore, targeting it early when teaching verbal behavior is critical. Sundberg and Michael (2001) recommended targeting the mand as one of the first, if not the first, operants when teaching verbal behavior to individuals with autism spectrum disorder (ASD). The rationale for this recommendation is that the mand directly benefits the speaker and, therefore, makes verbal behavior immediately functional for them. Additionally, targeting the mand capitalizes on the speaker's motivation, making teaching verbal behavior easier for the caregiver or instructional agent. A robust body of published literature includes extensive research on and conceptual analyses of the mand. These publications have yielded important information about the mand, including antecedent events that influence their emission and the consequences that maintain them.

It is important for program development to understand the unique interactive effects, the multiple control of the discriminative stimulus (S^D) and MO, and how each differentially contributes to the emission of the mand. Motivating operations are changes in some internal or external environmental event that exert two major influences. The first is that they influence the reinforcing or punishing value of a stimulus (or class of stimuli). The second is that they influence response classes that have produced those reinforcers and punishers in the past. The MO primarily influences the mand's form (Miguel, 2017; Skinner,

1957). For example, if an individual is food-deprived, the mand will be for food (e.g., banana, pizza). However, if the individual is deprived of warmth (i.e., feels cold), the mand will be for warmth (e.g., blanket, jacket, heater). Under the value-altering effect, the MO can either establish or abolish a stimulus as a reinforcer or punisher. For example, food deprivation will establish food as a reinforcer, and satiation will abolish the value of food as a reinforcer. A head-ache may establish music as a punisher but may simultaneously establish a cold cloth as a reinforcer. Under the behavior-altering effect, a response class that has produced those characteristic consequences in the past is either evoked or abated. If an individual's responding is under the influence of the MO of food deprivation and food is established as a reinforcer (value-altering effect), then response classes that have produced food in the past, like manding for food, are evoked (behavior-altering effect). As this individual's responding comes under the control of a different MO, like satiation, then food's value as a reinforcer is abolished (value-altering effect) and response classes that have produced food in the past, like manding for food, are abated (behavior-altering).

The S^D is correlated with the availability of reinforcement for a given mand and increases the probability of the mand. For example, if a child is deprived of fluids, this fluid deprivation functions as an MO, establishing a juice box as a reinforcer. Deprivation of fluids, however, does not increase the availability of the juice box. But the presence of the child's parent (the listener) will function as an S^D because manding for juice in their presence, in the past, has reliably produced juice, strengthening the probability that the child will emit the mand for "juice box" in the presence of their parent. The S^D and the MO exert multiple control, specifically convergent control, over the mand (Michael et al., 2011). For example, if a child has been deprived of sufficient stimulation and sees a board game, the stimulation deprivation will function as an MO (establishing *playing the game* as a reinforcer), and the sight of the boardgame and the pres-ence of a listener will function as S^Ds (both correlated with the availability of *playing the game*) and converge to influence the mand, "Let's play this board-game." This particular mand form requires the convergent influence of stimula-tion deprivation (the MO) and the presence of the game and a listener (the S^Ds) for emission. Given the substantial number of manding interactions in the typi-cal environment, most mands result from generalization across MOs and S^Ds.

In the remainder of this chapter, we will describe approaches to and con-siderations when assessing manding, including prerequisite skills and develop-ing treatment protocols related to assessment outcomes. We will then describe how to develop an effective mand program, including examples of appropriate response measurement systems and data collection sheets. We will also describe strategies for promoting the generalization of the mand in your programming. Finally, we will discuss common clinical challenges when teaching the mand and strategies for addressing them.

Assessing the Mand

Manding communicates something important about the state of the speaker to the listener, and it helps the speaker gain access to reinforcers. The benefits of initiating treatment with mand training include optimizing the effects of the learner's motivation, making verbal behavior training immediately functional for the learner, and making teaching verbal behavior easier for the instructional agent(s) (Sundberg & Michael, 2001). Some research has even suggested that starting with mand training may be the optimal approach for teaching a foreign language with respect to capitalizing on the learner's motivation, rate of acquisition, and emergence of other verbal operants (Wu & Lechago, 2019). To develop an effective manding program, thoughtfully designed assessments are indicated.

Communication Modality

One of the first things to consider is the communication modality of both the assessment(s) and the treatment program. Communication modality selection should be influenced by the learner's current skills, whether they are currently manding and the modality of those mands, and the probability of reinforcement for communicating with a given modality by the learner's predominant verbal communities. If the learner communicates using multiple modalities, mand assessments should be conducted using those modalities. For example, suppose you have a learner vocally manding and tacting some items and using a speech-generating device (SGD) to mand for and tact other items. In that case, the mand assessment should include mands emitted vocally *and* mands using the SGD (see Chapter 11 for further guidance on selecting communication modalities).

There will be learners for whom there is no established system of communication when they present for treatment. This is common with young and/or newly diagnosed individuals. If this is the case, it is important to do two things: (1) inquire with the caregiver about how the learner is currently getting their needs met (e.g., ask them what their child does when they want or need something), and (2) quickly establish a communication system. Establishing a functional communication system involves assessing a variety of skills, including their fine motor imitation (for sign language), visual scanning and discrimination (for visually-based and selection-based communication systems), oral-motor imitation and echoic skills (for vocal-verbal behavior), and matching pictures to objects (for selection-based communication systems). Assessing and identifying learner performance of these skills should guide the communication modality selected for initial treatment.

There are two different kinds of verbal behavior: selection-based and topography-based (Michael, 1985). Topography-based verbal behavior involves emitting responses that have varied and distinguishable topographies, like vocal-verbal behavior and sign language. Selection-based verbal behavior involves the same selection response from an array of stimuli. The stimuli associated with selection-based responses are usually pictures or printed words, used in systems like the Picture Exchange Communication System (PECS®) or voice output devices (VODs). There are multiple considerations when deciding between a topography-based and selection-based communication system. Some of these considerations include the learner's current skill sets, including vocal and motor imitation skills, visual discrimination skills, ease of response prompting for the instructional agent(s), and the probability that responding will be reinforced by the learner's predominant verbal communities. Petursdottir and Ingvarsson (2023) provided a conceptually shrewd evaluation of these considerations when comparing these two communication systems.

Teaching selection-based systems of communication like button pressing (talk blocks) is an effective way to establish an acceptable form of manding relatively quickly for some learners, especially those with robust visual discrimination skills and greater challenges with imitation. However, doing so does not preclude simultaneously teaching the prerequisite skills for or directly teaching topography-based forms of communication like sign language or vocal-verbal behavior. In fact, research supports the Total Communication (TC) approach, which involves assessing and teaching verbal behavior using vocal and other modalities of communication simultaneously (Carbone et al., 2006). It is critical to ensure that your learner relatively quickly has an acceptable way to communicate their needs to gain control over their reinforcers and environment and reduce the probability of problem behavior.

Cultural Considerations[2]

The learner's family is often their primary verbal community. It behooves practitioners to seriously consider the family's wishes and ideas concerning language, communication modality, and initial targets. Of course, this must be tempered with what you observe with your learner's current skills. It is not uncommon for families to want their child to engage in vocal-verbal conversations when it is clear that a variety of other skills must first be taught before more complex language-like conversations can be targeted. For example, a consumer's caregiver may want you to teach their child to tell them what they did at school during the day (recalling past events). After assessing the child's verbal behavior, you have determined that they cannot engage in intraverbals in the form of answering simple questions (e.g., "Where do you go to school?" "How old are you?"). These intraverbals are prerequisites to recalling past events (like recounting what happened at school). Therefore, you must gently communicate with the family about establishing these intraverbals before teaching recalling past events.

We recommend that you talk with the family to identify the language that will be selected for teaching. Some families speak a language in the home that is different from that spoken by the greater community. If your learner speaks or is consistently exposed to more than one language, conducting mand assessments in all languages is important. After assessments in all the relevant languages are completed, you will collaborate with your learner's family to determine which language might be best to teach manding different targets (maybe one or maybe multiple, depending on the relevant audiences). Another variable to consider during language selection is the learner's language preference (Aguilar et al., 2016; Kunze et al., 2019). Assessing learner preference for language contributes to the individualization of treatment, a hallmark of behavior-analytic approaches to teaching and treatment, and may enhance enjoyment for the child while learning (Aguilar et al., 2016).

Additionally, the heritage language may be preferred for those English language learners who use SGDs to communicate (Kunze et al., 2019). There is minimal research in ABA on this topic, but some research has suggested that targeting both (or multiple) languages is not detrimental to and can even benefit the learner's acquisition of verbal behavior (Ohashi et al., 2012). Effective communication between the learner and their family will result in multiple reinforcers for the learner and their family. Some of these reinforcers include the child participating in family events and cultural practices and the family meeting their child's needs.

For some families, there may be some discomfort with certain types of communication modalities as they may be viewed as cumbersome or stigmatizing. It is incumbent upon you as the therapist to work with the family to select a modality that is acceptable to the family (since they will be the verbal community that reinforces responding most of the time) and that also comports with the learner's current skills. This will require skilled and sensitive conversations with the family about why you may be recommending certain modalities. Initial manding targets should be related to the learner's existing reinforcers. Identifying those reinforcers will require working with the family to discuss the learner's daily schedule and preferences (food, activities, items, people), conducting structured preference assessments, and exposure to novel activities and items.

Additionally, it is important that you communicate with the family regarding their sentiments about withholding certain items. For example, withholding food may be unacceptable for some families or cultures. Ensure the items you plan to include when engaging in play or introducing novel toys and activities are familiar to the learner and acceptable to the family. For example, for some families, a Santa Claus or jack-o-lantern may not be something the learner is familiar with if the family does not celebrate Christmas or Halloween, respectively. We discuss the requirements for effective manding assessment trials below.

Features and Considerations of Manding Assessment Trials

The first part of this section will include the critical components of the mand trial to evaluate basic mands (e.g., mands for food or toys) and more advanced mands (e.g., mands for the removal of something or mands for information). After this, we will offer some strategies and resources for conducting mand assessments, though please note that the resources suggested in this chapter do not constitute an exhaustive list of possible assessment measures, and formal assessments for verbal behavior will be discussed in Chapter 2 in this volume.

The mand is a response (verbal operant) under the primary control of a relevant MO. Therefore, it is critical to assess (and train) to ensure the presence of the MO. To do this, you must conduct a structured preference assessment (SPA) to identify reinforcers (preferred items/edibles, activities). It is beyond the scope of this chapter to provide detailed descriptions of each type of structured preference assessment, but interested readers are directed to Carr et al. (2000), Ciccone et al. (2015), and Clay et al. (2021). The one you select will be predicated on your learner's skills (e.g., scanning an array of items) and tolerance for having an item taken away, among other variables. There are many empirically supported stimulus preference assessments (SPAs), and it may be challenging to determine which one will be the best for your learner. We recommend an article that describes a stimulus preference assessment decision-making system (SPADS) (Lill et al., 2021). In this publication, the authors synthesized the literature on SPAs and decision-making models regarding the selection of SPAs, and they developed their own a priori decision-making model to support practitioners in selecting the optimal SPA for their learners. The SPADS considers categories of variables, including (1) client, stimulus, and setting characteristics, (2) agreement across SPA procedures to help make context-specific selections, (3) stimulus dimensions like class and novelty, and (4) MOs. After identifying preferred items, activities, and/or foods, you will use these to select the mand target(s) and plan your assessment trials.

Strategies for Contriving the MO

Deprivation and Withholding. Begin the assessment by establishing some amount of deprivation for the reinforcers you will use to teach the mand. For example, if you want to use a cookie, you want to conduct assessment trials when your learner has not recently eaten, as this relative food deprivation—the MO—will make the cookie valuable as a reinforcer. Initially, you may want the learner to be food-deprived for 30–60 minutes before the session. If this is unacceptable to caregivers, you want to ensure that the learner has not eaten the target food (cookie) or other similar categories of food (baked goods) for at least 30–60 minutes prior to the session, even if they eat a light snack within this time frame. If the learner appears to be motivated for the cookie for only a few teaching trials, you may consider increasing cookie deprivation prior to the session (e.g., if 30 minutes does not work, you can extend it to 60 minutes). You may even start an assessment session by offering a small amount of time with or a small amount of the reinforcer (e.g., a quarter of the cookie). After taking back the reinforcer or allowing your learner to consume the reinforcer, you will withhold the reinforcer and wait to see if the learner mands for it (e.g., "cookie"). If the learner engages in indicating responses like pointing, reaching, or searching for the item/food, it indicates continued interest. We recommend a publication by Frampton and her colleagues on identifying indicating responses and their role in mand training (Frampton et al., 2024). It is important to verify that your learner remains interested in the reinforcer during the assessment because you do not want to count the absence of a mand as a skill deficit when what you might be observing is a motivational deficit. If your learner ceases to demonstrate interest in the item/food, do not continue to conduct assessment trials with those items/foods, and try again later in the session or on another day. In addition to verifying the MO, ensure that you and the learner are facing one another, that there are minimal items in front of the learner that could potentially distract them, and that you remain in control of the reinforcer(s) you are targeting during the mand assessment.

Barriers to Reinforcement. For more advanced mands, like mands for the removal of something (negatively reinforced mands), you may create a barrier to the reinforcer that requires the learner to mand for its removal. For example, you might turn on their favorite movie and then stand in front of or partially conceal the TV/tablet screen to see if the learner mands for some form of removal (e.g., "move," "get out of the way"). You might also use barriers to test for some mands for information (MFIs; Who? What? When? Where? How? Why?). For example, you might heat a preferred food (e.g., brownie) in the microwave, and when you take it out and place it on the table, and they reach for it, you might block them and say, "You have to wait before you can eat it" to see if they mand, "Why?".

Interrupted Behavior Chain Procedure. For mands for items and mands for information (MFI), you might have them engage in a preferred activity chain and hide a piece essential to chain completion to see if they mand for the item or the location of the item. For example, you might have them put together a Mr Potato Head and hide the eyes. When they get to the point where they need the eyes, they might either mand for its location ("Where are the eyes?") or the item ("eyes?"). If you are assessing MFIs and if they mand for the item, you might say that you hid the eyes somewhere to see if they mand, "Where?" If you are using an interrupted behavior chain procedure, it is important to verify that the terminal reinforcer for the chain functions as a reinforcer (e.g., they enjoy the completed Mr Potato Head and play with it) and that they are interested in playing with it at the time of the assessment.

Capturing the MO

The aforementioned procedures described contriving the MO during more formal or discrete trial assessment sessions. It is also helpful to assess for mands during more naturally occurring interactions. This is referred to as Natural Environment

Teaching (NET), a form of naturalistic teaching (Dufek & Schreibman, 2014). NET involves identifying, testing, and teaching opportunities during naturalistic play. For example, you and the learner may be playing and taking turns with the Play-Doh. When the learner reaches for the Play-Doh, you grab it and hold it just within reach, and ask, "What do you want?" to provide an opportunity for a mand for the Play-Doh (e.g., "Play-Doh") or the color of the Play-Doh (e.g., "green"). In this example, you would capture an assessment opportunity during play with the learner.

We recommend that the mand assessment include both formal discrete and NET trials. If the learner does not mand for the item, label it, and return the item to them for play (e.g., "Here's the Play-Doh! So squishy!"). When assessing the mand, in an effort to keep the therapeutic environment engaging for the learner and to reduce the probability of problem behavior, there are a few strategies you can employ. You want to ensure that you pair yourself and the therapeutic spaces with fun activities. This may involve the delivery of reinforcers and positive attention on a relatively frequent basis for desirable behaviors, including things like playing nicely, listening carefully, and working hard. An abundance of playful interactions with the learner is helpful and should be individualized to the learner's specific interests and preferences. For example, some learners enjoy physical play, like jumping on a trampoline or a lot of movement, while others may prefer quieter activities, like coloring and playing with stickers. You will also want to minimize negative experiences for the learner to circumvent or minimize escape-maintained (problem) behavior. Some negative experiences may include presenting too many demands during the session, a lot of physical prompting to sit or respond, especially if they are protesting or visibly distressed, and not offering sufficient breaks. While it may not be realistic to expect the learner to comply all the time during each session, it is imperative to ensure assent on their part as best as possible by creating environments rich with reinforcement, engagement, centering the learner's preferences, honoring requests or indications of needing rest or termination of an activity, and offering the learner choices as much as feasible (Morris et al., 2024).

Consequences during the Assessment

If the learner emits the mand, immediately deliver the reinforcer. If they mand for an item or food, provide the item or food immediately (within 1 minute). If they mand for the removal of a barrier, then remove the barrier (e.g., move out of the way of the TV screen). For MFIs, it is critical that the only thing you provide is the information (and not the corresponding item/activity/person). For example, if you give the learner a bowl of their favorite ice cream without the spoon and they mand for the location of the spoon ("Where is the spoon?"), it is imperative that you provide the information (e.g., "It is in the blue drawer") and not the item (e.g., spoon).

Response Requirements

Another important consideration for assessment and teaching is acceptable response forms. For vocal-verbal responding, the learner might not emit the entire word but might emit the sound of the first part or letter of the word (e.g., "c" or "coo" for the cookie). We suggest you accept approximations as long as they sound like or include the sounds of the target word and the learner emits the same approximation consistently (e.g., says "coo" each time during trials in which the cookie is the reinforcer). For MFIs, we suggest you accept the correct MFI form ("Where?") even in the absence of the complete frame ("Where is the spoon?"); however, we recommend working on teaching the full MFI frames as soon as possible (Palmer, 2015). For example, if an individual only emits the mand "Why?", then the listener would have to be privy to the learner's MO to reinforce the response (i.e., the listener would have to know why they are asking "Why?"). However, if an individual emits the full mand frame, "Why doesn't this computer turn on?", they substantially expand their pool of responsive listeners, increasing the probability of reinforcement for their mand for information. In terms of frames, we do not recommend that you require frames during the initial mand assessment ("I want cookie"); instead, you should accept the mand for the item ("cookie") and promptly deliver the reinforcer. However, if you teach your learner 5–10 one-word mands, research has suggested that subsequently teaching mand frames ("I want cookie") can increase response variability (Hernandez et al., 2007; Jessel & Ingvarsson, 2022).

With respect to communication modalities alternative to vocal-verbal responding, the aforementioned guidelines still apply. If a learner emits the correct sign, hands the correct card, or pushes the correct button on their device, deliver the reinforcer within 1 minute. If the learner's sign looks similar to the target sign (you must consider the learner's fine motor skills) and the learner emits the same approximation consistently, we suggest you accept this as an appropriate response form. We also suggest that you honor and reinforce omnibus mands ("toy," "play," "more"), especially for those learners with communication systems that involve pressing a button like the big mac or talk blocks. An omnibus mand is a low-effort response that produces the simultaneous delivery of several reinforcers. These are helpful when teaching a response to replace problem behavior, and they do not preclude the acquisition of mands for specific reinforcers ("baby doll," "trampoline," "more chips") (Ward et al., 2020). However, as soon as it is feasible, we suggest teaching increasingly discriminated manding (e.g., the specific name of the food or toy).

Maintaining Motivation during the Assessment

If the learner is not emitting mands during the assessment, this will result in multiple (if not all) trials that end in termination and non-delivery of the reinforcer(s).

This may negatively impact the assessment session, wherein your presence may be established as an s-delta or warning stimulus (your presence will signal failure to obtain the reinforcer and repeated trial termination), or the presentation of items to complete an activity chain may come to function as a conditioned motivating operation–reflexive (CMO-R) (Michael, 1982). The CMO-R is a condition that alters the value of its own removal or presence as a reinforcer or punisher. In this situation, the presentation of the materials may come to signal a worsening condition and may establish escape from the session or removal of the activity as a reinforcer. In other words, the learner will lose interest and may want to leave the session. To make and keep yourself and the session fun, there are some strategies you should employ. Make sure that you are engaging with the learner in play and preferred interactions between trials. These play interactions also represent good opportunities to deliver less preferred reinforcers (reinforcers not being targeted during the mand assessment) between assessment trials. If you are using activity chains, ensure you intersperse assessment trials with trials in which you provide the learner with all the items necessary to complete the chain so they can complete the chain and enjoy the terminal reinforcer (i.e., EO absent opportunities).

Prerequisite Skills for Advanced Mands

Before assessing advanced forms of manding, observing, or formally testing one-word mands is essential. Advanced forms of manding include manding for the removal of something, someone, or a situation ("No more food, please"), or mands that are under the influence of multiple MOs such as MFIs ("Where is the nurse's office?"). Also, mands that are longer than one word and involve mand frames (e.g., "I would like strawberry ice cream") may be considered more advanced. We do not recommend assessing or teaching advanced forms of manding if the learner cannot yet emit simple mands (e.g., one-word mands for foods or items). Below are some considerations in the assessment of more advanced forms of manding.

Mand Frames

A mand frame is a mand with an increased utterance length and often includes a subject, verb, and object. Mand frames are sensitive to contextual variables (e.g., specific verbal community, number of controlling MOs) and engender more precise responding on the part of the listener (Palmer, 2015). Most children start to emit two-word utterances (e.g., "more tickles") by age 2 years (American Speech-Language-Hearing Association, 2024). By 3 years old, most children can make utterances of three or more words (e.g., "I want tickles"). However, before children use mand frames, they emit multiple one-word mands. There is no definitive number of one-word-mands a learner must emit before mand frames are targeted. However, some researchers have suggested that after learning a few one-word mands, some learners might be ready to learn mand frames, which can promote response variability (e.g., Hernandez et al., 2007). If your learner is emitting verbal behavior that includes multiple-word utterances (e.g., tacts consisting of multiple words—"blue block," "I see ball"), this might indicate that it is appropriate to test for and then teach mand frames (e.g., "I want the __"). Some researchers suggest that teaching mand frames in conjunction with other procedures like extinction, scripting, and differential reinforcement can also increase response variability (Betz et al., 2011; Hernandez et al., 2007; Jessel & Ingvarsson, 2022). For more information on mand frames, we also recommend the literature review published by Shea et al. (2019).

Mands for Information (MFIs)

Between 3 and 4 years old, most children can emit all the MFIs (American Speech-Language-Hearing Association, 2024). Some important prerequisites for MFIs include manding for items they want and need, following 1+-step directions, uttering 2+ word phrases, following a simple sequence of events, and robust listener (receptive) skills. Mands for information that include the frame are composed of both the mand and an autoclitic frame. Autoclitics are verbal behaviors that describe or alter the value of other verbal behavior to produce more effective responding on the part of the listener (Skinner, 1957; Lechago, 2020). For example, if someone were to say, "Anjali hat," it may not be clear to the listener how the hat relates to Anjali. However, if they were to say, "Anjali's hat," this would denote to the listener that the hat belongs to Anjali, and now the listener can relate more effectively to the hat. The "'s" is an autoclitic frame that alters the other verbal behavior and denotes possession. Mands for information with full frames function similarly. For example, with the mand, "Where is the strainer?", the "*Where is the __*" portion of the mand is an autoclitic frame that has been reinforced under other similar conditions in which the speaker could not find something they needed. Therefore, when the speaker is experiencing a situation in which they cannot find something, this strengthens the probability of the emission of the autoclitic frame, "*Where is the __.*" This autoclitic frame helps the listener more precisely reinforce the speaker's response in relation to the strainer (i.e., they can provide them with the location of the strainer). The "*strainer*" portion of the sentence is the mand for the item, and emission of the item mand is under the influence of the MO that established the strainer as a reinforcer (e.g., they need to remove water from their pot of pasta). Multiple MOs influence this MFI, including strained pasta, which, by virtue of the conditioned motivating operation-transitive (CMO-T), establishes the strainer as a reinforcer and, in turn, information about the location of the strainer as a reinforcer. A

CMO-T is defined as an environmental variable that establishes the effectiveness of another event as a reinforcer or punisher (Michael, 1982). If one of those items, now established as a reinforcer, is missing, this will increase the probability of a response that has produced it in the past under similar conditions, like manding for information about the missing item (the strainer in this example). After the reinforcer, information about the location of the item (e.g., the strainer is in the red cabinet) is provided to the speaker, the speaker must be able to respond effectively to this information (e.g., go to the red cabinet to retrieve the strainer) for the MFI to be a functional response. The listener must be able to identify the strainer and the red cabinet. This is why MFIs are considered advanced forms of manding. If the learner cannot identify multiple items and locations, follow instructions, emit longer mand frames, or emit mands under the influence of multiple MOs, then they do not have the prerequisite skills to learn to successfully mand for information. If you want to assess MFIs, ensuring that your learner demonstrates the aforementioned skills might be helpful.

Assessment Resources and Intervention Guides

Often, the mand assessment constitutes one aspect of a more comprehensive verbal behavior assessment with your learner. Sometimes, it does not, depending on the structure of your clinic and your learner's goals. Either way, a more complete picture of your learner's skills will help determine your starting point with the mand assessment and teaching. Please refer to Chapter 2 in this volume for a discussion of commercially available, criterion-referenced assessments that would be useful to consider for conducting verbal behavior assessments.

When welcoming a new learner and their family to the clinic, we like to inquire about how the learner currently gets their needs met and become familiar with their skills and preferences. This involves conversations with the caregivers and learner, play, and careful observations. Do they play with toys and games, and can they take turns? Can they point to things, and do they look if I point at something? Do they write, draw, or look at pictures? Can they feed themselves or tap me on the arm if they need something? Can they imitate me, and do they appear to enjoy social interactions? How many people do they interact with each day, and who do they interact with each day? What activities do they engage in during the week? The starting points for assessing and teaching mands may differ between a learner who can tap your shoulder to gain and share your attention and a learner who is not yet sharing attention with you, referred to as joint attention (Holth, 2005). For example, we worked with a learner who was making minimal eye contact, not attempting to gain our attention, and not exhibiting joint attention. We presented a talk block (a colorful button that is easy to depress) and assessed whether she could look at it and depress it. After she did, we allowed her to interact with a preferred item, placed the talk block in front of her, took the item back, and observed whether she pressed the button to gain access to it. She did not do this independently initially, but then we physically prompted the block press and immediately delivered the preferred item. She quickly learned to press the button for preferred items independently, and we were able to teach picture matching and introduce a picture exchange system of communication shortly after that.

We have also served learners who could make eye contact, say a few words, and play turn-taking games. With them, we might have started playing a game they selected and withheld an item they needed to play the game to assess whether they would mand for it. During this assessment probe, we would also take the opportunity to observe other features of their responding such as whether they search for the item first, look at us when manding, whether they experience distress or exhibit problem behavior, or simply just stop and play with something else or mand to play with something else. These observations provide important information about their play skills, verbal behavior skills, and social interaction skills. It also provides information about situations that could evoke problem behavior. We recommend becoming familiar with your learner's skills and interests to take a strengths-based approach to treatment. A strengths-based approach highlights the skills rather than only focusing on the deficits when working with a learner and/or their family and community (Donaldson et al., 2017). A strengths-based approach to working with a learner and their family encourages an optimistic view of the child. It assists you in thinking about how everyone can benefit from their current skills and environments to assess and teach manding.

In addition to the formal criterion-referenced assessment tools described in Chapter 2 in this volume, there are other published assessments that might be useful for assessing manding. *Teaching Language to Children with Autism or Other Developmental Disabilities* (Sundberg & Partington, 1998, 2010) briefly introduces Skinner's (1957) analysis of verbal behavior and an introduction to the verbal operants. It includes a brief language assessment called the Brief Language Assessment Form (BLAF) and ideas for curriculum building. This tool is best used in conjunction with a more comprehensive assessment tool such as the Verbal Behavior Milestones Assessment and Placement Program (VB-MAPP; Sundberg, 2008). This is an excellent resource for developing your learner's verbal behavior program, including a manding program.

Learners might not mand for many different reasons. For example, they may have difficulty imitating an echoic model or simply cannot emit the mand. To cultivate programming that meets the learner's needs, Bourret et al. (2004) offered an excellent assessment for vocal manding to identify specific areas of need to inform treatment development. When teaching initial mands, for example, during functional communication training (FCT), it is important to consider the topography of the mand and to assess topographies that might be most appropriate for your learner. Kunnavatana et al. (2018) developed an approach for reducing the arbitrary selection of mand topographies and assessing preferences for response topographies in two adults with ASD who exhibited no functional communication skills. Another important consideration when assessing manding is the impact of the relevant MOs on responding. The influence of MOs and related reinforcers is not static, impacting the probability of manding. An excellent resource for consideration of MOs during the mand assessment was published by Boelter et al. (2011), wherein they varied access to the availability of concurrently available reinforcers with different MO manipulations to determine their effects on the emission of mands.

Interdisciplinary Collaborations

Individuals diagnosed with ASD are often diagnosed with other psychiatric or developmental disorders. These might include attention deficit hyperactivity disorder, anxiety disorders, and feeding disorders, to name a few. Due to the comorbidity of diagnoses common to this population, you will likely be one member of a larger team of service providers from various disciplines that will be working with the learner. Some multidiscipline teams comprise providers from various disciplines who provide treatment independently. Some multidisciplinary teams are interdisciplinary and employ a collaborative approach to treatment. We recommend that you communicate with the other professionals on the learner's team of service providers (especially the speech-language pathologist [SLP]) to discuss each of your assessments, treatment ideas, and recommendations for teaching verbal behavior (mands). This can increase cohesion in the treatment plan and ensure that treatment plans created by one provider do not represent a barrier to a treatment plan created by another provider. This also provides you all with the opportunity to enhance other's treatment recommendations with your respective professional expertise. Some of our most enriching professional experiences and effective treatment plan development occurred through collaboration with SLPs and occupational therapists (OTs) working with our learners. We also recommend reading Braga-Kenyon et al. (2015), which carefully detailed the need for multidisciplinary care, the role of the behavior analyst, and effective strategies for working within a multidiscipline team. Interdisciplinary collaborations have been formalized through such organizations as the Speech Pathology Applied Behavior Analysis Special Interest Group (SPABA SIG) (https://www .behavioralspeech.com/journals-books-and-websites.html) and *The Journal of Speech and Language Pathology–Applied Behavior Analysis* (https://psycnet .apa.org/PsycARTICLES/journal/slp/5/2). We also direct the reader to Chapter 14 in this volume for additional information related to collaborating with other service providers.

Procedures to Teach Manding

In this section, we will discuss multiple strategies for teaching manding. We will provide considerations and recommendations for teaching one-word mands, simple mand frames, negatively reinforced mands, and mands for information.

Antecedent Considerations

An essential feature of teaching manding is ensuring the presence of the relevant MO. Please refer to our previous section in this chapter on *assessing the mand*, which describes the role of the MO and ways to contrive or capture the MO during teaching sessions, as well as provides information about mand topographies. Once you have ensured the presence of a relevant MO and identified an appropriate communication modality, you can begin teaching mands. Keep in mind that it is important to consistently evaluate for what items there is a relevant MO in place, as preferences may change and could be impacted by multiple variables such as recent access to the item as well as the response effort of a task. For example, if you want to teach a learner to mand for an iPad®, to contrive the MO, you want to ensure the iPad has applications or easy access to videos in which the learner is interested. Additionally, you will want to ensure some period of deprivation (i.e., the learner has not had access to the iPad or the specific videos or applications for a while). The instructor may turn the iPad on but not play a specific video or game. Initial mands should consist of one-word (or an approximation), such as "iPad" or "Pah". Then, the instructor might increase the mand requirement to a simple frame such as "I want iPad."

Another form of mands is negatively reinforced mands (i.e., mands for the removal or termination of something). For example, "Stop please," "All done," or "Finished" are negatively reinforced mands. Practitioners may need to first work to identify stimuli to include as negative reinforcers. One way to do this is by administering the *Negative Reinforcement Rating Scale* (NRRS; Zarcone et al., 1999). The NRSS is a survey given to caregivers or instructors that helps identify situations that a learner might avoid (i.e., school tasks, self-care tasks); modified versions of this survey have also been created to include auditory, olfactory, and tactile items (Groskreutz et al., 2014). If you want to teach a mand for "stop please" to contrive the MO, you will want to set up a situation where the instructor blocks or modifies the learner's environment (e.g., play context) in a less preferred way (e.g., moving the learner's toys or playing with them in a slightly different manner) or set up a situation where the instructor presents an aversive stimulus (e.g., alarm).

When teaching MFIs, there are some important considerations specific to the MO. You will typically need to contrive or capture more than one MO per target MFI. For example, when teaching your learner to mand for the location of something (e.g., "Where is the tablet?"), there are two MOs you need to consider. It is important to ensure EOs are in place for the item and information related to the item's location (e.g., "it is in the office drawer"). Often, the value of one reinforcer, what we refer to as the distal reinforcer (the information about the location of the item), is related to the value of the other reinforcer, what we call the terminal or proximal reinforcer (the tablet). This is important because you want to ensure the presence of these two MOs when you develop your MFI teaching program. In the example, the tablet is the established reinforcer (as determined by observation and a structured preference assessment), so information about its location is also established as a reinforcer. Therefore, you will contrive a situation wherein the learner needs the information (distal reinforcer) to access the proximal reinforcer (tablet; e.g., hiding the tablet in an unusual location in the home). Another example we offer is when teaching the "How?" MFI. You need to ensure that the information about how to do something functions as a reinforcer. To do that, you may take a preferred activity (like playing a video game on a computer) and then create a barrier to that reinforcer (turn off the computer). Now, the learner has to turn on the computer and navigate to the site where the game is located. To contrive the MO for the information, you must: (1) ensure that playing the game functions as a reinforcer, (2) that the learner does not know how to turn on the computer and navigate to the game site, (3) you must turn off the computer, and (4) direct the learner to, "Play your game." This will create opportunities for you to teach your learner to mand, "How do I find my game?" Several publications describe strategies for teaching various MFIs (Cengher et al., 2022).

Considerations and Parameters for Mand Training

Manding allows learners to control the delivery of reinforcers. While manding aids in establishing the learner's role as a speaker, the mands might start as initial approximations. For example, let us say a child is interested in a swing at a local park. The child shows interest by watching others play on it, approaching it, and gesturing toward the swing. As such, the availability of the swing serves as an MO by increasing the value of the swing as a reinforcer. Next, we want to ensure we have a verbal response that the child can emit. Initially, the instructor should evaluate the learner's current skills and select a modality (please refer to the previous section on the selection of mand modalities).

Next, the instructor should select an initial behavior similar to the target mand in some way. An initial iteration of the target mand may consist of partial components of words (e.g., "ssss") or one single word (e.g., "swing"). The instructor should immediately reinforce the response when the learner emits the initial behavior(s). As the learner becomes more fluent with the initial targeted approximation, the instructor should gradually increase the criteria for reinforcement by shaping the mand and requiring a response closer to the terminal mand. More specifically, the instructor will require more complexity before reinforcement is provided. For example, if the initial behavior is a simple vocalization like "ssss," the instructor might next require the learner to vocalize a more complex sound (e.g., "suh" or "swuh") or a complete word related to the activity. This process of shaping more advanced approximations and reinforcing successive approximations continues until the learner emits the entire target mand consistently and accurately. In the same example, let us say that the child can echo the word "swing" so the instructor can ensure the swing is in sight/available and present an echoic prompt ("say, swing") as a one-word mand. Once the learner engages in a response, the instructor should reinforce the mand by providing access to the swing. For an example of shaping responses (e.g., manding for access to a swing), see Table 4.1. An important consideration when shaping mands is identifying the ultimate target word based on the range of audiences that the learner is likely to encounter and who might respond to (and reinforce) such verbal responses. The same considerations are also applicable for negatively reinforced mands, where a response may be shaped from an initial response (e.g., "break") to a more complete or terminal response (e.g., "Excuse me, can I take a break now?"). Instructors can also help develop data collection sheets for other therapists or caregivers to shape mands more easily. For an example of a data sheet, see Figure 4.1. The instructor may provide multiple approximations or list one specific target they want the trainers to work on.

After teaching some initial mands, we recommend teaching learners to approach people to emit mands, as it may be important that a child approaches a teacher or caregiver in a different room to mand. For example, a child may need to find a caregiver to ask for help with a homework assignment or to access a snack. Increasing the distance between the learner and their communication partner is a training step in the Picture Exchange Communication System (PECS®; Bondy & Frost, 2001), focused on persistence despite traveling a distance to mand. During this training step, the instructor (or communication partner) should slowly move

Table 4.1 Example Sequence of Shaping a Vocal Mand, "Swing"

Step	Mand
1	Sssss
2	Swww or Suh
3	Swuh
4	Swing
5	Swing me
6	Swing me please
7	Push me on the swing
8	Will you push me on the swing?
9	Excuse me, will you push me on the swing?

Date:_____ DC:_____ Session:_____ Condition:_____

Target Item	Current Vocal Approximation Target(s)	Independent	Prompted
Wagon	Wa		
	Wa- Ga		
	Wae-Gun		
	Other:		

Figure 4.1 Sample data collection sheet.

away from the learner to teach the learner to find the person and mand. It may also be necessary to have a second instructor available to help prompt responding when teaching distance and persistence.

Interrupted Behavior Chains

The interrupted behavior chain procedure is an effective way to contrive the MO to teaching manding. Interrupted behavior chains are used to teach complex sequences of behaviors and involve breaking down these complex sequences into smaller, manageable steps and providing prompts at each step, allowing opportunities for mand training. The term interrupted in this context means that the natural sequence of the behavior is paused at certain points as a strategy for teaching mands. For example, Albert et al. (2012) taught three children with ASD to complete behavior chains (e.g., making a sandwich, making art projects). Once the participants acquired the behavior chains, the chains were interrupted by removing an item needed to complete the chain. The final product of the chain (e.g., sandwich) served as the terminal reinforcer for which there was presumably an MO (e.g., food deprivation). A CMO-T was established for those items required to complete this behavior chain (bread, condiments, knife, etc.), thereby evoking behavior that produced those items under similar conditions in the past, like manding for the missing items. The interrupted-behavior chain procedure, in conjunction with prompting procedures, was used to successfully teach the participants in this study to mand for missing items.

The interrupted behavior chain procedure can be used to contrive the MO to teach MFIs. For example, you may teach your learner to complete all the steps to make an exploding volcano. You then present them with the items associated with the activity, direct them to "Make a volcano," and hide one of the items necessary to complete the activity (e.g., the spoon used to scoop baking soda). You can use the interruption of hiding the spoon to teach them to directly mand for the item ("spoon"), or you can use the interruption as an opportunity to teach them to MFI (for the location of the item, "Where is the spoon?" or "Who has the spoon?").

Orienting and Eye Contact as a Type of Mand

Observing responses (e.g., orienting, eye contact) often occur before a learner emits a mand. For example, a learner might need to look to identify a listener who can provide the specific type of reinforcer they might be seeking. However, children with ASD may not develop eye contact spontaneously and without more direct training. Methods to teach eye contact have included extinction and reinforcement (e.g., Carbone et al., 2013) and shaping (Fonger & Malott, 2019). In general, we recommend that instructors work closely with caregivers and learners to evaluate their preferences and potential cultural (or other) considerations when (or if) teaching eye contact. For example, you would begin by discussing with the caregivers and, if possible, the learner, their thoughts and feelings about eye contact. If eye contact is not a priority for the learner or their caregivers, the team might consider focusing on other social skills more aligned with their preferences, such as alternative ways for the learner to engage socially, like teaching other forms of social attention (e.g., gestures, verbal greetings) that are more appropriate or comfortable for the learner. Alternatively, ensuring an orienting response (e.g., the learner's body faces a relevant listener) may be an acceptable alternative to requiring eye contact.

Prompting Procedures

Prompt delay procedures are one way to teach manding after initially pairing the instructor with the delivery of reinforcers. After a learner has demonstrated an approach or indicating behavior (e.g., looking at the instructor, approaching or gesturing toward a preferred item), the instructor may insert a response interval (i.e., item not immediately delivered following an approach or indicating response) to allow an opportunity for the learner to mand. Initial prompt delays may be short, such as 2 seconds–10 seconds. A delay may lead to mands for some learners due to previous pairings of the item's name and its delivery. However, instructors might also need to provide prompts to occasion correct responses (or for more complex mands). We recommend that readers see Cengher et al. (2017) for a more detailed review of prompt-fading procedures during skill acquisition.

Stimulus Control Transfer Procedures

Stimulus control transfer procedures play a critical role in teaching mands as they assist learners in moving from dependence on prompts to producing independent responses. Various prompt types, such as textual, echoic, and tact, might be considered. A textual prompt may consist of providing a written or typed item name (e.g., putting the target answer, a portion of the answer, or a cue on an index card). Textual prompts should only be used for learners with basic reading skills (e.g., skills including receptive identification and visual discrimination, some initial text-to-behavior correspondence). For example, Shillingsburg et al. (2016) used textual prompts to teach an MFI ("Who?") to four children with ASD. In their investigation, the textual prompt consisted of an index card with the words, "Who has it?". Textual prompts could also be used to teach a variety of different mands. For example, the word "break" may be written or typed on a card and used for a card exchange during mand training to escape from a work task. Similar to textual prompts, scripts may also be used for mand training. Scripts might be textual, visual, or auditory. Auditory scripts might use a voice recorder button to record a voice message (e.g., "May I have the —"). Scripts have been shown to increase the occurrence of both scripted and novel responses (i.e., responses that include additional components such as verbs beyond the script or to promote variability in responding; Betz et al., 2011; Lee et al., 2007).

An additional way to teach mands is through vocal (echoic) prompts. Refer to the examples related to vocal shaping above. Relatedly, mand training might include concurrent echoic training. Kodak et al. (2009) evaluated the implementation of echoic training, where the target item was not initially present before manding trials. The instructor initiated the trial with an echoic prompt (e.g., the instructor stated or modeled the target, such as "music" or "say, music") up to two times. Following a correct echoic, the instructor provided the reinforcer. Mand training with the item present but out of reach was conducted following echoic training. This procedure demonstrated that concurrent echoic and mand training increased manding in a young child with ASD.

Ultimately, we recommend that instructors select the least intrusive but most effective prompt for their learners (e.g., Schnell et al., 2020; Seaver & Bourret, 2014). We also recommend that instructors provide prompts only when the learner is attending. More specifically, ensure the learner looks at the instructor or the target item for the mand trial. Finally, we recommend that instructors have a plan for prompt-fading (see the section below on *Promoting Efficiency, Emergence, Generalization, and Maintenance* for more information on prompt dependence and fading).

Teaching Modality

Teaching vocal mands may be a long-term socially valid strategy, as this modality is common across almost all verbal behavior communities. However, additional evidence-based modalities for mand training exist, such as augmentative and alternative communication (AAC; e.g., SGDs, PECS®, button presses) and sign language. Previous reviews have suggested that AAC does not impede vocal-verbal behavior or speech production. Moderate gains in vocal-verbal behavior (e.g., mands of a different topography) have been observed after teaching AAC to children with ASD (e.g., Schlosser & Koul, 2015; Schlosser & Wendt, 2008). However, the impact of AAC on vocal-verbal behavior can vary across individuals. While AAC might improve vocalizations for some, the primary focus might be finding the most efficient means of communication, which may or may not involve vocalizations for other learners.

There are multiple practical considerations for each mand training modality. We suggest that practitioners reference Valentino et al. (2019) for an overview of a prerequisite skills assessment to identify potential modalities to use with learners. For example, instructors should consider the learner's skills with motor imitation, identity matching, and vocal imitation (e.g., Early Echoic Skills Assessment in the VB-MAPP, Sundberg, 2008 or the Early Echoic Skills Assessment and Program Planner, Esch 2023; see Chapter 5 in this volume). Additionally, we direct readers to Chapter 11 (Augmentative and Alternative Communication [AAC]) in this volume.

Teaching Formats

As previously mentioned, we recommend establishing mands in a range of teaching contexts that vary in the degree to which they resemble the environment where those mands are ultimately expected to occur (the endpoints of this spectrum have been referred to as "artificial, 'work' setting" and "natural, 'play' setting"; LeBlanc et al., 2006, p. 52). Instructors should also consider individual learner needs and resources available to use these strategies together to provide the most comprehensive services. One of the main focuses of NET is capturing and contriving the learner's motivation (i.e., a learner showing interest by gesturing or approaching something; Gevarter & Zamani, 2021; Sundberg & Partington, 1998). Opportunities for naturalistic learning can be set up when learners explore and play with toys. For example, a therapist may set up a bubble machine, observe that the learner is interested in the bubbles, and then capture this opportunity to practice manding for bubbles. More structured opportunities can also be organized during discrete trial teaching. For example, manding trials may include the presentation of the S^D (e.g., "What do you want?"), a response interval is initiated, prompts are presented as needed, and the reinforcer is delivered after the mand is emitted. These trials may be repeated sequentially or interspersed with other skill acquisition programs (i.e., mixed operant teaching, e.g., listener responding, tacting; Kates-McElrath & Axelrod, 2006).

Promoting Efficiency, Emergence, Generalization, and Maintenance

Promoting efficiency, emergence, generalization, and maintenance is crucial for ensuring long-term success for the learners. This section will use the term generativity to encompass various types of novel responses or behavior changes that are not directly trained (LaFrance & Tarbox, 2020). Generalized behavior change has been considered one of the defining features of applied behavior analysis (Baer et al., 1968). Similar to other verbal operants, mands are most likely to result in reinforcement when listeners or environmental cues have also developed discriminative control over the mand (Miguel, 2017). A feature of the mand relation is that an MO, and even the strength of an MO, varies considerably from instance to instance (Miguel, 2017). For example, the recency with which a learner has interacted with a toy, if they have the same item at both home and another setting, if there are multiple iterations of a toy (i.e., different styles, colors, sizes), and if there is a partner or peer available to play with the toy are variables that influence the MO. Each of these variables might also impact mand generalization and should be considered when programming for generality.

Promoting the Generalization of Mands

Multiple strategies can be used to establish generality in the context of daily routines. Some key features include varying the setting, programming common stimuli, loosely structured trials, using varied stimuli, and delivery of naturalistic reinforcers (Cowan & Allen, 2007; Delprato, 2001; Koegel et al., 1999; Miranda-Linne & Melin, 1992). See Table 4.2 for an example of each of these components.

It is also important to vary your MOs when feasible. Instructors should cultivate the occurrence of mands under various MOs. For example, instructors can teach the learner to mand for a drink (e.g., "juice") after eating something salty (MO 1) and after running outside on a warm day (MO 2), and further evaluate whether that mand occurs under other novel, but relevant, MOs (i.e., generalization across MOs; e.g., after eating something spicy, after playing on the playground). In addition to MOs, instructors should also consider what to establish as the S^D when developing teaching trials. The conversation partner in an interaction should help signal the availability of specific reinforcers and from

Table 4.2 Components and Examples of Ways to Promote the Generalization of Mands

Component	Example
Varying the setting	Providing opportunities to practice the skill at the clinic, home, school, and community.
Programming common stimuli	Role play opportunities to prepare for a forthcoming play/musical.
Loosely structured or teaching loosely	Instructor varies their tone of voice, facial expression.
Varied stimuli	Using 2D and 3D stimuli, using multiple exemplars of each type.
Naturalistic reinforcers	Praise and attention.

whom to mand specific items. Instructors should teach learners when to direct mands toward peers (e.g., "Want to play cars?"), adults (e.g., "Can you help me with this math problem?"), or to both (e.g., "What's your name?"); and they should use multiple exemplars to promote generalization.

Multiple Exemplar Training and Multiple Exemplar Instruction

Multiple exemplar training (MET) and multiple exemplar instruction (MEI) play critical roles in promoting the generativity of behavior change. Some researchers have used these terms interchangeably (Byrne et al., 2014). However, the two procedures represent different arrangements under some conditions (LaFrance & Tarbox, 2020). MET involves teaching a skill or behavior using a variety of examples, stimuli, and contexts, as opposed to teaching using a single exemplar. MET is useful for promoting generativity as it increases the likelihood that the learner's responding comes under the control of stimuli considered relevant/critical rather than stimuli considered irrelevant/noncritical. To achieve such control, it is common for behavior analysts to select teaching stimuli that contain critical features that should come to control responding but vary in the presence of noncritical features, thereby creating a correlation between the presence of critical features and reinforcement (Horner et al., 1984; Kirby & Bickel, 1988; Song et al., 2021). For example, when teaching the mand "build blocks," different types of blocks might be used during teaching (e.g., Lego®, Duplo®, and Wooded Blocks) to program variation in noncritical features (e.g., block material [plastic, wood, etc.], size, color). Further, MET involves teaching until a predetermined mastery criterion is met, then conducting probes with stimuli not associated with teaching to evaluate generativity. Together, this highlights the importance of *planning for* and *assessing* generativity.

Another form of MET relates to teaching response generalization, in which the response varies across teaching trials or sessions (Holth, 2017; LaFrance & Tarbox, 2020). For example, when teaching a mand for attention, the targeted responses might include "Talk to me please," "Will you please talk with me?" and other responses that would likely result in the same type of reinforcement in the speaking environment. With MET, each response topography serves the same function (e.g., in this example, access to attention). The MET procedure is often used to systematically plan for generativity (Stokes & Baer, 1977).

MEI represents a different way to promote generativity by changing instructions that require various verbal operants and listener skills during a sequence of trials (LaFrance & Tarbox, 2020). Referencing back to the building block example above, the stimulus (blocks) could be taught across verbal and non-verbal operants, including a listener response (e.g., selecting a block from an array of stimuli when the therapist says, "block"), echoic (e.g., saying "block" after the therapist says "block"), tact (e.g., saying "block" when the therapist holds up a block), and mand (e.g., saying "block" when the therapist contrives or captures a relevant MO). The teaching procedures for MEI have typically included teaching the same target concurrently as multiple distinct verbal operants (Sidener et al., 2010.). The trial arrangement and discriminative stimuli (e.g., touch, say, match, presence of stimulus) vary across trials. It is typical to include probe data within MEI to indicate when untrained verbal operants emerge.

Increasing Variability

Variability in responding can help learners increase the chances of accessing preferred items or reinforcers and might help promote generality. Increasing variability of mands and other responses can contribute to important and more complex skill sets like problem-solving and social skills (Axe et al., 2019; Cooper et al., 2020). For example, if an individual engages in a response that does not lead to reinforcement (e.g., raising their hand to ask for help but no one notices or comes to assist during quiet work time), engaging in a varied response can have benefits (e.g., approaching the teacher's desk to ask). Multiple procedures can help promote mand variability. Variability in responses can lead to improved communication and understanding from the verbal community. By promoting mand variability, instructors can increase a learner's effectiveness to ensure their needs and wants are met in different situations.

Lag Schedules

One way to promote variability is by using a lag schedule of reinforcement. A lag schedule is a type of intermittent reinforcement schedule where reinforcement delivery is delayed (or "lagged") by a specified number of responses. Lag schedules can be based on a fixed or variable number of responses. In a fixed-response lag schedule, reinforcement is provided following a specific (i.e., fixed) number of responses varied from the previous responses. For example, a fixed-3 lag schedule means reinforcement would be provided after every third varied response. In a variable-response lag schedule, the number of responses necessary to receive access to a reinforcer varies. For example, a variable-3 lag schedule would indicate that reinforcement is provided after two varied responses on one occasion, four responses on another, and three responses on another. See Table 4.3 for an example of a Lag 2 fixed schedule.

Lag schedules have been used within mand training (Falcomata et al., 2018; Pokorski et al., 2022; Silbaugh et al., 2020). For example, Silbaugh et al. (2020) investigated the effects of FCT with a Lag 1 schedule (e.g., 'I want it,' 'Can I have it') on vocal manding variability for four children with ASD. Results suggested that FCT with the arrangement of the lag schedule increased mand variability and decreased challenging behavior. See Figure 4.1 for an example of a data sheet using a lag schedule with mand frames. The data sheet could

Table 4.3 Lag 2 Example

Child Response	Reinforcement?
I want car	Yes
I want car	No
Can I have the car?	Yes
May I have the car?	Yes
I want the car	Yes
I want to play with the car	Yes
I want to play with the car	No
I'd like to play with the car	Yes
I want to play with the car	No
May I play with the car?	Yes

include the possible frames or responses to help make the schedule salient for instructors.

Instructive Feedback

Instructive feedback is another way to promote the generality of language and involves the incorporation of additional non-target stimuli or learning targets into a trial when teaching other skills (Wolery et al., 1993). Instructive feedback is used to promote the efficiency of instruction, as learners are not required to respond to the incorporated instructive feedback component (secondary target) of the trials (Vladescu & Kodak, 2013). There are multiple ways that instructive feedback has been presented to learners, for example, in the antecedent portion of the trial, the consequence portion, or both. Instructive feedback can be presented in linked or unlinked formats, depending on how the additional information is related to the primary teaching target. Linked instructive feedback targets involve presenting additional information directly related to the target response being taught. Unlinked targets present information unrelated to the primary teaching target. Over time, learners may incorporate this additional information (i.e., secondary targets) into their responses, leading to a broader range of skills and more flexible responses. Presenting instructive feedback that includes novel or supplementary information may encourage the learner to engage in more varied responses. See the review by Nottingham et al. (2015) for more detailed information about instructive feedback, including common aspects, clinical recommendations, and suggestions for future research.

Overcoming Common Clinical Challenges

Teaching mands can present various challenges to instructors. The following section discusses common clinical challenges that may be encountered while teaching mands and provides a brief overview of strategies to address them. Behavior analysts and treatment team members can create a more effective environment for mand training by considering these challenges and conducting regular adjustments to procedures.

Antecedent Considerations

Antecedent strategies encompass approaches that are applied before an individual's response. As reviewed in this chapter, it is important to continuously identify and use preferred items when doing mand training. Practitioners should regularly evaluate items that learners are interested in and reassess using preference or reinforcer assessments. However, barriers may arise related to assessing and manipulating MOs. For example, lengthy pre-session assessments might not always capture moment-to-moment changes or fluctuations in MOs. Instructors can work to ensure that a learner is indicating interest in an item by checking that the learner engages in an indicating response, such as reaching for an item, pointing to it, saying yes, or nodding their head in agreement (e.g., Frampton et al., 2024; Shillingsburg & Valentino, 2011).

Some procedures might also be employed to manipulate MOs. Strategies might consist of removing access to specific preferred items for a determined amount of time prior to mand training trials (Davis et al., 2012), only conducting a predetermined number of trials in a row to help prevent satiation (van der Meer et al., 2012), or using an interrupted behavior chain procedure (Albert et al., 2012). Additionally, an instructor may also wish to provide a period of noncontingent access to allow a learner to contact reinforcing properties of the item, then remove all or part of the item (e.g., Jennett et al., 2008).

Mands for Information (MFIs)

Regarding MFIs, some issues might arise that weaken the MO. For example, during pretreatment assessments, there may be repeated trials that are terminated because the learner fails to emit the MFI that produces the information (reinforcer). Over time, this might establish stimuli (items) associated with teaching trials as a CMO-R, establishing escape from the trial or session as a reinforcer, and evoking problem or avoidance behavior. One way to prevent this is to intersperse trials during the pre-assessment and during teaching in which the learner has all the items they need to successfully engage in the activity (i.e., EO absent; e.g., Shillingsburg et al., 2013; Kahlow et al., 2019; Pyles et al., 2021). When teaching MFIs, multiple MOs must be contrived. You must ensure that the MOs for the terminal reinforcer and the items associated with obtaining the terminal reinforcer are present during assessment and training.

If using multi-step behavior chains to teach MFIs, we recommend hiding a few different items within the same activity chain to ensure that it is the missing item that is evoking the MFI (e.g., "Who has the cup?"), and that it is not simply the sight of the items associated with that activity chain that is evoking the MFI (because it would be the same missing item in each trial associated with that chain). Relatedly, it is important to incorporate MET and target the MFI under various conditions and using multiple activities. The common feature across the teaching situations evokes the MFI frame, and the specific item/idea/location/person will influence the specific tact (label) inserted in the frame. For example, when teaching "Where is ___?", a required or desired item that is missing from the situation should evoke the mand frame, "Where is ___?" and the items required for that specific situation evoke the last part of the MFI (e.g., cup when making a volcano chain) to evoke, "Where is the cup?"

Prompt-Fading Procedures

Using systematic prompt-fading procedures helps reduce the probability of establishing prompt-dependent behavior. When using prompt-fading, an instructor may initially provide an immediate prompt, then fade the prompt by manipulating the topography of the prompt or the delay until the prompt is provided. For example, the instructor might implement a partial physical prompt instead of providing a full physical prompt to evoke a mand on an SGD. As the learner emits increased independent responses, the instructor might further fade their prompt by providing less intrusive prompts, such as model or gestural prompts (i.e., less and less assistance until the learner responds independently or to naturally occurring discriminative stimuli). Even with systematic prompt-fading procedures, prompt dependence might occur for some learners (Cividini-Motta & Ahearn, 2013; Gorgan & Kodak, 2019; Oppenheimer et al., 1993). As such, practitioners might consider the use of extended response intervals (also sometimes referred to as unlimited delay to prompts; Walls et al., 1984) if this occurs. An extended response interval refers to the time the instructor waits before providing a prompt following the S^D or MO. Extended response intervals might consist of providing participants with extra time to emit the mand. Other methods to reduce prompt dependence include differential reinforcement and extinction. See the consequence section below for more information on these procedures.

Consequences

Differential Reinforcement

The consequences are a defining feature of mands. As such, delivery of reinforcers specific to the MO is critical. Differential reinforcement is a common procedure added during mand training to supplement the contingent delivery of reinforcers specific to the MO. There are multiple variations of differential reinforcement, including reinforcing the target response. For example, Paden et al. (2012) taught children with ASD to mand to peers with picture exchange systems using differential reinforcement plus prompting. During the intervention, adult-directed mands were placed on extinction, and the experimenter provided the least intrusive prompt to occasion a mand to a peer. Following peer-directed mands, the peer provided a preferred item to the participant. Other variations of differential reinforcement include setting up more substantial reinforcers (i.e., quantity or magnitude), denser reinforcement schedules, or higher-quality items (i.e., preference level) for independent responses in conjunction with providing less substantial quantity, leaner reinforcement schedules, or lower-quality items for prompted responses (see Johnson et al., 2017 and Cividini-Motta et al., 2024 for more information on these variations of differential reinforcement for skill acquisition procedures).

Identifying Opportunities to Teach

Insufficient opportunities for reinforcing mands also pose a clinical challenge. Practitioners must dedicate sufficient time and teaching trials to mand training each day. This means planning time daily to work on mand training using discrete trial teaching and identifying opportunities throughout the learner's regular daily activities for mand training using NET. Over time, these training opportunities should occur more often using NET. By embedding and training within routine activities or the natural environment, practitioners can ensure more practice opportunities and promote stronger stimulus control and the learner's ability to communicate in varied contexts. We recommend Tiger et al. (2008) for a practical guide to FCT that includes many features of mand training procedures for practitioners to consider.

Other Features of Training

Limited Variability

Another clinical challenge that might emerge is when learners demonstrate limited variability in their manding. Low variability in responses can also consist of repetitive manding, which might make it more challenging for an individual to communicate with their audience effectively. For example, repetitive manding might reduce the learner's ability to adapt their requests based on different contexts or audiences. When learners mand repetitively for one item, it indicates a lack of control by other relevant variables such as the availability of that item or the preferences of their communication partners. This is problematic as such children need to learn to adjust their mands to fit various social contexts and increase the likelihood of reinforcement. Additionally, a learner might learn to rely on a specific mand that has been reinforced in the past, leading to a lack of variability in their mand repertoire. See Rodriguez and Thompson (2015) for an in-depth review of behavior variability. Please refer to an earlier section in this chapter titled "Increasing Variability" for strategies to promote generalization of the mand. Ultimately, to help establish a more variable mand repertoire, it is important to ensure that the learner can engage in multiple varied responses that can each be consistently reinforced.

Response Requirement and Related Variables

An ongoing challenge that practitioners will potentially encounter is that learners might become less engaged or responsive as the effort required to access reinforcement increases. Previous researchers have suggested that challenging behavior is more likely to occur when the communicative response requires more response effort than challenging behavior (Horner & Day, 1991; Tiger et al., 2008). Thus, during initial communication training, practitioners should consider the response effort of the initial mands and then consider increasing the response effort (e.g., adding mand frames) to help promote generalization (Hernandez et al., 2007). When teaching new mands, practitioners should deliver the item requested immediately and frequently. However, that can sometimes be hard to maintain as the requested item may not always be available, or it may not be practical to reinforce at the desired schedule (Fisher et al., 2000; Sidener et al., 2006).

Mands for Information: Response Requirements and Resistance to Extinction. We recommend requiring the learner to emit the entire mand frame ("Where is the cup?") as opposed to the MFI in isolation ("Where?"). Doing this would ensure a larger pool of effective listeners likely to reinforce the MFI. If you teach a learner only to ask the MFI ("Where?"), the listener must be present and knowledgeable about all the contextual variables affecting the learner to respond to and reinforce the MFI effectively. Also, teaching the entire MFI frame from the start, especially if you target more than one MFI at a time or target MFIs and mands concurrently, promotes discriminated responding on the part of your learner from the start. Targeting more than one MFI or MFIs and other mands concurrently increases the likelihood that contextual variables (e.g., presence or absence of salient items or people, relevant MOs) differentially evoke the appropriate MFI (Somers et al., 2014). This also leads to enhanced maintenance and generalization of manding for information.

It is also important to teach persistence when emitting MFIs. In other words, teach your learner what to do when the person they first approach does not know the answer (e.g., does not provide the reinforcer). There is limited research on this. However, the research suggested programming for resistance to extinction (Carnett et al., 2020). After your learner emits MFI across situations and people, you can start teaching them to approach a second person if the first person says something like, "I don't know." It is important that if you do this, you intersperse trials in which the first person reinforces the MFI on some occasions (i.e., provides them with the information). After some time, you may add a third conversation partner and evaluate persistence when the first and second conversation partners do not know the answer or provide vague answers (e.g., "It's upstairs").

Scrolled Responses

One error pattern that may emerge is scrolled responses (e.g., saying multiple answers back-to-back). Scrolling behavior sometimes occurs when a learner is receiving training for multiple similar words simultaneously, and during training, they might scroll to "find" the correct response. The learner might 'scroll' by engaging in multiple incorrect verbal responses, sometimes sequentially or repetitively, before engaging in a correct response. For example, a learner might say multiple previously reinforced responses (i.e., orange, apple, banana) to access an item. One strategy practitioners can use is to ensure that the discriminative stimuli are salient, which might help the learner differentiate between the targeted words. Practitioners might also consider reducing the demands or the number of targets that are being trained at once. For example, they might present a smaller set of options or focus on a smaller target set at a time to help facilitate successful responses.

Manding is a critical skill and is purported to be one of the first verbal operants an individual develops (Schlinger, 1995). It allows listeners insight into the speaker's current conditions, and it allows the speaker to exert some control over their environment and experiences. Therefore, it behooves researchers to continue investigating strategies and concepts that continue to help us refine and develop more effective approaches to teaching manding. It is equally important for practitioners to continue to ensure that they are using research-supported approaches to teaching manding.

Notes

1 For some children, for example, those who are hard of hearing (HOH), manding in the form of gestures and sign language are reinforced. For now, we will discuss the development of manding in terms of vocalizations as this is the most common form of communication; however, we will discuss teaching manding using a variety of modalities later in this chapter. The reader is also directed to Chapter 11 in this volume for content specific to learners using alternative and augmentative communication devices.

2 The reader is also directed to Chapter 13 in this volume for additional considerations regarding the relevance of culture and diversity to language learning.

References

Aguilar, J. M., White, P. J., Fragale, C., & Chan, J. M. (2016). Preference for language of instruction of an English language learner with autism. *Developmental Neurorehabilitation*, *19*(3), 207–210. https://doi.org/10.3109/17518423.2015.1044133

Albert, K. M., Carbone, V. J., Murray, D. D., Hagerty, M., & Sweeney-Kerwin, E. J. (2012). Increasing the mand repertoire of children with autism through the use of an interrupted chain procedure. *Behavior Analysis in Practice*, *5*(2), 65–76. https://doi.org/ 10.1007/BF03391825

American Speech-Language-Hearing Association. (2024). *Typical speech and language development.* https://www.asha.org/public/speech/development/

Axe, J. B., Phelan, S. H., & Irwin, C. L. (2019). Empirical evaluations of Skinner's analysis of problem solving. *The Analysis of Verbal Behavior, 35*(1). 39–56. https://doi.org/10.1007/s40616-018-0103-4

Baer, D. M., Wolf, M. M., & Risley, T. R. (1968). Some current dimensions of applied behavior analysis. *Journal of Applied Behavior Analysis, 1*(1), 91–97. https://doi.org/10.1901/jaba.1968.1-91

Betz, A. M., Higbee, T. S., Kelley, K. N., Sellers, T. P., & Pollard, J. S. (2011). Increasing response variability of mand frames with script training and extinction. *Journal of Applied Behavior Analysis, 44*(2), 357–362. https://doi.org/10.1901/jaba.2011.44-357

Boelter, E. W., & Hagopian, L. P. (2011). Effects of preference on verification of discriminated mands. *Journal of Applied Behavior Analysis, 44*(4), 931–935. http://dx.doi.org.uhcl.idm.oclc.org/10.1901/jaba.2011.44-931

Bondy, A., & Frost, L. (2001). The picture exchange communication system. *Behavior Modification, 25*(5), 725–744. https://doi.org/10.1177/0145445501255004

Bourret, J., Vollmer, T. R., & Rapp, J. T. (2004). Evaluation of a vocal mand assessment and vocal mand training procedures. *Journal of Applied Behavior Analysis, 37*(2), 129–144. https://doi.org/10.1901/jaba.2004.37-129

Braga-Kenyon, P., Kenyon, S., & Guilhardi, P. (2015). The behavior analyst as a team member: Toward a cohesive multidisciplinary approach to treating individuals diagnosed with an Autism Spectrum Disorder (ASD). *International Journal of Behavior Analysis and Autism Spectrum Disorder, 1,* 18–29.

Byrne, B. L., Rehfeldt, R., & Aguirre, A. A. (2014). Evaluating the effectiveness of the stimulus pairing observation procedure and multiple exemplar instruction on tact and listener responses in children with autism. *The Analysis of Verbal Behavior, 30*(2), 160–169. https://doi.org/10.1007/s40616-014-0020-0.

Carbone, V. J., Lewis, L., Sweeney-Kerwin, E. J., Dixon, J., Louden, R., & Quinn, S. (2006). A comparison of two approaches for teaching VB functions: Total communication vs. vocal-alone. *The Journal of Speech and Language Pathology-Applied Behavior Analysis, 1,* 181–192. https://doi.org/10.1037/h0100199

Carbone, V. J., O'Brien, L., Sweeney-Kerwin, E. J., & Albert, K. M. (2013). Teaching eye contact to children with autism: A conceptual analysis and single case study. *Education and Treatment of Children, 36*(2), 139–159. https://doi.org/10.1353/etc.2013.0013

Carnett, A., Ingvarsson, E. T., Bravo, A., & Sigafoos, J. (2020). Teaching children with autism disorder to ask 'where' question using a speech-generating device. *Journal of Applied Behavior Analysis, 53*(3), 1383–1403. https://doi.org/10.1002/jaba.663

Carr, J. E., Nicolson, A. C., & Higbee, T. S. (2000). Evaluation of a brief multiple-stimulus preference assessment in a naturalistic context. *Journal of Applied Behavior Analysis, 33*(3), 353–357. https://doi.org/10.1901/jaba.2000.33-353

Cengher, M., Budd, A., Farrell, N., & Fienup, D. M. (2017). A review of prompt-fading procedures: Implications for effective and efficient skill acquisition. *Journal of Developmental and Physical Disabilities, 30,* 155–173. https://doi.org/10.1007/s10882-017-9575-8

Cengher, M., Budd, A., Farrell, N., & Fienup, D. M. (2018). A review of prompt-fading procedures: Implications for effective and efficient skill acquisition. *Journal of*

Developmental and Physical Disabilities, 30(2), 155–173. https://doi.org/10.1007/s10882-017-9575-8

Cengher, M., Bowman, M. D., Shawler, L. A., & Ceribo-Singh, M. S. M. (2022). A systematic review of mands for information. *Behavioral Interventions, 37*(3), 864–886. https://doi.org/10.1002/bin.1893

Ciccone, F. J., Graff, R. B., & Ahearn, W. H. (2015). Increasing the efficiency of paired-stimulus preference assessments by identifying categories of preference. *Journal of Applied Behavior Analysis, 48*(1), 221–226. https://doi.org/10.1002/jaba.190

Cividini-Motta, C., & Ahearn, W. H. (2013). Effects of two variations of differential reinforcement on prompt dependency. *Journal of Applied Behavior Analysis, 46*(3), 640–650. https://doi.org/10.1002/jaba.67

Cividini-Motta, C., Livingston, C., & Efaw, H. (2024). Systematic review of differential reinforcement in skill acquisition. *Behavior Analysis in Practice, 17*, 401–416. https://doi.org/10.1007/s40617-023-00903-z

Clay, C. J., Schmitz, B. A., Clohisy, A. M., Haider, A. F., & Kahng, S. (2021). Evaluation of free-operant preference assessment: Outcomes of varying session duration and problem behavior. *Behavior Modification, 45*(6), 962–987. https://doi.org/10.1177/0145445520925429

Cooper, J. O., Heron, T. E., & Heward, W. L. (2020). *Applied behavior analysis* (3rd ed.). Pearson.

Cowan, R. J., & Allen, K. D. (2007). Using naturalistic procedures to enhance learning in individuals with autism: A focus on generalized teaching within the school setting. *Psychology in the Schools, 44*(7), 701–715. https://doi.org/10.1177/0145445520925429

Davis, B. J., Kahng, S. W., & Coryat, K. (2012). Manipulating motivating operations to facilitate the emergence of mands for a child with autism. *The Analysis of Verbal Behavior, 28*(1), 145–150. https://doi.org/10.1007/BF03393116

Delprato, D. J. (2001). Comparisons of discrete-trial and normalized behavioral language intervention for young children with autism. *Journal of Autism and Developmental Disorders, 31*(3), 315–325. https://doi.org/10.1023/a:1010747303957

Donaldson, A. L., Krejcha, K., & McMillin, A. (2017). A strengths-based approach to autism: Neurodiversity and partnering with the autism community. *Perspectives, Sig 1 Language Learning and Education, 2*, 56–68. https://doi.org/10.1044/persp2.SIG1.56

Dufek, S., & Schreibman, L. (2014). Natural environment training. In J. Tarbox, D. R. Dixon, P. Sturmey, & J. L. Matson (Eds.), *Handbook of early intervention for autism spectrum disorders* (pp. 325–344). Springer.

Esch, B. E. (2023). *Early echoic skills assessment and program planner*. Different Roads.

Falcomata T. S., Muething C. S., Silbaugh B. C., Adami S., Hoffman K., Shpall C., & Ringdahl J. E. (2018). Lag schedules and functional communication training: Persistence of mands and relapse of problem behavior. *Behavior Modification, 42*(3), 314–334. https://doi.org/10.1177/0145445517741475

Fisher, W. W., Thompson, R. H., Hagopian, L. P., Bowman, L. G., & Krug, A. (2000). Facilitating tolerance of delayed reinforcement during functional communication training. *Behavior Modification, 24*(1), 3–29. https://doi.org/10.1177/0145445500241001

Fonger, A. M., & Malott, R. W. (2019). Using shaping to teach eye contact to children with autism spectrum disorder. *Behavior Analysis in Practice, 12*(1), 216–221. https://doi.org/10.1007/s40617-018-0245-9

Frampton, S. E., Axe, J. B., Davis, C. R., Meleshkevish, O., & Li, M. H. (2024). A tutorial on indicating responses and their importance in mand training. *Behavior Analysis in Practice, 17*, 1238–1249. https://doi.org/10.1007/s40617-024-00965-7

Gevarter, C., & Zamani, A. A. (2021). Naturalistic developmental behavioral interventions: The role of motivating operations. *Journal of Applied Behavior Analysis, 54*(3), 1060–1079. https://doi.org/10.1002/jaba.833

Gorgan, E. M., & Kodak, T. (2019). Comparison of interventions to treat prompt dependence for children with developmental disabilities. *Journal of Applied Behavior Analysis, 52*(4), 1049–1063. https://doi.org/10.1002/jaba.638

Groskreutz, N. C., Groskreutz, M. P., Bloom, S. E., & Slocum, T. A. (2014). Generalization of negatively reinforced mands in children with autism. *Journal of Applied Behavior Analysis, 47*(3), 560–579. https://doi.org/10.1002/jaba.151

Hernandez, E., Hanley, G.P, Ingvarsson, E. T., & Tiger, J. H. (2007). A preliminary evaluation of the emergence of novel mand forms. *Journal of Applied Behavior Analysis, 40*(1), 137–156. http://doi.org/10.1901/jaba.2007.96-05

Holth, P. (2005). An operant analysis of joint attention skills. *Journal of Early and Intensive Behavior Intervention, 2*(3), 160–175. http://doi.org/10.1037/h0100311

Holth, P. (2017). Multiple exemplar training: Some strengths and limitations. *The Behavior Analyst, 40*(1), 225–241. https://doi.org/10.1007/s40614-017-0083-z

Horner, R. H., Bellamy, G. T., & Colvin, G. T. (1984). Responding in the presence of nontrained stimuli: Implications of generalization error patterns. *Journal of the Association for Persons with Severe Handicaps, 9*(4), 287–295. https://doi.org/10.1177/154079698400900406

Horner, R. H., & Day, H. (1991). The effects of response efficiency on functionally equivalent competing behaviors. *Journal of Applied Behavior Analysis, 24*(4), 719–732. https://doi.org/10.1901/jaba.1991.24-719

Jennett, H. K., Harris, S. L., & Delmolino, L. (2008). Discrete trial instruction vs. mand training for teaching children with autism to make requests. *The Analysis of Verbal Behavior, 24*(1), 69–85. https://doi.org/10.1007/BF03393058

Jessel, J., & Ingvarsson, E. T. (2022). Teaching two children with autism to mand for known and unknown items using contrived motivating operations. *Behavioral Interventions, 37*(1), 139–152. http://doi.org/10.1002/bin.1777

Johnson, K. A., Vladescu, J. C., Kodak, T., & Sidener, T. M. (2017). An assessment of differential reinforcement procedures for learners with autism spectrum disorder. *Journal of Applied Behavior Analysis, 50*(2), 290–303. https://doi.org/10.1002/jaba.372

Kahlow, T. A., Sidener, T. M., Kisamore, A. N., & Reeve, K. F. (2019). Teaching the mand "When?" to children with autism spectrum disorder. *The Analysis of Verbal Behavior, 35*(2), 221–234. https://doi.org/10.1007/s40616-019-00115-z

Kates-McElrath, K., & Axelrod, S. (2006). Behavioral intervention for autism: A distinction between two behavior analytic approaches. *The Behavior Analyst Today, 7*(2), 242. https://doi.org/10.1037/h0100085

Kirby, K. C., & Bickel, W. K. (1988). Toward an explicit analysis of generalization: A stimulus control interpretation. *The Behavior Analyst, 11*(2), 115–129. https://doi.org /10.1007/bf03392465.

Kodak, T., Clements, A., & Ninness, C. (2009). Acquisition of mands and tacts with concurrent echoic training. *Journal of Applied Behavior Analysis, 42*(4), 839–843. https://doi.org/10.1901/jaba.2009.42-839

Koegel, R. L., Koegel, L. K., & Carter, C. M. (1999). Pivotal teaching interactions for children with autism. *School Psychology Review, 28*(4), 576–594. https://doi.org/10 .1080/02796015.1999.12085986

Kunnavatana, S. S., Wolfe, K., & Aguilar, A. N. (2018). Assessing mand topography preference when developing a functional communication training intervention. *Behavior Modification, 42*(3), 364–381.

Kunze, M., Drew, C., Machalicek, W., Safer-Lichtenstein, J., & Crowe, B. (2019). Language preference of a multilingual individual with disabilities using a speech generating device. *Behavior Analysis in Practice, 12*(4), 777–781. https://doi.org/10 .1007/s40617-019-00379-w

LaFrance, D. L., & Tarbox, J. (2020). The importance of multiple exemplar instruction in the establishment of novel verbal behavior. *Journal of Applied Behavior Analysis, 53*(1), 10–24. https://doi.org/10.1002/jaba.611

LeBlanc, L. A., Esch, J., Sidener, T. M., & Firth, A. M. (2006). Behavioral language interventions for children with autism: Comparing applied verbal behavior and naturalistic teaching approaches. *The Analysis of Verbal Behavior, 22*(1), 49–60. https://doi.org/10.1007/bf03393026

Lechago, S. A. (2020). Verbal Behavior. In S. Hupp & J. D. Jewell (Eds.), *The encyclopedia of child and adolescent development*. Wiley-Blackwell. https://doi.org /10.1002/9781119171492.wecad094

Lee, R. L., Sturmey, P., & Fields, L. (2007). Schedule induced and operant mechanisms that influence variability: A review and implications for future investigations. *The Psychological Record, 57*, 429–455. https://doi.org/10.1007/BF03395586

Lill, J. D., Shriver, M. D., & Allen, K. D. (2021). Stimulus preference assessment decision-making system (SPADS): A decision-making model for practitioners. *Behavior Analysis in Practice, 14*(4), 1144–1156. https://doi.org/10.1007/s40617-020 -00539-3

McGreevy, P., Fry, T., & Cornwall, C. (2012, 2014). *Essential for living*. Orlando: McGreevy.

Michael J. (1982). Distinguishing between discriminative and motivational functions of stimuli. *Journal of the Experimental Analysis of Behavior, 37*(1), 149–155. https://doi .org/10.1901/jeab.1982.37-149

Michael, J. (1985). Two kinds of verbal behavior plus a possible third. *The Analysis of Verbal Behavior, 3*, 1–4. https://doi.org/10.1007/BF03392802

Michael, J., Palmer, D. C., & Sundberg, M. L. (2011). The multiple control of verbal behavior. *Analysis of Verbal Behavior, 27*(1), 3–22. https://doi.org/10.1007/ BF03393089

Miguel, C. F. (2017). The generalization of mands. *Analysis of Verbal Behavior, 33*(2), 191–204.

Miranda-Linne, F., & Melin, L. (1992). Acquisition, generalization, and spontaneous use of color adjectives: A comparison of incidental teaching and traditional discrete-trial procedures for children with autism. *Research in Developmental Disabilities, 13*(3), 191–210. https://doi.org/10.1016/0891-4222(92)90025-2

Morris, C., Oliveira, J. P., Perrin, J., Federico, C. A., & Martasian, P. J. (2024). Toward a further understanding of assent. *Journal of Applied Behavior Analysis, 57*(2), 304–318. https://doi.org/10.1002/jaba.1063

Nottingham, C. L., Vladescu, J. C., & Kodak, T. M. (2015). Incorporating additional targets into learning trials for individuals with autism spectrum disorder. *Journal of Applied Behavior Analysis, 48*(1), 227–232. https://doi.org/10.1002/jaba.179

Ohashi, J. K., Mirenda, P., Marinova-Todd, S., Hambly, C., Fombonne, E., Szatmari, P., Bryson, S., Roberts, W., Smith, I., Vaillancourt, T., Volden, J., Waddell, C., Zwaigenbaum, L., Georgiades, S., Duku, E., & Thompson, A. (2012). Comparing early language development in monolingual- and bilingual-exposed young children with autism spectrum disorders. *Research in Autism Spectrum Disorders, 6*(2), 890–897. http://doi.org/10.1016/j.rasd.2011.12.002

Oppenheimer, M., Saunders, R. R., & Spradlin, J. E. (1993). Investigating the generality of the delayed prompt effect. *Research in Developmental Disabilities, 14*, 425–444. https://doi.org/10.1016/0891-4222(93)90036-J

Paden, A. R., Kodak, T., Fisher, W. W., Gawley-Bullington, E. M., & Bouxsein, K. J. (2012). Teaching children with autism to engage in peer-directed mands using a picture exchange communication system. *Journal of Applied Behavior Analysis, 45*(2), 425–429. https://doi.org/10.1901/jaba.2012.45-425

Palmer, D. C. (2015). Verbal behavior: What is the function of structure? *European Journal of Behavior Analysis, 8*, 161–175. https://doi.org/10.1080/15021149.2007.11434280

Petursdottir, A. I., & Ingvarsson, E. T. (2023). Re-visiting topography-based and selection-based verbal behavior. *The Analysis of Verbal Behavior, 39*(2), 169–189. https://doi.org/10.1007/s40616-023-00182-3

Pokorski, E. A., Todt, M. J., Willard, K. C., Barton, E. E., Martinez, A. P., & Lloyd, B. P. (2022). Effects of lag schedules of reinforcement on variable manding in preschoolers with disabilities. *Journal of Early Intervention, 45*(4), 370–390. https://doi.org/10.1177/10538151221137796

Pyles, M. L., Chastain, A. N., & Miguel, C. F. (2021). Teaching children with autism to mand for information using "Why?" as a function of denied access. *The Analysis of Verbal Behavior, 37*(1), 17–34. https://doi.org/10.1007/s40616-020-00141-2

Rodriguez, N. M., & Thompson, R. H. (2015). Behavioral variability and autism spectrum disorders. *Journal of Applied Behavior Analysis, 48*(1), 167–187. http://doi.org/10.1002/jaba.164

Sagi, A. (1981). Mothers' and non-mothers' identification of infant cries. *Infant Behavior and Development, 4*(1), 37–40. http://doi.org/10.1016/S0163-6383(81)80005-7

Schlosser, R. W., & Koul, R. K. (2015). Speech output technologies in interventions for individuals with autism spectrum disorders: A scoping review. *Augmentative and Alternative Communication, 31*(4), 285–309. https://doi.org/10.3109/07434618.2015.1063689

Schlosser, R. W., & Wendt, O. (2008). Effects of augmentative and alternative communication intervention on speech production in children with autism: A systematic review. *American Journal of Speech-Language Pathology, 17*(3), 212–230. https://doi.org/10.1044/1058-0360(2008/021)

Schlinger, H. D., Jr. (1995). *A behavior analytic view of child development.* Plenum Press.

Schnell, L. K., Vladescu, J. C., Kisamore, A. N., DeBar, R. M., Kahng, S., & Marano, K. (2020). Assessment to identify learner-specific prompt and prompt-fading procedures for children with autism spectrum disorder. *Journal of Applied Behavior Analysis, 53*(2), 1111–1129. https://doi.org/10.1002/jaba.623

Seaver, J. L., & Bourret, J. C. (2014). An evaluation of response prompts for teaching behavior chains. *Journal of Applied Behavior Analysis, 47*(4), 777–792. https://doi.org/10.1002/jaba.159

Shea, K. A., Sellers, T. P., Brodhead, M. T., Kipfmiller, K., & Sipila-Thomas, E. (2019). A review of mand frame training procedures for individuals with autism. *European Journal of Behavior Analysis, 20*(2), 1–14. http://doi.org/10.1080/15021149.2019.1661708

Shillingsburg, M. A., Bowen, C. N., & Valentino, A. L. (2013). Mands for information using "How" under EO-absent and EO-present conditions. *The Analysis of Verbal Behavior, 30*(1), 54–61. https://doi.org/10.1007/s40616-013-0002-7

Shillingsburg, M. A., Gayman, C. M., & Walton, W. (2016). Using textual prompts to teach mands for information using "who?". *Analysis of Verbal Behavior, 32*, 1–14.

Shillingsburg, M. A., & Valentino, A. L. (2011). Teaching a child with autism to mand for information using "How". *The Analysis of Verbal Behavior, 27*(1), 179–184. http://doi.org/10.1007/BF03393100

Sidener, T. M., Carr, J. E., Karsten, A. M., Severtson, J. M., Cornelius, C. E., & Heinicke, M. R. (2010). Evaluation of single and mixed verbal operant arrangements for teaching mands and tacts. *The Analysis of Verbal Behavior, 26*(1), 15–30. https://doi.org/10.1007/BF03393079.

Sidener, T. M., Shabani, D. B., Carr, J. E., & Roland, J. P. (2006). An evaluation of strategies to maintain mands at practical levels. *Research in Developmental Disabilities, 27*(6), 632–644. https://doi.org/10.1016/j.ridd.2005.08.002

Silbaugh, B. C., Swinnea, S., & Falcomata, T. S. (2020). Replication and extension of the effects of lag schedules on mand variability and challenging behavior during functional communication training. *Analysis of Verbal Behavior, 36*(1), 49–73. https://doi.org/10.1007/s40616-020-00126-1

Skinner, B. F. (1957). *Verbal behavior.* Appleton-Century-Crofts.

Somers A., Sidener, T.M., DeBar, R.M., & Sidener, D.W. (2014). Establishing concurrent mands for Items and mands for information about location in children with autism. *The Analysis of Verbal Behavior, 30*(1), 29–35. https://doi.org/10.1007/s40616-014-0007-x

Song, C. J., Vladescu, J. C., Reeve, K. F., Miguel, C. F., & Breeman, S. L. (2021). The influence of correlations between noncritical features and reinforcement on stimulus generalization. *Journal of Applied Behavior Analysis, 54*(1), 346–366. https://doi.org/10.1002/jaba.760

Stokes, T. F., & Baer, D. M. (1977). An implicit technology of generalization. *Journal of Applied Behavior Analysis, 10*(2), 349–367. http://doi.org/10.1901/jaba.1977.10-349

Sundberg, M. L. (2008). *VB-MAPP verbal behavior milestones assessment and placement program: A language and social skills assessment program for children with autism or other developmental disabilities.* AVB Press.

Sundberg, M. L., & Michael, J. (2001). The benefits of Skinner's analysis of verbal behavior for children with autism. *Behavior Modification, 25*(5), 698–724. https://doi.org10.1177/0145445501255003

Sundberg, M. L., & Partington, J. W. (1998). *Teaching language to children with autism or other developmental disabilities.* Behavior Analysts, Inc.

Sundberg, M. L., & Partington, J. W. (2010). *Teaching language to children with autism or other developmental disabilities.* AVB Press.

Tiger, J. H., Hanley, G. P., & Bruzek, J. (2008). Functional communication training: A review and practical guide. *Behavior Analysis in Practice, 1*(1), 16–23. https://doi.org/10.1007/BF03391716

Valentino, A. L., LeBlanc, L. A., Veazey, S. E., Weaver, L. A., & Raetz, P. B. (2019). Using a prerequisite skills assessment to identify optimal modalities for mand training. *Behavior Analysis in Practice, 12*(1), 22–32. https://doi.org/10.1007/s40617-018-0256-6

van der Meer, L., Sutherland, D., O'Reilly, M. F., Lancioni, G. E., & Sigafoos, J. (2012). A further comparison of manual signing, picture exchange, and speech-generating devices as communication modes for children with autism spectrum disorders. *Research in Autism Spectrum Disorders, 6*(4), 1247–1257. http://doi.org/10.1016/j.rasd.2012.04.005

Vladescu, J. C., & Kodak, T. M. (2013). Increasing instructional efficiency by presenting additional stimuli in learning trials for children with autism spectrum disorders. *Journal of Applied Behavior Analysis, 46*(4), 805–816. http://doi.org/10.1002/jaba.70

Walls, R. T., Dowler, D. L., Haught, P. A., & Zawlocki, R. J. (1984). Progressive delay and unlimited delay of prompts in forward chaining and whole task training strategies. *Education & Training of the Mentally Retarded, 19*(4), 276–284.

Ward, S. N., Hanley, G. P., Warner, C. A., & Gage, E. E. (2020). Does teaching an omnibus mand preclude the development of specifying mands. *Journal of Applied Behavior Analysis, 54*(1), 248–269. https://doi.org/10.1002/jaba.784

Wolery, M., Werts, M. G., & Holcombe, A. (1993). Reflections on 'effects of instructive feedback related and unrelated to target behaviors'. *Exceptionality, 4*, 117–123. https://doi.org/10.1207/s15327035ex0402_5

Wu, W., Lechago, S. A., & Rettig, Lisa A. (2019). Comparing mand training and other instructional methods to teach a foreign language. *Journal of Applied Behavior Analysis, 52*(3), 652–666. https://doi.org/10.1002/jaba.564

Zarcone, J. R., Crosland, K., Fisher, W. W., Worsdell, A. S., & Herman, K. (1999). A brief method for conducting a negative-reinforcement assessment. *Research in Developmental Disabilities, 20*(2), 107–124. http://doi.org/10.1016/ S0891-4222(98)00036-5

Chapter 5

Echoics

Barbara E. Esch and Catia Cividini-Motta

Introduction

Definition of Echoic Behavior

The echoic is a verbal operant under the control of a verbal discriminative stimulus with formal similarity and point-to-point correspondence (Skinner, 1957). In everyday terms, we could say it is repeating what is heard, either from others (*echoic*) or from one's own self (*self-echoic*). *Formal similarity* refers to two characteristics of stimuli. First, it means the *form* of the stimulus and the form of the response product (also a stimulus) are in the same sense mode. For example, both are auditory, visual, or tactile. Second, these stimuli resemble each other physically (Michael, 1993/2004). So, in the case of the echoic, there is an *auditory stimulus* and an *auditory response* product (i.e., similar form) and they both contain similar physical characteristics (e.g., soundwave frequencies, such as vowel energy peaks [*formants*]). *Point-to-point correspondence* means that each component of the stimulus aligns with the same-sequence component of the response. For example, in the auditory stimulus "cat," the "c" (/k/) sound is first, the "a" (/æ/) sound is next, and the "t" (/t/) sound is last. Likewise, the auditory response product has the same sequence of identical sounds: [k-æ-t] ("cat"). Thus, the individual components of the response and their sequence correspond to those of the evocative stimulus. It may simplify understanding to know that if a stimulus and response product have *form*al similarity, they necessarily also have point-to-point correspondence (Michael, 1982, 1993/2004).

From a *behavioral response* perspective, the formal similarity (with point-to-point correspondence) that characterizes an echoic (one type of *duplic* behavior; see Michael, 1982) is achieved because the speaker's vocal musculature is moving (responding) in comparable ways to that of the person providing the auditory stimulus. When the speaker's vocal musculature does *not* move in a similar way, we might observe what are commonly called articulation errors (e.g., "tat" for "cat," "thoup" for "soup"). The process of physically producing real-time speech is complicated (see Lindsey, 2020, for a video related to how vocal organs work), yet most people learn it without specialized training.

DOI: 10.4324/9781003433668-7

Echoic Role in Language Learning

Early echoic skills are usually observed in infants by 3–6 months old and are well-established by 9–12 months. This does not mean vocal imitation occurs with point-to-point precision to the adult model, but the skills needed to produce connected speech are in place: frequent vocalizations, syllables made up of consonants and vowels, variations in prosodic features (e.g., pitch), and multiple syllables rapidly produced on a single (exhaled) breath. This critical mass of vocalizations is the foundation for echoic skill acquisition, but how does it happen in the first place? Bijou and Baer (1965) suggested that both automatic and direct reinforcement may be responsible for the development of babbling in young children through the process known as autoshaping. Accordingly, verbal behavior may undergo autoshaping until it "achieves parity" with the vocal-verbal behavior of one's verbal community (Palmer, 1996). Additionally, it is likely that caregivers condition their own vocalizations as reinforcers when these co-occur with other stimuli that are related to caregiving interactions (e.g., feeding, physical contact, smiles). As a result, certain speech sounds (e.g., those spoken by caregivers) have a strong pairing history and, as such, they automatically strengthen the articulatory movements that produced them (i.e., automatic reinforcement; Palmer, 1996; Vaughan & Michael, 1982). Moreover, Skinner (1957) referenced automatic contingencies, specifically automatic reinforcement, in his description of babbling:

> The young child alone in the nursery may automatically reinforce his own exploratory vocal behavior when he produces sounds which he has heard in the speech of others. The self-reinforcing property may be merely an intonation or some other idiosyncrasy of a given speaker or of speakers in general.
> (p. 58)

Thus, automatic contingencies may be particularly relevant for the acquisition of verbal behavior, including echoics.

Echoics are critical, but they play a different role for beginning speakers than for those who are already language proficient. For early speech learners, echoics can act as a bridge (i.e., stimulus control transfer) to establish other language responses that produce more powerful reinforcement than simply approval for saying it right (Esch, 2024). For example, there is great benefit (and efficiency) in echoing an adult's speech to ask for and get what you want (i.e., the *mand* function; Skinner, 1957; see Chapter 4 in this volume); to comment on and share joint attention for objects and other non-verbal stimuli in the environment (i.e., the *tact* function; see Chapter 6 in this volume); and to react verbally to the verbal behavior of others (e.g., say/sing rhymes or fill-in-the-blank as beginning "conversation" skills; the *intraverbal* function; see Chapter 7 in this volume).

This perspective of echoic-as-bridge to other verbal skills underscores a critical point: that, for early speech learners, the echoic vis-à-vis articulatory precision can be less than perfect for quite some time while more critical language skills (fluency, longer, more complex syllable combinations) are being established as verbal behavior.

Echoics are also key to establishing foundational language repertoires involving listener and tact relations (e.g., *naming*, Horne & Lowe, 1996; *bidirectional naming*, Miguel, 2016, 2018) and joint control and the role of the self-echoic in delayed discriminations (Lowenkron, 1998, 2006). In learners with autism spectrum disorder (ASD), a self-echoic repertoire may enhance the emergence of listener behavior (Petursdottir & Carr, 2011). Underlying all these skills are the necessary and nearly nonstop vocal-verbal exchanges with early learners and their caregivers in "feedback cycles between two communication partners" (Moerk, 1990, p. 303), a sort of dance in which both individuals provide and respond imitatively to vocal models provided by the other (an excellent example is provided by Roy, 2011). This speaker-listener practice allows for ongoing modification of each other's echoic behavior to achieve closer and closer correspondence to a desired target (i.e., correct articulation).

For more sophisticated speakers, the foundational skills described above allow speakers to recruit, overtly or covertly, both echoic and self-echoic mediating behaviors to engage in more complex behaviors such as verbal problem-solving, remembering, categorization, imagery, and other perceptual behavior (see Axe et al., 2018; Kisamore et al., 2011; Schlinger & Blakely, 2024). A strong echoic repertoire can be used to increase response variability (e.g., Olin et al., 2020).

This chapter focuses on the echoic skill development of early speech learners. In addition to the importance of establishing early echoics (discussed above), we review approaches to assess and establish echoics and provide practical guidelines and recommendations for teaching echoics in applied settings. We also discuss strategies for overcoming common clinical challenges that may be encountered in working with early speech learners.

Echoic Assessment

Purpose

As with any type of speech-language evaluation, the goal of echoic assessment is to identify deficits and strengths to inform treatment. If assessment determines that the learner can echo some sounds, then intervention can target other operants related to these sounds while strengthening echoics for other sounds and syllable combinations. But before commencing any testing, we must identify if there is a need for an assessment at all. Several questions can help with this decision.

Preliminary Considerations for Assessment

First and most importantly, is speech (i.e., vocal-verbal behavior) a teaching priority (e.g., will sufficient time and appropriate expertise be allocated to teaching the learner to speak)? If yes, then it makes sense to assess vocal skills and determine the need for treatment. If speech is not a priority, see Sundberg and Partington (1998/2010, Chapter 4) and Chapter 11 in this volume. Next, does the learner have the prerequisite skills to participate in echoic testing? Chief among these is engaging with the adult to make back-and-forth speech responses when the activity is one of vocal imitation (i.e., *I say it, now you say it*). Parity with the model is not a requirement, but consistency in responding (e.g., nearly 1:1) is crucial. Otherwise, there may not be enough analyzable data to provide therapeutic direction. For learners who imitate only sporadically (or not at all), formal echoic testing is probably premature. Instead, clinicians can track vocalizations to provide periodic snapshots of emergent echoic skills (e.g., Early Echoic Skills Assessment and Program Planner [EESAPP] Pretest and/or a vocalization baseline; see Esch, 2024). Finally, does the learner already demonstrate strong echoics, such as easily repeating multiple syllables in a string, with accurate vowels and mostly accurate consonants? Even though articulation may not be perfect, such strong echoics suggest the learner is likely to benefit, without specialized teaching, from normal day-to-day vocal-verbal interactions in instructional settings. In this case, echoic testing may provide no additional information.

Assessment Focus

Because assessment should inform treatment, selecting the appropriate assessment tool first requires knowing what the intervention is intended to accomplish. Vocal imitation (echoic) tests generally fall into two distinct areas: (1) descriptions of topographic correctness (*articulation accuracy*) and (2) descriptions of response adequacy within a curricular context (*behavioral function*). Tests that focus on articulation (i.e., topography-only) can pinpoint information about the nature of errors (e.g., omissions, distortions, substitutions of phonemes and/ or syllables), and tests oriented to verbal behavior development (see *Function-Based Assessments* below) can reveal controlling variables for the various response topographies.

Topography-Based Assessments

These assessments, often referred to as articulation tests, may restrict administration to only qualified listeners (e.g., speech-language pathologists); therefore, guidelines for any particular instrument should be consulted. Traditional assessments of articulatory accuracy are typically *norm-referenced*, meaning that speech performance is compared to that of neurotypical learners of similar chronological age. The response of interest is topographic (i.e., response *form*). For example, when shown pictures and asked to name (i.e., tact) them, a learner might make these error responses: "thoup" for *soup*, "gween" for *green*, and "wabbit" for *rabbit*. If test results show a preponderance of these kinds of errors, then raw or scaled scores can be used to place a learner among a group of peers, either generally (e.g., normal versus delayed articulation) or more specifically (e.g., identify certain speech sound disorders; for example, distorted /r/ in initial and blend positions). Tests designed to yield a topographic speech sample may evoke those responses via echoic-only stimuli (e.g., Kaufman Speech Praxis Test; Kaufman, 1995), or, alternatively, they may employ multiple antecedent stimuli, including pictures and sentence fill-ins, in addition to an echoic model (e.g., Bankson-Bernthal Test of Phonology, 2020; Goldman-Fristoe Test of Articulation-3, 2015; Structured Photographic Articulation Test-3, Tattersall & Dawson, 2016).

Topographic-only descriptions lack contextual information about the type of errors made by the learner as well as information about the strength of the overall speech repertoire to support the development of other relevant skills (e.g., verbal behavior [language]). To address this, a different type of assessment is needed, namely to capture (report) the extant stimulus conditions under which particular responses were made and how those fit into the larger instructional and curricular format. It should be noted, though, that data from some topography-based tests have proven useful in behavioral training aimed at improving articulation (e.g., Aravamudhan & Awasthi, 2020; Eikeseth & Nesset, 2003). For the interested reader, a database is available (B. Esch et al., 2010) of many norm-referenced speech-language tests (including articulation tests) that analyzes test items for such putative stimulus control (i.e., verbal function).

Function-Based Assessments

Assessments with a functional-curricular focus are often *criterion-referenced*, in contrast to norm-referenced topography-based (articulation) assessments discussed above. This means that a learner's particular skills and skill sets can be evaluated without regard to or reference to the performance of other learners (although some may include norms as well, e.g., the Assessment of Basic Language and Learning Skills–Revised [ABLLS-R]; Partington, 2006). Assessments such as these probe performance in a hierarchy of requisite skills for each particular repertoire (e.g., vocal imitation) within a composite of related skill sets (e.g., language, math, reading, writing, safety/judgment, visual performance, play/leisure). As such, it is clear that the emphasis is on testing each particular skill for its contribution to a larger (curricular) whole.

An echoic assessment within this context aims to determine the strength of the repertoire with the assumption that it will be used to support the development of other vocal-verbal functions (e.g., mands, tacts, bidirectional naming, intra-verbals); in other words, speech responses that are topographically similar to those evoked echoically but under different or even multiple stimulus control (see *Introduction* discussion; also see Esch, 2024; Sundberg & Partington, 1998/2010; see Chapter 10 in this volume). In order to function thus, speaking skills must be at strength: (a) frequent and controlled, exhaled vocalizations with variation in prosody (e.g., pitch, loudness, duration) and (b) increasingly complex segments of consonants and vowels (i.e., syllable complexity; see Esch, 2024) that match the auditory model closely enough that they contact reinforcement. From this skill base (which is readily observable in typically developing early speech learners), additional speech characteristics can be assessed (e.g., phrase length). The following section discusses assessments that, in one way or another, evaluate the echoic with the focus on expanding it into non-echoic verbal behavior within a curricular paradigm.

Behavioral Assessments of Speech Performance. Speech tests in this category are usually designed to be administered and interpreted by a range of individuals, including teachers, parents, and behavior analysts. However, caveats are often included. For example, the Verbal Behavior Milestones Assessment and Placement Program (VB-MAPP; Sundberg, 2014) lists five skill sets that an assessor should have (e.g., knowledge of typical linguistic development and behavior analysis). Similarly, Esch (2024) stated that "successful administration [of the Early Echoic Skills Assessment] requires providing accurate vocal models and careful listening with a 'discerning ear'" (p. 26). As mentioned, echoic evaluation is not primarily to describe articulatory accuracy per se (as with topographic tests) but, more expansively, to identify a range of acceptable (not necessarily precise) speech components that can be reinforced as fledgling speaking skills. This begs the question: Is a perfect echoic needed for this to happen? Not at all. We only have to look at new speakers (e.g., toddlers) to know that the bar for perfect point-to-point correspondence is not essential, at least initially. As noted by Esch (2024),

> We don't expect early speech learners to speak perfectly, free of articulation errors. We test the echoic repertoire to determine how well the skill is being acquired, so that we know whether our learner can benefit from echoic prompts in establishing other critical verbal functions.
>
> (p. 21)

In other words, a new speaker's vocal imitative responses will be evaluated *during testing* for adherence to the model, but *outside* the testing situation, these responses only need to be similar enough to a model to be reinforced; accuracy will come with practice as vocal movements achieve precision. Thus, assessments that probe echoics are integral to a multi-skills evaluation. The following section discusses several tools that are designed from this perspective.

The ABLLS-R (Partington, 2006) is designed for use with children with ASD or other developmental disabilities. It evaluates 25 developmentally referenced learning domains (e.g., cooperation and reinforcer effectiveness; visual performance; motor imitation; requesting) that, together, comprise guidance for curricular decisions and skill tracking. The Echoic subtest is broad; it probes 20 vocal imitation task sets, from simple (e.g., imitates consonant-vowel combinations) to complex (e.g., imitates six-word phrases; matches pitch/tone; time-delayed echoic). Scoring grids make it easy to compare the echoics relative progress within and across the other skill areas.

The Essential for Living program (EFL; McGreevy & Fry, 2014) is a handbook and teaching protocol that encompasses curriculum and assessment needs for communication, behavior, and functional skills (a total of 18 areas). EFL is aimed at children and adults with moderate-to-severe disabilities and is designed to describe the functionality of skills needed for these individuals to successfully maneuver daily life, not to describe developmental sequences that they have or have not acquired. Speech (in the category *Spoken Words*) can be assessed via interview during a *Quick Assessment* and then subsequently confirmed with direct observation and assessment. *EFL* provides a rubric to identify whether a learner is an "effective speaker," assessing echoics as "spoken-word repetitions." EFL is unique in that it describes these repetitions according to their "stimulability" (consistency and appropriateness of occurrence); thus, vocal imitative responses are categorized as *controlled* (repeats when asked) or *uncontrolled* (echolalia). For learners with few or no echoics, the *EFL* assessment provides a plethora of alternatives to speaking (e.g., sign language, speech-generating devices) that, akin to speech, prioritizes the need for any communication modality to serve a functional purpose (e.g., get what you want; give/share important information).

The Motor and Vocal Imitation Assessment (MVIA; Aguirre & Gutierrez, 2019) evaluates different types of imitation skills (object, body, facial, and vocal) across two features: meaningful/nonmeaningful and producing sound/no sound. It was developed to identify patterns of performance that could guide intervention. In the subtest for *vocal* imitation (i.e., echoic), there are eight tasks across four areas: (1) vocal play (single consonant and vowel production), (2) canonical babbling of reduplicated syllables (e.g., "ba-ba"), (3) non-reduplicated syllables (e.g., "da-di"), and (4) true words (e.g., preferred items). Although the MVIA contains only eight test items for vocal imitation, it identifies that skill's rank in the hierarchy of other imitation skills, from simple (object, body) to complex (vocal, facial). Thus, treatments can be designed to reflect this hierarchy, for example, by sequencing or alternating task difficulty. (See next section, *Teaching Procedures*, for specific and detailed information about interventions.)

The Behavioral Language Assessment Form (BLAF; Sundberg & Partington, 1998) provides a quick description, using a 5-point scale, of 12 early skills in language and related areas (e.g., cooperation, request, social interaction, letters/numbers). Sundberg and Partington (1998) described the BLAF as "best suited for individuals who have very limited verbal skills" (p. 11). Vocal imitation (echoic) skills range from "cannot repeat any sounds or words" (1 point) to "will clearly repeat any word or even simple phrases" (5 points; Sundberg & Partington, 1998, p. 26). The BLAF also includes a pre-echoic section called *Vocal Play* that helps identify requisite vocal behaviors (e.g., frequent vocalizations; varied intonations) upon which a functional echoic repertoire can be built.

The VB-MAPP (Sundberg, 2014) is based on typical developmental milestones of learners from birth to four years old. It measures and tracks the acquisition of 170 critical language and learning skills, including the echoic. This skill (echoic) is evaluated within the VB-MAPP using a focused tool called the Early Echoic Skills Assessment (EESA; Esch, 2008/2014). The EESA assesses five groups of vocal imitative skills, from single-vowel syllables to two- and three-syllable combinations of vowels and consonants, as well as prosodic features of pitch, loudness, and duration. The purpose of EESA is to identify the necessary speech regularity and syllable complexity (observed in typical early speakers from birth to 30 months) to support connected speech and allow stimulus control to transfer from echoic to that of other verbal functions.

The VB-MAPP's EESA test for echoics (Esch, 2008/2014) has been expanded to the EESAPP (Esch, 2024). This comprehensive tool includes (a) the Early Echoic Skills Assessment-Revised (EESA-R),[1] containing 100 items across five increasingly complex skill groups and (b) a results analysis system to help users interpret test performances in order to design an appropriate initial verbal behavior (echoic-to-mand/tact) training program. Echoic skills tested by EESA-R are evaluated for articulatory accuracy and for their syllable complexity, defined by the number of syllables in the utterance, the number of different consonant sounds, and the number of different vowel sounds. For example, the syllable combination "mama" has two syllables, one consonant sound, and one vowel sound (syllable complexity total: 4). By contrast, the syllable combination "ma-mee" (*mommy*) has two syllables, one consonant sound, and two different vowel sounds (syllable complexity total: 5). Thus, EESA-R provides specific data about speech targets according to the potential influence of their syllable complexity on articulatory accuracy. That is, higher syllable complexity numbers may decrease accuracy, which, of course, decreases the likelihood that the response can be reinforced (understood) by the learner's verbal community. Syllable complexity information is important because it can guide not only the *selection* but also the *sound sequencing* as well, of appropriate speech targets.

In addition to the EESA-R assessment, the EESAPP (Esch, 2024) contains an echoic pretest, which can be used to determine a learner's consistency in responding imitatively when asked. Low-frequency responding suggests a formal assessment is premature, at least until the learner makes some speech response (even if inaccurate) on a consistent basis. The point is an important one because it emphasizes the need to pinpoint the learner's skill base along a continuum or hierarchy of vocal skills, to determine readiness to participate in echoic assessment and, in turn, in a vocal language program if indicated.

In general, echoics are acquired along a progression from (a) no response to a vocal model, then to (b) sporadic or inconsistent responding, then (c) consistent but inaccurate responding, and finally to responding that has (d) point-to-point correspondence with the speech model (Esch, 2024; McGreevy & Fry, 2014; Sundberg & Partington, 1998/2010). As we pointed out earlier, echoic testing for (a) and (b) is unlikely to provide enough echoic data for program decision-making. However, responding described by (c) should yield analyzable information. Tests that focus on behavioral function are particularly useful because they highlight that even less-than-perfect responses (from an articulation perspective) still have functionality. More specifically, they capture components of reinforceable speech responses that align perfectly with normal speech development: fluent, connected strings of syllable combinations that do not necessarily achieve topographic perfection before they come under the control of the contingencies of reinforcement as functional units of behavior.

Assessment–Intervention Link

A comprehensive assessment of echoics can be invaluable to support speech acquisition program development and intervention. As a start, treatment guidance can come from assessment information that answers a variety of questions (see Esch, 2024, Chapter 4). First, are sufficient vocalizations occurring on a regular basis so as to contact reinforcement as fledgling speech skills? If not, can their frequency be increased? Next, how accurate and consistent were vowel sounds on the assessment (vowel accuracy is prioritized over consonant accuracy)? Then, if consonants were part of the echoic model, were those included in the echoic response? If not, all information to a listener (who could provide reinforcement for the utterance) would be lost. Therefore, even a consonant misarticulation would be preferred over an omission, because it could function as a placeholder while other articulation skills were being acquired. Can the learner echo up to six syllables as a connected unit (even if the consonants are somewhat imprecise)? This skill (multiple syllables on one breath, without syllable deletions) makes it more likely that non-echoic verbal operants can be easily programmed and strengthened (e.g., fill-in phrases; answering "WH" questions; asking for information, or giving instructions).

Echoic assessments can help inform specific treatments. For example, Aravamudhan and Awasthi (2020) included echoic tasks as part of evaluating auditory discrimination, a prerequisite skill critical to *vocal imitation training* (VIT). Echoics (and self-echoics) are also integral to acquiring generalized verbal repertoires such as bidirectional naming (Miguel, 2016, 2018), categorization (Kobari-Wright & Miguel, 2014; Miguel et al., 2008), joint control and remembering (Lowenkron, 1998), and listener behavior (Petursdottir & Carr,

2011; also see J. Esch et al., 2010, 2013). When echoic assessment (or pre-test) failures deem speech training premature, those data help point the way to preliminary interventions for developing a critical mass of vocalizations, for example, stimulus-stimulus pairing (Carroll & Klatt, 2008; Esch et al., 2005, 2009; Miguel et al., 2002) or vocal variability training (Esch, J. et al., 2009; Koehler-Platten et al., 2013). Alternatively, when assessment outcomes indicate beginner-level echoics (i.e., several accurately-echoed vowels and a few conso-nants, regardless of accuracy), then these syllable building blocks can be used to launch a program of echoic shaping toward more intelligible targets—for exam-ple, possible steps to shape the word *computer*: (1) uh-tuh, (2) puh-tuh, (3) poo-tuh, (4) kuh-poo-tuh, (5) kum-poo-tuh, and (6) kum-pyoo-tuh. It should be noted that, in cases when interim approximations to the target response are deemed acceptable, the vocal model provided should remain the terminal target response (e.g., say "computer"), not the interim approximated response. Moreover, echoic "drill" without additional functional benefit for the speaker (e.g., as a mand or tact) is probably contraindicated for early speech learners, due to the likely nega-tive history already in place from unsuccessful speaking attempts. For this rea-son, echoic targets for early speakers should be within echoic-and-mand (or tact) contexts. Drill-like intervention (echoic-only) can then be reserved for learners who are already fluent speakers able to emit a wide range of syllable complexity (i.e., multiple different consonants/vowels), but who need to improve specific articulatory precision.

Teaching Procedures

Our discussion in this chapter focuses on echoics for *early* speech learners. The requisite foundation for this is a critical mass of easily (rapidly) produced multi-syllable strings with varied consonants and vowels and natural-sounding pro-sodic features (e.g., pitch, loudness). With that repertoire available, teaching can commence, but to what end? The purpose of strengthening echoics (with early speakers) is so that these same topographies can be recruited (under echoic stimulus control) and then, via stimulus control transfer, as more complex verbal behavior (e.g., mand, tact, intraverbal).

As described earlier, automatic reinforcement facilitates the acquisition of vocalizations, including echoics. Therefore, numerous studies aimed at increas-ing rates of vocalizations have employed procedures designed to condition vocalizations as reinforcers (see Interventions to Increase Vocalizations section below). Additionally, given that neurotypical children acquire a large repertoire of recognizable syllabic vocalizations (i.e., canonical babbling; Lang et al., 2019), as support for acquisition of echoics, previous research targeting acqui-sition of echoics has appropriately sought to increase vocalizations first, and then employed procedures to establish echoic control over these responses (e.g., Carroll & Klatt, 2008).

In this section, we provide an overview of interventions that have been shown to lead to an increase in rates of overall vocalizations and procedures aimed at teaching echoics. Sample teaching protocols based on published research and datasheets are available in Appendix A (available at www.routledge.com /9781032560625). However, it is important to note that clinicians must individualize the teaching protocols based on their learner's needs (e.g., decrease the number of trials per session, increase the duration of reinforcement). Additionally, no intervention appears to be universally effective. That is, interventions shown to be effective for some participants and responses do not necessarily have the same effect on other participants or with other responses (e.g., see Shillingsburg et al., 2015 for examples of conflicting outcomes related to the SSP procedure). Therefore, clinicians must be prepared to evaluate multiple procedures prior to identifying the one that is effective for their learner. Alternatively, clinicians could concurrently evaluate the impact of multiple interventions to determine efficacy (see Carroll et al., 2015 as an example).

Interventions to Increase Vocalizations

There are two main categories of interventions used to increase rates of vocalizations. The first category consists of interventions that aim to condition vocalizations as reinforcers by pairing them with other conditioned or unconditioned reinforcers (i.e., respondent conditioning). Examples include stimulus-stimulus pairing (SSP; Sundberg et al., 1996) and response-contingent pairing (RCP; Dozier et al., 2012). The other category of interventions involves the delivery of a reinforcer contingent on the occurrence of vocalizations (i.e., operant conditioning). An example of a procedure that entails direct reinforcement of vocalizations is contingent vocal imitation (CVI; Pelaez et al., 2018). Independent of the procedure chosen, to determine if the procedures are effective, clinicians must compare baseline levels (e.g., rate of target vocalizations prior to the intervention) to levels of vocalizations obtained throughout the intervention (e.g., record data during intervention sessions or following each session; see Carroll & Klatt, 2008 as an example) and/or to levels attained following the completion of the intervention (e.g., after a specified number of intervention sessions are completed; see Chance et al., 2021 as an example).

Stimulus-Stimulus Pairing (SSP)

The SSP procedure, also known as a response-independent pairing, involves the pairing of a neutral vocal stimulus with an already reinforcing stimulus (e.g., edibles, toys, or social stimuli). Usually, the target vocal stimulus is presented multiple times during each pairing trial (e.g., five times), and the reinforcing stimulus is provided after the first but before the last presentation of the target vocal stimuli. The first investigation of the effects of SSP on independent vocalizations was completed by Sundberg et al. (1996), and in this study, the pairing procedure resulted in at least some novel vocalizations for all the participants. However, other studies investigating the effects of the SSP procedure have produced conflicting results. For instance, Stock et al. (2008) compared SSP, echoic training (i.e., modified VIT procedure in which the target sound was presented five times per trial), and a control condition in which the sound and reinforcer were presented but not in temporal proximity. The SSP procedure was effective in increasing rates of vocalizations for only one out of three participants.

Numerous modifications have been made to the SSP procedure to attempt to increase its efficacy, including interspersing pairing trials (S+) with non-pairing (S-, vocal stimulus presentation only) trials (e.g., Esch et al., 2009), the addition of an observing prompt (i.e., "look"; Esch et al., 2009), and the use of an exaggerated prosodic pattern (i.e., motherese) when presenting the target sounds (e.g., Esch et al., 2009). Moreover, there are several variables (e.g., the number of presentations of the target vocalization [i.e., number of pairings] per trial; the type of reinforcing stimulus [e.g., social stimuli; food; toys] presented during each trial) that clinicians planning to implement SSP must consider. Regarding some of these variables, results of the literature review completed by Shillingsburg et al. (2015) indicated that, in general, SSP had larger effects sizes with children who were 5 years or younger, children without a functional vocal repertoire, when edibles were delivered during the pairing trials, when delayed conditioning was employed, and when procedures (e.g., delivery of reinforcing stimulus was delayed or withheld) were implemented to minimize adventitious reinforcement of vocalizations. Additionally, the number of presentations of the target sound per trial did not influence effect sizes. Therefore, clinicians might want to consider evaluating an SSP iteration based on the outcomes of this review, and if the procedure is ineffective, making procedural modifications or evaluating another conditioning procedure.

Response-Contingent Pairing (RCP)

The RCP procedure is similar to SSP in that both entail the pairing of a neutral stimulus (e.g., a vocalization) with a reinforcing stimulus. However, these procedures differ in that in RCP, the implementer presents the paired neutral stimulus and the reinforcing stimulus contingent on the learner's emission of a specified response (e.g., disk sorting; Dozier et al., 2012). Results of previous studies indicate that the RCP procedure may be more effective (i.e., increased target responses to higher levels) than SSP (Lepper & Petursdottir, 2017) and that RCP was effective at establishing vocalizations as reinforcers and increasing rates of vocalizations for some participants (Chance et al., 2021).

Operant Discrimination Training (ODT)

The ODT procedure, as described by Lepper et al. (2013), is like RCP in a few ways. Both procedures entail the pairing of the target vocalization with a reinforcer and in both cases, the pairing of the vocalization and the reinforcer occurs contingent on the emission of a specific response by the learner (e.g., disk sorting with RCP; Dozier et al., 2012; arm raising with ODT; Lepper et al., 2013). However, in the case of ODT, the reinforcer is only provided when the specified response (e.g., arm raising) occurs in the presence of a particular stimulus (the discriminative stimulus; S^D) and not when the stimulus is absent (S^Δ). Therefore, when using ODT to condition vocalizations, the S^D is a target vocalization whereas the S^Δ consists of non-target vocalizations (e.g., Lepper et al., 2013). In other words, when using ODT, the target vocalization acquires reinforcing properties because it signals the availability of a reinforcer for a particular response (i.e., the target vocalization becomes an S^D). More specifically, in the study completed by Lepper et al., each session included trials in which a target vocalization or a non-target vocalization was presented by the experimenter three times; arm raising, the specified response, was reinforced only when it occurred during the presentation of the target vocalization. Moreover, during target trials, if the participant did not raise their arm independently during the presentation of the target vocalization, the experimenter prompted arm raising and then delivered the preferred stimulus. In this study, both SSP and ODT led to an increase in the rate of vocalizations for the three participants, but results of the concurrent-chains preference assessment indicated that all participants preferred ODT over SSP and the control condition (i.e., presentation of target sound and delivery of preferred stimulus were separated by 20 seconds).

Observational Conditioning (OC)

According to Greer and Singer-Dudek (2008), OC is a type of observational learning, the process by which a learner acquires new skills through the observation of another person engaging in that response and contacting reinforcement (Greer et al., 2006). Consequently, OC results from observing another person receiving that stimulus contingent on the occurrence of a target response. Previous research has demonstrated that OC is effective at establishing neutral stimuli (e.g., plastic disks; Greer & Singer-Dudek, 2008) as reinforcers, but there are few studies evaluating the impact of OC on the conditioning of vocalizations. One exception is the study completed by Chance et al. (2021). In this study, during the OC conditioning sessions, the participant observed the experimenter emit the target vocalization five times contingent on the emission of a correct response by the confederate; no consequences were provided for any responses emitted by the participant. Results indicated that, for some of the participants, the OC procedure established the target vocalization as a reinforcer and that it led to an increase in rates of vocalizations. It is important to note that previous research has identified four prerequisites for observational learning: attending to a model, imitation, delayed imitation, and consequence discrimination (MacDonald & Ahearn, 2015); thus, it is plausible that OC may not be effective for learners lacking these skills.

Contingent Vocal Imitation (CVI)

As the name implies, during CVI, the learner's vocalization is imitated by another person, usually a caregiver or another adult (e.g., Neimy et al., 2020). That is, the implementer echoes the learner's vocalizations. This intervention appears to have its origins in the observation of caregiver-child interactions, which indicate that caregivers often emit vocalizations and respond to their child's vocalizations with an echoic response (i.e., imitation of the vocalization) or with motherese speech (e.g., Pelaez et al., 2011a, 2011b). Moreover, it has been suggested that the caregiver's vocalization likely acquired reinforcing properties and their presentation, contingent on the occurrence of the child's vocalization, reinforces the children's vocalization (Pelaez et al., 2018). However, one potential drawback to this intervention is the fact that pairing trials are initiated by the learner, which could lead to very few instances of pairings per day. A few studies have evaluated the impact of CVI on the occurrence of vocalizations. For instance, in a study completed by Fiani et al. (2021), which included children diagnosed with Down syndrome, CVI led to an increase in the rate of vocalizations (e.g., English syllables with vowels) and a decrease in babbling for the three participants.

Interventions to Establish Echoic Control

Once a learner has a repertoire of vocalizations, independent of the size or complexity of the repertoire, the next step is to establish echoic control over these vocalizations. That is, we must ensure that the learner emits these vocalizations in response to the presentation of a vocal S^D (i.e., a vocal model) by another person. Vocal imitation training (VIT) is likely the most commonly used intervention for establishing echoics. Other examples include mand-model (MM; Cividini-Motta et al., 2017), shaping (e.g., Lovaas et al., 1966), and chaining (e.g., Tarbox et al., 2009). Moreover, at least in some cases, procedures commonly employed to increase the rate of vocalizations (e.g., SSP, CVI) have led to an increase in echoics.

Vocal Imitation Training (VIT)

This procedure, which is sometimes referred to as echoic training (e.g., Stock et al., 2008), involves presenting a model of the target vocalization to the learner and delivering a reinforcer contingent on the learner's emission of the same vocalization (i.e., learner's imitation of the vocalization; emission of an echoic) within a specified interval (e.g., within 5 seconds). In other words, this intervention consists of direct reinforcement of echoics. Results of previous studies have shown that VIT is effective at establishing echoics (e.g., Baer et al., 1967; Carroll & Klatt, 2008; Cividini-Motta et al., 2017). For instance, Carroll and Klatt (2008) employed the SSP procedure to increase the frequency of a known target vocalization and then VIT (i.e., referred by the authors as procedure five) to bring the target vocalization under echoic control for one of their participants. However, in this study, SSP led to increase in the frequency of only one target vocalization for the first participant (i.e., Mary), and it did not increase the frequency of the target vocalizations of the second participant (i.e., Max). In the study by Cividini-Motta et al. (2017), which compared SSP, MM, and VIT, the VIT procedure led to an increase in at least some of the target echoics for three of the five participants.

Mand-Model (MM)

The MM procedure, which was first described by Rogers-Warren and Warren (1980), has been employed to teach a variety of skills including echoics (e.g., Cividini-Motta et al., 2017) and graphic symbol combinations (e.g., Nigam et al., 2006). According to LeBlanc et al. (2006), the procedure can be used to shape more complex vocal responses (e.g., longer phrases); it is most appropriate for learners who "initiate language at low rates" (p. 55), and its name does not refer to acquisition of a mand by the learner but instead of the behavior of the implementer, who mands for a response. Although procedural variations exist, in general, when using the MM procedure, the implementer must first identify preferred items to deliver as consequences for correct vocalizations. Additionally, the implementer must identify target vocalizations, and, if using the procedure to shape more complex responses, determine the criterion for reinforcement. During an instruction trial, the implementer presents the preferred stimulus to the learner and a vocal prompt, in the form of a mand, for the target response (e.g., "What do you want?"). If the learner emits the target vocalization, the implementer provides access to the preferred stimulus. If the learner does not respond, additional prompts are usually provided, including, for instance, another vocal prompt for the target response (e.g., "Tell me what you want?"; Cividini-Motta et al., 2017; "Ask me in a full sentence."; LeBlanc et al., 2006), and if necessary, a model of the target response (e.g., "Say ball"). Examples of modifications to the procedure including the use of preferred stimuli that include the target sound in their name (e.g., "p" for peppermint) and restricting access to the preferred stimulus prior to sessions (e.g., no access to the item for at least 1 hour; Cividini-Motta et al., 2017).

Shaping

Shaping consists of reinforcement of successive approximations to the target response (Newman et al., 2009). That is, a reinforcer is provided if the learner emits a response that is equal to a predetermined acceptable response or better (i.e., closer to the target response), and other responses are placed on extinction. Shaping has been used to establish novel responses in persons with disabilities since the early days of behavior analysis. For instance, Lovaas et al. (1966) used shaping, in combination with prompting, to establish echoics in two children with schizophrenia. In this study, during the first step, all vocalizations emitted by the participant produced access to a reinforcer; next, only vocalizations emitted within 6 seconds of the vocal model presented by the therapist; finally, during the last step reinforcers were delivered only when the participant emitted a vocalization, within 6 seconds of the model, that matched the vocalization presented by the therapist. In a more recent study, Drash et al. (1999) used shaping to establish mands, echoics, and tacts. In this study, the authors first established a manding repertoire by contriving establishing operations (EOs) for specific reinforcers. Specifically, the experimenter presented the preferred stimulus out of reach of the participant, and then provided a vocal prompt for a response (e.g., "Do you want this?"; "What do you want?"). Initially, any vocalization other than a scream or cry produced access to the preferred item, whereas during subsequent sessions, specific sounds were reinforced and specific sounds were paired with specific reinforcers (e.g., "mmm" was reinforced with access to an M&M). Moreover, as training progressed, the experimenter began to echo the participant's response, requiring the participant to emit the response once again (i.e., imitate the implementer). As a result, the participant's response was multiply controlled by the EO for the specific reinforcer, the non-verbal stimulus (i.e., the sight of the preferred stimulus), and the verbal stimulus (i.e., the vocal model presented by the experimenter). In this study, the MM procedure led to the acquisition of mands and echoics for the three participants and tacts for two of the participants.

Chaining

In the context of teaching echoics, chaining entails dividing vocalizations into smaller units (e.g., phonemes; syllables) and employing modeling and reinforcement of correct responses (i.e., VIT) to teach each unit and the target echoic (Tarbox et al., 2009). For instance, Tarbox et al. (2009) target echoics divided into two components (e.g., "Ball" was separated into two parts, "b" and "all"). Training sessions consisted of five presentations of the target echoic, and each presentation of the target echoic included a sequence of three trials, presented in rapid succession. During the first trial of the sequence the experimenter presented a model of the initial component (e.g., "say b") and correct imitation of the response by the participant resulted in reinforcement (i.e., a preferred stimulus and praise) and immediate presentation of a model of the second component (e.g., "say all"); correct imitation of the second component produced reinforcement and the presentation of a model of the target echoic (e.g., say "ball"). If the participant emitted an incorrect response, the experimenter presented the trial once again and then proceeded with the sequence. In this study, the three participants acquired the three target echoics within 5–35 sessions, and echoic responding persisted when the intervention was withdrawn (i.e., maintenance phase). Moreover, similar results were attained by Mallory et al. (2019), who employed similar procedures to increase the complexity of echoics of two children with ASD. However, as noted by Tarbox et al., the procedures employed in this study included the delivery of a reinforcer following correct imitation of each component of the chain and the presentation of the entire chain during the last trial of the sequences, which are not components usually included in behavioral chains. Thus, these authors indicated that their procedure should be considered a modified chaining or chaining-like procedure.

It should be noted that echoic training procedures that separate consonants from the vowel (which is requisite to define any English syllable entity) may not produce the natural-sounding (fluently produced) syllable strings that are typical of normal speech. Early speech learners progress from cooing sounds to *canonical babbling*, characterized by a consonant and a vowel-like part, rapidly produced in longer and more phonetically complex strings. As Lang et al. (2019) stated:

> The rapid transition between consonants and vowels is a defining feature of the difference between precanonical and canonical syllable productions. Infants gradually develop the oral-motor skills necessary to produce adult-like consonant-vowel-syllables, which, in turn, are the prerequisite to uttering conventional words.
>
> (p. 111)

Therefore, when choosing speech targets for early speech learners, any consonant sound should be in syllable form (i.e., with a vowel attached).

Tactics for Promoting Efficiency, Emergence, Generalization, and Maintenance

There are numerous ways to increase the efficiency of programs targeting acquisition, generalization, and maintenance of vocalizations and echoics. One potential way to increase the efficiency of the instructional procedures is to synthesize them. For instance, instead of attempting to isolate the effects of conditioning and direct reinforcement, in clinical settings, where the goal is to facilitate the emergence of vocalizations and echoics, it is appropriate to pair vocalizations with reinforcement and ensure that vocalizations contact direct reinforcement (e.g., combine SSP with VIT). Additionally, clinicians should consider prompting, reinforcing, and pairing vocalizations with reinforcers throughout the entire day, as this would be analogous to what normally occurs during the early development of vocalizations in infants (e.g., caregivers speak to them frequently and throughout daily routine activities, such as feeding, pair vocalizations with reinforcers). For example, the therapist could emit a target vocalization concurrently with the delivery of a reinforcer for correct responding. Moreover, whenever possible, clinicians should employ instructional procedures that may result in the acquisition of multiple operants (e.g., MM; see Drash et al., 1999). Therefore, in clinical settings, it may be advantageous to pair each echoic response with a particular preferred stimulus, show the preferred stimulus to the participant while presenting the vocal model of the target echoic, and then reinforce echoic responses with access to the specific preferred stimulus. Then, in cases when the target echoic consists of a component of the tact or mand (e.g., "pop" instead of "popcorn") and the participant acquires the vocalization as a tact and a mand for the specified preferred stimulus, shaping and/or chaining can be used to teach the complete response (e.g., "popcorn").

Regarding maintenance and generalization of echoics, there are a few things clinicians should consider. First, given that mands allow the learner to specify their reinforcers, clinicians should target the acquisition of mands related to newly acquired echoics by using echoic prompts and targeting the acquisition of mands whose names include the newly acquired echoic. Therefore, echoic targets should include at least the minimal number of components of an actual word. This means that a single consonant would not be an appropriate target, because, in English, there are no words made up of a single consonant sound. In addition, in cases when the newly acquired echoics are not incorporated as prompts for the acquisition of other operants, to ensure maintenance of the response, the clinician must provide the learner with opportunities to practice the newly acquired echoic (e.g., intersperse mastered echoics into sessions targeting the acquisition of other echoics or responses). Second, clinicians should conduct periodic probes to determine if the learner has maintained the skills; if not, retraining could be provided. Third, regarding generalization of the newly acquired echoic, instructional programs must be designed to foster generalization (e.g., include common stimuli; target sufficient exemplars; introduce naturally occurring contingency; Stokes & Baer, 1977). For instance, training could incorporate multiple and, if possible, familiar people and stimuli available in the learner's natural environment, and should continue until the learner's responses have generalized to novel people and environmental contexts. Finally, the goal of every echoic program should be to establish a repertoire of generalized echoics. That is, the learner should be able to echo novel vocal stimuli without requiring training. To accomplish this goal, clinicians must train multiple exemplars and probe whether the learner can echo novel vocal models.

Strategies for Overcoming Clinical Challenges

Helping a learner acquire, strengthen, and maintain vocal-verbal skills can present many challenges. In this section, we identify and briefly discuss four of the most common issues in clinical practice and suggest strategies for dealing with these. Due to overlaps among the areas discussed, strategies in one section may apply to issues in other sections as well.

Learner is Resistant to Teaching Sessions

A learner may be resistant to instruction. For instance, they may not comply with an instruction to emit a vocalization (i.e., do not attempt to emit a vocalization), or they may not comply with an instruction to move to the area designed for teaching sessions, or they may engage in disruptive behavior when an instruction to emit a vocalization is provided. If resistance occurs during teaching sessions in which vocal responding is required, this may signal the learner's history of failure with speaking attempts. This negative learning experience may have occurred for related reasons. First, it is possible that the performance targets may have been set too high (e.g., a requirement for precise articulation in the absence of established foundational speech skills). At the same time, past reinforcement schedules (during speech training) may have been too thin. For example, the learner's speaking attempts may have been met often with "try again" instead of with differential reinforcement for small, incremental improvements. Other issues may be infrequent and lengthy sessions (e.g., twice weekly for 30 minutes) instead of short and frequently spaced practice sessions (e.g., 2 minutes each, 30 times a day). Note: The latter more closely aligns with the speaking experiences of most early speech learners, whose chatter (i.e., practice) seems to occur nearly incessantly. Here are some strategies to reduce resistance to vocal-verbal teaching sessions:

- Keep the reinforcement schedule rich in the beginning. Provide high-preference outcomes for nearly every speech attempt at first.
- Match the performance requirement (i.e., antecedent stimulus) to the learner's skill level, or close to that level. Then, as soon as consistent (not necessarily accurate) responding is occurring, increase response requirements in small, reachable steps. Ensure teaching targets are appropriate. Broadly, early speech learners who vocalize infrequently or weakly first need to establish basic vocal speech skills before they can match the precise articulation of an echoic model. Several fundamental skills are typically in place within the first 12 months: (a) vocalizing on exhaled, not inhaled, breaths, (b) fluently producing multiple syllables on one breath, and (c) emitting rapid, connected syllable strings that consist of vowels and consonants. Together, these competencies ensure that the early speech learner has mastered (and

can sustain) the requisite coordinated adjustments of the vocal musculature to support the emission of reinforceable speech responses. (Note: these prerequisite skills underscore why, for early speech learners, targets should not focus on producing single consonant sounds alone. It is critical that syllables (vowels, or vowels plus consonants) are prioritized over consonant-only precision. For further information, see Esch, 2024, p. 7.)

- Conduct more frequent, shorter-duration teaching sessions, such as 2–3 minutes, 30–50 times a day, instead of 30 minutes once a day. This establishes vocal responding as a teaching priority and provides the multitude of vocal-verbal practice opportunities that are more akin to those of typical early speakers.
- Some considerations appropriate for an assessment environment (e.g., cooperation, test environment, materials, reinforcers) are applicable to treatment sessions as well (see Sundberg & Partington, 1998/2010, pp. 9–11 for a discussion).

Unrealistic Performance Expectations

The problem of unrealistic expectations for speech learner performance may stem from the clinician's unfamiliarity with *typical* speech and language development (see American Speech-Language-Hearing Association, n.d. for resources related to speech and language developmental norms), such that tackling *atypical* repertoires seems daunting. The atypical repertoires we refer to are those of learners who have failed to keep pace with their speech-learning peers, and the task is one of habilitating their weak repertoire, by contrast with *re*habilitating a damaged one. Thus, it is critical to know which early milestones should be in place and to pinpoint those that are missing. When important foundational skills (milestones) are overlooked, it can lead to setting program targets that are too difficult, out of sequence, or unnecessary.

In thinking about our expectations for early speech milestones, consider how speech typically progresses, from no skill at birth to sophisticated speaking repertoires within just a few years (Esch, 2024):

> Infants practice sound-making and babbling, providing critical practice in breath control that coordinates with basic tongue movements. Babies and toddlers expand the skill with tongue movement practice…in longer and longer syllable strings (baby talk), thus perfecting jaw control, vocal cord movement, and other actions of the speech musculature. This fluency in producing strings of syllables is achieved long before pinpointed accuracy. Think function over form at these early stages. Eventually, children refine articulation skill through nearly nonstop practice until, as older children and adults, they can emit more sophisticated and complex vocalizations.
>
> (p. vii)

It is important to underscore this hierarchy of increasingly complex speech skills. If we observe new speakers, we can see that their first skills are not those of articulation precision but, rather, of rapidly producing more and more syllables of more and more complexity (i.e., connected speech). Syllable complexity can be defined in terms of three components: (1) number of syllables in a phrase or syllable string, (2) number of *different* consonant sounds, and (3) number of *different* vowel sounds (see Esch, 2024, Chapter 2). For example, the word "taco" has two syllables, two different consonant sounds ("t" and "k"), and two different vowel sounds ("ah" and "oh"); by contrast, the word "tooth" has one syllable, two different consonant sounds ("t" and "th") and one vowel sound ("oo"). We can sum these component numbers to identify the relative complexity of the utterances (taco = 6; tooth = 4).

By focusing on elements of syllable complexity instead of specific articulation, instructors can pinpoint, track, and target the same skill progression of neurotypical speech learners, who first master rapidly produced utterances with varied vowels and consonants (i.e., canonical babbling; Goldstein et al., 2003; Goldstein & Schwade, 2008) long before articulation precision is achieved. In other words, articulatory accuracy comes after, not before, these long strings of easily-produced, connected syllables of vowel-consonant sound combinations. To illustrate, we know that "baby-talk" and consonant misarticulations are commonly accepted by a child's verbal community for years. These misarticulations occur exactly because they yield to the higher priority of rapidly produced speech. The verbal community provides reinforcement for fluent, "acceptably imprecise" early speech, and, at the same time, frequently provides echoic models of the requisite syllable complexity components; together, these support improved articulation (Esch, 2024; Lang, 2019).

Problems Understanding Learner's Vocal Responses

Speech is fleeting. This momentary salience is, of course, an inherent characteristic of all sound-based stimuli, and for speech signals, it goes both ways: the auditory stimulus is short-lived for the listener but also for the speaker. Let us consider various issues vis-à-vis the salience of spoken (auditory) response products from the perspectives of the early speech learner and that of the teacher/clinician.

Early Speaker

If the speaker is a "newbie" (i.e., just learning to talk), their speech may be weak (e.g., auditory stimuli produced are low volume [quiet], unclear, infrequent, or inconsistent). Speech responses that produce low-salience auditory stimuli are at risk of not contacting reinforcement that would otherwise strengthen these responses. In the case of *automatic reinforcement* ("that sounds right!"; see

Palmer, 1996, 2018; Vaughan & Michael, 1982), the auditory stimulus must be strong enough to impact the speaker's own receptors; if it is not, response strengthening may fail to occur. In addition, "other-provided" (i.e., differential) reinforcement, programmed in training settings, may be less likely to follow a weak response than a stronger one, either because it was not clearly heard or because it was deemed wrong (i.e., did not meet the reinforcement requirement). In this situation, it is critical to provide strong positive consequences for almost any speech sounds until vocalizing is consistent enough that asking the learner to repeat does not result in avoidance behavior. Then, when vocal responding is consistent, asking a learner to self-echo ("Huh?" "What'd you say?") is acceptable and helps establish their skills in attending to their own vocal behavior (see J. Esch et al., 2010).

Teacher-as-Listener

From an instructor's perspective, it can be difficult to determine the reinforceability of a particular spoken response. We may not have clearly heard it or be able to transcribe it quickly enough to take note of it, or we may be unsure exactly which response to reinforce. Each of these has its own challenges and possible solutions. If a response was unclear, it is perfectly fine to ask the learner to repeat, but there are some caveats. First, be aware of the learner's tolerance for repetition (i.e., low or no reinforcement) and keep requests to "say it again" to a minimum. Also, it may be possible to table that item and return to it later. For example, an activity of "pick-a-card" can provide repeated speech opportunities when the materials include multiples of the same item. For instance, a teacher could arrange a display of assorted pictures (e.g., five dogs, five trees, five cars) on a board that the learner can see but not reach. The learner could mand/tact a desired picture from the teacher's display to match-to-sample on a grid in front of the learner, with the goal of filling each grid cell with its matching picture (e.g., Bingo).

If recording a response is a challenge, it may help to immediately echo, and, if necessary, to self-echo (echo it again) what was heard. This extends the salience of the auditory stimulus, perhaps long enough to transcribe the utterance. It also serves to increase the teacher's skill in echoing the learner, which facilitates target identification (i.e., *What did they say and is that what I'm targeting?*). Another strategy for fast, accurate recording is to use the International Phonetic Alphabet (IPA; https://www.internationalphoneticalphabet.org). Familiarity with IPA transcription is particularly helpful to accurately identify vowel sounds; this simplifies target selection because it pinpoints speech sounds, not arbitrary letters that represent sounds.

When teachers are unsure which vocal response to reinforce, the issue may be related more to uncertainty about the speech targets themselves. In this case, it is helpful to understand how speech is normally acquired (see Unrealistic Performance Expectations section above) and then to identify (and reconsider, if necessary) the current teaching focus and whether it fits into a logical curricular sequence. A specific strategy may simplify the task of pinpointing which response to reinforce: speech trials can be arranged with a limited number of response options (e.g., minimal contrasts). For example, in an echoic-mand-tact context, a teacher could ask, "Do you want the (picture of) 'dog' or 'log,' 'zipper' or 'kipper,' 'beet' or 'boat?'" This effectively reduces the likelihood of other responses and allows the teacher to listen for echoic accuracy of (either) specific phoneme (e.g., "ee" or "oh") presented in the auditory stimulus. Finally, sometimes teachers fail to reinforce what turns out to be the "best response" (i.e., a previous one). This is not crucial because, if vocalizing is consistent, such a response is likely to occur again. Moreover, recognizing these missed opportunities suggests that the teacher's skill in observing response differences is improving, and thus they can provide differential reinforcement more effectively in the future.

Interprofessional Concerns

There can be significant differences in clinical perspective and priorities among professionals of different backgrounds and training (see Chapter 14 in this volume). Difficulties can arise when team members fail to agree on responsibilities and priorities for the teaching targets. Additionally, a "team" consisting of a single individual may effectively stall decision-making to the extent that the provider is unsure how to proceed with building a functional vocal-verbal repertoire.

In terms of teamwork, a consensus-building perspective is that we are all members of a learner's verbal community; therefore, each of us (e.g., parents, relatives, caregivers, teachers, neighbors) can feel comfortable assuming some responsibility for encouraging early speech learners to talk and communicate. Also, when planning for early speech learners, it is useful for the team to agree on how neurotypical learners acquire foundational speech skills (i.e., developmental sequences) and *that the same sequences apply to those who have not yet acquired these skills* (thus, a shared focus that the task is one of habilitation and not *re*habilitation; see Unrealistic Performance Expectations section above). These two shared perspectives ensure team activities that are defined within an orderly curricular sequence of goals, objectives, and vocal-verbal targets. These can be summarized as: (a) each team member can contribute to assessment and program planning in terms of their specific knowledge base; (b) acquisition of foundational (early) speech skills follows the same progression for most learners: speaking on exhaled breath, extensive vocal practice with vowels and vowel-consonant combinations, and producing longer and longer syllable strings made up of increasingly complex components (of consonant and vowel sounds); and (c) speech is acquired within a context of functional language skills; thus, for early speech learners, echoic-only drill should not take precedence over teaching within non-echoic contexts (e.g., mands, tacts). If team members can agree on these basics, it is likely they can align their clinical roles according to their specific scope of practice (i.e., skill sets).

A final concern is that of multilingual situations. Target prioritization may be unclear when a learner's family speaks one language at home and the school provides instruction in a different language. In this case, the family's priorities must be considered (see also Chapter 13 in this volume). In the United States, many families will endorse English for school instruction, while communicating at home in their native language. If the learner is currently non-vocal (or low-vocal), it is useful to seek consensus on which language environment can and will provide the bulk of vocal-verbal instruction.

Summary

Echoics are fundamental to developing vocal-verbal behavior, commonly called spoken language. The echoic repertoire supports the acquisition of many complex language skills including mand, tact, intraverbal, self-echoic/tact behavior, listener-speaker behavior, verbal problem-solving, and perceptual behavior. There are many tools to assess echoics and, not surprisingly, they yield different information. Topography-focused tests are typically used to identify specific types of speech sound disorders; this tends to lead to treatments that focus on improving specific articulation errors (or phonological). Echoic assessments with a behavioral focus usually emphasize integrating the echoic into other language skills (e.g., asking for things), with less insistence on precise topography in favor of strengthening any recognizable (reinforceable) response. Treatments focus on two areas: (1) establishing a critical mass of vocalizations that can come under contingencies of reinforcement as verbal operants and (2) implementing operant conditioning procedures to strengthen these skills. A rich repertoire of fluently produced vocalizations is a prerequisite for echoic skill acquisition. We discussed several procedures for increasing vocalizations and establishing echoics (see Table 5.1).

It is important to base treatments on research when available, but clinical judgment must play a role as well, particularly in cases where there may be little guidance from research or when a learner fails to respond to certain intervention protocols. Early speech learners who are just beginning to (accurately) echo the speech of others, by definition, lack a strong history of reinforcement for vocalizing, so clinicians should ensure they arrange contingencies of reinforcement that mirror those available in the natural environment for neurotypical learners. This means frequent reinforcement for most vocal attempts, with

Table 5.1 Overview of Teaching Procedures

KEY AR = Arbitrary response **Cq** = Consequence **PS** = Preferred stimulus **Proc** = Procedure **Rfcr** = Reinforcer **Voc** = Vocalization

Proc	Trial initiator	Trial onset	Models per trial	Cq for Voc/Echoic	Cq for NR/Error	Example
SSP	(T)eacher	Vocal model	Multiple	Withhold rfcr	Continue trial	T emits model (e.g., *ah, ah, ah, ah, ah*). T delivers rfcr between 1st and 5th presentation if L does not emit target voc.
RCP	(L)earner	AR	Multiple	End trial	Continue trial/ end trial	L emits AR (e.g., presses button). T emits vocal model (e.g., *ah, ah, ah*) and delivers reinforcer during 3rd presentation of vocal model; end trial if L emits any voc.
ODT	(T)eacher	Vocal instruction	Single	None	None	T presents to L and C the vocal instruction for AR; when C emits a correct response T presents vocal model of target response. No Cq for responses emitted by L.
OC	(C)onfederate	AR	Multiple	None	None	C emits AR. T emits vocal model (e.g., "ah", "ah", "ah", "ah"). No Cq for responses emitted by L.
CVI	(L)earner	Voc	Single	T echoes response	N/A	L says *ah*. T immediately echoes vocalization ("ah").
VIT	(T)eacher	Vocal model	Single	Deliver rfcr	Withhold rfcr	T says *Say ah*; L emits "ah" within 5 s. T delivers Rfcr.

(Continued)

Table 5.1 (Continued)

KEY AR = Arbitrary response **Cq** = Consequence **PS** = Preferred stimulus **Proc** = Procedure **Rfcr** = Reinforcer **Voc** = Vocalization

Proc	Trial initiator	Trial onset	Models per trial	Cq for Voc/Echoic	Cq for NR/Error	Example
MM	(T)eacher	PS+prompt	Single	Deliver rfcr	2nd prompt/withhold rfcr	T presents PS and prompt (e.g., *What do you want?*). L emits target voc within 5 s; T delivers rfcr. If L does not respond, T provides additional prompts (e.g., *Tell me what you want*).
Shaping	(T)eacher	Vocal model	Single	Deliver rfcr	Represent trial	T presents vocal model (e.g., *Monday*). If L emits acceptable approximation (e.g., "Muhday") within 5 s, T delivers rfcr.
Chaining	(T)eacher	Vocal model Component 1	Single Each component and target	Deliver rfcr model Component 2	Represent trial	IM presents vocal model (e.g., *mon*). L emits target response (e.g., "mon") within 5 s, T presents vocal model (e.g., *day*), learner emits target response (e.g., "day") within 5 s, T delivers rfcr. T presents vocal model (e.g., *Monday*), L emits target response (e.g., "Monday") within 5 s, T delivers rfcr.

Note: SSP = stimulus–stimulus pairing; RCP = response-contingent pairing; ODT = operant discrimination training; OC = observational conditioning; CVI = contingent vocal imitation; VIT = vocal imitation training; MM = mand-model.

attainable increments that "set the bar" toward terminal vocal-verbal targets. Practical adjustments to formal protocols that may promote acquisition include synthesizing (pairing) components of the learn unit (e.g., reinforcers follow most vocalizations), and programming multiple stimulus control to establish combined operants (e.g., echoic-mand, echoic-tact). Maintenance and generalization can be enhanced by prioritizing topographies that (1) specify reinforcers (i.e., mands), (2) contain requisite components of real words (i.e., avoid training a single consonant without an attached vowel), and (3) include mastered echoics that are programmed for reinforcement, even though these may only approximate the terminal target. In addition, periodic probes can alert clinicians to any decrement in echoics. Finally, instructional programs should include components to foster generalization, such as naturally occurring contingencies and settings and people that the learner encounters regularly. We identified four common challenges to vocal-verbal instruction and discussed strategies for overcoming these issues: (1) Learner is resistant to teaching sessions; (2) Unrealistic expectations for learner performance; (3) Problems understanding learner's vocal responses; and (4) Interprofessional concerns.

There is great individual, societal, and cultural benefit for speech learners to become skilled at repeating what they hear. *Atomic repertoires* (Palmer, 2012), such as the echoic, are the seeds that engender a myriad of complex human skills, and the unique stimuli (auditory) produced by echoics can disperse quite easily discriminations of all kinds. Therefore, the overarching goal of echoic training should be to establish generalized echoics, a fundamental skill that supports not only foundational language repertoires discussed throughout this chapter, but also is essential to broader, more complex verbal behavior such as self-editing (Skinner, 1957), awareness of parity (i.e., "judgments of similarity," Palmer, 2012, p. 68), and, by extension, reasoning and evaluative behavior (see Skinner, 1953, 1969).

Note

1 An abbreviated version of the EESA-R is included in the recent VB-MAPP update.

References

Aguirre, E. E., & Gutierrez, A. (2019). An assessment and instructional guide for motor and vocal imitation. *Journal of Autism and Developmental Disorders, 49*(6), 2545–2558. https://doi.org/10.1007/s10803-019-04008-x

American Speech Language Hearing Association. (2024, January 7). Developmental norms for speech and language. *ASHA.* https://www.asha.org/slp/schools/prof-consult/norms/

Aravamudhan, S., & Awasthi, S. (2020). Behavioral interventions to treat speech sound disorders in children with autism. *Behavior Analysis in Practice, 13*(1), 174–185. https://doi.org/10.1007/s40617-019-00362-5

Axe, J. B., Phelan, S. H., & Irwin, C. L. (2018). Empirical evaluations of Skinner's analysis of problem solving. *The Analysis of Verbal Behavior, 35*(1), 39–56. https://doi.org/10.1007/s40616-018-0103-4

Baer, D. M., Peterson, R. F., & Sherman, J. A. (1967). The development of imitation by reinforcing behavioral similarity to a model. *Journal of the Experimental Analysis of Behavior, 21*(5), 405–416. https://doi.org/10.1901/jeab.1967.10-405

Bankson, N. W., & Bernthal, J. E. (2020). *Bankson-bernthal test of phonology*. Pro-Ed.

Bijou, S., & Baer, D. M. (1965). *Child development: II. Universal stage of infancy*. Appleton-Century-Crofts.

Carroll, R. A., Joachim, B. T., St. Peter, C. C., & Robinson, N. (2015). A comparison of error-correction procedures on skill acquisition during discrete-trial instruction. *Journal of Applied Behavior Analysis, 48*(2), 257–273. https://doi.org/10.1002/jaba.205

Carroll, R. A., & Klatt, K. P. (2008). Using stimulus-stimulus pairing and direct reinforcement to teach vocal verbal behavior to young children with autism. *The Analysis of Verbal Behavior, 24*(1), 135–146. https://doi.org/10.1007/BF03393062

Chance, S., Cividini-Motta, C., & Livingston, C. (2021). Assessing the effects of observational conditioning and response-contingent pairing on the vocalizations of children with autism spectrum disorder. *The Analysis of Verbal Behavior, 37*(1), 194–216. https://doi.org/10.1007/s40616-021-00157-2

Cividini-Motta, C., Scharrer, N., & Ahearn, W. H. (2017). An assessment of three procedures to teach echoic responding. *The Analysis of Verbal Behavior, 33*(1), 41–63. https://doi.org/10.1007/s40616-016-0069-z

Dozier, C. L., Iwata, B. A., Thomason-Sassi, J., Worsdell, A. S., & Wilson, D. M. (2012). A comparison of two pairing procedures to establish praise as a reinforcer. *Journal of Applied Behavior Analysis, 45*(4), 721–735. https://doi.org/10.1901/jaba.2012.45-721

Drash, P. W., High, R. L., & Tudor, R. M. (1999). Using mand training to establish an echoic repertoire in young children with autism. *The Analysis of Verbal Behavior, 16*(1), 29–44. https://doi.org/10.1007/BF03392945

Eikeseth, S., & Nesset, R. (2003). Behavioral treatment of children with phonological disorder: The efficacy of vocal imitation and sufficient-response-exemplar training. *Journal of Applied Behavior Analysis, 36*(3), 325–337. https://doi.org/10.1901/jaba.2003.36-325

Esch, B. E. (2014). Early Echoic Skills Assessment (EESA). In M. L. Sundberg (Ed.), *Verbal behavior milestones assessment and placement program*. AVB Press.

Esch, B. E. (2024). *Early echoic skills assessment and program planner*. Different Roads.

Esch, B. E., Carr, J. E., & Michael, J. (2005). Evaluating stimulus-stimulus pairing and direct reinforcement in the establishment of an echoic repertoire of children diagnosed with autism. *The Analysis of Verbal Behavior, 21*(1), 43–58. https://doi.org/10.1007/BF03393009

Esch, B. E., Carr, J. E., & Grow, L. L. (2009). Evaluation of an enhanced stimulus-stimulus pairing procedure to increase early vocalizations of children with autism. *Journal of Applied Behavior Analysis, 42*(2), 225–241. https://doi.org/10.1901/jaba.2009.42-225

Esch, B. E., LaLonde, K. B., & Esch, J. W. (2010). Speech and language assessment: A verbal behavior analysis. *The Journal of Speech-Language Pathology and Applied Behavior Analysis, 5*(2), 166–191. https://doi.org/10.1037/h0100270

Esch, J. W., Esch, B. E., & Love, J. R. (2009). Increasing vocal variability in children with autism using a lag schedule of reinforcement. *The Analysis of Verbal Behavior*, *25*(1), 73–78. https://doi.org/10.1007/BF03393071

Esch, J. W., Esch, B. E., McCart, J. D., & Petursdottir, A. I. (2010). An assessment of self- echoic behavior in young children. *The Analysis of Verbal Behavior*, *26*(1), 3–13. https://doi.org/10.1007/ BF03393078

Esch, J. W., Mahoney, A. M., Kestner, K. M., & Esch, B. E. (2013). Echoic and self-echoic responses in children. *The Analysis of Verbal Behavior*, *29*(1), 117–123. https://doi.org/10.1007/BF03393129

Fiani, T., Izquierdo, S. M., & Jones, E. A. (2021). Effects of mother's imitation on speech sounds in infants with Down syndrome. *Research in Developmental Disabilities*, *119*(1), 104118. https://doi.org/10.1016/j.ridd.2021.104118

Goldman, R., & Fristoe, M. (2015). *Goldman fristoe test of articulation – 3*. Pearson.

Goldstein, M. H., King, A. P., & West, M. J. (2003). Social interaction shapes babbling: Testing parallels between birdsong and speech. *Proceedings of the National Academy of Sciences (PNAS)*, *100*(13), 8030–8035. https://doi.org/10.1073/pnas.1332441100

Goldstein, M. H., & Schwade, J. (2008). Social feedback to infants' babbling facilitates rapid phonological learning. *Psychological Science*, *19*(5), 515–523. https://doi.org/10.1111/j.1467-9280.2008.02117.x

Greer, R. D., & Singer-Dudek, J. (2008). The emergence of conditioned reinforcement from observation. *Journal of the Experimental Analysis of Behavior*, *89*(1), 15–29. https://doi.org/10.1901/jeab.2008.89-15

Greer, R. D., Singer-Dudek, J., & Gautreaux, G. (2006). Observational learning. *International Journal of Psychology*, *41*(6), 486–499. https://doi.org/10.1080/00207590500492435

Horne, P. J., & Lowe, C. F. (1996). On the origins of naming and other symbolic behavior. *Journal of the Experimental Analysis of Behavior*, *65*(1), 185–241. https://doi.org/10.1901/jeab.1996.65-185

Kaufman, N. R. (1995). *Kaufman speech praxis test for children (KSPT)*. Wayne State University Press.

Kisamore, A. N., Carr, J. E., & LeBlanc, L. A. (2011). Training preschool children to use visual imagining as a problem-solving strategy for complex categorization tasks. *Journal of Applied Behavior Analysis*, *44*(2), 255–278. https://doi.org/10.1901/jaba.2011.44-255

Kobari-Wright, V. V., & Miguel, C. F. (2014). The effects of listener training on the emergence of categorization and speaker behavior in children with autism. *Journal of Applied Behavior Analysis*, *47*(2), 431–436. https://doi.org/10.1002/jaba.115

Koehler-Platten, K., Grow, L. L., Schulze, K. A., & Bertone, T. (2013). Using a lag reinforcement schedule to increase phonemic variability in children with autism spectrum disorders. *The Analysis of Verbal Behavior*, *29*(1), 71–83. https://doi.org/10.1007/BF03393125

Lang, S., Bartl-Pokorny, K. D., Pokorny, F. B., Garrido, D., Mani, N., Fox-Boyer, A. V., ...Marschik, P. B. (2019). Canonical babbling: A marker for earlier identification of late detected developmental disorders? *Current Developmental Disorders Reports*, *6*(1), 111–118. https://doi.org/10.1007/s40474-019-00166-w

LeBlanc, L. A., Esch, J. W., Sidener, T. M., & Firth, A. E. (2006). Behavioral language interventions for children with autism: comparing applied verbal behavior and naturalistic teaching approaches. *Analysis of Verbal Behavior*, *22*(1), 49–60. https://doi.org/10.1007/BF03393026

Lepper, T. L., & Petursdottir, A. I. (2017). Effects of response-contingent stimulus pairing on vocalizations of nonverbal children with autism. *Journal of Applied Behavior Analysis*, *50*(4), 756–774. https://doi.org/10.1002/jaba.415

Lepper, T. L., Petursdottir, A. I., & Esch, B. E. (2013). Effects of operant discrimination training on the vocalizations of nonverbal children with autism. *Journal of Applied Behavior Analysis*, *46*(3), 656–661. https://doi.org/10.1002/jaba.55

Lindsey, G. (2020, May 11). *An introduction to the vocal organs-with MRI video* [Video]. YouTube. https://www.youtube.com/watch?v=SVKR3ESdAk8.

Lovaas, O. I., Berberich, J. P., Perloff, B. F., & Schaeffer, B. (1966). Acquisition of imitative speech by schizophrenic children. *Science*, *151*(3711), 705–707. https://doi.org/10.1126/science.151.3711.705

Lowenkron, B. (1998). Some logical functions of joint control. *Journal of the Experimental Analysis of Behavior*, *69*(3), 327–354. http://dx.doi.org/10.1901/jeab.1998.69-327

Lowenkron, B. (2006). An introduction to joint control. *The Analysis of Verbal Behavior*, *22*(1), 123–127. https://doi.org/1007/BF03393034

MacDonald, J., & Ahearn, W. (2015). Teaching observational learning to children with autism. *Journal of Applied Behavior Analysis*, *48*(4), 800–816. https://doi.org/10.1002/jaba.257

Mallory, R., Bernier, S., & Park, H. L. (2019). The effectiveness of chaining to increase complexity of echoics in children with autism spectrum disorder and language delay. *Journal of Multidisciplinary Graduate Research*, *1*(1), 1–13.

McGreevy, P., & Fry, T. (2014). *Essential For Living. A communication, behavior and functional skills curriculum, assessment and professional practitioner's handbook.* Essential for Living.

Michael, J. (1982). Skinner's elementary verbal relations: Some new categories. *The Analysis of Verbal Behavior*, *1(1)*, 1–3. https://doi.org/10.1007/BF03392791

Michael, J. L. (1993/2004). *Concepts & principles of behavior analysis.* Association for Behavior Analysis International.

Miguel, C. F. (2016). Common and intraverbal bidirectional naming. *The Analysis of Verbal Behavior*, *32*(2), 125–138. https://doi.org/10.1007/s40616-016-0066-2

Miguel, C. F. (2018). Problem-solving, bidirectional naming, and the development of verbal repertoires. *Behavior Analysis: Research and Practice*, *18*(4), 340–353. https://doi.org/10.1037/bar0000110

Miguel, C. F., Carr, J. E., & Michael, J. (2002). The effects of a stimulus-stimulus pairing procedure on the vocal behavior of children diagnosed with autism. *The Analysis of Verbal Behavior*, *18*(1), 3–13. https://doi.org/10.1007/BF03392967

Miguel, C. F., Petursdottir, A. I., Carr, J. E., & Michael, J. (2008). The role of naming in stimulus categorization by preschool children. *Journal of the Experimental Analysis of Behavior*, *89*(3), 383–405. http://dx.doi.org/10.1901/jeab.2008-89-383

Moerk, E. L. (1990). Three-term contingency patterns in mother-child verbal interactions during first-language acquisition. *Journal of the Experimental Analysis of Behavior*, *54*(3), 293–305. http://dx.doi.org/10.1901/jeab.1990.54-293

Neimy, H., Pelaez, M., Monlux, K., Carrow, J., Tarbox, J., & Weiss, M. J. (2020). Increasing vocalizations and echoics in infants at risk of autism spectrum disorder. *Behavior Analysis in Practice*, *13*(2), 467–472. https://doi.org/10.1007/s40617-020-00413-2

Newman, B., Reinecke, D., & Ramos, M. (2009). Is a reasonable attempt reasonable? Shaping versus reinforcing verbal attempts of preschoolers with autism. *The Analysis of Verbal Behavior*, *25*(1), 67–72. https://doi.org/10.1007/BF03393070

Nigam, R., Schlosser, R. W., & Lloyd, L. L. (2006). Concomitant use of the matrix strategy and the mand-model procedure in teaching graphic symbol combinations. *Augmentative and Alternative Communication*, *22*(3), 160–177. https://doi.org/10.1080/07434610600650052

Olin, J., Sonsky, A., & Howard, M. (2020). Using a lag schedule of reinforcement to increase response variability in children with autism spectrum disorders. *The Analysis of Verbal Behavior*, *36*(1), 169–179. https://doi.org/10/1007/s40616-020-00129-y

Palmer, D. C. (1996). Achieving parity: The role of automatic reinforcement. *Journal of the Experimental Analysis of Behavior*, *65*(1), 289–290. https://doi.org/10.1901/jeab.1996.65-289.

Palmer, D. C. (2012). The role of atomic repertoires in complex behavior. *The Behavior Analyst*, *35*(1), 59–73. https://doi.org/10.1007/BF03392266

Palmer, D. C. (2018, August 9). *The role of automatic reinforcement in shaping speech* [Video]. National Autism Conference Archives. https://legacy.wpsu.org/live/2012_player/69508.

Partington, J. W. (2006). *The assessment of basic language and learning skills – revised (ABLLS-R)*. Behavior Analysts, Inc.

Pelaez, M., Borroto, A. R., & Carrow, J. (2018). Infant vocalizations and imitation as a result of adult contingent imitation. *Behavioral Development*, *23*(1), 81–88. https://doi.org/10.1037/bdb0000074

Pelaez, M., Virués-Ortega, J., & Gewirtz, J. L. (2011a). Contingent and non-contingent reinforcement with maternal vocal imitation and motherese speech: Effects of infant vocalizations. *European Journal of Behavior Analysis*, *12*(1), 277–287. http://doi.org/10.1080/15021149.2011.11434370

Pelaez, M., Virués-Ortega, J., & Gewirtz, J. L. (2011b). Reinforcement of vocalizations through contingent vocal imitation. *Journal of Applied Behavior Analysis*, *44*(1), 33–40. http://doi.org/10.1901/jaba.2011.44-33

Petursdottir, A. I., & Carr, J. E. (2011). A review of recommendations for sequencing receptive and expressive language instruction. *Journal of Applied Behavior Analysis*, *44*(4), 859–876. https://doi.org/10.1901/jaba.2011.44-859

Rogers-Warren, A., & Warren, S. F. (1980). Mands for verbalization: Facilitating the display of newly trained language in children. *Behavior Modification*, *4*(3), 361–382. https://doi.org/10.1177/0145445580430

Roy, D. (2011, May). *The birth of a word* [Video]. TED Conferences. https://www.ted.com/talks/deb_roy_the_birth_of_a_word?language=en#.

Schlinger, H. D. Jr., & Blakely, E. (2024). A mediational theory of equivalence relations and transformation of function. *Journal of the Experimental Analysis of Behavior*, *122*(2), 207–223. https://doi.org/10.1002/jeab.4204

Shillingsburg, M. A., Hollander, D. L., Yosick, R. N., Bowen, C., & Muskat, L. R. (2015). Stimulus-stimulus pairing to increase vocalizations in children with language delays: A review. *The Analysis of Verbal Behavior, 31*(1), 215–235. https://doi.org/10.1007/s40616-015-0042-2

Skinner, B. F. (1953). *Science and human behavior.* New York: Macmillan.

Skinner, B. F. (1957). *Verbal behavior.* Prentice-Hall, Inc. https://doi.org/10.1037/11256-000

Skinner, B. F. (1969). *Contingencies of reinforcement: A theoretical analysis.* Appleton-Century-Crofts.

Stock, R. A., Schulze, K. A., & Mirenda, P. (2008). A comparison of stimulus-stimulus pairing, standard echoic training, and control procedures on the vocal behavior of children with autism. *The Analysis of Verbal Behavior, 24*(1), 123–133. https://doi.org/10.1007/BF03393061

Stokes, T. F., & Baer, D. M. (1977). An implicit technology of generalization. *Journal of Applied Behavior Analysis, 10*(2), 349–367. https://doi.org/10.1901/jaba.1977.10-349

Sundberg, M. L. (2014). *The verbal behavior milestones assessment and placement program: The VB-MAPP* (2nd ed.). AVB Press.

Sundberg, M. L., Michael, J., Partington, J. W., & Sundberg, C. A. (1996). The role of automatic reinforcement in early language acquisition. *The Analysis of Verbal Behavior, 13*(1), 21–37. https://doi.org/10.1007/BF03392904

Sundberg, M. L., & Partington, J. W. (1998/2010). *Teaching language to children with autism or other developmental disabilities.* AVB Press.

Tarbox, J., Madrid, W., Aguilar, B., Jacobo, W., & Schiff, A. (2009). Use of chaining to increase complexity of echoics in children with autism. *Journal of Applied Behavior Analysis, 42*(4), 901–906. https://doi.org/10.1901/jaba.2009.42-901

Tattersall, P. J., & Dawson, J. I. (2016). *SPAT-D 3: The structured photographic articulation test featuring dudsberry* (3rd ed.). Pro-Ed.

Vaughan, M. E., & Michael, J. L. (1982). Automatic reinforcement: An important but ignored concept. *Behaviorism, 10*(2), 217–227. https://www.jstor.org/stable/27759007

Chapter 6

Tacts

Nicole M. Rodriguez, Maya J. Fallon, and Todd M. Owen

A tact is a verbal operant occasioned by a non-verbal stimulus and maintained by generalized conditioned reinforcement (e.g., acknowledgment, praise, or continued interaction with the listener; Skinner, 1957). In layman's terms, "label" is often synonymous with "tacts," and although frequently discussed in terms of the control exerted by visual stimuli, the entire physical environment is a source of stimulus control for tacts, including other sensory modalities such as olfactory, auditory, gustatory, and tactile stimuli (e.g., Bergmann & Kodak, 2023; Dass et al., 2018; Hanney et al., 2019; Rajagopal et al., 2021). Examples of tacts include stating, "It's raining" in response to the sight or feeling of raindrops, "Ambulance" in response to the sight or sound of an ambulance, and "That's huge!" in response to the sight of an oversized cake.

Because accurate tacting is foundational in developing a robust language repertoire, tact training is essential to language intervention programs. Tacts allow one to communicate about stimuli in their environment. They are, therefore, primarily beneficial to the listener, particularly when they allow the listener to extend their contact with stimuli that they have not experienced or cannot access (e.g., Skinner, 1957; Sundberg, 2015). Moreover, other forms of verbal behavior, like mands (see Chapter 4 in this volume) and intraverbals (see Chapter 7 in this volume), could be limited without a strong tact repertoire. For example, a learner who can accurately tact objects and events in their environment is better positioned to learn to mand and engage in intraverbals about those objects and events. An example of tact-to-mand transfer can be seen when a child who has learned to tact a desired musical toy as "music" is then able to request that toy by saying "music" when the proper motivating conditions are present (e.g., Wallace et al., 2006). This transfer demonstrates the relation between tacts and mands in language development (Sundberg & Partington, 1998). In terms of language intervention programs, tacts can be used to teach other verbal operants (e.g., intraverbals; May et al., 2013) and are often part of multiply controlled responses (Michael et al., 2011), including joint control (Lowenkron, 1998). Thus, tacts are fundamental to effective communication and social interactions and play a pivotal role in supporting other types of verbal behavior.

DOI: 10.4324/9781003433668-8

In this chapter, we will review different types of tacts, approaches to establishing them, and provide practical guidelines and recommendations for teaching tacts. In doing so, we will primarily focus on vocal-verbal behavior (we refer readers to Chapter 11 in this volume for more information on how language intervention programs can be adapted for non-vocal children).

Assessment

Before teaching, instructors should assess the learner's prerequisite skills and existing tact repertoire to determine what responses are strong, weak, or missing. Some researchers have suggested that stimulus control transfer procedures tend to be more effective when echoic and mand repertoires are established prior to teaching tacts (LeBlanc et al., 2009). Thus, assessments of echoics and mands can uncover potential barriers that may impede tact development. For example, if echoic control is weak, one might first focus on establishing an echoic repertoire, as echoic prompts can be incorporated into stimulus control transfer procedures to establish tacts (e.g., Barbera & Kubina, 2005; Bloh, 2008; Kodak et al., 2009).

The Assessment of Basic Language and Learning Skills–Revised (ABLLS-R; Partington, 2010) and the Verbal Behavior Milestones Assessment and Placement Program (VB-MAPP; Sundberg, 2008) are criterion-referenced assessments that allow instructors to track development via repeated administration (see Chapter 2 in this volume for more information on assessments of verbal behavior). Both include a range of skills to comprehensively assess a learner's tact repertoire, such as tacting reinforcing items, tacting actions, responding "yes" or "no" to identify a tact, as well as tacting the features, functions, and classes of items. One of the advantages of these assessments is that they guide the selection of targets for intervention; however, these assessment tools should be used as just that, guides, as they are not intended to form the basis of curricula. The selection of targets should be based on what is relevant for the learner and their family (e.g., what is common in their environment). Cultural responsiveness (see Chapter 13 in this volume) enhances the assessment of a learner's tact repertoire and social validity of outcomes by ensuring evaluations are accurate, unbiased, and respectful of language diversity, with family and community involvement critical to this process (Kristiansen, 2023). This approach, along with collaboration with speech and language professionals (see Chapter 14 in this volume), complements the use of ABLLS-R and VB-MAPP in tracking and assessing skills.

Teaching Procedures

Whereas neurotypically developing children generally acquire tacts through incidental teaching, children with autism spectrum disorder (ASD) often need direct and systematic instruction with repeated exposure to prompts and reinforcement to acquire new skills (Sundberg & Michael, 2001). Perhaps the most direct way of teaching tacts is through the transfer of stimulus control procedures. To arrange for the transfer of stimulus control, one must first select a controlling prompt, in other words, a prompt that will reliably occasion the target response when presented. Echoic prompts, if effective, can be a convenient method of occasioning a specific vocal response. For example, if the target is to tact a toy airplane, the instructor may hold up or point to the object and immediately state, "airplane" or "say, 'airplane.'" The learner's correct prompted response (i.e., echoing "airplane") would then be reinforced. Using an errorless approach, in subsequent presentations of the object, the instructor might introduce a delay to the prompt (e.g., 2 s). As stimulus control is transferred from the prompt to the presentation of the object, the learner should begin to independently respond, "airplane," before the prompt needs to be delivered, after which the learner's independent response would contact reinforcement. Other methods of fading the echoic prompt may include immediately presenting a partial echoic prompt (e.g., "airpl..." or "air...") before introducing a delay to the prompt in subsequent trials. The ease with which echoic prompts can be used to teach tacts is one reason why instructors may consider prioritizing establishing a strong echoic repertoire before beginning to work on tacts. However, articulation need not be perfect before initiating tact training; prompting and reinforcing vocal approximations (e.g., "tuck" instead of "truck" or "buh-buh" instead of "bubbles") can be an effective method of progressing through language training while considering developmentally appropriate vocalizations as well as the likely effect of those vocalizations on the listener (i.e., whether the vocalization is understandable, albeit only when in the presence of the object being tacted; see Chapter 5 for some additional information on vocal approximations).

Another important consideration is the context in which teaching will occur. For example, whereas discrete-trial instruction involves a highly structured approach that allows for a high dose of teaching, naturalistic approaches (e.g., play-based teaching) tend to occur in less-structured environments and prioritize capitalizing on the learner's interests and creating an engaging environment (e.g., Charlop-Christ et al., 1999; see Chapter 3 in this volume). As an example, Pisman and Luczysnki (2020) illustrated how tacts and mands could be taught during play, with caregivers as the implementers of the target play-based strategies, without disrupting the children's preference for the play context.

The transfer of stimulus control procedures described above can be embedded into either discrete-trial instruction or naturalistic approaches, and progress can be monitored via continuous or discontinuous data collection (e.g., "cold probes" in which acquisition of a target is assessed under baseline contingencies prior to each instructional session). Ultimately, effective teaching of tacts to learners with ASD likely involves a combination of structured and naturalistic approaches, with an emphasis on individualization and generalization. Other approaches, namely those that promote emergent responding, are described below.

Tactics for Promoting Efficiency and Emergence

In the context of language training programs for learners with ASD, the focus on efficiency and emergence is paramount. Efficiency in language training ensures that the limited time for developmental gains is maximized. At the same time, the emergence aspect emphasizes the functional development of language skills in a manner that may more closely represent typical development. This dual emphasis is not just a theoretical ideal but a practical necessity. The focus on efficiency and emergence guides instructors in designing interventions tailored to each learner's needs and is embedded within a framework that fosters robust, functional language skills. Below, we discuss various tactics for promoting efficiency in acquiring two types of tacts.

Novel Tacts

The emergence of verbal behavior entails a response under the controlling conditions of one verbal operant (e.g., a mand) and transfers to the control of another verbal operant (e.g., tact) without direct teaching. For a more in-depth discussion of behavioral concepts and methods for promoting emergent verbal behavior, we refer readers to Chapter 9 in this volume. Here, we briefly expand on three relatively common strategies for facilitating the emergence of novel tacts.

Multiple Exemplar Instruction. Multiple exemplar instruction is a teaching approach that involves targeting different verbal operants and listener behavior (e.g., echoics, mands, tacts, intraverbals, intraverbal tacts, match, point to) that are intermixed and presented in consecutive trials, often surrounding the same set of stimuli. For example, when teaching a learner to respond to the stimulus, "crayon," an instructor may present a crayon and provide generalized reinforcement for the tact, "crayon." The learner may later be asked to respond as a listener when a therapist instructs, "Hand me the crayon," when presented among an array of various utensils. During a mand trial, the instructor could contrive a motivating operation by, for example, presenting a coloring task with all materials aside from crayons, in which a correct response would result in the manded item. This process continues across new stimulus sets until data indicate that teaching only one operant leads to the emergence of untrained operants for the same response form (LaFrance & Tarbox, 2020). This teaching approach contrasts with developing separate programs targeting only one verbal operant per program, which may or may not include similar sets of stimuli (e.g., with the same response form) across programs.

Multiple exemplar instruction can be used to establish functional interdependence between speaker and listener repertoires whereby teaching one results in the emergence of the other and vice versa (technically referred to as bidirectional naming; see Chapters 9 and 10 in this volume for a more detailed review). Other approaches involve collecting baseline measures of speaker and listener behavior, teaching one (e.g., tacts) to mastery, and testing for the emergence of the other (e.g., listener behavior). Although results may vary across participants, research suggests that tact training is more likely to result in the emergence of listener responding than vice versa (e.g., Delfs et al., 2014; Petursdottir & Carr, 2011).

Matrix Training. As conceptualized by Goldstein (1983), matrix training is a teaching method that organizes stimuli into a structured grid-like matrix, facilitating the acquisition of combinations of concepts and fostering recombinative generalization. Specifically, in the realm of tacts, this method employs a matrix in which one dimension represents objects/people/places while another denotes actions or attributes. By initially teaching specific tact combinations directly—such as "fast car" and "slow train"—the goal is that learners subsequently tact untaught combinations like "slow car" and "fast train."

Several pivotal procedural decisions underlie the process of arranging matrices. First, the instructor should determine the number of dimensions and the matrix size. The number of dimensions is contingent on the desired discrimination, whether two-term (e.g., "fast car") or three-term (e.g., "fast red car"). Meanwhile, the matrix size hinges on the number of stimuli. Figure 6.1 shows an example of a 3 x 3 matrix with three nouns and three verbs, resulting in nine noun-verb combinations. Second, the instructor should determine whether they will incorporate known targets, unknown targets, or a combination of both. Including known targets may be the most conservative approach as it ensures the learner has the prerequisite skills for learning combinations; by contrast, including unknown targets may be more efficient (Frampton & Axe, 2023). Failure to achieve recombinative generalization when solely teaching combinations may indicate the need to go back and teach individual targets. Third, the instructor should choose the training layout, for example, diagonal versus overlap training (see review by Curiel et al., 2020). In diagonal training, procedures are applied to targets along the diagonal, with the remaining stimuli used to evaluate emergence (see Figure 6.1). This approach is advisable when stimuli are known (Curiel et al., 2020; Kemmerer et al., 2021). Conversely, overlap training involves teaching two cells from each row along the diagonal in a systematic manner, which can be particularly beneficial when matrices contain unknown targets, as it may result in incidental teaching of individual targets (see Figure 6.2; Curiel et al., 2020; Kemmerer et al., 2021). These procedural decisions underscore the intricacies of matrix training and its potential efficacy in promoting the acquisition and generalization of tact relations.

Instructive Feedback. Instructive feedback entails presenting secondary targets (also referred to as non-targets) during instructional trials for primary targets (e.g., Delmolino et al., 2013; Vladescu & Kodak, 2013). Whereas primary targets are directly taught using prompts and differential consequences, secondary targets are not. Instead, the instructor presents information regarding secondary targets without prompts or differential consequences for responding to the information presented (i.e., the instructive feedback). Instructive feedback may be

	Singing	Eating	Reading	Driving
Parrot	Parrot-Singing	Parrot-Eating	Parrot-Reading	Parrot-Driving
Hippo	Hippo-Singing	Hippo-Eating	Hippo-Reading	Hippo-Driving
Giraffe	Giraffe-Singing	Giraffe-Eating	Giraffe-Reading	Giraffe-Driving
Tiger	Tiger-Singing	Tiger-Eating	Tiger-Reading	Tiger-Driving

Figure 6.1 Matrix example—diagonal training.
Note: Along the vertical axis are known nouns (animals), and the horizontal axis reflects known verbs (actions) for twelve noun-verb combinations. The diagonal targets (shaded in dark grey) are taught (trained), while nondiagonal targets are assessed for emergence (untrained).

presented before or after instructional trials for primary targets. However, when presented after, it is usually presented following the delivery of reinforcement for correct responding to primary targets. For example, during a trial in which a learner correctly tacts a toy race car, the instructor may respond, "Yeah! That is a race car! Race cars are fast!" or "Nice job! This is a boat" (while presenting a picture of a boat). Instructive feedback might also facilitate generalization across stimuli (e.g., Schnell et al., 2018). For example, the instructor may state, "This is also a race car," while presenting a different exemplar of a race car. Instructional efficiency is improved when the learner acquires secondary targets in the absence of direct reinforcement (e.g., "fast" in response to questions about race cars or "boat" in response to being shown a picture of a boat).

A consideration for instructors is whether to require an echoic response during instructive feedback. For example, following the selection of a fire truck, the instructor may say, "That's it, you touched the fire truck. Fire trucks are red [in the United States]. Say, 'red.'" Some research suggests echoic responding can play a functional role in emergent tact control (e.g., Horne & Lowe, 1996), whereas other research indicates it does not (e.g., Haq et al., 2017; Petursdottir et al., 2020). It is also recommended to provide multiple exposures to stimulus pairings between the discriminative stimulus and the secondary tact response

	Singing	Eating	Reading	Driving
Parrot	Parrot-Singing	Parrot-Eating	Parrot-Reading	Parrot-Driving
Hippo	Hippo-Singing	Hippo-Eating	Hippo-Reading	Hippo-Driving
Giraffe	Giraffe-Singing	Giraffe-Eating	Giraffe-Reading	Giraffe-Driving
Tiger	Tiger-Singing	Tiger-Eating	Tiger-Reading	Tiger-Driving

Figure 6.2 Matrix example—overlap training.

Note: Along the horizontal axis are animals and the vertical axis reflects actions. Dark grey shading indicates stimuli trained down the diagonal of the matrix. Light grey shading OV indicates the combination trained in the overlap training sequence. All other combinations (i.e., other squares) were used to assess for emergence.

(Gavidia et al., 2022; Petursdottir et al. (2020). Finally, the frequency of testing secondary targets may interact with the efficacy of instructive feedback. As an extreme example, the probability of a learner attending to instructive feedback may be negatively affected if the learner is never tested on the secondary targets.

Intraverbal Tacts

Thus far, we have discussed basic tacts (i.e., pure tacts or tacts prompted by a supplemental question such as "What is it?"). However, learners should also be able to answer different questions about the same object or picture. For example, a caregiver might hold up a toy truck and ask a number of questions (e.g., What is it? What color? What does it do? What sound does it make?). To contact reinforcement, the response must be under the control of the relevant property of the physical stimulus (tact) and the content of the question (intraverbal); this type of response is sometimes referred to as an intraverbal tact (Rodriguez et al., 2022). Below, we describe two approaches to programming for the emergence of intraverbal tacts using the example of different questions (e.g., "What color?", "What shape?") regarding colored shapes displayed in Table 6.1. Additional examples

Table 6.1 Sample Target Compound and Simple Stimuli for Teaching Intraverbal Tacts

Compound Stimuli	Simple Stimuli

of potential target compound stimuli are included in Table 6.2. We recommend starting with different questions about elements (features) of a compound stimulus before progressing to questions about the category (class) or function, as well as starting with less complex visual stimuli (e.g., colored shapes vs. picture scenes).

Sequencing of Component Skills. One approach to teaching intraverbal tacts is to teach a set of component skills and then test for the emergence of intraverbal tacts. Rodriguez et al. (2022) provided preliminary evidence regarding the relevance of several component skills: element tact, category tact, intraverbal categorization, and multiply controlled listener response. Since then, research has suggested that element tact and intraverbal categorization should be sufficient for the emergence of intraverbal tacts (Pantano, 2022). Given our clinical experience, we suspect that there are multiple paths to success. In what follows, we highlight one recommended sequence of teaching component skills and briefly touch upon others. We refer readers to Michael et al. (2011) and Rodriguez et al. for an in-depth discussion of the conceptual underpinnings.

First, to evaluate the efficacy of teaching a sequence of component skills, it is recommended that instructors collect baseline probes of intraverbal tacts before and after the teaching of specific component skills. Because emergent responding is of general importance, collecting preteaching and postteaching data on each of the skills listed in Table 6.3 can also be valuable. To be able to rule out the effects of a history of direct reinforcement, it is customary to test for emergent responding when no differential reinforcement is in place for correct responding to target stimuli. However, because learners with ASD are often accustomed to receiving reinforcers for correct responding when learning new skills and not contacting reinforcement for correct responding may interfere with learning, we suggest including differential reinforcement for correct responses to target stimuli and, instead, looking at first trial performance as a

Table 6.2 Examples of Target Intraverbal Tacts

Question	Visual Compound Stimuli
"What [animal/letter]?"	
"What [color/shape/feeling]?"	
"What animal?" "What does it say?"	
"Who?" "Where?" "What doing?"	

measure of emergent responding. To facilitate visual discrimination of first trial performance for intraverbal-tact probes, we suggest presenting each combination of the single elements with each question (e.g., a red triangle with "What shape?") no more than once per session and looking for large shifts in the level of correct responding (e.g., from 50% to 94% or 100% correct). For the targets listed in Table 6.1, presenting each compound stimulus with each question ("What color?" vs. "What shape?") would result in 18 trials of target stimuli

Table 6.3 Sample shape trial for each component skill

Skill	Question/ Instruction	Visual Sample Stimulus	Visual Comparison Stimuli	Target Response	Teaching Prompt
Element Tact	"What is it?"	Simple Stimulus	—	Label element (e.g., "triangle")	Vocal Model
Category Tact	"This is a type of …"	Simple Stimulus	—	Label category (e.g., "shape")	Vocal Model
Intraverbal Categorization	"Tell me some shapes"	—	—	List elements (e.g., "triangle, square, circle")	Picture
Element Listener	"Touch triangle"	—	6-card array (not grouped by category) *	Touch	Point
Category Listener	"Touch shapes"	—	6-card array (grouped by category) *	Touch corresponding category sheet or pull sheet closer	Point

(Continued)

Table 6.3 (Continued)

Skill	Question/ Instruction	Visual Sample Stimulus	Visual Comparison Stimuli	Target Response	Teaching Prompt
Intraverbal Categ.- Listener	"Touch all shapes"	—	6-card array	Touch	Point
Multiply Controlled Selection Response	"Show me shape"	Compound stimulus	6-card array	Touch	Point
Matching[a]	"Match"	Simple stimulus	3-card array	Touch	—

Note: Comparison stimuli are outlined in a box to indicate that it is suggested that they are grouped by category. The position of elements within the category should be randomized across sessions, and the position of the categories should be randomized across trials. Asterisks denote the correct selection response. For the multiply controlled selection response, the comparison stimuli are grouped by category, but the correct selection response is to touch the element (e.g., triangle) within the category.

[a]Matching might be considered a pre-requisite. We propose testing it during a pre-assessment or as part of troubleshooting should intraverbal errors persist.

per session. Mastered tact targets (other than the target colors and shapes) should also be interspersed at a rate that ensures overall continued responding (e.g., every 2–3 trials), particularly under conditions in which correct responding is expected to be low (i.e., before the teaching of any component skills). Further, to decrease the likelihood that errors are due to a lack of attending to the keyword in the question, instructors should prompt a differential observing response that requires the learner to repeat the keyword in the question (e.g., repeat "color" or "shape"; e.g., Kisamore et al., 2016). However, once emergence is observed, maintenance of correct responding should be evaluated in the absence of the differential observing response prompt.

After collecting preteaching data, the next step is teaching unmastered element tacts. This is important for ensuring that the target properties of the visual stimulus (e.g., color, shape) exert control over the target tact (e.g., red, blue, green, triangle, square, circle). Next, to ensure that the keyword in the question exerts divergent control over the target intraverbals (e.g., color: red, blue, green; shape: triangle, square, circle; e.g., Michael et al., 2011), instructors should teach intraverbal categorization (see Appendix A for a sample protocol available at www.routledge .com/9781032560625; see Chapter 10 in this volume for more information on divergent and convergent control). Once element tacts and intraverbal categorization are mastered, intraverbal tacts may emerge (Pantano, 2022). Upon testing for the emergence of intraverbal tacts, one might also find that the remaining component skills have also emerged (e.g., element listener, category listener). However, an exception is noted in the case of category tact, which can be conceptualized as an intraverbal tact in which a different question is asked about the same picture (e.g., "This is a type of __" when prompting a category tact vs. "What is it?" when prompting an element tact). If intraverbal tacts do not emerge and there are missing component skills, then a reasonable next step is to teach each unmastered component skill one at a time and retest the emergence of intraverbal tacts. For example, if the multiply controlled listener response remains unmastered, teaching this skill, which is the listener counterpart to the intraverbal tact, may be sufficient for transfer across listener and speaker repertoires as it, too, requires both the visual compound stimulus and the keyword in the question to exert stimulus control but over a selection response. See Appendix B (available at www.routledge.com /9781032560625) for a sample protocol for teaching multiply controlled listener response. See the "Strategies for Overcoming Common Clinical Challenges" section for additional suggestions.

Teaching Autoclitic Frames. An alternative approach to establishing intraverbal tacts involves prompting the learner to produce the correct response within an autoclitic frame (e.g., degli Espinosa et al., 2021; Meleshkevich et al., 2021). For example, when presented with a red triangle and asked, "What color?" the learner is prompted to respond, "Color red," and when asked, "What shape?" the learner is prompted to respond, "Shape triangle." Such prompts are then faded using a progressive prompt delay. In this example, the autoclitic frame is "color ___ " and "shape ___," respectively. This autoclitic frame is essentially a verbal structure that includes the keyword from the instructor's question and is designed to foster a history of contiguous usage in hopes of establishing divergent intraverbal control akin to the intraverbal categorization procedures described above. In other words, as a function of prompting the keyword from the question with the corresponding element tact occasioned by the visual stimulus (e.g., "shape triangle," "shape square," "shape circle"), the keyword may come to exert divergent intraverbal control over a variety of responses (e.g., "shape: triangle, square, circle"). As such, a potentially important aspect of the procedures described by degli Espinosa et al. (2021) is that if the learner omitted the frame but otherwise answered correctly (e.g., "triangle" instead of "shape triangle"), the instructor represented the question immediately followed by a frame prompt but without the target intraverbal tact (e.g., "What shape? Shape …"). If the learner omitted the autoclitic frame again, the instructor repeated the question, followed by a full verbal prompt (e.g., "What shape? Shape triangle").

Finally, to test for emergent responding, one can include generalization sets that feature different combinations of colors and shapes, the elements of which have been shown to be mastered when presented as simple stimuli (see Table 6.3 for procedures for testing element tacts). For example, if there are six colors and six shapes, then each combination of three of those colors and shapes can be used as teaching stimuli in which correct responding with the autoclitic frame is directly prompted and reinforced. All remaining combinations could then be used as generalization targets in which the question is presented with the compound stimulus, but no prompts or differential reinforcement for correct responding are provided (e.g., see Figures 1 and 2 in degli Espinosa et al., 2021).

Tactics for Promoting Generalization and Maintenance

Generalization of tacts involves ensuring that the skills learned in a clinical setting are applicable and used in other environments. Strategies recommended for promoting generalization include blending structured training with natural teaching sessions, testing whether tacts transfer to settings outside clinical settings, selecting socially valid and common targets in the learner's environment, and using social reinforcement (LeBlanc et al., 2009). Teaching tacts with targets familiar to the learner, such as everyday objects from their home, school, or community, is believed to increase the likelihood of maintenance and generalization. In what follows, we focus on strategies for obtaining generalization across targets from the same stimulus class or concept, defined as a group with common features or attributes (Layng, 2019; Tiemann & Markle, 1990).

When teaching tacts, the goal is for the tact to generalize across all members of the concept after teaching with a subset of exemplars. All members of the concept contain shared critical, or "must-have," features as well as unshared variable, or "can have," features that may vary across exemplars (Layng, 2019; Tiemann

& Markle, 1990). For example, when teaching a learner to tact vehicles, critical features would include a method of locomotion (e.g., wheels) and a space for an organism or materials to be transported (e.g., a seat); variable features could include the number of wheels, the number of seats, the color of the frame or body of the vehicle, the presence of windows, and the shape of the vehicle. When preparing stimuli for teaching, Tennyson et al. (1972), as well as Tiemann and Markle (1990), recommend creating sets of stimuli that have no shared variable features across the target exemplars, referred to as a fully divergent set (or sets with high disparity)—for example, a yellow bus, a blue sedan, and a red bicycle.

For the learner to accurately discriminate between critical and variable features, teaching sets should include thoughtfully selected nonexamples. It may be beneficial to start teaching using nonexamples that are missing more than one critical feature and do not share variable features (i.e., far-out nonexamples with high disparity) before gradually moving to nonexamples with only one missing critical feature and shared variable features (i.e., close-in nonexamples with low disparity; Halbur et al., 2020; Lawrence, 1952; Tiemann & Markle, 1990). Tiemann and Markle (1990) suggested including at least one close-in nonexample for each critical feature of the concept for each set of teaching stimuli. Presenting pairs of stimuli in which the example and close-in nonexample share variable features may aid learners in discriminating between variable and critical features, in that the only difference between the stimuli is the missing critical feature in the nonexample (Merrill & Tennyson, 1992; Tennyson et al., 1972). When one uses a fully divergent range of examples and at least one close-in nonexample for each critical feature, it is referred to as teaching the general case (Engelmann & Carnine, 1991).

Practically speaking, the extent to which the instructor goes through the formal process of identifying critical features, variable features, far-out examples, and close-in examples may depend on how much variability exists among exemplars of a concept (e.g., cat vs. dog) or the presence or probability of undesirable generalization based on a learner's history. Nevertheless, general case programming can serve as a useful heuristic. Further, the learner's repertoire should play an important role in considering including close-in examples. For example, one might start by teaching highly disparate stimuli and then systematically decrease the disparity among the stimuli in the target set by introducing stimuli that contain one but not all critical variables (Halbur et al., 2021).

Strategies for Overcoming Common Clinical Challenges

Social Reinforcement

Under typical conditions, the motivation to tact is often to share information or an experience with a listener, and this behavior is maintained by the response from that listener (e.g., acknowledgment, continued social interaction; Skinner,

1953). However, social attention can be of limited reinforcement value for learners with ASD (Lovaas et al., 1966). Thus, although training under social reinforcement contingencies is believed to increase the likelihood of generalization (e.g., across settings and people) and maintenance, for some learners, it may be necessary to incorporate tangible reinforcers (e.g., toys or food items) during tact training. As targets are acquired, the schedule of reinforcement should be gradually thinned to promote maintenance under reinforcement contingencies that are present outside of the teaching context.

Spontaneous Tacts

Neurotypically developing children experience a sudden expansion in their vocabulary around 16–24 months old (Goodman, 1997; Fenson et al., 1994). During this time, it is common to observe children spontaneously tacting various mundane objects in their environment. Caregivers, in turn, greet the child's tacts with enthusiasm and praise (e.g., "You are right! That is a train!" as the child brings them a toy train). However, over time, spontaneous tacting of mundane objects begins to dissipate, perhaps as a function of the changing social and cultural contingencies. As Skinner (1957) noted, "familiar objects lose their control because the community eventually withholds reinforcement except under special conditions" (p. 89). Rather than tact objects or events that are familiar or mundane, the verbal community may be more likely to reinforce tacting of objects or events that are novel or unusual. As Skinner described, "A pool table at the bottom of a swimming pool, a fire hydrant in the parlor, or a seal in the bedroom are more likely to evoke tacts than the same objects under commonplace conditions" and added, "Obviously, what is novel for the speaker may not be so for the listener, so that rule is not uniformly applicable" (p. 90).

Because of delays associated with their diagnosis, children with ASD are not likely to engage in a language explosion at an age that is as likely to occasion the desired response from their verbal community, which may partially explain the absence of a similar, albeit delayed, language explosion in children with ASD. One potential solution may be to instruct the child's communities of reinforcement (parents, teachers, etc.) to attend to spontaneous tacts. Indeed, it would be valuable to reinforce such occurrences in early language development to establish and maintain an expanded vocabulary. However, it is unclear whether the spontaneous tacting described above is a prerequisite for more sophisticated use of tacts. If the main advantage of a language explosion in early child development is to provide an opportunity to reinforce the rapid expansion of a child's vocabulary, then it may be acceptable to shift the focus of treatment for children with ASD to achieve a similar outcome via more contrived methods, namely, through (a) direct prompting and reinforcement of specific tacts or (b) programming for emergent responding (e.g., transfer across operants or listener skills).

Additionally, we might conduct a more thorough analysis of the conditions under which tacts typically occur and teach under those conditions. For example, in children, spontaneous tacts may be more likely to contact communities of reinforcement during play (e.g., "I'm making a snake" as the child needles Play-Doh), when looking at a picture book, or during a trip to the zoo (e.g., "Look! A tiger!"). Children should also tact stimuli when presented with a vocal prompt or question (e.g., "What is it?" or "What are you doing?"), as such questions are common occasions for tacting. However, to avoid teaching a tact repertoire entirely under the control of a vocal prompt, one should also consider bringing tacts under the control of non-verbal prompts, such as when someone holds up or points to an object or picture (e.g., Marchese et al., 2012). Marchese et al. (2012) suggested that the sporadic use of a vocal prompt (e.g., "What is it?") may also confer advantages for individuals who engage in echolalia (i.e., repeat parts of the question before, or instead of, tacting). If tacts appear to depend on a vocal prompt or question, one might consider introducing a prompt delay to transfer control from the vocal prompt, "What is it?" to, for example, pointing to an object.

Persistent Intraverbal Errors When Teaching Intraverbal Tacts

A common error when learners are first introduced to varying questions about the same picture or item is that the learner will tact the same property of the visual stimulus on every trial, regardless of the question being asked. For example, when presented with different colored shapes and rotating questions about their color versus shape, learners will often respond with the corresponding color each trial, even when the question is about the shape (e.g., responding "green" when presented with a green triangle and asked, "What shape?"). This type of error (i.e., intraverbal error) tends to occur even when all relevant element tacts have been mastered. In such cases, the learner's response is likely under the control of at least one property of the visual stimulus but not the accompanying question; teaching intraverbal categorization or responding within an autoclitic frame, as described above, may be sufficient for bringing the target response under the joint control of the visual stimulus and the keyword in the question.

Even still, intraverbal errors may persist, particularly when this is the first time intraverbal tacts are being addressed in a learner's language training program. The persistence of intraverbal errors might indicate a lack of sufficient control by the keyword in the question when presented with the visual stimulus (e.g., due to overshadowing or blocking; Rodriguez et al., 2022; Dinsmoor, 1995) or an absence of effective joint control. The same is true for two-component errors in which the learner responds by tacting both components of a compound stimulus rather than just one (e.g., "red triangle" rather than "triangle" when asked "What shape?"). To tackle this issue, research has shown the efficacy of strategies such as teaching the learner to repeat the keyword in the question followed by the corresponding intraverbal categorization (e.g., "shape: triangle, square, circle") or to rehearse this response multiple times before answering (e.g., "shape: triangle, square, circle, triangle, square, circle, triangle, square, circle" (Aragon et al., 2024). The self-rehearsal could be taught within separate sessions (see Aragon et al., 2024). Once the self-rehearsal is mastered, the instructor should reintroduce the target compound stimuli, presenting the visual stimulus just before the learner emits the third rehearsal. When emitted in this context, this repetition might amplify the probability that the auditory stimulus is exerting divergent control concurrently with the visual stimulus, thus fostering joint control (e.g., "circle" evoked by the visual stimulus and "circle" evoked by "shape" in the question).

Another potential issue that may explain intraverbal errors is that the learner's behavior is not under the discriminative control of each element of the target compound stimulus. To ensure that the learner is responding discriminatively toward the individual elements of the target compound stimuli, one should test for matching (see Table 6.3). If correct responding is low or at chance levels, one might consider restarting using more salient or discriminable elements within the compound stimulus as target intraverbal tacts before progressing to potentially more complex targets.

References

Aragon, M. A., Rodriguez, N. M., Luczynski, K. C., & McKeown, C., (2024). Facilitating the emergence of intraverbal-tact in autistic children via joint control. *Journal of Applied Behavior Analysis*, *57*(3), 784–797. https://doi.org/10.1002/jaba.1072

Barbera, M. L., & Kubina, R. M. (2005). Using transfer procedures to teach tacts to a child with autism. *The Analysis of Verbal Behavior*, *21*, 155–161. https://doi.org/10.1007/BF03393017

Bergmann, S., & Kodak, T. (2023). The tact is being emitted by the child: Replicating and extending parity research with English-speaking, typically developing children. *The Analysis of Verbal Behavior*. Advance online publication. https://doi.org/10.1007/s40616-023-00188-x

Bloh, C. (2008). Assessing transfer of stimulus control procedures across learners with autism. *The Analysis of Verbal Behavior*, *24*, 87–101. https://doi.org/10.1007/BF03393059

Charlop-Christy, M. H., LeBlanc, L. A., & Carpenter, M. H. (1999). Naturalistic Teaching Strategies (NaTS) to teach speech to Children with Autism: Historical perspective, development, and current practice. *California School Psychologist*, *4*, 30–46. https://doi.org/10.1007/BF03340868

Curiel, E. S., Axe, J. B., Sainato, D. M., & Goldstein, H. (2020). Systematic review of matrix training for individuals with autism spectrum disorder. *Focus on Autism and Other Developmental Disabilities*, *35*(1), 55–64. https://doi.org/10.1177/10883576198812

Dass, T. K., Kisamore, A. N., Vladescu, J. C., Reeve, K. F., Reeve, S. A., & Taylor-Santa, C. (2018). Teaching children with autism spectrum disorder to tact olfactory stimuli. *Journal of Applied Behavior Analysis, 51*(3), 538–552. https://doi.org/10.1002/jaba .470

degli Espinosa, F., Wolff, K., & Hewett, S. (2021) A comparison of two teaching procedures to establish generalized intraverbal-tacting in children with autism. *Journal of Applied Behavior Analysis, 54*(4), 1468–1487. https://doi.org/10.1002/jaba .869

Delfs, C. H., Conine, D. E., Frampton, S. E., Shillingsburg, M. A., & Robinson, H. C. (2014). Evaluation of the efficiency of listener and tact instruction for children with autism. *Journal of Applied Behavior Analysis, 47*(4), 793–809. https://doi.org/10 .1002/jaba.166

Delmolino, L., Hansford, A. P., Bamond, M. J., Fiske, K. E., & LaRue, R. H. (2013). The use of instructive feedback for teaching language skills to children with autism. *Research in Autism Spectrum Disorders, 7*(6), 648–661. https://doi.org/10.1016/j.rasd .2013.02.015

Dinsmoor, J. A. (1995). Stimulus control: Part II. *The Behavior Analyst, 18*(2), 253–269. https://doi.org/10.1007/BF03392712

Engelmann, S., & Carnine, D. (1991). *Theory of instruction* (Rev. ed.). National Institute for Direct Instruction.

Fenson L., Dale P. S., Reznick J. S., Bates E., Thal D. J., & Pethick S. J. (1994). Variability in early communicative development. *Monographs of the Society for Research in Child Development, 59*(5), 1–173. https://doi.org/10.2307/1166093

Frampton, S. E., & Axe, J. B. (2023). A tutorial for implementing matrix training in practice. *Behavior Analysis in Practice, 16*(1), 334–345. https://doi.org/10.1007/ s40617-022-00733-5

Frampton, S. E., & Shillingsburg, M. A. (2020). Promoting the development of verbal responses using instructive feedback. *Journal of Applied Behavior Analysis, 53*(2), 1029–1041. https://doi.org/10.1002/jaba.659

Gavidia, V. L., Bergmann, S., & Rader, K. A. (2022). The use of instructive feedback to promote emergent tact and intraverbal control: A replication. *The Analysis of Verbal Behavior, 38*(2), 95–120. https://doi.org/10.1007/s40616-022-00171-y

Goldstein, H. (1983). Recombinative generalization: Relationships between environmental conditions and the linguistic repertoires of language learners. *Analysis and Intervention in Developmental Disabilities, 3*(4), 279–293. https://doi.org/10 .1016/0270-4684(83)90002-2

Goodman, E. B. J. C. (1997). On the inseparability of grammar and the lexicon: Evidence from acquisition, aphasia and real-time processing. *Language and Cognitive Processes, 12*(5–6), 507–584. https://doi.org/10.1080/016909697386628

Halbur, M., Kodak, T., Williams, X. A., Reidy, J., & Halbur, C. (2021). Comparison of sounds and words as sample stimuli for discrimination training. *Journal of Applied Behavior Analysis, 54*(3), 1126–1138. https://doi.org/10.1002/jaba.830

Halbur, M. E., Caldwell, R. K., & Kodak, T. (2020). Stimulus control research and practice: Considerations of stimulus disparity and salience for discrimination training. *Behavior Analysis in Practice, 14*, 272–282. https://doi.org/10.1007/s40617-020 -00509-9

Hanney, N. M., Carr, J. E., & LeBlanc, L. A. (2019). Teaching children with autism spectrum disorder to tact auditory stimuli. *Journal of Applied Behavior Analysis, 52*(3), 733–738. https://doi.org/10.1002/jaba.605

Haq, S. S., Zemantic, P. K., Kodak, T., LeBlanc, B., & Ruppert, T. E. (2017). Examination of variables that affect the efficacy of instructive feedback. *Behavioral Interventions, 32*(3), 206–216. https://doi.org/10.1002/bin.1470

Horne, P. J., & Lowe, F. (1996). On the origins of naming and other symbolic behavior. *Journal of the Experimental Analysis of Behavior, 65*(2), 185–241. https://doi.org/10.1901/jeab.1996.65-185

Kemmerer, A. R., Vladescu, J. C., Carrow, J. N., Sidener, T. M., & Deshais, M. A. (2021). A systematic review of the matrix training literature. *Behavioral Interventions, 36*(2), 473–495. https://doi.org/10.1002/bin.1780

Kisamore, A. N., Karsten, A. M., & Mann, C. C. (2016). Teaching multiply controlled intraverbals to children and adolescents with autism spectrum disorders. *Journal of Applied Behavior Analysis, 49*(4), 826–847. https://doi.org/10.1002/jaba.344

Kodak, T., Clements, A., & Ninness, C. (2009). Acquisition of mands and tacts with concurrent echoic training. *Journal of Applied Behavior Analysis, 42*(4), 839–843. https://doi.org/10.1901/jaba.2009.42-839

Kristiansen, S. V. (2023). A Summary of the recommendations to increase cultural responsiveness in the field of applied behavior analysis. *International Electronic Journal of Elementary Education, 15*(3), 233–245. https://www.iejee.com/index.php/IEJEE/article/view/2058

LaFrance, D. L., & Tarbox, J. (2020). The importance of multiple exemplar instruction in the establishment of novel verbal behavior. *Journal of Applied Behavior Analysis, 53*(1), 10–24. https://doi.org/10.1002/jaba.611

Lawrence, D. H. (1952). The transfer of a discrimination along a continuum. *Journal of Comparative Physiological Psychology, 45*, 511–516. https://doi.org/10.1037/h0057135

Layng, T. J. (2019). Tutorial: Understanding concepts: Implications for behavior analysts and educations. *Perspectives on Behavior Science, 42*, 345–363. https://doi.org/10.1007/s40614-018-00188-6

LeBlanc, L. A., Dillon, C. M., & Sautter, R. A. (2009). Establishing mand and tact repertoires. In R. A. Rehfeldt & Y. Barnes-Holmes (Eds.), *Derived relational responding: Applications for learners with autism and other developmental disabilities* (pp. 79–108). New Harbinger Publications.

Lovaas, O. I., Freitag, G., Kinder, M. I., Rubenstein, B. D., Schaffer, B., & Simmons, J. Q. (1966). Establishment of social reinforcers in two schizophrenic children on the basis of food. *Journal of Experimental Child Psychology, 4*(2) 109–125. https://doi.org/10.1016/0022-0965(66)90011-7

Lowenkron, B. (1998). Some logical functions of joint control. *Journal of the Experimental Analysis of Behavior, 69*(3), 327–354. https://doi.org/10.1901/jeab.1998.69-327

Marchese, N. V., Carr, J. E., LeBlanc, L. A., Rosati, T. C., & Conroy, S. A. (2012). The effects of the question "What is this?" on tact-training outcomes of children with autism. *Journal of Applied Behavior Analysis, 45*(3), 539–547. https://doi.org/10.1901/jaba.2012.45-539

May, R. J., Hawkins, E., & Dymond, S. (2013). Brief report: Effects of tact training on emergent intraverbal vocal responses in adolescents with autism. *Journal of Autism and Developmental Disorders, 43*, 996–1004. https://doi.org/10.1007/s10803-012-1632-7

Meleshkevich, O., Axe, J. B., & degli Espinosa, F. D. (2021). Effects of time delay and requiring echoics on answering questions about visual stimuli. *Journal of Applied Behavior Analysis, 54*(2), 725–743. https://doi.org/10.1002/jaba.790

Merrill, D., & Tennyson, R. (1992). *Teaching concepts: An instructional design guide.* Educational Technology Publications.

Michael, J., Palmer, D. C., & Sundberg, M. L. (2011). The multiple control of verbal behavior. *The Analysis of Verbal Behavior, 27*(1), 3–22. https://doi.org/10.1007/bf03393089

Pantano, N. (2022). *A sequence to facilitate the emergence of intraverbal tacts in children with autism spectrum disorder* [Unpublished doctoral dissertation]. Caldwell University.

Partington, J. W. (2010). *The ABLLS-R—The assessment of basic language and learning skills-revised.* Behavior Analysts, Inc

Petursdottir, A. I., & Carr, J. E. (2011). A review of recommendations for sequencing receptive and expressive language instruction. *Journal of Applied Behavior Analysis, 44*(4), 859–876. https://doi.org/10.1901/jaba.2011.44-859

Petursdottir, A. I., Neaves, S. M., & Thomas, O. N. (2020). Emergent tact control following stimulus pairing: Comparison of procedural variations. *The Analysis of Verbal Behavior, 36*, 193–214. https://doi.org/10.1007/s40616-020-00132-3

Pisman, M. D., & Luczynski, K. C. (2020). Caregivers can implement play-based instruction without disrupting child preference. *Journal of Applied Behavior Analysis, 53*(3), 1702–1725. https://doi.org/10.1002/jaba.705

Rajagopal, S., Nicholson, K., Putri, T. R., Addington, J., & Felde, A. (2021). Teaching children with autism to tact private events based on public accompaniments. *Journal of Applied Behavior Analysis, 54*(1), 270–286. https://doi.org/10.1002/jaba.785

Rodriguez, N. M., Aragon, M. A., McKeown, C. A., & Glodowski, K. R. (2022). Facilitating the emergence of intraverbal tacts in children with autism spectrum disorder: A preliminary analysis. *Journal of Applied Behavior Analysis, 55*(2), 412–429. https://doi.org/10.1002/jaba.898

Schnell, L. K., Vladescu, J. C., Kodak, T., & Nottingham, C. L. (2018). Comparing procedures on the acquisition and generalization of tacts for children with autism spectrum disorder. *Journal of Applied Behavior Analysis, 51*(4), 769–783. https://doi.org/10.1002/jaba.480

Skinner, B. F. (1953). *Science and human behavior.* New York: Macmillan.

Skinner, B. F. (1957). *Verbal behavior.* Appleton-Century-Crofts. https://doi.org/10.1037/11256-000

Sundberg, M. L. (2008). *VB-MAPP: Verbal behavior milestones assessment and placement program.* AVB Press.

Sundberg, M. L. (2015). The most important verbal operant. *VB News, 14*(2), 3–5.

Sundberg, M. L., & Michael, J. (2001). The benefits of Skinner's analysis of verbal behavior for children with autism. *Behavior Modification, 25*(5), 698–724. https://doi.org/10.1177/0145445501255003

Sundberg, M. L., & Partington, J. W. (1998). *Teaching language to children with autism and other developmental disabilities*. Behavior Analysts.

Tennyson, R. D., Woolley, F. R., & Merrill, M. D. (1972). Exemplar and nonexampler variables which produce correct concept classification behavior and specified classification errors. *Journal of Educational Psychology*, *63*(2), 144–152. https://doi.org/10.1037/h0032368

Tiemann, P. W., & Markle, S. M. (1990). Effects of varying interactive strategies provided by computer-based tutorials for a software application program. *Performance Improvement Quarterly*, *3*(2), 48–64. https://doi.org/10.1111/j.1937–8327.1990.tb00457.x

Vladescu, J. C., & Kodak, T. M. (2013). Increasing instructional efficiency by presenting additional stimuli in learning trials for children with autism spectrum disorders. *Journal of Applied Behavior Analysis*, *46*(4), 805–816. https://doi.org/10.1002/jaba.70

Wallace, M. D., Iwata, B. A., & Hanley, G. P. (2006). Establishment of mands following tact training as a function of reinforcer strength. *Journal of Applied Behavior Analysis*, *39*(1), 17–24. https://doi.org/10.1901/jaba.2006.119-04

Chapter 7

Intraverbal Behavior
Toward Complex Language Development

Andresa A. De Souza and Adrienne M. Jennings

Language is essential in our daily functioning and plays a strong role in the educational experience of children. Language makes "socially significant" behavior possible, such as engaging in academic tasks, problem-solving, social interactions, participation in the community, and developing independence. Children with autism spectrum disorder (ASD) and developmental disabilities commonly present with persistent impairments in language (American Psychiatric Association, 2013), which can negatively affect various aspects of their lives at home, school, and in the community. Approximately 63% of children diagnosed with ASD experience language difficulties (Georgiou & Spanoudis, 2021). Moreover, it has been observed that more than half of those diagnosed with ASD exhibit deficits in various aspects of language structure, including phonology, grammar, and semantics (Boucher, 2012; Lord et al., 2018).

Taking a behavioral approach to language, Skinner (1957) established a taxonomy of verbal operants in his analysis of verbal behavior. Early verbal operants include the mand, echoic, tact, textual, transcriptive, copying text, and intraverbal (Sundberg & Michael, 2001). Although listener behavior is not considered a verbal operant, Skinner suggested that we need to include listener responses for a complete account of verbal behavior. Once early learners become advanced learners, practitioners must program for teaching opportunities that promote the acquisition of complex verbal behavior, in other words, multiply controlled verbal responses (see Chapter 10 in this volume). All verbal operants can occur under simple and multiply controlled conditions; however, the intraverbal is potentially the operant class with more implications in the case of multiply controlled verbal behavior than some of the other operant classes (e.g., tacts, echoics).

Most of a person's daily verbal interaction involves intraverbal relations. Intraverbals are also commonly required in the school environment in the form of answering questions, telling stories, solving problems, describing events, and

DOI: 10.4324/9781003433668-9

engaging in reciprocal interactions with peers. Take, for example, the following dialogue between two 6-year-old children at school:

Josi: Hey, Marcelo! Look at my new dino toy!
Marcelo: Cool! Can I see?
Josi: Sure, here it is. It roars! Rawwwr...
Marcelo: Awesome! I wish I had one. What does it eat?
Josi: It pretends to eat leaves and trees, but it's not real.
Marcelo: I saw a movie with a friendly dino, Arlo.
Josi: Me too! Arlo and Spot were best friends. Maybe we could have dino
          friends one day!
Marcelo: (Dreamily) That'd be cool!

The successful interaction between Josi and Marcelo is possible due to a verbal repertoire consisting of generalized mands, tacts, echoics, and, most definitely, multiply controlled intraverbals. Based on the fundamental principles of behavior, each instance of a verbal response becomes stronger when accompanied by reinforcement in the presence of its immediate antecedents (Skinner, 1957). As verbal behavior predominantly occurs in dialogues, intraverbal control (see description in the next section), in conjunction with various other influencing variables, undergoes constant operant conditioning. Because intraverbals and other verbal responses are continually conditioned throughout the speaker's verbal interactions, some traces of intraverbal relations likely contribute subtly to virtually everything one says (Palmer, 2016).

An extensive repertoire of multiply controlled intraverbals supports the acquisition and emergence of other verbal and non-verbal responses (Sundberg & Michael, 2001) as these readily available responses provide a basis upon which to respond to various verbal antecedent stimuli rapidly and proficiently. Failure to acquire an extensive intraverbal repertoire limits a child's potential for academic success. In addition, opportunities for social engagement are limited, provided most social interactions require back-and-forth verbal interactions that include mainly intraverbals, as in the example above. Therefore, it is crucial to program strategies for the acquisition of intraverbals as it can promote academic achievement and the development of social skills.

This chapter will focus on the intraverbal repertoire as a verbal operant class. We will provide an overall definition of intraverbals and describe the variables controlling this verbal operant. We will present empirically supported strategies to develop simple (i.e., verbal responses under the control of a single antecedent stimulus) and complex (i.e., verbal responses under the control of multiple antecedent stimuli) intraverbals, to promote the emergence of novel responses and to increase the variability of responses (see Table 7.1). Finally, we will offer practical guidelines for practitioners focused on language development programming.

Table 7.1 Intraverbal-Related Terms and Concepts

Term	Definition	Example
Simple	Verbal responses under the control of a single antecedent stimulus	Fill-in words in phrases (e.g., "You sleep in a ___")
Complex	Verbal responses under the control of multiple antecedent stimuli (i.e., multiply controlled intraverbals)	Answers to the questions "What clothing do we wear during the winter?" vs. "What clothing do we wear during the summer?"
Broad definition	Any verbal response evoked by a dissimilar verbal antecedent stimulus	All examples below would be considered an intraverbal under the broad definition
Narrow definition	Any verbal response evoked by a dissimilar verbal antecedent stimulus due to a history of reinforcement for contiguous usage under similar conditions.	Word-word association (e.g., pen–paper); fill-in words in songs (e.g., "Baby shark ___")
Intraverbal control	When a verbal antecedent stimulus requires the emission of other behaviors (emitted overtly or covertly) to evoke a verbal response.	Answering the question "What did buy at the store today?"

Note: See Axe (2008), Palmer (2016), and Sundberg (2016) for further discussion on these definitions.

Intraverbal Behavior and Intraverbal Control

Skinner (1957) defined the intraverbal as a verbal response under the control of a verbal antecedent stimulus and maintained by generalized conditioned reinforcement. A defining feature of the intraverbal is that the verbal antecedent stimulus and the verbal response bear no point-to-point correspondence. A verbal operant has point-to-point correspondence when the beginning, the middle, and the end of the verbal antecedent stimulus match the beginning, the middle, and the end of the verbal response. For example, if the verbal antecedent stimulus is "socks," a verbal response that shares point-to-point correspondence would be "socks." This example would not meet the definition of an intraverbal. In the case of the intraverbal, a verbal antecedent stimulus must evoke a verbal response without point-to-point correspondence. For example, if the verbal antecedent stimulus is "socks," the verbal response should differ from socks, such as "shoes." There are no formal similarity requirements in intraverbals. That is, the verbal antecedent stimulus and the verbal response may or may not be of the same modality (i.e., vocal, written, or sign language).

According to Palmer (2016), Skinner's definition of verbal operants allows for interpreting the intraverbal under broad and narrow definitions (see Table 7.1).

Under the broad definition, any verbal response evoked by a dissimilar verbal antecedent stimulus will meet the definition of an intraverbal. Any reinforced verbal response following a dissimilar verbal stimulus, such as word associations, answers to questions, or remarks on someone else's comments, would qualify as intraverbals. Under the narrow definition, an intraverbal is defined as "a verbal response directly under the control of a prior verbal stimulus as the result of a history of reinforcement for emitting that response in the presence of that stimulus" (Palmer, 2016, p. 97). In other words, an intraverbal is any verbal response evoked by a dissimilar verbal antecedent stimulus due to a history of reinforcement for contiguous usage under similar conditions. For example, a child who responds to the question "What can you drink?" is engaging in an intraverbal under the narrow definition if saying "milk," "water," or "orange juice" in the presence of the question was reinforced by their verbal community in the past. However, if the child were to say, "That's a silly question. I'm not thirsty," we would call it an intraverbal in the broad sense. That is, the response is clearly "evoked" by the question, but it has never been specifically reinforced in the presence of the question. We need a much more complex explanation for such instances of verbal behavior.

Only a small subset of the intraverbals a person emits in their daily verbal interactions likely result from a history of direct reinforcement for contiguous usage. The narrow definition is helpful to differentiate directly reinforced intraverbals from those controlled by multiple antecedent stimuli, as they are often more important in early intervention programs for children with ASD (Aguirre et al., 2016; Jennings et al., 2021). Developing instructional programs to teach a child to respond to word-word associations (e.g., "chair and table"), words in a song (e.g., "Five little monkeys jumping on the __"), questions about personal information (e.g., "What's your mom's name?"), and social situations (e.g., "How are you?") are essential to establish a repertoire of simple intraverbals and a history of social reinforcement. However, most of a person's verbal interactions are likely not a result of a history of direct reinforcement. Consider the response to the question, "What did you think about the movie last night?" This question will likely evoke a novel verbal response that has never been reinforced. Therefore, from the perspective of the narrow definition, this would not be considered an intraverbal. We should interpret the function of these verbal responses with greater discrimination (Palmer, 2016).

Generally, the behavior-analytic community and literature have more often adopted the broader definition, thereby classifying the kinds of responses above as intraverbals. That is, if a verbal response evoked by a verbal antecedent stimulus is not an echoic, textual, or transcription, it must be an intraverbal (Palmer, 2016). Interpreting the answer to the question above under the broad intraverbal definition implies we can determine the verbal antecedent stimulus that evokes the verbal response. That is, the question, "What did you think about the movie last night?" functions as a unit to evoke an intraverbal. For most of our daily exchanges, that is not a sufficient explanation. In reality, responding to this question involves a complex interaction of behaviors (e.g., intraverbals, tacts, visual imagining) and subsequent stimuli produced by the speaker that, when combined, serve to evoke a reinforceable response.

Furthermore, a verbal response is rarely under the control of a single antecedent (verbal or non-verbal) stimulus. According to Michael et al. (2011), outside of the controlled environment of experimental conditions, verbal responses, particularly intraverbals, are controlled by multiple antecedent stimuli. To respond to the question above, one needs to consider several components of the question: (a) "What did you think…" is an autoclitic[1] that changes the function of the question to imply one's impression of something; (b) "movie," could occasion a covert non-verbal stimulus (i.e., visual imagining of the movie) and therefore evokes a tact response; (c) "last night," also an autoclitic that changes the function of the question; and (d) the person asking the question, a non-verbal stimulus that serves as the audience to whom one's verbal response should conform to contact reinforcement or avoid punishment. Successfully answering the question, "What did you think about the movie last night?" requires (a) responding to multiple verbal and non-verbal antecedent stimuli; (b) engaging in a variety of covert (sometimes overt) behaviors; and (c) responding to stimuli produced by these behaviors. Suppose a practitioner fails to identify the constellation of controlling variables for this kind of unique response. In that case, they risk teaching more rote or robotic responses, lacking the "meaning" that can be attributed to the myriad of controlling variable interactions. "To call a multiply determined response an intraverbal is to give the illusion of explaining the response when we have not done so, and the practice tends to close off inquiry into the role of other controlling variables" (Palmer, 2016, p. 99).

Palmer (2016) suggested that we should refer to *intraverbal control* (see Table 7.1) when a verbal response, otherwise classified as an intraverbal, is controlled by multiple antecedent stimuli *and* the speaker's overt or covert behavior (e.g., mediating responses). That is, when a verbal antecedent stimulus is sufficient to evoke an intraverbal (e.g., "What can you drink?") due to its history of reinforcement for contiguous usage, we should refer to this response as an intraverbal. However, when a verbal antecedent stimulus requires the emission of other behaviors (emitted overtly or covertly) to evoke a verbal response (e.g., "What did you think about the movie last night?"), then we should refer to intraverbal control as one of the variables controlling the response.

The distinction between intraverbal and intraverbal control is particularly important in the context of teaching multiply controlled verbal behavior. Practitioners should consider the verbal skills required to emit intraverbals (those responses evoked explicitly by the verbal antecedent stimulus only and a history of reinforcement for contiguous usage) and the skills needed to emit mediating responses under intraverbal control, which may interact with other antecedent variables to occasion novel, multiply controlled verbal responses.

It is important to note that intraverbal control embraces more than discrete responses, such as words or phrases that tend to be evoked by characteristic stimuli typically observed in educational and clinical settings (Palmer, 2016). Most verbal responses involving grammar inflection (i.e., grammatical frames) are controlled by various antecedent (sometimes unidentified) stimuli and thus influenced by intraverbal control. In this chapter, we use the term "intraverbal" in the ordinary sense, in which there is a relatively discrete and identifiable target response and a reasonably discrete antecedent stimulus or stimuli (usually under multiple control and often under conditional stimulus control). As with any other verbal operant, intraverbal classes can only be identified through the relation between the antecedents, the response, and the consequences.

Multiple Control of the Intraverbal

Most of our daily verbal interactions result from many variables that interact among themselves (Michael et al., 2011). That is, verbal responses are, for the most part, multiply controlled by antecedent stimuli. Skinner (1957) introduced the notion of multiple control of verbal behavior:

> Two facts emerge from our survey of the basic functional relations in verbal behavior: (1) the strength of a single response may be, and usually is, a function of more than one variable and (2) a single variable usually affects more than one response.
>
> (p. 227)

Michael et al. (2011) identified two types of multiple control involved in verbal behavior: *convergent* and *divergent* control. In convergent control, two or more antecedent variables evoke a single response. For example, a child manding "cookie" is likely not only under the antecedent control of a motivating operation but also the discriminative control of the cookie's presence and their grandmother's presence. Conversely, in divergent control, a single antecedent variable evokes several verbal responses. In the same example, the smell of baking cookies could evoke the mand, "Can I have a cookie?" or the tact, "It smells like cookies." In the case of the intraverbal, the antecedent variables exerting convergent and divergent control over the response are verbal stimuli.

Sundberg (2016) discussed different types of verbal stimulus control involved in evoking intraverbals: simple, compound, conditional, and function-altering. In verbal simple discriminations, the intraverbal is evoked by a single-component verbal antecedent stimulus. Word associations and fill-ins are good examples of verbal simple discriminations. In verbal compound discriminations, two or more components of a verbal antecedent stimulus come together to evoke a particular intraverbal that would be different with a different configuration of those components. For example, the questions "What is a green vegetable?" and

"What is a green fruit?" should evoke different intraverbals due to the summation[2] effect of the different components (green, vegetable, and fruit). In verbal conditional discriminations, a verbal antecedent stimulus changes the function of another verbal antecedent stimulus. For example, asking the questions "When do you sleep?" and "Where do you sleep?" will evoke the responses "at night" and "in the bedroom," respectively. In this example, the verbal antecedent stimuli "when" and "where" change the function of the verbal antecedent stimulus "sleep," thus evoking distinct intraverbals. Finally, verbal function-altering stimuli (Schlinger & Blakely, 1994) change the function of another stimulus at a later time. The verbal antecedent stimulus, "Hey," by itself might have no evocative effect on a child's behavior, but if the teacher says, "When I say Hey, you say Ho," it would likely evoke the intraverbal, "Ho" but only when the teacher says, "Hey." Identifying and classifying the different types of verbal stimulus control involved in evoking intraverbals is useful for developing interventions when a learner presents with intraverbal deficits (e.g., the child can respond to verbal simple discriminations but struggles with verbal compound and conditional discriminations). See Sundberg (2016) for an extended discussion of verbal stimulus control and intraverbals.

It is not uncommon for children with ASD to demonstrate responses under restricted stimulus control of a single verbal antecedent stimulus (Dube & McIlvane, 1999). Failure to respond to an antecedent that contains multiple variables leads to rote intraverbals, as observed when the child answers a question under the control of a single variable (e.g., answering "monkey" for both questions "Tell me a jungle animal" and "Tell me a farm animal"). Developing complex language requires a repertoire of responding under different types of verbal stimulus control. Interventions for the acquisition of multiply controlled intraverbals and intraverbal control should consider the assessment of the child's repertoire in relation to variables controlling verbal behavior and the careful arrangement of stimuli in each teaching opportunity (e.g., Axe, 2008; Sundberg & Sundberg, 2011).

The Development of Intraverbals

The development of verbal behavior starts in infancy (Bijou, 1993; Schlinger, 1995). Early verbal responses involve vocalizations with social intent (e.g., mands for attention or access to an item) and are shaped into echoics. Around the same time, vocal mands and tacts emerge alongside listener behavior (Horne & Lowe, 1996). By 18 months, children are expected to have an initial repertoire of mands, tacts, listener responses, and echoics. Early intraverbals are relatively simple and commonly observed in children without developmental delays around 18–24 months (Sundberg & Sundberg, 2011). By this age, children learn to respond to their names, fill in words of songs, and make simple word associations. Complex intraverbals, including conversation skills, are not yet established, but children already possess extensive listener and speaker repertoires, including echoics, mands, and tacts. Around this age, children also develop tracking, attending to items, identity matching, motor imitation, and listener responding involving function, feature, and class of stimuli. These foundational skills support the quick development of language between the ages of 2 and 3, emphasizing intraverbals. Finally, by age 5, children demonstrate an extensive intraverbal repertoire and respond correctly to questions involving multiple controlling variables.

Intraverbals can range from simple to complex and can be of an unlimited number (Sundberg, 2014). Early intraverbals are likely acquired through a child's verbal community (e.g., caregivers, preschool teachers) and direct reinforcement of fill-in words in social games and songs (e.g., "Ready, set, …go!", "Mary had a little…lamb"), word associations (e.g., "Cats and … dogs"), and fill-ins involved in daily routines (e.g., "You play the… piano"). Most of these intraverbals involve simple discriminations, as the child's response is likely under the control of a single part of the antecedent stimulus. As the child's visual and auditory conditional discrimination skills become more refined, so do their verbal conditional discriminations. At this time, children can respond to most WH questions. They can also answer questions involving multiple components under convergent control (e.g., "What's the name of your brother?" vs. "What's the name of your dad?") and provide multiple answers to a question under divergent control (e.g., "What are some animals from the zoo?"). A repertoire of multiply controlled intraverbals supports the emergence of novel responses (DeSouza et al., 2019; Jennings et al., 2023) and pre-academic repertoires such as answering questions after listening to a passage of a book or retelling past events (Sundberg, 2014).

It is not uncommon for children with ASD to have a generalized tact and listener repertoire but demonstrate a restricted or complete lack of an intraverbal repertoire (Sundberg & Michael, 2001). That is likely because most intraverbals require verbal conditional discriminations and the presence of other mediating processes (i.e., intraverbal control). Sundberg and Sundberg (2011) conducted a descriptive analysis to evaluate intraverbal development as determined by age. To assess participants' intraverbal skills, the authors used an assessment comprised of 80 intraverbals that started with responses under simple stimulus control and progressed to complex forms of stimulus control (e.g., compound, conditional). Participants were 110 children; 39 had no diagnoses and were between the ages of 2 and 5 years, and 71 were children with a diagnosis of ASD between the ages of 2 and 15 years. Data for neurotypical children demonstrated a general correlation between their age and their intraverbal assessment scores. That is, as their ages increased, their intraverbal scores also increased. The data for children with ASD did not demonstrate a correlation between age and intraverbal score, showing their intraverbal learning progressed more slowly than neurotypical children.

Sundberg and Sundberg's (2011) results do not come as a surprise, as language and communication delays are a common occurrence in children with ASD. The more interesting finding from this research involved their error analysis. This analysis showed that children with ASD tended to make the same types of errors made by children without ASD who scored at the same level. That is, children with a similar total score on the assessment made the same types of errors throughout the assessment regardless of age or diagnosis. These errors typically involved providing answers under the control of only one part of the question, for example, answering "hair" for both "What grows on your head?" and "What grows outside?"

The outcomes of Sundberg and Sundberg (2011) are important because (a) they showed that children with and without ASD make mistakes involving verbal conditional discriminations, and (b) they suggested that the development of an intraverbal repertoire depends upon the acquisition of other verbal skills rather than simply the passage of time. Sundberg and Sundberg suggested several important prerequisite skills for developing multiply controlled intraverbals. First, children should respond as a speaker (i.e., tact) and as a listener (i.e., listener responding) in the presence of specific stimuli and classes of stimuli; next, children should demonstrate intraverbals under divergent control; and finally, children should respond as a listener to discriminations involving convergent control. Understanding the role of these prerequisites can facilitate the development of intraverbals and promote complex language development.

DeSouza et al. (2019) conducted a study to evaluate if the prerequisite skills suggested by Sundberg and Sundberg (2011) would facilitate the emergence of novel, multiply controlled intraverbals (e.g., "A mammal from the savanna is a __," "A bird from the savanna is a __"). Four children with ASD between 4 and 5 years participated in the study. They were taught a sequence of four skills related to two sets of targets with overlapping classes and features: multiple tact, multiple listener, intraverbal categorization, and listener compound discrimination. Results showed that all participants required exposure to all prerequisite skills before they demonstrated the emergence of convergent intraverbals at the criterion level. In other words, these prerequisite skills seem sufficient to promote the emergence of novel, multiply controlled intraverbals. These results are consistent with the assumptions made by Sundberg and Sundberg regarding prerequisite verbal skills that should facilitate the emergence of intraverbals under multiple control.

Establishing Intraverbals

Various strategies have been demonstrated to establish intraverbals in research and clinical settings. Intraverbals may be directly taught using transfer of stimulus control procedures. Alternatively, they might emerge (without direct instruction) due to instruction of other verbal behaviors (e.g., tact training, listener tasks). Researchers have also assessed auditory stimulus pairing (e.g., Carnerero & Pérez-González, 2015; Carnerero et al., 2019) to produce intraverbals.

In a recent intraverbal literature review, Jennings et al. (2021) identified intraverbal teaching with echoic prompts as the most common method researchers use to establish intraverbals. With intraverbal teaching, the clinician teaches intraverbals using transfer of stimulus control procedures. Dickes and Kodak (2015) demonstrated the effects of a progressive prompt delay to transfer stimulus control from echoic to intraverbal control to establish intraverbals and reverse relations with children with ASD. During initial intraverbal teaching, trials were presented with an immediate echoic prompt. After the researcher said, "A crow says __" the researcher would immediately say "caw-caw" and wait for the participant to repeat "caw-caw." The echoic prompt was systematically delayed contingent on consecutive correct responses. After teaching intraverbals to verbal antecedents such as, "A crow says __" and "A seal says __," reverse probes were conducted with trials such as, "Caw-caw says the __" and "Arf says the __." The results demonstrated that, in general, this procedure was effective in establishing intraverbals and was sufficient to produce emergent intraverbals for most participants.

Alternatively, stimulus control can be transferred from a tact to an intraverbal. For example, consider teaching a response to the question, "What do you eat for breakfast?" Initially, the clinician could immediately present a picture of cereal or show the learner an actual cereal box as a tact prompt. A progressive prompt delay can be used to fade the prompt so the verbal antecedent stimulus controls the intraverbal "cereal." Kay et al. (2020) compared intraverbal acquisition using echoic or tact prompts with children with ASD. Both strategies were found to be effective. Similar to previous findings (e.g., Coon & Miguel, 2012; Roncati et al., 2019), the prompt type to which the participant was more recently exposed was found to be more efficient. In other words, the difference in efficiency was related to the participant's learning history. This line of research aligns with our recommendations for establishing simple intraverbals (see Figure 7.1). Additionally, the studies highlighted above illustrate the role of echoic and tact repertoires as necessary to facilitate intraverbal acquisition.

Other strategies employed to promote the acquisition of intraverbals involve teaching a response and then assessing emergent intraverbals. For example, researchers have demonstrated the emergence of intraverbals by teaching related tacts. May et al. (2013) taught adolescents with ASD two tacts (e.g., the name of a character [Rocky], the character's preferred food [apple]). Following the acquisition of tacts, the researchers assessed bidirectional intraverbals[3] (e.g., "What food does Rocky eat?", "Which monster eats apples?") and found that they emerged for all participants. In another example, using group instruction and choral responding, May et al. (2019) taught young children first- and second-language tacts (e.g., "What is this in English?" ["hospital"], "What is this in Welsh?" ["Ysbyty"]). Following the intervention, half of the participants demonstrated

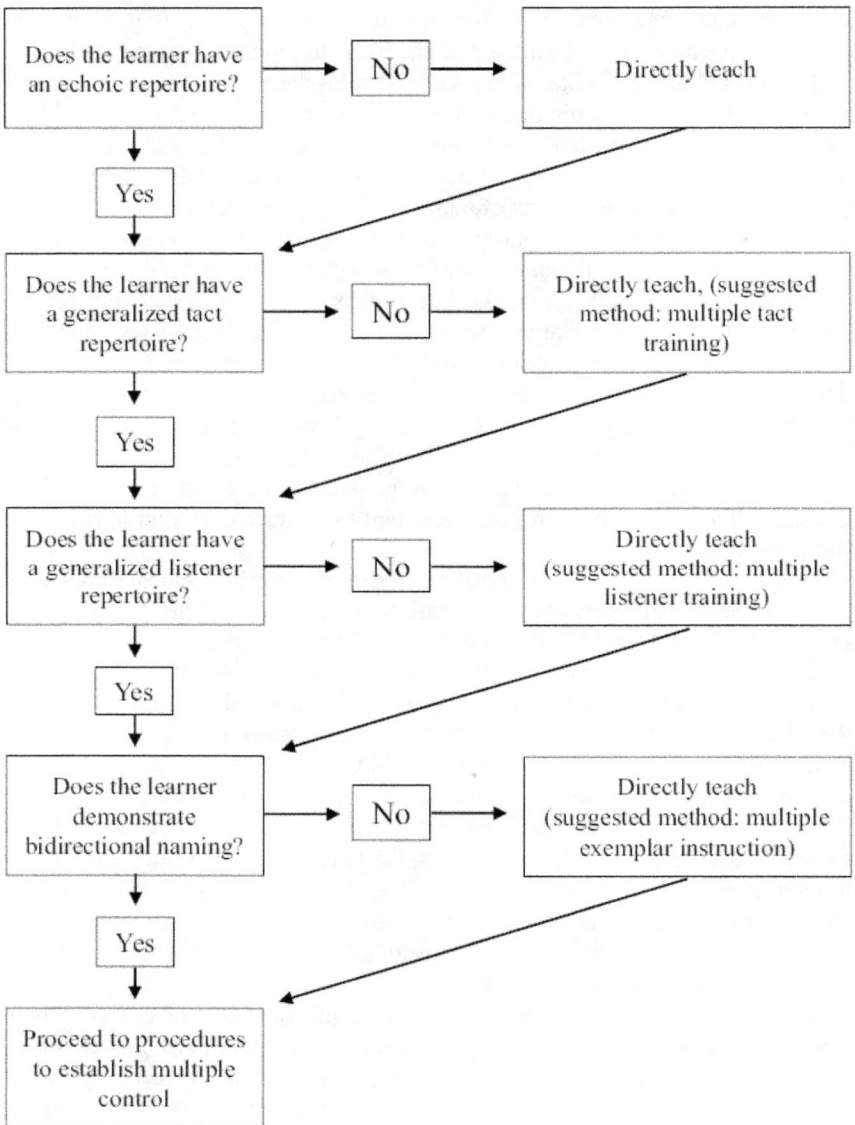

Figure 7.1 Sequence to establish early verbal behavior repertoire.

emergent intraverbals (e.g., "What is hospital in Welsh?" ["Ysbyty"], "What is ysbyty in English?" ["Hospital"]).

Another strategy that can facilitate the emergence of intraverbals is teaching listener responding. Smith et al. (2016) taught participants to select the corresponding stimulus from an array when presented with questions (e.g., selecting the bird when asked, "What's an animal that flies?", selecting the elephant when asked, "What's an animal that's gray?"). This procedure was evaluated by assessing intraverbals (e.g., "What's an animal that flies?", "What's an animal that's gray?"). Listener teaching was effective in promoting the emergence of intraverbals for four of the five participants, whereas one participant required additional tact teaching before intraverbals emerged. Equivalence-based instruction (EBI; see also Chapter 10 in this volume) is another way listener responding can promote the emergence of intraverbals. LaFond et al. (2021) taught children using matching-to-sample training to establish conditional discriminations for equivalence classes of caregiver contact information. Participants first learned to select the printed name of their caregivers (from an array of names) when shown their photos. The next conditional discriminations included selecting the caregivers' phone numbers in the presence of their photos and selecting their printed workplaces when their photos were shown. Subsequently, participants emitted correct intraverbals when asked questions such as, "What's your mom's phone number?" or "Where does your dad work?"

Other demonstrations that have produced emergent intraverbals have specifically sequenced verbal operant instruction, such as establishing tacts and listener responses prior to testing for intraverbals. An effective teaching sequence used by Shillingsburg et al. (2018) started by establishing listener feature/function relations (e.g., selecting the picture of a fish when asked, "Who lives in the sea?"). Next, tact feature/function relations were taught (e.g., saying "sea" when shown a picture of a fish and asked, "Where does this one live?"). Bidirectional intraverbals (e.g., "Where does a fish live?" ["sea"], "Who lives in the sea?" ["fish"]) were taught if necessary. Intraverbals emerged for subsequent sets after exposure to the teaching sequence with the first set. Relatedly, Shillingsburg and Frampton (2019) presented a varied sequence of mastered targets for related skills (tact, tact function, listener, listener by function). To illustrate this sequence using the target "book," the first trial might require the participant to tact "book." The next trial could assess the listener response (pointing to the book in an array). The following trial could assess tacting function by showing a picture of a book and asking, "What do you do with a book?" Another trial would assess listener by function by presenting an array of stimuli and asking, "What do you read?" Exposure to this varied sequence of verbal operant instruction produced emergent item-function and function-item intraverbals (e.g., "What do you do with a book?" and "What do you read?"). In another combination of procedures, Vallinger-Brown and Rosales (2014) compared listener-responding teaching (e.g., selecting a dime when asked, "What coin is worth

10 cents?") to stimulus-stimulus pairing (i.e., no overt response was required). During the stimulus-stimulus pairing condition, an auditory stimulus (e.g., "A penny is worth one cent") was presented simultaneously as a visual stimulus. The condition in which listener responding was taught was slightly more effective at producing emergent intraverbals (e.g., responding "dime" when asked, "What coin is worth 10 cents?"). Still, transfer of stimulus control procedures were necessary to facilitate mastery.

When deciding which teaching procedures to use to establish intraverbals, it is important to consider the learner's current verbal repertoire. If the learner has strong echoic skills, echoic-to-intraverbal transfer of stimulus control procedures may be effective. Suppose the learner has more robust listener behavior instead. In that case, selection-based instruction may be useful to establish a simple intraverbal repertoire while interventions target strengthening other speaker behaviors (e.g., echoics, tacts).

Practical Guidelines

Background Information

Our recommendations for practitioners designing instructional programs to establish intraverbals are based on the literature, which suggests a sequence of prerequisite skills for complex verbal behavior, such as intraverbals. These guidelines provide an overview of empirical findings that support our suggested framework for establishing intraverbals.

A developmental sequence for intraverbals has been suggested in the behavior-analytic literature, starting with some of the earliest intraverbal research (e.g., Poon & Butler, 1972). Furthermore, the role of multiply controlled speaker behavior in facilitating intraverbals is not a new concept. Results from Partington and Bailey's (1993) Experiment 2 show that teaching tacts for stimuli, along with the class they belong to (e.g., "apple" and "fruit"), can facilitate intraverbals. However, as described above, Sundberg and Sundberg (2011) expanded on previous findings, and their data support the suggestion that there is a set of prerequisite skills that should be established before multiply controlled intraverbals emerge (see Figures 7.1 and 7.2). The following guidelines are our recommendations based on the intraverbal literature.

1.   Program for the Acquisition of Early Verbal Behavior Repertoire

Establishing simple intraverbals (Axe, 2008) can be relatively straightforward with systematic planning, assuming the learner has an echoic repertoire. Transfer of stimulus control procedures can be used with a prompting procedure, such as a progressive prompt delay, to produce simple intraverbals errorlessly (e.g., Dickes & Kodak, 2015; Kay et al., 2020).

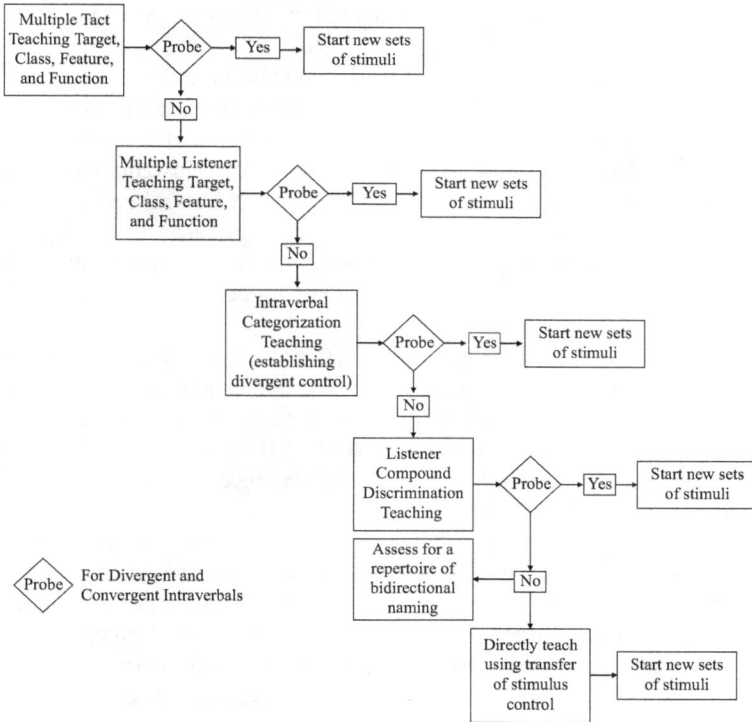

Figure 7.2 Sequence skills to establish multiply controlled intraverbals.

For children who make discrete sounds, practitioners should focus on developing a repertoire of generalized echoic behavior (Esch, 2023). A repertoire of generalized echoics can facilitate the acquisition of intraverbals (Alzrayer, 2023) and self-rehearsal skills (e.g., Vosters & Luczynski, 2020), essential for the development of problem-solving strategies (e.g., Harman et al., 2021; Kisamore et al., 2011). A repertoire of generalized tacts and listener responding might promote bidirectional naming, which appears essential for developing multiply controlled intraverbals (DeSouza et al., 2019; Miguel, 2018).

While the ultimate aim of intraverbal programs should be to establish intraverbal control, it is crucial to establish generalized speaker and listener repertoires and simple intraverbals before progressing to multiply controlled intraverbals. Consider how intraverbals are not assessed in the Verbal Behavior Milestones Assessment and Placement Program (VB-MAPP; Sundberg, 2014) until Level 2. As described above, transfer of stimulus control procedures are recommended for developing an extensive repertoire of simple intraverbals. Practitioners may benefit from reviewing preschool curricula for ideas for simple intraverbals, which include nursery rhymes, animal sounds, and word associations.

2.   Assess for Skills That Can Facilitate the Emergence of Intraverbals

When conducting assessments, the focus is typically on evaluating the discrete skills of the learner and identifying any deficits. It is crucial to consider how we can assess the learner's skills in relation to conditions that promote generative language. The VB-MAPP (Sundberg, 2014) offers insights into a child's prerequisite skills related to verbal operants. However, this assessment does not directly evaluate the presence of generative language capabilities. Some skills essential for generative language are bidirectional naming (see Chapters 9 and 10 in this volume), mediating responses (see Chapter 10 in this volume) and incidental learning.

The presence of a repertoire of bidirectional naming can be assessed by teaching a set of stimuli for listening responding and another set for speaker (i.e., tacts) and probing for the emergence of speaker and listener responses, respectively (Greer et al., 2005; Lowe et al., 2005; Salomonsen & Eldevik, 2024). Correct responses during probes suggest the presence of bidirectional naming (Hawkins et al., 2018).

When assessing mediating responses, one can observe occurrences of differential observing responses (DORs), such as repeating the relevant part of the antecedent stimulus (e.g., Kisamore et al., 2016), self-echoic behavior where the child repeats their own verbal behavior (e.g., Esch et al., 2010) to problem-solve tasks, and unprompted tacts during listener responding tasks (e.g., DeSouza et al., 2019). It is important to note that these responses may be emitted covertly, making direct observation challenging.

Additionally, consideration must be given to skills that enable children to learn in their natural environment without explicit teaching (Palmer, 2005). Incidental learning can promote language acquisition in situations where there are no consequences mediated by other people. Children who learn incidentally can profit from their teachers' instructions in school settings. Furthermore, a repertoire of observational learning (MacDonald & Ahearn, 2015; Zaltzman et al., 2022) can allow children to learn from their peers and others in their natural environment.

3.   Ensure a Repertoire of Bidirectional Naming and the Emergence of Novel Responses

The concept of bidirectional naming (originally termed naming; Miguel, 2016) was introduced by Horne and Lowe (1996) as a behavioral process that the authors considered to be the basis for developing symbolic behavior and the emergence of new operants. Horne and Lowe based their account on the operant analysis of verbal behavior described by Skinner (1957) and the knowledge from developmental psychology. Horne and Lowe defined naming as a bidirectional behavior relation in which the acquisition of one response as a listener presupposes the presence of the same response as a speaker and vice versa. For example, if a child learns to select a toy car when asked, "Give me the car," they will also tact it in the presence of the toy car when someone asks, "What is it?"

Research has suggested that children who do not learn how to tact after listener teaching and vice versa may be able to do so after multiple exemplar instruction (MEI; e.g., Greer et al., 2005; Lechago et al., 2015). MEI involves teaching an instructional target across different operants in rapid and random rotation across consecutive trials (LaFrance & Tarbox, 2020). MEI should include at least two operants, but it can involve the teaching of three or more operants at the same time. MEI should not be confused with multiple exemplar training (MET), which involves rotating different exemplars of a specific target across the same operant.

As a behavioral process, bidirectional naming seems to support children's incidental acquisition of most of their listener and speaker responses (Fiorile & Greer, 2007). In the absence of bidirectional naming, children would depend on explicit instructions to develop their listener and speaker repertoires. As such, bidirectional naming seems to facilitate the acquisition of new operants without direct instruction and thus could be the key to fast acquisition and the emergence of novel operants (e.g., Frampton et al., 2017; Shillingsburg et al., 2018).

In addition to ensuring a repertoire of bidirectional naming, there are numerous demonstrations of procedures that result in emergent verbal behavior (e.g., Conine et al., 2023; Jennings et al., 2021; Petursdottir, 2018; Raaymakers et al., 2019). For example, decades of research have demonstrated that teaching speaker behavior often results in the emergence of listener behavior (e.g., Contreras et al., 2020; Petursdottir & Carr, 2011). Additionally, multiple tact training has been shown to produce visual categorization (e.g., Ribeiro & Miguel, 2020). Depending on a given learner's skill set, it is possible to use procedures such as those described in the *Establishing Intraverbals* section to promote the emergence of tacts, listener responses, and intraverbals.

4.   Teach Mediating Responses

Beyond establishing prerequisite skills, teaching mediating responses to facilitate the acquisition of intraverbals may also be beneficial. Requiring a response to the antecedent stimulus has been shown to be an effective strategy for producing discriminated responding when presented with conditional discriminations (e.g., Kisamore et al., 2013, 2016). One way to establish mediating responses is through DORs. Adding a DOR by having learners either repeat the verbal antecedent (Kisamore et al., 2013) or the relevant components (Kisamore et al., 2016) has been found to be an effective strategy to increase the accuracy of responding or as a modification when the acquisition of new verbal responses is stagnant.

DORs require the learner to respond differentially to the antecedent stimulus, thus increasing the sensory contact with the stimulus (Grow & LeBlanc, 2013). To maintain the benefits of DORs, gradual, systematic withdrawal is necessary (Farber & Dickson, 2023). Practitioners interested in using DORs should review the recommendations provided by Farber and Dickson (2023).

Responding as both a speaker and listener to a variety of autoclitic frames might be a prerequisite skill or at least be helpful in facilitating intraverbal acquisition. degli Espinosa et al. (2021) found that responding to questions such as "What shape?" or "What number?" with autoclitic frames such as "shape square" or "number two" was more effective and efficient for some participants compared to the acquisition of intraverbals without autoclitic frames. Autoclitic frames provide additional context that can assist discrimination. For example, during multiple tact training described by DeSouza et al. (2019), participants learned to respond with either "mammal" or "bird" after hearing the frame "*It's a —.*" Participants also learned to respond with "savanna" or "rainforest" after hearing the frame "*From the __.*" The frame "it's a" is a cue that the child's response should refer to a category of animals, whereas the frame "from the" is a cue that the child's response should refer to a location.

5.   Follow a Sequence from Simple to Multiply Controlled Responses

Establishing multiply controlled intraverbals is a multi-step process requiring more than just an echoic repertoire and a few tacts. Based on the initial findings (DeSouza et al., 2019; Jennings et al., 2023; Rodriguez et al., 2022), the sequence of skills suggested by Sundberg and Sundberg (2011) appears to serve as the framework for producing multiply controlled intraverbals (see Figure 7.2).

To illustrate the sequence suggested by Sundberg and Sundberg (2011), consider the example of teaching categories of utensils and tools. Before presenting the discriminative stimulus, "A type of utensil used for spreading is a __" or "A type of tool used for cutting is a __," we would first need to establish the categories of tools, utensils, and items for spreading and cutting. The instructional program would start by teaching tacts for utensils and tools under multiple control. In other words, we would need to teach the tact for the item (e.g., spatula, knife, trowel, saw), the tacts for how the item is used (e.g., spreading, cutting), and the tact for the category (e.g., utensil, tool). After these speaker responses are established, the next step would be to teach (if necessary) multiply controlled listener behavior. For example, when presented with an array of utensils and tools (e.g., spatula, knife, trowel, saw), the learner should select the correct stimulus or stimuli when presented with questions such as, "Point to the utensils" or "Point to things for spreading." The next skill in the sequence would involve categorizing the stimuli in the absence of a visual stimulus, in other words, intraverbal categorization or divergent stimulus control. For example, responding "knife, saw" when asked, "Tell me some things for cutting" or "trowel, saw" when

asked, "Tell me some tools." The final[4] skill in the sequence is listener responding under convergent control, also referred to as listener compound discrimination. An example of a correct response for this skill would be selecting the
spatula from an array of stimuli after the discriminative stimulus, "Point to the
utensil used for spreading." Teaching each of these skills, multiply controlled
speaker and listener behavior, speaker behavior under divergent control, and
listener behavior under convergent control, should result in an emergence of
intraverbals under convergent control. In other words, the responses to the discriminative stimuli, "A type of utensil used for spreading is a __" or "A type of
tool used for cutting is a __," would emerge.

A handful of studies have evaluated this sequence of skills (DeSouza et al.,
2019; Jennings et al., 2023; Rodriguez et al., 2022). The results of DeSouza et
al. (2019) provide preliminary evidence suggesting that each of these skills (i.e.,
multiple tact, multiple listener, intraverbal categorization, listener compound
discrimination) serves as a prerequisite, yet exactly which skills must be directly
taught for a given learner may vary. In a related evaluation, Rodriguez et al.
(2022) investigated a similar sequence of skills to establish tacts under intraverbal control. In line with the aim to produce multiply controlled verbal behavior,
the sequence of component skills included multiple tact training (element tact
and category tact), intraverbal categorization, and the selection response. One of
the experimental manipulations included changing which component skill was
presented last to shed light on the necessity of the component skills and different combinations. The findings were similar to those of DeSouza et al. (2019)
in that participants only demonstrated the emergence of tacts under intraverbal
control when proficiency across all component skills was also observed. These
data are particularly useful as the altered sequence supports the necessity of each
component skill.

To better understand the underlying mechanisms of this sequence, Jennings
et al. (2023) conducted a translational evaluation of the emergence of convergent intraverbals following the teaching of the sequence of component skills
outlined by Sundberg and Sundberg (2011) and evaluated by DeSouza et al.
(2019). Across a series of experiments, the results supported previous findings.
Emergent convergent intraverbals were only observed when participants demonstrated proficiency in multiple tact, multiple listener, intraverbal categorization, and listener compound discrimination. However, similar to DeSouza et
al. (2019), teaching was not required for each skill for each participant. More
research is necessary to determine precisely which skills are necessary and
which skills may result in the emergence of others. Additionally, more research
is needed to determine the relevant variables and learner characteristics present when component skills emerge. In the meantime, we recommend clinicians
conduct frequent probes for intraverbals throughout the teaching of component
skills, as teaching for each may not be required.

Final Considerations

Intraverbals should be established early. Intraverbals are essential for a child to become a proficient speaker and develop academic and social skills. Neurotypical children learn simple intraverbals such as fill-in-the-blank responding (e.g., "ready, set, __," "1, 2, __") within their first years. Establishing responding that does not share point-to-point correspondence while other verbal operants are acquired is crucial. If a learner has a long history of echoics, adjusting to responding that does not share point-to-point correspondence can require extensive teaching (let alone responses that are also multiply controlled). Once intraverbals are established, the intervention should progress with programming to produce intraverbal control.

Practitioners should continue building upon early intraverbal repertoires and shifting to establishing multiply controlled intraverbals and responding in line with intraverbal control. A repertoire of simple and complex intraverbals is ultimately required for effective communication and conversation skills in academic and social environments. Various procedures and ways to sequence instruction can produce emergent verbal behavior. We encourage clinicians to adopt procedures focusing on prerequisite and component skills with probes for target behaviors to maximize teaching efficiency and produce flexible repertoires.

In conclusion, this chapter described effective strategies for teaching intraverbals to children with ASD, addressing various levels of individual functioning. At the early functioning levels, the emphasis has been on the importance of "narrow" intraverbals, characterized by consistent antecedent variables and predictable responses, which are crucial for enhancing communication in individuals with limited verbal abilities. At the other extreme, we find the central role of mediating responses, intraverbal control, and intraverbal frames, particularly autoclitic frames, in producing novel and multiply controlled verbal responses, constructing sentences, and exhibiting grammatical behavior. The complexity of interweaving intraverbal frames with other terms, especially in articulating past or future events, highlights the intricate nature of language development. While we did not thoroughly discuss intraverbal fames and autoclitics in this chapter, we recognize their importance in language development. As we envision future horizons for the field, mastery of novel grammatical sentences emerges as an ideal goal representing the highest functioning levels. It becomes evident that the intraverbal as a response class and source of control is, in fact, integral to navigating the complexities of linguistic behavior, underscoring its enduring importance in the realm of autism intervention and language development.

Acknowledgments

We thank Anna Ingeborg Petursdottir and David Palmer for their valuable input and critical review of earlier versions of this chapter.

Notes

1 Skinner (1957) defined *autoclitics* as "behavior which is based upon or depends upon other verbal behavior" (p. 315). Autoclitics are responses emitted by the speaker that change the function of the speaker's verbal behavior. In the example above, "What did you think…" changes the function of the speaker's verbal behavior to imply a question about someone's opinion.

2 The summation effect (Skinner, 1957, p. 228) refers to the additive strength of stimulus control when presented with an antecedent that contains multiple controlling variables (e.g., Oliveira et al., 2023). The strength of the stimulus control increases with added controlling variables.

3 Review Miguel (2016) for an extended discussion on intraverbal bidirectional naming.

4 More data are needed to determine the exact sequence of these skills. Recent findings (DeSouza et al., 2019; Jennings et al., 2023; Rodriguez et al., 2022) suggest these skills are more accurately tacted as component skills as it is still to be determined the optimal sequence and if it is actually necessary to teach each skill. Each of these skills may not need to be directly taught, and for some learners, teaching one or two of these component skills may result in the remaining skills emerging. The reference here to this being the final skill is based on Sundberg and Sundberg's (2011) original suggestion and the preliminary research on this sequence.

References

Aguirre, A. A., Valentino, A. L., & LeBlanc, L. A. (2016). Empirical investigations of the intraverbal: 2005-2015. *The Analysis of Verbal Behavior, 32*(2), 139–153. https://doi.org/10.1007/s40616-016-0064-4

Alzrayer, N. M. (2023). Comparing the effect of echoic and listener responding in the development of complex intraverbals. *Behavior Analysis in Practice, 17*, 189–198. https://doi.org/10.1007/s40617-023-00822-z

American Psychiatric Association. (2013). *Diagnostic and statistical manual of mental disorders* (5th ed.). https://doi.org/10.1176/appi.books.9780890425596

Axe, J. B. (2008). Conditional discrimination in the intraverbal relation: A review and recommendations for future research. *The Analysis of Verbal Behavior, 24*(1), 159–174. https://doi.org/10.1007/BF03393064

Bijou, S. W. (1993). *Behavior analysis of child development* (2nd Rev. ed.). Context Press.

Boucher, J. (2012). Research review: Structural language in autistic spectrum disorder-characteristics and causes. *Journal of Child Psychology and Psychiatry and Allied Disciplines, 53*(3), 219–233. https://doi.org/10.1111/j.1469-7610.2011.02508.x.

Carnerero, J. J., & Pérez-González, L. A. (2015). Emergence of naming relations and intraverbals after auditory stimulus pairing. *The Psychological Record, 65*(3), 509–522. https://doi.org/10.1007/s40732-015-0127-2

Carnerero, J. J., Pérez-González, L. A., & Osuna, G. (2019). Emergence of naming relations and intraverbals after auditory stimulus pairing: Effects of probing the listening skill first. *The Psychological Record, 69*(3), 239–252. https://doi.org/10.1007/s40732-019-00336-7

Conine, D. E., Frampton, S. E., Buote, K. A., & Keller, C. E. (2023). A scoping review of empirical research on emergent intraverbal behavior. *Behavioral Interventions, 39*(2), e1986. https://doi.org/10.1002/bin.1986

Contreras, B. P., Cooper, A. J., & Kahng, S. (2020). Recent research on the relative efficiency of speaker and listener instruction for children with autism spectrum disorder. *Journal of Applied Behavior Analysis, 53*(1), 584–589. https://doi.org/10.1002/jaba.543

Coon, J. T., & Miguel, C. F. (2012). The role of increased exposure to transfer-of-stimulus control procedures on the acquisition of intraverbal behavior. *Journal of Applied Behavior Analysis, 45*(4), 657–666. https://doi.org/10.1901/jaba.2012.45-657.

degli Espinosa, F., Wolff, K., & Hewett, S. (2021). A comparison of two teaching procedures to establish generalized intraverbal-tacting in children with autism. *Journal of Applied Behavior Analysis, 54*(4), 1468–1487. https://doi.org/10.1002/jaba.869

DeSouza, A. A., Fisher, W. W., & Rodriguez, N. M. (2019). Facilitating the emergence of convergent intraverbals in children with autism. *Journal of Applied Behavior Analysis, 52*(1), 28–49. https://doi.org/10.1002/jaba.520

Dickes, N. R., & Kodak, T. (2015). Evaluating the emergence of reverse intraverbals following intraverbal training in young children with autism spectrum disorder. *Behavioral Interventions, 30*(3), 169–190. https://doi.org/10.1002/bin.1412

Dube, W. V., & McIlvane, W. J. (1999). Reduction of stimulus overselectivity with nonverbal differential observing responses. *Journal of Applied Behavior Analysis, 32*(1), 25–33. https://doi.org/10.1901/jaba.1999.32-25

Esch, B. E. (2023). *EESA: Early echoic skills assessment and program planner set.* Different Roads to Learning.

Esch, J. W., Esch, B. E., McCart, J. D., & Petursdottir, A. I. (2010). An assessment of self-echoic behavior in young children. *The Analysis of Verbal Behavior, 26*(1), 3–13. https://doi.org/10.1007/BF03393078

Farber, R. S., & Dickson, C. A. (2023). The classification and utility of the differential observing response. *Behavior Analysis: Research and Practice, 23*(3), 179–194. https://doi.org/10.1037/bar0000272

Farber, R. S., Dickson, C. A., & Dube, W. V. (2017). Reducing overselective stimulus control with differential observing responses. *Journal of Applied Behavior Analysis, 50*(1), 87–105. https://doi.org/10.1002/jaba.363.

Fiorile, C. A., & Greer, R. D. (2007). The induction of naming in children with no prior tact responses as a function of multiple exemplar histories of instruction. *The Analysis of Verbal Behavior, 23*, 71–87.

Frampton, S. E., Robinson, H. C., Conine, D. E., & Delfs, C. H. (2017). An abbreviated evaluation of the efficiency of listener and tact instruction for children with autism. *Behavior Analysis in Practice, 10*(2), 131–144. https://doi.org/10.1007/s40617-017-0175-y

Georgiou, N., & Spanoudis, G. (2021). Developmental language disorder and autism: Commonalities and differences on language. *Brain Sciences, 11*(5), 589. https://doi.org/10.3390/brainsci11050589

Greer, R. D., Stolfi, L., Chavez-Brown, M., & Rivera-Valdes, C. (2005). The emergence of the listener to speaker component of naming in children as a function of multiple exemplar instruction. *The Analysis of Verbal Behavior*, *21*, 123–134. https://doi.org /10.1007/bf03393014

Grow, L., & LeBlanc, L. (2013). Teaching receptive language skills: Recommendations for instructors. *Behavior Analysis in Practice*, *6*(1), 56–75. https://doi.org/10.1007/ BF03391791

Harman, M. J., Kodak, T., Bohl, L., & Mayland, T. (2021). The effects of competing verbal behavior on performance in a math task. *The Analysis of Verbal Behavior*, *37*(1), 57–76. https://doi.org/10.1007/s40616-021-00145-6

Hawkins, E., Gautreaux, G., & Chiesa, M. (2018). Deconstructing common bidirectional naming: A proposed classification framework. *The Analysis of Verbal Behavior*, *34*(1–2), 44–61. https://doi.org/10.1007/s40616-018-0100-7

Horne, P. J., & Lowe, C. F. (1996). On the origins of naming and other symbolic behavior. *Journal of the Experimental Analysis of Behavior*, *65*(1), 185–241. https://doi.org/10 .1901/jeab.1996.65-185

Jennings, A. M., Vladescu, J. C., Miguel, C. F., Reeve, K. F., & Sidener, T. M. (2021). A systematic review of empirical intraverbal research: 2015–2020. *Behavioral Interventions*, *37*(1), 79–104. https://doi.org/10.1002/bin.1815

Jennings, A. M., Vladescu, J. C., Miguel, C. F., Reeve, K. F., & Sidener, T. M. (2023). A translational evaluation of component skills for the establishment of multiply controlled intraverbals. *Journal of the Experimental Analysis of Behavior*, *119*(3), 513–528. https://doi.org/10.1002/jeab.837

Kay, J. C., Kisamore, A. N., Vladescu, J. C., Sidener, T. M., Reeve, K. F., Taylor-Santa, C., & Pantano, N. A. (2020). Effects of exposure to prompts on the acquisition of intraverbals in children with autism spectrum disorder. *Journal of Applied Behavior Analysis*, *53*(1), 493–507. https://doi.org/10.1002/jaba.606

Kisamore, A. N., Carr, J. E., & LeBlanc, L. A. (2011). Training preschool children to use visual imagining as a problem-solving strategy for complex categorization tasks. *Journal of Applied Behavior Analysis*, *44*(2), 255–278. https://doi.org/10.1901/jaba .2011.44-255

Kisamore, A. N., Karsten, A. M., & Mann, C. C. (2016). Teaching multiply controlled intraverbals to children and adolescents with autism spectrum disorders. *Journal of Applied Behavior Analysis*, *49*(4), 826–847. https://doi.org/10.1002/jaba.344

Kisamore, A. N., Karsten, A. M., Mann, C. C., & Conde, K. A. (2013). Effects of a differential observing response on intraverbal performance of pre- school children: A preliminary investigation. *The Analysis of Verbal Behavior*, *29*(1), 101–108. https:// doi.org/10.1007/BF03393127

LaFond, T. R., Reeve, K. F., Day-Watkins, J., Reeve, S. A., Vladescu, J. C., & Jennings, A. M. (2021). Using stimulus equivalence-based instruction to teach young children their caregivers' contact information. *Behavioral Interventions*, *36*(1), 105–125. https://doi.org/10.1002/bin.1742

LaFrance, D. L., & Tarbox, J. (2020). The importance of multiple exemplar instruction in the establishment of novel verbal behavior. *Journal of Applied Behavior Analysis*, *53*(1), 10–24. https://doi.org/10.1002/jaba.611

Lechago, S. A., Carr, J. E., Kisamore, A. N., & Grow, L. L. (2015). The effects of multiple exemplar instruction on the relation between listener and intraverbal categorization repertoires. *The Analysis of Verbal Behavior*, *31*(1), 76–95. https://doi.org/10.1007/ s40616-015-0027-1

Lord, C., Elsabbagh, M., Baird, G., & Veenstra-Vanderweele, J. (2018). Autism spectrum disorder. *Lancet, 392*(10146), 508–520. https://doi.org/10.1016/s0140 -6736(18)31129-2.

Lowe, C. F., Horne, P. J., & Hughes, J. C. (2005). Naming and categorization in young children: III. Vocal tact training and transfer of function. *Journal of the experimental analysis of behavior, 83*(1), 47–65. https://doi.org/10.1901/jeab.2005.31-04

MacDonald, J., & Ahearn, W. H. (2015). Teaching observational learning to children with autism. *Journal of Applied Behavior Analysis, 48*(4), 800–816. https://doi.org /10.1002/jaba.257

May, R. J., Chick, J., Manuel, S., & Jones, R. (2019). Examining the effects of group-based instruction on emergent second-language skills in young children. *Journal of Applied Behavior Analysis, 52*(3), 667–681. https://doi.org/10.1002/jaba.563

May, R. J., Hawkins, E., & Dymond, S. (2013). Brief report: Effects of tact training on emergent intraverbal vocal responses in adolescents with autism. *Journal of Autism and Developmental Disorders, 43*(4), 996–1004. https://doi.org/10.1007/s10803-012 -1632-7

Michael, J., Palmer, D. C., & Sundberg, M. L. (2011). The multiple control of verbal behavior. *The Analysis of Verbal Behavior, 27,* 3–22. https://doi.org/10.1007/ BF03393089

Miguel, C. F. (2016). Common and intraverbal bidirectional naming. *The Analysis of Verbal Behavior, 32*(2), 125–138. https://doi.org/10.1007/s40616-016-0066-2

Miguel, C. F. (2018). Problem-solving, bidirectional naming, and the development of verbal repertoires. *Behavior Analysis: Research and Practice, 18*(4), 340–353. https:// doi.org/10.1037/bar0000110

Oliveira, J. S. C. D., Cox, R. E., & Petursdottir, A. I. (2023). Summation in convergent multiple control over selection-based verbal behavior. *The Analysis of Verbal Behavior.* https://doi.org/10.1007/s40616-023-00194-z

Palmer, D. C. (2005). Ernst Moerk and the puzzle of zero-trial learning. *The Analysis of Verbal Behavior, 21*(1), 9–12. https://doi.org/10.1007/BF03393006

Palmer, D. C. (2016). On intraverbal control and the definition of the intraverbal. *The Analysis of Verbal Behavior, 32*(2), 96–106. https://doi.org/10.1007/s40616-016 -0061-7

Partington, J. W., & Bailey, J. S. (1993). Teaching intraverbal behavior to preschool children. *The Analysis of Verbal Behavior, 11,* 9–18. https://doi.org/10.1007/ BF03392883

Petursdottir, A. I. (2018). The current status of the experimental analysis of verbal behavior. *Behavior Analysis: Research and Practice, 18*(2), 151–168. https://doi.org /10.1037/bar0000109

Petursdottir, A. I., & Carr, J. E. (2011). A review of recommendations for sequencing receptive and expressive language instruction. *Journal of Applied Behavior Analysis, 44*(4), 859–876. https://doi .org/10.1901/jaba.2011.44-859

Poon, W., & Butler, K. G. (1972). Evaluation of intraverbal responses in five-to-seven year-old children. *Journal of Speech and Hearing Research, 15*(2), 303–307. https:// doi.org/10.1044/jshr.1502.303

Raaymakers, C., Garcia, Y., Cunningham, K., Krank, L., & Nemer-Kaiser, L. (2019). A systematic review of derived verbal behavior research. *Journal of Contextual Behavioral Science, 12,* 128–148. https://doi.org/10.1016/j.jcbs.2019.02.006

Ribeiro, D. M., & Miguel, C. F. (2020). Using multiple-tact training to produce emergent visual categorization in children with autism. *Journal of Applied Behavior Analysis, 53*(3), 1768–1779. https://doi.org/10.1002/jaba.687

Rodriguez, N. M., Aragon, M. A., McKeown, C. A., & Glodowski, K. R. (2022). Facilitating the emergence of intraverbal tacts in children with autism spectrum disorder: A preliminary analysis. *Journal of Applied Behavior Analysis, 55*(2), 412–429. https://doi.org/10.1002/jaba.898

Roncati, A. L., Souza, A. C., & Miguel, C. F. (2019). Exposure to a specific prompt topography predicts its relative efficiency when teaching intraverbal behavior to children with autism spectrum disorder. *Journal of Applied Behavior Analysis, 52*(3), 739–745. https://doi.org/10.1002/jaba.568

Salomonsen, R., & Eldevik, S. (2024). Effects of serial multiple exemplar training on bidirectional naming in children with autism. *The Analysis of Verbal Behavior, 40,* 28–52. https://doi.org/10.1007/s40616-024-00203-9

Schlinger, H. D., Jr. (1995). *A behavior analytic view of child development.* Plenum Press. https://doi.org/10.1007/978-1-4757-8976-8

Schlinger, H. D., Jr., & Blakely, E. (1994). A descriptive taxonomy of environmental operations and its implications for behavior analysis. *The Behavior Analyst, 17*(1), 43–57. https://doi.org/10.1007/BF03392652

Shillingsburg, M. A., & Frampton, S. E. (2019). The effects of the interspersal of related responses on the emergence of intraverbals for children with autism spectrum disorder. *The Analysis of Verbal Behavior, 35*(2), 172–195. https://doi.org/10.1007/s40616-019-00110-4

Shillingsburg, M. A., Frampton, S. E., Cleveland, S. A., & Cariveau, T. (2018). Clinical applications of procedures to promote the emergence of untrained intraverbal relations with children with autism. *Learning and Motivation, 62,* 51–66. https://doi.org/10.1016/j.lmot.2017.02.003

Skinner, B. F. (1957). *Verbal behavior.* Prentice Hall.

Smith, D. P., Eikeseth, S., Fletcher, S. E., Montebelli, L., Smith, H. R., & Taylor, J. C. (2016). Emergent intraverbal forms may occur as a result of listener training for children with autism. *The Analysis of Verbal Behavior, 32*(1), 27–37. https://doi.org/10.1007/s40616-016-0057-3

Sundberg, M. L. (2014). *VB-MAPP: Verbal behavior milestones assessment and placement program* (2nd ed.). AVB Press

Sundberg, M. L. (2016). Verbal stimulus control and the intraverbal relation. *The Analysis of Verbal Behavior, 32*(2), 107–124. https://doi.org/10.1007/s40616-016-0065-3

Sundberg, M. L., & Michael, J. (2001). The benefits of Skinner's analysis of verbal behavior for children with autism. *Behavior Modification, 25,* 698–724. https://doi.org/10.1177/0145445501255003

Sundberg, M. L., & Sundberg, C. A. (2011). Intraverbal behavior and verbal conditional discriminations in typically developing children and children with autism. *The Analysis of Verbal Behavior, 27*(1), 23–44. https://doi.org/10.1007/BF03393090

Vallinger-Brown, M., & Rosales, R. (2014). An investigation of stimulus pairing and listener training to establish emergent intraverbals in children with autism. *The Analysis of Verbal Behavior*, *30*(2), 148–159. https://doi.org/10.1007/s40616-014 -0014-y

Vosters, M. E., & Luczynski, K. C. (2020). Emergent completion of multistep instructions via joint control. *Journal of Applied Behavior Analysis*, *53*(3), 1432–1451. https://doi .org/10.1002/jaba.670

Zaltzman, T. R., Parry-Cruwys, D., MacDonald, J., & Sweeney-Kerwin, K. E. (2022). An examination of observational learning using Skinner's taxonomy of verbal behavior. *Behavioral Interventions*, *37*(1), 153–169. https://doi.org/10.1002/bin.1819

Chapter 8

Listener Behavior

Samantha Bergmann, Tiffany Kodak, and Haven S. Niland

Skinner (1957) offered a taxonomy of verbal behavior that categorized behavior by operants based on the associated antecedents and consequences (see Chapter 1 in this volume). Skinner did not include listener behavior as a verbal operant, yet effective listener behavior may require individuals to engage in other verbal operants (often covertly) and is a commonly targeted behavior during behavioral intervention for individuals with autism spectrum disorder (ASD) who display language deficits. Thus, it is important to define listener behavior, describe how this behavior is established during behavioral intervention, and discuss practical guidelines when teaching listener behavior.

What Is Listener Behavior?

Skinner (1957) described listener behavior as behavior that is controlled by, and mediates reinforcement for, a speaker's behavior. For example, a mother who asks her son to "Grab my purse on your way out, please" receives the reinforcer when he brings her purse out to the car. The child's listener behavior may also be reinforced when his mom gives him a piece of gum from her purse. Thus, it is easy to understand why listener behavior is important to one's functioning and everyday interactions with others, and why deficits in listener behavior are necessary to address with behavioral intervention.

Listener behavior is a repertoire that is established in early development and expands and becomes more complex as one acquires more verbal behavior. For example, a child may acquire early listener behavior through natural interactions with a caregiver when the caregiver provides vocal instructions (e.g., "Find the car," "Where's your nose," "Pick up the toy") and delivers praise and other social interactions when the child engages in the specified behavior. Over time, the listener repertoire becomes more advanced as multiple antecedent stimuli acquire control over listener responses, such as when a child responds correctly after his teacher says, "Stand up and get in line by the door when I call your table number." Although neurotypical children acquire listener behavior through natural interactions with others and incidental teaching opportunities, children

DOI: 10.4324/9781003433668-10

with ASD often require specialized instruction to acquire simple and more complex listener behavior.

Different terms are used to refer to listener behavior and the interventions used to teach listener behavior such as receptive language, receptive identification, receptive labels, and/or receptive discriminations (Grow & LeBlanc, 2013). Nevertheless, these terms generally refer to teaching listener behavior in response to auditory stimuli. Because listener behavior is frequently targeted in early-intervention and skill-acquisition programs for children and adolescents with ASD, it is necessary to provide a thorough description of listener behavior and the conditions that occasion and reinforce it.

Control by Auditory Stimuli

Auditory stimuli like spoken words and sounds can acquire control over a learner's responding. That is, the learner behaves differentially in the presence and absence of the words and sounds that they hear. A history of contacting reinforcement by responding in particular ways in the presence of some auditory stimuli and not others is the process by which this outcome occurs. One of the first listener discriminations acquired is responding to one's name—a particularly important auditory stimulus in one's environment. Responding to one's name (i.e., looking toward the direction of the speaker) emerges between 5 and 10 months of age in typical development (Gerber et al., 2010), and failure to orient to name by 12 months of age is a developmental red flag (Center for Disease Control [CDC], 2023). In responding to one's name, hearing one's own name becomes a discriminative stimulus (S^D) and other names become s-deltas (S^Δ). That is, Mohamed has contacted reinforcers if he looks at the teacher when they say "Mohamed" (S^D) but not if he looks when they say "Grace" (S^Δ). Responding to one's name is often important for responding to bids for joint attention, following instructions, responding in an emergency, and accessing other social interactions. Deficits in responding to one's name can be one of the first indicators of ASD (Conine et al., 2020). Difficulties in responding to name may be described as part of a "developmental cascade" because deficits contribute to reduced social engagement and increased safety risks (Conine et al., 2020, p. 744).

Listener discriminations are commonly referred to as "following instructions." Following instructions is an important developmental milestone often delayed in children with ASD. Auditory stimuli likely first begin controlling responding by 12 months of age when children stop what they are doing briefly after hearing, "No." (CDC, 2023). At first, following instructions may be under the control of both auditory and visual stimuli; that is, the child may complete requested actions when the spoken instructions are accompanied by gestures. For example, a toddler may go to the bathroom after hearing, "Let's go potty," only if the caregiver also points in the direction of the bathroom.

Many neurotypical children will follow instructions with gestures by about 15 months, and they will follow instructions without gestures by 18 months (CDC, 2023). That is, at 18 months, they should now reliably walk to the bathroom after "Let's go potty" without their caregiver pointing to the bathroom. By 24 months, many children can follow two-step instructions like, "Hug the doll and feed the doll" (American Speech-Language-Hearing Association [ASHA], n.d.). By 30 months, an auditory stimulus like "It's time for dinner" can evoke a sequence of behaviors (CDC, 2023); that is, children can begin to follow multi-step routines without receiving an instruction for each step in the sequence. Thus, rather than needing to tell their child to wash their hands, go to the table, sit at their chair, get a napkin, etc., the child completes the chain following only the instruction to begin.[1]

Control by Auditory and Visual Stimuli

There are also many instances of responding that are controlled by both auditory and visual or textual stimuli, and the acquisition of auditory-visual discriminations is an important developmental milestone. Eye gaze is likely one of the first behaviors to come under the control of both auditory and visual stimuli. By 15 months, most children will scan their environment and look at a familiar object after hearing its name (CDC, 2023). For example, a toddler may scan her environment until she sees the cat after hearing, "Kitty!" Around this same period (i.e., 13–18 months), children are likely to begin identifying at least one of their body parts when asked (e.g., touching nose after hearing, "nose;" ASHA, n. d.). For many children, this repertoire quickly expands beyond eye gaze and body-part identification to include pointing, grabbing, reaching for, and selecting common nouns in books, pictures, and their environment after hearing the item's name by 2 years old (CDC, 2023). For example, a 2-year-old child may touch the picture of a train when their caregiver says, "train," but not when they say, "tree." Listener behavior controlled by auditory and visual stimuli expands to more complex relations like prepositions (e.g., "Put the toy *in* the box" vs. "Put the toy *on* the box"), wh-questions (e.g., "Which animal has a tail?", "Where is the ball?"), and information about the stimuli (i.e., feature [parts of an item like elements, color, shape, texture], function [what one can do with an item], class [category]; Sundberg & Partington, 1998).

Types of Discriminations

Sundberg (2016) explained the importance of acquiring and expanding a listener-discrimination repertoire to support the acquisition of verbal operants like tacts and intraverbals. He categorized verbal stimuli that evoke listener behavior into four categories based on their stimulus configurations and effects: simple, compound, verbal conditional, and verbal function-altering.[2]

Simple Discriminations or Discriminated Operants

A simple discrimination or discriminated operant (Eikeseth & Smith, 2013) involves a response that is reinforced when it occurs in the presence of a stimulus (i.e., S^D) and not in its absence or in the presence of another stimulus (i.e., S^Δ). In an example of a simple discrimination, a learner who raises their arms would receive reinforcement if their teacher says, "lift arms," but not "touch tummy" nor "lift legs." The outcome of this contingency is that the instruction, "lift arms," will become an S^D for arm raising and an S^Δ for other responses.[3] A simple discrimination is a three-term contingency: S^D, response, and reinforcer. Regarding listener behavior, simple discriminations include motor behavior that occurs in the presence of auditory stimuli without additional antecedent stimuli like pictures such as responding to one's name and following instructions.

Compound Discriminations

A compound discrimination includes two or more S^Ds that occasion a different response because they are presented together instead of separately (Eikeseth & Smith, 2013; Sundberg, 2016). An example of a compound listener discrimination involves responding differentially to the instructions, "pat tummy," "rub tummy," "pat elbow," and "rub elbow." The stimuli "pat," "rub," "tummy," and "elbow" all evoke responses on their own. However, when they are presented in combinations, the listener must behave differently to each one to respond correctly. That is, after hearing "pat tummy," the listener must pat, rather than rub, their stomach and not touch their elbow. In this compound-discrimination example, multiple S^Ds evoke a response, which is different from that which is emitted in the presence of the stimuli presented in isolation. Thus, understanding convergent multiple control is critical to programming compound discriminations. Convergent multiple control is when one response is evoked by more than one variable (Michael et al., 2011). Convergent multiple control is also critical to understanding conditional discriminations.

Conditional Discriminations

As described above, a simple discrimination consists of three terms: the S^D, response, and consequence. A conditional discrimination adds at least one antecedent to form a four-term contingency: the conditional stimulus, S^D (S+), response, and consequence. In a conditional discrimination, that additional stimulus—the conditional stimulus—changes whether other antecedent stimuli function as S^D (S+) or S^Δ (S−). That is, the three-term contingency of S^D, response, and consequence comes under contextual control (Eikeseth & Smith, 2013). A common example of a conditional discrimination is selecting pictures or objects after spoken words (auditory-visual conditional discrimination [AVCD]).

Consider a scenario wherein a young child is playing with food, utensils, and serving dishes in a toy kitchen. When the caregiver says, "Put it in the bowl," responding toward the bowl (S+) will be reinforced whereas responding toward the plate will not (S−). However, if the caregiver says, "Put it on the plate," the roles of the dishes change; now, responding toward the plate (S+) will be reinforced whereas responding to the bowl will not (S−). In this example, whether the bowl or plate will be an S+ or an S− is conditional (i.e., dependent) upon what the caregiver says; said another way, the caregiver's instructions determine the function of the other stimuli in the environment.

Listener discriminations can include verbal conditional stimuli (Eikeseth & Smith, 2013). In a verbal conditional discrimination, portions of the auditory stimulus modify the function of the rest of the auditory stimulus. To illustrate listener behavior under the control of a verbal conditional discrimination, consider a classroom wherein a teacher calls the children to line up for recess in a variety of ways. When the teacher says, "Line up if your name starts with the letter *a*," Alonzo, Annalise, Avery, and Amina are permitted to line up (reinforcer) whereas Tariq, Javier, Louisa, and Zoey must wait. In this example, "if your name starts with the letter *a*" modifies the function of the instruction such that "line up" is an S^D for students whose names begin with the letter *a* and is an S^Δ for students whose names start with all other letters.

Compound discriminations can be embedded within conditional discriminations if the conditional stimulus or S^D contains at least two elements (Eikeseth & Smith, 2013). To illustrate this, consider a learner who is acquiring AVCDs of fruits and vegetables of different colors after learning to select stimuli based on color and category. In front of the learner, four different toy foods are placed: a green apple, a green broccoli floret, a red pear, and a red pepper. These items represent the comparison array, and each one is an S+ and an S− based on the words spoken by the teacher. The learner has already acquired selecting apple and pear after "fruit," broccoli and pepper after "vegetable," pear and pepper after "red," and apple and broccoli after "green." Now, if the teacher alternates between instructions that include both the feature (red, green) and class (fruit, vegetable) like, "green fruit," "red fruit," "green vegetable," and "red vegetable," then this could be a compound-conditional discrimination.

The conditional stimulus could also include additional verbal stimuli like "Which is a fruit that is red?" and "Which is a vegetable that is green?" Something to be aware of is that presenting a conditional stimulus with multiple words that include features (e.g., color, shape), objects, or categories does not automatically create a compound-conditional discrimination (Eikeseth & Smith, 2013). There must be overlapping features or objects presented as conditional stimuli and comparison stimuli. If the red and green vegetables example described above included only one fruit or one exemplar that was green, the listener would not need to respond to both elements of the S^D to respond correctly. That is, only the category or color would control selection.

In the example described above, the learner had previously acquired selecting the stimuli after hearing the feature (color) and class (food group) before the compound-conditional discrimination was introduced. Compound-conditional discriminations are likely to require the learner to respond to various features, functions, and categories or classes of stimuli. Thus, it is important to teach the learner to identify stimuli in conditional-discrimination preparations before introducing compounds. For example, before teaching a learner to identify green fruits, green vegetables, red fruits, and red vegetables from an array that includes all those combinations, the learner should first learn to identify the items (e.g., apple, broccoli), their categories (e.g., fruits, vegetables), and their features (e.g., green, red; Eikeseth & Smith, 2013). A teacher could address this skill in several ways including teaching the learner to select features and categories as AVCDs (e.g., selecting the fruit after hearing "fruit" in an array that includes only one fruit), or teaching the learner to match by feature or category (e.g., match apple and pear together after hearing "match fruit").

Conditional discriminations by feature, function, or class, often require a learner to respond to the same stimulus following a variety of auditory stimuli—convergent control—mainly with respect to responses under tact-intraverbal (e.g., in the presence of a yellow cylindrical block, saying, "yellow" after hearing "What color?" and saying, "cylinder" after hearing "What shape?" degli Espinosa, 2022) or intraverbal control (DeSouza et al., 2019). For example, in DeSouza et al. (2019) the terminal target response was naming the correct item or animal in the presence of compound auditory antecedent stimuli like saying "zebra" in the presence of, "A mammal from the savanna is a _____." DeSouza et al. included two listener discrimination tasks in their study. The first was a multiple-listener procedure in which the learner had to select the correct corresponding visual stimulus (S+) in the presence of a variety of antecedent stimuli (e.g., point to zebra, point to all mammals). This task is similar to the skill on the Verbal Behavior Milestones Assessment and Placement Program (VB-MAPP, Sundberg, 2014) which requires the learner to identify the correct visual stimulus in the presence of rotating wh- questions (e.g., selecting a beanie hat when asked, "Where is the hat?", "Which one do you wear in the cold?", "What can you wear on your head?"). The second listener task in DeSouza et al. was a compound discrimination that required the learner to select the correct stimulus that was evoked by multiple elements of the conditional stimulus (e.g., select zebra after hearing, "Point to the mammal from the savanna" from an array with other mammals that do not live in the savanna and non-mammals that do live in the savanna). Although these tasks were described in the context of teaching intraverbals, considering a similar sequence of instruction for compound-conditional discriminations controlled by auditory and visual stimuli is warranted.

Approaches to Teaching Listener Behavior and Practical Guidelines

To teach listener behavior to individuals with ASD, researchers and practitioners can use discrete trial as well as naturalistic teaching arrangements. Conducting preference assessments and in-the-moment reinforcer assessments are recommended to provide consequences that will likely function as reinforcers to establish control by auditory and visual stimuli. Researchers and practitioners can use a variety of prompts (e.g., hand-over-hand or physical guidance, gestural), prompt-fading procedures (e.g., prompt delay, least-to-most hierarchies, errorless), and error-correction procedures to teach listener behavior (see Bergmann & Kodak, 2023, for descriptions of instructional components for listener discriminations). Efficacious and efficient prompts, prompt-fading procedures, and error-correction procedures can be idiosyncratic or learner-specific (e.g., McGhan & Lerman, 2013). Thus, the current chapter will not focus on general teaching arrangements, per se, but will instead describe arrangements of particular importance for teaching listener behavior to learners with ASD.

During discrete-trial instruction, behavior analysts can require a trial-initiation response to signal to the instructor that the child is ready for the S^D to be presented. A trial-initiation response involves the learner engaging in a discrete behavior (e.g., touch card, eye contact with instructor) to initiate the start of the learning trial, which may increase the likelihood that they attend to the antecedents. Incorporating a trial-initiation response may be especially helpful when teaching listener responses because auditory stimuli are transient in the environment, meaning the sound is no longer observable after it has been presented.

Behavior analysts should consider the disparity of auditory and visual stimuli included in instruction. Stimulus disparity refers to the magnitude or intensity of the difference between stimuli. High-disparity stimuli have a large degree of difference from one another (i.e., sound or look very different), whereas low-disparity stimuli have a small degree of difference (i.e., sound or look very similar). Selecting auditory stimuli for conditional stimuli and S^D that do not have overlapping sounds, do not rhyme, and have different pitches can increase the disparity of these stimuli (e.g., Halbur, Caldwell, & Kodak, 2021); arranging visual comparison stimuli that differ in color, features, size, and saturation can increase disparity (e.g., Hannula et al., 2020). Listener-behavior instruction could begin with highly disparate auditory and visual stimuli, and the disparity of these stimuli can decrease gradually over time.

Behavior analysts should also consider the salience of auditory and visual stimuli included in instruction. Stimulus salience refers to the difference between the S^D and the background environment (Halbur, Caldwell, & Kodak, 2021). Loosely speaking, salience refers to how much an S^D stands out from other stimuli in the environment. Manipulating the pitch, volume, duration, or number of repetitions can increase the salience of auditory stimuli (e.g., Summers et al.

1993). Manipulating the color, intensity, or size can increase the salience of visual stimuli (e.g., Lorah & Karnes, 2016). Behavior analysts should be cautious that manipulating stimulus features to increase salience may result in control by irrelevant stimulus features if one is unable to fade the manipulations and maintain the terminal skill (Halbur, Caldwell, & Kodak, 2021). Differential observing responses (DOR; described below) may be a better option to increase stimulus salience and decrease the likelihood of faulty stimulus control.

Control by Auditory Stimuli

Go/No-Go Procedures

A go/no-go procedure can be used to assess and teach simple auditory discriminations. In a go/no-go procedure, a learner emits a response in the presence of one auditory stimulus and does not emit the response in its absence or in the presence of a different auditory stimulus (i.e., S^{Δ}). For example, Serna et al. (1992) taught two adult women with intellectual disabilities to touch a shape on a screen when the computer said, "touch." After the participants were reliably touching the screen only in the presence of "touch" and not its absence (i.e., presence vs. absence discrimination), Serna et al. introduced a second auditory stimulus, the word "wait," as an S^{Δ} (i.e., quality discrimination). Serna et al. and other preparations of go/no-go have used a visual stimulus as a manipulandum (e.g., card touch in Bergmann et al., 2021a; Kodak et al., 2015), which is available to the learner throughout all trials. The learner receives reinforcement for engaging with the item in the presence of one and only one auditory stimulus, and they may also receive reinforcement for *not* engaging with the item in the absence of that stimulus or the presence of another (Saunders & Williams, 1998). For example, learners in Kodak et al. (2015) received reinforcement if they touched a white card on the table when they heard a cat meowing and received reinforcement if they refrained from touching the card for 5 s when they heard a horn honking. However, a manipulandum is not required for a go/no-go procedure. Instead, a learner could receive reinforcement for emitting a motor response in the presence of one auditory stimulus and not in its absence. For example, a learner receives reinforcement for raising their hand only when they hear a tone, or they receive reinforcement for orienting toward a speaker only when their name is called.

Practical Considerations. To teach learners to respond correctly in a go/no-go procedure, behavior analysts can consider using errorless-teaching procedures (Serna et al., 1992) or prompt-delay procedures (Bergmann et al., 2021a; Kodak et al., 2015). In an errorless teaching procedure, the training begins with the S^D only, and the S^{Δ} is introduced for very brief periods. Contingent on no response during the S^{Δ} interval, the S^D is presented. The duration of the S^{Δ} presentation is gradually increased based on success until the S^D and S^{Δ} intervals are equal in duration. When using a prompt-delay procedure, instruction begins with a 0-s prompt delay wherein the target response is prompted immediately upon the presentation of the S^D and that response is reinforced. After several trials with a 0-s prompt delay, the behavior analyst increases the delay between the presentation of the antecedent stimulus and the prompt either in stages (i.e., progressive prompt delay, e.g., 0 s, 3 s, 5 s) or all at once (i.e., constant prompt delay, e.g., 5 s) until the terminal delay is reached.

A go/no-go procedure can be beneficial to assess and teach simple discriminations controlled by auditory stimuli, and it can be designed to progress from discriminations that are likely easier (i.e., presence vs. absence) to those that are increasingly harder (i.e., quality discriminations with words that become less and less disparate; e.g., environmental sounds, environmental sounds vs. nonsense words, words vs. nonsense words, words with no overlapping sounds, words with overlapping sounds; Greer & Ross, 2008; Serna, 2016). However, the go/no-go procedure is not without its limitations. First, learning histories and demands of the assessment or intervention context may create a predisposition to "go" (Serna, 2016). That is, learners may be very likely to engage with the manipulandum or emit the motor response no matter which auditory stimulus is present; therefore, it could be difficult to establish auditory control. For example, in Bergmann et al. (2021a), three of the five participants—two with ASD—touched the card whenever an auditory stimulus was present. If this is a concern for a learner, then a go-left/go-right procedure might be more appropriate (Serna, 2016). Second, when the absence of an auditory stimulus is used as an S^Δ rather than another stimulus, then it can be unclear when a trial has begun. Thus, it could be beneficial to program an additional antecedent stimulus that signals the start of the stimulus-presentation interval. For example, Schlund (2000) presented a light at the onset of every trial, regardless of whether the S^D and S^Δ were programmed. Third, this procedure may have limited social validity given that it looks quite different from the conditions typically considered "following instructions." That is, the learner receives reinforcement for responding in the presence of only one auditory stimulus and essentially not responding in the presence of all others. Therefore, it may be beneficial to progress quickly from a go/no-go procedure to one that focuses on discriminated operants.[4]

Discriminated Operants or Do-This/Do-That Procedure

In a discriminated operant or do-this/do-that procedure, a learner is taught to behave one way following one auditory stimulus and a different way following another auditory stimulus. Bergmann et al. (2021a) referred to this procedure as do this/do that to make the requirement of topographically distinct behaviors salient, as "doing this" in the presence of one stimulus is reinforced, whereas "doing that" in the presence of a different stimulus is reinforced. For example, the learner receives reinforcement if they raise their hand after "raise hand" and stomp their feet after "stomp feet." Simple auditory discriminations can require the learner to engage with visual materials in different ways based on the S^D provided. For example, a student learning to draw has a marker and a blank piece of paper on their desk. When the teacher says, "triangle," the response that will be reinforced is picking up the marker and drawing a three-sided shape on the paper. Drawing a four-sided shape after the instruction, "triangle" would not be reinforced. If the teacher says, "square" instead, then drawing four sides of equal length would be reinforced and drawing a three-sided figure would not.

Practical Considerations. A key component of teaching discriminated operants is to include more than one auditory stimulus (S^D) and target response within a set. That is, the learner should be working on several targets at one time rather than only one at a time in massed-trial instruction. For example, a single session could include alternating trials of "stomp feet," "touch toes," and "clap hands" (Grow & LeBlanc, 2013) and not only "stomp feet." If only one instruction is presented at a time, a learner does not have to attend to the auditory stimulus to emit the reinforced response because other features of the teaching arrangement (e.g., teacher, desk, reinforcers, movement of the teacher's lips) could evoke the correct response. Therefore, it is critical to begin instruction with more than one target, and the recommended minimum is to include at least three to decrease the likelihood of problematic sources of stimulus control (e.g., biases, scrolling; Grow & LeBlanc, 2013).

When beginning instruction in discriminated operants, it is recommended that the instructor provide brief spoken instructions that contain only the stimuli necessary to differentially behave in their presence (Grow & LeBlanc, 2013). This recommendation is to reduce overlapping stimuli in the S^Ds. Thus, rather than saying "Show me touching nose" and "Show me clapping hands," a teacher should begin with "nose" and "clap" to increase the likelihood that the relevant auditory stimulus evokes the action. As control by auditory stimuli expands to include many responses, then the teacher may include overlapping words like "show me" and vary instructions when discrimination of different actions becomes a relevant goal (e.g., "point to nose," "scratch your nose," "wipe nose"). Additionally, initial instruction should include stimuli that sound very different from one another (i.e., highly disparate; Halbur, Kodak, et al., 2021) before progressing to auditory stimuli with similar phonemes. For example, initial instruction could include "tummy" and "head," whereas later instruction could include "hand" and "head."

Control by Auditory and Visual Stimuli

No matter which specific arrangement is used to teach children with ASD to respond based on what they hear and see in the environment, some general strategies may help facilitate acquisition. To improve attending to auditory and visual stimuli during AVCD instruction, behavior analysts can modify when stimuli are presented during the trial. The auditory stimulus may be presented before (sample-first presentation), at the same time as (simultaneous presentation), or after (comparison-first presentation) the visual stimuli. The best order of presentation may be specific to each learner (e.g., Bergmann et al., 2021b). To make visual stimulus presentation manageable for instructors, a divider (e.g., posterboard) can be lifted, stimuli can be affixed to a flat surface that is flipped, or printed on sheets in a binder that are turned to reveal the comparison array.

Echoing the auditory stimulus is another way to secure attending and increase stimulus salience. Learners who engage in overt or covert self-echoics may be more likely to echo or partially echo auditory stimuli, making the stimulus present in the environment for longer and increasing the likelihood of a correct response (Farber & Dickson, 2023). For learners who may be less likely to echo, instructors can increase stimulus salience by repeating the auditory stimuli at regular intervals (e.g., every 2 s) until the learner responds (e.g., Bergmann et al., 2021b). If the learner has an echoic repertoire, an echoic DOR is recommended to increase stimulus salience.

Observing responses and DORs can be used to increase stimulus salience and attending to instructional stimuli and their relevant features (Dinsmoor, 1995a). An observing response involves the learner emitting the same discrete behavior (e.g., raising a hand) following the presentation of each S^D, which indicates to the instructor that they have observed (i.e., seen, heard) what was presented. A DOR involves the learner emitting a unique behavior (e.g., hand raise for S^{D1} and knock for S^{D2}) or the same response according to different reinforcement schedules (e.g., four knocks for S^{D1} and two knocks for S^{D2}) presented during the session for every S^D. This behavior indicates to the instructor that the learner has observed the S^D and can respond differentially to it and other S^Ds (Farber & Dickson, 2023; Grow & LeBlanc, 2013). Several studies have evaluated echoic DORs in teaching listener responses and observed improved accuracy in AVCDs and multicomponent instructions (e.g., Charlop, 1983; Koegel et al., 1981). For learners without vocal-verbal or echoic repertoires, manual sign or written DORs have also been shown to be effective in supporting the acquisition of listener responses (e.g., Elias & Goyos, 2013; Stromer et al., 1996).

Simple-to-Conditional and Conditional-Only Procedures

When teaching AVCDs, a common goal is for the learner to identify the correct item or picture (S+) from increasingly large arrays, and teaching AVCDs to children with ASD is often described in curricula for early intervention. Some of those resources describe massed trials of one target before subsequently introducing distractors and other targets (e.g., Leaf & McEachin, 1999; Lovaas, 2003). This is often referred to as a simple-to-conditional method of instruction. If using the simple-to-conditional method to teach a learner to identify three AVCDs in an array of three—the minimum number of conditional and comparison stimuli recommended (Green, 2001; Grow & LeBlanc, 2013)—the teacher will implement a 9-step program (see Figure 8.1). The program begins by teaching the learner to touch a single visual stimulus after hearing the spoken stimulus (e.g., a picture of a triangle after hearing "triangle") in Step 1 and ends with all three stimuli presented and alternated across trials (e.g., triangle, circle, and diamond are all S+ and S−) in Step 9 until the learner meets a predetermined mastery criterion (e.g., 100% for two consecutive sessions).

Instruction in the simple-to-conditional method is designed to teach in a scaffolded manner such that simple discriminations prepare the learner to respond conditionally. Although the rationale for the simple-to-conditional method is strong, research (e.g., Grow et al., 2011; Lin & Zhu, 2020) suggests that training conditionally (i.e., Step 9 only) from the outset can be efficacious, more efficient, prevent or lessen problematic sources of stimulus control (e.g., position or stimulus biases, win-stay error pattern), improve maintenance, and facilitate generalization. Favorable outcomes for learners with the conditional-only procedure persist even when the simple-to-conditional method is modified to exclude the steps in which the stimuli are introduced in isolation (i.e., Steps 1, 2, and 6 in Figure 8.1; Grow & Van Der Hijde, 2017; Yuan et al., 2023). Thus, the evidence base supports the use of a conditional-only method to teach AVCDs (see Lin & Zhu, 2020; Fisher et al., 2019 for potential advantages of a simple-to-conditional method for early learners). If a learner is struggling to acquire AVCDs, rather

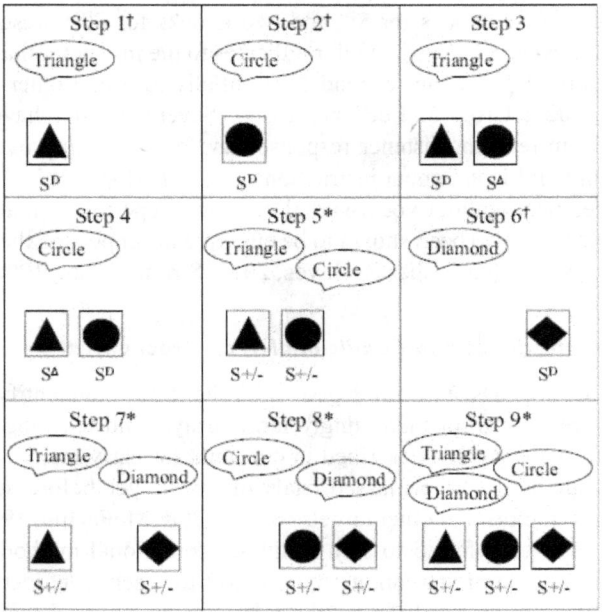

Figure 8.1 Steps of the simple-to-conditional training method to teach AVCDs.

than defaulting to the simple-to-conditional method, it could be beneficial to assess and teach putative prerequisite skills.

Prerequisite Skills for Control by Auditory and Visual Stimuli in Conditional Discriminations

Emitting a correct response that is under the joint control of an auditory stimulus and a visual stimulus is a composite skill that likely requires several component behaviors. Instead of introducing visual and auditory stimuli in isolation and adding distractors in the simple-to-conditional method, teaching component skills or learning-to-learn skills could facilitate the acquisition of more complex repertoires like AVCDs (Green, 2001). Repertoires that include simple and conditional visual and auditory discriminations are likely necessary to benefit from AVCD instruction. Thus, a behavior analyst could assess skills like visual discrimination, matching-to-sample, and auditory discrimination prior to beginning AVCD instruction as a proactive strategy or once little to no progress has been made with conditional-only programming as a reactive strategy.

One option is the Assessment of Basic Learning Abilities (ABLA, Kerr et al., 1977; Martin & Yu, 2000); a behavior analyst can use the ABLA to help identify "the ease or difficulty" (Martin et al., 2008, p. 228) with which a learner will acquire simple and conditional discriminations. The ABLA has six levels that build to an AVCD, and research supports that mastery of previous levels predicts whether a learner will pass subsequent levels (Kerr et al., 1977; Martin et al., 2008). The ABLA assesses imitation (Level 1: place object in container following model), position discrimination (Level 2: place object in container on the left no matter which container), visual discrimination (Level 3: place object in particular container no matter the position), match-to-sample (Level 4: matching objects with containers of same color), auditory discrimination (Level 5: place object in container with fixed position based on auditory stimulus; this is equivalent to a go-left/go-right procedure and is a conditional discrimination [left container is S+ based on one auditory stimulus and is an S− based on the other]), and auditory-visual conditional discrimination (Level 6: place object in container based on auditory stimulus and containers switch positions). To administer the ABLA, inexpensive materials, including a can, a box, wooden blocks, and a piece of foam, are required. The ABLA can be administered in a relatively short period of time based on the number of prompted and independent trials per level. That is, each level of the ABLA begins with a three-step sequence: (1) demonstrate the correct response, (2) prompt the correct response, and (3) provide an independent opportunity for the learner to emit the correct response. If the learner emits a correct independent response, then the examiner assesses performance for that level with opportunities to respond independently until the learner passes (i.e., eight correct responses in a row) or fails (i.e., eight total errors). If a learner fails a level, the behavior analyst could design a program to teach that skill before readministering the assessment and progressing to AVCD instruction.

Another option is based on a prerequisite assessment developed by Kodak et al. (2015, 2022) in which five skills are assessed: (1) imitation of selection response (i.e., pointing), (2) simple visual discrimination, (3) visual match-to-sample, (4) scanning (assessed during match-to-sample), and (5) auditory discrimination. In the imitation task, the instructor pointed to one of three pictures on the tabletop and provided reinforcement if the learner pointed to the same picture. In the simple visual discrimination task, one of three pictures was the S^D across all trials, so the instructor provided reinforcement if the learner pointed to only that picture. In the visual match-to-sample task, the instructor provided a picture that was identical to one of the three pictures on the table and provided reinforcement if the learner matched the pictures. During the match-to-sample task, the instructor recorded whether the learner looked at each stimulus for the scanning task. The final task assessed auditory discrimination, and the procedure used differed across publications. Kodak et al. (2015) used a go/no-go task wherein the instructor placed a card on the tabletop and played two different sounds (e.g., cat meowing and horn honking) and provided reinforcement if the learner touched the card in the presence of one sound and refrained from touching the card for 5 s in the presence of the other. Kodak et al. (2022) used an auditory match-to-sample task wherein the instructor played a sound that matched one of three buttons with audio recordings on the table and provided reinforcement if the learner selected the button with the matching sound. Contrary to the ABLA, in which the levels are assessed in an ascending order, the Kodak et al. assessments used a multielement design in which all tasks are completed concurrently in a randomized order. Each task continued until the participant reached a mastery criterion (i.e., 80% correct for two consecutive sessions of the same task) or a discontinuation criterion (i.e., 10 sessions without an increasing trend). Although the assessment accurately predicted whether 78% (Kodak et al., 2015) and 71% (Kodak et al., 2022) of participants would benefit from AVCD instruction, researchers need to evaluate whether the skills assessed are prerequisites. That is, further research is required to evaluate whether teaching missing repertoires leads to the acquisition of AVCDs.

Differential-Outcomes Procedure

During discrete-trial instruction, the instructor may elect to deliver putative reinforcers by rotating through different preferred items randomly or as the learner's behavior indicates that MOs have changed (e.g., mands for a different item/activity, no interaction with the item). It is also possible to deliver the same reinforcer across targets and trials. If the same consequence is provided across trials, this is sometimes referred to as a common-outcomes procedure. Although the common-outcomes procedure can be efficacious for many learners, the discriminability of antecedent stimuli could be enhanced if the differential-outcomes procedure (DOP; sometimes called stimulus-specific reinforcement procedures) is used instead. The DOP involves arranging different reinforcers (or outcomes) for each correct target response in a set. For example, a DOP to teach discriminated responding to "touch toes" and "pat tummy" might involve reinforcing touching toes with stickers and patting tummy with a doll. In a common-outcomes procedure, a correct response to both "touch toes" and "pat tummy" would be reinforced with the doll only.

In empirical comparisons of common- and differential-outcomes procedures to teach conditional discriminations, the DOP usually resulted in faster acquisition and fewer errors for many learners, including children with ASD (Estévez et al., 2001; McCormack et al., 2019). These findings of relatively better efficiency and accuracy have been termed the differential-outcomes effect, which occurs most often for learners who acquire conditional discriminations slowly or with many errors. Learners who acquire discrimination skills at a steady pace with common procedures may have little room for improvement and not benefit from the DOP (McCormack et al., 2019).

Practical Considerations

When identifying potential reinforcers for the DOP, behavior analysts should select items that vary in dominant color, size, texture, and/or shape. If tokens are used, they should be different from one another and used to exchange for different sets of backup reinforcers. For example, participants in Estévez et al. (2001) earned green tokens to exchange for different toys and red tokens to exchange for different foods. After selecting different items, behavior analysts should conduct preference assessments (e.g., paired stimulus preference assessment, Fisher et al., 1992) to identify enough items, edibles, and activities that are of relatively equal preference. Selecting items of relatively equal preference for the DOP can prevent problematic patterns of responding such as bias toward one response to access a more highly preferred consequence or incorrect/no responding to terminate certain trials with less-preferred consequences (Litt & Schreibman, 1981; McCormack et al., 2019).

During instruction, behavior analysts should use enhanced data sheets (e.g., include the target and designated reinforcer for each trial) to make it more likely that the instructor always delivers the correct reinforcer following target responses (Halbur et al., 2024; LeBlanc et al., 2020; see Figure 8.2. Additionally, behavior analysts should program prompting and prompt-fading strategy during instruction (Schnell et al., 2023). The prompting procedure should include a period of non-differential reinforcement so that each target response is paired with the response-specific reinforcer (McCormack et al., 2019). The DOP relies on the learner engaging in consequence discrimination following each target response, and failure to do so may result in increased errors during acquisition

AVCD Set 1 Date: _____ Child: _____ Prompt Delay: _____ Session #____ Initials: ____

Trial	Left	Middle	Right	Reinforcer	Indep.	Prompted
1.	Snake	Fish	**Bird**	DOLL	+ / - / NR	+ / - / NR
2.	Bird	Snake	**Fish**	BLOCKS	+ / - / NR	+ / - / NR
3.	**Fish**	Bird	Snake	BLOCKS	+ / - / NR	+ / - / NR
4.	Fish	Bird	**Snake**	CAR	+ / - / NR	+ / - / NR
5.	Fish	**Bird**	Snake	DOLL	+ / - / NR	+ / - / NR
6.	**Bird**	Snake	Fish	DOLL	+ / - / NR	+ / - / NR
7.	Bird	**Snake**	Fish	CAR	+ / - / NR	+ / - / NR
8.	Snake	**Fish**	Bird	BLOCKS	+ / - / NR	+ / - / NR
9.	**Snake**	Fish	Bird	CAR	+ / - / NR	+ / - / NR

AVCD Set 1 Date: _____ Child: _____ Prompt Delay: _____ Session #____ Initials: _____

Trial	Left	Middle	Right	Reinforcer	Indep.	Prompted
1.	**Snake**	Fish	Bird	CAR	+ / - / NR	+ / - / NR
2.	Fish	Bird	**Snake**	CAR	+ / - / NR	+ / - / NR
3.	**Bird**	Snake	Fish	DOLL	+ / - / NR	+ / - / NR
4.	Snake	**Fish**	Bird	BLOCKS	+ / - / NR	+ / - / NR
5.	Snake	Fish	**Bird**	DOLL	+ / - / NR	+ / - / NR
6.	**Fish**	Bird	Snake	BLOCKS	+ / - / NR	+ / - / NR
7.	Fish	**Bird**	Snake	DOLL	+ / - / NR	+ / - / NR
8.	Bird	Snake	**Fish**	BLOCKS	+ / - / NR	+ / - / NR
9.	Bird	**Snake**	Fish	CAR	+ / - / NR	+ / - / NR

Figure 8.2 Example of enhanced data sheets for the differential-outcomes procedure.

(Davison & Nevin, 1999). Behavior analysts may enhance consequence discrimination by delivering the different tangible reinforcers in a consistent location (e.g., Fisher et al., 2014) or stating the reinforcer as it is delivered.

Program for Generalization

Multiple Exemplar Training

Multiple exemplar training (MET) involves identifying the range of exemplars that comprise a stimulus class and teaching a subset of those stimuli. The goal of MET is to produce correct responses to novel stimuli that share features of the trained exemplars (i.e., stimulus generalization; Marzullo-Kerth et al., 2011). The selection of exemplars to include in teaching could be based on a consideration of critical (i.e., must-have) attributes and variable (i.e., can-have) attributes (Johnson & Bulla, 2021; Twyman & Hockman, 2021). The critical attributes are those that define and are present in all exemplars that comprise the stimulus class. The variable attributes can co-occur with the critical attributes but often differ across exemplars of the stimulus class. For example, the critical attributes of the stimulus class "cell phone" include a device that (1) uses a wireless connection and cellular network to make calls, (2) has a unique phone number associated with it, and (3) contains a rechargeable battery. Some variable attributes of a cell phone include whether it is a smartphone as well as the color, size, and brand. The exemplars selected to establish cell phone as a stimulus class would include different variable attributes (e.g., a red iPhone, a gray flip phone, a silver Samsung Galaxy Z fold, a black EasyPhone Prime [not a smartphone]). In addition, the nonexamples during listener training should include far-out nonexamples (i.e., stimuli that share none of the critical attributes in common with a cell phone such as a laptop computer) and close-in nonexamples (i.e., stimuli that share some but not all the critical attributes, such as a walkie-talkie).

Practical Considerations. Due to overlapping variable attributes in exemplars and nonexamples of a stimulus class, it is important to consider stimulus disparity. The magnitude of difference between stimuli during AVCD instruction would be low if the array includes a cell phone, walkie-talkie, and landline phone. Although these stimuli may be helpful to include in later instruction to assist the learner in responding differentially to close-in nonexamples and exemplars of the stimulus class, initial instruction could include stimuli with a higher magnitude of difference (i.e., high-disparity stimuli) that have fewer overlapping features such as a cell phone, a laptop computer, and a television.

Matrix Training

Matrix training is an instructional arrangement that can lead to a type of generative responding called recombinative generalization. In recombinative generalization, a learner responds correctly to novel combinations of known components. Although most studies on matrix training have included speaker skills, others have taught listener discriminations with children with ASD (e.g., Curiel et al., 2018; Jimenez-Gomez et al., 2019). For example, Curiel et al. (2018) arranged matrices with action-object combinations (e.g., shake dog, give me llama) and taught three toddlers with ASD or other language delays to emit a subset of the actions with the objects and probed others for recombinative generalization. After training six targets directly, the participants responded to the untrained combinations with varying degrees of accuracy. Two of the participants showed recombinative generalization to all or nearly all untrained targets, but one participant showed limited generalization. Arranging motor responses along one axis and items along another would create combinations of listener discriminations, and the size of the matrix could be adjusted based on the learner's repertoire (see Figure 8.3 for an example matrix). Using matrix training to teach listener discriminations could be an efficient teaching strategy that leads to a recombinative repertoire, which is important for flexible responding in the natural environment.

	Cup	Block	Hat	Spoon
Slide	Slide Cup	Slide Block	Slide Hat	Slide Spoon
Shake	Shake Cup	Shake Block	Shake Hat	Shake Spoon
Tap	Tap Cup	Tap Block	Tap Hat	Tap Spoon
Lift	Lift Cup	Lift Block	Lift Hat	Lift Spoon

Figure 8.3 Example matrix for teaching listener discriminations.
Note: The components are arranged along the horizontal (e.g., objects) and vertical axes (e.g., actions). A selection of the combinations is taught; this figure shows non-overlap training or diagonal training with the shaded cells. If using overlap training, an additional diagonal would be added to training (e.g., "slide block," "shake hat," "tap spoon," and "lift cup"). When presented with an array of the four items and the spoken instructions (e.g., "slide cup"), the learner should select the correct item from the array and manipulate it. After meeting mastery with the shaded cells, the remaining combinations in unshaded cells are presented in recombinative generalization probes.

Practical Considerations. Matrix training is not a specific way to teach skills; rather, it is a framework for organizing, teaching, and probing stimuli. Therefore, behavior analysts using matrix training to teach listener behavior must select what and how to teach. When selecting listener-behavior targets, behavior analysts should select ones that have separable components that can be combined and recombined in meaningful ways (Frampton & Axe, 2023). A number of discriminated operants (i.e., following instructions) and AVCDs could be good candidates for matrix training including completing actions with objects (see Figure 8.3; Curiel et al., 2018; Jimenez-Gomez et al., 2019), completing or identifying preposition-object relations (e.g., the ball on the box, the ball in the hat), identifying adjective-object relations (e.g., red square, green circle, red circle), and spelling (e.g., mat, cat, mop, cop; Tanji & Noro, 2011). After selecting what to teach, behavior analysts should decide on a matrix-training variation. The two most common arrangements are nonoverlap (i.e., diagonal training; see Figure 8.3) and overlap training. In nonoverlap training, each component is trained in only one combination. In overlap training, each component is trained in at least two combinations. The training history of the components should be used to guide variation selection. If the matrix includes known components, then nonoverlap training is recommended (Frampton & Axe, 2023). If the matrix includes unknown components, behavior analysts should consider using overlap training (Frampton & Axe, 2023) or training the components along with the nonoverlap combinations (i.e., simultaneous training; Bergmann et al., 2022). When teaching the combinations, behavior analysts can use whichever skill-acquisition procedures are efficacious for their learner (i.e., prompts, prompt-fading, error correction, differential reinforcement). After the learner's responding meets the mastery criterion, the behavior analyst should probe untrained combinations to assess recombinative generalization. If recombinative generalization is observed, the behavior analyst may consider assessing responding to a generalization matrix (i.e., a matrix of similar known components wherein none of the combinations have been taught directly). In addition to the practical considerations listed above, researchers and practitioners are encouraged to read the matrix-training tutorial by Frampton and Axe (2023).

Functional Interdependence of Verbal Operants

Bidirectional Naming

Many children acquire listener behavior through interactions with adults in their everyday environment. As adults draw attention to everyday objects and model their names for the child, the child subsequently learns their names. After very few teaching interactions, the child can identify those objects as a listener (i.e., point to, pick up) and a speaker (i.e., tact). For example, an adult may say, "This is my hat" while showing the hat to the child and putting it on their head. The child may echo, "hat" while watching the adult. Later, the adult says, "Find my hat," and the child points to the adult's hat. Also, upon seeing the hat again, the child says, "hat." Horne and Lowe (1996) conceptualized the emergence of the untrained verbal behavior in their theory of naming, and subtypes of naming were later proposed to better understand which verbal operants emerged and the conditions under which they emerged (Hawkins et al., 2018; Miguel, 2016).

The amount of language a child needs to acquire exceeds what is possible to teach during behavioral intervention; therefore, establishing bidirectional naming (BiN; Miguel et al., 2018) is worthwhile to develop a robust and complex language repertoire. Common bidirectional naming (C-BiN; Miguel et al., 2018) is the process in which the same stimulus comes to evoke speaker and listener behavior. For example, a child who is taught to tact "hat" in the presence of the hat can subsequently point to the hat upon hearing "hat" without any additional instruction. The process of incidental bidirectional naming (Hawkins et al., 2018) is such that the child learns speaker and/or listener responses to the same stimulus by observing another person's speaker or listener responses, not through direct instruction. For example, the child learns to tact "hat" after only hearing an adult tact "hat" in the presence of the hat. BiN supports rapid language acquisition by creating the opportunity for listener behavior to emerge after only training speaker behavior or from incidental teaching interactions (LaFrance & Tarbox, 2020). BiN has been referred to as a behavioral cusp because it expands the child's language repertoire in such a way that they are exposed to new contingencies, which accelerate learning (LaFrance & Tarbox, 2020; Rosales-Ruiz & Baer, 1997).

Children with ASD often require direct intervention to acquire BiN; however, the mechanisms by which BiN are established are not universally agreed upon (see LaFrance & Tarbox, 2020 for a review). Studies on BiN suggest that tacts, echoics, and listener behavior are the building blocks of BiN (Greer et al., 2005). Multiple exemplar instruction (MEI) has been successful in establishing BiN for children with ASD and other developmental delays (LaFrance & Tarbox, 2020). MEI involves rotating consecutive trials of varied operants (e.g., mands, echoics, tact, listener responses) with the same set of stimuli until mastery is met for all operants in the set.

Assess BiN Repertoire. It is important to assess whether the learner can demonstrate BiN before conducting MEI, as MEI may not be necessary. To do this, the behavior analyst should probe tacts and AVCDs with target stimuli. From these probes, they should teach targets that the learner does not respond to correctly on pure-tact and intraverbal-tact trials and targets to which responding was at or below chance for AVCD-probe trials. The number of targets in a set will depend on the learner's history of successfully acquiring multiple targets at a time. Once targets are selected, identity-matching trials wherein the instructor tacts the S+ during the trials (e.g., "match square") can be used to assess joint incidental BiN (Fiorile & Greer, 2007; Greer et al., 2005). In the matching trials, the learner is not required to echo the tact. This arrangement may mimic incidental-teaching interactions in which the learner hears an adult tact a stimulus with which they are interacting, and that item subsequently acquires joint control over their speaker and listener behavior.

After the matching trials, responding during pure-tact, intraverbal-tact, and AVCD probes should be reassessed. If the learner demonstrates correct responding on all response types, this performance may be indicative of BiN. The behavior analyst should repeat this process with additional sets of stimuli to confirm. If the learner engages in low levels of correct responding after matching, behavior analysts should provide instruction for one verbal operant and then re-evaluate whether the learner can emit untrained responses. For example, the behavior analyst first teaches pure tacts of the target stimuli to mastery—the mastery criterion should depend on the learner's history of instruction and maintenance of tacts. Thereafter, the behavior analyst probes AVCDs with the same targets to assess for listener unidirectional naming. If the learner displays BiN, their responding on probe trials will be at or near-mastery. If this occurs, repeat the teach-probe sequence several times for confirmation while continuing to assess for joint incidental BiN. If the learner does not display joint incidental BiN after displaying listener unidirectional naming for several sets of stimuli, MEI is recommended to try to induce BiN. Similarly, responding at or near chance levels on probes for unidirectional listener naming indicates that the learner does not demonstrate BiN, and behavior analysts can move forward with MEI.

Conduct MEI. Although occasionally confused, MEI is not the same as MET (see LaFrance & Tarbox, 2020). Rather than programming for stimulus generalization, MEI involves teaching varied speaker and listener responses to mastery with one set of stimuli and probing BiN with other, untrained sets. The responses typically include pure tact, intraverbal tact (impure tact), echoic, AVCD, and identity matching see Figure 8.4. (Fiorile & Greer, 2007 Greer et al., 2005; Olaff et al., 2017). For example, the learner may learn to say "kite" simultaneously as an intraverbal tact (when asked, "What is it" while seeing a kite), pure tact (i.e., after seeing a picture of a kite), and an echoic (i.e., after hearing "kite"); the learner may point to kite as a listener (i.e., after hearing "kite" and in the presence of a visual array), and match the picture of the kite to an identical picture. Instructors vary the order of the responses and the target stimulus for each trial to reduce practice effects (Figure 8.4). Learners should be encouraged to echo the names of target stimuli on AVCD trials because requiring echoics during MEI increases the likelihood of BiN (e.g., Hawkins et al., 2009; Olaff et al., 2017).

Practical Considerations. Before beginning MEI to establish BiN, it is important to consider whether the learner's repertoire includes prerequisite skills that could support the acquisition of BiN. For example, learners should be able to echo the target stimuli, but it is not clear whether a generalized echoic repertoire

MEI Set 1 Date: ____ Child: _____ Prompt Delay: _____ Session # ____ Initials: ____

Trial	Operant	S^D			Independent	Prompted
1.	Echoic	"Ball"			+ / - / NR	+ / - / NR
2.	IV Tact	"What is it?" + *Juice image*			+ / - / NR	+ / - / NR
3.	Match	Juice	Kite	**Ball**	+ / - / NR	+ / - / NR
4.	Pure Tact	*Kite image*			+ / - / NR	+ / - / NR
5.	Listener	Kite	**Ball**	Juice	+ / - / NR	+ / - / NR
6.	Echoic	"Kite"			+ / - / NR	+ / - / NR
7.	Match	**Juice**	Ball	Kite	+ / - / NR	+ / - / NR
8.	IV Tact	"What is it?" + *Kite image*			+ / - / NR	+ / - / NR
9.	Listener	Ball	**Juice**	Kite	+ / - / NR	+ / - / NR
10.	IV Tact	"What is it?" + *Ball image*			+ / - / NR	+ / - / NR
11.	Listener	Ball	Juice	**Kite**	+ / - / NR	+ / - / NR
12.	Echoic	"Juice"			+ / - / NR	+ / - / NR
13.	Pure Tact	*Ball image*			+ / - / NR	+ / - / NR
14.	Match	**Kite**	Juice	Ball	+ / - / NR	+ / - / NR
15.	Pure Tact	*Juice image*			+ / - / NR	+ / - / NR

Figure 8.4 Example of an enhanced data sheet for multiple exemplar instruction.

is necessary for BiN (Cao et al., 2018; Greer & Longano, 2010). Echoics confirm the child can differentiate between different sounds, which is necessary for the establishment of appropriate stimulus control by auditory stimuli (Bergmann & Kodak, 2023; Green, 2001). Echoics are also integral for teaching tacts, as echoic prompts are often used to transfer control to the visual stimulus. Learners should also be able to differentiate between visual stimuli used in AVCD and tact trials. Identity-matching trials can confirm visual discrimination of target stimuli (e.g., Fiorile & Greer, 2007; Hawkins et al., 2009). Finally, learners should have demonstrated acquisition of some listener skills with a reliable pointing or selection response (e.g., hand S+ to the instructor, place S+ in bin) prior to beginning MEI.

Establish Joint Control

Although we have exclusively described listener behavior in response to another speaker's behavior, sometimes the listener and speaker reside within the same skin. In other words, people respond as a listener to their own behavior. A self-listener repertoire is important for other verbal behavior, including self-echoics, self-editing, reading, and verbal thinking, among others. For example, when someone provides vocal directions to a new location, the listener may echo those directions (e.g., repeat, "right at the bank, take the second left at the grocery store") and then engage in self-echoic behavior (i.e., repeatedly echoing one's own rehearsal of the directions) until completing all the steps of the directions. Responding to oneself as a listener produces automatic reinforcement, such as when engaging in self-echoics of directions is reinforced when the person successfully finds the location.

Self-echoic behavior is necessary to respond effectively as a listener in many circumstances, such as responding to instructions following a delay. If an adult says, "Pick up your book and papers and put them in your backpack by the door," the child must echo and continue to self-echo these instructions during the delay to walk from their current location to the location of the books, papers, and backpack. Joint control is required to respond correctly as a listener to delayed instructions (Vosters & Luczynski, 2020). Joint control is defined as a change in control when a stimulus that is rehearsed by engaging in self-echoic behavior is emitted in the presence of a second stimulus (e.g., a covert tact of the item), and the combined control of those stimuli evokes a response (Lowenkron, 1998). From our example of the adult telling the child to pick up a book and papers to put in a backpack by the door, the auditory instructions are rehearsed while the child walks into and scans a room to find the book and papers. While continuing to self-echo the instructions, the child covertly tacts items in the room while scanning (e.g., "sweatshirt, pencils...") until the tact "book" occurs, which matches the stimulus being rehearsed. This match between the stimulus being rehearsed and the tact is the onset of joint control. The child then picks up the book and continues to engage in self-echoics and tacts of items in the room until the tact "papers" occurs and matches the rehearsed stimulus, which evokes the response of picking up the papers. Finally, the child continues to rehearse "Put them in your backpack by the door" while walking with the book and papers to the door, and the covert tact of "backpack" occurs in the presence of the visual stimulus of the backpack. The onset of joint control again evokes a response of putting the book and papers in the backpack.

Despite the importance of self-echoics in listener responding and joint control, children with ASD show reduced levels of self-echoic behavior in comparison to their neurotypical peers (Esch et al., 2010). Therefore, behavior analysts have devised teaching strategies to increase self-echoics and improve responding to delayed instructions in children with ASD. For example, Vosters and Luczynski (2020) taught three children with ASD to engage in self-echoics to rehearse auditory stimuli presented in two-step instructions during the delay to walk between rooms to complete the instructions. Once participants correctly engaged in self-echoics during the delay and could tact the stimuli associated with the instructions, they engaged in correct delayed listener responding. Following teaching, participants demonstrated emergent performance of novel instructions evoked by joint control.

Practical Considerations. Behavior analysts should consider teaching self-echoic behavior during behavioral intervention to children with ASD due to the importance of this repertoire for effective listener behavior and the deficits associated with self-echoics for children with ASD. Instruction to engage in echoics and self-echoics of auditory stimuli could begin during AVCD instruction. For example, the learner could be prompted to echo the auditory stimulus (e.g., "apple") and continue to overtly self-echo the auditory stimulus while scanning the array of comparison stimuli. When the self-echoic of the auditory stimulus occurs in the presence of the matching visual stimulus in the array, the learner could be taught to overtly tact that stimulus (i.e., say, "That's apple") and then point to the apple. Learning to engage in echoics, self-echoics, and tacts of stimuli during AVCD instruction teaches the necessary repertoires of behavior for joint control and may result in the emergence of other operants. For example, engaging in a tact of the stimulus while pointing to it during AVCD instruction may result in the emergence of tacts thereafter (Kobari-Wright & Miguel, 2014).

Once self-echoics consistently occur during AVCD instruction, behavior analysts should ensure the learner continues to emit self-echoics during delays to engage in listener behavior. Behavior analysts can use intervention procedures similar to Vosters and Luczynski (2020) to teach children with ASD to engage in self-echoics during delays to completing one-step and multi-step instructions. In addition, self-echoics could be prompted during instruction for other skills for which this repertoire is necessary to independently engage in listener behavior (e.g., making food from a recipe, repeating what one has said when asked, "What did you say?").

Conclusion

Listener behavior is an important repertoire for individuals to function success-fully across environments. If learners have delayed or weak listener behavior repertoires, intervention should be designed to evaluate the type(s) of discrimi-nation currently in the learner's repertoire and expand to more advanced dis-criminations. To design effective interventions for listener behavior, behavior analysts must be familiar with the types of discriminations reviewed in this chapter and refrain from attempting to teach advanced discriminations before prerequisite skills are established. Furthermore, behavior analysts can maxi-mize instructional time during service delivery by teaching a subset of skills and measuring the emergence of untrained repertoires (e.g., matrix training, MEI) and teaching a subset of targets and assessing stimulus generalization (e.g., MET). Using the procedures described in this chapter will help behavior ana-lysts evaluate and design effective and efficient interventions to establish listener behavior in learners with ASD.

Notes

1 Although auditory stimulus control may be observed by a child's completion of tasks following spoken instructions, caregivers are certainly familiar with the fact that observed auditory stimulus control at one time does not guarantee completion of the requested tasks at another time. Auditory stimulus control increases the likelihood that the child will engage in the desired response, but other variables like motivating opera-tions (MOs) and a history of differential reinforcement will affect the probability of the response occurring. Of course, given other variables like MOs and competing stimuli in the environment (e.g., a television playing a show, the ring of a doorbell, the arrival of another family member), providing the instruction one time at the beginning of the chain will not guarantee the child will complete it without reminders or instructions for specific steps. Thus, it is not only important to create a learning history wherein auditory stimuli control responding, but it is also important to create an environment wherein the learner is motivated to complete the requested actions.

   In addition to orienting to name and following instructions, differential behavior in the presence of auditory stimuli is important for academic skills. Auditory dis-crimination also plays an important role in speaker behavior such as the emission of echoics, self-echoics, and intraverbals.

2 A discrimination type suggested by Schlinger and Blakely (1994) and discussed by Sundberg (2016) includes function-altering verbal stimuli. These verbal stimuli change the function of stimuli at another point in time. That is, the effect of these stimuli on the listener's behavior is not observed immediately following their pres-entation but later in the presence of relevant stimuli. For example, a teacher may say, "When the timer goes off, go get your snack." If a child attempts to go to their cubby to grab their snack before the timer goes off, they are likely to be told to put it back and return to their seat. When the timer goes off, the child is permitted to go get and eat their snack. The verbal stimulus, "When the timer goes off, go get your snack" changes the function of the timer, which rings later in time, such that the timer becomes an S^D for getting their snacks. This can be referred to as rule-governed behavior (Skinner, 1969), and the verbal stimulus may be called a

contingency-specifying stimulus (Schlinger & Blakely, 1994). Although this chapter focuses primarily on listener behavior controlled by auditory stimuli in simple, compound, and conditional discriminations, interested readers can refer to Schlinger and Blakely (1987, 1994) as well as Sundberg (2016) for a breakdown of how verbal function-altering stimuli create motivating operations and future S^Ds (pp. 115–116).

3 Although the S^D in the "Lift your arms" example consists of multiple words, it is still a simple discrimination. A simple discrimination is not called simple because it only includes one word or a single auditory stimulus; rather, the discrimination is simple because there is one S^D (i.e., multiple stimuli can function as one unit, Eikeseth & Smith, 2013; Skinner, 1957; referred to as a "single-component verbal stimulus" by Sundberg, 2016). However, multiple auditory stimuli and other antecedents like pictures may not function as single units and require multiple control (i.e., convergent control, joint control) like compound stimuli and conditional discriminations.

4 There are additional procedures that can be used to assess and teach auditory stimulus control. These procedures include go-left/go-right procedures and auditory identity matching/auditory match-to-sample. Interested readers are referred to Bergmann and Kodak (2023) for a review of both Greer and Ross (2008) and Salem et al. (2014) for auditory matching, and Serna (2016) for go-left/go-right procedures.

References

American Speech-Language-Hearing Association. (n.d.). *Communication milestones: Age ranges.* https://www.asha.org/public/developmental-milestones/communication-milestones/

Bergmann, S., Van Den Elzen, G., Kodak, T, Niland, H., & Dawson, D. (2022). Comparing matrix training procedures with children with autism spectrum disorder. *The Analysis of Verbal Behavior, 38*(1), 24–53. https://doi.org/10.1007/s40616-022-00167-8

Bergmann, S., & Kodak, T. (2023). Auditory-visual discriminations: Stimulus control, teaching procedures, and considerations. In J. L. Matson (Ed.), *Handbook of applied behavior analysis* (Autism and Child Psychopathology Series, pp. 211–233). Springer. https://doi.org/10.1007/978-3-031-19964-6_13

Bergmann, S., Kodak, T., Van Den Elzen, G., Jones, T., & Benitez, B. (2021a). Efficacy and efficiency of auditory discrimination procedures for children with autism spectrum disorder and typical development: A preliminary investigation. *European Journal of Behavior Analysis, 22*(1), 74–100. https://doi.org/10.1080/15021149.2020.1795556

Bergmann, S., Turner, M., Kodak, T., Grow, L., Meyerhofer, C., Niland, H., & Edmonds, K. (2021b). Replicating stimulus-presentation orders in discrimination training. *Journal of Applied Behavior Analysis, 54*(2), 793–812. https://doi.org/10.1002/jaba.797

Cao, Y., & Greer, R. D. (2018). Mastery of echoics in Chinese establishes bidirectional naming in Chinese for preschoolers with naming in English. *The Analysis Verbal Behavior, 34*, 79–99. https://doi.org/10.1007/s40616-018-0106-1

Centers for Disease Control and Prevention. (2023, June 6). *CDC's developmental milestones.* https://www.cdc.gov/ncbddd/actearly/milestones/index.html

Charlop, M. H. (1983). The effects of echolalia on acquisition and generalization of receptive labeling in autistic children. *Journal of Applied Behavior Analysis, 16*(1), 111–126. https://doi.org/10.1901/jaba.1983.16-111

Conine, D. E., Vollmer, T. R., & Bolívar, H. A. (2020). Response to name in children with autism: Treatment, generalization, and maintenance. *Journal of Applied Behavior Analysis, 53*(2), 744–766. https://doi.org/10.1002/jaba.635

Curiel, E. S., Sainato, D. M., & Goldstein, H. (2018). Matrix training for toddlers with autism spectrum disorder and other language delays. *Journal of Early Intervention, 40*(3), 268–284. https://doi.org/10.1177/1053815118788060

Davison, M., & Nevin, J. A. (1999). Stimuli, reinforcers, and behavior: An integration. *Journal of the Experimental Analysis of Behavior, 71*(3), 439–482. https://doi.org/10.1901/jeab.1999.71-439

degli Espinosa, F. (2022). Teaching generalized question-discrimination skills to children with autism: Conceptual and applied considerations. *Behavioral Interventions, 37*(1), 43–55. https://doi.org/10.1002/bin.1825

DeSouza, A. A., Fisher, W. W., & Rodriguez, N. M. (2019). Facilitating the emergence of convergent intraverbals in children with autism. *Journal of Applied Behavior Analysis, 52*(1), 28–49. https://doi/org/10.1002/jaba.520de

Dinsmoor, J. A. (1995). Stimulus control: Part II. *The Behavior Analyst, 18*, 253–269. https://doi.org/10.1007/BF03392712

Eikeseth, S., & Smith, D. P. (2013). An analysis of verbal stimulus control in intraverbal behavior: implications for practice and applied research. *The Analysis of Verbal Behavior, 29*(1), 125–135. https://doi.org/10.1007/BF03393130

Elias, N.C., & Goyos, C. (2013). Mimetic relation as matching-to-sample observing response and the emergence of speaker relations in children with and without hearing impairments. *The Psychological Record, 63*, 131–140. https://doi.org/10.11133/j.tpr.2013.63.1.010

Esch, J. W., Esch, B. E., McCart, J. D., & Petursdottir, A. I. (2010). An assessment of self-echoic behavior in young children. *The Analysis of Verbal Behavior, 26*(1), 3–13. https://doi.org/10.1007/BF03393078

Estévez, A., Fuentes, L., Mari-Beffa, P., Gonzalez, C., & Alvarez, D. (2001). The differential outcome effect as a useful tool to improve conditional discrimination learning in children. *Learning and Motivation, 32*(1), 48–64. https://doi.org/10.1006/lmot.2000.1060

Farber, R. S., & Dickson, C. A. (2023). The classification and utility of the differential observing response. *Behavior Analysis: Research and Practice, 23*(3), 179–194. https://doi.org/10.1037/bar0000272

Fiorile, C. A., & Greer, R. D. (2007). The induction of naming in children with no prior tact responses as a function of multiple exemplar histories of instruction. *The Analysis of Verbal Behavior, 23*(1), 71–87. https://doi.org/10.1007/BF03393048.

Fisher, W. W., Pawich, T. L., Dickes, N., Paden, A. R., & Toussaint, K. (2014). Increasing the saliency of behavior-consequence relations for children with autism who exhibit persistent errors. *Journal of Applied Behavior Analysis, 47*(4), 738–748. https://doi.org/10.1002/jaba.172

Fisher, W., Piazza, C. C., Bowman, L. G., Hagopian, L. P., Owens, J. C., & Slevin, I. (1992). A comparison of two approaches for identifying reinforcers for persons with severe and profound disabilities. *Journal of Applied Behavior Analysis, 25*(2), 491–498. https://doi.org/10.1901/jaba.1992.25-491

Fisher, W. W., Retzlaff, B. J., Akers, J. S., DeSouza, A. A., Kaminski, A. J., & Machado, M. A. (2019). Establishing initial auditory-visual conditional discriminations and emergence of initial tacts in young children with autism spectrum disorder. *Journal of Applied Behavior Analysis, 52*(4), 1089–1106. https://doi.org/10.1002/jaba.586

Frampton, S. E., & Axe, J. B. (2023). A tutorial for implementing matrix training in practice. *Behavior Analysis in Practice, 16*(1), 334–345. https://doi.org/10.1007/s40617-022-00733-5

Gerber, R. J., Wilks, T., & Erdie-Lalena, C. (2010). Developmental milestones: Motor development. *Pediatrics in Review, 31*(7), 267–277. https://doi.org/10.1542/pir.31-7-267

Green, G. (2001). Behavior analytic instruction for learners with autism: Advances in stimulus control technology. *Focus on Autism and Other Developmental Disabilities, 16*(2), 72–85. https://doi.org/10.1177/108835760101600203.

Greer, R. D., & Longano, J. (2010). A rose by naming: How we may learn how to do it. *The Analysis of Verbal Behavior, 26*(1), 73–106. https://doi.org/10.1007/BF03393085.

Greer, R. D., & Ross, D. E. (2008). *Verbal behavior analysis: Inducing and expanding new verbal capabilities in children with language delays.* Pearson Education.

Greer, R. D., Stolfi, L., Chavez-Brown, M., & Rivera-Valdes, C. (2005). The emergence of the listener to speaker component of naming in children as a function of multiple exemplar instruction. *The Analysis of Verbal Behavior, 21*(1), 123–134. https://doi.org/10.1007/BF03393014.

Grow, L., & LeBlanc, L. (2013). Teaching receptive language skills. *Behavior Analysis in Practice, 6*(1), 56–75. https://doi.org/10.1007/BF03391791

Grow, L. L., Carr, J. E., Kodak, T. M., Jostad, C. M., & Kisamore, A. N. (2011). A comparison of methods for teaching receptive labeling to children with autism spectrum disorders. *Journal of Applied Behavior Analysis, 44*(3), 475–498. https://doi.org/10.1901/jaba.2011.44-475

Grow, L. L., & Van Der Hijde, R. (2017). A comparison of procedures for teaching receptive labeling of sight words to a child with autism spectrum disorder. *Behavior Analysis in Practice, 10*(1), 62–66. https://doi.org/10.1007/s40617-016-0133-0

Halbur, M., Caldwell, R. K., & Kodak, T. (2021). Stimulus control research and practice: Considerations of stimulus disparity and salience for discrimination training. *Behavior Analysis in Practice, 14*(1), 272–282. https://doi.org./10.1007/s40617-020-00509-9

Halbur, M., Kodak, T., Williams, X., Reidy, J., & Halbur, C. (2021). Comparisons of sounds and words as sample stimuli for discrimination training. *Journal of Applied Behavior Analysis, 54*(3), 1126–1138. https://doi.org/10.1002/jaba.830

Halbur, M., Reidy, J., Kodak, T., Cowan, L., & Harman, M. (2024). Comparison of enhanced and standard data sheets on treatment fidelity and data collection for tact training. *Behavior Analysis in Practice, 17*(2), 533–543. https://doi.org/10.1007/s40617-023-00869-y

Hannula, C., Jimenez-Gomez, C., Wu, W., Brewer, A. C., Kodak, T., Gilroy, S. P., Hutsell, B. A., Alsop, B., & Podlesnik, C. A. (2020). Quantifying errors of bias and discriminability in conditional-discrimination performance in children diagnosed with autism spectrum disorder. *Learning and Motivation, 71,* Article 101659. https://doi.org/10.1016/j.lmot.2020.101659

Hawkins, E., Gautreaux, G., & Chiesa, M. (2018). Deconstructing common bidirectional naming: A proposed classification framework. *The Analysis of Verbal Behavior, 34,* 44–61. https://doi.org/10.1007/s40616-018-0100-7

Hawkins, E., Kingsdorf, S., Charnock, J., Szabo, M., & Gautreaux, G. (2009). Effects of multiple exemplar instruction on naming. *European Journal of Behavior Analysis, 10*(2), 265–273. https://doi.org/10.1080/15021149.2009.11434324

Horne, P. J., & Lowe, C. F. (1996). On the origins of naming and other symbolic behaviors. *Journal of the Experimental Analysis of Behavior, 65*(1), 185–241. https://doi.org/10.1901/jeab.1996.65-185.

Jimenez-Gomez, C., Rajagopal, S., Nastri, R., & Chong, I. M. (2019). Matrix training for expanding the communication of toddlers and preschoolers with autism spectrum disorder. *Behavior Analysis in Practice, 12*(2), 375–386. https://doi.org/10.1007/s40617-019-00346-5

Johnson, K., & Bulla, A. J. (2021). Creating the components for teaching concepts. *Behavior Analysis in Practice, 14*(3), 785–792. https://doi.org/10.1007/s40617-021-00626-z

Kerr, N., Myerson, L., & Flora, J. A. (1977). The measurement of motor, visual, and auditory discrimination skills. *Rehabilitation Psychology, 24*(3), 95–112. https://doi.org/10.1037/h0090912

Kobari-Wright, V. V., & Miguel, C. F. (2014). The effects of listener training on the emergence of categorization and speaker behavior in children with autism. *Journal of Applied Behavior Analysis, 47*(2), 431–436. https://doi.org/10.1002/jaba.115

Kodak, T., Bergmann, S., Cordeiro, M. C., Bamond, M., Eisenhower, R. W., & Fiske, K. E. (2022). Replication of a skills assessment for auditory-visual conditional discrimination training. *Journal of Applied Behavior Analysis, 55*(2), 622–638. https://doi.org/10.1002/jaba.909

Kodak, T., Clements, A., Paden, A. R., LeBlanc, B., Mintz, J., & Toussaint, K. A. (2015). Examination of the relation between an assessment of skills and performance on auditory-visual conditional discriminations for children with autism spectrum disorder. *Journal of Applied Behavior Analysis, 48*(1), 52–70. https://doi.org/10.1002/jaba.160

Koegel, R. L., Dunlap, G., Richman, G. S., & Dyer, K. (1981). The use of specific orienting cues for teaching discrimination tasks. *Analysis and Intervention in Developmental Disabilities, 1*(2), 187–198. https://doi.org/10.1016/0270-4684(81)90031-8

LaFrance, D., & Tarbox, J. (2020). The importance of multiple exemplar instruction in the establishment of novel verbal behavior. *Journal of Applied Behavior Analysis, 53*(1), *10–24.* https://doi.org/10.1002/jaba.611

Leaf, R., & McEachin, J. (1999). *A work in progress.* DRL Books.

LeBlanc, L. A., Sump, L. A., Leaf, J. B., & Cihon, J. (2020). The effects of standard and enhanced data sheets and brief video training on implementation of conditional discrimination training. *Behavior Analysis in Practice, 13*(1), 53–62. https://doi.org/10.1007/s40617-019-00338-5

Lin, F. Y., & Zhu, J. (2020). Comparison of two discrimination methods in teaching Chinese children with autism. *Journal of Applied Behavior Analysis, 53*(2), 1145–1152. https://doi.org/10.1002/jaba.652

Litt, M. D., & Schreibman, L. (1981). Stimulus-specific reinforcement in the acquisition of receptive labels. *Analysis and Intervention in Developmental Disabilities, 1*(2), 171–186. https://doi.org/10.1016/0270-4684(81)90030-6

Lorah, E. R. & Karnes, A. (2016). Evaluating the Lagrange Builder$_{TM}$ application in the acquisition of listener responding in young children with autism. *Journal of*

Developmental and Physical Disabilities, *28*, 255–265. https://doi.org/10.1007/s10882-015-9464-y

Lovaas, O. I. (2003). *Teaching individuals with developmental delays: Basic intervention techniques*. Pro-Ed.

Lowenkron, B. (1998). Some logical functions of joint control. *Journal of the Experimental Analysis of Behavior*, *69*(3), 327–354. https://doi.org/10.1901/jeab.1998.69-327

Martin, G. L., Thorsteinsson, J. R., Yu, C. T., Martin, T. L., & Vause, T. (2008). The assessment of basic learning abilities test for predicting learning of persons with intellectual disabilities: A review. *Behavior Modification*, *32*(2), 228–247. https://doi.org/10.1177/0145445507309022

Martin, G. L., & Yu, C.T. (2000). Overview of research on the assessment of basic learning abilities tests. *Journal on Developmental Disabilities*, *7*(2), 10–36. https://psycnet.apa.org/record/2002-10669-001

Marzullo-Kerth, D., Reeve, S. A., Reeve, K. F., & Townsend, D. B. (2011). Using multiple exemplar training to teach a generalized repertoire of sharing to children with autism. *Journal of Applied Behavior Analysis*, *44*(2), 279–294. https://doi.org/10.1901/jaba.2011.44-279

McCormack, J. C., Elliffe, D., & Virues-Ortega, J. (2019). Quantifying the effects of the differential outcomes procedure in humans: A systematic review and a meta-analysis. *Journal of Applied Behavior Analysis*, *52*(3), 870–892. https://doi.org/10.1002/jaba.578.

McGhan, A. C., & Lerman, D. C. (2013). An assessment of error-correction procedures for learners with autism. *Journal of Applied Behavior Analysis*, *46*(3), 626–639. https://doi.org/10.1002/jaba.65

Michael, J., Palmer, D. C., & Sundberg, M. L. (2011). The multiple control of verbal behavior. *The Analysis of Verbal Behavior*, *27*(1), 3–22. https://doi.org/10.1007/BF03393089

Miguel, C. F. (2016). Common and intraverbal bidirectional naming. *The Analysis of Verbal Behavior*, *32*(1), 125–138. https://doi.org/10.1007/s40616-016-0066-2.

Miguel, C. F. (2018). Problem-solving, bidirectional naming, and the development of verbal repertoires. Behavior Analysis: Research and Practice. 18(4), 340–353. https://doi.org/10.1037/bar0000110.

Olaff, H. S., Ona, H. N., & Holth, P. (2017). Establishment of naming in children with autism through multiple response-exemplar training. *Behavioral Development Bulletin*, *22*(1), 67–85. https://doi.org/10.1037/bdb0000044.

Rosales-Ruiz, J., & Baer, D. M. (1997). Behavioral cusps: A developmental and pragmatic concept for behavior analysis. *Journal of Applied Behavior Analysis*, *30*(3), 533–544. https://doi.org/10.1901/jaba.1997.30-533.

Salem, S., Martin, T., Martin, G., Yu, C. T., Dodson, L., & Wightman, J. (2014). Teaching auditory-auditory identify matching to persons with intellectual disabilities and children with autism: A pilot study. *Journal on Developmental Disabilities*, *20*(3), 57–70.

Saunders, K. J., & Williams, D. C. (1998). Stimulus-control procedures. In K. A. Lattal & M. Perone (Eds.), *Handbook of research methods in human operant behavior* (pp. 193–228). Springer US. https://doi.org/10.1007/978-1-4899-1947-2_7

Schlinger, H. D., & Blakely, E. (1987). Function-altering effects of contingency-specifying stimuli. *The Behavior Analyst*, *10*, 41–45. https://doi.org/10.1007/BF03392405

Schlinger, H. D., & Blakely, E. (1994). A descriptive taxonomy of environmental operations and its implications for behavior analysis. *The Behavior Analyst, 17,* 43–57. https://doi.org/10.1007/BF03392652

Schlund, M. W. (2000). When instructions fail: The effects of stimulus control training on brain injury survivors' attending and reporting during hearing screenings. *Behavior Modification, 24*(5), 658–672. https://doi.org/10.1177/0145445500245003

Schnell, L. K., Cengher, M., & Kisamore, A. N. (2023). Prompt and prompt-fading procedures. In J. L. Matson (Ed.), *Handbook of applied behavior analysis* (Autism and Child Psychopathology Series, pp. 161–170). Springer. https://doi.org/10.1007/978-3-031-19964-6_9

Serna, R. W. (2016). Recent innovations in the assessment of auditory discrimination abilities in non-speaking individuals with intellectual disabilities. In M. Romski & R. Sevcik (Eds.). *Communication interventions for individuals with severe disabilities: Exploring research challenges & opportunities* (pp. 235–258). Paul H. Brookes.

Serna, R. W., Stoddard, L. T., & McIlvane, W. J. (1992). Developing auditory stimulus control: A note on methodology. *Journal of Behavioral Education, 2*(4), 391–403. https://doi.org/10.1007/BF00952356

Skinner, B. F. (1957). *Verbal behavior.* Copley Publishing Group.

Skinner, B. F. (1969). *Contingencies of reinforcement: A theoretical analysis.* Prentice Hall, Inc.

Stromer, R., Mackay, H. A., & Remington, B. (1996). Naming, the formation of stimulus classes, and applied behavior analysis. *Journal of Applied Behavior Analysis, 29*(3), 409–431. https://doi.org/10.1901/jaba.1996.29-409

Summers, J. A., Rincover, A., & Feldman, M. A. (1993). Comparison of extra and within-stimulus prompting to teach prepositional discriminations to preschool children with developmental disabilities. *Journal of Behavioral Education, 3,* 287–298. https://doi.org/10.1007/BF00961556

Sundberg, M. L. (2014). *VB-MAPP: Verbal behavior milestones assessment and placement program: A language and social skills assessment program for children with autism or other developmental disabilities.* AVB Press.

Sundberg, M. L. (2016). Verbal stimulus control and the intraverbal relation. *The Analysis of Verbal Behavior, 32*(2), 107–124. https://doi.org/10.1007/s40616-016-0065-3

Sundberg, M. L., & Partington, J. W. (1998). *Teaching language to children with autism or other developmental disabilities.* AVB Press.

Tanji, T., & Noro, F. (2011). Matrix training for generative spelling in children with autism spectrum disorder. *Behavioral Interventions, 26*(4), 326–339. https://doi.org/10.1002/bin.340

Twyman, J. S., & Hockman, A. (2021). You have the big idea, concept, and some examples ... Now what? *Behavior Analysis in Practice, 14,* 802–815. https://doi.org/10.1007/s40617-021-00638-9

Vosters, M. E., & Luczynski, K. C. (2020). Emergent completion of multistep instructions via joint control. *Journal of Applied Behavior Analysis, 53*(3), 1432–1451. https://doi.org/10.1002/jaba.670

Yuan, C., Deng, X., Zhu, J., & Wang, C. (2023). Comparing a modified simple-conditional with the conditional-only methods in teaching Chinese children with autism. *Journal of Applied Behavior Analysis, 56*(3), 696–704. https://doi.org/10.1002/jaba.1006

Chapter 9

Generative and Emergent Verbal Behavior

Sarah E. Frampton and Caio F. Miguel

Language learning has been described as "virtually inevitable" (Hoff, 2006, p. 55) in neurotypical children living within responsive social contexts. The generality of this finding points to a genetic basis for language acquisition (Stromswold, 2001). However, the variability observed across stages of development implicates the role of environmental and social variables (Hoff, 2006). Some theories of language development place a strong emphasis on *internal* drivers, focusing on the contributions of various brain structures in the acquisition process (Chomsky, 1965). This perspective considers the child as an active agent in their language learning, consistent with a constructivist view of development (Bruner, 1983).

In contrast, a behavior-analytic view strongly emphasizes operant conditioning as the primary mechanism for language learning (LaFrance & Miguel, 2024). Thus, environmental variables such as antecedents (e.g., the number of words heard by the child; Hart & Risley, 1995) and consequences (e.g., caregiver responsiveness to language attempts; Tamis-LeMonda et al., 2001) are crucial for language development, which suggests that language is sensitive to the same variables as any other operant behavior. For this reason, Skinner (1957) referred to language and communication as *verbal behavior*, defining it as any behavior whose consequences are mediated by another organism acting as the listener. Moreover, the listener must have learned to react to the behavior of the speaker (Skinner, 1957). This suggests that language evolves because members of a specific verbal community have shaped, prompted, and reinforced the behavior of saying, writing, signing, etc., in a specific language (e.g., English). Thus, verbal behavior develops from the interactions between individuals who can both speak and understand. This further suggests that to be considered "verbal," organisms must be listeners and speakers at the same time or speak with understanding (Miguel, 2016). Over several decades, Skinner's analysis has influenced hundreds of empirical evaluations (e.g., DeSouza et al., 2017; Petursdottir & Devine, 2017) and has led to effective assessment and intervention for children with language delays (LaFrance & Miguel, 2024; Sundberg & Michael, 2001).

DOI: 10.4324/9781003433668-11

Skinner (1957) classified distinctive types of verbal behaviors based on their specific function (i.e., controlling variables) as *verbal operants*. These operants might initially develop *independently* (e.g., learning the mand for "cup" does not produce a tact for the same object), but later into childhood, might become *interdependent* in that the acquisition of one (e.g., mand) might lead to the establishment of another (e.g., tact; Kelley et al., 2007; Finn et al., 2012). Moreover, words the child reacted to as a listener begin to occur as tacts, and vice versa (e.g., Delfs et al., 2014; Sprinkle & Miguel, 2012). This functional interdependence accounts for a toddler's rapid language expansion (Horne & Lowe, 1996).

In the context of daily activities and routines, language learning continues to accelerate to include more sophisticated grammatical structures (Brown, 1973). By approximately 24 months, words to describe objects and actions are rapidly acquired (Waxman et al., 2013). As these new words are learned in isolation, they might be recombined to form novel phrases and sentences (Goldstein, 1983). For example, after the child points to a toy sheep and says, "Sheep," the parent might respond, "Yes, a fluffy sheep." In future instances, the child might tact the sheep by both its name ("sheep") and feature ("fluffy"). With estimated multi-millions of opportunities to listen to adult speech in early childhood (Hart & Risley, 1995), language learning exponentially accelerates such that by age six, children emit thousands of words in varied, complex sentences (Visser-Bochane et al., 2020).

Language Development in Children with Autism Spectrum Disorder

However, for children diagnosed with autism spectrum disorder (ASD), language development might not follow the same trajectory. Research suggests that as many as 65%–75% of children diagnosed with ASD present with moderate-to-severe delays in speech production (Anderson et al., 2007; Tager-Flusberg & Caronna, 2007). For example, children with ASD might not produce their first word until 38 months (Howlin, 2003). Eaves and Ho (2004) reported that 50% of the children (mean age 33 months) with ASD in their study presented with no spoken functional communication. From the same sample, 70% of the children with ASD presented with listener and speaker skills below the norms expected of a 12-month-old. Similarly, Luyster et al. (2007) reported that, on average, their sample of children with ASD at 30 months understood 75 spoken words and produced only 25 words with understanding. These impairments in development are particularly troubling, as language skills predict vocational, educational, and social outcomes (Tager-Flusberg et al., 2011).

Verbal Behavior Interventions

Effective early intervention for young children with ASD should aim at aggressively addressing these disparities to minimize compounding language delays in later years. A practitioner serving a child diagnosed with ASD will begin with a thorough language assessment (see Chapter 2 in this Volume). Behavior-analytic assessments such as the Verbal Behavior Milestones Assessment and Placement Program (VB-MAPP; Sundberg, 2008) and the Assessment of Basic Language and Learning Skills–Revised (ABLLS-R; Partington, 2010) pinpoint specific operants needing intervention. Early intervention should begin with instruction for these respective verbal operants (e.g., echoics, mands, tacts) using evidence-based practices like errorless teaching procedures compounded with differential reinforcement (LaFrance & Miguel, 2024). In these early stages, practitioners work to identify instructional approaches that result in (a) acquisition of responses, (b) discrimination between responses within the same operant, and (c) generalization across novel exemplars, instructors, and settings (Sundberg, 2008). Gains in each operant should be monitored, and changes should be made to instructional approaches until learning consistently and steadily occurs across operants (i.e., mid-Level 2 on the VB-MAPP).

However, practitioners must be careful to avoid "teaching to the test." That is, teaching isolated verbal operants that result in increased assessment scores but minimal lasting impact on the individual's life.[1] An integrated verbal behavior intervention focuses less on teaching young children with ASD to learn specific content (i.e., isolated verbal operants) and focuses instead on teaching behavioral cusps.[2] A cusp has been defined as "a behavior change that has consequences for the organism beyond the change itself, some of which might be considered important" (Rosales-Ruiz & Baer, 1997, p. 534). These consequences bring behavior into contact with new contingencies and controlling variables in new environments, resulting in continued opportunities for learning. The development of cusp skills might also lead to the development of additional cusp skills as these new contexts for learning are encountered. As noted by Rosales-Ruiz and Baer (1997), for a behavior change to be consistent with a cusp, it must lead to "widespread further changes or to important further changes" (p. 537).

Regarding verbal behavior intervention, critical cusps that meet this definition involve accelerating learning and serve as a foundation for developing more complex skills (Hixson, 2004; Palmer, 2005, 2012). In other words, they result in learning how to learn. For example, upon learning to imitate novel actions by varied instructors across settings (i.e., a generalized imitation repertoire), a learner might acquire a variety of related motor skills without specific instruction (e.g., learning to dance after watching a video, learning to kick a ball by watching a peer). Learning to echo any spoken word (i.e., generalized echoic repertoire) might result in the child demonstrating new phrases and songs overheard during Circle Time. However, learning unrelated, isolated targets in distinct operants (e.g., tact "giraffe," mand "cracker," say "blue" when hearing "what color is the sky?") will not result in radical, repertoire-altering changes for the client. Thus, once foundational skills in each operant have been established, the practitioner must shift their attention to teaching cusps in a developmentally oriented, logical sequence that will establish a firm foundation for complex repertoires of social, academic, and vocational importance (Bosch & Hixson, 2004; Hixson, 2004).

Learning-to-learn cusp skills (e.g., generalized echoic and imitative repertoires) present an elevated level of challenge for assessment as one must determine what was learned and under what conditions it was learned (Hixson, 2004). To do so requires tighter control over variables related to instruction to limit the likelihood of extraneous variables from influencing outcomes (like instruction in other contexts). Assessing cusps necessitates a multi-step approach involving an initial pre-assessment, a learning experience aligned with the cusp, and a post-assessment (see Figure 9.1). The pre-assessment determines the status of targets to be included in the evaluation as either known (i.e., the client consistently emits a correct response) or unknown (i.e., the client does not emit a response, responses are inconsistent or incorrect). At this stage, targets will be selected or excluded based on the parameters of each learning assessment. Next, the learning experience element of the assessment is conducted. The procedures of the learning experience will differ by cusp, and multiple variations might be appropriate. Finally, when the learning experience is concluded, the post-assessment will be repeated with procedures identical to the pre-assessment to evaluate the effects of the learning experience (Hixson, 2004).

In the following sections, we will describe several learning-to-learn cusp skills relevant to verbal behavior. The cusps described include bidirectional naming, the emergence of intraverbals, recombinative generalization, and problem-solving. Though these are not an exhaustive list of all potentially important cusps, these are areas well established in the applied behavior analysis (ABA) literature with direct implications for verbal behavior intervention in practice. For each, we will provide (a) an introduction to the underlying conceptual framework, (b) findings from the applied literature, and (c) procedures for assessing and intervening on the cusp.

Cusp: Bidirectional Naming (BiN)

When individuals talk, they produce auditory stimuli that affect listeners whose behavior has been shaped by their verbal community to respond to these stimuli in specific ways. Thus, when a child asks for a puzzle piece (i.e., a speaker response), the parents can understand what the child says, as evidenced by their behavior of fetching the puzzle piece (i.e., a listener response), which will serve to strengthen the child's behavior as a mand. Moreover, if the child has also learned to locate the puzzle piece when others ask for it (behave as a listener), then the auditory stimulus produced by the mand, "give me the puzzle piece," will affect not only the parents but also the child who can react to the auditory products of their own verbal behavior. Said another way, the child can speak with understanding, or in a more technical way, the child can behave as a listener

	Bidirectional naming (BiN)	Intraverbal Emergence (IV-E)	Recombinative Generalization (RCG)
Pre-assessment	Probe targets as both object-name tacts and name-object listener responses.	Probe targets as both name-feature/function and feature/function-name intraverbals.	Probe targets within interior of the matrix.
Learning Experience Variations	1)Teach targets as either object-name tacts or name-object listener responses. 2)Dictate object-name tact without a client response requirement.	1) Teach either object-name tact or name-object listener response. Then, teach object-feature/function tact or feature/function-object listener response. 2) Teach object-name tact and dictate object-feature/function as instructive feedback.	1) Teach non-overlapping or overlapping targets within matrix interior.
Post-assessment	Same as pre-assessment.		
Intervention Variations	1) Require explicit collateral responses during instruction. 2) Use multiple exemplar instruction.	1) Progressively train additional relations within and across targets. 2) Use MEI.	1) Train additional targets within matrix interior. 2) Train across matrices.
	Repeat assessment process until cusp demonstrated.		

Figure 9.1 Cusp assessment and intervention pathways.

to their own speaker behavior. The concept of bidirectional naming (BiN; Horne & Lowe, 1996; Miguel, 2016) describes the relation between speaker and listener behaviors and the history of reinforcement that leads children to behave as both.

Performances consistent with BiN involve *both* speaker and listener responding with respect to the same object. For example, a client might participate in ABA services and learn to point to keys when instructed (e.g., "Point to keys"). However, when presented later with the keys and asked, "What are these?" the auditory stimulus might not adequately set the occasion for the tact, "keys." In this case, the client does respond in accordance with BiN, as the keys do not evoke speaker behavior. When BiN has been established, listener instruction will result in learning tacts, and tact instruction will result in learning listener relations. More importantly, both speaker and listener relations might eventually be learned simply from observing objects paired with their names (Horne & Lowe, 1996; Miguel, 2016). The ability to learn language incidentally, specifically tacting an object after hearing others name it, has been the subject of much research (Brown et al., 2023)

The independence of speaker and listener behavior might be observed in early development and persist into later years for children with ASD (Petursdottir et al., 2018). This failure to demonstrate BiN has several troubling ramifications for these individuals. First, if tact training fails to produce listener relations (and vice versa), twice as much instruction is required to support vocabulary development related to relevant topics. Second, research findings suggest that BiN might be necessary to develop more advanced skills, such as sorting by category, analogical reasoning, and problem-solving (e.g., Jennings & Miguel, 2017; Lee et al., 2015; Zhirnova et al., 2025). BiN has also been implicated in the emergence of intraverbals (Conine et al., 2024), discussed later in this chapter. Finally, BiN has been associated with language explosion, in that children might be able to learn incidentally only after all behaviors associated with BiN have been established (see Miguel, 2018). Thus, establishing BiN should be considered a high priority in clinical services.

Findings from Applied Research

Questions related to the efficiency of tact vs. listener instruction have been of interest in the applied literature for decades (Contreras et al., 2020; Petursdottir & Carr, 2011). Several studies have directly compared the effects of tact and listener instruction within learners with ASD and found that tact training is more likely to result in learning listener relations than the reverse (Delfs et al., 2014; Frampton et al., 2017; Sprinkle & Miguel, 2012). This is likely because, during tact training, vocal behavior is echoically prompted and reinforced in the presence of the non-verbal stimulus (e.g., picture). Thus, during tact instruction, children hear and then repeat the name of the picture while looking at it. Reinforcement is contingent on correct vocalizations but also strengthens attending to the picture. After many repetitions, the name of the picture (spoken by the therapist and the child) becomes discriminative for looking at the picture itself, which is a form of listener behavior that is functionally equivalent to the behavior of pointing or selecting (Miguel, 2016). Thus, listener behavior might be adventitiously reinforced during tact training.

Moreover, when a transfer from listener to speaker behavior is observed, it is likely because the child echoes during the instruction (Carneiro et al., submitted; Horne & Lowe, 1996; Miguel, 2016). When a therapist asks a child to point to a picture, and the child echoes the instruction (i.e., the name of the picture) while pointing at the picture, then reinforcement delivered contingent upon the pointing response (i.e., listener behavior) will also strengthen vocalizing the name of the object in its presence (i.e., speaker behavior). Thus, the picture itself might become a discriminative stimulus for saying its name (i.e., a tact) over several trials.

Thus, one way to induce BiN is by teaching children to echo the stimulus name during listener (i.e., auditory-visual conditional discrimination) trials. Carneiro et al. (submitted) investigated whether requiring echoic responses during listener instruction would facilitate the emergence of tacts and, ultimately, BiN in children with ASD. Three participants, aged 3–5 years, underwent listener instruction under two conditions: one requiring echoics and the other not. Results showed that the echoic condition led to slightly faster mastery of listener behavior for two participants, while both conditions produced similar outcomes in terms of the emergence of tacts. However, participants echoed at similar rates in both conditions, suggesting that echoics might have played a role in the emergence of tacts. In another unpublished study with neurotypical children, Engell (2024) showed that children could tact names of arbitrary pictures after hearing an adult talk about them with more accuracy when asked to echo these pictures' names while looking at them, as opposed to when not asked to echo, or asked to sing a song.

Several studies have demonstrated the effectiveness of multiple exemplar instruction (MEI) in producing BiN and generative verbal behavior across a variety of participants. This procedure involves the rapid and random rotation of instructions targeting different operants, such as listener behavior and tacts, across a series of consecutive trials (LaFrance & Tarbox, 2020). For instance, when teaching a child to respond to the stimulus "dog," the child might be instructed to engage in different types of responses, like finding a picture of a dog (listener behavior) and labeling a picture of a dog (tact). The antecedents and consequences vary to evoke the correct response for each operant, with generalized conditioned reinforcement following correct responses. MEI is especially noted for promoting functional interdependence between speaker and listener repertoires and across verbal operants, facilitating generativity, or the emergence of untaught verbal behaviors.

Greer et al. (2005) worked with three participants with language and developmental delays, showing that MEI led to bidirectionality between speaker and listener repertoires, with generalization to untrained stimuli. Nuzzolo-Gomez and Greer (2004) studied four participants aged 3–7 years, including both neurotypical children and those with ASD. They found that MEI facilitated the emergence of untaught mands and tacts, outperforming single-exemplar instruction (SEI). Olaff et al. (2017) replicated these findings with three children with ASD and developmental disabilities, demonstrating that BiN only emerged after MEI, even when other common teaching methods were used. In a similar study, Hawkins et al. (2009) exposed participants to a matching task during which stimuli were named by the experimenters (e.g., "Match [name]."). MEI resulted in elevated rates of correct tact and listener responding during probes. However, mastery was not attained until the procedures were adapted to incorporate echoics for one participant and signs for another. Even though MEI might strengthen the bidirectionality of these repertoires, participants were likely echoing the instruction while selecting the stimuli in an arrangement similar to Carneiro et al. (submitted).

As mentioned before, once children behave as listeners and speakers, they can learn incidentally. One procedure investigated for this purpose is the stimulus pairing observation procedure (SPOP). In a study by Solares and Fryling (2019), researchers presented stimuli to participants while labeling them by name. Each stimulus was presented during 15 trials within the condition before probes for tact and listener relations were conducted. They found that SPOP led to mastery-level responding for both speaker and listener trials with all three participants with ASD. When SPOP alone did not yield substantial gains in tact and listener responding, the addition of MEI, which would have served to establish BiN, led to the incidental acquisition of experimental targets.

Research has also shown that when stimuli occasion the same speaker and listener behaviors, participants would categorize them as the same. For example, oranges, apples, and bananas would all evoke the word "fruit" (speaker behavior), and such a word would also make a child orient toward these objects (listener behavior). Thus, when presented with a novel object (a durian) and told it is a fruit, a child would categorize it as such by putting it in the fruit bowl. Moreover, if the child likes fruits and has learned to eat them, they will try to do the same with the durian. In other words, the common name "fruit" has transformed the function of that object. A series of studies (e.g., Kobari-Wright & Miguel, 2014; Miguel & Kobari-Wright, 2013; Lee et al., 2015; Ribeiro & Miguel, 2020) has shown that it is not until children have acquired both speaker and listener behaviors that they can categorize. In Lee et al. (2015), four preschool children learned to select pictures of dogs when hearing their category names (e.g., hound dog, work dog, toy dog), after which they were tested to see whether they could tact each picture by category and visually match (categorize) them. After listener training, two children could not tact or categorize the pictures. In other words, the two components of BiN were not established. However, after they were taught how to tact the pictures by category (speaker), they could match them. These results support the notion that BiN is a necessary skill for the establishment of visual categorization (e.g., Miguel et al., 2008)

Assessment and Intervention on BiN Cusp

Practitioners might initially detect deficits related to BiN as they administer criterion-referenced assessments such as the VB-MAPP (Sundberg, 2008). When reviewing the tact and listener domains, they might note elevated performance in the listener domain compared to the tact domain or vice versa. These data would suggest that tact and listener repertoires remain independent. In other words, the child might not be speaking with understanding. The absence of BiN might also be detected through clinical record review. For example, targets might be mastered in the listener training program and then evaluated in the baseline for the tact program. If targets are mastered in the tact baseline, this is suggestive of BiN; if not, BiN appears absent. Importantly, as many variables might be unaccounted for from record review alone, we recommend directly evaluating BiN.

Before evaluating BiN, we recommend practitioners establish effective and efficient procedures to teach tacts and listener responding. If tacts cannot be readily established via transfer of stimulus control procedures, it is unlikely they will emerge following only listener training. Furthermore, suppose a high volume of trials is required. This suggests underlying barriers to learning that should be addressed before evaluating BiN (e.g., auditory-visual conditional discrimination errors, faulty echoics). Once tacts and listener responses can be quickly established through direct teaching, practitioners could simply probe new sets of stimuli as both tacts and listener responses prior to instruction (see Figure 9.1).

If teaching tacts is not followed by the emergence of listener behavior, or vice versa, the use of MEI is recommended (e.g., Greer et al., 2005; Fiorile & Greer, 2007) and integration of explicit requirements to echo during instruction (e.g., Carneiro et al., submitted; Hawkins, 2009), as described above. Once listener behavior emerges from tact instruction, and vice versa, BiN should be evaluated as a product of incidental learning (i.e., SPOP). If a child does not learn to tact and respond as a listener to stimulus targets simply by hearing others name the object, MEI should be used to establish this critical form of BiN. Importantly, this evaluation and intervention process should continue until BiN occurs in contexts common in early childhood education (e.g., story time, show and tell).

When BiN has been firmly established with object-name relations, practitioners can evaluate whether categorization and other cognitive skills are demonstrated. In these cases, programming would include teaching the child category names such as "This is a puzzle, it is a toy," and probing for sorting by category (Ribeiro & Miguel, 2020). Analogical reasoning related to categories might be targeted next. In a recent study by Zhirnova et al. (2025), typical preschool children developed simple visual analogies such as truck is to bus as dress is to pants (using an MTS task) after learning to tact each pair of stimuli as either "same" or "different." Interestingly, knowing how to label the individual pictures by name and category was insufficient for them to pass analogy tests. They needed to learn how pictures were related so that when seeing a pair consisting of a truck and a bus, children could tact them as being the same, the product of which occasioned the selection of the other pair whose members were also "same," in this case, dress and paint. Thus, the interrelation between speaker and listener repertoires seems crucial for developing higher-order cognitive skills.

Cusp: Intraverbal Emergence (IV-E)

As children learn the names of objects and their features, functions, and classes, intraverbals relating these stimuli might emerge without direct teaching (Conine et al., 2024). For example, when shown a picture of a bear, a child might be taught to respond "bear" when asked, "What is it?" and "berries" when asked, "What does it eat?", then subsequently respond correctly in the absence of the picture when asked, "What does a bear eat?" and "Who eats berries?" Conine et al. (2024) noted that the occurrences of these new responses cannot be attributed to either stimulus or response generalization. The emergence of new responses can be attributed to instruction in skills related to the same object. Skinner (1957) discussed the occurrence of contiguous verbal behaviors occurring in the same context and the potential for substitutability between said responses. Thus, responding "bear" and "berries" in the presence of the same picture might occur due to contiguous usage.

These responses might also have been established during initial tact training. When presented with the bear and asked, "What does it eat?" the child might have been covertly tacting the bear (a skill already established in their repertoire) such that the reinforcement provided for "berries" functioned to strengthen both responses. This conceptualization is consistent with the effects of BiN (Horne & Lowe, 1996; Miguel, 2016, 2018) and could also account for intraverbals emerging from listener instruction. After learning to select the bear picture when asked, "Which animal has cubs?" the child might later emit an intraverbal in response to the same question if they tacted "bear" in the presence of the picture. The reinforcement ostensibly provided for the selection response would function to strengthen this verbal response under the control of the question, leading to IV-E.

In neurotypical children, intraverbals of varying levels of complexity correspond with age (Sundberg & Sundberg, 2011). However, in children with ASD, age alone is not strongly predictive of the development of intraverbal complexity (Sundberg & Sundberg, 2011). Deficits in emitting intraverbals following training in related speaker and listener skills have been reported across the behavior analytic literature (Conine et al., 2024). These challenges are troubling, given the emphasis on intraverbals in the context of daily social interactions and academic instruction (Palmer, 2016; Skinner, 1957; Sundberg & Sundberg, 2011).

Though various efficacious strategies might be deployed to teach intraverbals directly (Jennings et al., 2022), this approach is resource-intensive and might result in isolated instructional gains. If intraverbals are directly taught and controlled by verbal stimuli, they might lack a connection to the physical world. A child might answer "What does a bear have?" with "claws" without having previously seen a picture of the bear or its claws. Though classification as an intraverbal requires control by antecedent verbal stimuli, the participation of the verbal stimuli within a broad class that includes a variety of stimulus forms is important for the response to be meaningful. Ultimately, the stimulus "bear" should occasion a wide variety of verbal and perceptual responses, not just one isolated target response.

Importantly, responses narrowly defined as intraverbals have a specific instructional history in which the verbal behavior was established under the control of a verbal antecedent with contingent reinforcement (Palmer, 2016). Thus, answering "bear" following specific training. However, verbal responses that occur under the control of a verbal antecedent without a specific training history are more accurately described as occurring under intraverbal control (Palmer, 2016). Intraverbal responses that emerge from the training of other conditional discriminations might align with this interpretation, as they have no specific reinforcement history.

Findings from Applied Research

Applied research evaluating IV-E has accelerated over the past decade (Conine et al., 2024; Jennings et al., 2022). Tact training has been applied to establish the emergence of intraverbals with participants with ASD in several studies (e.g., Conine et al., 2021; Grannan & Rehfeldt, 2012; Lee et al., 2022; May et al., 2013). In one study with two adolescents with ASD, May et al. (2013) taught two different tact responses in the presence of the same pictures of made-up monsters ("What is the name of this monster?" and "What does this monster eat?"). Once these tact responses were mastered, the researchers evaluated related intraverbals (e.g., "What does [name] eat?" and "Which monster eats [food]?") and observed mastery-level responding. Teaching participants to tact the name and a feature, function, or class for the same stimulus (also referred to as multiple tact training) was effective when combined with a matching-to-sample procedure in a study by Grannan and Rehfeldt (2012). Two young children with ASD were taught to tact the names of objects presented in pictures (e.g., "What is it?" and the child says "[name]") and their category (e.g., "What is a [name]?" and the child says "[category]"). Then, participants were taught to match members of the same categories. Following the combined intervention package, participants correctly listed members of respective categories when asked, "What are four [category]?" Lee et al. (2022) replicated and extended these results in a group format with three children with ASD. Collectively, these results suggest that tact training might result in IV-E for some individuals with ASD.

Listener training has also successfully established IV-E for participants with ASD (e.g., Conine et al., 2021; Smith et al., 2016; Vallinger-Brown & Rosales, 2014). In an example by Smith et al. (2016), participants were taught to select a picture from the array when a feature or function was dictated by the researcher (e.g., "What's a [category] that's [feature]?" or "What do you [function]?"). Following listener training, four of the five participants with ASD emitted correct intraverbals consisting of the object's name when asked the same question without the pictures. Importantly, all participants could tact the stimuli by name prior to the listener training. Vallinger-Brown and Rosales (2014) reported similar findings following listener training with three children with ASD. Results from these studies suggest that listener training might result in IV-E for individuals with ASD. However, when directly compared, Conine et al. (2021) found that tact training more reliably produced emergent intraverbals than listener training with three children with ASD.

Several studies have reported IV-E without direct teaching of the related features and functions (e.g., Frampton & Shillingsburg, 2020; Gavidia et al., 2022; Tullis et al., 2022; Vallinger-Brown & Rosales, 2014). Frampton and Shillingsburg (2020) incorporated instructive feedback related to features/functions into maintenance trials for previously mastered listener targets with two children with ASD. For example, after the participants pointed to an outline of Tennessee, the researcher provided praise and stated the capital (e.g., "The capital of that state is Nashville"). Following three sessions in which the IF was provided three times per target, probes for listener responding by feature, tact feature, name-feature, and feature-name intraverbals were conducted. For both participants, IF resulted in IV-E. These results have been replicated and extended by Gavidia et al. (2022) and Tullis et al. (2022).

Assessment and Intervention on IV-E Cusp

Practitioners might initially detect barriers to IV-E from disparities in domains on the VB-MAPP. For example, the VB-MAPP scores in Levels 2 and 3 might be observed for the tact, listener, and listener responding by feature, function, and class (LRFFC) domains, while scores in the intraverbal domain lag. These differential performances suggest that tact and listener instruction in object names, features, functions, and classes have not resulted in subsequent IV-E. Practitioners might also indirectly identify IV-E through a review of clinical records. Tact and listener responses might be mastered for object names and features, functions, and classes, yet when related intraverbals are evaluated in baseline, no correct responses are observed.

When directly evaluating IV-E, practitioners should begin by developing appropriate instructional targets with aligned discriminative stimuli (see Figure 9.2). For example, if teaching responses related to forest animals, researchers should select consistent features to instruct for teaching targets (e.g., claws for the bear and antlers for the deer). Then, they should review the verbal antecedent stimuli for consistency between programs. Listener responding by feature questions could match directly with feature-name intraverbal questions (e.g., "What has claws?" and the child touches the bear picture for the listener or says "bear" for the intraverbal). Tact feature questions could match closely with name-feature intraverbal questions with only the substitution of the animal's name (e.g., "What does it have?" vs. "What does a bear have?"). This approach

Template		
Target	**Antecedents**	**Response**
Listener Name-Object	"Point to [name]"	Points to object
Tact Object-Name	"What is it?" + show object	"[Name]"
Listener Feature-Object	"What has [feature]?"	Points to object
Tact Object-Feature	"What does it have?" + show object	"[Feature]"
Intraverbal Name-Feature	"What does [name] have?"	"[Feature]"
Intraverbal Feature-Name	"What has [feature]?"	"[Name]"

Example		
Target	**Antecedents**	**Response**
Listener Name-Object	"Point to *bear*"	Points to *bear*
Tact Object-Name	"What is it?" + show *bear*	"*Bear*"
Listener Feature-Object	"What has *claws*?"	Points to *bear*
Tact Object-Feature	"What does it have?" + show *bear*	"*Claws*"
Intraverbal Name-Feature	"What does *a bear* have?"	"*Claws*"
Intraverbal Feature-Name	"What has *claws*?"	"*Bear*"

Figure 9.2 Aligned listener, tact, and intraverbal targets for object-name and object-feature targets.

has been used across several applied studies with learners with and without disabilities (e.g., Frampton & Shillingsburg, 2020; May et al., 2013; Shillingsburg et al., 2018).

Next, practitioners should systematically train relations and periodically probe to determine if intraverbals have emerged (see Figure 9.2). Shillingsburg et al. (2018) progressively introduced listener, tact, and then intraverbal training across sets of clinically relevant stimuli with six children with ASD. Participants could tact and select stimuli by name prior to the evaluation. Listener training related to a feature/function was introduced, and effects on related tacts and intraverbals were probed. Next, tacts for the same feature/function were taught, and intraverbals were probed. When intraverbals were not emitted at high levels, they were directly trained. Following intervention with Set 1, the procedures were repeated with a second set and, in some cases, a third. By the study's conclusion, intraverbals emerged to some degree for all six participants following listener and/or tact training.

If progressively teaching listener responses and tacts does not eventually result in IV-E, practitioners could consider using MEI to establish the cusp (see Figure 9.1). When tact and listener training related to features/functions failed to produce emergent intraverbals, Shillingsburg and Frampton (2019) employed a version of MEI with two children with ASD. The researchers presented mastered tact and listener responses for names and features/functions in rapid and random alternation prior to probes for the related intraverbals. For example, prior to an intraverbal probe for the book target (e.g., "What do you read?" and the child says "book"), the researchers presented a tact trial (e.g., "What is it?" and the child says "book"), a listener responding by function trial (e.g., "What do you read" and the child points to book), a tact feature trial (e.g., "What do you do with this?" and the child says read), and listener by name trial (e.g., "Point to book" and the child points to book). For two participants, the interspersal procedure led to the mastery of the related intraverbals without any direct teaching, and effects on untreated intraverbals were also reported. Hewett and Hawkins (2023) reported similar successes using MEI after initial training failed to produce IV-E.

Once direct training of tact and listener relations consistently results in the emergence of intraverbals, practitioners could consider shifting to procedures that rely on dictation, such as instructive feedback (see Figure 9.1). With this approach, the primary target will relate to the object's name, and the instructive feedback will include the related feature or function. So, the client will tact the bear, and then the implementer will say, "Great! It has claws." Probes for secondary targets (i.e., tact object-feature relation) and IV-E would be conducted after several sessions with IF. If IF does not result in IV-E, practitioners can simply train the intraverbals that did not emerge and repeat the process with a new set of stimuli. This approach was adopted by Tullis et al. (2017), and eventually, IF alone was sufficient to produce IV-E.

Cusp: Recombinative Generalization

Recombinative generalization (RCG) has been defined as "the process of producing or responding to novel utterances when familiar stimuli are recombined in novel ways" (Goldstein & Mousetis, 1989, p. 346). For example, a child might say, "Dog jumping" upon seeing their pet engaging in the corresponding action. In the case of recombinative generalization, this noun-verb response will not have a history of explicit prompting and reinforcement. The "dog" and "jumping" responses might each have a prior instructional history as isolated targets. These are components that make up the combined composite response. As more component skills are learned (e.g., colors, adjectives), they will be recombined into more complex combined utterances like "The brown dog is jumping high." Combined utterances have been reported in the developmental literature beginning at approximately 2–3 years of age (Brown, 1973). For children with ASD, delays in word combinations have been reported (Paul, 2007). Once established, RCG has the potential to exponentially increase the efficiency of instruction in content areas relevant to verbal behavior intervention, including (a) expanding tact repertoires to phrase and sentence length with varied parts of speech (e.g., nouns, verbs, adjectives, adverbs, prepositions, and pronouns) and (b) following instructions as a listener that include varied parts of speech, reading, academic skills (e.g., time, math, money skills), and play (Curiel et al., 2020; Kemmerer et al., 2021).

Findings from Applied Research

Matrix training approaches have been used to evaluate RCG in children with ASD (see Curiel et al., 2020; Kemmerer et al., 2021). A matrix is a grid with instructional targets arranged on the x- and y-axis (see Figure 9.3). The targets within the interior of the matrix will be a composite of each of the targets on the axes. These are considered the priority for assessment and intervention (see Figure 9.1). For example, Axe and Sainato (2010) developed a matrix with nouns and verbs as the component skills on the axes. They evaluated the composite skill of following instructions, including both components (e.g., "Circle the star.").

Frampton et al. (2019) evaluated the RCG of colors and shapes using a matrix training approach. Prior to the initial baseline, participants could tact the colors and shapes that make up the matrix in isolation (e.g., tacting "red" when shown a red card and tacting "circle" when shown an outline of the shape). The researchers created three matrices with these known components, each with three known colors and three known shapes. In baseline, all the interior combined targets were probed (e.g., a red circle, a blue star, a blue circle, a red star). Low levels of correct responding were observed, suggesting that mastery of the component skills in isolation was insufficient for RCG. Three nonoverlapping targets on the diagonal of Matrix 1 were selected for tact training (see

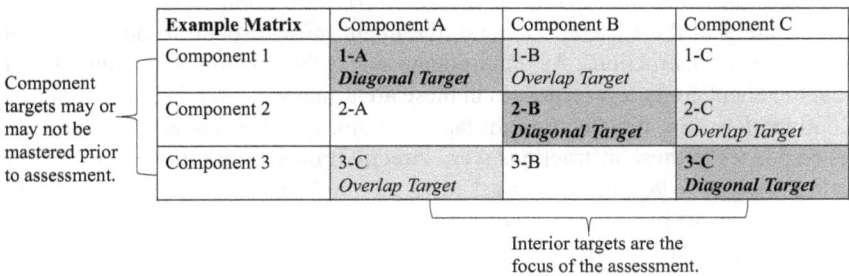

	Example Matrix	Component A	Component B	Component C
	Component 1	**1-A** *Diagonal Target*	1-B *Overlap Target*	1-C
Component targets may or may not be mastered prior to assessment.	Component 2	2-A	**2-B** *Diagonal Target*	2-C *Overlap Target*
	Component 3	3-C *Overlap Target*	3-B	**3-C** *Diagonal Target*

Interior targets are the focus of the assessment.

Figure 9.3 Matrix diagram.

Figure 9.3). These targets were considered nonoverlapping as each component skill was presented once with only one other component from the other axis of that matrix. Following mastery, three participants emitted high levels of correct responding with all targets within Matrix 1, consistent with RCG. Correct responses were also observed for Matrices 2 and 3, from which no targets were trained. However, three participants failed to demonstrate sustained, high levels of correct responding in the post-test. Additional training with the nonoverlapping targets was conducted for these participants, and robust improvements were observed across all matrices. Similar outcomes have been reported in studies evaluating RCG with noun-verb listener responses (e.g., Axe & Sainato, 2010), vocal tacts (e.g., Frampton et al., 2016), and tacts on a speech-generating device (SGD; Marya et al., 2021).

In some instances, training additional targets within the interior of the matrix has been necessary for RCG to develop. When teaching object-preposition tacts, Pauwels et al. (2015) found that nonoverlap training led to high levels of correct responding on the interior matrix targets for two participants. Additionally, correct responses were observed for the exterior components (i.e., the objects and the prepositions) that were initially unknown. Additional overlap training (see Figure 9.3) was necessary for the third participant before improved responding was observed for interior and exterior targets. The overlap approach resembles multiple exemplar training (MET), as the components are presented in various combinations and might prevent multicomponent responses from being acquired as a single unit. For example, the tact "strainer under box" might occur under the control of the presence of the strainer alone, regardless of its relative position to the box. Training responses in which the same object is in multiple locations (e.g., "strainer above box") might serve to bring responding appropriately under the control of both relevant stimuli (i.e., the object and the position).

Assessment and Intervention on RCG Cusp

Practitioners might initially detect challenges with RCG as they conduct the VB-MAPP (Sundberg, 2008). For a full score on Milestone 9 in the Tact Domain, the client must emit 50 noun-verb or verb-noun tacts. Similarly, on Milestone 9 in the Listener Domain, the client must respond to 50 verb-noun or noun-verb instructions. As practitioners assess these items, they might detect that the client emits few responses in these areas that were not directly trained as combinations. So, the client might tap the drum, spin the top, and roll the ball, as responses to these instructions were directly trained within clinical programming, but fail to respond when asked to tap the ball and roll the top as these combinations were not explicitly trained.

Direct assessment of RCG will follow the steps shown in Figure 9.1, tailored to meet the client's needs (Frampton & Axe, 2023). First, practitioners should select clinically appropriate or educationally relevant learning targets that align with client goals. Targets on the interior of the matrix should be evaluated in a pre-assessment probe followed by systematic instruction on strategically selected targets—either overlapping or nonoverlapping within the matrix (see Figure 9.1). Effects of instruction should be evaluated in a post-assessment probe, identical to pre-assessment. If high levels of correct responding are observed with the untrained targets, this outcome suggests the RCG cusp has been established. If poor performance is observed, the RCG cusp requires intervention. Intervention might include remedial training for the selected targets (e.g., Frampton et al., 2019), training additional targets within the matrix (e.g., Pauwels et al., 2015), or training across matrices (e.g., Frampton et al., 2016; Marya et al., 2021).

Cusp: Problem-Solving

Specific instructional histories alone are insufficient to account for the rich diversity of verbal responses emitted by neurotypical children. For example, a caregiver might ask their child, "What's your teacher's favorite color?" when shopping for a gift. As the child has never specifically been asked this question, it would be impossible to account for the subsequent response, "green," as a product of a training history. Skinner (1953, 1984) conceptualized questions of this nature as a type of problem and detailed a variety of precurrent responses that might occur to produce a solution. These precurrent responses function to produce new discriminative stimuli, which in turn evoke new responses until the terminal solution, or response, occurs and is reinforced (Skinner, 1953, 1984). These precurrent responses might take any variety of forms, "acting in any way which helps in the recalling of a previously learned answer" (Skinner, 1984, p. 583), and occur overtly or covertly (Axe et al., 2019; Palmer, 1991).

Precurrent responses play a crucial role in the emission of responses under intraverbal control (Palmer, 2016; Miguel, 2018). For example, if asked, "What is in your refrigerator?" an individual might pause to visually imagine the contents of their refrigerator and recall recently prepared meals. These precurrent behaviors (Skinner, 1984) provide additional sources of stimulus control that influence the answer on a day-to-day basis. These responses must be carefully differentiated from other types of intraverbals, as these multiply controlled responses must be sensitive to shifting environmental contingencies. For example, the answer to the question will change on Saturday after a pizza party on Friday night. Collectively, behaving to solve problems might account for many of the generative, complex performances observed across the lifespan (Skinner, 1984).

The preponderance of research with children with and without disabilities in problem-solving has been conducted within the framework of executive functioning (Hill, 2004; Zelazo et al., 1997). Research findings suggest that, over time, children demonstrate increasingly sophisticated problem-solving skills (Zelazo et al., 1997). However, findings with children diagnosed with ASD indicate delays and dysfunctions across a number of related measures (Hill, 2004). Importantly, these evaluations of problem-solving are not in alignment with Skinner's (1953, 1984) analysis, limiting the conclusions for behavior analytic research and practice.

Findings from Applied Research

Children with ASD have been taught to solve problems by engaging in several variations of precurrent responding to answer novel, unknown questions (Axe et al., 2019). Unknown questions have been conceptualized as establishing operations (EOs) as they evoke precurrent responding such that the solution and contingent reinforcement might be produced. In contrast, questions the participants can readily answer, referred to as known questions, are presented to function as abolishing operations (AOs) for precurrent responding. The questions exert sufficient discriminative control over responding that the solution response should be immediately occasioned, such that precurrent responding is not evoked (Axe et al., 2019). To answer questions about nearby social partners, Landa et al. (2020) taught children with ASD to mand for information as the precurrent response strategy. After being asked an unknown question (e.g., "What is Robin's favorite movie?"), participants were taught to approach the named social partner and mand for the information (e.g., "What's your favorite movie?"). The social partner responded (e.g., "Con Air"), and the experimenter repeated the original question to determine if the participant responded discriminatively given the dictated information. Reinforcers were provided contingent upon correct responding to both known and unknown questions. Across the series of studies, Landa et al. found that mands for social information were consistently occasioned as a form of precurrent responding, mands for information occurred more consistently on unknown question trials, and generalization across social partners reliably occurred.

Similar outcomes were observed in a series of studies evaluating a precurrent response in the form of a mand directly to the experimenter who presented the unknown question (e.g., "I don't know, please tell me"; Carnett & Ingvarsson, 2016; Ingvarsson & Hollobaugh, 2010). In this series of studies with children with ASD who were both vocal communicators and SGD users, participants eventually began to respond correctly to the previously unknown questions such that precurrent responding was no longer required.

Researchers have also evaluated forms of material manipulation to answer unknown questions. Levingston et al. (2009) taught students to manipulate a presented worksheet to answer mathematical word problems. Following a series of verbal instructions, participants learned to identify critical components of the word problems and translate them into an equation on the worksheet. Once in equation form, participants readily solved the math problems, and generalization to novel problems was observed. Frampton and Shillingsburg (2018) taught children with

ASD to sort and sequence picture cards to answer questions about how to do familiar activities (e.g., "How do you play bowling?). Participants were first trained to tact all the actions depicted in pictures of the routines. When minimal effects on explaining how were observed, participants were taught to sort out the pictures for the named activity and then sequence them in order of completion. Participants were then prompted to emit autoclitics as they tacted the mastered actions (e.g., "First…Next…Then…Last"). After correct responding was observed with the pictures present, the experimenter removed the materials and presented the same question as an intraverbal probe without any pictures present. After the training, participants correctly explained how to complete the targeted activities. The precurrent responses, sorting and sequencing, generalized across activities such that correct responding began to occur after only tact actions training.

Precurrent responding in the form of visual imagining has also been identified as a useful means of responding to unknown questions. Kisamore et al. (2011) taught neurotypical children to follow a series of steps related to listing members of various categories. When participants failed to list many exemplars, indicating a problem, participants were trained to emit intraverbal rules related to the precurrent response strategy, to tact pictures of members of each category, and to visually imagine the members within a relevant context. Once provided with a reminder to engage in the precurrent response chain when presented with the problem (i.e., rule prompts), high levels of correct responding were observed across categories. Keesey-Phelan et al. (2022) taught a child with ASD to engage in visual imagining as part of a precurrent response chain to answer recall questions about daily activities. During the target activities, an adult took pictures that would later be used to support visual imagining. Later in the day, a different adult asked the participant questions about the activities. When the participant had difficulty answering the questions, suggesting they were a problem, the adult taught the child a chain of precurrent responses involving visually imagining using the pictures. When prompts and visual supports were faded, the participant demonstrated greater recall across activities, settings, and adults. Though preliminary, these results suggest that visual imagining might be another viable means to teach children with ASD to solve problems (Miguel, 2018).

Assessment and Intervention on Problem-Solving Cusp

The conceptualization provided by Skinner (1953, 1984) and outcomes of empirical research (Axe et al., 2019) provide a framework that permits the flexible adaptation of problem-solving intervention into practice (see Figure 9.4). When assessing problem-solving, practitioners should begin by identifying personally relevant, ecologically valid problem contexts that the client experiences in daily life through a combination of interview and observation (see Figure 9.4). Examples might include specific daily living activities or structured learning tasks. Within these contexts, practitioners should identify the types of problems that commonly arise in the context that might be easily (and safely) arranged. Practitioners should consider the types of problems evaluated in the literature (e.g., Axe et al., 2019), problem-solving strategies used by others to solve this type of problem, strategies that are relevant for the learner, and the procedures commonly used to arrange EOs (Frampton et al., 2024).

When a problem is presented, like missing toothpaste during the toothbrushing routine, the practitioner should observe any behavior that occurs that modifies the environment so that a solution might eventually be evoked. For example, when the toothpaste is missing, does the participant search for it, mand for it, or mand for the location of more toothpaste? When a problem is presented in the form of a question with an unknown answer, does the client mand for information from the practitioner or a peer, manipulate the materials by flipping over the stimulus card to find the answer, or use a reference tool (e.g., tablet, smartphone, book)? Evaluating responding under these problem conditions can connect to particular Milestones on the VB-MAPP, such as searching for missing items (Play Milestone 6), mands for missing items (Mand Milestone 6), mands for actions (Mand Milestone 7), mands for information (Mand Milestone 11), and mands for termination (Mand Milestone 12). Notably, several Milestones on the VB-MAPP inherently require precurrent responses such as scanning complex arrays and referencing models (e.g., Visual Performance and Matching-to-Sample Milestones 11 and 23). Collectively, these might be conceptualized as forms of precurrent responses expected to occur when problem conditions are present (EO in place) and function to make the solution response more probable.

Based on the client's skills, the practitioner should match appropriate forms of precurrent responding to the targeted problems (e.g., manding, searching, use of tools). Discussions with the client and caregivers should inform what forms of precurrent response(s) would be appropriate and likely reinforced. For example, some caregivers might desire their child to learn to use stools to reach items on high shelves, while others would prefer the child mand for assistance.

As relevant problems and precurrent responses are selected, practitioners should thoughtfully sequence trials across problem variations and intermittently include abolishing operation (AO) trials (see Figure 9.4). Targeting multiple variations of problems (e.g., empty toothpaste, missing toothbrush) creates more opportunities for teaching and programs for generality from the outset. Including multiple problem variations also permits an evaluation of functional control, as responses on empty toothpaste trials can be compared to responses on missing toothbrush trials (Frampton et al., 2024). Including AO trials allows for an ongoing assessment of functional control over the precurrent response (Landa et al., 2020).

Once mastery of a precurrent response type is observed with a problem, practitioners should evaluate generality across problems and contexts. Once the client can mand for missing items related to toothbrushing, the same precurrent responses could be evaluated during a craft. New problems might also be introduced into the original contexts, and new forms of precurrent responding

Problem Context Template			
Problems	**Variation 1**	**Variation 2**	**Variation 3**
[Establishing Operation 1]			
Precurrent Response(s)			
[Establishing Operation 2]			
Precurrent Response(s)			
[Establishing Operation 3]			
Precurrent Response(s)			
None (Abolishing Operation)	*No precurrent responses should occur*		

Problem Context Example: Toothbrushing			
Problems	**Variation 1**	**Variation 2**	**Variation 3**
All items present except one is missing	Toothbrush	Toothpaste	Floss
Precurrent Response(s)	*Search drawers, mand to caregiver for missing item, mand to caregiver for assistance*		
Item is sabotaged	Toothbrush is gross	Toothpaste is empty	Floss is stuck
Precurrent Response(s)	*Search linen cabinet for replacement, mand to caregiver for new item, order replacement on app*		
None (Abolishing Operation)	*No precurrent responses should occur*		

Figure 9.4 Problem planning grid.

might be taught under the control of the established problem variations. Perhaps problems related to empty or missing floss might be introduced, and the client might be taught to search nearby drawers (see Lora et al., 2020 for related examples during vocational skills training). Ultimately, practitioners should personalize their approaches to teaching problem-solving to meet client needs while incorporating best practices identified in empirical evaluations and adhering to Skinner's (1953, 1984) conceptual analysis.

Integrating Cusps into ABA Practice

When instruction is designed for isolated operants, there are many opportunities for inefficiencies and redundancies. The same household items might be explicitly taught as listener targets, then later as tacts and intraverbals. As a result, the client might be exposed to unnecessary instruction. It might also be the case that the client is learning household items in one operant and exotic animals in another. This type of disparate instruction does not resemble the instructional practices clients will encounter in less restrictive settings, nor does it replicate how neurotypical children learn (Horne & Lowe, 1996). In early childhood education, similar learning targets are presented across numerous contexts within the daily routine, such as crafts, stories, and games (Bergeron et al., 1996; Kostelnik, 1991), so children learn the function of these objects while talking about them. For example, children in a preschool classroom might learn about winter by making snowman hats and having a pretend snowball fight at free play. In the contexts of these activities, the children will have ongoing opportunities to behave as a listener as they respond to instructions and as a speaker as they answer questions about the theme, mand for materials and actions related to the activities, etc. Verbal operants are integrated throughout the day as related content is taught.

As ABA programming progresses from assessing to establishing learning-to-learn behavior cusps as described above, the forms of standard instruction must also evolve. Instructional practices should be adapted to work in concert with these developing cusps and integrate them into regular programming. Suppose a client demonstrates a critical cusp such as BiN in tightly controlled analog assessment and intervention conditions (e.g., with three-picture sets). This finding must be extended to "everyday" learning contexts (e.g., household items while completing daily routines). Programming might become less tightly controlled as the practitioner identifies relevant content areas for instruction that might be presented as either tact or listener targets across exemplars. For example, a child who enjoys crafting might be taught the names of various tools (e.g., scissors, brush) and materials (e.g., paint, paper) while creating beautiful art projects. In comparison, a child who enjoys playing with dinosaurs might be taught the names of various species during play. Ongoing probes might be used to determine mastery in both speaker and listener operants. The assessment results of learning-to-learn behavioral cusps must be actively integrated into ongoing programming to maximize client outcomes and prepare them for instruction in less restrictive contexts.

Delivering high-quality, effective instruction for isolated verbal operants is a critical first step in developing programming for clients with ASD. Once efficacious instructional methodologies acceptable to the client have been established, practitioners must shift their priorities to establishing learning-to-learn cusps. Programming for these cusps will (a) promote the interdependence of verbal operants, (b) lead to the development of complex, composite responses, (c) result in more efficient mastery of content targets, and (d) prepare clients to eventually access instruction in less restrictive settings that do not offer intensive, isolated verbal operant instruction. Decades of applied research have paved the way by repeatedly demonstrating how these cusps might be assessed and remediated as needed. Adopting these practices into ongoing service delivery is consistent with the mission of providing effective treatment to clients (Van Houten et al., 1988). We hope this chapter serves to synthesize findings from across studies and guides application in clinical contexts.

Notes

1 It is the authors' hypothesis that this type of faulty instructional design stems from inadequate training on the use of verbal behavior assessment tools (Padilla, 2020), over-emphasis on establishing pure verbal operants (Michael et al., 2011), and inadequate practitioner training on procedures used to produce generative learning (Critchfield, 2018).
2 LaFrance and Miguel (2024) noted that the approach is not a new approach but a part of an evolution of empirical findings supporting Skinner's (1957) analysis of verbal behavior (e.g., Miguel, 2018), executed within the context of clinical care (e.g., Shillingsburg et al., 2020; Sundberg & Partington, 1998).

References

Anderson, D. K., Lord, C., Risi, S., Dilavore, P. S., Shulman, C., Thurm, A., et al. (2007). Patterns of growth in verbal abilities among children with autism spectrum disorder. *Journal of Consulting and Clinical Psychology, 75,* 594–604. https://doi.org/10.1037/0022-006x.75.4.594.

Axe, J. B., Phelan, S. H., & Irwin, C. L. (2019). Empirical evaluations of Skinner's analysis of problem solving. *The Analysis of Verbal Behavior, 35*(1), 39–56. https://doi.org/10.1007/s40616-018-0103-4

Axe, J. B., & Sainato, D. M. (2010). Matrix training of preliteracy skills with preschoolers with autism. *Journal of Applied Behavior Analysis, 43*(4), 635–652. https://doi.org/10.1901/jaba. 2010. 43- 635

Bergeron, B. S., Weemuth, S., Rhodes, M., & Rudenga, E. A. (1996). Language development and thematic instruction: Supporting young learners at risk. *Childhood Education, 72*(3), 141–145. https://doi.org/10.1080/00094056.1996.10521618

Bosch, S., & Hixson, M. D. (2004). The final piece to a complete science of behavior: Behavior development and behavioral cusps. *The Behavior Analyst Today, 5*(3), 244–254. https://doi.org/10.1037/h0100033

Brown, K., Rosales, R., Garcia, Y., & Schneggenburger, S. (2023). A review of applied Research on pairing procedures to facilitate emergent language. *The Psychological Record, 73*(1), 1–16. https://doi.org/10.1007/s40732-023-00543-3

Brown, R. (1973). *A first language: The early stages.* George Allen & Unwin.

Bruner, J. (1983). *Children's talk: learning to use language.* Norton & Company.

Carneiro, A., Cortez, M. D., & Miguel., C. F. (submitted). *The effects of requiring echoic responses during listener instruction on the emergence of tacts in children with autism.* Manuscript submitted for publication.

Carnett, A., & Ingvarsson, E. T. (2016). Teaching a child with autism to mand for answers to questions using a speech-generating device. *The Analysis of Verbal Behavior*, *32*(2), 233–241. https://doi.org/10.1007/s40616-016-0070-6

Chomsky, N. (1965). *Aspects of the theory of syntax*. Massachusetts Institute of Technology

Conine, D. E., Frampton, S. E., Buote, K. A., & Keller, C. E. (2024). A scoping review of empirical research on emergent intraverbal behavior. *Behavioral Interventions*, *39*(2), e1986. https://doi.org/10.1002/bin.1986

Conine, D. E., Vollmer, T. R., Dela Rosa, C. M., & Slanzi, C. M. (2021). The effects of listener and tact training on the emergence of intraverbals among children with autism. *Behavior Analysis: Research and Practice*, *21*(1), 26–41. https://doi.org/10.1037/bar0000201

Contreras, B. P., Cooper, A. J., & Kahng, S. (2020). Recent research on the relative efficiency of speaker and listener instruction for children with autism spectrum disorder. *Journal of Applied Behavior Analysis*, *53*(1), 584–589. https://doi.org/10.1002/jaba.543

Critchfield, T. S. (2018). Efficiency is everything: Promoting efficient practice by harnessing derived stimulus relations. *Behavior Analysis in Practice*, *11*, 206–210. https://doi.org/10.1007/s40617-018-0262-8

Curiel, E. S., Axe, J. B., Sainato, D. M., & Goldstein, H. (2020). Systematic review of matrix training for individuals with autism spectrum disorder. *Focus on Autism & Other Developmental Disabilities*, *35*(1), 55–64. https://doi.org/10.1177/1088357619881216

Delfs, C. H., Conine, D. E., Frampton, S. E., Shillingsburg, M. A., & Robinson, H. C. (2014). Evaluation of the efficiency of listener and tact instruction for children with autism. *Journal of Applied Behavior Analysis*, *47*(4), 793–809. https://doi.org/10.1002/jaba.166

DeSouza, A. A., Akers, J. S., & Fisher, W. W. (2017). Empirical application of Skinner's verbal behavior to interventions for children with autism: A review. *The Analysis of Verbal Behavior*, *33*(2), 229–259. https://doi.org/10.1007/s40616-017-0093-7

Eaves, L. C., & Ho, H. H. (2004). The very early identification of autism: Outcome to age 41/2–5. *Journal of Autism and Developmental Disorders*, *34*(4), 367–378. https://doi.org/10.1023/B:JADD.0000037414.33270.a8

Engell, T. S. (2024). The role of the echoic in the acquisition of tacts. [Unpublished master's thesis]. California State University, Sacramento.

Finn, H. E., Miguel, C. F., & Ahearn, W. H. (2012). The emergence of untrained mands and tacts in children with autism. *Journal of Applied Behavior Analysis*, *45*(2), 265–280. https://doi.org/10.1901/jaba.2012.45-265

Fiorile, C. A., & Greer, R. D. (2007). The induction of naming in children with no prior tact responses as a function of multiple exemplar histories of instruction. *The Analysis of Verbal Behavior*, *23*(1), 71–87. https://doi.org/10.1007/BF03393048

Frampton, S. E., & Axe, J. B. (2023). A tutorial for implementing matrix training in practice. *Behavior Analysis in Practice*, *16*(1), 334–345. https://doi.org/10.1007/s40617-022-00733-5

Frampton, S. E., Davis, C. R., Meleshkevich, O., & Axe, J. B. (2024). A clinical tutorial on methods to capture and contrive establishing operations to teach mands. *Behavior Analysis in Practice*, *17*(4), 1270–1282. https://doi.org/10.1007/s40617-024-00985-3

Frampton, S. E., Robinson, H. C., Conine, D. E., & Delfs, C. H. (2017). An abbreviated evaluation of the efficiency of listener and tact instruction for children with autism. *Behavior Analysis in Practice, 10*(2), 131–144. https://doi.org/10.1007/s40617-017 -0175-y

Frampton, S. E., & Shillingsburg, M. A. (2018). Teaching children with autism to explain how: A case for problem solving? *Journal of Applied Behavior Analysis, 51*(2), 236– 254. https://doi.org/10.1002/jaba.445

Frampton, S. E., & Shillingsburg, M. A. (2020). Promoting the development of verbal responses using instructive feedback. *Journal of Applied Behavior Analysis, 53*(2), 1029–1041. https://doi.org/10.1002/jaba.659

Frampton, S. E., Thompson, T. M., Bartlett, B. L., Hansen, B., & Shillingsburg, M. A. (2019). The use of matrix training to teach color shape tacts to children with autism. *Behavior Analysis in Practice, 12*(2), 320–330. https://doi.org/10.1007/s40617-018 -00288-4

Frampton, S. E., Wymer, S. C., Hansen, B., & Shillingsburg, M. A. (2016). The use of matrix training to promote generative language with children with autism. *Journal of Applied Behavior Analysis, 49*(4), 869–883. https://doi.org/10.1002/jaba.340

Gavidia, V. L., Bergmann, S., & Rader, K. A. (2022). The use of instructive feedback to promote emergent tact and intraverbal control: A replication. *The Analysis of Verbal Behavior, 38*(2), 95–120. https://doi.org/10.1007/s40616-022-00171-y

Goldstein, H. (1983). Recombinative generalization: Relationships between environmental conditions and the linguistic repertoires of language learners. *Analysis and Intervention in Developmental Disabilities, 3*(4), 279–293. https://doi.org/10 .1016/0270-4684(83)900022

Goldstein, H., & Mousetis, L. (1989). Generalized language learning by children with severe mental retardation: Effects of peers' expressive modeling. *Journal of Applied Behavior Analysis, 22*(3), 245–259. https://doi.org/10.1901/jaba.1989.22-245

Grannan, L., & Rehfeldt, R. A. (2012). Emergent intraverbal responses via tact and match-to-sample instruction. *Journal of Applied Behavior Analysis, 45*(3), 601–605. https://doi.org/10.1901/jaba.2012.45-601

Greer, R. D., Stolfi, L., Chavez-Brown, M., & Rivera-Valdes, C. (2005). The emergence of the listener to speaker component of naming in children as a function of multiple exemplar instruction. *The Analysis of Verbal Behavior, 21*(1), 123–134. https://doi .org/10.1007/BF03393014

Hart, B., & Risley, T. R. (1995). *Meaningful differences in the everyday experiences of young American children.* Paul H. Brookes Publishing.

Hawkins, E., Kingsdorf, S., Charnock, J., Szabo, M., & Gautreaux, G. (2009). Effects of multiple exemplar instruction on naming. *European Journal of Behavior Analysis, 10*(2), 265–273. https://doi.org/10.1080/15021149.2009.11434324

Hewett, K., & Hawkins, E. (2023). The use of multiple exemplar instruction to induce emergent listener discriminations and emergent intraverbal vocal responses in autistic children. *The Analysis of Verbal Behavior, 40*(1), 63–75. https://doi.org/10.1007/ s40616-023-00199-8

Hill, E. L. (2004). Executive dysfunction in autism. *Trends in Cognitive Sciences, 8*(1), 26–32. https://doi.org/10.1016/j.tics.2003.11.003

Hixson, M. D. (2004). Behavioral cusps, basic behavioral repertoires, and cumulative-hierarchical learning. *The Psychological Record*, *54*(3), 387–403. https://doi.org/10.1007/BF03395481

Hoff, E. (2006). How social contexts support and shape language development. *Developmental Review*, *26*(1), 55–88. https://doi.org/10.1016/j.dr.2005.11.002

Horne, P. J., & Lowe, C. F. (1996). On the origins of naming and other symbolic behavior. *Journal of the Experimental Analysis of Behavior*, *65*(1), 185–241. https://doi.org/10.1901/jeab.1996.65-185

Howlin, P. (2003). Outcome in high-functioning adults with autism with and without early language delays: Implications for the differentiation between autism and Asperger syndrome. *Journal of Autism and Developmental Disorders*, *33*(1), 3–13. https://doi.org/10.1023/A:1022270118899

Ingvarsson, E. T., & Hollobaugh, T. (2010). Acquisition of intraverbal behavior: Teaching children with autism to mand for answers to questions. *Journal of Applied Behavior Analysis*, *43*(1), 1–17. https://doi.org/10.1901/jaba.2010.43-1

Jennings, A. M., Miguel, C. F. (2017). Training intraverbal bidirectional naming to establish generalized equivalence class performances. *Journal of the Experimental Analysis of Behavior*, *108*(2), 269–289. https://doi.org/10.1002/jeab.277

Jennings, A. M., Vladescu, J. C., Miguel, C. F., Reeve, K. F., & Sidener, T. M. (2022). A systematic review of empirical intraverbal research: 2015–2020. *Behavioral Interventions*, *37*(1), 79–104. https://doi.org/10.1002/bin.1815

Keesey-Phelan, S. H., Axe, J. B., & Williams, A. L. (2022). The effects of teaching a problem-solving strategy on recalling past events with a child with autism. *The Analysis of Verbal Behavior*, *38*(2), 190–198. https://doi.org/10.1007/s40616-018-0103-4

Kelley, M. E., Shillingsburg, M. A., Jicel Castro, M., Addison, L. R., & LaRue Jr., R. H. (2007). Further evaluation of emerging speech in children with developmental disabilities: Training verbal behavior. *Journal of Applied Behavior Analysis*, *40*(3), 431–445. https://doi.org/10.1901/jaba.2007.40-431

Kemmerer, A. R., Vladescu, J. C., Carrow, J. N., Sidener, T. M., & Deshais, M. A. (2021). A systematic review of the matrix training literature. *Behavioral Interventions*, *36*(2), 473–495. https://doi.org/10.1002/bin.1780

Kisamore, A. N., Carr, J. E., & LeBlanc, L. A. (2011). Training preschool children to use visual imagining as a problem-solving strategy for complex categorization tasks. *Journal of Applied Behavior Analysis*, *44*(2), 255–278. https://doi.org/10.1901/jaba.2011.44-255

Kobari-Wright, V. V., & Miguel, C. F. (2014). The effects of listener training on the emergence of categorization and speaker behavior in children with autism. *Journal of Applied Behavior Analysis*, *47*(2), 431–436. https://doi.org/10.1002/jaba.115

Kostelnik, M. (1991*). Teaching young children using themes*. Good Year Books.

LaFrance, D. L., & Miguel, C. F. (2024). Teaching verbal behavior to children with autism spectrum disorder. In D. R. Dixon, P. Sturmey, & J. L. Matson (Eds.). *Handbook of early intervention for autism spectrum disorders: research, policy, and practice* (2nd ed., pp. 343–378). Springer.

LaFrance, D. L., & Tarbox, J. (2020). The importance of multiple exemplar instruction in the establishment of novel verbal behavior. *Journal of Applied Behavior Analysis*, *53*(1), 10–24. https://doi.org/10.1002/jaba.611

Landa, R. K., Frampton, S. E., & Shillingsburg, M. A. (2020). Teaching children with autism to mand for social information. *Journal of Applied Behavior Analysis, 53*(4), 2271–2286. https://doi.org/10.1002/jaba.733

Lee, G. P., Miguel, C. F., Darcey, E. K., & Jennings, A. M. (2015). A further evaluation of the effects of listener training on derived categorization and speaker behavior in children with autism. *Research in Autism Spectrum Disorders, 19*, 72–81. https://doi.org/10.1016/j.rasd.2015.04.007

Lee, G. T., Hu, X., & Shen, C. (2022). Brief report: Increasing intraverbal responses to subcategorical questions via tact and match-to-sample instruction. *Journal of Autism and Developmental Disorders, 54*(1), 4740–4751. https://doi.org/10.1007/s10803-022-05827-1

Levingston, H. B., Neef, N. A., & Cihon, T. M. (2009). The effects of teaching precurrent behaviors on children's solution of multiplication and division word problems. *Journal of Applied Behavior Analysis, 42*(2), 361–367. https://doi.org/10.1901/jaba.2009.42-361

Lora, C. C., Kisamore, A. N., Reeve, K. F., & Townsend, D. B. (2020). Effects of a problem-solving strategy on the independent completion of vocational tasks by adolescents with autism spectrum disorder. *Journal of Applied Behavior Analysis, 53*(1), 175–187. https://doi.org/10.1002/jaba.558

Luyster, R., Lopez, K., & Lord, C. (2007). Characterizing communicative development in children referred for autism spectrum disorders using the MacArthur-Bates Communicative Development Inventory (CDI). *Journal of Child Language, 34*(3), 623–654. https://doi.org/10.1017/S0305000907008094

Marya, V., Frampton, S., & Shillingsburg, A. (2021). Matrix training to teach tacts using speech generating devices: Replication and extension. *Journal of Applied Behavior Analysis, 54*(3), 1235–1250. https://doi.org/10.1002/jaba.819

May, R. J., Hawkins, E., & Dymond, S. (2013). Brief report: Effects of tact training on emergent intraverbal vocal responses in adolescents with autism. *Journal of Autism and Developmental Disorders, 43*(4), 996–1004. https://doi.org/10.1007/s10803-012-1632-7

Michael, J., Palmer, D. C., & Sundberg, M. L. (2011). The multiple control of verbal behavior. *The Analysis of Verbal Behavior, 27*, 3–22. https://doi.org/10.1007/BF03393089

Miguel, C. F. (2016). Common and intraverbal bidirectional naming. *The Analysis of Verbal Behavior, 32*(2), 125–138. https://doi.org/10.1007/s40616-016-0066-2

Miguel, C. F. (2018). Problem-solving, bidirectional naming, and the development of verbal repertoires. *Behavior Analysis: Research and Practice, 18*(4), 340–353. https://doi.org/10.1037/bar0000110

Miguel, C. F., & Kobari-Wright, V. V. (2013). The effects of tact training on the emergence of categorization and listener behavior in children with autism. *Journal of Applied Behavior Analysis, 46*(3), 669–673. https://doi.org/10.1002/jaba.62

Miguel, C. F., Petursdottir, A. I., Carr, J. E., & Michael, J. (2008). The role of naming in stimulus categorization by preschool children. *Journal of the Experimental Analysis of Behavior, 89*(3), 383–405. https://doi.org/10.1901/jeab.2008-89-383

Nuzzolo-Gomez, R., & Greer, R. D. (2004). Emergence of untaught mands or tacts of novel adjective-object pairs as a function of instructional history. *The Analysis of Verbal Behavior, 20*, 63–76. https://doi.org/10.1007/BF03392995

Olaff, H. S., Ona, H. N., & Holth, P. (2017). Establishment of naming in children with autism through multiple response-exemplar training. *Behavioral Development Bulletin, 22*(1), 67. https://doi.org/10.1037/bdb0000044

Padilla, K. L. (2020). Global assessment use and practices in applied behavior analysis: Surveying the field. *Research in Autism Spectrum Disorders, 79*, 1–12. https://doi.org /10.1016/j.rasd.2020.101676

Palmer, D. C. (1991). A behavioral interpretation of memory. In L. J. Hayes & P. N. Chase (Eds.), *Dialogues on verbal behavior: The first international institute on verbal relations* (pp. 261–279). Context Press.

Palmer, D. C. (2005). Ernst Moerk and the puzzle of zero-trial learning. *The Analysis of Verbal Behavior, 21*(1), 9–12. https://doi.org/10.1007/BF03393006

Palmer, D. C. (2012). The role of atomic repertoires in complex behavior. *The Behavior Analyst, 35*, 59–73. https://doi.org/10.1007/BF03392266

Palmer, D. C. (2016). On intraverbal control and the definition of the intraverbal. *The Analysis of Verbal Behavior, 32*(2), 96–106. https://doi.org/10.1007/s40616-016 -0061-7

Partington, J. W. (2010). *The assessment of basic language and learning skills–revised.* Behavior Analysts, Inc.

Paul, R. (2007). Communication and its development in autism spectrum disorders. In F. R. Volkmar (Ed.), *Autism and pervasive developmental disorders* (2nd ed., pp. 129– 155). Cambridge University Press. https://doi.org/10.1017/CBO9780511544446.005

Pauwels, A. A., Ahearn, W. H., & Cohen, S. J. (2015). Recombinative generalization of tacts through matrix training with individuals with autism spectrum disorder. *The Analysis of Verbal Behavior, 31*(2), 200–214. https://doi.org/10.1007/s40616-015 -0038-y

Petursdottir, A. I. (2018). The current status of the experimental analysis of verbal behavior. *Behavior Analysis: Research and Practice, 18*(2), 151. https://doi.org/10 .1037/bar0000109

Petursdottir, A. I., & Carr, J. E. (2011). A review of recommendations for sequencing receptive and expressive language instruction. *Journal of Applied Behavior Analysis, 44*(4), 859–876. https://doi.org/10.1901/jaba.2011.44-859

Petursdottir, A. I., & Devine, B. (2017). The impact of verbal behavior on the scholarly literature from 2005 to 2016. *The Analysis of Verbal Behavior, 33*(2), 212–228. https://doi.org/10.1007/s40616-017-0089-3

Ribeiro, D. M., & Miguel, C. F. (2020). Using multiple-tact training to produce emergent visual categorization in children with autism. *Journal of Applied Behavior Analysis, 53*(3), 1768–1779. https://doi.org/10.1002/jaba.687

Rosales-Ruiz, J., & Baer, D. M. (1997). Behavioral cusps: A developmental and pragmatic concept for behavior analysis. *Journal of Applied Behavior Analysis, 30*(3), 533–544. https://doi.org/10.1901/jaba.1997.30-533

Shillingsburg, M. A., & Frampton, S. E. (2019). The effects of the interspersal of related responses on the emergence of intraverbals for children with autism spectrum disorder. *The Analysis of Verbal Behavior, 35*(2), 172–195. https://doi.org/10.1007/ s40616-019-00110-4

Shillingsburg, M. A., Frampton, S. E., Cleveland, S. A., & Cariveau, T. (2018). A clinical application of procedures to promote the emergence of untrained intraverbal relations with children with autism. *Learning and Motivation, 62,* 51–66. https://doi.org/10.1016/j.lmot.2017.02.003

Skinner, B. F. (1953). Some contributions of an experimental analysis of behavior to psychology as a whole. *American Psychologist, 8*(2), 69–78. https://doi.org/10.1037/h0054118

Skinner, B. F. (1957). *Verbal behavior.* Appleton-Centruy-Crofts.

Skinner, B. F. (1984). An operant analysis of problem solving. *Behavioral and Brain Sciences, 7*(4), 583–591. https://doi.org/10.1017/S0140525X00027412

Smith, D. P., Eikeseth, S., Fletcher, S. E., Montebelli, L., Smith, H. R., & Taylor, J. C. (2016). Emergent intraverbal forms may occur as a result of listener training for children with autism. *The Analysis of Verbal Behavior, 32*(1), 27–37. https://doi.org/10.1007/s40616-016-0057-3

Solares, L., & Fryling, M. J. (2019). Further evaluation of the stimulus pairing observation procedure with children with autism spectrum disorder. *The Analysis of Verbal Behavior, 35*(1), 85–93. https://doi.org/10.1007/s40616-018-0101-6

Sprinkle, E. C., & Miguel, C. F. (2012). The effects of listener and speaker training on emergent relations in children with autism. *The Analysis of Verbal Behavior, 28*(1), 111–117. https://doi.org/10.1007/BF03393111

Stromswold, K. (2001). The heritability of language: A review and metaanalysis of twin, adoption, and linkage studies. *Language,* 647–723. https://www.jstor.org/stable/3086845

Sundberg, M. (2008). *VB-MAPP Verbal Behavior Milestones Assessment and Placement Program: A language and social skills assessment program for children with autism or other developmental disabilities: Guide.* AVB Press.

Sundberg, M. L., & Michael, J. (2001). The benefits of Skinner's analysis of verbal behavior for children with autism. *Behavior Modification, 25*(5), 698–724. https://doi.org/10.1177/0145445501255003

Sundberg, M. L., & Partington, J. W. (1998). *Teaching language to children with autism or other developmental disabilities.* Behavior Analysts, Inc.

Sundberg, M. L., & Sundberg, C. A. (2011). Intraverbal behavior and verbal conditional discriminations in typically developing children and children with autism. *The Analysis of Verbal Behavior, 27*(1), 23–44. https://doi.org/10.1007/BF03393090

Tager-Flusberg, H., & Caronna, E. (2007). Language disorders: autism and other pervasive developmental disorders. *Pediatric Clinics of North America, 54*(3), 469–481. https://doi.org/10.1016/j.pcl.2007.02.011

Tager-Flusberg H., Edelson L., & Luyster R. (2011). Language and communication in autism spectrum disorders. In D. Amaral, G. Dawson, & D. Geschwind (Eds.), *Autism spectrum disorders* (pp. 172–185). Oxford University Press.

Tamis-LeMonda, C. S., Bornstein, M. H., & Baumwell, L. (2001). Maternal responsiveness and children's achievement of language milestones. *Child Development, 72*(3), 748–767. https://doi.org/10.1111/1467-8624.00313

Tullis, C. A., Frampton, S. E., Delfs, C. H., & Shillingsburg, M. A. (2017). Teaching problem explanations using instructive feedback. *The Analysis of Verbal Behavior, 33*(1), 64–79. https://doi.org/10.1007/s40616-016-0075-1

Tullis, C. A., Gibbs, A. R., Priester, J., & Tillem, A. (2022). Emergence of verbal responses using instructive feedback: A replication and extension. *Behavioral Interventions, 37*(2), 271–289. https://doi.org/10.1002/bin.1836

Vallinger-Brown, M., & Rosales, R. (2014). An investigation of stimulus pairing and listener training to establish emergent intraverbals in children with autism. *The Analysis of Verbal Behavior*, *30*(2), 148–159. https://doi.org/10.1007/s40616-014 -0014-y

Van Houten, R., Axelrod, S., Bailey, J. S., Favell, J. E., Foxx, R. M., Iwata, B. A., & Lovaas, O. I. (1988). The right to effective behavioral treatment. *Journal of Applied Behavior Analysis*, *21*(4), 381–384. http://dx.doi.org/10.1901/jaba.1988.21-381

Visser-Bochane, M. I., Reijneveld, S. A., Krijnen, W. P., Van der Schans, C. P., & Luinge, M. R. (2020). Identifying milestones in language development for young children ages 1 to 6 years. *Academic Pediatrics*, *20*(3), 421–429. https://doi.org/10 .1016/j.acap.2019.07.003

Waxman, S., Fu, X., Arunachalam, S., Leddon, E., Geraghty, K., & Song, H. J. (2013). Are nouns learned before verbs? Infants provide insight into a longstanding debate. *Child Development Perspectives*, *7*(3), 155–159. https://doi.org/10.1111/cdep.12032

Zelazo, P. D., Carter, A., Reznick, J. S., & Frye, D. (1997). Early development of executive function: A problem-solving framework. *Review of General Psychology*, *1*(2), 198–226. https://doi.org/10.1037/1089-2680.1.2.198

Zhirnova, T., Miguel, C. F., & Cordeiro, M. C. (2025). The role of bidirectional naming in the emergence of analogical reasoning in children. *Journal of the Experimental Analysis of Behavior*, *123*(2), 324–336. https://doi.org/jeab.70003

Chapter 10

The Role of Multiple Control in Teaching Verbal Behavior

Vincent J. Carbone and David Roth

Dedication

To my Grandsons,

Kellen and Noah,

my primary sources.

VJC

To all practitioners interested in the molecular details of their practice.

DJR

Throughout previous chapters of this book, you have read detailed descriptions of Skinner's elementary verbal operant classes, in which each operant class is defined specifically by its unique antecedent controlling variable. Early in acquiring primary verbal operants, especially with autistic learners, rigid functional independence between operants is typically demonstrated. According to Skinner (1957), "When the response *Doll!* has been acquired as a mand, however, we do not expect that the child then spontaneously possesses a corresponding tact of a similar form" (p. 187). Based on this notion of functional independence among operants, one might conclude that, for individuals who do not acquire verbal behavior in a typical manner as their peers, every verbal response and its meaning would need to be explicitly taught. Of course, this would be impractical and, frankly, impossible.

The controlling variables for each of the primary verbal operant classes are simple and discrete. However, the controlling variables involved in the everyday responses that we tend to classify as "mands," "tacts," "intraverbals," etc., are more complex and extensive than what has been discussed thus far. Skinner (1957) addressed this issue in depth in Chapters 9–11, but he also warned the reader early in the book that verbal behavior is not usually acquired under simple stimulus control. He explained,

DOI: 10.4324/9781003433668-12

Once a repertoire of verbal behavior has been set up, a host of new problems arise from the interaction of its parts. Verbal behavior is usually the effect of *multiple causes*. Separate variables combine to extend their functional control, and new forms of behavior emerge from the recombination of old fragments.

(p. 10)

Given the complexities of verbal behavior in typical language development, there are several questions one should ask when programming interventions for individuals with verbal deficits: What methods produce responses that have never been directly taught? What accounts for the complexity of verbal responding demonstrated by individuals without verbal deficits? What should be included in verbal behavior programs to support a repertoire of complex responding, including conversational skills, talking about past and future events, responding to the novel verbal responses of others, speaking in grammatically correct sentences, reading and comprehending what is read, and describing the feelings and emotions of oneself and others?

Two Types of Multiple Control

Skinner's (1957) discussion of multiple causation emphasizes two general types of multiple control.

Two facts emerge from our survey of the basic functional relations in verbal behavior: (1) the strength of a single response may be, and usually is, a function of more than one variable, and (2) a single variable usually affects more than one response (p. 227).

Michael et al. (2011) classified these two categories as (a) convergent multiple control and (b) divergent multiple control.

Figures 10.1–10.3 illustrate the differences between an emitted elementary operant (not under multiple control), divergent multiple control, and convergent multiple control. Within these diagrams, we differentiate between responses emitted in the presence of a stimulus (indicated by solid arrows) and responses merely strengthened by a stimulus (indicated by dashed arrows). For instance, in the elementary tact example (Figure 10.1), the presentation of the dog evokes the child's spoken response, "dog."

However, individuals with increasingly complex verbal repertoires eventually learn multiple responses to a single image. For instance, in one context, a child might respond to the picture by saying, "dog" (e.g., when asked, "What type of animal is it?"). In another context, the child might respond by saying, "woof" (e.g., when asked, "What does this animal say?"). These are examples of the type of multiple control called *conditional discriminations*. When the child has learned multiple responses to a single stimulus, the mere presentation of the stimulus may divergently increase the strength of each of those responses

Figure 10.1 The elementary tact.
Note: The picture of the dog functions as a non-verbal discriminative stimulus that directly evokes the spoken response, "Dog."

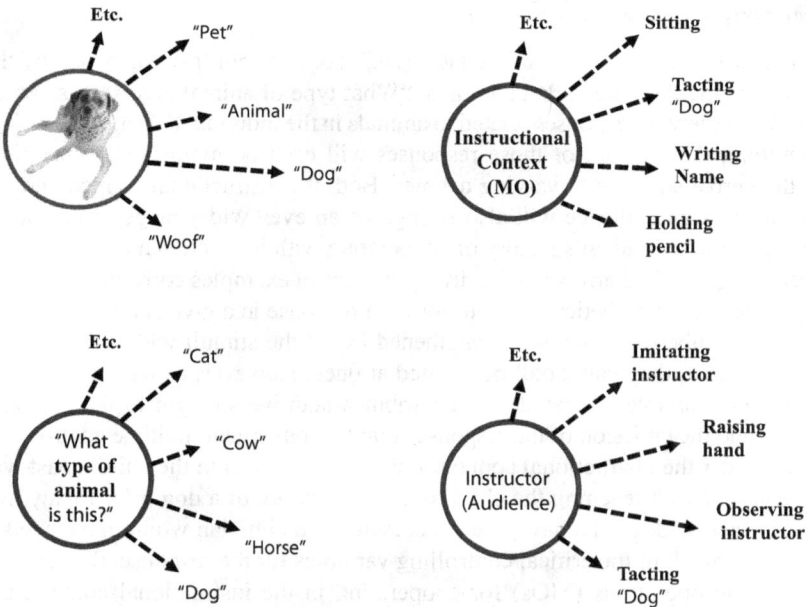

Figure 10.2 Divergent control.
Note: Owing to a history of reinforcement for several different responses to a given discriminative stimulus, the presentation of each variable independently increases the strength of several responses within the individual's repertoire.

momentarily, even if the responses are not emitted at that time (Palmer, 2009, 2021). Figure 10.2 illustrates how various stimuli within an instructional context each divergently strengthens a range of behaviors independently of one another.

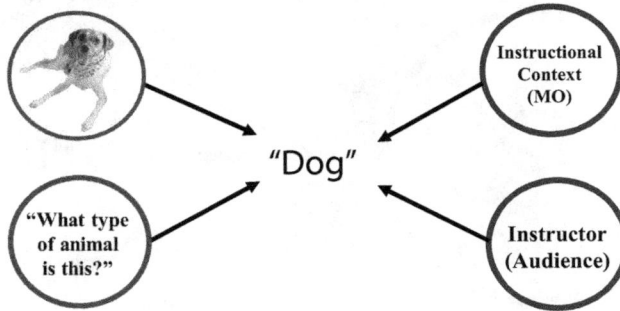

Figure 10.3 Convergent multiple control.
Note: The additive effects of the non-verbal discriminative stimulus (i.e., picture of dog), the verbal discriminative stimulus (i.e., "What type of animal is this?"), the audience variable (i.e., the instructor), and the motivating operation (i.e., the instructional context) multiply control the emitted response, "Dog."

For instance, in addition to the tacts (i.e., "dog," "woof") strengthened by the picture of the dog, the verbal stimulus, "What type of animal is this?" has occasioned a variety of responses related to animals in the individual's learning history. Therefore, the strength of those responses will each be momentarily increased by the verbal stimulus to varying degrees. Both the instructional context and the instructor as an audience will also strengthen an even wider range of responses related to the individual's history of cooperating with instructional tasks. The different lengths of the arrows in the divergent control examples correspond to varying degrees of hypothetical strength for each response in a given context. Despite the vast number of responses strengthened by all the stimuli within the instructional context, they cannot all be emitted at once. However, as we see in Figure 10.3, each variable independently contributes additive strength to the response "dog," and the emission of the response is under convergent multiple control.

Consider the instructional context in which a clinician in the child's past was once tasked with teaching the child to tact the picture of a dog prior to any history of tacting dogs. To have been successful, the clinician would have needed to recognize all of the critical controlling variables for the response: the relevant motivating operations (MOs) for cooperating in the instructional context, the non-verbal discriminative stimulus for the specific tact, and the appropriate verbal stimulus designed to evoke observational behavior to the relevant properties of the non-verbal stimulus (i.e., when asked, "What type of animal is this?" the child should respond to the properties of the picture that evoke the response, "dog," in contrast to the properties controlling a response to, "What does this animal say?"). Regarding the audience variable in controlling complex behavior, it is important to note that audience control is nearly ubiquitous in the multiple control of verbal responses. For instance, a speaker's verbal repertoire is differentially strengthened by the mere presence of any listener and weakened by the absence of one. However, audiences also exert more refined discriminative control in everyday life. For instance, children will typically respond to their teachers differently from how they speak with their parents or peers. For this reason, clinicians should analyze the audience variables that control differentiated responding between adults and the child's age-related peers. Once all of the critical variables were carefully accounted for, the clinician might have provided an echoic prompt in the presence of those conditions and then faded the prompt such that only the relevant controlling variables within the child's typical verbal environments came to control the response. Incorporating an analysis of the multiple variables that control verbal behavior in typical environments is important when teaching verbal behavior (Carr & Miguel, 2013, p. 335).

All of this suggests to the clinician that a thorough analysis of the multiple variables that control verbal responses in typical environments must be fully accounted for when designing and implementing instructional interventions. Failure to do so might preclude the opportunity for the autistic person to respond under the relevant sources of control and to acquire novel, untrained responses, referred to by Alessi (1987) as "generative responses." Generative responding is the critical alternative to rote responding when building verbal repertoires. degli Espinosa (2022) suggested that "…teaching strategies from Skinner's analysis of multiple causation offers clinicians a toolbox of procedures to overcome rote learning and discrimination errors, and to produce generative responding" (p. 53).

Multiply Controlled Verbal (and Non-Verbal) Responses

As the above example illustrates, verbal behavior observed in our everyday environments is usually the result of multiple variables.

> Skinner's discussion of multiple control is easily overlooked. Readers sometimes fail to recognize that pure forms of the respective verbal operants are rare outside the laboratory or instructional contexts, and a common preoccupation of students is to try to classify utterances as one or another verbal operant on the assumption that the example must be exclusively one type.
>
> (Michael et al., 2011, p. 4)

Skinner's taxonomy of the elementary verbal operant classes provides a critical foundation for analyzing complex circumstances that generate multiply controlled behavior. When we classify a response as a member of a given verbal operant class (e.g., "mand," "tact," or "intraverbal"), our classification also functions as an explanation for the response (Palmer, 2016). For example, if we observe a young boy point to a dog and say to his parent, "dog," we might classify the response as a tact. In doing so, we can also be said to explain why the response occurred at that moment: the child's response was evoked by the sight of the dog as a non-verbal discriminative stimulus due to a history of generalized reinforcement for the response when it has been emitted in the presence of other dogs. Similarly, if the parent said to him, "Woof says a ___," his response, "dog," in this context would be classified *and* explained as an intraverbal directly evoked by the verbal discriminative stimulus.

But more often than not, we observe responses emitted by both children and adults that lack a history of reinforcement in the presence of the observed antecedent stimuli, and therefore, they cannot be accurately explained as elementary verbal operants. For instance, suppose a teacher tells the child, "Yesterday, I took my pet outside on a leash. When a squirrel ran by, my pet barked and chased after it. Can you guess what kind of animal my pet is?" He would likely say, "dog," which might superficially appear to be an intraverbal evoked by the question. But, considering that the arrangement of antecedent verbal stimuli is completely novel to the child, there is no history of reinforcement to explain the response as an intraverbal. Palmer (2016) proposed that instead of classifying a verbal response to a *novel* arrangement of verbal stimuli as an intraverbal, behavior analysts should identify such responses as multiply controlled responses under several sources of *intraverbal control*. It is unlikely that the question alone would have evoked the response "dog." In other words, an explanation of the child's response to the novel arrangement of stimuli recognizes that among the relevant controlling variables, the intraverbal relations, which the verbal response *dog* shares with the verbal stimuli *leash, pet, bark,* and *chase*, play a critical role in controlling the terminal response to the question. The distinction between an intraverbal and an *intraverbally controlled* response can also be effectively extended to the other verbal operant classes. For instance, a behavior analysis of a multiply controlled response for which motivational variables exert the strongest control (e.g., a novel request to a listener) will benefit from being classified as a response mainly under *mand control* rather than as a mand. An analysis of a multiply controlled response for which non-verbal discriminative stimuli exert the most salient control (e.g., a description of a novel event) will be significantly improved by being identified as a response mainly under *tact control* instead of as a tact. It is important to recognize that when we identify a response as mand-controlled, tact-controlled, or intraverbally controlled, we have not yet identified *all* of the multiple variables that exert control over the response. When designing verbal behavior interventions for autistic learners, it is imperative to analyze as many of the variables that control a target response as possible. In the following, we share examples of behavior in the instructional environment under mand, tact, and intraverbal control.

Mand Control

Kate mands for and tacts many items when they are visibly present in the classroom. The classroom team has decided to program a manding-for-missing-items program. They begin by teaching Kate to independently execute a variety of behavior chains that lead to a terminal reinforcer (e.g., making a peanut butter and jelly sandwich). Once Kate acquired several of these chains, the instructors contrived situations in which specific items needed to complete a step in the chain were missing (e.g., while Kate was preparing the sandwich, the knife was no longer where it was usually located). When Kate arrives at the step in the chain that requires the missing item, she will engage in some searching behavior, but because she has only manded for visible items, she does not mand for the missing item. When motivation is evident, the instructors hold up the missing item to evoke the response (e.g., "knife!"). After Kate emits the response, the instructor briefly hides it again to transfer the response to the missing-item condition (e.g., "What did you say?"). The knife is delivered as a reinforcer to complete the chain when the response is emitted again. After many exemplars of this teaching style across a wide range of behavior chains, Kate begins to emit mand-controlled responses for missing items, which she has never been taught to mand for without the items visibly present. Each occasion in which Kate is presented with the dilemma of needing a missing item to complete a task requires multiple variables to evoke the mand-controlled response: the stimuli from the completed steps of the behavior chain, a listener who might know where the item is located, the motivating variables for the completion of the step, and any of Kate's own speaker-as-listener behavior acquired from previous mand training (speaker-as-listener behavior will be discussed in further detail below).

Tact Control

Alex has been taught elementary tacts for about one hundred different items (e.g., "pencil") and about 25 different actions (e.g., "tapping"). His instructor introduces a procedure to teach Alex to describe both the action and the items when an action is demonstrated with the item. When the instructor taps the pencil, she says, "What am I tapping?" while pointing to the pencil as a tact prompt. After Alex tacts the pencil, the instructor asks again without pointing to the pencil, "What am I tapping?" Reinforcement is provided for the correct response. The instructor then models the action again and says, "What am I doing?" If Alex says "tapping," a small amount of a reinforcer is provided. If he emits the complex tact-controlled response, "tapping pencil," the instructor differentially reinforces the response. After several opportunities to acquire different action-item tacts, Alex begins to emit untrained tact-controlled responses by combining the action tact and item tact. Additionally, Alex's tacts are emitted within the "grammatical frame" commonly accepted by Alex's verbal community (i.e., *action[ing] noun*), even if he has never been taught to do so with those tacts. The "grammatical frame" is technically classified as an *autoclitic frame*, which will be discussed later in this chapter.

Intraverbal Control

John has acquired hundreds of tacts of items and actions and can emit untrained action-object tact-controlled responses. John also has a repertoire of making hundreds of directly trained intraverbals to questions and fill-in statements. To teach John to respond with untrained intraverbally controlled responses, his instructor models actions involving specific items, such as cutting paper with scissors. While cutting the paper, the instructor says, "What do you cut?" while gesturing toward the paper being cut. After John accurately tacts the paper, the instructor removes the items and asks again, "What do you cut?" John's response "paper" is followed by reinforcement. Within the same teaching session, the instructor provides the same scenario but asks, "What do you cut *with*?" and gestures to the scissors. After several exemplars of directly teaching intraverbals in this manner, John eventually acquires a repertoire of emitting untrained intraverbally controlled responses to the questions, "What do you (action)?" and "What do you (action) with?" The variables that account for John's performance during novel presentations of these questions entail the instructor's presence as an audience, the questions as arrangements of discriminative stimuli, and John's own behavior in recalling previously acquired tact responses related to action-item stimulus presentations. An example of John's own behavior serving as a controlling variable may include covert imagining of prior teaching scenarios in which accurately tacting an instructor's behavior of cutting with scissors was reinforced.

In addition to the above examples of multiply controlled verbal behavior, it is important for us to consider the following type of multiply controlled behavior in which the individual's final non-verbal performance is partially controlled by listening to his own verbal responses.

Listener-Response Control

Nick has acquired a wide range of tacts and listener discriminations for objects and pictures. He has also been taught to follow instructions to perform a single action when given an item (e.g., when given a marker and told, "Show me tapping," Nick will tap the marker on his desk). Nick's instructors decided to teach him to perform a specified action when given a two-component instruction. Nick's instructors lay out an array of items, including multiple examples of items that can be spun. Nick's instructor then tells Nick to "spin the crayon." Nick repeats back the instruction to himself and scans the array, when he sees the crayon, he stops scanning, picks it up, and spins it. Multiple variables within the context control Nick's behavior of spinning the crayon. After being told to "spin the crayon," his echoic of the instruction played an important role in "remembering" the instructional stimulus while scanning the array. Nick's behavior of bypassing the nonexamples and "recognizing" the crayon (i.e., stimulus discrimination) participated in the selection of the item. Finally, it is plausible that Nick privately repeated the instruction to himself one final time before spinning it on the table. Although Nick's terminal response is non-verbal, it is important to acknowledge that such complex performances are frequently mediated by the individual's own verbal behavior.

The examples above illustrate commonplace utterances in which the responses are novel in the presence of observed discriminative stimuli and motivating operations (i.e., there is no reinforcement history to explain the correlation between the stimulus and the response). Certain practices in applied behavior analysis have focused on multiple exemplar training procedures, which occasionally (though not inevitably) result in relevant novel responses. These responses have been described as "derived relational responses" in the literature on stimulus equivalence and relational frame procedures. Within these behavior-analytic paradigms, such novel responses are described as "emerging" from the stimuli as "generalized operants" in the absence of any supplemental mediating behavior on the part of the participant or client. In contrast, we interpret such performances through a molecular lens in this chapter. Therefore, to explain a novel response to presented stimuli, we cannot classify the observed stimulus-response relation as "an operant." Instead, we must look for other controlling variables often produced by the individual's own behavior. As the evidence cited by Michael et al. (2011) demonstrated, "The acquisition of derived relations is clearly facilitated by verbal mediation" (p. 17).

Problem-Solving and Verbal and Non-verbal Mediation

As discussed, tightly controlled experimental or instructional environments are rare and do not reflect the daily contingencies that verbal organisms experience. The so-called real world outside the classroom often includes circumstances in which motivational variables are in place but discriminative stimuli to evoke the relevant behavior are lacking. Skinner (1969) identified such circumstances as "problems" and said that to solve such problems, the individual "must change either himself or the situation until a response occurs. The behavior which brings about the change is properly called problem solving and the response it promotes a solution" (p. 133). The kinds of behavior that participate in problem-solving are critical skills which may be referred to as *behavioral cusps,* which, according to Rosales-Ruiz and Baer (1997), expose "the individual's repertoire to new environments, especially new reinforcers and punishers, new contingencies, new responses, new stimulus controls, and new communities of maintaining and destructive contingencies" (p. 534). Sundberg (2020a) suggested, "A cusp can facilitate subsequent learning by being a prerequisite or a component of a more complex behavior" (p. 4). The behavioral repertoires we call cusps comprise the mediating behaviors that account for multiply-controlled verbal responses and are the subject of this chapter. Most of the cusps we discuss below are examples of problem-solving repertoires that make untrained and multiply-controlled verbal behavior possible. These problem-solving repertoires are usually acquired without instruction for neurotypical children but must be taught directly to many autistic children.

Multiple Control and Problem-Solving

Palmer (1991) provided an analysis of recall as an example of problem-solving consistent with Skinner's (1969) analysis above. When we momentarily forget a person's name and need to recall it, or when trying to remember what we need to pick up at the store, we face problems common in daily experience. Palmer (1991) expanded on Skinner's description of a "problem" by providing a technical definition with three features (p. 271):

1. A target response (or set of responses) is part of the organism's repertoire under one or more stimulus conditions.
2. Discriminative stimuli are present indicating that the response is scheduled for reinforcement.
3. The response is not under direct control of current discriminative stimuli.

Familiarizing ourselves with these three features of problems and recognizing the roles that cusps play in solving them may be critical to our conceptual and procedural toolbox as practitioners.

Verbal and Non-verbal Mediation and Multiple Control

In every verbal interaction, we can assume the participation of both a speaker and a listener. But when we observe speakers behaving verbally by themselves to solve a problem, who are their listeners? When verbal organisms speak (or sign), they produce sounds (or sights) in the immediate environment, which can function as discriminative stimuli for their own subsequent behavior. In other words, when speakers respond to the stimulus products of their own behavior, they effectively serve as their *own* listeners (Palmer, 1998). Consequently, when emitting multiply controlled verbal behavior, an individual is an active participant in which additional sources of control for a response are generated by the individual, leading to the response that is scheduled for reinforcement (correct response). In the classroom, these repertoires of verbal mediation are critical to solving problems related to answering novel questions (intraverbal control), selecting named items from novel books or arrays (listener-response control), requesting information from others (mand control), answering questions by describing features, functions, and classes of items (intraverbal-tact control), and acquiring tacts after engaging in listener-selection tasks. Related to such tasks, Skinner (1957) stated, "The speaker's own verbal behavior automatically supplies stimuli for echoic, textual, or intraverbal behavior, and these in turn generate stimuli for further response" (p. 439). Sundberg (2018) explained it this way "...verbal behavior can produce products that function as causal variables that may participate in evoking other forms of verbal behavior" (p. 602).

The speaker's non-verbal behavior might also supplement verbal mediation (Ratkos & Camacho, 2023; Ratkos et al., 2023). For instance, in the classroom, a child might be asked to retrieve several specific items needed for an arts and crafts activity (e.g., glue, scissors, and paper). In addition to reciting "glue, scissors, paper" to herself, she might also engage in the perceptual behavior (discussed later) of imagining the arts and crafts closet and the specific shelves on which those items are located. Failure to develop this repertoire of engaging in verbal or non-verbal "precurrent" (Skinner, 1953) behavior limits a child's acquisition of multiply controlled and untrained verbal and non-verbal responses. Farrell (2017) has offered methods to teach this important speaker-as-listener repertoire to learners who do not acquire it typically. The following section will discuss the role of verbal and non-verbal mediation in developing behavioral cusp repertoires.

Behavioral Cusps

Bidirectional Naming

Bidirectional naming (BiN) (Horne & Lowe, 1996; Miguel, 2016, 2018) is a behavioral cusp leading to unprogrammed multiply controlled responses. "Naming is present when the child learns word-object relations incidentally with few exposures to these relations in their environment" (Farrell, 2017, p. 11). BiN represents a type of verbal mediation for a learner with a speaker-as-listener repertoire. This repertoire contains the kinds of responses which mediate performances of multiply controlled and untrained verbal behavior. BiN can take the form of *common bidirectional naming* (C-BiN) when tacts or listener responses are acquired incidentally. *Intraverbal bidirectional naming* (I-BiN) and even *visual bidirectional naming* (V-BiN) repertoires might also be acquired. In tests of the verbal mediating effects of I-BiN during match-to-sample tasks, individuals have been taught to intraverbally "link" verbal stimuli by saying something like, "The *ball* goes with the *red triangle*." When subsequently asked to match the ball with the correct figure within an array, a child might tact the ball and then say the self-generated rule, "The *ball* goes with the *red triangle*." In this case, the correct response would be mediated by the "match" (i.e., joint control) between the last two words in the child's spoken rule and the complex tact of the red triangle within the array (Carp & Petursdottir, 2015; Díaz et al., 2020; Jennings & Miguel, 2017; Ma et al., 2016; Santos et al., 2015; Sundberg et al., 2018).

BiN generally constitutes the merging of speaker and listener behavior and might account for the explosion of listener and speaker behavior observed around three years old in neurotypical children (Longano & Greer, 2010, p. 74). It appears that children learn vocabulary at a rate of 4–10 times faster once the naming repertoire is acquired (Greer & Ross, 2008). Skinner (1957) might have been the first to identify this important mediating repertoire through his example of how one might "pick up" novel tact- and listener-controlled responses by simply listening to an electrician talk about a "jones-plug" in the course of their work (p. 360). Nevertheless, Horne and Lowe (1996) identified this important verbal unit and called it the "naming" relation. "Naming appears to be *a*, or *the*, stage in children's development, a stage that makes it possible for children to come to learn language incidentally" (Greer & Longano, 2010, p. 74). Individuals with a naming repertoire acquire untrained tact-controlled responses after learning a listener response and untrained listener responses after acquiring the tact (Greer & Ross, 2008; Greer & Speckman, 2009). For example, learning to tact an object as a "ball" might lead to the untrained listener selection of this object when the auditory stimulus "ball" is presented. Conversely, learning the listener response might lead to the untrained tact. Convergent multiple control occurs in the case of the incidental acquisition of the tact and divergent multiple control in the case of the simultaneous acquisition of the listener response, respectively. Moreover, the acquisition of listener, tact, echoic, and speaker-as-own listener repertoires by about three years old makes possible the learning of untrained tact- and listener-controlled responses by observing and listening to others speak about objects in the everyday environment (Carnerero & Pérez-González, 2015; Pérez-González, Cereijo-Blanco et al., 2014).

> Through a history of listener, echoic and tact training in early childhood, a child may hear a caregiver tact a nonverbal stimulus, orient to the nonverbal stimulus, echo the verbal response made by the caregiver, and then tact a similar stimulus in the future.
>
> (Dressel, 2019, p. 114)

Many autistic learners might not acquire this repertoire without special teaching in the form of multiple exemplar instruction (MEI; Fiorile & Greer, 2007; Gilic & Greer, 2011; Greer & Ross, 2008; LaFrance & Tarbox, 2020). MEI usually includes an instructor presenting four or five target object stimuli and rotating through tact, listener, and match-to-sample trials with each target stimulus.

BiN facilitates the development of speaking with "understanding" (Miguel, 2018). More technically, "…naming involves not only tacting, but also reacting to the (auditory) stimulus produced by the tact as a listener" (Miguel, 2016, p. 128). Some consider this to be the definition of what it means to be "truly verbal" (Greer & Speckman, 2009). Many important verbal and non-verbal skills are facilitated once this repertoire is acquired.

Ordinary child-caregiver interactions are usually sufficient to produce C-BiN with neurotypical children. If a caregiver frequently interacts with a child by engaging with objects while tacting them, the child is more likely to act as both a speaker and a listener related to those items without programmed instruction. In the example below, a parent might point to a toy and say its name during a typical playful interaction with a child. Following several opportunities of experiencing this type of interaction, the child may learn to orient toward the object (listener behavior) when they hear the name spoken. When the child orients toward the toy, she may echo the parent's verbal response. The child might then learn the tact as a listener to her own speaker behavior. In this case, all of the variables necessary to acquire listener behavior and the tact have occurred incidentally, and as shown below, the tact may be acquired through this single verbal episode. Autistic learners frequently require contrived instructional scenarios, including MEI, to acquire such repertoires.

See Figure 10.4 for a demonstration of how a "generalized" echoic repertoire functions as a behavioral cusp mediating listener-to-tact BiN mediated by joint control.

Another example below demonstrates the role of BiN and joint control in which a child is taught to select an item by feature, function, or class to produce untrained intraverbals. The learner tacts the item while selecting it as a listener during instruction and then subsequently emits the appropriate intraverbal when the antecedent vocal stimulus is presented in the absence of the item. Figure 10.5 illustrates this point with a learner who uses manual sign as her form of verbal behavior.

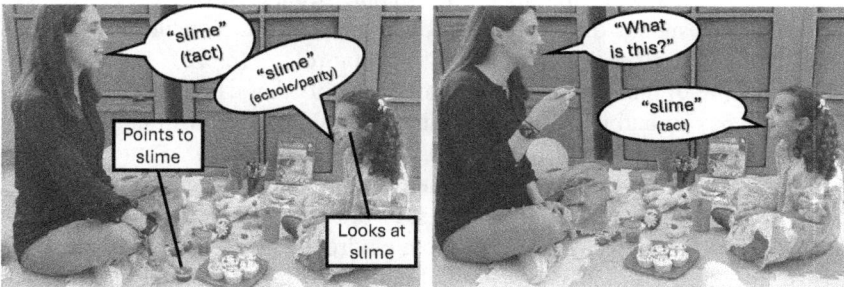

Figure 10.4 Example of listener-to-tact biN.
Note: The role of the bidirectional naming repertoire in acquiring a tact response incidentally.

Figure 10.5 Example of tact to intraverbal bidirectional naming.
Note: Acquisition of the tact to intraverbal in a learner who has acquired the BiN repertoire.

Joint Control

As discussed, we face a *problem* when a response is required of us, but the relevant controlling stimuli are momentarily absent, such as when there is an unavoidable delay between the stimulus and the response. For instance, when we are searching for something in the grocery store, in our living room, or through a list of names or items. When faced with such problems, we often learn to "hold onto the stimulus" by listening to our own self-echoic of the stimulus. When we finally find the item we are looking for, we have a sort of aha! moment in which we discriminate a "jump" in the strength of our rehearsed response (Palmer, 2006). This noticeable jump in response strength, arising from the sudden overlapping topographies between our self-echoic and the tact of the item, ends our search and controls our selections of the item.

Joint control responding is an important behavioral cusp that has been demonstrated to play a substantial role in teaching multiply controlled listener and speaker behavior to autistic learners (for a review of applications with learners with autism and language acquisition see Ampuerro & Miklos, 2019; Hozella et al., 2024). Michael et al. (2011) pointed out, "Joint control is the convergent control of a response of a particular topography by two concurrent variables and is therefore a special case of multiple control..." (p. 12). The following is an example of the confluence of verbal operants that can produce untrained listener behavior and illustrates the nature of joint control with autistic learners. Sam can tact and identify hundreds of items as a listener. Sam has no difficulty emitting the target response when asked to, "Find (item)" from a small array of pictures. However, if Sam is asked to find multiple items from a large array or somewhere within the classroom environment, he is unable to find the items, despite the fact that he can find pictures of the same items in a small array. Sam's instructors have identified that he is not "remembering" the items as he hunts for them. Sam's instructors coach Sam to rehearse to himself the names of the items as he looks for them. When Sam implements this strategy (e.g., repeating "broom, dustpan, paper towel" after being told to retrieve those items), he will continue to scan the environment until his self-echoic of each of the items' names (e.g., "broom") converges with a momentary tact of each of the corresponding items (e.g., the sight of the broom evokes, "broom"). For each item, both the self-echoic and the tact jointly control a sudden increase in response strength, which in turn evokes Sam's behavior of selecting the item (Palmer, 2006). Lowenkron (1998) offered this account to explain the acquisition of mainly untrained listener and some speaker behavior. Joint control is essential to mediating tasks such as the one described above, but it also may play a fundamental role in mediating bidirectional naming tasks.

Joint Control or Bidirectional Naming?

The naming relation has garnered substantial attention in the applied literature as an important repertoire to explain many instances of convergent and divergent multiple control with autistic learners (Greer & Ross, 2008; Horne & Lowe, 1996; Miguel, 2016, 2018). A similar account of merging the speaker and listener repertoires can be found in the literature on joint control (Miguel, 2016). Lowenkron (1996) agreed with Horne and Lowe (1996) that the interaction of the listener, tact, echoic, and self-echoic repertoires leads to word-object bidirectionality. In other words, BiN and joint control appear to explain the same phenomenon. However, Lowenkron claimed that Horne and Lowe do not provide a cogent analysis of the mechanism that accounts for the word-object bidirectionality other than to assert that it occurs. Lowenkron stated that a joint control analysis is necessary to clearly specify the evocative stimulus for the emergence of novel relations. He claimed that the source of stimulus control that accounts for the transfer from the tact to an untrained listener selection response, as seen in BiN, is the discriminable event of simultaneously emitting two verbal operants (tact and self-echoic) of the same form. Lowenkron claimed that this type of bidirectional responding would not be possible without one's discrimination of joint control. Remaining consistent with the literature, we will use the terms BiN and joint control where appropriate and cited in the literature to explain the merging of speaker and listener behavior as an explanatory cusp. However, we reiterate Michael's (1996) warning about introducing a term (e.g., BiN) that represents the interaction of several variables more fully described as a composite of mediating responses involving joint control.

Autoclitic Behavior

In addition to the roles that speaker-as-listener behavior play in bidirectional naming and joint control activity, another important speaker-as-listener variable for us to consider is what Skinner (1957) classified as *autoclitics*. Skinner (1957) described autoclitics as "behavior which is based upon or depends upon other verbal behavior" (p. 315). We have discussed the various elementary (or primary) verbal operant classes. Autoclitic responses *depend upon* elementary operants brought to strength by a given context, so we can classify the autoclitic as a secondary verbal operant class.

Returning to the example of the child tacting the dog for his parents, we can imagine a different scenario in which he observes the dog running in circles after its own tail. He might emit the following response, "That *dog* is chasing its *tail*." This tact-controlled response includes an example of an important type of autoclitic, which Skinner identified as an *autoclitic frame*. When an individual contacts a contingency that requires a description of a complex scenario, "the relational aspects of the situation strengthen a frame, and specific features of the situation strengthen the responses fitted into it" (Skinner, 1957, p. 336). The responses *dog* and *tail* are separate elementary tacts embedded within the autoclitic frame *X is chasing Y*. Additionally, the pronouns *that* and *its* are also autoclitics controlled by subtle stimulus features of the context. A further autoclitic function within this complex utterance includes ordering the primary verbal operants within the autoclitic frame (Palmer, 2007, 2023). Notice that the child didn't say, "That *tail* is chasing its *dog*," and when a typical speaker makes such mistakes, the response is usually interrupted by the speaker and corrected, "That tail is chasing… I mean, that dog is chasing its tail." Palmer (2023) revealed that behavior analysts still have work to do to account for the subtle speaker-as-listener shifts in stimulus control, which account for the accurate emission of primary verbal operants within autoclitic frames. Although Skinner has laid the groundwork for an analysis of autoclitic behavior, an application of this analysis to the treatment of autistic learners has only scratched the surface.

Imagining

Each of us has access to a small portion of the environment that is uniquely private (Skinner, 1957). In fact, "Some verbal behavior … is under the control of stimuli to which the speaker alone is able to react" (Skinner, 1957, p. 130). Many private and covert behaviors contribute substantially to the emission of multiply controlled verbal behavior. These covert behaviors might take the form of self-questioning, echoics, elicited responses of smooth muscles and glands, and even *imagining*. For example, intraverbally controlled behavior of recalling past events is usually under the control not only of a question from someone but also private stimuli that are generated by one's non-verbal responses to the question (Aguirre & Rehfeldt, 2015; Axe et al., 2019; Frampton & Shillingsburg, 2018; Keesey-Phelan et al., 2022; Kisamore et al., 2011; Palmer, 2016; Sautter et al., 2011). These non-verbal mediating behaviors are examples of problem-solving that produce additional stimuli leading to the response scheduled for reinforcement (Kisamore et al., 2011; Sautter et al., 2011). For example, Palmer (2016) concluded that a response to the question, "Name an animal with antlers?" would be controlled partly by the question and partly by imagining reindeer, moose, and other antlered animals generated by the question. Miguel (2018) made an interesting observation about sensory imagining on a related topic. He suggested that there is a bidirectional relationship between imagining and one's reaction to it. He suggested it is analogous to speaking and reacting to your own behavior as a listener. Imagining as a mediating response appears to be an important behavioral cusp that might produce untrained, multiply controlled verbal behavior.

Specifically, in the case of imagining, individuals respond to the private stimulus products of their perceptual behavior (e.g., visual, auditory, olfactory) in ways that are similar to how they react to perceptual stimuli in the public environment. Since perceptual behavior is sensitive to contingencies of rein-forcement, it can take the form of private operant behavior controlled by non-verbal and verbal stimuli in everyday environments (Horne & Lowe, 1996; Miguel, 2018). "… when a person sees a person or place in his imagination, he may simply be doing what he does in the presence of the person or place" (Skinner, 1974, p. 82). Skinner referred to this as "seeing in the absence of the thing seen" (p. 82). In other words, one might see an object when it is present, but they can also "see" it when it is no longer present under weaker stimulus con-trol. For example, upon arriving home from school, a child might be asked by an interested parent, "Who did you play with during recess today?" The response to this question is unlikely to be solely under the control of the question because there is inevitably no history of reinforcement for an accurate response to this question. Additionally, the stimuli present during recess (e.g., peers, playground activities) are not present in the current environment (i.e., home). Therefore, the question might evoke a series of private responses, including "seeing and hearing" their playmates during recess. The child might then list off the names of their playmates from recess. This list of names is multiply controlled by intra-verbal behavior *and* the imagining products. In the absence of imagining and other types of mediating behavior, untrained complex verbal responding might not be possible. In a later section of this chapter, we will provide references to several studies in which imagining mediates untrained multiply controlled ver-bal responding through programmed instruction.

Atomic Repertoires

So far, we have demonstrated a number of examples of previously trained response forms that can be controlled by antecedent stimuli which have never controlled the response in the past. We call these responses "novel" because, in such circumstances, they have never been evoked by the observed antecedent. For example, the child has a history of saying "dog" in the presence of dogs, but the instance of saying "dog" in response to the question, "Can you guess what kind of animal my pet is?" was completely novel. Another example of behavior we might call "novel" is one in which the form of a response itself has never been explicitly trained.

Returning one last time to the example of the child who tacts "dog" to his parent, suppose the dog was an unfamiliar breed to the child. This might produce motivative variables which evoke a mand-controlled response for information, such as, "Mommy, what kind of dog is that?" The mother might reply, "That is a Shiba Inu." We can then imagine a little girl approaching the boy who emits the new tact-controlled response to her, "That's a Shiba Inu!" (listener-to-speaker bidirectional naming). Not only has he never said this dog's breed in this par-ticular context before, but this is also the first time the child has ever been heard to produce the specific arrangement of syllables: shee-bah ee-noo. Because the child has a strong speaker-as-listener repertoire, he contacts automatic reinforcement for his attempt by recognizing that his response matches, or *achieves parity* with, the spoken model provided by his mother (Palmer, 1996). The child's novel arrangement of response elements is possible only because of an atomic echoic repertoire.

Throughout Skinner's (1957) *Verbal Behavior*, he identified a wide range of examples of what he calls minimal units or minimal repertoires. "Minimal" in this sense is synonymous with the term "atomic," which Skinner appeared to prefer in his later writings (Skinner, 1969, 1980). The term "atomic repertoires" has been formally classified by Palmer (2012) and defined as "A set of fine-grained units of behavior, each under control of a distinctive stimulus, that can be evoked in any permutation by the arrangement of corresponding stimuli" (p. 61). In addition to an atomic echoic repertoire, Skinner (1957) and Palmer (2012) have also identified atomic imitation repertoires, textual repertoires, transcriptive repertoires, tact repertoires, and rule-governed repertoires.

Given that behavior analysts have identified the various repertoires that account for incidental novel behavior in typical development, behavior analysts and educators are now in an optimal position to design instructional sequences for autistic learners by directly training these repertoires. We have identified the above repertoires as cusps whose mediating behaviors explain many occurrences of novel responding that open the individual to an incalculable number of life-enhancing contingencies of reinforcement. What is important for practitioners to note is that these repertoires are teachable. Systematically designing our instructional procedures with a focus on verbal behavioral cusps will ultimately permit our students with verbal deficits to acquire increasingly complex repertoires in the absence of explicit instruction.

An Example of Problem-Solving and Behavioral Cusps

Let us take an example of problem-solving in which many behavioral cusps interact with one another to eventually produce a solution. Imagine an autistic child who has been taught a wide range of generative skills, including those covered in this chapter. Suppose the child is invited on a class trip to an air and space museum and sees a very interesting and novel space vehicle for which he does not have a tact at strength. He is faced with a *problem* that contains all the three features of Palmer's definition: (1) The child has a repertoire of the relevant phonemes under other sources of control, (2) the discriminative and motivational elements of the vehicle and the presence of an audience indicate that a tact of the item is likely to be reinforced, and (3) the novel elements of the space vehicle do not momentarily function as a discriminative stimulus for the tact response. The child might solve the initial part of the problem by gaining his teacher's attention and pointing in the direction of the vehicle (i.e., attaining *joint attention* with the teacher). Once the teacher attends to the vehicle, the child might emit the mand-controlled response, "What is that called?" The teacher responds, "That's called a Mars rover." The child echoes "marz roh-ver" while observing the visual elements of the vehicle. The child continues to listen to his own *self-echoic* of the string of phonemes while contacting automatic reinforcement by *achieving parity/joint control* with the verbal stimuli produced by the teacher's response. When the child's vocal responses contact reinforcement in the presence of the stimulus properties of the vehicle, the vehicle eventually acquires tact control over the verbal response, "Mars rover." Now, the child is in a position to respond to a peer's mand-controlled response, "What is that thing called?" by saying, "That is called a Mars Rover!" (emitting the elementary tact within the *autoclitic frame*: "That is called X."). This entire sequence of events in which the child listened to his teacher's spoken responses and eventually acquired the speaker response for himself illustrates the phenomenon known as *listener-to-tact bidirectional naming*.

Assessment

As emphasized, many autistic learners fail to acquire the behavioral cusps outlined throughout this chapter, which explains why they often do not experience the explosion of verbal behavior that occurs with most young children. However, proper identification and assessment of the skills required to develop novel responding might be the first step toward teaching these important repertoires, which heretofore have been overlooked in many behavioral language training programs.

Assessing a learner's skill level across verbal operant categories is indeed a crucial first step in developing a comprehensive language training program. However, this approach alone might not be sufficient, especially when considering the importance of teaching multiply controlled complex verbal behavior. A consideration of the repertoires outlined in this chapter is critical to this process. Once again, these repertoires and their effects are referred to as behavioral cusps. "A cusp can facilitate subsequent learning by being a prerequisite or a component of a more complex behavior" (Sundberg, 2020b, p. 4). For example, the acquisition of the behavioral cusps of C-BiN, I-BiN, or joint control facilitates the acquisition of echoics, tacts, listener responses, and intraverbals after hearing another person tact an item in view of the child (Sundberg, 2020b).

Verbal Behavior Milestones Assessment and Placement Program (VB-MAPP)

The VB-MAPP (Sundberg, 2008) provides the practitioner with a comprehensive method to assess the acquisition of verbal behavior within the context of Skinner's categories of language development. (For a detailed description of the VB-MAPP and how to score it, see Chapter 2 in this volume). Scoring the VB-MAPP provides a baseline and ongoing measurement of a learner's important verbal and non-verbal skills corresponding to the typically developing repertoires of children from birth to four years old. The results of this type of assessment are necessary for the implementation of a comprehensive language and basic skill development program. The instrument serves as both an assessment and curriculum that sequences the ordering of skills to be taught.

More recently, Sundberg (2020b) suggested that the VB-MAPP might also provide a guide to the identification of behavioral cusps responsible for generative and untrained multiply controlled responding. Skinner (1957) pointed out that multiply controlled novel responses only occur after a large repertoire of elementary verbal operants is acquired. The elementary verbal operants are the skills that are typically learned within the first two levels of the VB-MAPP and correspond to the period when novel and untrained responding begins to occur in earnest. Sundberg (2020b) suggested that these skills include verbal behavior (e.g., mands, echoics, imitation of signs, tacts, and intraverbals), non-verbal behavior (e.g., visual-perceptual skills, listener discrimination, imitation of non-verbal behavior, scanning, and reinforcing speakers), and a rich history of speaker-listener interactions (Hart & Risley, 1995). "The combination of speaker, listener, and match to sample repertoires can produce especially powerful generative effects through multiple control..." (Sundberg, 2020a p. 51).

Following Sundberg's lead, we suggest that the VB-MAPP has the additional function of assisting in the identification and acquisition of behavioral cusps. Although the VB-MAPP does not directly identify behavioral cusps, it does help practitioners identify the skills that directly implicate a variety of behavioral cusps. Identification of these skills during the assessment process can permit the practitioner to exploit them for their instructional value, or if there is no evidence of these skills, the practitioner can then know there is a need to teach behavioral cusps directly. If conducting the VB-MAPP and you do not observe and record untrained responses in several VB-MAPP milestones, this indicates that essential behavioral cusps have not been acquired. If a practitioner continues to teach rote skills within these milestones rather than focusing on establishing and identifying behavioral cusps, it will not likely produce a desirable outcome. Using the VB-MAPP to identify and teach behavioral cusps may avoid unproductive treatment time, potentially years, spent teaching rote skills that may never lead to untrained and generative responding, which is crucial for the most effective outcome.

Figure 10.6 displays a VB-MAPP grid (Sundberg, 2020b) and shows how it can support the teaching of complex multiply controlled verbal behavior within a language training program.

The milestones colored in red represent the acquisition of skills that support the development of behavioral cusps and complex stimulus control responding. The milestones colored in green represent the untrained skills resulting from multiply controlled responding. Skills acquired within the green-colored milestones indicate that a learner has acquired a behavioral cusp repertoire responsible for acquiring untrained responses within this milestone. An analysis of the multiple variables responsible for the incidental acquisition of these skills will lead one to the identification of a behavioral cusp. The aim of every language training program for autistic learners is to support the development of the green-colored repertoires so that immersion in a stimulating everyday verbal environment will lead to the incidental acquisition of complex verbal behavior. Some of the responses within the untrained repertoires, identified on the VB-MAPP in Figure 10.6, result from multiply controlled generative responding. In the case of autistic learners, some cusps might be acquired without instruction, but in most cases, they will require planned instruction within a language training program.

Table 10.1 was developed to assist the practitioner in using the VB-MAPP to assess important milestones *and* behavioral cusp repertoires. The table provides the practitioner with a list of some of the milestones identified as generative

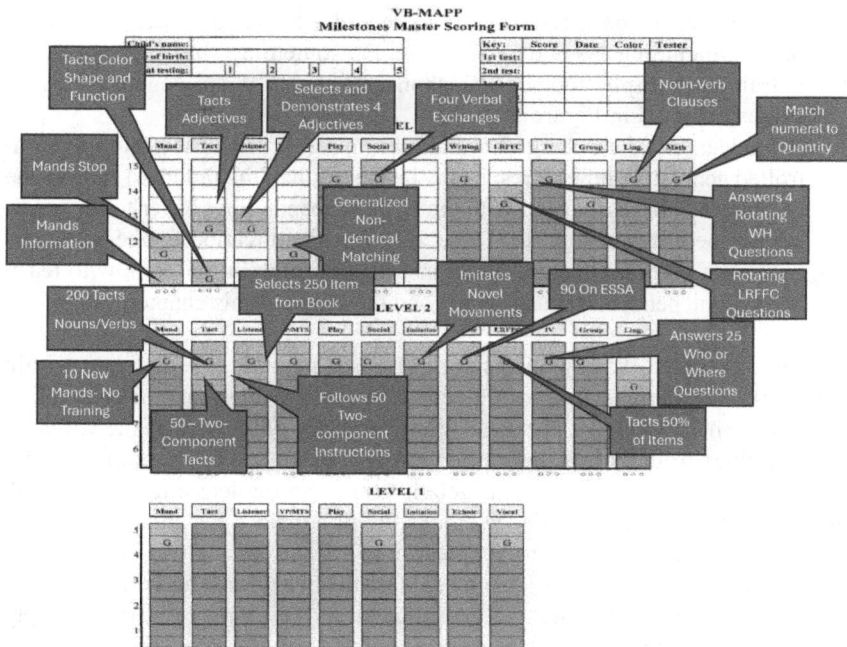

Figure 10.6 VB-MAPP milestones grid.
Note: The VB-MAPP grid displays the milestones that include multiply-controlled responses. The design of this figure was derived from a similar figure contained in a presentation by Sundberg (2020b).

repertoires and, therefore, suggests that a behavioral cusp might be responsible for any untrained skills within the milestone. In addition, the table contains a description of the type of operant control involved in the multiply controlled skill, the VB-MAPP milestone description, an example of the skill, and the interpreted mediating repertoires that account for the emergence of the untrained responses.

To derive the greatest clinical benefit from this table, the practitioner should do the following:

1. Conduct the VB-MAPP assessment with an autistic learner according to the manual's instructions.
2. Probe for novel untrained skills within the green-colored generative milestones. The probe should be designed to be consistent with an analysis of the variables (mediating repertoires) that account for the untrained responding. For example, teach tacts and then probe for untrained corresponding listener responses within a book (Level 2, Milestone 10). Probe for untrained mand-controlled responses for information (Level 3, Milestone 11) by arranging the conditions under which information about location would be a reinforcer and record whether a "where" response occurs, including the autoclitic frame. Do something similar to check for untrained multiply controlled responses in each of the generative milestones depicted in Figure 10.6.
3. If the learner fails to emit untrained responses in any of the multiply controlled generative repertoires, it may be the result of the failure to acquire the behavioral cusp associated with that type of responding. Refer to the mediating repertoires section of Table 10.1 for identification of the advanced repertoire that may require direct instruction. Information on how to teach each of the behavioral cusps is beyond the scope of this chapter.

It should be noted that the cusps comprised of mediating repertoires within Table 10.1 are derived from a molecular analysis of the relevant controlling variables. The analysis of the controlling variables differentiates the explanatory variables from a mere description of the procedures. For example, procedures to teach intraverbals might include arranging the learning environment (teaching procedures) to produce verbal conditional discriminations. However, the procedures do not provide an explanation. Instead, an analysis that includes verbal and non-verbal mediation may explain the behavior. The analysis guides and informs the development of the procedures. Teaching complex multiply controlled behavior requires a precise analysis of the moment-to-moment interaction of behavioral variables. This table provides the experienced practitioner with a guide for teaching complex verbal behavior to learners who would not acquire these skills otherwise.

Table 10.1 Mediating Repertoires for Multiply Controlled VB-MAPP Responses

Type of Operant Control	VB-MAPP Level (L), Milestone (M), and Skill	Example	Mediating Repertoires (Cusps)
Mand Control	Mand—L2 M10: Emits new mands without explicit training Mand—L3 M11: Mands for Information	Asks for "spatula" during a cooking activity after being only explicitly taught the tact	Acquired when relevant MOs are present during tact acquisition
Says, "Where are my shoes?" in order to be told their location	Mands emitted within autoclitic frames		**Tact Control**
	Tact—L2 M9: Emits untrained combinations of actions (verbs) and items (nouns)	Says "dog barking" when shown a barking dog and asked, "What do you see?" or says, "kicking ball," when asked "What am I doing?" while kicking a ball	
Emits tacts of items and actions within relevant autoclitic frames: (noun) (verb)ing or (verb)ing (noun)			
	Tact—L2 M10: Labels untrained items and actions, or features, functions, or classes of items	When shown various photos from a new book, child responses to questions, such as, "what does this toy do?," "what is this a type of?," or "what size is this one?"	

(Continued)

Table 10.1 (Continued)

Type of Operant Control	VB-MAPP Level (L), Milestone (M), and Skill	Example	Mediating Repertoires (Cusps)
	Tact—L3 M12: Describes color, shape, and function of objects when presented in a novel mixed order format	When shown a picture of a brown dog in an array of animals, the child will say "woof woof" when asked, "What does it say?", and "brown," when asked, "What color?"	Joint control between intraverbal response to one's own autoclitic frame and one's own tact of the related properties of the item
	Tact—L3 M13: Untrained tacts of adjectives and adverbs (Not color or shape)	When shown a turtle walking in an aquarium and asked, "What color?" or "How is it moving?", the child says "brown" or "slow"	
Listener-Response Control	Listener—L2 M9: Follows untrained two-component instructions	Follows instruction to "spin the crayon" when the crayon is presented with other objects that can also be spun	Atomic listener behavior, and self-echoic and tact mediated joint control
	Listener—L2 M10: Selects untrained items from book	Follows direction to "touch the flower" from a photo in a new book	Tact-to-Listener BiN, Verbal and non-verbal problem-solving, which may be mediated by joint control
	Listener—L3 M13: Selects (and tacts) untrained adjectives and adverbs and demonstrates adverbs	Finds and tacts an item when told, "Show me the loud toy" or demonstrates an action when told, "Show me slow walking"	Joint control between intraverbal response to one's own autoclitic frame and one's own tact of the related item in environment

(Continued)

Table 10.1 (Continued)

Type of Operant Control	VB-MAPP Level (L), Milestone (M), and Skill	Example	Mediating Repertoires (Cusps)
	LRFFC—L2 M10 & L3 M14: Tacts photo or item when selecting it by feature, function, or class	Touches and tacts the picture of a ball from an array when asked, "What do you throw?"	
Visual-Perceptual Control	VP/MTS—L2 M10: Matching non-identical objects to novel photos ("generalized" matching)	Matches a toy car to a photo of a dissimilar car	
	VP/MTS—L3 M12: Matches items in novel arrays, which include similar stimuli ("generalized" matching)	Matches new items within a messy array	Verbally and/or non-verbally (e.g., imagining) mediated joint control responding
	Math—L3 M15: Engages in untrained matching between numerals and quantities ("generalized" matching)	Matches the numeral 3 to a cup containing three bears	
Imitative Control	Imitation L2 M10: Imitates novel movements ("generalized" imitation) ("generalized" matching)	Imitates a modeled sequence of pushing buttons on a microwave	Atomic imitative behavior and joint control between one's discriminated actions and the model's
Echoic Control	Echoic—L2 M10: Echoes novel words, short phrases, volume, pitch, and prosody ("generalized" echoic)	Imitates the novel utterance, "The polka-dot monster ate all of my cereal!!!"	Atomic echoic behavior joint control between one's discriminated vocals and the model's

(Continued)

Table 10.1 (Continued)

Type of Operant Control	VB-MAPP Level (L), Milestone (M), and Skill	Example	Mediating Repertoires (Cusps)
Intraverbal Control	Intraverbal—L2 M10: Answers untrained who or where questions	"Where is your hat?" controls "In the closet."	Verbal and non-verbal problem-solving, which may be mediated by joint control
	Intraverbal—L3 M15: Untrained responses to rotating "WH" questions on single topic	Accurate responses to questions, such as, "Where do you play baseball?," "What position do you play?," and "Who do you play with?"	
	Social—L3 M15: Engages in untrained verbal exchanges	Children talk back-and-forth about different properties of an ongoing activity, such as building a house with blocks	Emitting intraverbal-, mand-, tact-, and listener-controlled responses maintained by joint attention as a reinforcer
Autoclitic Control	Vocal—L1 M5: Spontaneously vocalizes whole words with rhythm and intonation	During independent play activities, the child emits tact and mand forms with similar vocal properties as her mother and father	Repertoire acquired by automatic reinforcement from achieving parity with verbal community
	Linguistic—L3 M15: Combines noun and verb phrases grammatically correctly	Describing a novel event as "The boy waved to the girl."	Emitting elementary operants within autoclitic frames and achieving parity

Note: The table lists several multiply controlled verbal and non-verbal operants within the VB-MAPP Milestones Assessment and the mediating repertoires that account for their emission.

Curriculum Considerations for Multiple Control

We have discussed how the VB-MAPP can serve as an assessment tool for identifying developmental milestones related to critical generative repertoires for autistic learners. We have also outlined behavioral cusps responsible for these repertoires. When designing systematic programming for developing generative repertoires, it may be necessary to view an established curriculum through a behavior-analytic lens to effectively teach mediating behaviors for complex responses. There are language-based curricula that provide systematic developmental sequencing of skills, but these developmental curricula often fail to account for the explanatory mediating repertoires.

As practitioners pursue an analysis of curriculum design within the scope of behavioral cusps at the level presented within this chapter, readers may find it useful to reference a diagram of skills sequencing from Francesca degli Espinosa's (2011) doctoral dissertation and in a PowerPoint presentation on "learning how to learn" (degli Espinosa, 2017). Chapter 4 of the dissertation provides a detailed account of a sequence of verbal behavior programming consistent with a molecular analysis of behavioral cusps. Some fundamental generative repertoires emphasized throughout the document include two types of bidirectional naming skills: listener-to-speaker (e.g., self-echoic mediated listener-to-tact transfer) and speaker-to-speaker (e.g., self-tact mediated listener-to-intraverbal transfer). Studies within the dissertation support procedures for training these repertoires. The full details of degli Espinosa's analysis are beyond the scope of the present chapter; however, we recommend reading Chapter 6 of degli Espinosa (2011) for an example of a joint control teaching procedure in which degli Espinosa demonstrated robust results in training a listener-to-tact naming repertoire to participants who failed to acquire the repertoire incidentally through listener selection training alone.

All of the participants in the study who failed to emit untrained tact-controlled responses following successful listener-selections of those items eventually acquired a repertoire of tacting novel items following accurate corresponding listener-selections after the systematic naming protocol was implemented. This particular protocol might be useful to teach a repertoire of the kinds of listener-to-tact naming skills (mediated by joint attention and joint control) that are commonly observed in less-structured environments.

Teaching Multiply Controlled Verbal and Non-Verbal Responding

The taxonomy of verbal operant classes offered by Skinner is elegant and quickly draws the attention of the reader interested in the practical application of the analysis. That fact is not offered without some precautions. "… our task is not necessarily to classify behavior but to identify its controlling variables"

(Palmer, 2016, p. 98). Moreover, the design of a language treatment program that fails to consider multiple controlling variables for each operant would have little chance of producing the complex verbal responding that results from the interaction of controlling variables in the real world. "... If one fails to consider multiple control, one's interpretations of verbal behavior are likely to be conspicuously inadequate." (Michael et al., 2011, p. 4). Recent advances in the application of Skinner's analysis of verbal behavior have acknowledged the role of multiple control in the development of complex responding and have called for increased research activity in this area (Aguirre et al., 2016; DeSouza et al., 2017; Stauch et al., 2017). Complex responding requires a flexible repertoire in which responses to novel stimuli result from previous exposure to related stimuli.

The literature has clearly shifted toward identifying the multiple variables that account for complex verbal responses (DeSouza et al., 2017). The following tables provide the practitioner with a guide to past and current research on teaching multiply controlled verbal behavior across several operant categories. The authors of the following studies have used one or more of the behavioral cusps identified in this chapter.

Mand Control

The teaching of tacts will sometimes produce mand control. Skinner (1957) acknowledged the occasional interdependence of operants when he stated, "The speaker commonly starts with a tact and then appears to possess a corresponding mand" (p. 188). Skinner offered an example of a child in a store asking the name of a toy, and when told "doodler," he immediately emitted the mand-controlled response, "Buy me a doodler" (p. 188). Skinner added the caveat that this may only occur with a particular history of reinforcement. He suggested that all mands may, in fact, be tacts of momentarily desired items. Further, mands always produce a state of affairs or items that may produce related tact control at a later date.

Research on Mand Control. Teaching tacts to individuals with substantial mand and tact repertoires might produce untrained mand control. This incorporates divergent multiple control in the form of a tact-to-mand transfer procedure (see Table 10.2).

Skinner (1957) defined question-asking (i.e., mand-controlled responses for information) as mands for verbal action. In other words, the reinforcers that maintain the repertoires of mand-controlled responding for information are verbal discriminative stimuli that control subsequent responding from the asker (see Table 10.3). Mand-controlled responding for information is a complex response usually not acquired by children until three years of age (Sundberg, 2008). This skill is often taught explicitly to autistic learners (Cengher et al., 2022). Acquisition of this skill can be valuable since it provides access to

Table 10.2 Tact-to-Mand Transfer Procedures

Study/Article	Research Type (R) and Participant Type (P)	Skills Addressed	Mediating Repertoires (Cusps)
Finn et al., 2012	R: Empirical P: Autistic	Novel requesting (i.e., mand-controlled) behavior	Verbal and non-verbal problem-solving, which may be mediated by joint control; Emitting mands within autoclitic frames
Hall & Sundberg, 1987	R: Empirical P: Intellectually Disabled, Deaf	Novel requesting (i.e., mand-controlled) behavior	Verbal and non-verbal problem-solving, which may be mediated by joint control
Nuzzolo-Gomez & Greer, 2004	R: Empirical P: Developmenatally Disabled, Autistic	Novel requesting (i.e., mand-controlled) behavior	Verbal and non-verbal problem-solving, which may be mediated by joint control; Emitting mands within autoclitic frames
Petursdottir et al., 2005	R: Empirical P: Neurotypical	Novel requesting (i.e., mand-controlled) behavior	Verbal and non-verbal problem-solving, which may be mediated by joint control
Ribeiro et al., 2010	R: Empirical P: Intellectually Disabled	Novel requesting (i.e., mand-controlled) behavior	Verbal and non-verbal problem-solving, which may be mediated by joint control
Sigafoos, 1990	R: Empirical P: Intellectually Disabled	Novel requesting (i.e., mand-controlled) behavior	Verbal and non-verbal problem-solving, which may be mediated by joint control
Wallace et al., 2006	R: Empirical P: Autistic	Novel requesting (i.e., mand-controlled) behavior	Verbal and non-verbal problem-solving, which may be mediated by joint control

Note: Research describing procedures to teach mand control after tact control training.

Table 10.3 Mand-Controlled Responses for Information

Study/Article	Research Type (R) and Participant Type (P)	Skills Addressed	Mediating Repertoires (Cusps)
Cengher et al., 2022: Mand control for *what, where, when, how, which, why, who*	**R:** Review **P:** Autistic	Novel requesting (i.e., mand-controlled) behavior	Emitting mands within relevant autoclitic frames
Lechago & Lowe, 2015	**R:** Review **P:** Autistic	Novel requesting (i.e., mand-controlled) behavior	Emitting mands within relevant autoclitic frames
Lechago et al., 2010	**R:** Empirical **P:** Autistic	Novel requesting (i.e., mand-controlled) behavior	Emitting mands within relevant autoclitic frames

Note: Conceptual papers and research describing methods to teach mand control for information.

information that might provide opportunities to contact other forms of reinforcement (Cengher et al., 2022). The protocols for teaching this repertoire involve scenarios that establish information (i.e., verbal discriminative stimuli) as a reinforcer and then prompting the mand for information with an autoclitic frame appropriate to the motivation (e.g., "What is X?," "How do I X?," "Where is X?," etc.).

Tact Control

Tacts are often under the multiple control of an audience, a verbal antecedent ("What is it?"), and a non-verbal stimulus (Sundberg & Partington, 1998). Most research on teaching tact control has used stimulus control transfer procedures, such as echoic or textual prompts (DeSouza et al., 2017). Although these procedures typically require the ongoing teaching of each response, DeSouza et al. (2017) pointed out that there is a growing body of research on teaching untrained, tact-controlled responses. MEI, along with instructive feedback, matrix training, and listener training, have all exploited covert precurrent verbal mediating responses to teach multiply controlled generative tact control.

Research on Tact Control. Multiply controlled, untrained tact control has resulted from MEI in which tact, listener, and match-to-sample trials are interspersed among several non-verbal stimuli (photos or objects, see Table 10.4). MEI has been demonstrated to produce C-BiN repertoires, which account for the production of untrained tact-controlled responses in some autistic learners.

Table 10.4 Multiple Exemplar Instruction May Facilitate Tact-Controlled Responding

Study/Article	Research Type (R) and Participant Type (P)	Skills Addressed	Mediating Repertoires (Cusps)
Delfs et al., 2014; Delfs & Frampton, 2014; Fiorile & Greer, 2007; Frampton et al., 2017; Gilic & Greer, 2011; Greer & Keohane, 2005; Greer et al., 2005; Greer & Ross, 2008; Hawkins et al., 2009; Nuzzolo-Gomez & Greer, 2004; Olaff et al., 2017; Olaff & Holth, 2020; Yoon et al., 2023	R: Empirical P: Autistic	Tact-controlled responding	Listener-to-tact bidirectional naming; Verbal and non-verbal problem-solving, which may be mediated by joint control

Note: MEI research papers that have demonstrated the production of untrained tacts.

By correlating in time, the presentation of a non-verbal stimulus with the corresponding tact, individuals have subsequently produced the tact even without a requirement to respond or socially-mediated reinforcement. This method has been identified as Stimulus Pairing Observation Procedure (SPOS, see Table 10.5).

A strategy similar to SPOS, Instructive Feedback, has been found to be effective in producing tact control. In these studies, tacts were modeled in the presence of a non-verbal stimulus and embedded during instruction of other skills without a requirement to respond to the modeled stimulus (see Table 10.6).

Responding to stimuli containing more than one element is a challenge for many autistic learners (Eikeseth & Smith, 2013). For example, tacts of objects containing multi-stimulus elements such as size, shape, color, actions, or noun-action sequences, such as "kicking ball," present difficulties for many autistic learners. As demonstrated in the example in Figure 10.7, matrix training is an arrangement of targets in which teaching the tacts "dog drinking," "bear jumping," and "alligator eating" result in the acquisition of several untrained responses (see also Table 10.7).

Mand control training might produce untrained and tact-controlled responses (see Table 10.8). The presence of a non-verbal stimulus during mand control training may implicitly train tact control (Petursdottir et al., 2005).

Table 10.5 SPOS May Lead to Tact-Controlled Responding

Study/Article	Research Type (R) and Participant Type (P)	Skills Addressed	Mediating Repertoires (Cusps)
Boelens et al., 2007; Byrne et al., 2014; Hawkins et al., 2018; Lobato & de Souza, 2020; Pérez-González, et al., 2014; Petursdottir et al., 2020; Rosales et al., 2012; Solares & Fryling, 2019; Vallinger-Brown et al., 2014	**R:** Empirical **P:** Autistic and Neurotypical	Tact-controlled responding	Listener-to-tact bidirectional naming; Verbal and non-verbal problem-solving, which may be mediated by joint control

Note: SPOS research papers that have demonstrated the teaching of untrained tact-controlled responses.

Table 10.6 Instructive Feedback May Produce Tact-Controlled Responding

Study/Article	Research Type (R) and Participant Type (P)	Skills Addressed	Mediating Repertoires (Cusps)
Al-Sharif, 2023; Carrol & Kodak, 2015; Dass et al., 2018; Delmolino et al., 2013; Dressel et al., 2019; Ferguson et al., 2020; Frampton & Shillingsburg, 2020; Gavidia et al., 2022; Haq et al., 2017; Leaf et al., 2017; Loughrey et al., 2014; Nottingham et al., 2017; Nottingham et al., 2020; Reichow & Wolery, 2011; Tullis et al., 2017, 2019, 2021, 2022b; Vladescu & Kodak, 2013	R: Empirical P: Autistic	Tact-controlled responding	Listener-to-tact bidirectional naming; Verbal and non-verbal problem-solving, which may be mediated by joint control

Note: Research papers that have demonstrated the teaching of untrained tact control through instructive feedback.

	DRINKING	JUMPING	EATING
DOG	**"Dog drinking"** **(trained response)**	"Dog jumping" (untrained response)	"Dog eating" (untrained response)
BEAR	"Bear drinking" (untrained response)	**"Bear jumping"** **(trained response)**	"Bear eating" (untrained response)
ALLIGATOR	"Alligator drinking" (untrained response)	"Alligator jumping" (untrained response)	**"Alligator eating"** **(trained response)**

Figure 10.7 Example of a matrix grid to teach multielement tact-controlled responding. *Note:* This example demonstrates the benefit of matrix training in producing untrained tact-controlled responses.

Listener selection training has been demonstrated to produce tact responding (see Table 10.9). In this type of training, a learner is asked to select an item from an array of objects or photos when told its name (Grow & LeBlanc, 2013). This is sometimes referred to as auditory-visual conditional (AVCD) discrimination training (Bergmann & Kodak, 2023).

Listener-Response Control

Complex listener responding might involve AVCDs (Kodak et al., 2015, 2022). Michael et al. (2011) defined conditional discrimination as one in which "the effect of a discriminative stimulus depends on other stimuli" (p. 37). Complex conditional discriminations occur whenever the product of an auditory stimulus alters the evocative effect of a visual stimulus regarding performance or selection. Kodak et al. (2022) pointed out that "Many everyday tasks require an AVCD, and this type of discrimination (also referred to as receptive identification, receptive labeling, and listener responses) is frequently targeted in comprehensive behavioral intervention programs…" (p. 623). For example, tasks such as asking a learner to select the photo of an elephant from a page of a book that includes zoo animals require a composite of multiply controlled discriminations. The instructor asks the learner to "point to the elephant" in the presence of the complex scene in Figure 10.8.

Table 10.7 Matrix Training May Lead to Complex Tact-Controlled Responses

Study/Article	Research Type (R) and Participant Type (P)	Skills Addressed	Mediating Repertoires (Cusps)
Curiel et al., 2020;	R: Review P: N/A	Tact-controlled responding	Emits tacts of items and actions/ adjectives within relevant autoclitic frames: (adjective) (noun) or (noun) (verb)ing
Frampton & Axe, 2023;	R: Tutorial P: N/A	Tact-controlled responding	N/A
Kemmerer et al., 2021;	R: Review P: N/A	Tact-controlled responding	Atomic echoic and tact behavior
Bergman et al., 2022; Curiel et al., 2016, 2018 Curiel & Curiel, 2021 Frampton et al., 2016; Frampton et al., 2019; Jimenez-Gomez, et al., 2019; Kohler & Malott, 2014, 2015; Marya et al., 2021; Naoi et al., 2006; Pauwels et al., 2015	R: Empirical P: Autistic and Neurotypical	Tact-controlled responding	Emits tacts of items and actions/ adjectives within relevant autoclitic frames: (adjective) (noun) or (noun) (verb)ing

Note: Research demonstrating methods to teach untrained tact control.

Table 10.8 Mand Control Training May Lead to Tact-Controlled Responses

Study/Article	Research Type (R) and Participant Type (P)	Skills Addressed	Mediating Repertoires (Cusps)
Albert et al., 2012; Finn et al., 2012; Nuzzolo-Gomez & Greer, 2004; Petursdottir et al., 2005	**R:** Empirical **P:** Autistic	Tact-controlled responding	Listener-to-tact bidirectional naming; Verbal and non-verbal problem-solving, which may be mediated by joint control

Note: Research has demonstrated that teaching mand control may produce untrained tact-controlled responses.

Table 10.9 Listener Selection May Produce Tact-Controlled Responses

Study/Article	Research Type (R) and Participant Type (P)	Skills Addressed	Mediating Repertoires (Cusps)
Fisher et al., 2019; Keintz et al., 2011; Ribeiro et al., 2010	**R:** Empirical **P:** Intellectually Disabled	Tact-controlled responding	Listener-to-tact bidirectional naming; Verbal and non-verbal problem-solving, which may be mediated by joint control

Note: Research studies have demonstrated that listener selection training may produce untrained tact-controlled responses.

Discriminative Stimulus	Evoked Response	Consequence
(1) "Point to the elephant"	(2) Echoing "elephant" while scanning the array of photos	(3) Scanning stops and is reinforced by seeing the elephant while simultaneously echoing and tacting "elephant"
(4) Sight of elephant	(5) Pointing to the elephant	(6) Instructional reinforcement

Figure 10.8 Description of the controlling relations in listener selection responses.
Note: Responses and functional relationships within listener selection activities

Verbal mediation plays an important role in listener selection responding. Further, listener responding might also involve following multiple-step directions or matching to a sample that includes a delay between the presentation of the instruction and the completion of all of the steps of the task.

Research on Listener-Response Control. Multiply controlled untrained listener-responding has resulted from MEI in which tact, listener, and match-to-sample trials are interspersed among several non-verbal stimuli (photos or objects; see Table 10.10). MEI has been demonstrated to produce C-BiN repertoires.

Table 10.10 Multiple Exemplar Instruction May Facilitate Multiply Controlled Listener Responses

Study/Article	Research Type (R) and Participant Type (P)	Skills Addressed	Mediating Repertoires (Cusps)
Fiorile & Greer, 2007; Gilic & Greer, 2011; Greer et al., 2005; Greer et al., 2007; Hawkins et al., 2009; Nuzzolo et al., 2001; Olaff et al. 2017; Olaff & Holth, 2020; Yoon et al., 2023	**R:** Empirical **P:** Autistic	Untrained listener-selections	Tact-to-listener bidirectional naming; Verbal and non-verbal problem-solving, which may be mediated by joint control

Note: MEI research papers have demonstrated the production of untrained listener responses.

Further, recent studies have investigated whether speaker or listener behavior more efficiently results in untrained multiply controlled responses. It appears that speaker behavior frequently mediates the acquisition of listener behavior in the form of AVCDs and other listener responses, including direction-following (see Table 10.11).

The studies in Table 10.12 document the acquisition of listener behavior in the form of multiply controlled untrained direction-following, multiple selection responses, and match-to-sample following the training of speaker behavior.

Intraverbal Control

Several reviews of the literature on verbal behavior over the years have documented the increasing number of studies that have focused on teaching intraverbals (DeSouza et al., 2019; Oah & Dickinson, 1989; Petursdottir, 2018; Petursdottir & Devine, 2017; Sautter & LeBlanc, 2006). These reviews demonstrate the evolution of teaching intraverbals controlled by a single verbal antecedent control to the current trend of teaching intraverbally controlled behavior. Palmer's (2016) analysis of intraverbal control led to a greater interest in teaching complex intraverbal behavior, as documented in recent literature reviews (Aguirre et al., 2016; Jennings et al., 2022).

Many autistic learners fail to acquire a complex intraverbal repertoire (Sundberg & Sundberg, 2011). It appears that the complexity of stimulus control contributes to this difficulty. Generally, the multiple control involved in

Table 10.11 Speaker Training Facilitates the Acquisition of Multiply Controlled Listener Selection Responses

Study/Article	Research Type (R) and Participant Type (P)	Skills Addressed	Mediating Repertoires (Cusps)
Bergman & Kodak, 2023	**R:** Book Chapter **P:** N/A	Untrained listener-selections	Tact-to-listener bidirectional naming; Verbal and non-verbal problem-solving, which may be mediated by joint control
Contreras et al., 2020	**R:** Review **P:** N/A	Untrained listener-selections	Tact-to-listener bidirectional naming; Verbal and non-verbal problem-solving, which may be mediated by joint control
Petursdottir & Carr, 2011	**R:** Review **P:** N/A	Untrained listener-selections	Tact-to-listener bidirectional naming; Verbal and non-verbal problem-solving, which may be mediated by joint control
Bao et al., 2017	**R:** Empirical **P:** Autistic	Untrained listener-selections	Tact-to-listener bidirectional naming; Verbal and non-verbal problem-solving, which may be mediated by joint control
Delfs et al., 2014	**R:** Empirical **P:** Autistic	Untrained listener-selections	Tact-to-listener bidirectional naming; Verbal and non-verbal problem-solving, which may be mediated by joint control
Delfs & Frampton, 2014	**R:** Empirical **P:** Autistic	Untrained listener-selections	Tact-to-listener bidirectional naming; Verbal and non-verbal problem-solving, which may be mediated by joint control
Díaz et al., 2020	**R:** Empirical **P:** Neurotypical	Untrained listener-selections	Tact-to-listener bidirectional naming; Verbal and non-verbal problem-solving, which may be mediated by joint control

(Continued)

Table 10.11 (Continued)

Study/Article	Research Type (R) and Participant Type (P)	Skills Addressed	Mediating Repertoires (Cusps)
Fisher et al., 2019	**R:** Empirical **P:** Autistic	Untrained listener-selections	Tact-to-listener bidirectional naming; Verbal and non-verbal problem-solving, which may be mediated by joint control
Frampton et al., 2017	**R:** Empirical **P:** Autistic	Untrained listener-selections	Tact-to-listener bidirectional naming; Verbal and non-verbal problem-solving, which may be mediated by joint control
Ingvarsson et al., 2012	**R:** Empirical **P:** Autistic	Untrained listener-selections	Tact-to-listener bidirectional naming; Verbal and non-verbal problem-solving, which may be mediated by joint control
Jennings & Miguel, 2017	**R:** Empirical **P:** Neurotypical	Untrained listener-selections	Tact-to-listener bidirectional naming; Verbal and non-verbal problem-solving, which may be mediated by joint control
Kodak & Paden, 2015	**R:** Empirical **P:** Autistic	Untrained listener-selections	Tact-to-listener bidirectional naming; Verbal and non-verbal problem-solving, which may be mediated by joint control
Moustakis & Mellon, 2018	**R:** Empirical **P:** Dev. Disabled and Neurotypical	Untrained listener-selections	Tact-to-listener bidirectional naming; Verbal and non-verbal problem-solving, which may be mediated by joint control
Luoma et al., 2024	**R:** Empirical **P:** Neurotypical	Untrained listener-selections	Intraverbal bidirectional naming; Verbal and non-verbal problem-solving, which may be mediated by joint control

(Continued)

Table 10.11 (Continued)

Study/Article	Research Type (R) and Participant Type (P)	Skills Addressed	Mediating Repertoires (Cusps)
Sprinkle & Miguel, 2012	**R:** Empirical **P:** Autistic	Untrained listener-selections	Tact-to-listener bidirectional naming; Verbal and non-verbal problem-solving, which may be mediated by joint control
Sundberg & Sundberg, 1990	**R:** Empirical **P:** Intellectually Disabled	Untrained listener-selections	Tact-to-listener bidirectional naming; Verbal and non-verbal problem-solving, which may be mediated by joint control
Sundberg et al., 2018	R: Empirical P: Dev. Disabled and Neurotypical Adults	Untrained listener-selections	Tact-to-listener bidirectional naming; Verbal and non-verbal problem-solving, which may be mediated by joint control
Wraikat et al., 1991	**R:** Empirical **P:** Dev. Disabled	Untrained listener-selections	Tact-to-listener bidirectional naming; Verbal and non-verbal problem-solving, which may be mediated by joint control

Note: Research papers demonstrating the acquisition of untrained listener-selections following speaker training.

intraverbal responding requires verbal conditional discriminations (VC^D). "That is, one discriminative stimulus alters the evocative effect of a second stimulus in the same antecedent (or vice versa), and they collectively evoke a response." (Sundberg & Sundberg, 2011, p. 25) This is a type of discrimination in which the correct response depends upon at least two stimuli converging to evoke a correct response. For example, failure to emit responses under divergent control results in the response "truck" to the question, "Name some vehicles?"

Palmer (2016) suggested that the analysis of multiply controlled and untrained intraverbal control based on VC^{D}s might not account for all complex intraverbal behavior. In fact, it might only account for responses with a prior history of responding to the specific antecedent stimuli. More often, responses to questions such as, "What did you do last evening?" result from mediating responses

Table 10.12 Multiply Controlled Direction-Following, Multiple Selection Responses, and Match-to-Sample Responding

Study/Article	Research Type (R) and Participant Type (P)	Skills Addressed	Mediating Repertoires (Cusps)
Causin et al., 2013	**R:** Empirical **P:** Autistic	Untrained listener-selections	Tact-to-listener bidirectional naming; Verbal and non-verbal problem-solving, which may be mediated by joint control
Clough et al., 2016	**R:** Empirical **P:** Neurotypical	Untrained listener-selections	Tact-to-listener bidirectional naming; Verbal and non-verbal problem-solving, which may be mediated by joint control
DeGraff & Schlinger, 2012	**R:** Empirical **P:** Neurotypical	Untrained listener-selections	Tact-to-listener bidirectional naming; Verbal and non-verbal problem-solving, which may be mediated by joint control
Gutierrez, 2006	**R:** Empirical **P:** Neurotypical	Untrained listener-selections	Verbal and non-verbal problem-solving, which may be mediated by joint control
Hozella et al., 2022	**R:** Empirical **P:** Autistic	Untrained listener-selections	Tact-to-listener bidirectional naming; Verbal and non-verbal problem-solving, which may be mediated by joint control
Ratkos et al., 2016	**R:** Empirical **P:** Autistic	Untrained listener-selections	Verbal and non-verbal problem-solving, which may be mediated by joint control
Sidener, 2006	**R:** Empirical **P:** Autistic	Untrained listener-selections	Tact-to-listener bidirectional naming; Verbal and non-verbal problem-solving, which may be mediated by joint control

(Continued)

Table 10.12 (Continued)

Study/Article	Research Type (R) and Participant Type (P)	Skills Addressed	Mediating Repertoires (Cusps)
Tu, 2006	**R:** Empirical **P:** Autistic	Untrained listener-selections	Verbal and non-verbal problem-solving, which may be mediated by joint control
Vosters & Luczynski, 2020	**R:** Empirical **P:** Autistic	Untrained listener-selections	Tact-to-listener bidirectional naming; Verbal and non-verbal problem-solving, which may be mediated by joint control

Note: Research papers demonstrating the effects of speaker behavior on the acquisition of untrained listener responses.

evoked by the antecedent stimulus (see Intraverbal Control section above). Palmer suggested that covert intraverbals and visual imagining might provide supplemental stimulation beyond the verbal antecedent to evoke the response scheduled for reinforcement.

Research on Intraverbal Control. Several recent conceptual papers and literature reviews on intraverbal control have provided the practitioner with a comprehensive overview of the variables that must be considered when teaching intraverbal control to learners who do not acquire this repertoire typically (see Table 10.13). Most important is the distinction between intraverbals and intraverbal control (Palmer 2016).

The research studies in Table 10.14 demonstrate the role of verbal and non-verbal problem-solving repertoires in the production of responses under intraverbal control. Procedures that include differential observing responses, self-questioning, and visual and auditory imagining are included.

A growing body of research has demonstrated that teaching related or components operant responses (e.g., tact, multiple tact, listener, and intraverbals) might result in untrained intraverbal control. The research studies in Table 10.15 demonstrated multiply controlled intraverbal responses generated by teaching related operants.

Several prerequisite skills taught in a sequence might produce multiply controlled and untrained intraverbal control (Sundberg & Sundberg, 2011). When related multiple tacts, multiple listener responses, intraverbal categorization, and listener compound discriminations are acquired, there is an interplay among these

Table 10.13 Conceptual and Review Papers on Teaching Intraverbal Control

Study/Article	Research Type (R) and Participant Type (P)	Skills Addressed	Mediating Repertoires (Cusps)
Aguirre et al., 2016	**R**: Review **P**: N/A	Intraverbal Control	N/A
Axe, 2008	**R**: Conceptual **P**: N/A	Conditional Discriminations-Intraverbal Control	N/A
Eikeseth & Smith, 2013	**R**: Conceptual **P**: N/A	Compound Stimuli-Intraverbal Control	N/A
Jennings et al., 2022	**R**: Review **P**: N/A	Intraverbal Control	N/A
Palmer, 2016	**R**: Conceptual **P**: N/A	Intraverbal Control	Verbal and non-verbal problem-solving, which may be mediated by joint control
Stauch et al., 2017	**R**: Review **P**: N/A	Intraverbal Control	N/A
Sundberg, 2016	**R**: Conceptual **P**: N/A	Conditional Discriminations-Intraverbal Control	N/A

Note: Conceptual and review papers describing the acquisition of untrained intraverbal responses.

components skills that produce untrained intraverbal control (see Table 10.15; e.g., DeSouza et al., 2019; Jennings et al., 2023).

Intraverbal-Tact Control

Most objects and other stimuli in the environment contain several dimensions or properties, including shape, color, and size, along with the identity or the name that the verbal community has established as a tact. For example, the object in the sketch in Figure 10.9 below is something we tact as a "ball." Its properties include its orange color and round shape.

If asked to tact the item in response to the question, "What is it?" or to tact any of the dimensions of the ball with questions such as, "What shape?" or "What color?" many autistic learners experience difficulty (degli Espinosa, 2022; Rodriguez et al., 2022; Aragon et al., 2024). They might respond with the name of the item when asked, "What color?" or the color when asked, "What is it?" A multiply controlled response is required for a correct response. Both the

Table 10.14 Conceptual and Empirical Papers on the Role of Problem-Solving

Study/Article	Research Type (R) and Participant Type (P)	Skills Addressed	Mediating Repertoires (Cusps)
Axe et al., 2019	R: Conceptual P: Autistic	Problem-solving methods	N/A
Brinkerhoff et al., in press	R: Empirical P: Autistic	Intraverbally controlled responses to questions about missing items	Verbal and non-verbal problem-solving, which may be mediated by joint control
Frampton & Shillingsburg, 2018	R: Empirical P: Autistic	Answer novel "how" questions	Verbal and non-verbal problem-solving, which may be mediated by joint control
Keesey-Phelan et al., 2022	R: Empirical P: Autistic	Answer questions about past events	Verbal and non-verbal problem-solving, which may be mediated by joint control
Kisamore et al., 2011	R: Empirical P: Neurotypical	Respond to questions by naming items in a category (e.g. "Name a bunch of animals?")	Verbal and non-verbal problem-solving, which may be mediated by joint control
Kisamore et al., 2013	R: Empirical P: Neurotypical	Answering antonym- and synonym-based questions	Verbal and non-verbal problem-solving, which may be mediated by joint control
Kisamore et al., 2016	R: Empirical P: Autistic	Answer novel noun-adjective questions (e.g., "What's a vehicle that's red?")	Verbal and non-verbal problem-solving, which may be mediated by joint control
Mellor et al., 2015	R: Empirical P: Neurotypical	Answer questions about animal or object sounds	Verbal and non-verbal problem-solving, which may be mediated by joint control
McGee et al., 2024	R: Empirical P: Neurotypical	Visual-Visual Match-to-Sample	Verbal and non-verbal problem-solving, which may be mediated by joint control

(Continued)

Table 10.14 (Continued)

Study/Article	Research Type (R) and Participant Type (P)	Skills Addressed	Mediating Repertoires (Cusps)
Sautter et al., 2011	**R**: Empirical **P**: Neurotypical	Respond to questions by naming items in a category (e.g., "Tell me some farm animals?")	Verbal and non-verbal problem-solving, which may be mediated by joint control

Note: Conceptual papers describing the role of problem-solving in teaching intraverbal control.

Table 10.15 Teaching Related Operants Leads to Multiply Controlled Intraverbal Responding

Study/Article	Research Type (R) and Participant Type (P)	Skills Addressed	Mediating Repertoires (Cusps)
Allan et al., 2015; Almås et al., 2022; Alzrayer, 2020; Bellos-Diaz et al., 2015; Conine et al., 2021; DeSouza et al., 2019; Devine et al., 2016; Dickes & Kodak, 2015 Grannan & Rehfeldt, 2012; Jennings et al., 2023; Keintz et al., 2011; Miguel et al., 2005; Pérez-Gonzáles et al., 2007; Pérez-Gonzáles et al., 2018; Petursdottir et al., 2008; Kodak & Paden, 2015; Shillingsburg et al., 2018; Smith et al., 2016; Thakore & Petursdottir, 2022 Vallinger-Brown et al., 2014	**R**: Empirical **P**: Autistic & Neurotypical	Various untrained intraverbally controlled responses	Contiguous usage; Verbal and non-verbal problem-solving, which may be mediated by joint control

Note: Research reports demonstrating that teaching relevant operants may produce untrained intraverbal response.

Figure 10.9 Example stimulus illustrating multiple control in intraverbal–tact responding. The verbal antecedent question and the nonverbal stimulus specified by the question must jointly control the response (e.g., "ball," "orange," or "round").

verbal antecedent question and the non-verbal stimulus specified by the question must ultimately control the response (Michael et al., 2011).

Research on Intraverbal-Tact Control. Researchers have used different methods and posed different analyses to describe the mediating repetoires that account for the acquisition of intraverbal-tact responses (see Table 10.16).

Within one study, Rodriguez et al. (2022) demonstrated that teaching a sequence of related components skills (DeSouza et al., 2019; Jennings et al., 2023) produced multiply controlled intraverbal-tact responses in some autistic learners. A follow-up study by Aragon et al. (2024) examined the variables that might have accounted for the failure of some autistic individuals in the Rodriguez et al. study to acquire intraverbal-tact responses. Teaching a differential observing response (DOR), along with requiring either divergent intraverbal responses to the question or echoic rehearsal of the divergent intraverbals, produced intraverbal-tact responses in participants who failed to acquire the responses through other methods. In similar performances, degli Espinosa (2022) demonstrated the role of problem-solving and autoclitic frames in teaching multiply controlled intraverbal-tact responding.

Equivalence-Based Instruction

Equivalence-based instruction (EBI) has its roots in the seminal work of Sidman and Tailby (1982). The methods are derived from the principles of stimulus

Table 10.16 Teaching Multiply Controlled Intraverbal-Tact Responding

Study/Article	Research Type (R) and Participant Type (P)	Skills Addressed	Mediating Repertoires (Cusps)
degli Espinosa, 2022	**R:** Conceptual **P:** N/A	Intraverbal-tact Control (question answering)	N/A
degli Espinosa, Gerosa et al., 2021 ; degli Espinosa, Wolff et al., 2021; Meleshkevich et al., 2021	**R:** Empirical **P:** Autistic	Intraverbal-tact Control (question answering)	Verbal and non-verbal problem-solving, which may be mediated by joint control; Emitting elementary verbal operants within relevant autoclitic frames
Rodriguez et al., 2022	**R:** Empirical **P:** Autistic	Intraverbal-tact Control (question answering)	Verbal and non-verbal problem-solving, which may be mediated by joint control; Interplay of component skills
Aragon et al., 2024	**R:** Empirical **P:** Autistic	Intraverbal-tact Control (question answering)	Verbal and non-verbal problem-solving, which may be mediated by joint control: Emitting DOR; divergent intraverbal responses and echoic rehearsal

Note: Research papers demonstrating research methods to teaching untrained intraverbal-tact responses.

equivalence. Using a match-to-sample conditional discrimination procedure, contingencies are arranged such that the stimuli involved are said to be "…treated as interchangeable for one another within a particular context, in the absence of any physical similarity among them and in the absence of a reinforcement history of treating them as such" (Carp & Petursdottir, 2015, p. 104). Interest in EBI has been generated by claims that it can produce untrained responding after teaching only a few stimulus relations. Figure 10.10 shows an example of the benefits of this approach.

When you teach a verbally competent individual to select the photo of a cat from an array of objects when asked to do so (B → A) and to also select a photo of a cat when they see the written word cat (C → A), as indicated by the solid lines in this diagram, all the untrained relations depicted by the dashed lines

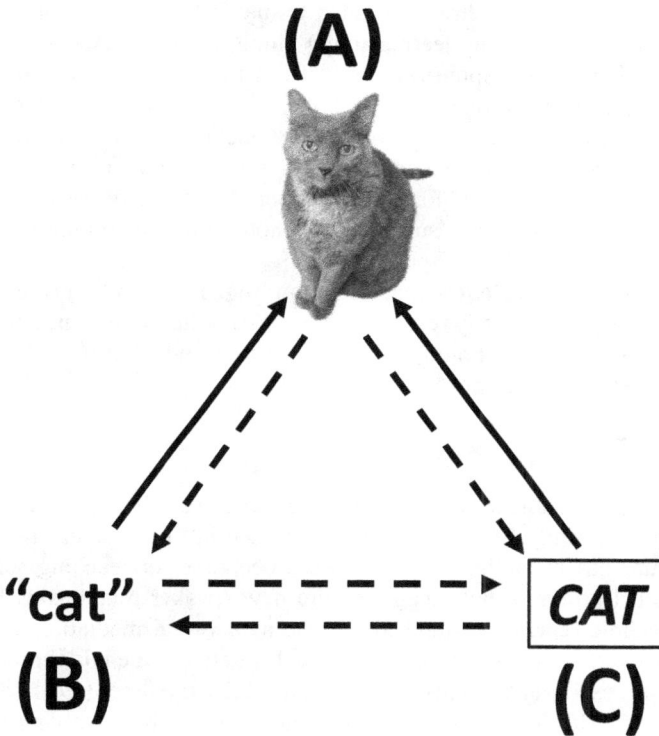

Figure 10.10 Stimulus equivalence example.
Note: Arrangement of stimuli within a stimulus equivalence example.

might result without any additional teaching. For instance, following the training described above, we might observe the individual say cat when shown the photo (A → B; tact control), match the photo of the cat to the written word (A → C; match-to-sample), select the written word cat when the word is heard (B → C; textual selection), and say the word cat when shown the written word (C → B; textual control). While there is disagreement about the behavioral mechanisms that account for the multiply controlled responding generated by EBI, verbal mediation appears to be a fundamental controlling variable (Eikseth & Smith, 1992; Schlinger & Blakely, 2024; Sprinkle & Miguel, 2012).

> Stimulus induction on the basis of a "relation" presents no difficulty in a natural science if the relation can be described in physical terms. Where this appears to be the case, we have to turn to other possibilities for example, ... mediating behavior....
>
> (Skinner, 1953, p. 138)

For example, after being directly trained to match the photo of the cat to the written word (C → A), the learner might simultaneously respond (overtly or covertly) with a verbal response such as, "The written word goes with the photo of the cat." During an untrained test trial, the individual might be presented with the written word *CAT* and an array of pictures, including a photo of the cat. The incidentally acquired verbal response might mediate a novel jointly controlled matching response scheduled for reinforcement (A → C). Non-verbal mediation during the test trial, such as visualizing the photo of the cat, might also contribute to developing untrained responses.

Research on Equivalence-Based Responding. The term EBI (Fienup et al., 2010) is now used to identify research that uses stimulus equivalence procedures to teach verbal behavior and other skills to children and adults (see Table 10.17 for examples of this literature).

Closing Remarks

Joint control and bidirectional naming are central to mediating many problem-solving tasks in daily life. As we have discussed in this chapter, the behavioral literature has capitalized on effective procedures for teaching self-echoic rehearsal to learners to help them acquire new speaker relations as listeners. The self-echoic repertoire might also serve as a verbal mediation strategy to "hold on to a stimulus" when faced with a delay between the initial problem and the terminal response. With respect to such problems, Palmer (1991, 2006) and Skinner (1957, 1980) have identified commonplace problem-solving scenarios in which joint control mediates the solution but where self-echoic rehearsal fails to account for the problem-solving strategy. For instance, when we try to recall the name of a person we happen to see in the grocery store, the eventual and sudden *aha!* moment does not occur because of a self-echoic of the person's name. Due to the very nature of the problem, the person's name is not even available as an echoic stimulus. This particular aspect of multiple control is ubiquitous in our daily lives, yet we may not have scratched the surface in its applied or experimental research in behavior analysis.

Implications for Future Directions on Multiple Control and Problem-Solving

How can we teach autistic learners to mediate problem-solving tasks when the actual "solving" is inherently covert to the instructor (and perhaps even covert to the learner)? Skinner did not overlook this problem. In his autobiography, he described a dilemma in which his daughter Deborah was eating a candy bar with her friend and lost her orthodontic retainer because she "forgot" that it was on her lap. One solution to help prevent forgetting could have been to teach her to "hold on to the stimulus" by engaging in self-echoic rehearsal (e.g., "retainer

Table 10.17 Equivalence-Based Instruction to Teach Multiply Controlled Verbal Behavior

Study/Article	Research Type (R) and Participant Type (P)	Skills Addressed	Mediating Repertoires (Cusps)
Blair & Dorsey, 2020	**R:** Book Chapter **P:** N/A	N/A	N/A
Díaz et al., 2023	**R:** Review **P:** Neurotypical	Food Portion Estimates (Speaker and listener responses)	N/A
Pilgrim, 2022	**R:** Book Chapter **P:** N/A	N/A	N/A
Shawler et al., 2023	**R:** Review **P:** N/A	N/A	N/A
Tullis & Gibbs, 2022	**R:** Book Chapter **P:** N/A	N/A	N/A
Belisle et al., 2023	**R:** Empirical **P:** Autistic	Verbal and non-verbal responses related to employee names, jobs and responsibilities	Verbal and non-verbal problem-solving, which may be mediated by joint control
Benitez & Domeniconi, 2023	**R:** Empirical **P:** Autistic	Textual Behavior	Verbal and non-verbal problem-solving, which may be mediated by joint control
Benjo et al., 2018	**R:** Empirical **P:** Autistic	Verbal responses and non-verbal selections	Verbal and non-verbal problem-solving, which may be mediated by joint control
Carp & Petursdottir, 2012	**R:** Empirical **P:** Neurotypical	Intraverbally controlled responses	Verbal and non-verbal problem-solving, which may be mediated by joint control
Ferguson et al., 2022	**R:** Empirical **P:** Autistic Neurotypical	Speaker and listener behavior	Verbal and non-verbal problem-solving, which may be mediated by joint control
Giannakokos et al., 2021	**R:** Empirical **P:** Neurotypical	Safety Skills	Verbal and non-verbal problem-solving, which may be mediated by joint control

(Continued)

Table 10.17 (Continued)

Study/Article	Research Type (R) and Participant Type (P)	Skills Addressed	Mediating Repertoires (Cusps)
Groskreutz et al., 2010	**R:** Empirical **P:** Autistic	Tact- and intraverbally controlled responses	Verbal and non-verbal problem-solving, which may be mediated by joint control
Keintz et al., 2011	**R:** Empirical **P:** Autistic	Verbal responses and non-verbal selections	Verbal and non-verbal problem-solving, which may be mediated by joint control
LaFond et al., 2021	**R:** Empirical **P:** Neurotypical	Caregiver Information (Match-to-sample and intraverbally controlled response)	Verbal and non-verbal problem-solving, which may be mediated by joint control
Pérez-González et al., 2008	**R:** Empirical **P:** Autistic	Intraverbally controlled responses	Verbal and non-verbal problem-solving, which may be mediated by joint control
Rosales et al., 2014	**R:** Empirical **P:** Autistic and Neurotypical	Verbal responses and non-verbal selections	Verbal and non-verbal problem-solving, which may be mediated by joint control
Silva et al., 2018	**R:** Empirical **P:** Autistic	Intraverbally controlled responses	Verbal and non-verbal problem-solving, which may be mediated by joint control
Stanley et al., 2018	**R:** Empirical **P:** Autistic	Academic Skills (Speaker and listener)	Verbal and non-verbal problem-solving, which may be mediated by joint control
Still et al., 2015	**R:** Empirical **P:** Autistic	Mand-controlled responses	Verbal and non-verbal problem-solving, which may be mediated by joint control

(Continued)

Table 10.17 (Continued)

Study/Article	Research Type (R) and Participant Type (P)	Skills Addressed	Mediating Repertoires (Cusps)
Tullis et al., 2019	**R:** Empirical **P:** Autistic	Tact- and intraverbally controlled responses	Verbal and non-verbal problem-solving, which may be mediated by joint control
Zaring-Hinkle et al., 2016	**R:** Empirical **P:** Neurotypical	Intraverbally controlled responses	Verbal and non-verbal problem-solving, which may be mediated by joint control

Note: Research papers demonstrating the effectiveness of EBI to teach untrained verbal behavior to autistic and typical learners.

on lap," "retainer on lap," etc.) as she ate her candy bar, but that would hardly be a practical strategy, given that the rehearsal would compete with enjoying the candy bar and time with her friend. (And we would still be faced with the problem of getting her to engage in the self-echoic strategy in the first place.) Regarding this problem, Skinner (1983) speculated the following:

> This kind of forgetting involves "holding on to a stimulus"—remaining under the control of the retainer-in-the-lap until the time comes to get up, *while scarcely responding to it meanwhile.* A set of materials for teaching machines might be designed to encourage: (1) remembering what it is you are looking for, (2) remembering several things at once, any of which may suddenly be important (cf. the card game "Concentration"), and (3) remembering directions until the opportunity arises to follow them.
>
> (p. 172)

In Skinner's (1953) book *Science and Human Behavior*, he wrote, "In a scientific analysis it is seldom possible to proceed directly to complex cases. We begin with the simple and build up to the complex, step by step" (p. 24). Skinner's (1957) analysis emulated this scientific practice by interpreting basic units of verbal behavior known as the verbal operant classes as an initial step toward a scientific understanding of language and communication. Since Skinner's 1957 publication, behavior analysis has produced a rich body of applied and conceptual research on elementary verbal operants, resulting in an improved understanding of human behavior and an improved quality of life for countless autistic individuals. As behavior analysis continues to build up to more complex cases of verbal behavior, the importance of Skinner's analysis of multiple control appears to be taking center stage. Throughout this chapter, we have provided an overview of the current analytic landscape within both the conceptual and applied domains of multiple control. Skinner's anecdote about the problem with his daughter's retainer is important because it highlights one of many critical aspects of multiple control for which there is still much work to be done. We hope this chapter provides students, professors, practitioners, and researchers with additional tools as they continue to investigate the vast terrain of unexplored areas for research on multiple control and new applications for improving the repertoires of all learners.

References

Aguirre, A. A., & Rehfeldt, R. A. (2015). An evaluation of instruction in visual imagining on the written spelling performance of adolescents with learning disabilities. *The Analysis of Verbal Behavior, 31*(1), 118–125. https://doi.org/10.1007/s40616-015-0028-0

Aguirre, A. A., Valentino, A. L., & LeBlanc, L. A. (2016). Empirical investigations of the intraverbal: 2005–2015. *The Analysis of Verbal Behavior, 32*(2), 139–153. https://doi.org/10.1007/s40616-016-0064-4

Albert, K. M., Carbone, V. J., Murray, D. D., Hagerty, M., & Sweeney-Kerwin, E. J. (2012). Increasing the mand repertoire of children with autism through the use of an interrupted chain procedure. *Behavior Analysis in Practice, 5*(2), 65–76. https://doi.org/10.1007/BF03391825

Alessi, G. (1987). Generative strategies and teaching for generalization. *The Analysis of Verbal Behavior, 5*(1), 15–27. https://doi.org/10.1007/BF03392816

Allan, A. C., Vladescu, J. C., Kisamore, A. N., Reeve, S. A., & Sidener, T. M. (2015). Evaluating the emergence of reverse intraverbals in children with autism. *The Analysis of Verbal Behavior, 31*(1), 59–75. https://doi.org/10.1007/s40616-014-0025-8

Almås, I. K., Smith, D. P., Eldevik, S., & Eikeseth, S. (2022). Emergent intraverbal and reverse intraverbal behavior following listener training in children with autism spectrum disorder. *The Analysis of Verbal Behavior, 38*(1), 1–23. https://doi.org/10.1007/s40616-021-00164-3

Al-Sharif, D. (2023). *Evaluating the effects of instructive feedback on the emergence of verbal behavior* [Unpublished doctoral dissertation]. The Chicago School of Professional Psychology.

Alzrayer, N. M. (2020). The impact of an intraverbal webbing procedure on the emergence of advanced intraverbal skills in children with autism spectrum disorder. *Behavior Analysis in Practice, 13*(4), 914–923. https://doi.org/10.1007/s40617-020-00410-5

Ampuero, M. E., & Miklos, M. (2019). The effect of joint control training on the performance of multiply controlled behavior: A systematic literature review relevant to children with autism spectrum disorder and other developmental disabilities. *The Analysis of Verbal Behavior, 35*(2), 149–171. https://doi.org/10.1007/s40616-019-00116-y

Aragon, M. A., Rodriguez, N. M., Luczynski, K. C., & McKeown, C. A. (2024). Facilitating the emergence of intraverbal tacts by autistic children via joint control. *Journal of Applied Behavior Analysis*, *57*(3), 784–797. https://doi.org/10.1002/jaba.1072

Axe, J. B. (2008). Conditional discrimination in the intraverbal relation: A review and recommendations for future research. *The Analysis of Verbal Behavior*, *24*(1), 159–174. https://doi.org/10.1007/BF03393064

Axe, J. B., Phelan, S. H., & Irwin, C. L. (2019). Empirical evaluations of Skinner's analysis of problem solving. *The Analysis of Verbal Behavior*, *35*(1), 39–56. https://doi.org/10.1007/s40616-018-0103-4

Bao, S., Sweatt, K. T., Lechago, S. A., & Antal, S. (2017). The effects of receptive and expressive instructional sequences on varied conditional discriminations. *Journal of Applied Behavior Analysis*, *50*(4), 775–788. https://doi.org/10.1002/jaba.404

Belisle, J., Burke, R., Janota, T., Dennis, L., & Taylor, S. (2023). Promoting the emergence of vocational knowledge through equivalence-based instruction with a young adult with autism. *Behavior Analysis in Practice*, *16*, 1216–1221. https://doi.org/10.1007/s40617-023-00814-z

Belloso-Díaz, C., & Pérez-González, L. A. (2015). Effect of learning tacts or tacts and intraverbals on the emergence of intraverbals about verbal categorization. *The Psychological Record*, *65*(4), 749–760. https://doi.org/10.1007/s40732-015-0145-0

Benitez, P., & Domeniconi, C. (2023). Equivalence-based instruction to teaching reading by families and teachers students with autism and/or intellectual disabilities. *Behavioral Interventions*, *38*(3), 861–880. https://doi.org/10.1002/bin.1932

Benjo, H. Johansson, S. & Romnero, J (2018) Emergent language responses following match-to-sample training among children with autism spectrum disorder. *International Journal of Psychology and Psychological Therapy*, *18*, 1–14.

Bergmann, S., & Kodak, T. (2023). Auditory-visual discriminations: stimulus control, teaching procedures and considerations. In J. L. Matson (Ed.), *ABA Handbook of behavior analysis: Integrating Research into Practice* (Vol. 1, pp. 211–234). Springer International Publishing. https://doi.org/10.1007/978-3-031-19964-6_13

Bergmann, S., Van Den Elzen, G., Kodak, T., Niland, H., & Daw-Son, D. (2022). Comparing matrix training procedures for children with autism spectrum disorder. *Analysis of Verbal Behavior*, *38*(1), 24–53.

Blair, B., & Dorsey M. (2020). Equivalence-based instruction (EBI). In F. Volkmar (Ed.), *Encyclopedia of autism spectrum disorders* (pp. 1–7). Springer. https://doi.org/10.1007/978-1-4614-6435-8_102286-1

Boelens, H., Hofman, B., Tamaddoni, T., & Eenink, K. (2007). Specific effect of modeling on young children's word productions. *The Psychological Record*, *57*, 145–166. https://doi.org/10.1007/ BF03395569

Brinkerhoff, S., Carbone, V., O'Rouke, S., & Basfer, C. (in press). A preliminary analysis of joint control procedures to teach children with autism spectrum disorder to report missing items. *Behavior Analysis in Practice*.

Byrne, B. L., Rehfeldt, R. A., & Aguirre, A. A. (2014). Evaluating the effectiveness of the stimulus pairing observation procedure and multiple exemplar instruction on tact and listener responses in children with autism. *The Analysis of Verbal Behavior*, *30*(2), 160–169. https://doi.org/10.1007/s40616-014-0020-0

Carnerero, J. J., & Pérez-González, L. A. (2015). Emergence of naming relations and intraverbals after auditory stimulus pairing. *The Psychological Record, 65*(3), 509–522. https://doi.org/10.1007/s40732-015-0127-2

Carp, C. L., & Petursdottir, A. I. (2012). Effects of two training conditions on the emergence of novel intraverbals: An extension of Peréz-González et al. (2008). *The Psychological Record, 62*(2), 187–205. https://doi.org/10.1007/bf03395797

Carp, C. L., & Petursdottir, A. I. (2015). Intraverbal naming and equivalence class formation in children. *Journal of the Experimental Analysis of Behavior, 104*(3), 223–240. https://doi.org/10.1002/jeab.183

Carr, J. E., & Miguel, C. F. (2013). The analysis of verbal behavior and its therapeutic applications. In *APA handbook of behavior analysis, Vol. 2: Translating principles into practice* (pp. 329–352). American Psychological Association. https://doi.org/10.1037/13938-013

Carroll, R. A., & Kodak, T. (2015). Using instructive feedback to increase response variability during intraverbal training for children with autism spectrum disorder. *The Analysis of Verbal Behavior, 31*(2), 183–199. https://doi.org/10.1007/s40616-015-0039-x

Causin, K. G., Albert, K. M., Carbone, V. J., & Sweeney-Kerwin, E. J. (2013). The role of joint control in teaching listener responding to children with autism and other developmental disabilities. *Research in Autism Spectrum Disorders, 7*(9), 997–1011. https://doi.org/10.1016/j.rasd.2013.04.011

Cengher, M., Bowman, M. D., Shawler, L. A., & Ceribo-Singh, M. S. M. (2022). A systematic review of mands for information. *Behavioral Interventions, 37*(3), 864–886. https://doi.org/10.1002/bin.1893

Clough, C. W., Meyer, C. S., & Miguel, C. F. (2016). The effects of blocking and joint control training on sequencing visual stimuli. *The Analysis of Verbal Behavior, 32*(2), 242–264 https://doi.org10.1007/s40616-016-0067-1

Conine, D. E., Vollmer, T. R., Dela Rosa, C. M., & Slanzi, C. M. (2021). The effects of listener and tact training on the emergence of intraverbals among children with autism. *Behavior Analysis: Research and Practice, 21*(1), 26–41. https://doi.org/10.1037/bar0000201

Contreras, B. P., Cooper, A. J., & Kahng, S. (2020). Recent research on the relative efficiency of speaker and listener instruction for children with autism spectrum disorder. *Journal of Applied Behavior Analysis, 53*(1), 584–589. https://doi.org/10.1002/jaba.543

Curiel, E. S., & Curiel, H. (2021). Teaching receptive money identification skills using matrix training: A preliminary investigation. *Behavioral Interventions, 36*(3), 572–582. https://doi.org/10.1002/bin.1794

Curiel, E. S., Sainato, D. M., & Goldstein, H. (2016). Matrix training of receptive language skills with a toddler with autism spectrum disorder: A case study. *Education and Treatment of Children, 39*, 95–109. https://doi.org/10.1177/1053815118788060

Curiel, E. S. L., Axe, J. B., Sainato, D. M., & Goldstein, H. (2020). Systematic review of matrix train- ing for individuals with autism spectrum disorder. *Focus on Autism and Other Developmental Disabilities, 35*(1), 55–64. https://doi.org/10.1177/1088357619881216

Curiel, E. S. L., Sainato, D. M., & Goldstein, H. (2018). Matrix training for toddlers with autism spectrum disorder and other language delays. *Journal of Early Intervention, 40*(3), 268–284. https://doi.org/10.1177/1053815118788060

Dass, T. K., Kisamore, A. N., Vladescu, J. C., Reeve, K. F., Reeve, S. A., & Taylor-Santa, C. (2018). Teaching children with autism spectrum disorder to tact olfactory stimuli. *Journal of Applied Behavior Analysis*, *51*(3), 538–552. https://doi.org/10.1002/jaba.470

degli Espinosa, F. (2011). *Verbal behaviour development for children with autism* [Unpublished doctoral dissertation]. University of Southampton.

degli Espinosa, F. (2017). *Teaching "learning how to learn": A functional analysis of curriculum programming for children with autism* [PowerPoint slides]. National Autism Conference, Penn State University. https://storage.outreach.psu.edu/autism /16.%20and%2028.%20Presentation_0.pdf

degli Espinosa, F. (2022). Teaching generalized question-discrimination skills to children with autism: Conceptual and applied considerations. *Behavioral Interventions*, *37*(1), 43–55. https://doi.org/10.1002/bin.1825

degli Espinosa, F., Gerosa, F., & Brocchin-Swales, V. (2021a). Teaching multiply controlled tacting to children with autism. *European Journal of Behavior Analysis*, *22*(2), 173–193. https://doi.org/10.1080/15021149.2020.1737407

degli Espinosa, F., Wolff, K., & Hewett, S. (2021b). A comparison of two teaching procedures to establish generalized intraverbal-tacting in children with autism. *Journal of Applied Behavior Analysis*, *54*(4), 1468–1487. https://doi.org/10.1002/jaba .869

DeGraaf, A., & Schlinger, H. D., Jr. (2012). The effect of joint control training on the acquisition and durability of a sequencing task. *The Analysis of Verbal Behavior*, *28*(1), 59–71. https://doi.org/10.1007/BF03393107

Delfs, C. H., Conine, D. E., Frampton, S. E., Shillingsburg, M. A., & Robinson, H. C. (2014). Evaluation of the efficiency of listener and tact instruction for children with autism. *Journal of Applied Behavior Analysis*, *47*(4), 793–809. https://doi.org/10 .1002/jaba.166

Delfs, C. H., & Frampton, S. E. (2014). Practical implications of evaluating the efficiency of listener and tact instruction for children with autism. *Journal of Applied Behavior Analysis*, *47*(4), 810–813. https://doi.org/10.1002/jaba.176

Delmolino, L., Hansford, A. P., Bamond, M. J., Fiske, K. E., & Larue, R. H. (2013). The use of instructive feedback for teaching language skills to children with autism. *Autism Spectrum Disorders*, *7*(6), 648–661.

DeSouza, A. A., Akers, J. S., & Fisher, W. W. (2017). Empirical application of Skinner's Verbal Behavior to interventions for children with autism: A review. *The Analysis of Verbal Behavior*, *33*(2), 229–259. https://doi.org/10.1007/s40616-017-0093-7

DeSouza, A. A., Fisher, W. W., & Rodriguez, N. M. (2019). Facilitating the emergence of convergent intraverbals in children with autism. *Journal of Applied Behavior Analysis*, *52*(1), 28–49. https://doi.org/10.1002/jaba.520

Devine, B., Carp, C. L., Hiett, K. A., & Petursdottir, A. I. (2016). Emergence of intraverbal responding following tact instruction with compound stimuli. *The Analysis of Verbal Behavior*, *32*(2), 154–170. https://doi.org/10.1007/s40616-016-0062-6

Diaz, J. E., Luoma, S. M., & Miguel, C. F. (2020). The role of verbal behavior in the establishment of comparative relations. *Journal of the Experimental Analysis of Behavior*, *113*(2), 322–339. https://doi.org/10.1002/jeab.582

Díaz, M., Garcia, Y., & Mahoney, A. (2023). A review on equivalence-based procedures to teach food-portion estimation skills. *Behavioral Interventions*, *38*(2), 477–493. https://doi.org/10.1002/bin.1934

Dickes, N. R., & Kodak, T. (2015). Evaluating the emergence of reverse intraverbals following intraverbal training in young children with autism spectrum disorder. *Behavioral Interventions*, *30*(3), 169–190. https://doi.org/10.1002/bin.1412

Dressel, A., Nicholson, K., Albert, K. M., & Ryan, V. M. (2019). The effect of a mediation-blocking task on the acquisition of instructive feedback targets. *The Analysis of Verbal Behavior*, *35*(2), 113–133. https://doi.org/10.1007/s40616-019-00119-9

Eikeseth, S., & Smith, T. (1992). The development of functional and equivalence classes in high-functioning autistic children: The role of naming. *Journal of the Experimental Analysis of Behavior*, *58*(1), 123–33. https://doi.org/10.1901/jeab.1992.58-123

Eikeseth, S., & Smith, D. P. (2013). An analysis of verbal stimulus control in intraverbal behavior: implications for practice and applied research. *The Analysis of Verbal Behavior*, *29*(1), 125–135. https://doi.org/10.1007/BF03393130

Farrell, C. (2017). *An investigation into the speaker-as-own-listener repertoire and reverse intraverbal responding* [Unpublished doctoral dissertation]. Columbia University.

Ferguson, J. L., Cihon, J. H., Majeski, M. J., Milne, C. M., Leaf, J. B., McEachin, J., & Leaf, R. (2022). Toward efficiency and effectiveness: Comparing equivalence-based instruction to progressive discrete trial teaching. *Behavior Analysis in Practice*, *15*(4), 1296–1313. https://doi.org/10.1007/s40617-022-00687-8

Ferguson, J. L., Majeski, M. J., McEachin, J., Leaf, R., Cihon, J. H., & Leaf, J. B. (2020). Evaluating discrete trial teaching with instructive feedback delivered in a dyad arrangement via telehealth. *Journal of Applied Behavior Analysis*, *53*(4), 1876–1888. https://doi.org/10.1002/jaba.773

Fienup, D. M., Covey, D. P., & Critchfield, T. S. (2010). Teaching brain-behavior relations economically with stimulus equivalence technology. *Journal of Applied Behavior Analysis*, *43*(1), 19–33. https://doi.org/10.1901/jaba.2010.43-19

Finn, H. E., Miguel, C. F., & Ahearn, W. H. (2012). The emergence of untrained mands and tacts in children with autism. *Journal of Applied Behavior Analysis*, *45*(2), 265–280. https://doi.org/10.1901/jaba.2012.45-265

Fiorile, C. A., & Greer, R. D. (2007). The induction of naming in children with no prior tact responses as a function of multiple exemplar histories of instruction. *The Analysis of Verbal Behavior*, *23*(1), 71–87. https://doi.org/10.1007/BF03393048

Fisher, W. W., Retzlaff, B. J., Akers, J. S., DeSouza, A. A., Kaminski, A. J., & Machado, M. A. (2019). Establishing initial auditory-visual conditional discriminations and emergence of initial tacts in young children with autism spectrum disorder. *Journal of Applied Behavior Analysis*, *52*(4), 1089–1106. https://doi.org/10.1002/jaba.586

Frampton, S., & Axe, J. B. (2023). A tutorial for implementing matrix training in practice. *Behavior Analysis in Practice*, *16*(1), 334–345. https://doi.org/10.1007/s40617-022-00733-5

Frampton, S. E., Robinson, H. C., Conine, D. E., & Delfs, C. H. (2017). An abbreviated evaluation of the efficiency of listener and tact instruction for children with autism. *Behavior Analysis in Practice*, *10*(2), 131–144. https://doi.org/10.1007/s40617-017-0175-y

Frampton, S. E., & Shillingsburg, M. A. (2018). Teaching children with autism to explain how: A case for problem solving?: Explaining how. *Journal of Applied Behavior Analysis*, *51*(2), 236–254. https://doi.org/10.1002/jaba.445

Frampton, S. E., & Shillingsburg, M. A. (2020). Promoting the development of verbal responses using instructive feedback. *Journal of Applied Behavior Analysis*, *53*(2), 1029–1041. https://doi.org/10.1002/jaba.659

Frampton, S. E., Thompson, T. M., Bartlett, B. L., Hansen, B., & Shil-Lingsburg, M. A. (2019). The use of matrix training to teach color-shape tacts to children with autism. *Behavior Analysis in Practice*, *12*(2), 320–330.

Frampton, S. E., Wymer, S. C., Hansen, B., & Shillingsburg, M. A. (2016). The use of matrix training to promote generative language with children with autism: *Journal of Applied Behavior Analysis*, *49*(4), 869–883. https://doi.org/10.1002/jaba.340

Gavidia, V. L., Bergmann, S., & Rader, K. A. (2022). The use of instructive feedback to promote emergent tact and intraverbal control: A replication. *The Analysis of Verbal Behavior*, *38*(2), 95–120. https://doi.org/10.1007/s40616-022-00171

Giannakakos, A. R., Vladescu, J. C., Reeve, K. F., Kisamore, A. N., Fienup, D. M., & Carrow, J. N. (2021). Using behavioral skills training and equivalence-based instruction to teach children safe responding to dangerous stimuli: A proof of concept. *The Psychological Record*, *71*(1), 119–131. https://doi.org/10.1007/s40732-020-00380-8

Gilic, L., & Greer, R. D. (2011). Establishing naming in typically developing two-year-old children as a function of multiple exemplar speaker and listener experiences. *The Analysis of Verbal Behavior*, *27*(1), 157–177. https://doi.org/10.1007/BF03393099

Grannan, L., & Rehfeldt, R. A. (2012). Emergent intraverbal responses via tact and match-to-sample instruction. *Journal of Applied Behavior Analysis*, *45*(3), 601–605. https://doi.org/10.1901/jaba.2012.45-601

Greer, R. D., & Keohane, D.-D. (2005). The evolution of verbal behavior in children. *Behavioral Development Bulletin*, *12*(1), 31–47. https://doi.org/10.1037/h0100559

Greer, R. D., & Longano, J. (2010). A rose by naming: how we may learn how to do it. *The Analysis of Verbal Behavior*, *26*(1), 73–106. https://doi.org/10.1007/BF03393085

Greer, R. D., & Ross, D. E. (2008). *Verbal behavior analysis: Inducing and expanding complex communication in children with severe language delays*. Allyn & Bacon.

Greer, R. D., & Ross, D. E. (2008). *Verbal behavior analysis: Inducing and expanding new verbal capabilities in children with language delays*. Pearson.

Greer, R. D., & Speckman, J. (2009). The integration of speaker and listener responses: A theory of verbal development. *The Psychological Record*, *59*(3), 449–488. https://doi.org/10.1007/bf03395674

Greer, R. D., Stolfi, L., Chavez-Brown, M., & Rivera-Valdes, C. (2005b). The emergence of the listener to speaker component of naming in children as a function of multiple exemplar instruction. *The Analysis of Verbal Behavior*, *21*(1), 123–134. https://doi.org/10.1007/BF03393014

Greer, R. D., Stolfi, L., & Pistoljevic, N. (2007). Emergence of naming in preschoolers: A comparison of multiple and single exemplar instruction. *European Journal of Behavior Analysis*, *8*(2), 109–131. https://doi.org/10.1080/15021149.2007.11434278

Groskreutz, N. C., Karsina, A., Miguel, C. F., & Groskreutz, M. P. (2010). Using complex auditory-visual samples to produce emergent relations in children with autism. *Journal of Applied Behavior Analysis*, *43*(1), 131–136. https://doi.org/10.1901/jaba.2010.43-131

Grow, L., & LeBlanc, L. (2013). Teaching receptive language skills: Recommendations for instructors. *Behavior Analysis in Practice, 6*(1), 56–75. https://doi.org/10.1007/BF03391791

Gutierrez, R. D. (2006). The role of rehearsal in joint control. *The Analysis of Verbal Behavior, 22*(1), 183–190. https://doi.org/10.1007/BF03393038

Hall, G., & Sundberg, M. L. (1987). Teaching mands by manipulating conditioned establishing operations. *The Analysis of Verbal Behavior, 5*(1), 41–53. https://doi.org/10.1007/BF03392819

Haq, S. S., Zemantic, P. K., Kodak, T., LeBlanc, B., & Ruppert, T. E. (2017). Examination of variables that affect the efficacy of instructive feedback. *Behavioral Interventions: Theory & Practice in Residential & Community-Based Clinical Programs, 32*(3), 206–216. https://doi.org/10.1002/bin.1470

Hart, B., & Risley, T. R. (1995). *Meaningful differences in the everyday experience of young American children.* Paul H Brookes Publishing.

Hawkins, E., Gautreaux, G., & Chiesa, M. (2018). Deconstructing common bidirectional naming: A proposed classification framework. *The Analysis of Verbal Behavior, 34*(1–2), 44–61. https://doi.org/10.1007/s40616-018-0100-7

Hawkins, E., Kingsdorf, S., Charnock, J., Szabo, M., & Gautreaux, G. (2009). Effects of multiple exemplar instruction on naming. *European Journal of Behavior Analysis, 10*(2), 265–273. https://doi.org/10.1080/15021149.2009.11434324

Horne, P. J., & Lowe, C. F. (1996). On the origins of naming and other symbolic behavior. *Journal of the Experimental Analysis of Behavior, 65*(1), 185–241. https://doi.org/10.1901/jeab.1996.65-185

Hozella, W., Ampuero, M. E., & Miklos, M. (2024). A tutorial on the applications of lowenkron's joint control to language acquisition programs. *Perspectives on Behavior Science, 47*(4), 783–802. https://doi.org/10.1007/s40614-024-00424-2

Hozella, W., Garcia, Y. A., Ackerlund Brandt, J. A., & Mahoney, A. (2022). Using joint control to teach activities of daily living and vocational tasks to students with autism. *Behavioral Interventions, 37*(1), 123–138. https://doi.org/10.1002/bin.1850

Ingvarsson, E. T., Cammilleri, A. P., & Macias, H. (2012). Emergent listener responses following intraverbal training in children with autism. *Research in Autism Spectrum Disorders, 6*(2), 654–664. https://doi.org/10.1016/j.rasd.2011.09.009

Jennings, A. M., & Miguel, C. F. (2017). Training intraverbal bidirectional naming to establish generalized equivalence class performances. *Journal of the Experimental Analysis of Behavior, 108*(2), 269–289. https://doi.org/10.1002/jeab.277

Jennings, A. M., Vladescu, J. C., Miguel, C. F., Reeve, K. F., & Sidener, T. M. (2022). A systematic review of empirical intraverbal research: 2015–2020. *Behavioral Interventions, 37*(1), 79–104. https://doi.org/10.1002/bin.1815

Jennings, A. M., Vladescu, J. C., Miguel, C. F., Reeve, K. F., & Sidener, T. M. (2023). A translational evaluation of component skills for the establishment of multiply controlled intraverbals. *Journal of the Experimental Analysis of Behavior, 119*(3), 513–528. https://doi.org/10.1002/jeab.837

Jimenez-Gomez, C., Rajagopal, S., Nastri, R., & Chong, I. M. (2019). Matrix training for expanding the communication of toddlers and preschoolers with autism spectrum disorder. *Behavior Analysis in Practice, 12*(2), 375–386. https://doi.org/10.1007/s40617-019-00346-5

Keesey-Phelan, S. H., Axe, J. B., & Williams, A. L. (2022). The effects of teaching a problem-solving strategy on recalling past events with a child with autism. *The Analysis of Verbal Behavior*, *38*(2), 190–198. https://doi.org/10.1007/s40616-022-00176-7

Keintz, K. S., Miguel, C. F., Kao, B., & Finn, H. E. (2011). Using conditional discrimination training to produce emergent relations between coins and their values in children with autism. *Journal of Applied Behavior Analysis*, *44*(4), 909–913. https://doi.org/10.1901/jaba.2011.44-909

Kemmerer, A. R., Vladescu, J. C., Carrow, J. N., Sidener, T. M., & Deshais, M. A. (2021). A systematic review of the matrix training literature. *Behavioral Interventions*, *36*(2), 473–495. https://doi.org/10.1002/bin.1780

Kisamore, A. N., Carr, J. E., & LeBlanc, L. A. (2011). Training preschool children to use visual imagining as a problem-solving strategy for complex categorization tasks. *Journal of Applied Behavior Analysis*, *44*(2), 255–278. https://doi.org/10.1901/jaba.2011.44-255

Kisamore, A. N., Karsten, A. M., & Mann, C. C. (2016). Teaching multiply controlled intraverbals to children and adolescents with autism spectrum disorders. *Journal of Applied Behavior Analysis*, *49*(4), 826–847. https://doi.org/10.1002/jaba.344

Kisamore, A. N., Karsten, A. M., Mann, C. C., & Conde, K. A. (2013). Effects of a differential observing response on intraverbal performance of preschool children: A preliminary investigation. *The Analysis of Verbal Behavior*, *29*(1), 101–108. https://doi.org/10.1007/BF03393127

Kodak, T., & Paden, A. R. (2015). A comparison of intraverbal and listener training for children with autism spectrum disorder. *The Analysis of Verbal Behavior*, *31*(1), 137–144. https://doi.org/10.1007/s40616-015-0033-3

Kodak, T., Bergmann, S., Cordeiro, M.C., Bamond, M., Isenhower, R.W., & Fiske, K.E. (2022). Replication of a skills assessment for auditory-visual conditional discrimination training. *Journal of Applied Behavior Analysis*, 55(2), 622-638. https://doi.org/10.1002/jaba.909.

Kohler, K. T., & Malott, R. W. (2014). Matrix training and verbal generativity in children with autism. *The Analysis of Verbal Behavior*, *30*(2), 170–177. https://doi.org/10.1007/s40616-014-0016-9

Kohler, K. T., & Malott, R. W. (2015). Erratum to: Matrix training and verbal generativity in children with autism. *The Analysis of Verbal Behavior*, *31*(2), 280. https://doi.org/10.1007/s40616-015-0046-y

LaFond, T. R., Reeve, K. F., Day-Watkins, J., Reeve, S. A., Vladescu, J. C., & Jennings, A. M. (2021). Using stimulus equivalence-based instruction to teach young children their caregivers' contact information. *Behavioral Interventions*, *36*(1), 105–125. https://doi.org/10.1002/bin.1742

LaFrance, D. L., & Tarbox, J. (2020). The importance of multiple exemplar instruction in the establishment of novel verbal behavior. *Journal of Applied Behavior Analysis*, *53*(1), 10–24. https://doi.org/10.1002/jaba.611

Leaf, J. B., Cihon, J. H., Alcalay, A., Mitchell, E., Townley-Cochran, D., Miller, K., Leaf, R., Taubman, M., & McEachin, J. (2017). Instructive feedback embedded within group instruction for children diagnosed with autism spectrum disorder. *Journal of Applied Behavior Analysis*, *50*(2), 304–316. https://doi.org/10.1002/jaba.375

Lechago, S. A., Carr, J. E., Grow, L. L., Love, J. R., & Almason, S. M. (2010). Mands for information generalize across establishing operations. *Journal of Applied Behavior Analysis, 43*(3), 381–395. https://doi.org/10.1901/jaba.2010.43-381

Lechago, S. A., & Low, A. (2015). A review of the mand-for-information training research literature. *International Journal of Behavior Analysis & Autism Spectrum Disorders, 1*(1), 35–54.

Lobato, D. F., & de Souza, D. G. (2020). Bidirectional naming in children with autism: Effect of stimulus pairing observation procedure and multiple exemplar instruction. *Revista Brasileira de Educação Especial, 26*, 503–518.

Loughrey, T. O., Betz, A. M., Majdalany, L. M., & Nicholson, K. (2014). Using instructive feedback to teach category names to children with autism. *Journal of Applied Behavior Analysis, 47*(2), 425–430. https://doi.org/10.1002/jaba.123

Lowenkron, B. (1996). Joint control and word-object bidirectionality. *Journal of the Experimental Analysis of Behavior, 65*(1), 252–255. https://doi.org/10.1901/jeab .1996.65-252

Lowenkron, B. (1998). Some logical functions of joint control. *Journal of the Experimental Analysis of Behavior, 69*(3), 327–354. https://doi.org/10.1901/jeab.1998.69-327

Luoma, S. M., Miguel, C. F., LaFrance, D. L., & Lee, V. N. (2024). The role of intraverbal bidirectional naming in the establishment of comparative relations. *Journal of the Experimental Analysis of Behavior, 122*(2), 158–181. https://doi.org/10.1002/jeab .4207

Ma, M. L., Miguel, C. F., & Jennings, A. M. (2016). Training intraverbal naming to establish equivalence class performances. *Journal of the Experimental Analysis of Behavior, 105*(3), 409–426. https://doi.org/10.1002/jeab.203

Marya, V., Frampton, S., & Shillingsburg, A. (2021). Matrix training to teach tacts using speech generating devices: Replication and extension. *Journal of Applied Behavior Analysis, 54*(3), 1235–1250. https://doi.org/10.1002/jaba.819

McGee, R. E., Roberts, C. R., & Petursdottir, A. I. (2024). Effects of instructed visual imagining on emergent conditional discriminations. *Journal of the Experimental Analysis of Behavior, 122*(2), 182–194. https://doi.org/10.1002/jeab.4205

Meleshkevich, O., Axe, J. B., & Espinosa, F. D. (2021). Effects of time delay and requiring echoics on answering questions about visual stimuli. *Journal of Applied Behavior Analysis, 54*(2), 725–743. https://doi.org/10.1002/jaba.790

Mellor, J. R., Barnes, C. S., & Rehfeldt, R. A. (2015). The effects of auditory tact and auditory imagining instructions on the emergence of novel intraverbals. *The Analysis of Verbal Behavior, 31*(2), 236–254. https://doi.org/10.1007/s40616-015-0036-0

Michael, J. (1996). Seperate repertoires or naming? *Journal of the Experimental Analysis of Behavior, 65*(1), 296–298. https://doi.org/10.1901/jeab.1996.65-296

Michael, J., Palmer, D. C., & Sundberg, M. L. (2011). The multiple control of verbal behavior. *The Analysis of Verbal Behavior, 27*(1), 3–22. https://doi.org/10.1007/ BF03393089

Miguel, C. F. (2016). Common and intraverbal bidirectional naming. *The Analysis of Verbal Behavior, 32*(2), 125–138. https://doi.org/10.1007/s40616-016-0066-2

Miguel, C. F. (2018). Problem-solving, bidirectional naming, and the development of verbal repertoires. *Behavior Analysis Research and Practice. 18*(4), 340–353. https:// doi.org/10.1037/bar0000110

Miguel, C. F., Petursdottir, A. I., & Carr, J. E. (2005). The effects of multiple-tact and receptive-discrimination training on the acquisition of intraverbal behavior. *The Analysis of Verbal Behavior*, *21*(1), 27–41. https://doi.org/10.1007/BF03393008

Moustakis, I. S., & Mellon, R. C. (2018). Transitivity as Skinnerian problem solving controlled by self-constructed relational stimuli. *Journal of the Experimental Analysis of Behavior*, *110*(3), 451–473. https://doi.org/10.1002/jeab.473

Naoi, N., Yokoyama, K., & Yamamoto, J. (2006). Matrix training for expressive and receptive two-word utterances in children with autism. *Japanese Journal of Special Education*, *43*, 505–518. https://doi.org/10.6033/tokkyou.43.505

Nottingham, C. L., Vladescu, J. C., Debar, R. M., Deshais, M., & Dequinzio, J. (2020). The influence of instructive feedback presentation schedule: A replication with children with autism spectrum disorder. *Journal of Applied Behavior Analysis*, *53*(4), 2287–2302. https://doi.org/10.1002/jaba.706

Nottingham, C. L., Vladescu, J. C., Kodak, T., & Kisamore, A. N. (2017). Incorporating multiple secondary targets into learning trials for individuals with autism spectrum disorder. *Journal of Applied Behavior Analysis*, *50*(3), 653–661. https://doi.org/10.1002/jaba.396

Nuzzolo-Gomez, R., & Greer, R. D. (2004). Emergence of untaught mands or tacts of novel adjective-object pairs as a function of instructional history. *The Analysis of Verbal Behavior*, *20*(1), 63–76. https://doi.org/10.1007/BF03392995

Oah, S. Z., & Dickinson, A. M. (1989). A review of empirical studies of verbal behavior. *The Analysis of Verbal Behavior*, *7*(1), 53–68. https://doi.org/10.1007/BF03392837

Olaff, H. S., & Holth, P. (2020). The emergence of bidirectional naming through sequential operant instruction following the establishment of conditioned social reinforcers. *The Analysis of Verbal Behavior*, *36*(1), 21–48. https://doi.org/10.1007/s40616-019-00122-0

Olaff, H. S., Ona, H. N., & Holth, P. (2017). Establishment of naming in children with autism through multiple response-exemplar training. *Behavioral Development Bulletin*, *22*(1), 67–85. https://doi.org/10.1037/bdb0000044

Palmer, D. C. (1991). A behavioral interpretation of memory. In L. J. Hayes & P. N. Chase (Eds.), *Dialogues on verbal behavior: The first international institute on verbal relations* (pp. 261–279). Context Press.

Palmer, D. C. (1996). Achieving parity: The role of automatic reinforcement. *Journal of the Experimental Analysis of Behavior*, *65*(1), 289–290. https://doi.org/10.1901/jeab.1996.65-289

Palmer, D.C. (1998). The Speaker as listener: The interpretation of structural regularities in verbal behavior. *The Analysis of Verbal Behavior*, *15*, 3–16. https://doi.org/10.1007/BF03392920

Palmer, D. C. (2006). Joint control: A discussion of recent research. *The Analysis of Verbal Behavior*, *22*, 209–215. https://doi.org/10.1007/BF03393040

Palmer, D. C. (2007). Verbal behavior: What is the function of structure? *European Journal of Behavior Analysis*, *8*(2), 161–175. https://doi.org/10.1080/15021149.2007.11434280

Palmer, D. C. (2009). Response strength and the concept of the repertoire. *European Journal of Behavior Analysis*, *10*(1), 49–60. https://doi.org/10.1080/15021149.2009.11434308

Palmer, D. C. (2012). The role of atomic repertoires in complex behavior. *The Behavior Analyst, 35*(1), 59–73. https://doi.org/10.1007/BF03392266

Palmer, D. C. (2016). On intraverbal control and the definition of the intraverbal. *The Analysis of Verbal Behavior, 32*(2), 96–106. https://doi.org/10.1007/s40616-016 -0061-7

Palmer, D. C. (2021). On response strength and the concept of response classes. *Perspectives on Behavior Science, 44*(2–3), 483–499. https://doi.org/10.1007/s40614 -021-00305-y

Palmer, D. C. (2023) Toward a behavioral interpretation of english grammar. *Perspectives on Behavior Science, 46*, 521–538. https://doi.org/10.1007/s40614-023-00368-z

Pauwels, A. A., Ahearn, W. H., & Cohen, S. J. (2015). Recombinative generalization of tacts through matrix training with individuals with autism spectrum disorder. *Analysis of Verbal Behavior, 31*(2), 200–214. https://doi.org/10.1007/s40616-015-0038-y

Pérez-González, L. A., Cereijo-Blanco, N., & Carnerero, J. J. (2014). Emerging tacts and selections from previous learned skills: A comparison between two types of naming. *The Analysis of Verbal Behavior, 30*(2), 184–192. https://doi.org/10.1007/s40616-014 -0011-1

Pérez-González, L. A., García-Asenjo, L., Williams, G., & Carnerero, J. J. (2007). Emergence of intraverbal antonyms in children with pervasive developmental disorder. *Journal of Applied Behavior Analysis, 40*(4), 697–701. https://doi.org/10 .1901/jaba.2007.697-701

Pérez-González, L. A., Herszlikowicz, K., & Williams, G. (2008). Stimulus relations analysis and the emergence of novel intraverbals. *The Psychological Record, 58*(1), 95–129. https://doi.org/10.1007/bf03395605

Pérez-González, L. A., Pastor, A., & Carnerero, J. J. (2014). Observing tacting increases uninstructed tacts in children with autism. *The Analysis of Verbal Behavior, 30*(1), 62–68. https://doi.org/10.1007/s40616-013-0003-6

Pérez-González, L. A., Salameh, J., & García-Asenjo, L. (2018). Emergence of intraverbals with categories as responses after learning intraverbals with elements in reverse stimulus-response functions. *European Journal of Behavior Analysis, 19*(1), 72–89. https://doi.org/10.1080/15021149.2018.1465755

Petursdottir, A. I. (2018). The current status of the experimental analysis of verbal behavior. *Behavior Analysis: Research and Practice, 18*(2), 151–168. https://doi.org /10.1037/bar0000109

Petursdottir, A. I., & Carr, J. E. (2011). A review of recommendations for sequencing receptive and expressive language instruction. *Journal of Applied Behavior Analysis, 44*(4), 859–876. https://doi.org/10.1901/jaba.2011.44-859

Petursdottir, A. I., Carr, J. E., & Michael, J. (2005). Emergence of mands and tacts of novel objects among preschool children. *The Analysis of Verbal Behavior, 21*(1), 59–74. https://doi.org/10.1007/BF03393010

Petursdottir, A. I., & Devine, B. (2017). The impact of Verbal Behavior on the scholarly literature from 2005 to 2016. *The Analysis of Verbal Behavior, 33*(2), 212–228. https://doi.org/10.1007/s40616-017-0089-3

Petursdottir, A. I., Neaves, S. M., & Thomas, O. N. (2020). Emergent tact control following stimulus pairing: Comparison of procedural variations. *The Analysis of Verbal Behavior, 36*(2), 193–214. https://doi.org/10.1007/s40616-020-00132-3

Petursdottir, A. I., Olafsdittur, A. R. & Aradottir, B. (2008). The effects of tact and listener training on the emergence of bidirectional intraverbal relations. *Journal of Applied Behavior Analysis, 41*(3), 411–415. https://doi.org/10.1901/jaba.2008.41-411

Pilgrim, C. (2022). Equivalence-based instruction. In J. Cooper, T. Heron, & W. Heward (Eds.), *Applied behavior analysis* (pp. 452–496). Pearson.

Ratkos, T., & Camacho, M. (2023). The effects of vocal blocking on sequencing visual and tactile stimuli. *The Analysis of Verbal Behavior, 39*(2), 226–246. https://doi.org /10.1007/s40616-023-00187-y

Ratkos, T., Camacho, M., & O'Dell, K. (2023). Disrupting delayed matching-to-sample performance with varied distractor tasks. *European Journal of Behavior Analysis, 24*(1–2), 139–153. https://doi.org/10.1080/15021149.2023.2267345

Ratkos, T., Frieder, J. E., & Poling, A. (2016). Accurate delayed matching to sample responding without rehearsal: An unintentional demonstration with children. *The Analysis of Verbal Behavior, 32*, 69–77. https://doi.org/10.1007/s40616-016-0052-8

Reichow, B., & Wolery, M. (2011). Comparison of progressive prompt delay with and without instructive feedback. *Journal of Applied Behavior Analysis, 44*(2), 327–340. https://doi.org/10.1901/jaba.2011.44-327

Ribeiro, D. M., Elias, N. C., Goyos, C., & Miguel, C. F. (2010). The effects of listener training on the emergence of tact and mand signs by individuals with intellectual disabilities. *The Analysis of Verbal Behavior, 26*(1), 65–72. https://doi.org/10.1007 /BF03393084

Rodriguez, N. M., Aragon, M. A., McKeown, C. A., & Glodowski, K. R. (2022). Facilitating the emergence of intraverbal tacts in children with autism spectrum disorder: A preliminary analysis. *Journal of Applied Behavior Analysis, 55*(2), 412–429. https://doi.org/10.1002/jaba.898

Rosales, R., Maderitz, C., & Garcia, Y. A. (2014). Comparison of simple and complex auditory-visual conditional discrimination training: Discrimination training. *Journal of Applied Behavior Analysis, 47*(2), 437–442. https://doi.org/10.1002/jaba.121

Rosales, R., Rehfeldt, R. A., & Huffman, N. (2012). Examining the utility of the stimulus pairing observation procedure with preschool children learning a second language. *Journal of Applied Behavior Analysis, 45*(1), 173–177. https://doi.org/10.1901/jaba .2012.45-173

Rosales-Ruiz, J., & Baer, D. M. (1997). Behavioral cusps: A developmental and pragmatic concept for behavior analysis. *Journal of Applied Behavior Analysis, 30*(3), 533–544. https://doi.org/10.1901/jaba.1997.30-533

Santos, P. M., Ma, M. L., & Miguel, C. F. (2015). Training intraverbal naming to establish matching-to-sample performances. *The Analysis of Verbal Behavior, 31*(2), 162–182. https://doi.org/10.1007/s40616-015-0040-4

Sautter, R. A., & Leblanc, L. A. (2006). Empirical applications of Skinner's analysis of Verbal Behavior with humans. *The Analysis of Verbal Behavior, 22*, 35–48. https:// doi.org/10.1007/BF03393025

Sautter, R. A., LeBlanc, L. A., Jay, A. A., Goldsmith, T. R., & Carr, J. E. (2011). The role of problem solving in complex intraverbal repertoires. *Journal of Applied Behavior Analysis, 44*(2), 227–244. https://doi.org/10.1901/jaba.2011.44-227

Schlinger, H. D., Jr, & Blakely, E. (2024). A mediational theory of equivalence relations and transformation of function. *Journal of the Experimental Analysis of Behavior*, *122*(2), 207–223. https://doi.org/10.1002/jeab.4204

Shillingsburg, M. A., Frampton, S. E., Cleveland, S. A., & Cariveau, T. (2018). Clinical applications of procedures to promote the emergence of untrained intraverbal relations with children with autism. *Learning and Motivation*, *62*, 51–66. https://doi.org/10.1016/j.lmot.2017.02.003.

Shawler, L. A., Zhelezoglo, K. N., Miguel, C. F., & Brand, D. (2023). Procedural parameters in equivalence-based instruction with individuals diagnosed with autism: A call for systematic research. *Journal of Applied Behavior Analysis*, *56*(3), 520–533. https://doi.org/10.1002/jaba.998

Sidener, D. W. (2006). Joint control for dummies: An elaboration of lowenkron's model of joint (stimulus) control. *The Analysis of Verbal Behavior*, *22*(1), 119–122. https://doi.org/10.1007/bf03393033.

Sidman, M., & Tailby, W. (1982). Conditional discrimination vs. matching to sample: An expansion of the testing paradigm. *Journal of the Experimental Analysis of Behavior*, *37*(1), 5–22. https://doi.org/10.1901/jeab.1982.37-5

Sigafoos, J., Reichle, J., Doss, S., Hall, K., & Pettitt (1990). "Spontaneous" transfer of stimulus control from tact to mand contingencies. *Research in Developmental Disabilities*, *11*, 165–176. https://doi.org/10.1016/0891-4222(90)90033-5

Silva, A. M., Keuffer, S.C., de Oleviera, J. C., & Barros, R. S. (2018) Acquisition of intraverbal repertoire via equivalence-based instruction in children with autism spectrum disorder. *Trends in Psychology*, *26*(3), 1173–1188. https://doi.org/10.9788/TP2018.3-02Pt

Skinner, B. F. (1953). *Science and human behavior*. The MacMillan Company.

Skinner, B. F. (1957). *Verbal behavior*. Prentice Hall. https://doi.org/10.1037/11256-000

Skinner, B. F. (1969). *Contingencies of reinforcement: A theoretical analysis*. Prentice Hall.

Skinner, B. F. (1974). *About behaviorism*. Alfred A. Knopf.

Skinner, B. F. (1980). *Notebooks*. Prentice-Hall.

Skinner, B. F. (1983). *Matter of consequences*. Alfred A. Knopf.

Smith, D. P., Eikeseth, S., Fletcher, S. E., Montebelli, L., Smith, H. R., & Taylor, J. C. (2016). Emergent intraverbal forms may occur as a result of listener training for children with autism. *The Analysis of Verbal Behavior*, *32*(1), 27–37. https://doi.org/10.1007/s40616-016-0057-3

Solares, L., & Fryling, M. J. (2019). Further evaluation of the stimulus pairing observation procedure with children with autism spectrum disorder. *The Analysis of Verbal Behavior*, *35*(1), 85–93. https://doi.org/10.1007/s40616-018-0101-6

Sprinkle, E. C., & Miguel, C. F. (2012). The effects of listener and speaker training on emergent relations in children with autism. *The Analysis of Verbal Behavior*, *28*(1), 111–117. https://doi.org/10.1007/BF03393111

Stanley, C. R., Belisle, J., & Dixon, M. R. (2018). Equivalence-based instruction of academic skills: Application to adolescents with autism. *Journal of Applied Behavior Analysis*, *51*(2), 352–359. https://doi.org/10.1002/jaba.446

Stauch, T., LaLonde, K., Plavnick, J. B., Savana Bak, M. Y., & Gatewood, K. (2017). Intraverbal training for individuals with autism: The current status of multiple control.

The Analysis of Verbal Behavior, 33(1), 98–116. https://doi.org/10.1007/s40616-017-0079-5.

Still, K., May, R. J., Rehfeldt, R. A., Whelan, R., & Dymond, S. (2015). Facilitating derived requesting skills with a touchscreen tablet computer for children with autism spectrum disorder. *Research in Autism Spectrum Disorders, 19*, 44–58. https://doi.org/10.1016/j.rasd.2015.04.006

Sundberg, C. T., & Sundberg, M. L. (1990). Comparing topography-based verbal behavior with stimulus selection-based verbal behavior. *The Analysis of Verbal Behavior, 8*(1), 31–41. https://doi.org/10.1007/BF03392845

Sundberg, C. T., Sundberg, M. L., & Michael, J. (2018). Covert verbal mediation in arbitrary matching to sample. *Journal of the Experimental Analysis of Behavior, 109*(3), 600–623. https://doi.org/10.1002/jeab.434

Sundberg, M. L. (2008). *The verbal behavior milestones assessment and placement program: The VB-MAPP.* AVB Press.

Sundberg, M. L. (2016). Verbal stimulus control and the intraverbal relation. *The Analysis of Verbal Behavior, 32*(2), 107–124. https://doi.org/10.1007/s40616-016-0065-3

Sundberg, M. L. (2020a). *Generative verbal learning and children with autism* [PowerPoint slides]. Michigan Autism Conference, Kalamazoo, MI.

Sundberg, M. L. (2020b). Establishing generative verbal learning for children with language delays [PowerPoint slides]. Ohio State University, Columbus, OH.

Sundberg, M. L., & Partington, J. W. (1998). *Teaching language to children with autism or other developmental disabilities.* AVB Press.

Sundberg, M. L., & Sundberg, C. A. (2011). Intraverbal behavior and verbal conditional discriminations in typically developing children and children with autism. *The Analysis of Verbal Behavior, 27*(1), 23–43. https://doi.org/10.1007/BF03393090

Thakore, A., & Petursdottir, A. I. (2022). Acquisition and generalization of divergent intraverbal responses in children diagnosed with autism spectrum disorder. *Behavioral Interventions, 37*(1), 105–122. https://doi.org/10.1002/bin.1796

Tu, J. C. (2006). The role of joint control in the manded selection responses of both vocal and non-vocal children with autism. *The Analysis of Verbal Behavior, 22*, 191–207. https://doi.org/10.1007/bf03393039

Tullis, C. A., Frampton, S. E., Delfs, C. H., Greene, K., & Reed, S. (2021). The effects of instructive feedback and stimulus equivalence procedures on group instructional outcomes. *Journal of Behavioral Education, 30*(1), 1–21. https://doi.org/10.1007/s10864-019-09349-2

Tullis, C. A., Frampton, S. E., Delfs, C. H., & Shillingsburg, M. A. (2017). Teaching problem explanations using instructive feedback. *The Analysis of Verbal Behavior, 33*(1), 64–79. https://doi.org/10.1007/s40616-016-0075-1

Tullis, C. A., & Gibbs, A. R. (2022). Equivalence-based instruction for people with autism spectrum disorder. In J. L. Matson & P. Sturmey (Eds.), *Handbook of autism and pervasive developmental disorder, autism and child psychopathology series.* Springer. https://doi.org/10.1007/978-3-030- 88538-0_39.

Tullis, C. A., Gibbs, A. R., Priester, J., & Tillem, A. (2022b). Emergence of verbal responses using instructive feedback: A replication and extension. *Behavioral Interventions, 37*(2), 271–289. https://doi.org/10.1002/bin.1836

Tullis, C. A., Marya, V., & A. M. Shillingsburg, (2019). Enhancing instruction via instructive feedback for a child with autism using a speech-generating device. *The Analysis of Verbal Behavior*, *35*(1), 103–112. https://doi.org/10.1007/s40616-018 -0096-z

Vallinger-Brown, M., & Rosales, R. (2014). An investigation of stimulus pairing and listener training to establish emergent intraverbals in children with autism. *The Analysis of Verbal Behavior*, *30*(2), 148–159. https://doi.org/10.1007/s40616-014 -0014-y

Vladescu, J. C., & Kodak, T. M. (2013). Increasing instructional efficiency by presenting additional stimuli in learning trials for children with autism spectrum disorders: Increasing instructional efficiency. *Journal of Applied Behavior Analysis*, *46*(4), 805– 816. https://doi.org/10.1002/jaba.70

Vosters, M. E., & Luczynski, K. C. (2020). Emergent completion of multistep instructions via joint control. *Journal of Applied Behavior Analysis*, *53*(3), 1432–1451. https://doi .org/10.1002/jaba.670

Wallace, M. D., Iwata, B. A., & Hanley, G. P. (2006). Establishment of mands following tact training as a function of reinforcer strength. *Journal of Applied Behavior Analysis*, *39*(1), 17–24. https://doi.org/10.1901/jaba.2006.119-04

Wraikat, R., Sundberg, C. T., & Michael, J. (1991). Topography-based and selection-based verbal behavior: A further comparison. *The Analysis of Verbal Behavior*, *9*(1), 1–17. https://doi.org/10.1007/BF03392856

Yoon, J. S., Greer, R. D., Virk, M., & Fienup, D. M. (2023). The establishment of incidental bidirectional naming through multiple exemplar instruction: A systematic replication. *The Analysis of Verbal Behavior*, *39*(1), 86–98. https://doi.org/10.1007/ s40616-023-00181-4

Zaring-Hinkle, B., Carp, C. L., & Lepper, T. L. (2016). An evaluation of two stimulus equivalence training sequences on the emergence of novel intraverbals. *The Analysis of Verbal Behavior*, *32*(2), 171–193. https://doi.org/10.1007/s40616-016-0072-4

Chapter 11

Augmentative and Alternative Communication

Lilith M. Reuter-Yuill, Tamara S. Kasper, Lina M. Slim, and M. Alice Shillingsburg

Communication is an inherent human right (Communication Bill of Rights, Brady et al., 2016). It is a shared social responsibility to protect the participation and inclusion of all people, including marginalized communities such as individuals with severe and profound disabilities. It is the professional obligation of practitioners such as Board Certified Behavior Analysts (BCBA®) and speech-language pathologists/therapists (SLPs/SLTs) to protect these rights (ASHA Ethics, 2023; BACB, 2020) and support the communication and social engagement of individuals with complex communication needs. The term "complex communication needs" refers to a diverse population of individuals for whom vocal-verbal repertoires (i.e., speech) alone cannot meet daily communication needs. This includes the estimated 30% of learners with autism spectrum disorder (ASD)[1] with little to no functional speech despite intervention (Rose et al., 2016; Wodka et al., 2013). These learners represent a subset of individuals with complex communication needs as they present with persistent impairments in social communication and social interactions (American Psychiatric Association, 2022). That is, social stimuli may inadequately function as discriminative stimuli (failing to occasion behavior) and may also fail to reinforce, shape, or maintain communicative response forms (failing to reinforce behavior). Researchers using eye-tracking software have demonstrated that children with ASD visually attend to non-social stimuli (i.e., object and object movement) over social stimuli such as faces (Jones et al., 2023; Klin et al., 2009) and caregiver voices (Pierce et al., 2023). These autistic learners face challenges to communication that require specific intervention not only to acquire an initial communicative response form(s) but also to increase communicative initiation, reciprocity of social interactions, integration of communicative response forms (e.g., gesture combined with vocalization and eye contact), and flexibility of communication across verbal operants. Consequently, these learners are considered strong candidates for augmentative and alternative communication (AAC).

To adequately address each learner's unique communication support needs, components of the AAC intervention must be tailored to the individual. This tailoring includes both the assessment-information selection of the AAC

DOI: 10.4324/9781003433668-13

modality and the AAC instructional practice. This process of individualization has been mentioned in the literature by different names, including personalized AAC interventions, customized AAC supports, and precision AAC (Beukelman et al., 2016; Light et al., 2021). Importantly, each learner also exists in a unique, dynamic social system. Therefore, the service delivery model must also be adequately responsive to the presenting needs of the individual's social environment. The approach is well known in applied behavior analysis as identifying environment-behavior relations to guide function-based treatments (i.e., individualized interventions) and is the cornerstone of this science. Supporting the communication of individuals with ASD in the current state of AAC presents a unique and exciting opportunity for interprofessional collaboration between BCBAs and SLPs. The purpose of this chapter is twofold. First, we will define and describe AAC as an area, a communication modality, and an instructional practice. Second, we will present research-informed recommendations for AAC assessment and the design of successful AAC interventions. The chapter closes with strategies to overcome common clinical challenges through interprofessional collaboration between BCBAs and SLPs.

AAC as an Area

The term "AAC" may be a source of confusion. It is sometimes used to designate a specific but shared area of applied research and clinical practice that addresses communication needs. It is more commonly used as a hypernym to refer to a myriad of verbal behavior topographies (i.e., communication modalities) that are traditionally organized into *aided* and *unaided* categories. AAC is *augmentative* when used to supplement speech and *alternative* when used in place of speech as an intermediary or terminal response form(s) (adapted from Beukelman & Light, 2020). Designing AAC interventions requires attention to the AAC modality and the AAC instructional practice (Figure 11.1).

> *Importantly, AAC is not synonymous with a single communication modality such as speech-generating device (SGD) nor is it specific to a single manualized protocol such as the Picture Exchange Communication System (PECS®). Consequently, it would be correct to say, "Allison uses AAC" or "Allison is an AAC user." The sentence could be improved by including additional relevant detail such as, "Allison is an AAC user. She uses manual sign in coordination with vocalizations in the home environment with her parents but also uses a static 2x3 grid display using Proloquo2Go on her iPad mini at school." It would be incorrect to say, "Allison uses an AAC"*

Figure 11.1 Clarifying the appropriate use of the term AAC user and the importance of specifying communication modalities and contexts.

What Do We Mean by AAC Modality?

Team members must be familiar with the available AAC modality options to make informed decisions. The traditional AAC taxonomy organizes communicative forms and modalities into *unaided* and *aided* categories (ASHA, 2023). It may be well complemented by *topography-based (TB)* and *stimulus-selection-based (SB)* categories (Michael, 1985) to understand better the advantages and limitations of a particular AAC modality for a specific learner. In this section, we provide an overview of the available communicative forms through this combined lens with examples of the different ways they may be used to support communication.

Unaided versus Aided

Unaided modes of communication do not require supplemental tools or equipment and include modalities such as conventional and unconventional gestures, manual signs, and idiosyncratic vocalizations (ASHA, 2023). Social gestural behaviors, such as pointing and reaching that indicate interest in a preferred item, action, or ongoing interaction, are sometimes referred to as behavioral indications (Drasgow et al., 1996), potential communicative acts (Sigafoos et al., 2000), and indicating responses (Kasper, 2021; Shillingsburg et al., 2020; Sundberg, 2008). Indicating responses were further defined by Kasper and Kaufman (2024) and noted by Brady et al. (2012) to occur in clusters, such as eye gaze/alternating eye gaze, facial expressions produced in close temporal proximity to word approximations, and other distinctive gestures. For example, an individual with complex communication needs might indicate interest in an item or activity by gazing at the item, reaching toward the item, or taking a caregiver's hand and placing it on the item. Indicating responses are an often overlooked but important communicative response form and should be considered an unaided AAC modality.

Manual signs include a range of visual-motor and gestural communicative forms consisting of handshapes, positions, body movements, and facial expressions representing phonemes, words, expressions, letters, or numbers (Frolli et al., 2022). Manual signs were the first form of unaided AAC introduced for nonspeaking learners with developmental disabilities (Bondy & Frost, 2011). Manual signs encompass idiosyncratic forms called home signs and borrowed signs from American Sign Language, the language of the (D)eaf community with its own grammar and syntax. They also include a range of manually coded English systems that more closely approximate the grammar and syntax of spoken English, such as Signed Exact English (SEE), Conceptually Accurate Signed English (CASE), and Linguistics of Visual English (LOVE). Manual gestures can also augment and improve speech sound production via phonetic hand cues (Kasper & Kaufman, 2024). Phonetic hand cues are a system of hand gestures that are modeled by the instructor, paired with the vocal production of a sound, and in some cases, also executed by the learner as they produce the sound. For example, for the /p/ phoneme, a single fist is held near the chin, which opens while the instructor models the /p/ phoneme. This manual sign may serve as a prompt for "p" in words within which "p" was previously omitted or produced in error. Using manual signs, individuals with ASD have successfully learned to tact objects and pictures (Carr et al., 1978; Remington & Clarke, 1983; Schepis et al., 1982), mand for preferred items (Achmadi et al., 2014; Carr & Kologinsky, 1983; Schepis et al., 1982; van der Meer et al., 2013), and respond to intraverbal questions with yes/no responses (Schepis et al., 1982; van der Meer et al., 2013). Further, instructor-modeled and learner-produced signs, in conjunction with speech, have been effectively used to improve the rate of acquisition of tacts and increase sentence length. Carbone et al. (2006) compared the effect of manual sign and speech (e.g., signing "ball" and saying "ball") to speech-only training (saying "ball") on the vocal-verbal tact responses of a child with autism, with results demonstrating nearly four times as many vocal-verbal tact responses during sign and speech training (i.e., multimodal tacts) than during speech-only training in less than half the number of teaching trials. Barrett and Sisson (1987) also found benefits in providing signs and speech combined as prompts when compared to speech only as prompts. For some learners, multimodal responding with sign and speech results in improved acquisition of verbal vocal targets.

Unaided AAC modalities require varying degrees of motor control from the learner, ranging from "early handshapes" such as B, S, A, 1, C, 0, 5 to signs with higher fine motor requirements such as F or signs that require coordinated movement (e.g., fingerspelling or lexicalized sign) or different handshapes from both hands (Valli et al., 2020). Additionally, communication partner(s) may require specific education and training to instruct, detect, and reinforce these communicative forms. A noteworthy advantage of unaided AAC modalities is that they do not necessitate the management, upkeep, or transport of an external device or hardware, which minimizes the AAC user's and communication partners' response effort in ensuring communication access. It has also been suggested that unaided AAC modalities may be advantageous since they share commonalities with speech (Frolli et al., 2022; Sundberg & Sundberg, 1990).

Aided AAC communication modalities require an external tool or device that ranges in technological sophistication. Low or light-technology modalities such as writing with a pen and paper, pointing to pictures or words on a board, exchanging a picture icon, and activating a microswitch or BIGmack require very little technology for implementation. In contrast, a speech-generating device (SGD), previously referred to as a voice output communication aid, represents a high-technology option. SGDs electronically generate voice output after selecting a symbol from a grid or visual scene display. Grid displays typically arrange symbols into rows and columns, while visual scenes depict particular locations (e.g., classroom, kitchen) or activities (e.g., shopping). These may be designed as static (fixed) or dynamic (navigating to other pages) displays, typically accessed by the AAC user through contact between their finger and the screen. To begin AAC intervention, emergent communicators with ASD may benefit from high iconicity (e.g., strong resemblance between the symbol and its referent) symbols and low navigation demands to establish initial communicative response forms (Gevarter et al., 2014). Said another way, accessing and navigating the AAC modality should entail a low response effort for the learner and include symbols that share a high degree of formal similarity with the stimulus (i.e., color photos would be considered to have higher iconicity than an X to represent "no"). Although beyond this chapter's scope, alternative access methods can be utilized for learners with motor or vision support needs.[2]

The proliferation of commercially available mobile technology has significantly increased the accessibility and popularity of SGDs (Light et al., 2019). The range of options and customizability features may be overwhelming and an additional source of confusion or conflict among team members (Figure 11.2).

To date, only a small percentage of different types and applications of SGDs have been concurrently compared in published peer-reviewed research articles to determine efficacy with individuals with ASD (Lorah et al., 2022). Table 11.1 is a non-exhaustive summary of these high-technology AAC options, including the manufacturer, device, application, vocabulary, and symbols. Aided AAC modalities require that AAC users upkeep and manage the device across settings, a disadvantage relative to unaided modalities. Advantages include potential access to a larger verbal community due to increased probability of reinforcement for adaptive communication across settings and communicative partners, increasing the likelihood of stimulus generalization (Brodhead et al., 2020).

There is an unfortunate trend in AAC that has kept the conversation stuck on finding "the right" high-tech device, "the right" application, "the right" vocabulary, "the right" symbols, and "the right" display. While these are certainly important considerations, well-designed instructional practices consistently implemented with procedural fidelity are more important (Ganz et al., 2017). Said another way, the form of the response (i.e., AAC modality) is less important than the AAC instructional practices that we use to teach it. A basketball player is not great because they were handed a basketball. To become proficient, they were surrounded by coaches and teammates that inspired them to play, learned the rules and techniques of the game, contrived opportunities for them to play and reinforced their improving skills. Teaching communication does not start and end with providing physical access to an appropriate tool.

Figure 11.2 Emphasizing that effective AAC instruction relies more on evidence-based teaching practices than on the device or modality itself.

Table 11.1 Examples of High-Technology AAC Options

Manufacturer	Device	Application	Vocabulary	Symbols
iOS	iPod Touch	Prologquo2Go	TouchChat— WordPower	Symbol Stix
Samsung	iPad	Sounding Board		Picture
Prentke Romich (PRC)		Easy VSD		
		My Choice Board		
		GoTalk NOW Lite		
		My Talkmobile		
		DECT.ilk		
		TouchChat		
		ChoiceBoard Creator		
		Vantage Lite		
		Springboard Lite		
		Sonoflex		

Note: The manufacturer, device, application, vocabulary, and symbols represent an incomplete list of the decisions required during the design of high-tech AAC. This list is adapted from Lorah et al. (2022).

Topography-Based versus Stimulus-Selection-Based

Team members must identify the discrimination and access demands of the AAC modality for the learner (i.e., the speaker) and the communication partner (i.e., the listener). Michael (1985) discussed two general categories of verbal behavior: *topography-based (TB)* and *stimulus-selection-based (SB)*. TB consists of unique response forms that come under the operant control of a discriminative stimulus. Said another way, the response products of TB look, sound, and feel different from one another. For instance, when you vocally say "cookie" versus "juice" in spoken English, the articulatory structures and musculature coordinate in different patterns to produce spoken words. Similarly, when you sign COOKIE and JUICE in American Sign Language, they are topographically different, with their unique combination of sign language parameters, including palm orientation, movement, handshape, location, and non-manual features. Contrastingly, SB are nondistinctive response forms that share a common response topography. For example, when a motivating operation (MO) is in effect for a toy dinosaur, a child may point to a dinosaur among several items on the shelf. They point to a toy dinosaur when they want the dinosaur, and they point to a bear when they desire the bear. The pointing is a shared topography in response to a particular MO (e.g., establishing operation and evocative effect) and a particular antecedent stimulus (e.g., a toy dinosaur or a toy bear) in the presence of other stimuli (e.g., toys on a shelf). Similarly, an AAC user may select a picture card from several options and exchange the card to mand for a preferred item or select a symbol from a static 2 x 3 grid display. These response forms (i.e., pointing, picture exchange, and touching a symbol on an SGD) are examples of SB because the response form (e.g., pointing, exchanging, touching) remains the same. Some researchers have suggested that TB forms may be advantageous as AAC modalities because the unique response forms resemble speech production and do not require a conditional discrimination like SB (Sundberg & Sundberg, 1990; Wraikat et al., 1991). Other researchers have suggested that SB may be acquired more efficiently and may be more widely preferred by AAC users (Barlow et al., 2013; Gevarter et al., 2013; Tincani, 2004). There is value in identifying the discrimination requirements and access demands of the AAC modality.

Socially significant communication needs, environmental supports, and barriers vary with each communicative context. Some learners may benefit from a single response form across contexts, while others might be best served via multimodal communication, where response forms are varied and individualized based on context (Light et al., 2019). Equally important in modality selection is the relative current and future value of a particular response form, the match between the strength profile of the learner and the skill set to be used, improved, or developed to access the AAC modality, and the individualized intervention strategies utilized.

What Do We Mean by AAC Instructional Practice?

A thorough understanding of the AAC modality as a communicative response form is insufficient information to guide effective AAC intervention. A comprehensive AAC taxonomy should include the form of communication and its function. Skinner (1957) argued that analyzing the controlling variables of verbal behavior is crucial for understanding its development and use. It follows that understanding the verbal operants, such as mands, tacts, echoics, and intraverbals, which are all understood in terms of their function (i.e., the antecedents and consequences maintaining the response; see Chapter 1 in this volume for a review), may be beneficial when applied to AAC. Specifically, it may be useful to identify the environmental variables that occasion and maintain a learner's current communication repertoire to guide the design of AAC interventions to teach various communication skills, including requesting (mands), commenting or labeling (tacts), and responding in conversation (intraverbals). As demonstrated in the previous section, there are unrealized benefits of combining behavior-analytic and speech/language perspectives to create precise descriptions of the AAC modality. The same applies to AAC instructional practice, the second component of AAC intervention.

The extant AAC literature contains several different instructional practices. This chapter organizes these techniques into two categories: *response-dependent* and *response-independent*. It is recommended that practitioners familiarize themselves with both approaches. Response-dependent AAC instructional practices are well known by behavior analysts and include the following key features of explicit teaching strategies: (a) systematic selection of response prompts or stimulus prompts that reliably occasion the communicative behavior of interest, (b) systematic transfer of stimulus control procedures such as prompt-fading or prompt delay to increase independence, and (c) use of reinforcers to increase the communicative behavior. Several recent reviews support the use of applied behavior analytic practices to promote the use of AAC (Logan et al., 2017). For example, Bondy and Frost (2011), the authors of the *Picture Exchange Communication System* (PECS®), outline specific prompt, prompt-fading, reinforcement, and error correction strategies across six phases of intervention. The learner begins in Phase 1: Learning How to Communicate by exchanging a picture with a communication partner to access a preferred item (e.g., indicating a response for the ball, being prompted to give a picture of the ball, and receiving the ball). Physical guidance is often used to support this initial mand but is systematically faded to increase independent communication. Communication is advanced through the stages and includes explicit teaching of social initiation by traveling to communication partners (Phase 2: Distance and Persistence), conditional discriminations (Phase 3: Picture Discrimination) to advanced selection-based tacts (Phase 6: Commenting) by selecting the relevant autoclitic frame and picture icon (i.e., hear motorcycle, select "I hear" + "motorcycle", contact social reinforcement) (Figure 11.3).

Similarly, initial SGD or sign language instruction often involves the identification of the most effective, least intrusive prompt(s), which are systematically faded (van der Meer & Rispoli, 2010). Motivation is captured or contrived, and prompt(s) are identified and used. Then, they are systematically faded within or across subsequent trials via less intrusive prompts, prompt delay, and delay to reinforcement. Recent advances have also shown that using physical prompts and prompt delay during an interrupted behavior chain are effective in teaching children to mand to peers using their SGD (Lorah et al., 2019). Lorah and Parnell (2017) used physical prompts and prompt delay to teach preschoolers with ASD to tact pictures during circle time on their SGDs. Gevarter et al.

A common error is to use "PECS" to refer to any pictures/symbols or use of picture symbols for visual schedules or communication boards. PECS® (Picture Exchange Communication System®) is an evidence-based manualized protocol with over 35 years of clinical validation. Thus, it would be correct to say we are teaching a learner to communicate with pictures via PECS®, but incorrect to say, we need to make more PECS for Jake's visual schedule.

Figure 11.3 Clarifying the correct use of the term PECS® and distinguishing it from the generic use of picture symbols or visual supports.

(2016) used delays to reinforcement, differential reinforcement, and response prompts to occasion subsequent vocalizations for learners with ASD using SGDs. These studies include AAC instructional practices that are categorized as response-dependent.

Response-independent AAC instructional practices encompass several different modeling-based procedures. In response-independent AAC instructional practices, the practitioner or communication partner models language using speech and AAC. They may do this by modeling the entire phrase or, more commonly, a keyword(s) with AAC at the same time as spoken language (synchronously) or after/before (asynchronously). One challenge in supporting the communication needs of AAC users is that these individuals may fail to receive language models using AAC and, as a result, realize less of their communicative potential relative to their peers who use vocal speech (Bruno & Trembath, 2006). Using modeling-based AAC strategies is a common recommendation from SLPs to offset the lack of natural models for AAC users (Drager et al., 2006). A key distinction of response-independent AAC instructional practices is that they are not response-driven. In other words, the instructor provides a model, and the learner may not immediately emit a contingent response. Therefore, the term "model" in response-independent instructional practices does not satisfy the definition of a prompt as it does not immediately occasion a contingent response from the learner. Response-independent instructional practices are familiar to SLPs but may be novel to behavior analysts.

Several different techniques meet the features of response-independent AAC instructional practices, including (a) the communication partner's speech is augmented by AAC, (b) modeling-based techniques are not response-driven, and (c) communicative responses are encouraged but not required from the learner. These techniques include Aided Language Modeling (Drager et al., 2006), Aided Language Stimulation (ALgS; Goossens, 1989), Natural Aided Language (Cafiero, 2001), System for Augmenting Language (SAL; Romski & Sevcik , 1992), Aided AAC Modeling (Binger & Light, 2007), and Augmented Input (Wandin et al., 2023). According to a recent scoping review, response-independent AAC instructional practices may result in positive communication outcomes, such as improved language comprehension and expression, for learners with ASD who use AAC (Wandin et al., 2023). For example, Drager et al. (2006) described an aided language modeling AAC intervention with two young children with ASD. The AAC intervention entailed three steps. First, the communication partner pointed to the target object (e.g., baby) during a play activity (e.g., dollhouse). Second, within 2 seconds, the communication partner pointed to the corresponding AAC symbol (e.g., a picture-based symbol of the baby) while simultaneously providing a speech model of the symbol (e.g., "baby"). In this procedure, symbol-object pairings occurred four times for each targeted object within each 15-min–20-min session. The intervention improved symbol comprehension and symbol production across three activities. Symbol comprehension was defined as selecting from an array of objects when presented with a spoken instruction and corresponding symbol (i.e., "Show me___" while holding up the corresponding symbol). Symbol production was defined as selecting the corresponding symbol from an array to label a presented object and instruction (i.e., "What's this?" while holding up the object). In practice, SLPs may recommend these techniques, calling them "modeling without expectations," "aided AAC modeling," "aided modeling," or "aided input." Though some promising research exists on these techniques, attention to identifying the specific variables that contribute to improvements in communication is needed, and better participant characterization would help clarify for whom these techniques might be beneficial. The majority of studies include additional secondary strategies such as expectant delay (i.e., time delay or delay to reinforcement), open-ended questions, contingent responding, direct prompting, or expansion/ recast (e.g., repeating or expanding on the child's utterance) with learners who have unknown baseline strengths or unreported skills in the areas of receptive language, symbol recognition, imitation, joint attention, or fast mapping (e.g., word learning through brief incidental exposure; Allen et al., 2017; Chazin et al., 2021; Wandin et al., 2023). For researchers, this is a call to action to include technological descriptions of procedures (e.g., dosage) and thorough descriptions of participant characteristics (e.g., age, prerequisite skills) that might moderate intervention outcomes.

These response-independent techniques commonly practiced by SLPs share commonalities with procedures in applied behavior analysis, including stimulus-stimulus pairing (Shillingsburg et al., 2015), instructional demonstrations (Hranchuk et al., 2019), and instructive feedback (Werts et al., 1995) that are used in interventions with individuals who speak or to promote speech. Valentino and Shillingsburg (2011) evaluated instructional demonstration or modeling without expectation to respond in the context of applied behavior analytic intervention for a child with ASD who communicated using signs. In this study, the child was engaged in preferred activities, and the clinician modeled the sign and simultaneously said the names of the items and the functions of the items. Later, with only exposure to the model, the child emitted mands, tacts, and intraverbals via signs. A combination of response-independent and response-dependent techniques can be implemented concurrently or sequentially, dispelling the misconception that one should occur to the exclusion of the other. Further, a collaboration between BCBAs and SLPs may be enhanced when there is a clear understanding of different approaches, and the intervention is guided by data-based decisions for a particular learner.

There are notable limitations in the current state of the literature on AAC instructional practices for AAC users with ASD. There is a narrow representation of interventions that target skills beyond early requesting or manding (Logan et al., 2017). Communicative responses are often limited to one-word utterances, and the majority of studies are completed with young children versus adolescents or adults (Wandin et al., 2023). When considering the evidence base for AAC instructional practices for learners with ASD who use SGDs, the scarcity of evidence relative to low-tech forms of AAC may give practitioners pause for consideration as to how to design AAC interventions with SGDs. However, a recent review suggests that many of the same evidence-based instructional practices that have been shown effective with low-tech and no-tech AAC modalities are also effective when using an SGD (Muharib et al., 2023). Specifically, reinforcers (i.e., specific to the motivating operation when manding and generalized when responding intraverbally or with tacts), prompting, prompt delay, interrupted behavior chains, and chaining procedures have all been used to teach SGD use to individuals with ASD. Although this literature base is in its infancy, if we view SGDs as a high-tech extension of picture-based AAC, practitioners may extend the evidence-based research for low-tech modalities and empirically supported instructional practices to the design and implementation of AAC interventions that use an SGD, albeit with some additional considerations such as aspects of the grid display, modeling on a device, and symbol iconicity. The emerging support for instructional practices to teach communication skills using SGDs primarily focuses on simple mand repertoires (Muharib et al., 2023). There is an urgency for research demonstrating effective techniques to teach complex communication skills, such as recalling past events and maintaining conversations with social partners. There is also a dearth of research on procedures to teach the complex response chains required to navigate through multiple folders within a communication device. Additionally, much of the existing AAC research focuses on instructional practices that directly teach responses rather than procedures that promote the emergence of flexible and generative responses (see Chapter 9 in this volume for further discussion of generative language). Innovation from the collaboration between BCBAs and SLPs in research and practice may help to address this need.

What Do We Mean by AAC Assessment?

The purpose of AAC assessment is *not* to identify the flashiest device with the newest features. The purpose is to gather information that should guide the design of AAC interventions for a specific learner. Attention to both the AAC modality and the AAC instructional practice is necessary for the individualization required to meet the needs of each learner (see Figure 11.1 for a visual reference of important elements of designing AAC intervention). The complementary expertise and skill sets of BCBAs and SLPs might enhance the assessment process. This section describes the typical process and underscores the distinctive advantages and unique benefits of interprofessional collaboration (Figure 11.4).

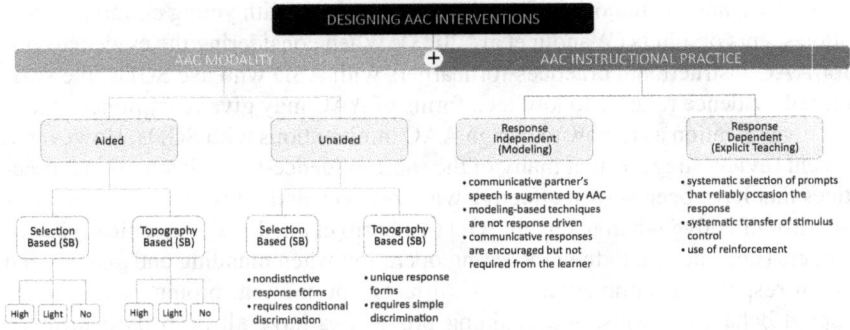

Figure 11.4 Designing AAC interventions.

AAC evaluations, typically conducted by a licensed SLP, guide AAC intervention and may be required for insurance to fund an SGD, a type of durable medical equipment. During an AAC assessment, SLPs are tasked with (a) identifying communication needs and priorities, (b) assessing ecological communication supports called opportunity barriers, and (c) completing a comprehensive assessment of the individual's current skills and abilities called access barriers (Beukelman & Light, 2020). Opportunity barriers include public perceptions and awareness of AAC; insurance policy requirements; federal or state practice regulations; or the knowledge and skill of the individual's caregiver or communication partners. Access barriers focus on the characteristics of the individual. The assessment of these types of ecological and individual variables is well-known in behavior analysis and may offer unique benefits when combined with the expertise of an SLP. Access barriers focus on the characteristics of the individual.

SLPs use indirect and direct assessment methods, including standardized norm-referenced assessments and criterion-referenced assessments, which may or may not be standardized. Direct assessments involve interacting with the individual or conducting observations in meaningful settings (e.g., school, home). Indirect assessments gather information from stakeholders such as parents, caregivers, teachers, paraprofessionals, or other support providers. Criterion-referenced assessments assess if an individual has achieved specific skills, benchmarks, or milestones. Norm-referenced assessments compare the individual's performance to same-age peers using a standard distribution/bell curve. A non-exhaustive list of examples of instruments and assessment methods is included in Table 11.2.

There are limitations of standardized and norm-referenced assessments for emergent communicators, minimally verbal, or nonspeaking individuals.

Table 11.2 Assessment Methods and Example Instruments

	Criterion-Referenced	Non-Referenced	Non-Standardized
Indirect	• Communication Matrix • Essential for Living (EFL)	• Communication and Symbolic Behavior Scales • Vineland Adaptive Behavior Scales Third Edition	• Functional Communication Profile • Dynamic AAC Goal Grid • Participation Inventory • Communication Needs Assessment
Direct	• Verbal Behavior Milestones Assessment and Placement Program (VB-MAPP) • Assessment of Basic Language and Learning Skills—Revised (ABLLS-R) • Rossetti Infant-Toddler Language Scale (Rossetti) • Early Denver Model Curriculum Checklist for Young Children with Autism	• Preschool Language Scales, Fifth Edition (PLS-5) • Clinical Evaluation of Language Fundamentals, Fifth Edition (CELF-5) • Peabody Picture Vocabulary Test Fifth Edition (PPVT-5)	• Functional Behavioral Assessment/ Descriptive Assessment/ Participation Analysis • Language/ Communication Sampling • Dynamic Assessment • Communication Complexity Scale

Note: This is a non-exhaustive list of instruments.

For example, assessments may lack flexible scoring to accommodate alternative modalities of communication and may erroneously assume that responses to a few items indicate a larger repertoire. According to Muller et al. (2020), the majority of SLPs reported dissatisfaction with some aspect of their current assessment method(s) and low levels of satisfaction with standardized methods used to assess communication in natural environments. Non-standardized assessments offering flexible scoring and administration may involve indirect assessment methods like unstructured interviews with a parent or direct observations/descriptive assessment of a learner's communication with peers across settings.[3] BCBAs, with their expertise in non-standardized assessment methods, can provide valuable information to SLPs and the team during the design of AAC interventions.

BCBAs may conduct a functional assessment of the verbal operants to identify existing environment-behavior relations that occasion and maintain particular communicative response forms. For example, a learner might reliably emit the sign for WATER in the presence of a glass filled with water, a non-verbal stimulus (i.e., a tact). However, they might unreliably emit the same sign under the control of an establishing operation to access water (i.e., a mand). In the aforementioned example, it might make sense to prioritize the learner's absent mand repertoire and utilize a tact-to-mand transfer approach to transfer skills from verbal operants of strength to the need area. Relatedly, Michael's (1982) extensions of duplics and codics are useful to assess key skill areas, such as imitation and matching, that may influence AAC acquisition.[4] Identifying which verbal relations are at strength at any given moment may help to guide the team's communication priorities and pieces of the AAC instructional practice.

Additionally, BCBAs might analyze stimulus-response patterns of communicative behavior by identifying both verbal and non-verbal sources of stimulus control (i.e., environmental inputs) and response requirements or demands from the learner (i.e., behavioral outputs). Team members must identify all potential sources of stimulus control to determine if and how they interact to the benefit or detriment of the learner (see Figure 11.2). For example, a learner may be unresponsive to a vocal-verbal instruction (i.e., auditory verbal stimulus) from the teacher; however, the same learner may respond when supplemental sources of stimulus control are added, such as the presentation of a picture card (static visual stimulus), sign (dynamic visual stimulus), or voice output from an SGD (auditory and visual stimulus). These techniques are consistent with response-independent AAC instructional practices (e.g., Augmented Input) that may be well-known to SLPs but less familiar to BCBAs. An interprofessional approach between BCBAs and SLPs has the potential to provide valuable information to guide individualized AAC interventions (Figure 11.5).

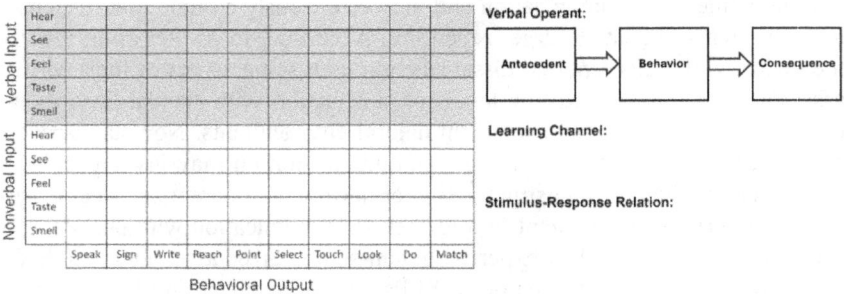

Figure 11.5 Assessment of verbal operant and stimulus-response relations.
Source: Modified from Haughton (1980)
Note: The Learning Channel Matrix is adapted from Haughton (1980) to include verbal and nonverbal stimuli to assist with the assessment of stimulus-response relations.

What Do We Mean by Being Effective?

When teaching communication skills to children with ASD who have significant delays in spoken language, directly teaching mands, tacts, and intraverbals is often an early step in intervention. However, instructional practices that promote emergent, flexible language skills are soon necessary. Emergent skills are new skills that occur seemingly without direct, explicit teaching. Emergent responses may result from the synthesis or combination of previously acquired component skills to generate novel, untaught responses or repertoires. Additionally, emergent responding is exemplified when a response taught as a speaker emerges as a listener response (and vice versa) or when a response acquired under one set of conditions emerges under another (e.g., a response learned as a mand is then emitted as a tact). For an in-depth review of emergent responding, the reader is directed to Chapter 9 of this book.

Researchers have begun to evaluate the efficacy of procedures shown effective in producing complex verbal behavior and emergent verbal behavior with speaking individuals with ASD, with autistic individuals who are nonspeaking. As a child's manding repertoire grows, intervention may evolve from targeting specific, single-word mands for items and activities to manding for information from others. Researchers have identified effective procedures to teach more complex mands for information to children and adolescents who speak (Cengher et al., 2022), and recently, several researchers have successfully used similar procedures to teach mands for information using speech-generating devices. For example, Carnett and Ingvarsson (2016) replicated and extended previous work (Ingvarsson & Hollobaugh, 2010) to teach a child with ASD to respond using his SGD, "I don't know, please tell me?" when posed a question he could not answer. Shillingsburg et al. (2019) replicated and extended previous studies and taught three children with ASD to use their SGDs to mand "who?" and "where?" to gain information regarding the location of missing preferred items. Most recently, Carnett et al. (2020) also taught children with ASD to mand "where?" on their SGDs during an interrupted behavior chain procedure. As with previous studies with speaking participants, the environmental arrangement involved contriving a motivating operation (MO) for needed information, prompting navigation to the appropriate icons or letters on the keyboard, followed by providing the requested information. Taken together, these studies support the notion that a more advanced manding repertoire can be taught using procedures similar to those that are effective with children with ASD who speak.

Recently, researchers have also begun to examine procedures that promote advanced, multi-word tact and intraverbal[5] phrases and procedures that promote generative responding for individuals who use AAC. Several procedures are effective in promoting emergent verbal behavior for children *with* ASD and other related developmental disabilities (Conine et al., 2023). Recently, some of these procedures have also been used effectively to promote emergent responding in those who use AAC to communicate. For example, Tullis et al. (2018) employed instructive feedback to promote emergent responding with an autistic child who typed on his SGD. Instructive feedback (IF) entails presenting incidental, extra information embedded during a teaching trial and examining whether the extra information is also learned. Tullis et al. taught the participant to identify a picture depicting a problem situation from an array of options. Once the problem situation was selected, secondary, extra information was provided by showing the participant the written explanation of why it was a problem. For example, if the problem selected was a pencil with a broken tip, the explanation for why it is a problem (i.e., because the broken pencil cannot write) was incidentally presented in the text.

Later, during probes, the participant typed the problem explanations on his SGD, which were never directly taught. An important consideration when using IF with individuals who use SGDs is whether the incidental information should be presented in the same form in which the person communicates. Tullis et al. presented the incidental information as text on a card because the participant communicated via typing. If the participant communicated via symbol selection on a dynamic grid display, incidental information could have been presented in this modality. This aligns with IF studies with speaking participants in which the incidental information provided is presented vocally but has yet to be empirically explored.

Matrix training is another well-established procedure that has been used to promote generative, novel responding in speaking individuals with ASD and has recently been shown effective in promoting generative responding with those who use SGDs. Matrix training is a method of arranging individual stimuli within a grid, such that different components are listed on the top and side axes, and the targeted combinations of those components are in the cells within the grid (see Frampton & Axe, 2022 for a tutorial). For example, if you are teaching tacts for color–shape combinations (e.g., red square, blue diamond), you would arrange the colors along the top axis of the grid and the shapes along the side axis. Within each cell, there would be a different color–shape combination. Once the matrix or grid is designed, the diagonal cells are taught directly. Once tacts for those color–shape combinations are learned, the other untaught cells are probed for recombinative generalization. Several studies with autistic individuals have shown that teaching in this manner results in acquiring all the targets in all the cells, even though only the diagonal targets were taught (see Curiel et al., 2020 for a review).

A few studies have examined matrix training to promote word combinations using AAC (e.g., Marya et al., 2021; Nigam et al., 2006). Only one study has examined matrix training with autistic individuals who use SGDs to teach multiword tacts requiring multi-step navigation on dynamic displays (Marya et al., 2021); see Figure 11.3 for an example matrix. In this study, three males with ASD (ages 3, 6, and 16 years) were taught to tact using noun-verb combinations to describe an agent performing an action, as demonstrated by the researcher. For example, the participant was shown a dog jumping and was asked, "What do you see?" to which the participant would navigate to the animals folder and select the icon "dog," then navigate to the actions folder and select the icon "jumping," and then touch the voice output icon such that the response "dog jumping" occurred. All three participants learned the directly taught targets (i.e., the diagonal targets) and produced novel, recombined noun-verb responses without direct teaching (i.e., non-diagonal cells). In addition, all three participants exhibited emergent noun-verb combinations to a generalization set of targets in which none of the combinations had been exposed to diagonal training. Although much more research is needed with this population, these results suggest that similar emergent responding can be expected when evidence-based instructional practices are used (Figure 11.6).

Procedures to promote intraverbal repertoires for autistic individuals who use AAC are also needed, particularly procedures that promote flexible responses to questions rather than rote ones. Although there is undoubtedly merit in teaching verbal repertoires that are under strict verbal antecedent control (e.g., What do you brush your teeth with? Toothbrush), there is concern that teaching specific answers to questions that could be answered in a variety of ways may limit one's verbal repertoire. For example, while there is likely only one answer to the question regarding brushing teeth, there are multiple answers to questions such as, "What do you wear to stay warm?" or "What did you eat for lunch?" Responses to questions such as these are emitted under multiple sources of control, and effective procedures to ensure one develops a flexible verbal repertoire to respond have been evaluated for children with ASD who speak (see Chapter 10 in this volume for a thorough discussion). Evaluating effective instructional practices to promote these skills for AAC users is just as important, though very

		Action		
		Jump	Eat	Sleep
Agent	Dog	Dog Jumping	Dog Eating	Dog Sleeping
	Cat	Cat Jumping	Cat Eating	Cat Sleeping
	Pig	Pig Jumping	Pig Eating	Pig Sleeping

Figure 11.6 Example matrix.
Note: The example matrix depicts nouns along the y-axis and verbs along the x-axis. Cells depict all possible noun-verb combinations.

little research exists. In one study, the authors used an error correction procedure consisting of physical and gestural prompts plus reinforcement for correct responses to teach three children with ASD to answer specific questions about activities they completed during the day (Shillingsburg et al., 2019). To establish responding under multiple control, the researchers randomly rotated through various activities in different physical locations throughout the day. At the end of the day, the participants were asked what activity they completed in each location. Correct responses had to correspond to the activity completed in each location on that particular day. Thus, intraverbals were emitted under the antecedent control of the verbal question and potentially private events evoked by the question (e.g., perhaps visually imagining the activities completed earlier in the day). Again, much more research in this area is necessary to build an evidence base for effective instructional practices to promote complex verbal repertoires for learners who use AAC.

Strategies for Overcoming Common Clinical Challenges

Behavior analysts and SLPs share the ethical responsibility to uphold an individual's right to communicate. To serve individuals with complex communication needs, they inevitably share space with stakeholders within and outside their respective disciplines. Unfortunately, the intra- and interprofessional collaboration required in AAC interventions is often perceived as a source of conflict or clinical challenge rather than a potential solution (Slim & Reuter-Yuill, 2021; Spencer et al., 2020). Realizing the untapped potential in the collaboration between BCBAs and SLPs can transform this clinical challenge in AAC interventions into a major source of strength. However, it is important to recognize that collaboration involves complex, interactive, and bidirectional processes between the individual and their environment across multiple systems—ecological, communicative context, communication partners, and the person (Reuter-Yuill et al., 2024). Reuter-Yuill et al. (2024) developed an Applied Model of Interprofessional Collaboration–Assessment (AMIC–A) to illustrate this process-based assessment approach through a combination of broader assessment and interprofessional collaboration. This chapter will focus on the "person" level to briefly describe an evidence-based collaborative process, highlighting the nature of the interactive process. Case scenarios will be used to demonstrate how various common clinical challenges can be identified and effectively addressed.

The collaboration process can be summarized in four stages. Recommendations represent an adaptation of the Conjoint Behavioral Consultation (Sheridan & Kratochwill, 2008) to guide collaboration between BCBAs and SLPs in AAC interventions. First, professionals and caregivers work together to evaluate the strengths and needs of the individual. During this initial step of *needs identification*, it is important to identify the person's existing communication and skill repertoires. Determining the knowledge, skills, and abilities of potential communication partner(s) is also valuable. Next, BCBAs, SLPs, other support service providers, and caregivers engage in joint and coordinated *needs analysis* by analyzing formal and informal assessment data. Together, they select intervention goals based on identified needs and team priorities. Assessment-supported communication strengths, component skills (e.g., imitation, symbolic recognition/matching-to-sample), and learning history guide the design of interventions tailored to address the person's unique needs. Following is *plan implementation*, wherein BCBAs often uniquely contribute to the fidelity of intervention via procedural fidelity checklists, education and training, and the development of data collection strategies and visual displays for *plan evaluation*. During plan evaluation, team members meet regularly, assess and analyze data, and engage in data-based decision-making according to agreed-upon acquisition criteria and timelines. This four-stage process is iterative, requiring ongoing assessment to determine the efficacy of the AAC intervention. A list of guiding questions for overcoming common clinical challenges through interprofessional collaboration, adapted from Sheridan et al. (2012), is provided in Table 11.3.

Table 11.3 Guiding Questions for Interprofessional Collaboration (IPC)

Interprofessional Collaboration (IPC)
Guiding Questions for Overcoming Common Clinical Challenges

	Yes	No	Resolution
Needs Identification	Yes	No	Resolution
Did the team identify what is happening prior to and after the priority skill(s)?			
Did the team identify and agree upon operational definitions for the selected priorities and goals?			
Did team members assess conventional and unconventional communication forms and patterns across communicative contexts (i.e., settings and communication partners)?			
Did team members assess and analyze conditions and idiosyncratic communication patterns that are observed prior to and after the selected behavior(s) across settings and contexts?			
Needs Analysis	Yes	No	Resolution
Did the team identify and agree upon operational definitions for the selected priorities and goals?			
Did the team select the initial steps or goal(s) that will support and enhance future communication skill repertoires?			
Did team members agree upon the priority goal(s) to address in the home and the community and across communication contexts?			
Did team members agree upon procedures to implement the intervention across conditions?			

(Continued)

Table 11.3 (Continued)

Interprofessional Collaboration (IPC)
Guiding Questions for Overcoming Common Clinical Challenges

Plan Implementation	Yes	No	Resolution
Were all relevant contextual and environmental supports identified and selected to meet the individual's needs and enhance strengths?			
Did team members utilize strategies based on existing skill strengths?			
Did team members implement intervention across contextual and communicative conditions/ functions?			
Did team members receive training on agreed-upon instructional practices?			
Did team members agree upon a system that ensures ongoing feedback, training supports, and troubleshooting when modifications need to be made?			
Did team members continuously review the data and progress made?			
Did team members actively make necessary adaptations and modifications as needed?			
Plan Evaluation	**Yes**	**No**	**Resolution**
Did the team identify whether the selected priorities and goals were met with considering the social, contextual, communicative, and individual factors?			
Were effective components of instructional practices identified?			
Were decisions for plan continuation, modifications, or discontinuation made?			
When present, were conflicts resolved in the best interest of the learner?			

Case Scenario: Frank

Frank is an easygoing, nonspeaking 15-year-old who uses an SGD with a 3 x 4 static grid display to mand for ten preferred items and activities identified by stimulus preference assessments. He independently performs daily living tasks, which were taught via task analyses. In the classroom, Frank does not regularly participate in lessons or overtly bid for attention from peers or staff; however, he approaches peer groups during less structured time and occasionally imitates their motor behavior (e.g., kicking snow). At home, he spends most of his time watching YouTube or playing video games in his room. He hovers in the kitchen when his caregivers are preparing meals. He does not engage in behaviors considered disruptive to peers or dangerous to himself or others.

Problem: Continuous advancement of AAC intervention is often overlooked in learners like Frank. An individual who possesses these skill strengths is capable of so much more! Often, emergent communicators are taught to mand for established reinforcers at the initiation of intervention; then, the emphasis shifts to focus on academically oriented skills. Older learners with limited communication repertoires and little disruptive or dangerous behaviors are underrepresented in AAC intervention studies, undereducated in AAC implementation, and illustrate the unexplored potential for greater communication and social interaction. General compliance or lack of overt demonstration of motivation is interpreted as the absence of unmet needs. This normalization of lack of progress in communication is concerning. AAC intervention team members must maintain a mindset of continuous improvement and growth for all learners.

Collaboration: In our scenario, a BCBA joins the team, which convenes in response to caregiver concerns that Frank is not communicating in the home environment and lacks essential skills to maximize autonomy and happiness. During *needs identification and needs analysis*, the team identified that Frank occasionally uses his SGD in the classroom and uses two schematic or activity-based displays during speech-language therapy. Frank has free access to most reinforcers in the home environment but will approach, hover, and gesture when desired items are visible but out of physical access. At restaurants, he points to pictures on menus or plates of other patrons to indicate desires. All team members are competent and motivated, but they were unaware of the inconsistent implementation of their communication device, unmet needs, and untapped interests. The team considers:

- The quality and quantity of reinforcers represented by symbols on his SGD
- Conventional/unconventional communication forms (i.e., approach, hover, point) across communicative contexts that indicate unmet needs, interests, and potential reinforcers
- Potential for conditioning additional reinforcers and teaching new behavior chains
- Use of current reinforcers and behavior chains to increase communication and social opportunities
- Use of dynamic displays to increase vocabulary and complexity of communication, as Frank's learning history includes mastery of 3-step behavior chains
- Selection of and training in the use of systematic teaching procedures across environments
- Environmental modifications and reallocation of time and resources to frequently and successively create and contrive communication opportunities with caregivers and peers

As the team interacts to explore and expand reinforcers beyond those depicted on his SGD, they define and use Frank's indicating responses to identify cooking, sports involving kicking, restaurants, Coldplay, and drumming. The team selects cooking and drumming as interests to develop for future use in contriving communication, peer interaction, and behavior chains. Existing behavior chains of swing setup and making microwave popcorn are targeted to establish the use of dynamic displays and promote peer interaction. During *plan implementation*, the BCBA provides training in behavior chain implementation with corresponding data collection and works with caregivers to increase communication opportunities in the home and community. The SLP and caregivers work jointly to adjust the SGD displays to meet Frank's growing home, school, and community needs. Team members meet regularly, assess and analyze data as part of *plan evaluation*, and modify training and intervention if progress lags. Frank is also included in a cooking class, leading to participation in an after-school baking group. Subsequently, he is included in bowling nights with this group. The collaborative process enhanced team member skills, improved team member satisfaction, and, most importantly, the continuous focus on improving Frank's communication skills improved his quality of life and made successful group home integration a reality.

Case Scenario: Carly

Carly is a 5-year-old nonspeaking girl with severe autism and suspected motor apraxia who has been receiving in-home ABA services for two years. The team has been attempting to teach her to exchange pictures via PECS® for 18 months during structured teaching. However, attempts to move beyond a single icon presented on the table have resulted in disruptive and dangerous behaviors. Observation reveals that Carly will exchange a picture for a presented item but will not consume it. In natural settings, she walks away when PECS® stimuli are presented. Her caregivers and SLP suggest an SGD in hopes that she will "like it" more, enabling her to communicate more effectively.

Problem: Often, when a learner fails to make progress, there may be an assumption that the communication modality is the issue. In reality, the variables that contribute to lack of progress may include any or all of the following: lack of sufficient or varied reinforcers, inadequate function of social stimuli as discriminative stimuli and reinforcers, lack of persistence in obtaining reinforcers (response effort weakens MO), failure to establish MO before prompting communication, failure to prompt immediately and fully during initial acquisition (prompt delay might weaken MO), failure to fade prompts consistently, lack of sufficient training trials, failure to individualize AAC modality selection based on learner skill set, failure to individualize AAC instructional practices based on learner skill set, failure to adjust the AAC intervention based on presenting needs of contexts and partners, failure to allocate sufficient time to education and training for communication partners, failure to use data-based decisions to monitor progress, poor procedural fidelity, schedule of reinforcement for AAC use is too lean and/or the schedule of reinforcement for functionally equivalent problem behavior occurs intermittently, failure to teach for generalization by assessing stimulus-response relations across learning channels, settings, and communication partners. Often, variables influencing lack of progress, prompt dependency, and overselectivity are not analyzed or modified in the search for "the right app," "the right device," or worse, lack of progress is attributed to the learner.

Collaboration: In this scenario, the team convenes to discuss the recommendation of an SGD by the SLP and the parent. The team engages in *needs identification and needs analysis* and notes that although Carly can match objects and pictures, she does not independently exchange a picture, even given months of training. She will approach specific staff to initiate idiosyncratic physical games, which result in giggles. She initiates with her parents by pulling them to the refrigerator for juice, pulling them to the bathtub for tubby time, bringing them a blanket to snuggle, and initiating a game of "Dancing with Daddy" by placing her feet on top of her dad's. During speech therapy, she activates a single BIGmack speech-generating switch to request recurrence (i.e., mand for repeat of tickles or push on a swing). ABA team members and caregivers are motivated to assist Carly and are well-intentioned but confess to a lack of formal training in implementing the PECS®. The SLP has formal training in PECS® and outlines the protocol for Phase 1. The ABA team shares that Carly's inconsistency in choice-making and resistance to the physical prompting necessary for the exchange have resulted in low training trials. The team is inspired to modify their intervention and improve her communication. The team considers:

- The quality and quantity of reinforcers are represented by the pictures compiled for communication. These items do not appear to function as reinforcers
- Conventional/unconventional communication forms (i.e., approach, pull, give item, idiosyncratic initiations of motor games via contact gestures) across communicative contexts that indicate unmet needs, interests, and potential reinforcers
- Potential for conditioning additional reinforcers
- Strengthening, shaping, and expanding indicating responses
- Selection of and training in the use of systematic teaching procedures across environments
- Environmental modifications and reallocation of time and resources to frequently and successively create and contrive communication opportunities with caregivers and peers

As part of *needs identification and needs analysis*, the team decides to observe, define, and inventory Carly's indicating responses during free-operant preference assessments and to further develop social behavior play chains like Dancing with Daddy. A list of these physical play routines, water play ideas, and preferred toys from speech therapy and home is compiled. The BCBA and SLP designed a data collection method for recording indicating responses for likes and dislikes. During *plan implementation*, the ABA team discontinues picture exchange instruction. They set a goal of developing 20 different toys, activities, or play chains across settings. They further establish a goal of conditioning touch and other social stimuli as discriminative stimuli (signaling the availability of reinforcement) and reinforcers (pairing with delivery of reinforcers). The team formally reassesses progress toward this goal by measuring her response to touch and proximity during weekly samples as well as reviewing indicating responses and reinforcers. Carly's pool of reinforcers increases systematically. The team views the PECS® training video, and the SLP monitors the initial reimplementation using new pictures representing current reinforcers. *Plan evaluation* confirms that Carly is moving quickly through the PECS® protocol and maintaining high degrees of social engagement. Concurrently, all team members have learned valuable skills by engaging in effective, open communication, joint decision-making, and establishing clear goals, procedures, and monitoring methods. These collaborative experiences establish harmonious partnerships between caregivers, behavior analysts, and SLPs as they share the social and ethical responsibility of promoting the highest communication opportunities for each individual with complex communication needs.

Summary

This chapter provides direction for the comprehensive, dynamic, ongoing process of assessing, designing, and implementing individualized, precise AAC interventions. It showcases research on effective AAC intervention from the fields of Behavior Analysis and Speech-Language Pathology. The combined research, knowledge, and skills of these two disciplines provide a unique and exciting opportunity to promote continuous improvement and growth in communication for autistic individuals who benefit from AAC intervention through interprofessional collaboration. This chapter is a call to action for these professionals to unite in safeguarding communication as a fundamental human right for all individuals.

Notes

1 It has been expressed by many autistic individuals that identity-first language is preferred. However, we also acknowledge that person-first language remains a preference for some individuals. The authors respect all perspectives of this diverse

community and will employ both person-first and identity-first language throughout this chapter.

2 SLPs make a distinction between direct and indirect access. Direct access is when there is contact between a person's body part (e.g., finger, hand, foot, head, eyes) and the device. Indirect access is when the AAC user activates a switch to make a selection using partner or technology-assisted scanning. There are also alternative access methods for individuals with motor or visual needs such as a joystick, trackball, mouth stick, eye gaze, sip and puff, etc. Each of these has different requirements or demands from the learner.

3 SLPs may use a non-standardized assessment method called dynamic assessment (DA). DA is a process-focused and flexible protocol that follows a test-teach-retest format (ASHA, 2023). This approach approximates typical progress monitoring in behavior analysis through baseline and ongoing measurement of targeted skills.

4 Michael (1982) defined the duplic relation with two key features: (a) the response form is controlled by a verbal stimulus, and (b) the response product has formal similarity with the controlling stimulus. Codics share point-to-point correspondence with the controlling stimulus, but there is no formal similarity. A better understanding of the relationship between AAC acquisition, imitation, and matching may start with a functional assessment of these skills.

5 Despite the common practice of identifying verbal behavior as one or another verbal operant. It is acknowledged that verbal behavior can be influenced by a combination of multiple antecedent and consequent stimuli, and the controlling variables can work simultaneously or interactively.

References

Achmadi, D., Sigafoos, J., van der Meer, L., Sutherland, D., Lancioni, G. E., O'Reilly, M. F., Hodis, F., Green, V. A., McLay, L., & Marschik, P. B. (2014). Acquisition, preference, and follow-up data on the use of three AAC options by four boys with developmental disability/delay. *Journal of Developmental and Physical Disabilities, 26*(5), 565–583. https://doi.org/10.1007/s10882-014-9379-z

Allen, A. A., Schlosser, R. W., Brock, K. L., & Shane, H. C. (2017). The effectiveness of aided augmented input techniques for persons with developmental disabilities: A systematic review. *Augmentative and Alternative Communication, 33*(3), 149–159. https://doi.org/10.1080/07434618.2017.1338752

American Psychiatric Association. (2013). *Diagnostic and statistical manual of mental disorders: DSM-5* (5th ed.).

American Speech-Language-Hearing Association. (2023). *Code of ethics* [Ethics]. www.asha.org/policy/.

Barlow, K. E., Tiger, J. H., Slocum, S. K., & Miller, S. J. (2013). Comparing acquisition of exchange-based and signed mands with children with autism. *The Analysis of Verbal Behavior, 29*(1), 59–69.

Barrett, R. P., & Sisson, L. A. (1987). Use of the alternating treatments design as a strategy for empirically determining language training approaches with mentally retarded children. *Research in Developmental Disabilities, 8*(3), 401–412. https://doi.org/10.1016/0891-4222(87)90022-9

Behavior Analyst Certification Board. (2020). *Ethics code for behavior analysts.* https://bacb.com/wp-content/ethics-code-for-behavior-analysts/

Beukelman, D. R., Bornman, J., & Light, J. C. (2016). Reflections from fellows of ISAAC. *Augmentative and Alternative Communication, 32*(4), 233–240. https://doi .org/10.1080/07434618.2016.1252947

Beukelman, D. R., & Light, J. C. (2020). *Augmentative & alternative communication: Supporting children and adults with complex communication needs.* Brookes Publishing Company.

Binger, C., & Light, J. (2007). The effect of aided AAC modeling on the expression of multi-symbol messages by preschoolers who use AAC. *Augmentative and Alternative Communication, 23*(1), 30–43. https://doi.org/10.1080/07434610600807470

Bondy, A., & Frost, L. (2011). *A picture's worth: PECS and other visual communication strategies in autism* (2nd ed., pp. xiv, 143). Woodbine House.

Brady, N. C., Bruce, S., Goldman, A., Erickson, K., Mineo, B., Ogletree, B. T., Paul, D., Romski, M. A., Sevcik, R., Siegel, E., Schoonover, J., Snell, M., Sylvester, L., & Wilkinson, K. (2016). Communication services and supports for individuals with severe disabilities: guidance for assessment and intervention. *American Journal on Intellectual and Developmental Disabilities, 121*(2), 121–138. https://doi.org/10.1352 /1944-7558-121.2.121

Brady, N., Fleming, K., Thiemann-Bourque, K., Olswang, L., Dowden, P., Saunders, M., & Marquis, J. (2012). Development of the communication Complexity Scale. *American Journal of Speech-Language Pathology, 21*(1), 16–28.

Brodhead, M. T., Brouwers, L. F., Sipila-Thomas, E. S., & Rispoli, M. J. (2020). A comparison of manual sign and speech generating devices in the natural environment. *Journal of Developmental and Physical Disabilities, 32*(5), 785–800. https://doi.org /10.1007/s10882-019-09720-1

Bruno, J., & Trembath, D. (2006). Use of aided language stimulation to improve syntactic performance during a weeklong intervention program. *Augmentative and Alternative Communication, 22*(4), 300–313. https://doi.org/10.1080/07434610600768318

Cafiero, J. M. (2001). The effect of an augmentative communication intervention on the communication, behavior, and academic program of an adolescent with autism. *Focus on Autism and Other Developmental Disabilities, 16*(3), 179–189. https://doi.org/10 .1177/108835760101600306

Carbone, V. J., Lewis, L., Sweeney-Kerwin, E. J., Dixon, J., Louden, R., & Quinn, S. (2006). A comparison of two approaches for teaching VB functions: Total communication vs. vocal-alone. *The Journal of Speech and Language Pathology – Applied Behavior Analysis, 1*(3), 181–192. https://doi.org/10.1037/h0100199

Carnett, A., & Ingvarsson, E. T. (2016). Teaching a child with autism to mand for answers to questions using a speech-generating device. *The Analysis of Verbal Behavior, 32*(2), 233–241. https://doi.org/10.1007/s40616-016-0070-6

Carnett, A., Ingvarsson, E. T., Bravo, A., & Sigafoos, J. (2020). Teaching children with autism spectrum disorder to ask "where" questions using a speech-generating device. *Journal of Applied Behavior Analysis, 53*(3), 1383–1403. https://doi.org/10.1002/jaba .663

Carr, E. G., Binkoff, J. A., Kologinsky, E., & Eddy, M. (1978). Acquisition of sign language by autistic children. I: Expressive labeling. *Journal of Applied Behavior Analysis, 11*(4), 489–501. https://doi.org/10.1901/jaba.1978.11-489

Carr, E. G., & Kologinsky, E. (1983). Acquisition of sign language by autistic children. II: Spontaneity and generalization effects. *Journal of Applied Behavior Analysis, 16*(3), 297–314. https://doi.org/10.1901/jaba.1983.16-297

Cengher, M., Bowman, M. D., Shawler, L. A., & Ceribo-Singh, M. S. M. (2022). A systematic review of mands for information. *Behavioral Interventions, 37*(3), 864–886. https://doi.org/10.1002/bin.1893

Chazin, K. T., Ledford, J. R., & Pak, N. S. (2021). A systematic review of augmented input interventions and exploratory analysis of moderators. *American Journal of Speech-Language Pathology, 30*(3), 1210–1223. https://doi.org/10.1044/2020_AJSLP-20-00102

Conine, D. E., Frampton, S. E., Buote, K. A., & Keller, C. E. (2023). A scoping review of empirical research on emergent intraverbal behavior. *Behavioral Interventions,* e1986. https://doi.org/10.1002/bin.1986

Curiel, E. S. L., Axe, J. B., Sainato, D. M., & Goldstein, H. (2020). Systematic review of matrix training for individuals with autism spectrum disorder. *Focus on Autism and Other Developmental Disabilities, 35*(1), 55–64. https://doi.org/10.1177/1088357619881216

Drager, K. D. R., Postal, V. J., Carrolus, L., Castellano, M., Gagliano, C., & Glynn, J. (2006). The effect of Aided Language Modeling on symbol comprehension and production in 2 preschoolers with autism. *American Journal of Speech-Language Pathology, 15*(2), 112–125. https://doi.org/10.1044/1058-0360(2006/012)

Drasgow, E., Halle, J. W., Ostrosky, M. M., & Harbers, H. M. (1996). Using behavioral indication and functional communication training to establish an initial sign repertoire with a young child with severe disabilities. *Topics in Early Childhood Special Education, 16*(4), 500–521. https://doi.org/10.1177/027112149601600408

Frampton, S. E., & Axe, J. B. (2022). A tutorial for implementing matrix training in practice. *Behavior Analysis in Practice, 16*(1), 334–345. https://doi.org/10.1007/s40617-022-00733-5

Frolli, A., Ciotola, S., Esposito, C., Fraschetti, S., Ricci, M. C., Cerciello, F., & Russo, M. G. (2022). AAC and autism: Manual signs and PECS, a comparison. *Behavioral Sciences, 12*(10), Article 10. https://doi.org/10.3390/bs12100359

Gevarter, C., O'Reilly, M. F., Kuhn, M., Mills, K., Ferguson, R., Watkins, L., Sigafoos, J., Lang, R., Rojeski, L., & Lancioni, G. E. (2016). Increasing the vocalizations of individuals with autism during intervention with a speech-generating device. *Journal of Applied Behavior Analysis, 49*(1), 17–33. https://doi.org/10.1002/jaba.270

Gevarter, C., O'Reilly, M. F., Rojeski, L., Sammarco, N., Lang, R., Lancioni, G. E., & Sigafoos, J. (2013). Comparing communication systems for individuals with developmental disabilities: A review of single-case research studies. *Research in Developmental Disabilities, 34*(12), 4415–4432. https://doi.org/10.1016/j.ridd.2013.09.017

Gevarter, C., O'Reilly, M. F., Rojeski, L., Sammarco, N., Sigafoos, J., Lancioni, G. E., & Lang, R. (2014). Comparing acquisition of AAC-Based mands in three young children with autism spectrum disorder using iPad® applications with different display and design elements. *Journal of Autism and Developmental Disorders, 44*(10), 2464–2474. https://doi.org/10.1007/s10803-014-2115-9

Goossens', C. (1989). Aided communication intervention before assessment: A case study of a child with cerebral palsy. *Augmentative and Alternative Communication, 5*(1), 14–26. https://doi.org/10.1080/07434618912331274926

Hranchuk, K., Greer, R. D., & Longano, J. (2019). Instructional demonstrations are more efficient than consequences alone for children with naming. *Analysis of Verbal Behavior, 35*(1), 1–20. https://doi.org/10.1007/s40616-018-0095-0

Ingvarsson, E. T., & Hollobaugh, T. (2010). Acquisition of intraverbal behavior: Teaching children with autism to mand for answers to questions. *Journal of Applied Behavior Analysis, 43*(1), 1–17. https://doi.org/10.1901/jaba.2010.43-1

Jones, W., Klaiman, C., Richardson, S., Aoki, C., Smith, C., Minjarez, M., Bernier, R., Pedapati, E., Bishop, S., Ence, W., Wainer, A., Moriuchi, J., Tay. S-W., & Klin, A. (2023). Eye-tracking-based measurement of social visual engagement compared with expert clinical diagnosis of autism. *JAMA, 330*(9), 854-865. https://doi.org/10.1001/jama.2023.13295

Kasper, T. S. (2021). The new professional and ethical compliance code for behavior analysts: an opportunity for renewed commitment to promoting functional communication. In A. Beirne & J. A. Sadavoy (Eds.), *Understanding ethics in applied behavior analysis* (2nd ed.). Routledge.

Kasper, T. S., & Kaufman, N. (2024). *Sign/select to talk* (2nd ed.). Northern Speech Services.

Klin, A., Lin, D. J., Gorrindo, P., Ramsay, G., & Jones, W. (2009). Two-year-olds with autism orient to nonsocial contingencies rather than biological motion. *Nature, 459*(7244), 257–261. https://doi.org/10.1038/nature07868

Light, J., Barwise, A., Gardner, A. M., & Flynn, M. (2021). Personalized early AAC intervention to build language and literacy skills: A case study of a 3-year-old with complex communication needs. *Topics in Language Disorders, 41*, 209–231.

Light, J., McNaughton, D., & Caron, J. (2019). New and emerging AAC technology supports for children with complex communication needs and their communication partners: State of the science and future research directions. *Augmentative and Alternative Communication, 35*(1), 26–41. https://doi.org/10.1080/07434618.2018.1557251

Logan, K., Iacono, T., & Trembath, D. (2017). A systematic review of research into aided AAC to increase social-communication functions in children with autism spectrum disorder. *Augmentative and Alternative Communication, 33*(1), 51–64. https://doi.org/10.1080/07434618.2016.1267795

Lorah, E. R., Holyfield, C., Miller, J., Griffen, B., & Lindbloom, C. (2022). A systematic review of research comparing mobile technology speech-generating devices to other AAC modes with individuals with autism spectrum disorder. *Journal of Developmental and Physical Disabilities, 34*(2), 187–210. https://doi.org/10.1007/s10882-021-09803-y

Lorah, E. R., Karnes, A., Miller, J., & Welch-Beardsley, J. (2019). Establishing peer manding in young children with autism using a speech-generating device. *Journal of Developmental and Physical Disabilities, 31*(6), 791–801. https://doi.org/10.1007/s10882-019-09679-z

Lorah, E. R., & Parnell, A. (2017). Acquisition of tacting using a speech-generating device in group learning environments for preschoolers with autism. *Journal of*

Developmental and Physical Disabilities, 29(4), 597–609. https://doi.org/10.1007/s10882-017-9543-3

Marya, V., Frampton, S., & Shillingsburg, A. (2021). Matrix training to teach tacts using speech generating devices: Replication and extension. *Journal of Applied Behavior Analysis, 54*(3), 1235–1250. https://doi.org/10.1002/jaba.819

Michael, J. (1982). Skinner's elementary verbal relations: Some new categories. *The Analysis of Verbal Behavior, 1,* 1–3.

Michael, J. (1985). Two kinds of verbal behavior plus a possible third. *The Analysis of Verbal Behavior, 3,* 1–4.

Muharib, R., Walker, V., & Dunn, W. (2023). Effects of interventions involving tablet-based speech-generating devices for individuals with ASD: A meta-analysis. *Journal of Autism and Developmental Disorders.* https://doi.org/10.1007/s10803-023-06173-6

Muller, K., Brady, N. C., Fleming, K. K., & Matthews, K. (2020). Communication assessment for individuals with minimal verbal skills: A survey of current practices and satisfaction. *American Journal of Speech-Language Pathology, 29*(4), 1997–2011. https://doi.org/10.1044/2020_AJSLP-19-00129

Nigam, R., Schlosser, R. W., & Lloyd, L. L. (2006). Concomitant use of the matrix strategy and the mand-model procedure inteaching graphic symbol combinations. *Augmentative and Alternative Communication, 22*(3), 160–177. https://doi.org/10.1080/07434610600650052

Pierce, K., Wen, T. H., Zahiri, J., Andreason, C., Courchesne, E., Barnes, C. C., Lopez, L., Arias, S. J., Esquivel, A., & Cheng, A. (2023). Level of attention to motherese speech as an early marker of autism spectrum disorder. *JAMA Network Open, 6*(2), e2255125. https://doi.org/10.1001/jamanetworkopen.2022.55125

Remington, B., & Clarke, S. (1983). Acquisition of expressive signing by autistic children: An evaluation of the relative effects of simultaneous communication and sign-alone training. *Journal of Applied Behavior Analysis, 16*(3), 315–327. https://doi.org/10.1901/jaba.1983.16-315

Reuter-Yuill, L. M., Slim, L. M., Kasper, T. S., Castaño, L., Dower, N. R., & Gevarter, C. B. (2024). An applied model of interprofessional collaboration-assessment (AMIC-A): A process-based approach to augmentative and alternative communication. *Seminars in Speech and Language, 45*(3), 194–212. https://doi.org/10.1055/s-0044-1787651

Romski, M. A., & Sevcik, R. A. (1992). Augmented language development in children with severe mental retardation. In Warren S. & Reichle J. (Eds.), Causes and effects of communication and language intervention (pp. 113–130). Paul Brookes.

Rose, V., Trembath, D., Keen, D., & Paynter, J. (2016). The proportion of minimally verbal children with autism spectrum disorder in a community-based early intervention programme. *Journal of Intellectual Disability Research, 60*(5), 464–477. https://doi.org/10.1111/jir.12284

Schepis, M. M., Reid, D. H., Fitzgerald, J. R., Faw, G. D., Van Den Pol, R. A., & Welty, P. A. (1982). A program for increasing manual signing by autistic and profoundly retarded youth within the daily environment. *Journal of Applied Behavior Analysis, 15*(3), 363–379. https://doi.org/10.1901/jaba.1982.15-363

Sheridan, S. M., Bovaird, J. A., Glover, T. A., Garbacz, S. A., Witte, A., & Kwon, K. (2012). A randomized trial examining the effects of conjoint behavioral consultation and the mediating role of the parent–teacher relationship. *School Psychology Review,* *41*, 23–46.

Sheridan, S. M., & Kratochwill, T. R. (2008). *Conjoint behavioral consultation:* *Promoting family-school connections and interventions* (2nd ed., pp. xv, 220). Springer Science + Business Media.

Shillingsburg, A., Marya, V., Bartlett, B., Thompson, T., & Walters, D. (2019). Teaching children with autism spectrum disorder to report past behavior with the use of a speech-generating device. *The Analysis of Verbal Behavior, 35*(2), 258–269. https:// doi.org/10.1007/s40616-019-00112-2

Shillingsburg, M. A., Frampton, S. E., Schenk, Y. A., Bartlett, B. L., Thompson, T. M., & Hansen, B. (2020). Evaluation of a treatment package to increase mean length of utterances for children with autism. *Behavior Analysis in Practice, 13*(3), 659–673. https://doi.org/10.1007/s40617-020-00417-y

Shillingsburg, M. A., Hollander, D. L., Yosick, R. N., Bowen, C., & Muskat, L. R. (2015). Stimulus-stimulus pairing to increase vocalizations in children with language delays: A review. *The Analysis of Verbal Behavior, 31*(2), 215–235. https://doi.org/10 .1007/s40616-015-0042-2

Shillingsburg, M. A., Marya, V., Bartlett, B. L., & Thompson, T. M. (2019). Teaching mands for information using speech generating devices: A replication and extension. *Journal of Applied Behavior Analysis, 52*(3), 756–771. https://doi.org/10.1002/jaba .579

Sigafoos, J., Woodyatt, G., Keen, D., Tait, K., Tucker, M., Roberts-Pennell, D., & Pittendreigh, N. (2000). Identifying potential communicative acts in children with developmental and physical disabilities. *Communication Disorders Quarterly, 21*(2), 77–86. https://doi.org/10.1177/152574010002100202

Skinner, B. F. (1957). *Verbal behavior.* Appleton-Century-Crofts. https://doi.org/10 .1037/11256-000

Slim, L., & Reuter-Yuill, L. M. (2021). A behavior-analytic perspective on interprofessional collaboration. *Behavior Analysis in Practice, 14*(4), 1238–1248.

Spencer, T., Slim, L., Cardon, T., & Morgan L. (2020). *ABAI interprofessional* *collaborative practice between behavior analysts and speech-language pathology.* Workgroup of ABAI Practice Board.

Sundberg, C. T., & Sundberg, M. L. (1990). Comparing topography-based verbal behavior with stimulus selection-based verbal behavior. *The Analysis of Verbal Behavior, 8*, 31–41.

Sundberg, M. L. (2008). *VB-MAPP Verbal Behavior milestones assessment and* *placement program: A language and social skills assessment program for children* *with autism or other developmental disabilities.* AVB Press.

Tincani, M. (2004). Comparing the picture exchange communication system and sign language training for children with autism. *Focus on Autism and Other Developmental Disabilities, 19*, 152–163. https://doi.org/10.1177/10883576040190030301

Tullis, C. A., Marya, V., & Alice Shillingsburg, M. (2018). Enhancing instruction via instructive feedback for a child with autism using a speech-generating device. *The Analysis of Verbal Behavior, 35*(1), 103–112. https://doi.org/10.1007/s40616-018 -0096-z

Valentino, A. L., & Shillingsburg, M. A. (2011). Acquisition of mands, tacts, and intraverbals through sign exposure in an individual with autism. *The Analysis of Verbal Behavior, 27*(1), 95–101. https://doi.org/10.1007/BF03393094

Valli, C., Lucas, C., Mulrooney, K. J., & Villanueva, M. (2020). *Linguistics of American sign language: An introduction* (5th ed.). Gallaudet University Press.

van der Meer, L. A. J., & Rispoli, M. (2010). Communication interventions involving speech-generating devices for children with autism: A review of the literature. *Developmental Neurorehabilitation, 13*(4), 294–306. https://doi.org/10.3109/17518421003671494

Van Der Meer, L., Kagohara, D., Roche, L., Sutherland, D., Balandin, S., Green, V. A., O'Reilly, M. F., Lancioni, G. E., Marschik, P. B., & Sigafoos, J. (2013). Teaching multi-step requesting and social communication to two children with autism spectrum disorders with three AAC options. *Augmentative and Alternative Communication, 29*(3), 222–234. https://doi.org/10.3109/07434618.2013.815801

Wandin, H., Tegler, H., Svedberg, L., & Johnels, L. (2023). A scoping review of aided AAC modeling for individuals with developmental disabilities and emergent communication. *Current Developmental Disorders Reports, 10*(2), 123–131. https://doi.org/10.1007/s40474-023-00275-7

Werts, M. G., Wolery, M., Holcombe, A., & Gast, D. L. (1995). Instructive feedback: Review of parameters and effects. *Journal of Behavioral Education, 5*(1), 55–75.

Wodka, E. L., Mathy, P., & Kalb, L. (2013). Predictors of phrase and fluent speech in children with autism and severe language delay. *Pediatrics, 131*(4), e1128–e1134. https://doi.org/10.1542/peds.2012-2221

Wraikat, R., Sundberg, C. T., & Michael, J. (1991). Topography-based and selection-based verbal behavior: A further comparison. *The Analysis of Verbal Behavior, 9*, 1–17.

Section 3

Professionalism

Chapter 12

The Importance of Basic and Translational Language Research

Anna Ingeborg Petursdottir

Behavior analysts have an ethical responsibility to maintain their competence through professional development (Behavior Analysis Certification Board, 2020), for example, by attending conferences and consuming relevant scholarly literature. Indeed, maintaining certification requires regular engagement in continuing education activities of this nature. These activities are considered important for practitioners, in part, because up-to-date knowledge of the discipline's evidence base may result in better-informed services to clients. When it comes to choosing which conference talks to attend, articles to read, or podcasts to listen to, practitioners likely often opt for content that has the potential to directly inform their everyday practice, such as applied research studies and "how-to" presentations. This is understandable. A practitioner's everyday work revolves around practical problem-solving, and seeking out data-based information to assist with that work should be encouraged as a matter of course. This chapter, however, makes the case that practitioners involved in teaching language and communication can *also* benefit from awareness of basic and translational research that addresses the conceptual foundations of behavior-analytic language intervention.

What Is Basic Research and Why Is It Important?

Characteristics of Basic Research

Basic research is generally understood as research that aims to provide knowledge "for knowledge's sake," rather than to accomplish practical goals. The Organisation for Economic Co-operation and Development (OECD), for example, defines basic research as "experimental or theoretical work undertaken primarily to acquire new knowledge of the underlying foundations of phenomena and observable facts, without any particular application or use in view" (OECD, 2015, p. 365). Because the focus is not directly on practical problems, basic research is sometimes mischaracterized in public discourse as having limited value to real-world problem-solving. However, basic research provides

DOI: 10.4324/9781003433668-15

information that may later prove useful in ways that scientists may or may not clearly anticipate at the time they perform the work. For example, the rapid development of SARS-CoV-2 vaccines during the COVID-19 pandemic was possible because of decades of research on artificial genes, the workings of messenger RNA, and the structure of coronaviruses (e.g., Halber, 2021; Moore & Wilson, 2021). Applied behavior analysis, of course, would hardly exist as an applied science and a profession had it not been for the basic operant research of B. F. Skinner and others.

Basic research is normally conducted under tightly controlled laboratory conditions to minimize unwanted variability and preserve *internal validity* (i.e., the extent to which the study design permits inferring functional relations between independent and dependent variables). In behavior analysis, basic research is sometimes conducted with nonhuman laboratory animals, such as rats or pigeons, and sometimes with human participants. An advantage of working with laboratory animals is that their histories and experiences outside of the experiment are largely known to the researchers, whereas human participants inevitably bring to the table long and mostly unknown learning histories that may affect their behavior in the experiment. That said, in the realm of language, there is an advantage to studying human participants that likely requires no explanation. Basic verbal behavior research is most often conducted with children or adults of typical development as participants, but has also included participants from clinical populations (Petursdottir & Devine, 2017). However, even in language research, there are examples of studies conducted with nonhuman animals that simulate aspects of human verbal behavior (e.g., Epstein et al., 1980; Kuroda et al., 2014; Wasserman et al., 2015). Such research, in fact, is important from a theoretical perspective, as it demonstrates a role of basic behavioral processes in producing behavior that shares striking similarities with aspects of human language.

In basic research on verbal behavior, establishment and testing of verbal relations may occur through interactions between the participant and an experimenter, or through interactions between the participant and a computer. The verbal stimuli and responses often consist of pre-experimentally meaningless syllables, and non-verbal stimuli may be unrepresentative of stimuli that a person is likely to encounter in the natural environment. To illustrate, Figure 12.1 shows a set of visual stimuli and nonsense words that were used in the present author's lab in a study with children. Participants in the study learned either to vocally tact each stimulus, or to respond as a listener to the spoken nonwords, in both cases followed by tests for *emergent* learning outcomes (i.e., responses that were not taught directly). The rationale for using contrived and arbitrarily related stimuli like these is that doing so may minimize the effects of individual histories on study outcomes. However, this practice is not universal. For example, Jennings and Miguel (2017) taught college students to tact pictures of various birds, trees, and reptiles, using their conventional species names, followed by additional training and tests. The participants did not enter the study with

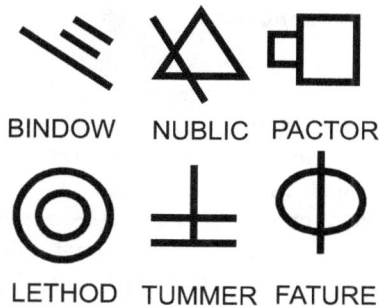

Figure 12.1 Example of a set of stimuli used in basic verbal behavior research.

most of the target tacts in their repertoires, but they likely had previous exposure to many of the names (e.g., "cardinal") and had surely encountered many visual exemplars of birds, trees, and reptiles in their lifetimes. Whereas using familiar types of stimuli may introduce unwanted variability into a study, it may increase a study's *ecological validity*; that is, the extent to which the results are likely to generalize to the world outside the laboratory.

Relevance of Basic Research to Practitioners

Behavior analysts who work in the domain of teaching language and communication use procedures and curricula that are grounded in theory and basic research. The procedures used to arrange reinforcement and establish stimulus control over verbal responses are, of course, derived from the basic experimental foundations of our field. Beyond that, the way we conceptualize the skills we teach, and how or when they should be taught, is based on conceptual analyses of language as a product of reinforcement contingencies that operate in the natural environment. The foundational theory in this context is Skinner's (1957) analysis of verbal behavior (see Chapter 1 in this volume). This analysis has informed the development of assessment tools and curricula that are widely used by practitioners working in early intervention settings with children diagnosed with autism spectrum disorder (ASD). One example is the *Verbal Behavior Milestones Assessment and Placement Program* (VB-MAPP; Sundberg, 2008); another is the *PEAK Relational Training System* (Dixon, 2014), which is additionally informed by theory and basic research on *derived stimulus relations* (i.e., relations among stimuli that arise without direct reinforcement). One important function of basic research is to evaluate the strengths and weaknesses of the theories that underlie clinical tools such as these. Therefore, familiarity with basic research may help practitioners become better-informed users who are able to critically evaluate the foundations of their practices.

Examples of Basic Verbal Behavior Research

Whereas basic research may not provide information of direct value to practitioners, it can provide information of substantial indirect value. This point will be illustrated by first describing two basic research studies, and then describing their implications for practitioners. Both studies were conducted in laboratory settings, with college students as participants.

The first study (Oliveira et al., 2023) addressed multiple control. Multiple control (see Chapter 10 in this volume) is an important analytic tool in Skinner's (1957) analysis of verbal behavior. One type of multiple control has been labeled *convergent* multiple control (Michael et al., 2011). Convergent control occurs when two or more antecedents that control the same verbal response form are present at the same time and increase the probability of occurrence of that response form over other response forms that might be at strength in the situation. For example, imagine someone asks you to name a vehicle and at the same time you hear a train horn in the distance. Although "car" might be your default intraverbal response to the verbal stimulus "vehicle," the stimulus may also evoke other intraverbal responses, such as "boat" and "train." Because the sound of the train horn (a source of control over the tact "train") contributes extra strength to that response, you might say "train" on this particular occasion. Note that you also might not have tacted the train out loud except because you were also asked to name a vehicle! The example may sound trivial, but the implications of convergent control are large. Skinner's (1957) analysis suggests, for example, that this type of multiple control (together with other verbal behavior referred to as autoclitic frames) is highly involved in verbal individuals emitting novel verbal behavior, such as sentences that have never been said before. This is aspect of language, often referred to as *productivity*, is tricky to explain in terms of prior reinforcement history, and in Skinner's (1957) account, convergent control is one of the keys to doing so.

Oliveira et al. (2023) set out to evaluate Skinner's (1957) proposal that convergent control results from the *summation* of stimulus control from two or more sources. Summation means that two stimuli that control the same response will exert a stronger evocative effect on that response than either stimulus in isolation, as illustrated in the train horn example above. To demonstrate summation, it is necessary to compare responding to a compound stimulus (e.g., saying "train" in the presence of the verbal stimulus "vehicle" combined with the sound of a train horn) to responding in the presence of each stimulus in isolation (e.g., saying "train" when presented only with the verbal stimulus "vehicle" or only with the sound of the train horn). Summation has been demonstrated in many basic research studies with humans and nonhumans, but not in the context of verbal behavior. The purpose of Oliveira et al. was to examine if summation could be demonstrated in a simulated verbal behavior situation, in which two stimuli controlled an overlapping response (as when "train" is controlled by both "vehicle" and the sound of the train horn), but each stimulus also controlled other verbal responses (just like "vehicle" might also exert intraverbal control over "car" and the train horn might exert tact control over "horn"). Participants were taught to select two different textual stimuli (e.g., "FA" and "ME") in the presence of each of several picture stimuli. Each picture, therefore, came to control the selection of two textual stimuli. In addition, training was arranged such that two pictures controlled the selection of each textual stimulus (e.g., selection of "FA" was one of the correct responses to two different pictures). In a final test, some trials presented the participants with a single picture stimulus, and other trials combined two pictures in a compound. Consistent with Skinner's (1957) proposal, participants were more likely to select each syllable in the presence of *both* of its controlling stimuli than in the presence of only one of the stimuli.

The second study (Ratkos et al., 2023) addressed descriptive autoclitics. Autoclitic behavior, according to Skinner (1957), is verbal behavior that is evoked by some aspect of the speaker's other verbal behavior. Autoclitics function to modify or sharpen the effects of the speaker's message (e.g., the mands and tacts and intraverbals they emit) upon the listener, by clarifying sources of stimulus control that are currently affecting the speaker. As with multiple control, autoclitic behavior serves an important function in Skinner's (1957) conceptual analysis. It plays a role in accounting for various aspects of complex verbal behavior, including much of the behavior of speaking grammatically. Along with multiple control, autoclitic behavior is key to accounting for language productivity in terms of reinforcement histories.

The descriptive autoclitic (one of several categories of autoclitic behavior) involves a speaker tacting some aspect of their own verbal behavior, such as the strength of their verbal response. For example, the "I think" in "I think the shovel is in the back yard" might tact weakness of "the shovel is in the back yard" (i.e., the speaker's certainty that this is so may be less than perfect under the current stimulus conditions). Few attempts have been made to empirically demonstrate functional relations between behavior of this sort and the controlling variables for descriptive autoclitics as per Skinner (1957). Ratkos et al. (2023), therefore, examined if variables likely to weaken a tact would increase the emission of response forms similar to "I think" in the previous example. Participants were shown images of common objects and asked to tact them vocally. Some images were clear and unambiguous, whereas others had been digitally distorted. The experimenters recorded the participants' vocal responses and coded them for the presence of possible weakness-tacting response forms (e.g., "I think," "I guess," or in the form of a question, such as "is it a ___?"). Consistent with Skinner's (1957) conceptualization, the more distorted the images, the more of these response forms were emitted.

The results of studies like Oliveira et al. (2023) and Ratkos et al. (2023) do not have *direct* implications for practice. For example, they do not tell us exactly how we might go about facilitating convergent multiple control or descriptive autoclitic behavior in the verbal behavior of children learning language skills. However, the results demonstrate that verbal behavior under controlled laboratory matches predictions of Skinner's (1957) account. By doing so, they provide valuable support for a theoretical analysis that underlies recommendations for practitioners, such as those found in Chapter 10 on multiple control in this volume. That is, they have the indirect benefit of helping validate the use of Skinner's (1957) account as a foundation for clinical practices and tools.

What Is Translational Research and Why Is It Important?

Functions of Translational Research

Basic research is often contrasted with applied research, which is generally understood to be research directed at solving practical problems. Within behavior analysis, applied research is often thought of in terms of Baer et al.'s (1968) seven dimensions of applied behavior analysis.[1] However, a lot of research is neither purely basic nor purely applied. Some research has most of the characteristics and functions of basic research, except that the end goal is clearly defined in terms of practical application. Other research may meet some or even all of the criteria described by Baer et al. (1968), but simultaneously contribute to foundational knowledge. These types of research activities are often described as *translational*.

Scientific translation is a bidirectional process (Austin, 2018; Rubio et al., 2010). That is, translational research transfers knowledge both from the laboratory to the field and from the field to the laboratory, or back to foundational knowledge. In the latter case, problems encountered or observations made in applied settings inspire controlled investigation that may ultimately serve to answer foundational knowledge questions. Translational research is not a discrete category of research that is fully separable from basic or applied research. Rather, there are different types or tiers of research activities that serve translational functions (Rubio et al., 2010). Kyonka and Subramaniam (2018) described a tiered model of translational research applied to the field of behavior analysis that will be used in this chapter to describe the role of translational activities in research on verbal behavior.

Five Tiers of Verbal Behavior

Table 12.1 lists the five tiers of research activity in behavior analysis described by Kyonka and Subramaniam (2018). At one end of the spectrum (Tier 0) is basic research as described in an earlier section of this chapter. Kyonka and Subramaniam labeled this tier "blue sky" basic research, in that it is motivated primarily by the pursuit of fundamental knowledge, without clear consideration of what the potential applications of that knowledge might be.

Table 12.1 Tiers of Basic and Translational Research Activity in Behavior Analysis (Kyonka & Subramaniam, 2018)

Tiers of Research	Function
Tier 0: Blue sky basic research	"Contributes new knowledge about the fundamental nature of behavior-environment relations" (p. 597)
Tier 1: Use-inspired research	"[I]nvestigates the fundamental nature of behavior-environment relations, but ... the results are relevant to a particular population or situation." (p. 599)
Tier 2: Solution-oriented research	Serves to "test and refine behavioral technology under relatively simplified, controlled circumstances" (p. 600)
Tier 3: Applied research	Applied behavior analysis as described by Baer et al. (1968) "emphasizes ecological and social validity in all respects." (p. 603)
Tier 4: Impact assessment	"[C]alculates the utility and cost-effectiveness of behavioral technology and specifies how it could be optimized for widespread use" (p. 605)

Tier 1 is use-inspired research. The research questions asked in Tier 1 may be similar to those asked in Tier 0, as the goal continues to be the acquisition of fundamental knowledge. However, the pursuit of knowledge in Tier 1 is guided by a need for that knowledge to solve a specific practical problem. Other than serving a clear translational function, Tier 1 research may look almost identical to Tier 0 research; for example, it is usually laboratory-based, and the subjects may or may not be human. In some cases, however, it includes features contributing to ecological validity, such as participants from relevant clinical populations (Kyonka & Subramaniam, 2018). The previous section on basic research described a basic (Tier 0) verbal behavior study (Oliveira et al., 2023) on convergent multiple control. Another laboratory study on the same topic by Jennings et al. (2023) may serve an example of Tier 1 activity. The participants were college students, and the stimuli were unfamiliar patterns and nonwords. However, the goal of the study was to follow up on previous applied research (DeSouza et al., 2019) on behavioral prerequisites for convergent control over intraverbal responding (e.g., when a statement like "A yellow fruit is a ..." evokes the response "banana" due to the combined influences of "yellow" and "fruit."). Jennings et al. sought to identify which other behavior involving the verbal stimulus elements ("yellow" and "fruit") might need to be established in a participant's repertoire in order for convergent control to be observed. This is a fundamental question about the operation of multiple control in verbal repertoires; however, it was also prompted by practical concerns: When teaching language to children with language delays, which skills need to be established before convergent multiple control can be expected?

Tier 2 is solution-oriented research conducted under controlled circumstances. This type of research focuses on potential solutions to practical problems and does not necessarily ask more fundamental questions about underlying processes. However, it is a step removed from applied research in that one or more aspects of ecological validity may be sacrificed for the purposes of increasing experimental control. For instance, the study might be conducted in a laboratory instead of a field setting, the stimuli or target behaviors might be low in social relevance, or the participants might not be drawn from a relevant population. To provide an example, Devine and Petursdottir (2022) asked if differential observing responses might facilitate teaching novel tacts that required difficult discriminations between visual stimuli. Specifically, before attempting to tact a complex visual stimulus, participants were required to match it to an identical stimulus (the differential observing response) in hopes of promoting attention to critical features that distinguished one stimulus from another. The study did not ask any fundamental questions of a conceptual nature; rather, its goal was to examine if there were practical benefits to incorporating differential observing responses into tact instruction. The participants in the study were preschoolers of typical development, which is a potentially relevant population insofar as children of typical development have a frequent need to acquire new tacts (e.g., in educational settings). However, the stimuli (e.g., made-up stick figures) and target vocal responses (nonsense syllables like "jid") were not of educational relevance to the participants, so the study might best fit the description of Tier 2. (For full disclosure, the study did not reveal a consistent effect of differential observing responses.)

Tier 3, according to Kyonka and Subramaniam (2018), is applied behavior analysis research similar to that described by Baer et al. (1968). It differs from Tier 2 in that it necessarily employs participants, settings, stimuli, and target behaviors of social relevance. At the same time, internal validity continues to be emphasized, for example, by employing rigorous experimental designs as also emphasized by Baer et al. Many studies in the verbal behavior literature are likely best described as Tier 3 studies, or in some cases, perhaps straddling the boundary between Tiers 2 and 3. To provide just one example of a Tier 3 study, Landa et al. (2017) evaluated a procedure for teaching children diagnosed with ASD to ask "when" questions, which were conceptualized as mands for time-related information. The participants had ASD diagnoses and received services in a program that focused on communication. The study was conducted in that setting, and the target behavior, which was successfully acquired by all participants, was of clear social relevance.

Tier 4, finally, consists of impact assessment as the applied endpoint of scientific translation. This category includes research activity aimed at evaluating potential larger-scale impacts and cost-effectiveness of behavioral interventions (Kyonka & Subramaniam, 2018). These goals can be accomplished, for example, through program-evaluation methodologies, by conducting multi-site clinical trials, or by conducting systematic reviews and meta-analyses to analyze data from multiple Tier 3 studies. Tier 4 research is perhaps scant in the verbal behavior literature, and examples exist primarily in the area of systematic reviews. For example, Tincani et al. (2020) systematically reviewed the literature on the use of speech-generating devices to teach communication skills. Their results suggested that a substantial evidence base exists for teaching children with neurodevelopmental disorders to use speech-generating devices to mand for preferred items placed within sight (i.e., responses potentially under partial mand and partial tact control). However, little research had demonstrated the establishment of other verbal operants or more complex verbal behavior.

Interactions between Tiers and Implications for Practitioners

It is hopefully clear from the examples provided in this and the previous section that the full spectrum of research activities that participate in the pathway of scientific translation is of relevance to the practice of behavior analysis. Some studies may be further removed from the "real world" than others, but ultimately our knowledge of effective practice depends on information that may be generated in each of the five tiers of research. Research that focuses on language learning under controlled circumstances may serve to evaluate the conceptual foundations of language interventions, as well as to provide insights into new ways of doing things. Such insights may then be tested under a range of circumstances, with some tests emphasizing internal validity and others emphasizing ecological validity. In turn, problems or successes encountered in applied settings may ultimately lead to more basic research on variables that influence verbal behavior, and so the cycle continues.

Basic and Translational Language Research in Behavior Analysis

The previous sections contained selected examples from the verbal behavior literature that served to illustrate the basic and translational functions of scientific research. However, a broader overview of the literature may be helpful to practitioners seeking to orient themselves to basic and translational findings of relevance to their work.

Historical Developments

Skinner's (1957) analysis of verbal behavior had little influence on empirical research in the first quarter century after its publication (McPherson et al., 1984). However, research that referenced Skinner or used Skinner's verbal operant terminology gradually began to increase in frequency (e.g., Dymond et al., 2006; Sautter & LeBlanc, 2006) with an exponential increase in the 21st century (Petursdottir & Devine, 2017). This increase was likely precipitated by growing interest in using Skinner's analysis to inform language interventions (Sundberg & Michael, 2001), along with other developments, such as the establishment of the journal *The Analysis of Verbal Behavior* in the 1980s. Although a large proportion of the research has been practically oriented (Dixon et al., 2007; Petursdottir, 2018), basic and translational functions have long been represented in this literature as well. For example, one of the very first studies clearly inspired by Skinner was a basic study on echoic control in the repertoires of human adults of typical development (Boe & Winokur, 1978). Studies that focused on fundamental questions about the variables influencing verbal behavior (i.e., Tier 0 and Tier 1 studies) accounted for 25% of all studies published between 2005 and 2016 that used concepts derived from Skinner's analysis (Petursdottir & Devine, 2017).

Independent of these developments, a body of research on stimulus equivalence (see Chapter 10 in this volume) and other derived stimulus relations came into existence in the late 20th century, inspired by the work of Murray Sidman and colleagues (e.g., Sidman, 1971; Sidman & Tailby, 1982). One reason this work generated so much interest is that it addressed the emergence, without direct reinforcement, of *symbolic* relations among stimuli, much like the relations between words and their non-verbal referents. As such, it seemed highly relevant to a behavioral analysis of language and its productive properties (Critchfield et al., 2018). Ultimately, research in this area led to the development of relational frame theory (Hayes et al., 2001), a behavior-analytic account of language and cognition that has been described as compatible with but going beyond Skinner (1957), and continues to be developed and refined (Barnes-Holmes & Harte, 2022). This theory extends the principles of stimulus equivalence to various derived relations among stimuli other than equivalence; for example, comparative relations (e.g., bigger than; smaller than), distinction (e.g., apples are different from oranges), and opposition (e.g., hot is the opposite of cold).

Relational frame theory and other theoretical perspectives on derived stimulus relations (e.g., Horne & Lowe, 1996; Sidman, 2000) have given rise to a wealth of basic and translational research. Basic studies examine variables that influence derived relations or test predictions of specific theories. Whereas translation of Skinner's (1957) analysis into application is most evident in the area of language intervention, translational research on derived stimulus relations has attended to a somewhat broader range of potential applications. Examples include, among others, instructional design in higher education (Brodsky & Fienup, 2018), treatment of anxiety (Dymond & Roche, 2009), and treatment of pathological gambling (Dymond & Roche, 2010).

Prominent Research Topics

Space does not permit a comprehensive overview of the entire literature, but a few prominent topics of verbal behavior research will be outlined briefly.

Derived Stimulus Control over Verbal Behavior

One way to establish verbal operants, such as tacts, mands, and intraverbals, is to reinforce a verbal response in the presence of the relevant antecedent stimulus (e.g., reinforce saying "car" in the presence of a car). However, antecedent stimuli may come to exert control over verbal responses in the absence of such a reinforcement history; that is, stimulus control consistent with a verbal operant may be derived from other experiences. How and under what circumstances this happens has been the topic of substantial investigation (Petursdottir, 2018). Researchers have investigated emergence of mands as a result of tact establishment or vice versa (e.g., Lamarre & Holland, 1985), emergence of intraverbal control as a result of tact instruction or vice versa (e.g., May et al., 2013), emergence of new intraverbal control as a result of reinforcing other intraverbals (e.g., Pérez-González et al., 2008), and various forms of derived control over verbal behavior based on other types of learning histories, such as establishment of listener relations (e.g., Lechago et al., 2015) or stimulus pairing (e.g., Petursdottir et al., 2020). Some of this work has been primarily theoretically motivated (i.e., Tier 0 or Tier 1 research). For example, Lamarre and Holland (1985) sought to demonstrate the functional independence of manding and tacting implied by Skinner's (1957) analysis, and Murphy and Barnes-Holmes (2010) sought to demonstrate derived manding based on the transformation of function, which is an important concept in relational frame theory. Other work has more directly focused on how derived stimulus control over verbal behavior might be promoted as a learning outcome, or asked under what circumstances that learning outcome is observed. For example, Smith et al. (2016) examined the effects of teaching relevant listener behavior on emergent intraverbals for children diagnosed with ASD, and Cortez et al. (2020) compared the effects of foreign-language tact and listener instruction on the emergence of foreign-language intraverbals in children of typical development.

Bidirectional Naming

Closely related to the research described in the previous section (and perhaps best thought of as a sub-area of that research), research on bidirectional naming (see Chapters 9 and 10 in this volume), focuses specifically on the emergence of bidirectional listener and speaker relations, such as responding to "car" by pointing to a car, and also tacting "car" upon seeing a car. The bidirectional naming literature contains two strands of research that ask somewhat different questions (Sivaraman & Barnes-Holmes, 2023). One strand of research has focused on variables that influence bidirectional naming, and interventions to establish it when absent. For example, a basic study (Sivaraman et al., 2021) examined if children of typical development under the age of two would demonstrate bidirectional naming following non-simultaneous stimulus pairing. As another example, a Tier 2 study (Hotchkiss & Fienup, 2020) evaluated different variations of intensive tact instruction as an intervention to induce bidirectional naming in special education students. The other strand of research has examined the role of bidirectional naming in stimulus equivalence, originally proposed by Horne and Lowe (1996). As an example, a basic study by Horne et al. (2004) demonstrated that after learning to select several different objects in response to the same verbal stimulus (a nonsense syllable, such as "vek"), young children were able to group those objects together only if tact control over relevant vocal responses (i.e., saying "vek"; upon seeing them) had also emerged. Other studies have extended similar demonstrations to other training scenarios (e.g., Jennings & Miguel, 2017; Petursdottir et al., 2015) and attended to translation of these findings into the design of generative teaching procedures for children diagnosed with ASD (e.g., Lee et al., 2015; Ribeiro & Miguel, 2020).

Problem-Solving and Mediating Functions of Verbal Behavior

A problem can be thought of as a situation in which no previously reinforced response is available that may directly serve to access reinforcement (Skinner, 1984). A problem may, however, evoke verbal and other behavior that serves to construct additional stimuli that, in turn, evoke effective behavior (see also Palmer, 2012). For most people, a question like "What is 39% of $12,541?" most likely does not immediately evoke the correct response ("$4,890.99"). Rather, the question evokes other behavior involving numbers (e.g., covert verbal behavior, paper-and-pencil calculation, or pulling up a calculator) that ultimately leads to the response "$4,890.99". At the basic level, research on verbal problem-solving focuses on demonstrating the effects of verbal behavior in problem situations, and at the translational level, it focuses on strengthening problem-solving repertoires (see Kieta et al., 2019, for a discussion of verbal problem-solving in educational settings). This area of research intersects with bidirectional naming, as it includes consideration of the involvement of verbal behavior in derived stimulus relations (Miguel, 2018). That is, a test for derived stimulus relations may be thought of as a problem-solving situation of sorts (Moustakis & Mellon, 2018), and accordingly, some of the basic research in this topic area has focused on the effects of verbal behavior on performance on such tests (e.g., Díaz et al., 2020; Moustakis & Mellon, 2018). However, other examples can be provided as well. Harman et al. (2021) conducted a study with college student participants who were instructed to solve math problems under several different conditions. One finding was that correct responding deteriorated when participants were instructed to recite the alphabet while solving the problems, suggesting this requirement interfered with covert verbal problem-solving. Sautter et al. (2011) demonstrated the effects of teaching a verbal problem-solving strategy on the intraverbal listing response of children with typical development, and Keesey-Phelan et al. (2022) taught a problem-solving strategy to a child diagnosed with ASD to increase recall of past events.

Rule-Governed Behavior

A rule can be defined as a verbal stimulus that states a reinforcement contingency (Skinner, 1984).[2] Rules permit verbal listeners to respond to reinforcement contingencies that they have never contacted in direct experience. For example, most drivers generally stop at a red light even if they have never experienced adverse consequences of running one, such as getting in an accident or being issued a ticket. Basic research on rule-governed behavior has examined the effects of instructions and self-generated rules on human responding on various schedules of reinforcement. Often, the focus is on the effects of inaccurate rules on sensitivity to actual reinforcement contingencies; that is, the tendency to follow a rule even when it inaccurately describes effective behavior on a particular schedule (e.g., Fox & Kyonka, 2017; Nergaard & Couto, 2021). This effect of rules on behavior has been hypothesized to be implicated in mental health problems, such as depression (e.g., Hayes & Gifford, 1997). That hypothesis, in turn, has led to translational research activity involving participants from relevant populations. For example, Hassoulas et al. (2017) compared the effects of rules on the schedule performance of individuals who scored high and low on a measure of obsessive-compulsive behavior, and McAuliffe et al. (2014) investigated the effects of different types of rules in a match-to-sample task with adolescents who displayed either higher or lower levels of depressive symptoms. A different strand of translational activity has focused on how to establish rule following in children diagnosed with ASD (e.g., Wymer et al., 2016). The literature on rule-governed behavior also has a link to the literature on derived stimulus relations (see Harte et al., 2020).

Other Topics and Future Directions

Previous sections of this chapter included examples of research on multiple control and autoclitic behavior and noted the relevance of research on these topics both to evaluating Skinner's (1957) behavioral analysis of language and to the design of teaching procedures. Both of these are emerging topics of current basic and translational research, although research on autoclitic behavior remains relatively rare. Certain types of autoclitic behavior, in Skinner's analysis, play an important role in explaining grammatical regularities in verbal behavior. A recent article by Palmer (2023) applies that analysis, along with the concept of *parity* (i.e., automatic reinforcement arising from the match between one's own verbal behavior and previously encountered verbal behavior of others), to a behavioral interpretation of grammar. Few empirical studies in the behavior-analytic literature have addressed grammar from this perspective. However, examples include a recent study on parity in children (Bergmann & Kodak, 2023) and a study on the use of multiple exemplar training to teach aspects of grammar (Speckman et al., 2012). Additional research on these topics could serve both to provide theoretically important information and practical insights into teaching grammatical behavior in language intervention or other relevant settings (e.g., second-language instruction).

Additional areas of research are also in need of strengthening. First, translational research on verbal behavior could be extended into more areas of potential application, including ones that involve typical adult verbal behavior (see e.g., Critchfield, 2010). Expertise arising from such research could ultimately expand employment opportunities for behavior analysts into new areas. Second, few behavior-analytic studies on language have been conducted with young children (e.g., 12–24 months) in their earliest stages of language acquisition. In one notable exception, an observational study of young toddlers and their caregivers (Cruvinel & Costa Hübner, 2013) found that caregivers were likely to arrange contingencies supporting acquisition of Skinner's (1957) verbal operants. This is potentially important information that may support the arrangement of similar contingencies in the context of language intervention. However, studies like these are few and far between, and more of them are needed to help evaluate behavior-analytic theories of language learning and justify their translation into practice.

Making Contact with the Basic and Translational Literature

How might practitioners go about making contact with the basic and translational literature on verbal behavior and derived stimulus relations? Practitioners may experience some general barriers when it comes to consuming scholarly literature in journal article form. These include a lack of time and contingencies to support the behavior of reading scholarly articles, and restricted access to academic journal content behind online paywalls. In a recent article, Briggs and Mitteer (2022) discuss these barriers and strategies for overcoming them. The authors provide suggestions for locating and accessing relevant journal content, and for integrating consumption of the scholarly literature into the culture of practice. The reader is referred to this resource for detailed information, but a few suggestions are worth reviewing.

In terms of access to journal articles, practitioners certified by the Behavior Analysis Certification Board (BACB) have complimentary access, through the BACB website certification gateway, to two major journals that often publish translational and basic work: the *Journal of Applied Behavior Analysis* and the *Journal of the Experimental Analysis of Behavior*. In addition, the full text of articles in journals published by the Association for Behavior Analysis International (e.g., *The Analysis of Verbal Behavior*, in which a number of studies cited in this chapter were published) becomes available without charge in the PubMed Central repository within 12 months of publication. Finally, as Briggs and Mitteer (2022) point out, researchers are usually happy to share their published work person-to-person, and some additionally post the full text of their recent articles on their personal websites or on social networking sites, such as ResearchGate (www.researchgate.net). In terms of time and contingencies, Briggs and Mitteer suggested, among other strategies, arranging a verbal community to support reading scholarly literature, for example, journal clubs.

When it comes to consuming research that is basic or translational in nature, many practitioners likely face an additional barrier. That is, many basic and translational research articles are not written with practitioners in mind as a target audience. They may employ concepts and terms with which practitioners with master's-level training may have had limited contact in their graduate courses, and describe unfamiliar experimental preparations. A reader's previous familiarity with an area of research may be assumed, and critical terms may be explained only cursorily (in part related to limits on the length of a typical journal article). The literature on verbal behavior and derived stimulus relations may be quite difficult in this regard. Not all graduate programs include an entire course on verbal behavior, but without such in-depth background, it may be next to impossible to decipher some of the research questions asked and the procedures used to answer them. Further, different terms are sometimes used to describe very similar phenomena, for example, depending on the theoretical perspective that guides the work. How can one acquire the background knowledge needed to learn more about research that initially may seem uninviting?

Ultimately, it is the responsibility of basic scientists to communicate their findings to broader audiences. With respect to dissemination to practitioners, such communication may often occur outside of the context of the empirical research articles themselves; for example, in conference talks and workshops, podcasts, in books or book chapters, or in review or discussion articles in applied journals. Practitioners attending professional conferences might seek out talks in which researchers provide an overview of a topic of basic or translational research, or tutorial-style presentations that aim to introduce a new audience to a particular topic. The annual convention of the Association for Behavior Analysis International, for example, regularly offers invited tutorials of relevance to verbal behavior, and pre-conference workshops sometimes offer training in conceptual foundations geared toward practitioner audiences. One annual conference is dedicated entirely to teaching verbal behavior; the *Verbal Behavior Conference* is held each year in Austin, Texas by the Central Texas Autism Center and can be attended virtually. This conference is largely practice-oriented, but also includes talks that are conceptual or introduce topics of basic research. Finally, practitioners who are involved in conference programming, for example, with their state or regional organizations, might consider making efforts to invite tutorial presentations or workshops on basic or translational research topics and ask that they be specifically designed to be accessible to a practitioner audience.

Table 12.2 lists selected online resources that may help familiarize readers with concepts and general problems studied in basic and translational research

Table 12.2 Resources Providing Background for Consuming Basic and Translational Research on Verbal Behavior

Topic	Author(s) and Title[a]	Format	Description	Access and Cost
Skinner's (1957) Verbal Behavior	Schlinger, H. (2022). VBC pre-workshop: An introduction to Skinner's Verbal Behavior.	Video	An eight-part course on Skinner's (1957) analysis of verbal behavior geared toward practitioners who did not have a course on this topic as part of their graduate training. Requires familiarity with basic behavioral principles, but no prior familiarity with verbal behavior is needed.	www.behaviorlive.com $70 for each part; CEUs available upon completion.
	Peterson, N. (2014). An introduction to verbal behavior.	Interactive web tutorial	An introductory tutorial that walks the student through major concepts presented in Skinner's (1957) Verbal Behavior. Requires familiarity with basic behavioral principles, but no prior familiarity with verbal behavior is needed.	www.foxylearning.com Open access version available, option to purchase access ($60) to earn CEUs for completion.
Multiple Control	Michael et al. (2011). The multiple control of verbal behavior.	Journal article	Reviews and explains the significance of the concept of multiple control in Skinner's (1957) analysis of verbal behavior. Requires prior familiarity with elementary verbal operants.	Full text available without charge in the PubMed Central archives. https://www.ncbi.nlm.nih.gov/pmc/; article ID PMC3139558 (type ID into search box to access).
	Palmer, D. C., and Sundberg, M. L. (2012). Multiple control.	Video	Covers similar ground as the article by Michael et al. (2011). Requires prior familiarity with elementary verbal operants.	https://legacy.wpsu.org/live/archive Open access provided by the National Autism Conference.

(Continued)

Table 12.2 (Continued)

Topic	Author(s) and Title[a]	Format	Description	Access and Cost
Stimulus Equivalence	Sidman, M. (2009). Equivalence relations and behavior: An introductory tutorial.	Journal article	Introduces principles of stimulus equivalence and explains experimental procedures used in the study of stimulus equivalence. It is helpful to have rudimentary familiarity with stimulus equivalence, but an in-depth background is not needed.	Full text available without charge in the PubMed Central archives. https://www.ncbi.nlm.nih.gov/pmc/; article ID PMC2779070 (type ID into search box to access).
	Pilgrim, C. (n.d.). An introduction to stimulus equivalence: What is it and why does it matter?	Video	Covers the basics of stimulus equivalence, findings from the stimulus equivalence literature, and its translation into equivalence-based instruction. Requires familiarity with basic behavioral principles, but no prior familiarity with stimulus equivalence is needed.	www.behaviorlive.com $10; CEUs available upon completion.
Relational Frame Theory	Fox, E. J. (n.d.). An introduction to relational frame theory.	Interactive web tutorial	An introductory tutorial that covers major concepts and philosophical foundations of relational frame theory. Requires familiarity with basic behavioral principles, but no prior familiarity with relational frame theory is needed.	www.foxylearning.com Open access version available, option to purchase access ($60) to earn CEUs for completion.

(Continued)

Table 12.2 (Continued)

Topic	Author(s) and Title[a]	Format	Description	Access and Cost
	Belisle, J. (n.d.). Relational frame theory and acceptance and commitment therapy.	Video	Provides an overview of relational frame theory and its translation into application. Requires familiarity with basic behavioral principles, but no prior familiarity with relational frame theory is needed.	www.behaviorlive.com $30; CEUs available upon completion.
Joint Control	Palmer, D. C. (2012). The role of joint control in behavior.	Video	Provides an overview of the concept of joint control (Lowenkron, 1998) and related basic and translational research. Requires familiarity with basic behavioral principles, and some prior familiarity with verbal behavior concepts is helpful.	https://legacy.wpsu.org/live/ archive Open access provided by the National Autism Conference.
Bidirectional Naming	Miguel, C. F. (2016). Common and intraverbal bidirectional naming.	Journal article	Summarizes major features of Horne and Lowe's (1996) conceptual analysis of naming along with joint control, describes relevant basic and translational research, and proposes terms to distinguish different types of naming. Requires prior familiarity with Skinner's (1957) analysis of verbal behavior and some familiarity with stimulus equivalence.	Full text available without charge in the PubMed Central archives. https://www.ncbi .nlm.nih.gov/pmc/; article ID PMC6381345 (type ID into search box to access).

(Continued)

Table 12.2 (Continued)

Topic	Author(s) and Title[a]	Format	Description	Access and Cost
Emergent Verbal Relations and Bidirectional Naming	Frampton, S. (2022). Learning by listening.	Video	Covers the concepts of bidirectional naming and its implications for practice. The presentation is practitioner-oriented but does require prior familiarity with Skinner's (1957) verbal operants.	https://autism.outreach.psu.edu/archive/ Open access provided by the National Autism Conference.
Problem-Solving and Bidirectional Naming	Miguel, C. F. (2019). Bidirectional naming and problem-solving	Video	Introduces the concept of bidirectional naming and its relevance to problem-solving in the form of matching-to-sample and categorization tasks, describes findings from basic and translational research, and implications for language intervention. Requires prior familiarity with Skinner's (1957) analysis of verbal behavior and some familiarity with stimulus equivalence.	https://uwf.behavior.org/courses/caio-f-miguel-bidirectional-naming-and-problem-solving/ $12; CEUs available upon completion.
Rule-Governed Behavior	Zapparoli et al. (2021). Rule-governed behavior: An ongoing RFT-based operant analysis.	Journal article	Provides an analysis of rule-governed behavior from a relational frame theory perspective and describes relevant basic research. Prior familiarity with stimulus equivalence and major concepts in relational frame theory is helpful.	https://www.revistaperspectivas.org/perspectivas/article/view/722/349 Open access

[a]Full references with direct URLs are provided in the chapter reference list and marked with an asterisk.

on verbal behavior and derived stimulus relations. Information is also provided on how to access each resource at the time this chapter is written, and on any background knowledge that may be needed to benefit from it. The resources do not necessarily include an extensive presentation of research findings (although some of them do include such content). However, they introduce and explain concepts that, in turn, may help consume other more data-based conference presentations and journal articles on basic and translational topics. In addition, of course, a number of chapters in the present volume also provide important background information.

In closing, the basic and translational literature on verbal behavior and derived stimulus relations is multifaceted and complex, and mastering it in its entirety may be an unachievable task (the present author, who has consumed vast amounts of this literature each year for over 20 years, is far from knowing all of it!). A practitioner whose primary responsibility is to deliver services to clients should not expect to become an expert on it overnight. However, familiarity with the foundations and key findings of this literature may help achieve a deeper understanding of problems that present themselves in practice.

Notes

1 According to Baer et al. (1968), research in applied behavior analysis is applied, behavioral, analytic, conceptually systematic, technological, effective, and has generality. Because the focus of the present chapter is on basic and translational research, these dimensions will not be discussed here, but the reader can consult the original article (Baer et al., 1968) or Chapter 1 in Cooper et al. (2019) for additional information. See also Critchfield and Reed (2017) for a critical evaluation of the appropriateness of these criteria for evaluating contemporary applied research in behavior analysis.

2 However, the behavior-analytic definition of a rule has been a matter of debate in the literature (see e.g., Harte et al., 2020; Schlinger, 1993).

References

*Resources listed in Table 12.2 (www.routledge.com/9781032560625)

Austin, C. P. (2018). Translating translation. *Nature Reviews Drug Discovery, 17*, 455–456. https://doi.org/10.1038/nrd.2018.27

Baer, D. M., Wolf, M. M., & Risley, T. R. (1968). Some current dimensions of applied behavior analysis. *Journal of Applied Behavior Analysis, 1*(1), 91–97. https://doi.org/10.1901/jaba.1968.1-91

Barnes-Holmes, D., & Harte, C. (2022). Relational frame theory 20 years on: The Odysseus voyage and beyond. *Journal of the Experimental Analysis of Behavior, 117*(2), 240–266. https://doi.org/10.1002/jeab.733

Behavior Analysis Certification Board. (2020). *Ethics code for behavior analysts.* https://www.bacb.com/wp-content/uploads/2022/01/Ethics-Code-for-Behavior-Analysts

Belisle, J. (n.d.). *Relational frame theory and acceptance and commitment therapy* [video]. Behavior Live. https://behaviorlive.com/courses/relational-frame-theory-and -acceptance-and-commitment-therapy

Bergmann, S., & Kodak, T. (2023). The tact is being emitted by the child: Replicating and extending parity research with English-speaking, typically developing children. *The Analysis of Verbal Behavior*. https://doi.org/10.1007/s40616-023-00188-x.

Boe, R., & Winokur, S. (1978). A procedure for studying echoic control in verbal behavior. *Journal of the Experimental Analysis of Behavior, 30*(2), 213–217. https://doi.org/10.1901/jeab.1978.30-213

Briggs, A., & Mitteer, D. R. (2022). Updated strategies for making regular contact with the scholarly literature. *Behavior Analysis in Practice, 15*(2), 541–552. https://doi.org/10.1007/s40617-021-00590-8

Brodsky, J., & Fienup, D. M. (2018). Sidman goes to college: A meta-analysis of equivalence-based instruction in higher education. *Perspectives on Behavior Science, 41*(1), 95–119. https://doi.org/10.1007/s40614-018-0150-0

Cooper, J. O., Heron, T. E., & Heward, W. L. (2019). *Applied behavior analysis* (3rd ed.). Pearson.

Cortez, M. D., dos Santos, L., Quintal, A. E., Silveira, M. L., & de Rose, J. C. (2020). Learning a foreign language: Effects of tact and listener instruction on the emergence of bidirectional intraverbals. *Journal of Applied Behavior Analysis, 53*(1), 484–492. https://doi.org/10.1002/jaba.559

Critchfield, T. S. (2010). Crucial issues in the applied analysis of verbal behavior: Reflections on *crucial conversations: Tools for talking when the stakes are high. The Analysis of Verbal Behavior, 26*(1), 133–145. https://doi.org/10.1007/BF03393087

Critchfield, T. S., Barnes-Holmes, D., & Dougher, M. J. (2018). Editorial: What Sidman did. Historical and contemporary significance of research on derived stimulus relations. *Perspectives on Behavior Science, 41*, 9–32. https://doi.org/10.1007/s40614 -018-0154-9

Critchfield, T. S., & Reed, D. D. (2017). The fuzzy concept of applied behavior analysis research. *The Behavior Analyst, 40*(1), 123–159. https://doi.org/10.1007/s40614-017 -0093-x

Cruvinel, A. C., & Hübner, M. M. (2013). Analysis of the acquisition of verbal operants in a child from 17 months to 2 years of age. *The Psychological Record, 63*, 735–750. https://doi.org/10.11133/j.tpr.2013.63.4.003

DeSouza, A. A., Fisher, W. W., & Rodriguez, N. M. (2019). Facilitating the emergence of convergent intraverbals in children with autism. *Journal of Applied Behavior Analysis, 52*(1), 28–49. https://doi.org/10.1002/jaba.520

Devine, B., & Petursdottir, A. I. (2022). Exploring effects of differential observing responses on vocal tact acquisition. *Behavioral Interventions, 37*, 29–42. https://doi.org/10.1002/bin.1782.

Diaz, J. E., Luoma, S. M., & Miguel. C. F. (2020). The role of verbal behavior in the establishment of comparative relations. *Journal of the Experimental Analysis of Behavior, 113*(2), 322–339. https://doi.org/10.1002/jeab.582

Dixon, M. R. (2014). *The PEAK relational training system*. Shawnee Scientific Press.

Dixon, M. R., Small, S. S., & Rosales, R. (2007). Extended analysis of empirical citations with Skinner's *Verbal Behavior*: 1984–2004. *The Behavior Analyst, 30*, 197–209.

Dymond, S., O'Hora, D., Whelan, R., & Donovan, A. (2006). Citation analysis of Skinner's Verbal Behavior: 1984–2004. *The Behavior Analyst, 29*(1), 75–88. https://doi.org/10.1007/BF03392118

Dymond, S., & Roche, B. (2009). A contemporary behavior analysis of anxiety and avoidance. *The Behavior Analyst, 32*(1), 7–27. https://doi.org/10.1007/BF03392173

Dymond, S., & Roche, B. (2010). The impact of derived relational responding on gambling behavior. *Analysis of Gambling Behavior, 4*(1), 38–53.

Epstein, R., Lanza, R. P., & Skinner, B. F. (1980). Symbolic communication between two pigeons. *Science, 207*, 543–545. https://doi.org/10.1126/science.207.4430.543

Fox, A. E., & Kyonka, E. G. E. (2017). Searching for the variables that control human rule-governed "insensitivity". *Journal of the Experimental Analysis of Behavior, 108*(2), 236–254. https://doi.org/10.1002/jeab.270

Fox, E. J. (n.d.). *An introduction to relational frame theory* [online tutorial]. Foxylearning. https://foxylearning.com/oer/an-introduction-to-relational-frame-theory/

Frampton, S. (2022). *Learning by listening* [video]. Penn State Outreach. https://autism.outreach.psu.edu/archive/conference-archive-2022/

Halber, D. (2021). Triumph of mRNA vaccines rests on decades of basic research at MIT. *Betterworld.mit.edu.* Retrieved November 28, 2023, from https://betterworld.mit.edu/triumph-of-mrna-vaccines-rests-on-decades-of-basic-research-at-mit/

Harman, M. J., Kodak, T., Bohl, L., & Mayland, T. (2021). The effects of competing verbal behavior on performance in a math task. *The Analysis of Verbal Behavior, 37*(1), 57–76. https://doi.org/10.1007/s40616-021-00145-6

Harte, C., Barnes-Holmes, D., Barnes-Holmes, Y., & Kissi, A. (2020). The study of rule-governed behavior and derived stimulus relations: Bridging the gap. *Perspectives on Behavior Science, 43*(2), 361–385. https://doi.org/10.1007/s40614-020-00256-w

Hassoulas, A., McHugh, L., Morris, H., Dickenson, E. R., & Reed, P. (2017). Rule-following and instructional control in obsessive-compulsive behavior. *European Journal of Behavior Analysis, 18*(2), 276–290. https://doi.org/10.1080/15021149.2017.1388608

Hayes, S. C., Blackledge, J. T., & Barnes-Holmes, D. (Eds.). (2001). *Relational frame theory: A post-Skinnerian account of human language and cognition*. Plenum.

Hayes, S. C., & Gifford, E. V. (1997). The trouble with language: Experiential avoidance, rules, and the nature of verbal events. *Psychological Science, 8*(3), 170–173. https://doi.org/10.1111/j.1467-9280.1997.tb00405.x

Horne, P. J., & Lowe, C. F. (1996). On the origins of naming and other symbolic behavior. *Journal of the Experimental Analysis of Behavior, 65*(1), 185–241. https://doi.org/10.1901/jeab.1996.65-185

Horne, P. J., Lowe, C. F., & Randle, V. R. L. (2004). Naming and categorization in young children: II. Listener behavior training. *Journal of the Experimental Analysis of Behavior, 81*(3), 267–288. https://doi.org/10.1901/jeab.2004.81-267

Hotchkiss, R. M., & Fienup, D. M. (2020). A parametric analysis of a protocol to induce bidirectional naming: Effects of protocol intensity. *The Psychological Record, 70*(3), 481–497. https://doi.org/10.1007/s40732-020-00383-5

Jennings, A. M., & Miguel, C. F. (2017). Training intraverbal bidirectional naming to establish generalized equivalence class performances. *Journal of the Experimental Analysis of Behavior, 108*(2), 269–289. https://doi.org/10.1002/jeab.277

Jennings, A. M., Vladescu, J. C., Miguel, C. F., Reeve, K. F., & Sidener, T. M. (2023). A translational evaluation of component skills for the establishment of multiply controlled intraverbals. *Journal of the Experimental Analysis of Behavior, 119*(3), 427–566. https://doi.org/10.1002/jeab.837

Keesey-Phelan, S. H., Axe, J. B., & Williams, A. L. (2022). The effects of teaching a problem-solving strategy on recalling past events with a child with autism. *The Analysis of Verbal Behavior, 38*(2), 190–198. https://doi.org/10.1007/s40616-022-00176-7

Kieta, A. R., Cihon, T. M., & Abdel-Jalil, A. (2019). Problem solving from a behavioral perspective: Implications for behavior analysts and educators. *Journal of Behavioral Education, 28*(2), 275–300. https://doi.org/10.1007/s10864-018-9296-9

Kuroda, T., Lattal, K. A., & García-Penagos, A. (2014). An analysis of an autoclitic analogue in pigeons. *The Analysis of Verbal Behavior, 30*, 89–99. https://doi.org/10.1007/s40616-014-0019-6

Kyonka, E. G. E., & Subramaniam, S. (2018). Translating behavior analysis: A spectrum rather than a road map. *Perspectives on Behavior Science, 41*(2), 591–613. https://doi.org/10.1007/s40614-018-0145-x

Lamarre, J., & Holland, J. G. (1985). The functional independence of mands and tacts. *Journal of the Experimental Analysis of Behavior, 43*(1), 5–19. https://doi.org/10.1901/jeab.1985.43

Landa, R. K., Hansen, B., & Shillingsburg, M. A. (2017). Teaching mands for information using 'when' to children with autism. *Journal of Applied Behavior Analysis, 50*(3), 538–551. https://doi.org/10.1002/jaba.387

Lechago, S. A., Carr, J. E., Kisamore, A. N., & Grow, L. L. (2015). The effects of multiple exemplar instruction on the relation between listener and intraverbal categorization repertoires. *Analysis of Verbal Behavior, 31*(1), 76–95. https://doi.org/10.1007/s40616-015-0027-1

Lee, G. P., Miguel, C. F., Darcey, E. K, & Jennings, A. M. (2015). A further evaluation of the effects of listener training on the emergence of speaker behavior and categorization in children with autism. *Research in Autism Spectrum Disorders, 19*, 72–81.

Lowenkron, B. (1998). Some logical functions of joint control. *Journal of the Experimental Analysis of Behavior, 69*(3), 327–354. https://doi.org/10.1901/jeab.1998.69-327

May, R. J., Hawkins, E., & Dymond, S. (2013). Brief report: Effects of tact training on emergent intraverbal vocal responses in adolescents with autism. *Journal of Autism and Developmental Disorders, 43*(4), 996–1004. https://doi.org/10.1007/s10803-012-1632-7

McAuliffe, D., Hughes, S., & Barnes-Holmes, D. (2014). The dark-side of rule governed behavior: An experimental analysis of problematic rule-following in an adolescent population with depressive symptomatology. *Behavior Modification, 38*(4), 587–613. https://doi.org/10.1177/0145445514521630

McPherson, A., Bonem, M., Green, G., Osborne, J. G. (1984). A citation analysis of the influence on research of Skinner's *Verbal Behavior. The Behavior Analyst, 7*, 157–167. https://doi.org/10.1007/BF03391898

Michael, J., Palmer, D. C., & Sundberg, M. L. (2011). The multiple control of verbal behavior. *The Analysis of Verbal Behavior, 27*, 3–22. https://doi.org/10.1007/BF03393089

Miguel, C. F. (2016). Common and intraverbal bidirectional naming. *The Analysis of Verbal Behavior*, *32*(2), 125–138. https://doi.org/10.1007/s40616-016-0066-2

Miguel, C. F. (2018). Problem-solving, bidirectional naming, and the development of verbal repertoires. *Behavior Analysis: Research and Practice*, *18*(4), 340–353. https://doi.org/10.1037/bar0000110

Miguel, C. F. (2019). *Bidirectional naming and problem solving* [video]. Center for Behavior Analysis, University of West Florida. https://uwf.behavior.org/courses/caio-f-miguel-bidirectional-naming-and-problem-solving/

Moore, J. P., & Wilson, I. A. (2021). Decades of basic research paved the way for today's 'warp speed' Covid-19 vaccines. *Stat+*. Retrieved November 28, 2023, from https://www.statnews.com/2021/01/05/basic-research-paved-way-for-warp-speed-covid-19-vaccines/

Moustakis, I. S., & Mellon, R. C. (2018). Transitivity as Skinnerian problem solving controlled by self-constructed relational stimuli. *Journal of the Experimental Analysis of Behavior*, *110*(3), 451–473. https://doi.org/10.1002/jeab.473

Murphy, C., & Barnes-Holmes, D. (2010). Establishing complex derived manding with children with and without a diagnosis of autism. *The Psychological Record*, *60*(3), 489–504.

Nergaard, S. K., & Couto, K. C. (2021). Effects of reinforcement and response-cost history on instructional control. *Journal of the Experimental Analysis of Behavior*, *115*(3), 679–701. https://doi.org/10.1002/jeab.680

OECD. (2015). *Frascati manual 2015: Guidelines for collecting and reporting data on research and experimental development*. OECD Publishing. https://doi.org/10.1787/9789264239012-en.

Oliveira, J. S. C. D., Cox, R. E., & Petursdottir, A. I. (2023). Summation in convergent control over selection-based verbal behavior. *The Analysis of Verbal Behavior*. https://doi.org/10.1007/s40616-023-00194-z

Palmer, D. C. (2012a). The role of atomic repertoires in complex behavior. *The Behavior Analyst*, *35*(1), 59–73. https://doi.org/10.1007/BF03392266

Palmer, D. C. (2012b). *The role of joint control in behavior* [video]. WPSU Penn State. https://legacy.wpsu.org/live/2012_player/59034

Palmer, D. C. (2023). Toward a behavioral interpretation of English grammar. *Perspectives on Behavior Science*. https://doi.org/10.1007/s40614-023-00368-z

Palmer, D. C., & Sundberg, M. L. (2012). *Multiple control* [video]. WPSU Penn State. https://legacy.wpsu.org/live/2012_player/49231

Pérez-González, L. A., Herszlikowicz, K., & Williams, G. (2008). Stimulus relations analysis and the emergence of novel intraverbals. *The Psychological Record*, *58*, 95–129. https://doi.org/10.1007/BF03395605

Peterson, N. (2014). *An introduction to verbal behavior* [online tutorial]. Foxylearning. https://foxylearning.com/oer/an-introduction-to-verbal-behavior/

Petursdottir, A. I. (2018). The current status of the experimental analysis of verbal behavior. *Behavior Analysis: Research and Practice*, *18*, 151–168. https://doi.org/10.1037/bar0000109

Petursdottir, A. I., Carp, C. L., Peterson, S. P., & Lepper, T. L. (2015). Emergence of visual-visual conditional discriminations following intraverbal training. *Journal of the Experimental Analysis of Behavior*, *103*, 332–348. https://doi.org/10.1002/jeab.136

Petursdottir, A. I., & Devine, B. (2017). The impact of *Verbal Behavior* on the scholarly literature from 2005 to 2016. *The Analysis of Verbal Behavior, 33*, 212–228. https://doi.org/10.1007/s40616-017-0089-3

Petursdottir, A. I., Neaves, S., & Thomas, O. (2020). Emergent tact control following stimulus pairing: Comparison of procedural variations. *The Analysis of Verbal Behavior, 36*(2), 193–214. https://doi.org/10.1007/s40616-020-00132-3

Pilgrim, C. (n.d.). *An introduction to stimulus equivalence: What is it and why does it matter?* [video]. Behavior Live. https://behaviorlive.com/courses/course-an-introduction-to-stimulus-equivalence-what-is-it-and-why-does-it-matte

Ratkos, T., McFayden, A., & Small, A. (2023). Stimulus clarity and the emission of descriptive autoclitics. *The Analysis of Verbal Behavior, 39*, 76–85. https://doi.org/10.1007/s40616-023-00184-1

Ribeiro, D. M., & Miguel, C. F. (2020). Using multiple-tact training to produce emergent visual categorization in children with autism. *Journal of Applied Behavior Analysis, 53*(3), 1768–1779. https://doi.org/10.1002/jaba.687

Rubio, D. M., Schoenbaum, E., Lee, L., Schteingart, D. E., Marantz, P., Anderson, K., Platt, L. D., Baez, A., & Esposito, K. (2010). Defining translational research: Implications for training. *Academic Medicine, 85*(3), 470–475. https://doi.org/10.1097/ACM.0b013e3181ccd618

Sautter, R. A., & LeBlanc, L. A. (2006). Empirical applications of Skinner's analysis of verbal behavior with humans. *The Analysis of Verbal Behavior, 22*, 35–48. https://doi.org/10.1007/BF03393025

Sautter, R. A., LeBlanc, L. A., Jay, A. A., Goldsmith, T. R., & Carr, J. E. (2011). The role of problem solving in complex intraverbal repertoires. *Journal of Applied Behavior Analysis, 44*(2), 227–244. https://doi.org/10.1901/jaba.2011.44-227

Schlinger, H. D. (1993). Separating discriminative and function-altering effects of verbal stimuli. *The Behavior Analyst, 16*(1), 9–23. https://doi.org/10.1007/BF03392605

Schlinger, H. (2022). *2022 VBC pre-workshop: An introduction to Skinner's Verbal Behavior* [video]. Behavior Live. https://behaviorlive.com/courses/vbc-pre-workshop-an-introduction-to-skinners-verbal-behavior

Sidman, M. (1971). Reading and auditory-visual equivalences. *Journal of Speech & Hearing Research, 14*(1), 5–13. https://doi.org/10.1044/jshr.1401.05

Sidman, M. (2000). Equivalence relations and the reinforcement contingency. *Journal of the Experimental Analysis of Behavior, 74*(1), 127–146. https://doi.org/10.1901/jeab.2000.74-127

Sidman, M. (2009). Equivalence relations and behavior: An introductory tutorial. *The Analysis of Verbal Behavior, 25*(1), 5–17. https://doi.org/10.1007/BF03393066

Sidman, M., & Tailby, W. (1982). Conditional discrimination vs. matching to sample: An expansion of the testing paradigm. *Journal of the Experimental Analysis of Behavior, 37*, 23–44. https://doi.org/10.1901/jeab.1982.37-5

Sivaraman, M., & Barnes-Holmes, D. (2023). Naming: What do we know so far? A systematic review. *Perspectives on Behavior Science.* https://doi.org/10.1007/s40614-023-00374-1

Sivaraman, M., Barnes-Holmes, D., & Royers, H. (2021). Nonsimultaneous stimulus presentations and their role in listener naming. *Journal of the Experimental Analysis of Behavior, 116*(3), 300–313. https://doi.org/10.1002/jeab.715

Skinner, B. F. (1957). *Verbal behavior*. Copley.

Skinner, B. F. (1984). An operant analysis of problem solving. *Behavioral and Brain Sciences, 7*(4), 583–613. https://doi.org/10.1017/S0140525X00027412

Smith, D. P., Eikeseth, S., Fletcher, S. E., Montebelli, L., Smith, H. R., & Taylor, J. C. (2016). Emergent intraverbal forms may occur as a result of listener training for children with autism. *The Analysis of Verbal Behavior, 32*(1), 27–37. https://doi.org/10.1007/s40616-016-0057-3

Speckman, J., Greer, R. D., & Rivera-Valdes, C. (2012). Multiple exemplar instruction and the emergence of generative production of suffixes as autoclitic frames. *The Analysis of Verbal Behavior, 28*, 83–99. https://doi.org/10.1007/BF03393109

Sundberg, M. L. (2008). *The verbal behavior milestones assessment and placement program: The VB-MAPP*. AVB Press.

Sundberg, M. L., & Michael, J. (2001). The benefits of Skinner's analysis of verbal behavior for children with autism. *Behavior Modification, 25*, 698–724. https://doi.org/10.1177/0145445501255003

Tincani, M., Miller, J., Lorah, E. R., & Nepo, K. (2020). Systematic review of verbal operants in speech generating device research from Skinner's analysis of verbal behavior. *Perspectives on Behavior Science, 43*(2), 387–413. https://doi.org/10.1007/s40614-020-00243-1

Wasserman, E. A., Brooks, D. I., & McMurray, B. (2015). Pigeons acquire multiple categories in parallel via associative learning: A parallel to human word learning? *Cognition, 136*, 99–122. https://doi.org/10.1016/j.cognition.2014.11.020

Wymer, S. C., Tarbox, J., Beavers, G. A., & Tullis, C. A. (2016). Teaching children with autism to follow rules specifying a behavior and a consequence. *The Analysis of Verbal Behavior, 32*(2), 265–274. https://doi.org/10.1007/s40616-016-0059-1

Zapparoli, H. B., Marin, R., & Harte, C. (2021). Rule-governed behavior: An ongoing RFT-based operant analysis. *Perspectivas em análise do comportamento, 12*(1), 197–213. https://doi.org/10.18761/PAC.2021.v12.RFT.09

Chapter 13

The Relevance of Culture and Diversity on Language Learning

Rocío Rosales, Samantha S. De Vasconcelos, and Gloria Leyla Fanning

The Relevance of Culture and Diversity on Language Learning

Families of all backgrounds are impacted by the increasing prevalence of autism spectrum disorder (ASD; Maenner et al., 2023; Shaw et al., 2023). Parallel to the increase in the prevalence of ASD, the racial, ethnic, and linguistic diversity of the U.S. population is projected to more than double in the next several decades (Vespa, 2021). According to recent estimates, between 350 and 430 different languages are spoken in homes in the United States, indicating that over 20% of children are being raised in a home where a language other than, or in addition to, English is spoken. In 2019, it was reported that 22% of individuals over the age of five spoke a language other than English at home, representing a 194% increase from 1980 (Dietrich & Hernandez, 2022).

A variety of terms are used to describe bilingual and multilingual learners. Bilingualism is broadly defined as the use of two or more languages (ASHA, 2017). If an individual is exposed to and acquires two languages starting in infancy, this is called *simultaneous* bilingualism; if learners are exposed to and learn a second language after their third birthday, this is called *sequential* bilingualism (Kangas, 2019). The second language may be English or any new language used outside the home environment.

There is also an essential distinction between *elective* and *circumstantial* bilinguals, or those individuals who learn a second language because they perceive a benefit in doing so, compared to individuals who immigrate to a country where their home language is not the majority and are therefore in a situation where learning a second language is a necessity (Rhodes et al., 2005). Circumstantial bilingual learners are also more likely to be called English Learners.

In the fields of education and special education, the terms *English Learner* (EL), *English Language Learner* (ELL), and *Limited English Proficient* (LEP) are used interchangeably (U.S. Department of Education, 2020), while the term *emergent bilingual* was introduced by Garcia (2009) to move away from a deficit model often used to describe learners acquiring a second language. More

DOI: 10.4324/9781003433668-16

recently, the term *culturally and linguistically diverse* (CLD) learner has been used to describe an individual exposed to a language other than English at home (Counts et al., 2018). English learner is the official term used by the U.S. Department of Education, but we will use the terms EL and CLD interchangeably in the remainder of the chapter.

The term EL describes an individual who meets four criteria: (a) aged 3–21 years old; (b) enrolled or preparing to enroll in elementary or secondary school; (c) was either not born in the United States or their native language is not English; is Native American or Alaska Native or resident of the outlying areas; comes from an environment where a language other than English had a significant impact on their English proficiency; or is migratory, native language is not English, and comes from an environment where a language other than English is dominant; and (d) has difficulty speaking, reading, writing, or understanding English enough to fail levels of achievement on State assessments, or succeed in a classroom where the language of instruction is English, or participate fully in society (Uro & Lai, 2019).

In the latest report prepared by the Council of the Great City Schools, it is estimated that five million ELs attend preschool, primary, or secondary school in the United States, and between 12%–14% of this population also receive special education services (Uro & Lai, 2019). There are also recent estimates reporting that approximately one in four children with ASD are being raised in a bilingual environment (Trelles & Castro, 2019). Thus, special educators and applied behavior analysts will likely encounter CLD learners on their caseload and need to decide the language of instruction for assessment and instruction. This highlights the importance of designing culturally and linguistically responsive interventions to support diverse learners and their families.

Language Difference or Disability?

One of the challenges faced by special educators and related personnel (e.g., behavior analysts) is that the behavior of ELs and learners with ASD and related disabilities may be difficult to discriminate. Reports of both overrepresentation and underrepresentation of CLD learners with disabilities (Zacarian, 2011) indicate that this population is sometimes *misdiagnosed* and other times *overlooked* when a disability is present. Practitioners must first identify how characteristics associated with developmental and learning disabilities may manifest in CLD learners. For example, learners may present with difficulties in both vocal (e.g., some language loss, difficulty following one or multiple-step instructions, understanding figurative language) and non-vocal communication (e.g., lack of joint attention). Learners may also display elevated levels of challenging behavior and isolation from peers. These difficulties may be related to acquiring a second language *or* be characteristics of ASD or a related disability. Thus, when such behaviors are observed during an assessment, the practitioner must consider that the function of these behaviors may be tied to second-language acquisition and not always a manifestation of a disability (or vice versa). Table 13.1 gives other examples of behaviors that may help differentiate between ELs and learners with disabilities.

Suppose a recipient of applied behavior analysis (ABA) services is identified as an EL or CLD. In that case, practitioners should consider the learner's history with English and the home language and their potential preference for a language of instruction. Additionally, the role that the language of instruction may have on challenging behavior(s) and skill acquisition, including listener (e.g., accurate responses to one-step instructions) and speaker responses (e.g., mands emitted with listeners in their verbal communities), must be considered. In the remainder of this chapter, we will: (a) provide a rationale for cultural and linguistic adaptations when working with ELs in the context of behavior analytic services; (b) review research in behavior analysis related to the impact of language of instruction on behaviors that interfere with learning, skill acquisition, and learner preference; and (c) provide recommendations for future research and practice when working with this population.

Rationale for Cultural and Linguistic Adaptations

A culturally responsive assessment and intervention will require more than a translation of a document or the presence of a trained interpreter. Bernal et al.

Table 13.1 Shared Characteristics between ELs and Learners with Disabilities

Behavior	English Learner	Learners with Disabilities
Language delay	Slow response due to processing English; often improves with exposure.	Consistent language delays across all languages, including the native language.
Attention	May appear distracted or off-task due to a lack of comprehension.	May be diagnosed with ADHD due to consistent attention difficulties regardless of the language.
Social interactions	Hesitant to engage in English but engages in native language; is susceptible to cultural misunderstandings.	Difficulty interpreting social cues, forming relationships, or reading emotions across all settings and languages.
Academic performance	They may struggle across academic subjects but improve with language support.	Inconsistent progress, with struggles in specific areas (e.g., reading comprehension, math reasoning).

Note: Adapted from Harris (2019).

(2009) defined a cultural adaptation as "the systematic modification of an evidence-based treatment or intervention protocol to consider language, culture, and context in such a way that it is compatible with the client's cultural patterns, meanings, and values" (p. 362). This definition helps distinguish between *superficial* adaptations (i.e., translations and interpretation) and adaptations that take into consideration the selection of goals, the profile of the individuals delivering the intervention, examples or materials used in the context of an intervention, among other variables (Barrera et al., 2013).

To gain a complete picture of a CLD learner's current repertoire, assessing language and related skills in both English and the learner's first language is critical. The Behavior Analyst Certification Board's (2020) *Ethics Code for Behavior Analysts* includes standards that can guide practitioners working with this population. For example, Standard 1.07: *Cultural Responsiveness and Diversity* encourages behavior analysts to seek out professional development related to cultural responsiveness and diversity and evaluation of biases; Standard 2.13: *Selecting, Designing, and Implementing Assessments* indicates the need for behavior analysts to select interventions and assessments that best meet the needs of diverse learners that are also consistent with behavioral principles and based on scientific evidence; and Standard 3.01: *Responsibility to Clients* highlights the need to act in the best interest of each learner. In education and special education, explicit legal mandates hold educators accountable for conducting assessments in multiple languages when working with ELs (U.S. Congress, 2003). Moreover, research in other related fields (e.g., speech-language pathology and early intervention) has shown that culturally and linguistically responsive language assessment and intervention improve learner outcomes (Dunst et al., 2016; Durán et al., 2016), procedural integrity (Durán et al., 2016), and overall family engagement and satisfaction (Larson et al., 2020).

Assessment practices from related disciplines can help to inform what behavior analysis practitioners do to evaluate the performance of learners with ASD and related disabilities who are also CLD. For example, a comprehensive guide developed by Rhodes et al. (2005) highlighted various methods school psychologists use to gather information about a student's language acquisition. An interview with parents and other caregivers is a first and critical step that includes considerations for preparing for the interview (e.g., Is an interpreter needed? Will the parent feel most comfortable if the interview is conducted in person? Which questions are most relevant to ask?). Suggested questions for the interview include those related to language exposure with adults and other children and educational history (see Table 13.2 for sample questions).

This form of indirect assessment should be followed by direct observation of the learner in their natural environment. A variety of behavioral language assessments that are commonly used will be described next.

Table 13.2 Sample Questions for Parent Interview

1. What language(s) do you use at home?
2. What language(s) is usually spoken at home?
3. At what age was your child first exposed to English?
4. What language(s) did your child first speak?
5. What language(s) do you speak to your child?
6. What language(s) does your child speak to you?
7. What language are you *most comfortable* using when communicating with your child?
8. What language(s) is heard on the radio and television at home?
9. What language(s) does your child use with other family members (e.g., grandparents, aunts, uncles, cousins)?
10. What language(s) do the adults in the family speak to each other?
11. What language(s) does your child use with friends?
12. Does your child participate in any community group experiences? If so, in which languages?
13. Has your child ever received English as a Second Language services? If yes, for how long have they been receiving these services?
14. Did your child attend a daycare or preschool? If yes, what language did the daycare or preschool use?
15. Does your child perform better when academics are presented in *English or* the home language?

Note: Adapted from Fahim (2014) and Peña et al. (2014).

Behavioral Language Assessments

When a learner is referred for ABA services, the intake process will include indirect assessments like an interview with caregivers and other assessments that help evaluate the skills in a learner's current repertoire. These assessments require direct observation or testing scenarios with the learner. Some assessments focus heavily on developmental skills, while others place a more significant emphasis on functional living skills. Although the specific behavioral assessment(s) used in practice will vary, they will likely include at least one or more *criterion-referenced assessments*. Criterion-referenced assessments differ from standardized or norm-referenced assessments in comparing a learner's skills to a predetermined learning goal or performance level instead of comparing them to other learners. According to a recent survey of behavior analysis practitioners (Padilla, 2020), the most commonly used criterion-referenced assessments that focus on developmental skills include the *Verbal Behavior Milestones Assessment and Placement Program* (VB-MAPP; Sundberg, 2008), the *Assessment of Basic Language and Learning Skills–Revised* (ABLLS-R; Partington, 2008); and *Promoting the Emergence of Advanced Knowledge* (PEAK) *Relational Training System* (Dixon, 2014a, 2014b, 2015). These assessments are grounded in Skinner's analysis of verbal behavior (1957), advances in verbal behavior research (Hayes et al., 2001), and established child developmental milestones.

The assessments evaluate a learner's current repertoire and identify relevant target goals for a treatment or individualized education plan. Importantly, these assessments are not intended to serve as a set curriculum but can guide curriculum goals and objectives along with information from collaborators such as the family, teachers, and other professionals working with the same learner. It is important to note that a recent review of the psychometric properties of these assessments showed that most also lack convincing evidence for validity and reliability (Padilla et al., 2023). These findings highlight the need for further research on this topic.

As noted above, translating documents is an example of a *superficial* cultural adaptation (Barrera et al., 2013). To date, all three behavioral language assessments referenced above been translated into a language other than English, but they have yet to be fully adapted for CLD learners. Enriquez et al. (2023) presented an option for a culturally and linguistically responsive assessment of functional language skills—the verbal operant experimental (VOX) analysis. The VOX (Mason, 2022) systematically manipulates learning trials to assess learners' verbal responses under different conditions (e.g., tact, mand, echoic, and intraverbal). This assessment is based on a functional analysis of verbal behavior first proposed by Lerman et al. (2005). Notably, the VOX excludes social norms often aligned with Westernized culture (e.g., sustained eye contact), and learner responses in English and the home language are accepted throughout the assessment.

Enriquez et al. (2023) evaluated the use of a VOX analysis and subsequent verbal behavior intervention with a 4-year-old boy diagnosed with ASD from a Spanish-speaking home. The assessment was conducted by clinicians who worked with the child and were fluent in English and Spanish; all instructions were presented in Spanish, which was identified as the participant's dominant language. The assessment began with an evaluation of the participant's tacting repertoire. Three preferred items were identified via a free-operant preference assessment followed by tact probes with the three most highly preferred items. The evaluator gave the participant brief access to one item at a time (to rule out mand control), followed by the evaluator pointing to the item and asking, "What is it?" During tact probes, the evaluator never said the item's name (to rule out echoic control) and did not provide any other verbal stimuli (to rule out intraverbal control). The evaluator repeated this process with each of the three preferred items. Next, the evaluator assessed the participant's mand repertoire using the same items. Following brief access to one of the preferred items, the evaluator removed the item from the participant's sight, did not name the item or provide any related verbal stimuli, and presented an opportunity for the participant to request (mand) the item with a verbal instruction (e.g., "What do you want?"

or "What are you looking for?"). This process was repeated until all three items were assessed for mand control. The evaluator assessed echoics next, followed by intraverbals. During the echoic probes, the evaluator presented one verbal stimulus corresponding to one of the preferred items in isolation. At the same time, the participant was engaged in an unrelated activity (e.g., if an item for the probe was a train set, the evaluator asked the participant to complete a coloring page unrelated to trains). Finally, during the intraverbal probes, the evaluator presented statements or questions related to each object (that was out of sight). As with the echoic probe, the participant was engaged in an unrelated activity during each probe, and the evaluator never named the items. For example, the evaluator presented fill-in-the-blank statements (e.g., "Choo, choo goes the ____") or asked simple questions (e.g., "What is a vehicle that rides on tracks?") to assess intraverbal control. In the VOX analysis, tact probes are always conducted first, followed by mand, echoic, and intraverbal probes—all presented in a counterbalanced order to help control sequence effects. Between two to four verbal episodes (e.g., one episode is the presentation of a tact, mand, echoic, and intraverbal probe for a single item) can be conducted in a single 60-minute session, making this assessment also practical for clinic and home use.

Enriquez et al. (2023) demonstrated the added value of the VOX analysis in developing a transfer of stimulus control procedure to expand the participant's verbal repertoire. That is, the prompting hierarchy individualized for the learner was informed by the results of the assessment. For example, since the participant presented with high levels of echoics and tacts but lower levels of mands and intraverbals, the intervention began with teaching mands by first briefly restricting access to a preferred item while showing the learner the item (tact control) and providing a vocal-verbal prompt (echoic control) as well as a fill-in-the-blank statement (intraverbal control). The systematic prompting procedure gradually faded until mand control was established with items out of sight. A similar procedure established stronger intraverbals to develop a more balanced repertoire across all four elementary verbal operants.

Replications demonstrating the benefit of the VOX for CLD learners are sorely needed. This experimental analysis can help determine functional language use in English and the learner's home language. As such, incorporating this assessment as routine practice when evaluating language skills may prove beneficial, like the utility of the analog functional analyses, in establishing the cause(s) of challenging behavior (Hanley, 2012). Future researchers should also aim to identify variables that account for language *selection* or language *preference* among this population and examine the extent to which these learners demonstrate functional differences across their first and second languages.

Once the assessment process is complete, practitioners are responsible for designing interventions to benefit each learner. An important variable to consider in developing behavior reduction and skill acquisition plans is that the language used during instruction may impact the overall effectiveness of any planned intervention. Moreover, learners may demonstrate a *preference* for instruction that is presented in English or their home language. The following sections of this chapter will summarize studies that have shown how to evaluate preference for language of instruction with CLD learners, the impact of language of instruction on skill acquisition, and the presence of challenging behavior.

Preference for Language of Instruction

Although the research is limited, some previous studies in behavior analysis have shown learner preference for language of instruction. For example, Aguilar (2017) assessed learner preference by evaluating the response of five participants during English and Spanish instruction delivery while controlling for task difficulty. Participants were 5–10 years old, came from homes where Spanish was the exclusively spoken language, and were diagnosed with a developmental disability. Two different tasks were presented: "difficult" tasks were skills the participants could not yet perform independently, while "easy" tasks were previously mastered. The experimenters presented a BIGmack communication device to give participants a way to indicate the choice of language of instruction, "work in English" or "trabajo en Español" or no auditory recording (a control condition). Pressing the communication device served as a link in the chain of three contingencies with three possible outcomes. The experimenter delivered one instruction trial in the respective language the participant activated and then gave access to the participant's preferred reinforcer for 30 seconds. If the participant did not select an auditory recording, the instructor waited 30 seconds without speaking or looking at the participant and proceeded to the subsequent trial. Response allocation was recorded for easy vs. difficult academic tasks using a reversal design with five participants. Results indicated that four of the five participants preferred the home language when tasks were *difficult,* and no participants indicated a preference when the task was *easy.* These results highlight the benefit of assessing the language of instruction when presenting new demands to improve the performance of CLD learners. A limitation of this study is that accuracy was not recorded, and the only communication modality evaluated was a selection-based response with the BIGmack communication device.

Kunze et al. (2019) aimed to extend the results of Aguilar (2017) by demonstrating a preference for language output (e.g., a therapist's voice) using speech-generating devices (SGDs) for a 10-year-old EL with Down Syndrome who was exposed to Spanish at home. An alternating-treatments design with an embedded concurrent-chain arrangement was used to compare the effects of three language conditions (English, Spanish, and control) on the choice of SGD language output. At the start of each session, a therapist walked into the room with a colored poster board displayed in the participant's line of vision, wearing a colored shirt that corresponded with the condition (e.g., green for English, orange for Spanish, purple for control). During the pre-session, the therapist delivered general verbal statements in the language specified for each condition every 15 seconds while the participant engaged with available toys. After 1 minute, the therapist removed all the toys, and the mand session began. Following the pre-session, the therapist presented three iPads® with colored cases that corresponded to a specific language and that were programmed to produce vocal output in either English or Spanish (or no vocal output for the control) at the same volume and using identical pictures of highly preferred edible items across all three conditions. Once the participant selected one of the iPads, the therapist removed all items and delivered the corresponding reinforcer. Manding sessions continued for 5 minutes. SGD voice output language and frequency of mands were coded during each session. Results showed that the participant emitted more mands per session in Spanish ($M = 25.57$) than in either English ($M = 3.86$) or the control ($M = 4.00$). Specifically, 76.50% of total mands were in Spanish, compared to 11.54% and 11.97% in English and the control, respectively. The authors suggested that future researchers should add measures of social validity to assess the acceptability of treatment, the families' views on the use of bilingual instruction, and the use of SGDs by parents of children who speak a language other than the cultural norm.

These studies provide valuable insights into the role of language preference in instructional settings for CLD learners with disabilities. By assessing learner preferences, Aguilar (2017) and Kunze et al. (2019) demonstrated the potential for tailoring interventions to enhance learner engagement and communication. While their findings highlight the benefits of incorporating the home language into instruction, they also underscore the need for further research to address critical gaps, such as measuring the accuracy of responses, exploring diverse communication modalities, and evaluating family perspectives on bilingual or multilingual interventions.

Impact of Language of Instruction on Skill Acquisition

Other studies within the behavior analysis literature have evaluated the impact of language of instruction on skill acquisition. Padilla Dalmau et al. (2011) evaluated whether differences in treatment effectiveness and language preference emerged across Spanish and English during functional communication training (FCT) for young children with developmental disabilities exposed to both languages in their home environment. Participants were two children (ages 5 and 6) with developmental disabilities (ASD and mild intellectual disability; spinal muscular atrophy and pervasive developmental disorder) who displayed destructive behavior. The effectiveness of FCT in Spanish vs. English was evaluated using a reversal design with an embedded multielement design across language types. Additionally, a concurrent schedule design was used to assess language preference during FCT sessions. During the intervention phase of the study, participants responded to a specific task followed by the opportunity to request a reinforcer (i.e., a brief 1–2-minute break) using a microswitch with an attached picture/word card. Each FCT session began with a 20–30-second play period during which preferred toys were available and either Spanish or English was spoken. During the play period, preferred toys were placed in front of the participant, followed by the presentation of a picture/word card with the word "trabajar," or "work," along with a corresponding verbal stimulus in the language of instruction designated for each condition (e.g., "es tiempo de trabajar" or "It's time to work"). The toys were then removed, and work materials were presented. The participants were prompted to complete one to four tasks using a 3-step least-to-most prompting procedure (verbal, model, physical). The task requirement increased to up to 20 tasks per session. Results suggested that FCT effectively increased both participants' manding and task completion (while reducing challenging behavior) regardless of the language used. The language in which demands were delivered, the language on the mand, and the language spoken by the implementor during reinforcement did not affect the intervention's effectiveness. Lastly, preference for the type of language did not emerge for either participant during FCT.

In a different evaluation of skill acquisition, Lim and Charlop (2018) evaluated both the preference for language and its impact on play behavior. This study assessed the effects of language of instruction on the play skills of four children, ages 8–12, with ASD who came from bilingual homes (Spanish or Korean in addition to English) and displayed deficits in play skills. Functional and interactive play behaviors were evaluated in sessions that were conducted in English compared to sessions conducted in the participant's home language (Spanish or Korean). Functional play was defined as the participant engaging with the toy in a way that aligned with its typical or intended use (e.g., bouncing a ball); interactive play was defined as the participant engaging in functional play *with* the experimenter (e.g., rolling a ball to the experimenter). The experimenters were all fluent in either Spanish or Korean. They provided verbalizations during all sessions related to different play instructions (e.g., "Pass me the ball" and "Build the train tracks") and play-related comments (e.g., "Playing with friends is fun!" and "The toys look like so much fun!") in the corresponding language for each condition. The selected verbalizations were based on the baseline assessment of each participant's play skills, interests, and vocalizations, and each vocalization was repeated twice in a 5-minute session with the order of presentation randomized. Results showed increased play behavior during both conditions for all participants but higher levels of play during the home language condition. In addition, occurrences of challenging behavior were measured, and results showed higher levels of challenging behavior during the English-only condition for one participant. A limitation of this study was the lack of a baseline during the home language condition. Thus, future researchers should aim to replicate these findings with an extended duration of play sessions.

Skill acquisition has also been focused on language development. In an early demonstration, Thordardottir et al. (1997) compared language intervention sessions conducted in two alternating conditions: English-only and a bilingual training condition (English and Icelandic) with a 4-year-old boy residing in the United States. The participant's language was severely delayed according to two norm-referenced assessments (i.e., The Peabody Picture Vocabulary Test and Preschool Boehm) conducted in both English and Icelandic. The results of these assessments placed the participant in the 1st percentile for English instruction and the 3rd percentile when the assessment was conducted in Icelandic. Training sessions were conducted during naturalistic play interactions and included a mix of vocal modalities (e.g., echoics, tacts, listener responses, and intraverbals). A unique stimulus set of "home" and "school" related vocabulary words was assigned to either English-only or bilingual instruction, and the dependent variable was the number of words emitted (as tacts) from each set in English. Overall, the acquisition of English was comparable in the two conditions, with a slight advantage observed in the bilingual condition. This early demonstration supports bilingual instruction for learners with documented language delays.

In a similar study, Pham et al. (2011) evaluated the effects of language of instruction (bilingual condition and English condition only) on vocabulary comprehension (number of items correctly identified) and attention to task (number of total responses) in a Vietnamese 3-year-old male child with a developmental delay and speech impairment. Results showed that the bilingual condition increased attention to the task at hand, and both the bilingual and English-only conditions increased receptive vocabulary in English. The client improved listener responses in both treatment conditions and in both languages.

León and Rosales (2018) also evaluated the effects of training when instruction was presented in English compared to a bilingual condition (English and Portuguese) for tact training. The participant was diagnosed with a communication disorder; his parents spoke Portuguese at home, and the family had expressed interest in their child learning more of their home language. Assessment of language was gathered via a parent questionnaire on exposure to English and the home language, as well as criterion (i.e., VB-MAPP) and standardized (i.e., Peabody Picture Vocabulary Test and Expressive One-Word Picture Vocabulary Test Fourth Edition) language assessments to determine the learner's repertoire in both languages at the start of the study. An adapted alternating treatment design was used to compare the acquisition rate in the two training conditions—English-only and bilingual. A contextual cue designated the language of instruction during each trial (e.g., blue background when stimuli were presented in English; yellow background when stimuli were presented in

Portuguese). Results showed that the participant emitted more correct responses during tact training in English than during the bilingual condition. However, performance was better on generalization and maintenance probes for the bilingual condition. This study did not isolate the effects of home language, and the participant had more prolonged exposure to English in academic settings and better performance in English on standardized language assessments. Thus, these results may not be generalizable to children in this population with a different history of language exposure.

Other demonstrations of skill acquisition when multiple languages are used in teaching include a study by Jimenez-Gomez et al. (2022), who evaluated the effects of instructive feedback to promote the acquisition of listener responses in both English and Spanish. Participants were three 4-year-old children with ASD who were exposed to Spanish at home and English in their academic community. Sessions consisted of five trials of a listener response task with relevant stimuli for each participant (e.g., food items, sports equipment, community helpers, tools). A therapist presented the participants with an array of three randomized stimuli and an instruction in English to select one of the items per trial. An errorless teaching procedure was used during acquisition trials along with stimulus-specific instructive feedback in Spanish for correct responses (e.g., "es la cinta de medir" following a correct response to the instruction "find measuring tape"), plus access to a preferred item for 30 seconds. Incorrect responses were followed by the end of the trial and a brief intertrial interval. Teaching sessions continued until the participant met the predetermined mastery criterion. Probes for listener responses in Spanish followed this. Results showed that 12 out of 18 potential Spanish listener targets were acquired without direct instruction. Thus, data indicate that instructive feedback enhances the efficiency of instruction. It is relevant to mention that the effectiveness of instruction feedback may depend on the participants' prerequisite skills (e.g., echoic and existing listener skills). However, this evaluation demonstrated the potential impact of instructive feedback in expanding the repertoires of children with ASD. This teaching approach can inform clinical programming to better serve the needs of individuals living in linguistically diverse environments. Replications of this methodology with additional diverse learners are needed.

Most recently, Hu et al. (2023) evaluated the effects of echoic-to-mand training to teach mands in English and the emergence of tact and listener responses. Participants were three Chinese-speaking preschool boys (4–5 years of age) with ASD and no prior learning history in English. Participants did not demonstrate bidirectional naming in Chinese as assessed by the Developmentally Based Behavior Assessment for Children with Autism (Feng & Sun, 2017). The teaching targets (food and toys) were selected based on observations of the learners' free play activities and parental reports. Pre- and post-training probes were conducted individually, while baseline, mand training in English, and generalization conditions were conducted in a group instruction format. The primary dependent variable was the percentage of accurate mands emitted by the child in English (the second language training condition). The percentage of tact and listener responses in English was scored as secondary dependent variables. Results showed that the training was effective in the acquisition of mand responses. Also, tacts and listener responses for the same vocabulary emerged without direct training. Future researchers should include other response types (e.g., intraverbal) and explore the underlying mechanism (e.g., bidirectional naming) responsible for emergent responses, evaluate the emergence of other types of verbal operants, and design more naturalistic opportunities for generalization.

Collectively, the results of these studies show that bilingual instruction does not necessarily impact or further restrict language development compared to instruction in English only. On the contrary, bilingual instruction can help avoid the negative aspects of eliminating a language that is part of a bilingual learner's verbal community. Results must be replicated with additional learners to demonstrate similarities and expected variability in responding with participants of diverse backgrounds, such as younger learners with a shorter learning history of more than one language and learners with different communication modalities.

Impact of Language of Instruction on Challenging Behaviors

As with skill acquisition, some studies in behavior analysis have shown the impact of language of instruction on challenging behavior for children with ASD and related disabilities. For example, Lang et al. (2011) delivered discrete trial instruction in English and Spanish to a child with ASD. They evaluated the effects of language on response accuracy and the presence of challenging behavior. Importantly, the child was simultaneously exposed to Spanish only at home and English exclusively at school. Relative to instructional sessions conducted in English, there were more correct responses and lower rates of challenging behavior in the Spanish language sessions. These findings suggest that different languages may be associated with different contingencies, reinforcer values, and motivating operations.

In a similar study, Rispoli et al. (2011) evaluated the influence of the language of implementation on functional analysis outcomes for a child with severe intellectual disability and cerebral palsy from a Spanish-speaking home. The study aimed to determine whether the functional analysis results would vary when the instructions presented in each condition were manipulated (Spanish vs. English). A series of 5-minute sessions was conducted in four conditions: attention, play-verbal (verbal praise on a fixed-time schedule), play-non-verbal (no verbal praise), and demand implementation in English and then in Spanish. Results showed that the highest levels of challenging behavior occurred during the attention and demand conditions in English. These results suggest that the language of instruction may influence the overall levels of challenging behavior within functional analysis conditions.

A recent study by Neely et al. (2020) focused on the impact of an English-only and Spanish-only intervention on challenging behavior and the potential for a resurgence of problem behavior. Resurgence or recurrence of a previously extinguished behavior may occur in learners from dual language homes when the communicative response contacts extinction, which may occur unintentionally. For example, suppose a learner is taught a functional communication response (FCR) in English at school, and the intervention functions as a replacement for a challenging behavior. However, the response is not reinforced in the home environment where adults primarily speak Khmer. In this case, the learner may start to engage in challenging behavior in both settings as a side effect of the extinction response in the home. The Neely et al. study participants were three learners (ages 4–5) who engaged in challenging behavior maintained by social reinforcement in both English and Spanish and lived in homes where Spanish was the dominant language. Sessions were conducted in an outpatient hospital-based clinic. The experimenter spoke in one language relevant to each session and wore a uniquely colored shirt for each condition (i.e., blue for English, red for Spanish). Researchers randomly determined the number of sessions for each condition (FCT-English and FCT-Spanish) and presented instructions with a least-to-most prompting hierarchy. If the participant engaged in the targeted challenging behavior, the experimenter prompted the participant to emit the FCR with a full vocal-verbal prompt (e.g., "end" or "fin"). The experimenter consequated both prompted and unprompted FCRs (in English and Spanish conditions) with a 10-second break from instruction. Challenging behavior resulted in extinction (i.e., the instruction continued). The conditions were taught sequentially, and results showed that the rate of challenging behavior immediately dropped to zero when FCT was implemented in Spanish for two of the three participants. These results suggest that FCRs learned in the participant's first language may lead to a resurgence of problem behavior. This may occur when the participant's first language FCRs do not contact reinforcement in the untaught language (e.g., Spanish). Two participants required additional teaching in the secondary language (Spanish), while the third participant eventually used Spanish FCRs in the Spanish condition without direct instruction.

Banerjee et al. (2022) aimed to replicate the results of Neely et al. (2020) with two participants (5- and 6-year-olds) with ASD. Both participants were exposed to Spanish in their home environment and spent at least 4 hours per day exposed to two different language environments (Spanish and English). Two experiments were conducted. In Experiment 1, the researchers assessed how FCT for Spanish mands influenced manding in English and Spanish under different conditions (English-only and Spanish-only). Therapists fluent in English but not Spanish conducted both language conditions, and Spanish probes always followed an

FCT-Spanish training condition. Therapists were trained to correctly pronounce relevant Spanish words before the onset of the study. Experiment 2 evaluated the effects of "repair the message" training on the occurrence of mands reinforced during no-prompt conditions. These results show additional support for the possible resurgence of challenging behavior when functional communication is only focused on one language (e.g., English) and the need to plan for intervention in multiple languages for CLD individuals receiving ABA services. Limitations of this study included a lack of formal assessment to evaluate participants' English and Spanish repertoires, only mands that conformed to the specific operational definitions were scored and reinforced, and the experimenters did not collect data on chained or mixed mands. In addition, therapists were not fluent in Spanish; thus, the ecological validity and generality were likely impacted.

Results of the studies that have evaluated the impact of language of instruction on challenging behavior collectively indicate the importance of considering this variable when working with CLD learners. Given the idiosyncratic results of the studies conducted to date, it is important to conduct direct and systematic replications of these procedures. Practitioners working with this population must evaluate the potential impact of language of instruction in all aspects of their work.

Recommendations for Research and Practice

The research reviewed in this chapter indicates that ELs or CLD individuals may exhibit a clear preference for a language of instruction. Furthermore, both skill acquisition and challenging behaviors can be affected when the language of instruction is manipulated. The impact of these variables is idiosyncratic, and there are noted limitations in the studies, necessitating direct and systematic replications to validate and extend findings. Future research should continue to investigate how language influences the value of social reinforcement, the intensity of challenging behaviors, and the skill acquisition process. The studies discussed in this chapter provide valuable methodologies for examining the effects of language implementation in learners with developmental disabilities from diverse linguistic backgrounds.

Future researchers could evaluate methodologies for presenting skill acquisition, including evaluating the effects of presenting instructional targets in English, the home language, or both. Approaches like pairing or instructive feedback could help support bilingual training conditions. Additionally, researchers might compare simultaneous instruction (delivering instruction in both English and the home language concurrently) to sequential instruction (delivering instruction first in the home language, then in English, or vice versa) to determine which condition yields the most favorable outcomes for individual learners. Cultural adaptations to behavioral language assessments also warrant further investigation. Replicating methodologies like those used by Enriquez et al. (2023) may address gaps in understanding learners' cultural and linguistic needs.

Finally, a systematic assessment of listener and speaker repertoires in English and the home language should be conducted when working with ELs. This is particularly important for individuals with limited vocal-verbal repertoires, as listener responding often precedes speaker development. This pattern also holds in second-language acquisition (IDEA [Individuals with Disabilities Education Act] and Research for Inclusive Settings [IRIS] Center, n.d.). Assessing these repertoires across multiple languages can provide a clearer picture of the learner's strengths and areas for growth. For example, a learner may have a more robust listener repertoire in English than a speaker repertoire or exhibit more robust skills in both listener and speaker repertoires in the home language.

Additionally, limited listener comprehension may increase task aversiveness, potentially leading to heightened challenging behavior. Similarly, the language of implementation may affect the quality of verbal reinforcement; for instance, praise delivered in English might be less reinforcing than praise in the learner's home language. Future research on these variables is essential to establish evidence-based guidelines and recommendations for practice.

The following guidelines and recommendations are offered as a starting point for applied researchers and practitioners working with linguistically diverse populations.

1. **Seek Input on the Family's Preferences.** Involving the family in the decision-making process is a critical first step. During intake, it is essential to clarify the child's language exposure at home and in the community and determine whether the family prefers English, the home language, or both for their child's instruction. These discussions can also provide opportunities to address family concerns about using their home language with their child (see Recommendation #3). Including questions like those outlined in Table 13.2 as part of the information-gathering process can help ensure a comprehensive understanding of the family's needs and preferences. Access to the home language also means access to culture. When professionals fail to support the home language in bilingual households, they risk denying learners a connection to an essential part of their cultural identity. Moreover, disregarding parents' preferences to raise their children bilingually contradicts best practice guidelines established by professional organizations such as the American Speech-Language-Hearing Association (ASHA, 2017) and the Behavior Analyst Certification Board (BACB, 2020).

2. **Determine Language of Assessment.** It is essential to conduct assessments in the learner's dominant language and/or incorporate culturally responsive tools to evaluate functional language skills as part of the intake process

(Enriquez et al., 2023). Family input is valuable in determining the most appropriate language for assessment, but practitioners should also consider utilizing standardized assessments available in multiple languages (e.g., the *MacArthur-Bates Communicative Development Inventories*, Fenson et al., 2006; *Receptive and Expressive One-Word Vocabulary Test*, Martin & Brownell, 2011a, 2011b) to develop a comprehensive profile of the learner's verbal repertoire. Gathering information about the learner's skills in their home language can provide critical insights that guide individualized treatment planning.

3. **Consider the Impact of Recommending "English Only."** Given that significant impairments in communication are a defining characteristic of autism, families often have questions and concerns about the effects of speaking their home language with their child. Recent reviews by independent research groups consistently indicate that exposure to two or more languages does not negatively impact language development in children with ASD (Lund et al., 2017). Moreover, bilingual children with language impairments tend to exhibit similar deficits across both languages (Valicenti-McDermott et al., 2013; Hambly & Fombonne, 2012). Despite these findings, studies also frequently report that parents receive advice from professionals recommending against bilingualism (Hambly & Fombonne, 2012; Lim & Charlop, 2018; Ohashi et al., 2012; Petersen et al., 2012; Valicenti-McDermott et al., 2013; Wang et al., 2019). Recommending an "English only" environment can significantly limit a learner's opportunities to engage meaningfully with members of their verbal community, such as parents, siblings, extended family members, and peers in community settings.

4. **Consider How Augmentative Communication Systems Can Be Adapted.** Augmentative communication systems, such as picture exchange systems, tablets, iPads, and other vocal output devices, offer flexibility to integrate multiple languages. However, there is limited empirical research on culturally responsive adaptations of these systems, though some case demonstrations have been documented (e.g., Al-Dawaideh & Al-Amayreh, 2013). Practitioners should avoid assuming that implementing an augmentative communication system will work uniformly across languages and cultures. For instance, challenges may arise in interpreting sentence structure for Japanese speakers when picture-based systems are designed exclusively for English sentence patterns (Nakamura et al., 1998). Similarly, the selection of graphic icons must be culturally relevant; for example, certain uncommon fruits in specific regions should be avoided when representing food items (Chompoobutr et al., 2013). Additional considerations include providing appropriate gender and language voice options and incorporating keyboards that support different languages (Dukhovny & Kelly, 2015).

5. **Collaborate with Other Professionals.** Collaboration with speech-language pathologists, multilingual teachers, and special and general education teachers is essential, as each professional brings valuable insights into treatment goals and strategies for working with ELs. Currently, behavior analysts lack a specific set of evidence-based practice guidelines for working with ELs with ASD. While including families in decision-making and seeking their input on language preferences and instructional needs aligns with best practices in the field, these recommendations do not offer a detailed framework for teaching language to this population. Therefore, consulting with and seeking input from interdisciplinary experts is crucial. Guidance on fostering effective interdisciplinary collaboration is available and can help behavior analysts navigate these professional relationships effectively (Brodhead, 2015).

6. **Include Parents as Change Agents.** The family's role in maintaining and promoting the generalization of behavior change procedures is integral to the work of behavior analysis practitioners. When working with families raising an EL, practitioners should support parents in using the home language with their child, particularly if the family has expressed a preference for doing so. If training sessions are conducted in English, practitioners can encourage parents to implement the same procedures in their home language. Treatment integrity data can be collected on nonvocal-verbal behaviors exhibited by parents and other caregivers, providing opportunities for feedback to enhance their interactions and adherence to intervention strategies.

7. **Recruit Bilingual Individuals into the Profession.** Although the number of bilingual behavior analysis practitioners has not been reported, there is documented underrepresentation of racial and ethnic diversity within the profession at the master's and doctoral levels and overrepresentation of individuals from racially and ethnically diverse groups in technician roles (Behavior Analyst Certification Board, n.d. n.d.). Several calls to increase diversity in the field have been made, with specific strategies outlined by Rosales et al. (2022). Recruiting bilingual individuals into the workforce offers numerous benefits, including fostering stronger relationships with families and multicultural communities and enhancing outreach to underserved populations.

When obtained with consent, respect, and sensitivity, information about a family's linguistic background and preferences enables clinicians to enhance the social and ecological validity of their interventions. Behavior analysis has a rich tradition of examining the influence of social environments and cultural factors on an individual's socially significant behaviors. The methodologies used in the studies reviewed in this chapter can be refined and applied to identify the conditions under which language and other cultural variables influence a learner's verbal behavior. Rather than treating cultural and linguistic knowledge as static facts, behavior analysts working with linguistically diverse populations should develop and test hypotheses about these variables. Hayes and Toarmino (1995) emphasized the importance of using individuals' cultural knowledge to formulate testable hypotheses about behavioral function rather than making broad assumptions or generalizations. Behavior analysts who adopt this approach can avoid overgeneralizing learners' behaviors based on cultural or linguistic characteristics and offer more precise, individualized interventions instead.

Raising a child with ASD can be challenging and stressful for parents (Giovagnoli et al., 2015). As practitioners, we are responsible for providing the highest quality of care. Given the current scarcity of empirical evidence and the absence of established evidence-based practices for language selection in ELs with ASD, recommendations regarding language use should be personalized. These recommendations must consider the learner's abilities, interests, familial preferences, and environmental contexts. Parents who express a desire or need to raise their children as bilingual should receive support and guidance to honor their decision and promote their child's developmental success.

References

Aguilar, J. M., Chan, J. M., White, P. J., & Fragale, C. (2017). Assessment of the language preferences of five children with autism from Spanish-speaking homes. *Journal of Behavioral Education, 26*, 334–347. https://doi.org/10.1007/s10864-017-9280-9

Al-dawaideh, A. M. & Al-Amayreh, M. M. (2013). The effectiveness of picture exchange communication system on learning request skills and the development of speech in Arabic-speaking children with autism. *Life Science Journal, 10*(2), 2139–2148. http://www.dx.doi.org/10.7537/marslsj100213.301

American Speech-Language-Hearing Association, & American Speech-Language-Hearing Association (ASHA). (2017). *Issues in ethics: Cultural and linguistic competence.* https://www.asha.org/practice/ethics/cultural-and-linguistic-competence/#sec1.3

Banerjee, I., Lambert, J. M., Copeland, B. A., Paranczak, J. L., Bailey, K. M., & Standish, C. M. (2022). Extending functional communication training to multiple language contexts in bilingual learners with challenging behavior. *Journal of Applied Behavior Analysis, 55*(1), 80–100. https://doi.org/10.1002/jaba.883

Barrera, M., Jr, Castro, F. G., Strycker, L. A., & Toobert, D. J. (2013). Cultural adaptations of behavioral health interventions: a progress report. *Journal of Consulting and Clinical Psychology, 81*(2), 196–205. https://doi.org/10.1037/a0027085

Behavior Analyst Certification Board. (n.d). *BACB certificant data.* Retrieved from https://www.bacb.com/BACB-certificant-data.

Behavior Analyst Certification Board. (2020). *Ethics code for behavior analysts.* https://bacb.com/wp-content/ethics-code-for-behavior-analysts/

Bernal, G., Jiménez-Chafey, M. I., & Domenech Rodríguez, M. M. (2009). Cultural adaptation of treatments: A resource for considering culture in evidence-based practice. *Professional Psychology: Research and Practice*, *40*(4), 361–368. https://doi.org/10.1037/a0016401

Brodhead, M. T. (2015). Maintaining professional relationships in an interdisciplinary setting: Strategies for navigating nonbehavioral treatment recommendations for individuals with Autism. *Behavior Analysis in Practice*, *8*(1), 70–78. https://doi.org/10.1007/s40617-015-0042-7

Chompoobutr, S., Potibal, P., Boriboon, M., & Phantachat, W. (2013). Perception and multi meaning analysis of graphic symbols for Thai picture-based communication system. *Disability and Rehabilitation: Assistive Technology*, *8*(2), 102–107. https://doi.org/10.3109/17483107.2012.737531

Counts, J., Antonis, K., & Whitford, D. K. (2018). Culturally and linguistically diverse learners in special education: English learners. *National Association of Secondary School Principals Bulletin*, *102*(1), 5–21. https://doi.org/10.1177/0192636515875594

Dietrich, S., & Hernandez, E. (2022). Language use in the United States: 2019. *American Community Survey Reports*.

Dixon, M. R. (2014a). *The PEAK relational training system: Direct training module*. Shawnee Scientific Press.

Dixon, M. R. (2014b). *The PEAK relational training system: Generalization module*. Shawnee Scientific Press.

Dixon, M. R. (2015). *The PEAK relational training system: Equivalence module*. Shawnee Scientific Press.

Dukhovny, E., & Kelly, E. B. (2015). Practical resources for provision of services to culturally and linguistically diverse users of AAC. *Perspectives on Communication Disorders and Sciences in Culturally and Linguistically Diverse (CLD) Populations*, *22*(1), 25–39. https://doi.org/10.1044/cds22.1.25

Dunst, C. J., Raab, M., & Hamby, D. W. (2016). Interest-based everyday child language learning. *Revista de Logopedia, Foniatria y Audiologia*, *36*(4), 153–161. https://doi.org/10.1016/j.rlfa.2016.07.003

Durán, L. K., Hartzheim, D., Lund, E. M., Simonsmeier, V., & Kohlmeier, T. L. (2016). Bilingual and home language interventions with young dual language learners: A research synthesis. *Language, Speech, and Hearing Services in Schools*, *47*(4), 347–371. https://doi.org/10.1044/2016_LSHSS-15-0030

Enriquez, J., Arechiga, N., Atherkode, S., Otero, M., Andrews, A., & Mason, L. (2023). Culturally responsive language assessment through a verbal operant experimental analysis. *Behavior Analysis: Research and Practice*, *23*(2), 165–178. https://doi.org/10.1037/bar0000269

Fahim, D., & Nedwick, K. (2014). Around the world: Supporting young children with ASD who are dual language learners. *Young Exceptional Children*, *17*(2), 3–20. https://doi.org/10.1177/1096250613477870

Feng, H., & Sun, W.-C. (2017). *Tzu-pi cheng fa chan pen wei ping liang hsi tung [Developmentally-based behavior assessment system for children with autism]*. Hua-Teng Publisher.

Fenson, L., Marchman, V. A., Thal, D. J., Dale, P. S., Reznick, J. S., & Bates, E. (2006). *MacArthur-bates communicative development inventories, (CDIs)* (2nd ed.). APA PsycTests. https://doi.org/10.1037/t11538-000

Garcia, O. (2009). Emergent bilinguals and TESOL: What's in a name? *TESOL Quarterly*, *43*(2), 322–326. http://www.jstor.org/stable/27785009

Giovagnoli, G., Postorino, V., Fatta, L. M., Sanges, V., De Peppo, L., Vassena, L., Rose, P. D., Vicari, S., & Mazzone, L. (2015). Behavioral and emotional profile and parental stress in preschool children with autism spectrum disorder. *Research in Developmental Disabilities*, *45–46*, 411–421. https://doi.org/10.1016/j.ridd.2015.08.006

Hambly, C., & Fombonne, E. (2012). The impact of bilingual environments on language development in children with autism spectrum disorders. *Journal of Autism and Developmental Disorders*, *42*(7), 1342–1352. https://doi.org/10.1007/s10803-011 -1365-z

Hanley, G. P. (2012). Functional assessment of problem behavior: Dispelling myths, overcoming implementation obstacles, and developing new lore. *Behavior Analysis in Practice*, *5*, 54–72. https://doi.org/10.1007/BF03391818

Harris, A. (2019). *Special topics in English learner programming: Difference vs. disability in English learners*. District of Columbia Office of the State Superintendent of Education. https://osse.dc.gov/sites/default/files/dc/sites/osse/documents/Separating %20Difference%20from%20Disability%20in%20English%20Learners.pdf

Hayes, S. C., Barnes-Holmes, D., & Roche, B. (Eds.). (2001). *Relational frame theory: A post-Skinnerian account of human language and cognition*. Kluwer Academic/ Plenum Publishers.

Hayes, S. C., & Toarmino, D. (1995). If behavioral principles are generally applicable, why is it necessary to understand cultural diversity? *The Behavior Therapist*, *18*, 21–23.

Hu, X., Lee, G. T., Pan, Q., Gilic, L., & Zeng, S. (2023). Effects of foreign mand training on the emergence of foreign tact and listener responses for Chinese-speaking children with autism spectrum disorder. *Behavioral Interventions*, *38*(2), 437–455. https://doi .org/10.1002/bin.1930

IRIS Center. (n.d.). *What does research say about teaching English language learners?* IRIS Center, Peabody College of Education, Vanderbilt University. https://iris .peabody.vanderbilt.edu/module/ell/cresource/q1/p02/

Jimenez-Gomez, C., Pichardo, J., & Ryan, V. (2022). Instructive feedback to expand listener skills in a second language in children with autism spectrum disorder. *Behavioral Interventions*, *37*(1), 19–28. https://doi.org/10.1002/bin.1843

Kangas, S. E. N. (2019). English learners with disabilities: Linguistic development and educational equity in jeopardy. In Gao, X. (Ed.), *Second handbook of English language teaching* (pp. 919–937). Springer International Handbooks of Education. Springer. https://doi.org/10.1007/978-3-030-02899-2_48.

Kunze, M., Drew, C., Machalicek, W., Safer-Lichtenstein, J., & Crowe, B. (2019). Language preference of a multilingual individual with disabilities using a speech generating device. *Behavior Analysis in Practice*, *12*(4), 777–781. https://doi.org/10 .1007/s40617-019-00379- w

Lang, R., Rispoli, M., Sigafoos, J., Lancioni, G., Andrews, A., & Ortega, L. (2011). Effects of language of instruction on response accuracy and challenging behavior in a child with autism. *Journal of Behavioral Education*, *20*(4), 252–259. https://doi.org /10.1007/s10864-011-9130-0

Larson, A. L., An, Z. G., Wood, C., Uchikoshi, Y., Cycyk, L. M., Scheffner Hammer, C., Escobar, K., & Roberts, K. (2020). Social validity in early language interventions for dual language learners: A systematic review of the literature. *Topics in Early Childhood Special Education, 40*(1), 39–51. https://doi.org/10.1177/0271121419901289

León, A. L., & Rosales, R. (2018). Effects of bilingual tact instruction for a child with communication disorder. *Journal of Behavioral Education, 27*(1), 81–100. https://doi.org/10.1007/s10864-017-9272-9

Lerman, D. C., Parten, M., Addison, L. R., Vorndran, C. M., Volkert, V. M., & Kodak, T. (2005). A methodology for assessing the functions of emerging speech in children with developmental disabilities. *Journal of Applied Behavior Analysis, 38*(3), 303–316. https://doi.org/10.1901/jaba.2005.106-04

Lim, N., & Charlop, M. H. (2018). Effects of English versus heritage language on play in bilingually exposed children with autism spectrum disorder. *Behavioral Interventions, 33*(4), 339–351. https://doi.org/10.1002/bin.1644

Lund, E. M., Kohlmeier, T. L., & Durán, L. K. (2017). Comparative language development in bilingual and monolingual children with autism spectrum disorder: A systematic review. *Journal of Early Intervention, 39*(2), 106–124. https://doi.org/10.1177/1053815117690871

Maenner, M. J., Warren, Z., Robinson Williams, A., Moakohene, E., Bakian, A. V., Bilder, D. A., Mrkin, M. S., Fitzgerald, R. T., Furnier, S. M., Hughes, M. M., Ladd-Acosta, C. M., McArthur, D., Pas, E. T., Salinas, A., Vehorn, A., Williams, S., Esler, A., Grzybowski, A., Hall-Lande, J., & Nguyen, R. H. N. (2023). Prevalence and characteristics of autism spectrum disorder among children aged 8 years -- autism and developmental disabilities monitoring network, 11 Sites, United States, 2020. *MMWR Surveillance Summaries, 72*(2), 1–14.

Martin, N. A., & Brownell, R. (2011a). *Expressive one word picture vocabulary test* (4th ed.). Academic Therapy Publications.

Martin, N. A., & Brownell, R. (2011b). *Receptive one word picture vocabulary test* (4th ed.). Academic Therapy Publications.

Mason, L., Otero, M., & Andrews, A. (2022). Cochran's Q test of stimulus overselectivity within the verbal repertoire of children with autism. *Perspectives on Behavior Science, 45*(1), 101–121. https://doi.org/10.1007/s40614-021-00319-6

Nakamura, K., Newell, A., Alm, N., & Waller, A. (1998). How do members of different language communities compose sentences with a picture-based communication system? —a cross–cultural study of picture–based sentences constructed by English and Japanese speakers. *Augmentative and Alternative Communication, 14*(2), 71–80.

Neely, L., Graber, J., Kunnavatana, S., & Cantrell, K. (2020). Impact of language on behavior treatment outcomes. *Journal of Applied Behavior Analysis, 53*(2), 796–810. https://doi.org/10.1002/jaba.626

Ohashi, J. K., Mirenda, P., Marinova-Todd, S., Hamby, C., Fombonne, E., Szatmari, P., Bryson, S., Roberts, W., Smith, I., Vaillancourt, T., Volden, J., Waddell, C., Zwaigenbaum, L., Georgiades, S., Duku, E., & Thompson, A. (2012). Comparing early language development in monolingual- and bilingual- exposed young children with autism spectrum disorders. *Research in Autism Spectrum Disorders, 6*(2), 890–897. https://doi.org/10.1016/j.rasd.2011.12.002

Padilla Dalmau, Y. C. P., Wacker, D. P., Harding, J. W., Berg, W. K., Schieltz, K. M., Lee, J. F., Breznican, G. P., & Kramer, A. R. (2011). A preliminary evaluation of functional communication training effectiveness and language preference when

Spanish and English are manipulated. *Journal of Behavioral Education*, *20*(4), 233–251. https://doi.org/10.1007/s10864-011-9131-z

Padilla, K. L. (2020). Global assessment use and practices in applied behavior analysis: Surveying the field. *Research in Autism Spectrum Disorder*, *79*, 101676. https://doi.org/10.1016/j.rasd.2020.101676

Padilla, K. L., Weston, R., Morgan, G. B., Lively, P., & O'Guinn, N. (2023). Validity and reliability evidence for assessments based in applied behavior analysis: A systematic review. *Behavior Modification*, *47*(1), 247–288. https://doi.org/10.1177/01454455221098151

Partington, J. W. (2008). *The assessment of basic language and learning skills–revised* (2nd ed). Behavior Analysts, Inc.

Peña, E. D., Gutiérrez-Clellen, V., Iglesias, A., Goldstein, B., & Bedore, L. (2014). *Bilingual English-Spanish Assessment (BESA)*. Brookes Publishing. https://products.brookespublishing.com/Bilingual-English-Spanish-Assessment-BESA-P1044.aspx

Petersen, J. M., Marinova-Todd, S. H., & Mirenda, P. (2012). Brief report: An exploratory study of lexical skills in bilingual children with autism spectrum disorder. *Journal of Autism and Developmental Disorders*, *42*(7), 1499–1503. https://doi.org/10.1007/s10803-011-1366-y

Pham, G., Kohnert, K., & Mann, D. (2011). Addressing clinician-client mismatch: A preliminary intervention study with a bilingual Vietnamese English preschooler. *Language, Speech, and Hearing Services in Schools*, *42*(4), 408–422. https://doi.org/10.1044/0161-1461/2011/10-0073.

Rhodes, R. L., Ochoa, S. H., & Ortiz, S. O. (2005). *Assessing culturally and linguistically diverse students: A practical guide*. New York: Guilford Publications.

Rispoli, M., O'Reilly, M., Lang, R., Sigafoos, J., Mulloy, A., Aguilar, J., & Singer, G. (2011). Effects of language of implementation on functional analysis outcomes. *Journal of Behavioral Education*, *20*, 224–232. https://doi.org/10.1007/s10864-011-9128-7

Rosales, R., León, I. A., & León-Fuentes, A. L. (2022). Recommendations for recruitment and retention of a diverse workforce: A report from the field. *Behavior Analysis in Practice*, *16*(1), 346–361. https://doi.org/10.1007/s40617-022-00747-z

Shaw, K. A., Bilder, D. A., McArthur, D., Robinson Williams, A., Amoakohene, E., Bakian, A. V., Durkin, M. S., Fitzgerald, R. T., Furnier, S. M., Hughes, M. M., Pas, E. T., Salinas, A., Warren, Z., Williams, S., Esler, A., Grzybowski, A., Ladd-Acosta, C. M., Patrick, M., Zahorodny, W., & Green, K. K. (2023). Early identification of autism spectrum disorder among children aged 4 years -- autism and developmental disabilities monitoring network, 11 Sites, United States, 2020. *MMWR Surveillance Summaries*, *72*(1/2), 3–15. https://doi.org/10.15585/mmwr.ss7202a1

Skinner, B. F. (1957). *Verbal behavior*. Appleton-Century-Crofts.

Sundberg, M. L. (2008). *VB-MAPP Verbal Behavior milestones assessment and placement program: A language and social skills assessment program for children with autism or other developmental disabilities*. AVB Press.

Thordardottir, E. T., Weismer, S. E., & Smith, M. E. (1997). Vocabulary learning in bilingual and monolingual clinical intervention. *Child Language Teaching and Therapy*, *13*(3), 215–227. https://doi.org/10.1177/026565909701300

Trelles, M. P., & Castro, K. (2019). Bilingualism in autism spectrum disorder: Finding meaning in translation. *Journal of the American Academy of Child and Adolescent Psychiatry, 58*(11), 1035–1037. https://doi.org/10.1016/j.jaac.2019.05.027

Uro, G., & Lai, D. (2019). English language learners in America's Great City Schools: Demographics, achievement, and staffing. *Council of the Great City Schools*. https://eric.ed.gov/?id=ED597915

U.S. Congress. (2003). *Individuals with disabilities education improvement act of 2004*, H.R. 1350, 108th Congress. https://www.congress.gov/bill/108th-congress/house-bill/1350/text

U.S. Department of Education. (2020, February 10). *Schools' civil rights obligations to English learner students and limited English proficient parents.* https://www.masslegalservices.org/content/schools-civil-rights-obligations-english-learner-students-and-limited-english-proficient

Valicenti-McDermott, M., Tarshis, N., Schouls, M., Galdston, M., Hottinger, K., Seijo, R., Shulman, L., & Shinnar, S. (2013). Language differences between monolingual English and bilingual English-Spanish young children with autism spectrum disorders. *Journal of Child Neurology, 28*(7), 945–948. https://doi.org/10.1177/0883073812453204

Vespa, J. (2021, October 8). *Demographic turning points for the United States: Population projections for 2020 to 2060*. Census.gov. Https://www.census.gov/ library/publications/2020/demo/p25-1144.html

Wang, B., Cao, F., & Boyland, J. T. (2019). Addressing autism spectrum disorders in China. *New Directions for Child & Adolescent Development, 163*, 137–162. https://doi.org/10.1002/cad.20266

Zacarian, D. (2011). The over- and under-identification of ELLs in special education. *Colorín Colorado*. https://www.colorincolorado.org/article/over-and-under-identification-ells-special-education

Chapter 14

Collaborating with Other Service Providers

Paula Braga Kenyon, Shawn Kenyon, Danielle LaFrance, and Beth Bellone

Intervention with individuals on the autism spectrum[1] will ideally come from multiple professionals across multiple disciplines, including but not necessarily limited to behavior analysis, psychology, special education, speech-language pathology, and occupational therapy. As part of an intervention package for autistic individuals, these disciplines will all likely be involved in supporting the language needs of individual clients.

Understanding the unique scopes of practice and training requirements of the aforementioned professions is likely to enhance interdisciplinary treatment (see LaFrance et al., 2019). This chapter reviews similarities and differences across select behavioral health professions. Additionally, it provides practical guidelines and recommendations for formative collaborative and cross-discipline relationships to enhance communication in individuals with autism who require intervention.

According to the Centers for Disease Control and Prevention (CDC), the current prevalence of autism spectrum disorder (ASD) in the United States is estimated to be approximately 1 in 36, which equates to approximately 2.8% of the country's total population (CDC, n.d.). This marks an increase from the previous estimate of 1 in 44, indicating a rise in diagnosed cases attributed to improved diagnostic methods and greater awareness, highlighting ASD as a worldwide health concern.

The complexity and prevalence of comorbidities among individuals with ASD and identified individual treatment needs often require interdisciplinary collaboration (e.g., Brodhead, 2015; Kelly & Tincani, 2013; Newhouse-Oisten et al., 2017). Communication and social deficits associated with ASD, combined with additional disorders, complicate clinical assessment and treatment. Due mainly to these challenges, nuanced assessments are crucial to ensuring effective intervention and cohesive collaboration across service professionals. This is particularly important with interdisciplinary treatment teams, which are critical for successful ethical treatment while achieving the best outcomes for autistic individuals.

DOI: 10.4324/9781003433668-17

Interdisciplinary intervention involves professionals from different disciplines working together in an integrated and cohesive manner (Mitchell et al., 2010). To this end, they collaborate to create a unified treatment plan, set common goals, and share responsibilities for the client's overall care. Professionals from different disciplines regularly communicate and collaborate in this interdisciplinary environment, integrating their expertise to develop and implement a coordinated treatment plan. Interdisciplinary teams often hold regular meetings, share observations and data, and collaboratively adjust treatment plans as the data indicate to coordinate care and address the client's evolving needs.

Communication is a pivotal skill for individuals to have autonomy and a good quality of life. Each profession contributes differently to assessing, evaluating, and treating communication skills in autistic individuals. To collaborate and maximize each professional's knowledge, one must understand the scope of competence and practice along with ethical guidelines for each profession (LaFrance et al., 2019).

We will discuss areas of overlap among a number of professions often involved in the care of autistic individuals and advocate for improved collaboration to maximize client outcomes. By highlighting the unique areas of expertise and skill sets within each profession, we hope to promote a broader understanding of an integrative approach to care. Additionally, we aim to increase awareness of the challenges to effective collaboration, sparking further discussion on this topic and eventually incorporating collaboration into course sequences, training programs, continuing education experiences, conference presentations, and clinical discussions.

Importance of Collaboration

Individuals with ASD are frequently diagnosed with multiple psychiatric disorders. Some of these diagnoses may include childhood anxiety disorders, depressive disorders, oppositional defiant and conduct disorders, attention deficit hyperactivity disorder (ADHD), tic disorders, obsessive-compulsive disorders, and mood disorders. One study examining 112 children aged 10–14 found that 70% had at least one comorbid disorder, and 40% had two or more (Simonoff et al., 2008). Nebel-Schwalm and Worley (2014) reported a 40%–70% prevalence of comorbidity in children and adolescents with ASD, including conditions such as encopresis, language disorders, and anxiety disorders. Another study by Khachadourian et al. (2023) found that 35.3% of children they studied who were diagnosed with ASD (n = 40,582) were also diagnosed with ADHD, as compared to only 16.8% of their non-ASD siblings (n = 11,389). Additionally, these authors found that the children with ASD were also frequently diagnosed with learning disability (23.5%) and intellectual disability (21.7%), making these the two most common comorbidities.

Beyond psychiatric disorders, ASD is also associated with other neurological comorbidities, such as motor impairments (including stereotypic behaviors, motor delays, dyspraxia, poor coordination, and gait problems), sleep dysfunction (difficulty with sleep onset and prolonged night awakenings), and epilepsy (Maski et al., 2011). Given this information, it seems clear that effective treatment for autistic individuals may require coordinated intervention with co-occurring behavioral health and/or medical conditions, as these may interact with each other (CASP, 2024). Common treatment goals are most likely to be met when there is a shared understanding, governance, and coordination of care among all treating healthcare providers and professionals.

Understanding the Roles and Expertise of Each Profession

Behavior analysts, psychologists, school psychologists, special education teachers, speech-language pathologists, and occupational therapists may all, among others, be involved in the assessment, evaluation, and treatment of individuals with ASD. Therefore, it is important to understand the role and contributions of each professional (LaFrance et al., 2019). As a follow-up to LaFrance et al. (2019), the following sections of this chapter summarize the scopes of practice, training, and competence of the above-mentioned six key professions that frequently provide concurrent services to individuals diagnosed with ASD.

Scopes of Practice

Behavior Analysis. A *Board Certified Behavior Analyst* (BCBA®) is an expert in behavior analysis, trained to assess, design, implement, and evaluate behavior intervention programs. The Behavior Analyst Certification Board® (BACB®) is a national nonprofit organization established in 1998 to certify practitioners. BACB® certification helps healthcare providers and their subscribers identify providers who meet entry-level competencies to practice applied behavior analysis (ABA). The BCBA® is a graduate-level certification in behavior analysis. Professionals certified at this level are independent practitioners who provide ABA services. Applicants for behavior analyst certification must meet eligibility requirements, including a master's degree or higher, defined graduate coursework in behavior analysis, and supervised practice or fieldwork before they are approved to take a professionally developed and scored examination. In addition, the certified practitioner must obtain ongoing continuing education and adhere to an ethics code to maintain certification.

Among many duties, behavior analysts supervise the work of others in the field, such as Board Certified Assistant Behavior Analysts® (BCaBAs®) and Registered Behavior Technicians® (RBTs®). Behavior Analysts may also provide services directly to patients and provide training to caregivers. The primary duties of a Behavior Analyst focus on assessing, designing, implementing, and evaluating behavior intervention plans to improve client behavior. Key responsibilities include:

1. Designing assessment and intervention activities: Behavior analysts conduct skills assessments using norm- and criterion-referenced assessments to determine the initial repertoire of the clients they serve (CASP, 2024). They also conduct functional assessments to determine the function of any interfering behaviors exhibited by their clients.
2. Developing *Behavior Intervention Plans* (BIPs): Based on assessment results, Behavior Analysts create individualized intervention plans to reduce interfering behaviors and promote socially significant behavior changes (i.e., replacement behaviors). They ensure the plan is grounded in evidence-based practices and adheres to the ethical guidelines of the Behavior Analyst Certification Board (BACB®, 2020).
3. Supervision and training: Behavior Analysts provide direct supervision and training to RBTs® and other staff implementing intervention strategies. They also train caregivers and family members to support the generalization of behavior change across settings.
4. Data collection and analysis: Accurate data collection is crucial in tracking client progress. Behavior Analysts regularly monitor and analyze data to make data-driven decisions and adjust treatment plans as necessary (Carr & Nosik, 2017). The Behavior Analyst continually reviews treatment goals and progress toward improving their patients' quality of life, independence, and autonomy.
5. Adhering to ethical guidelines: Behavior Analysts are responsible for maintaining ethical standards outlined by the BACB®. This includes ensuring that interventions are in the best interests of their clients and obtaining informed consent (BACB, 2020).
6. Consulting, collaborating with other professionals, and participating in interdisciplinary teams: Behavior Analysts work closely with other professionals, such as speech therapists, occupational therapists, and educators, to ensure cohesive and collaborative care.
7. Collaborating with, training, and supporting caregivers: Behavior Analysts involve their clients' families or guardians in the treatment plan by inviting them (and the client, when possible) to help with goal selection and provide training on treatment plan implementation.
8. Communicating client needs and progress with funders: Behavior Analysts report their clients' progress to stakeholders.

Directly related to the work that Behavior Analysts do with individuals on the autism spectrum, the Council of Autism Service Providers' Third Edition

Guidelines (CASP, 2024) highlighted the importance of individualized coordination of care focused on each patient's needs, along with additional services they have received, and the importance of documentation on the impact of coordination of care, which is suggested to be included in treatment plans.

Psychology. Psychologists bring an understanding of mental health, cognitive processes, and emotional well-being. They often provide diagnostic assessments and therapeutic interventions that complement behavior-analytic approaches. As summarized by LaFrance et al. (2019), the practice of psychology includes "the observation, description, evaluation, interpretation, and modification of human behavior by the application of psychological principles, methods, and procedures" (APA's Model Act, 2010, p. 2). Similar to Behavior Analysts, licensed psychologists seek to "a) prevent, eliminate, evaluate, assess, or predict symptomatic, maladaptive, or undesired behavior, and b) evaluate, assess, and/or facilitate the enhancement of individual, group, and/or organizational effectiveness, or c) assist in legal decision-making" (APA, 2010, p. 2). With this comes a host of different divisions represented in the American Psychological Association (APA; e.g., psychoanalytic and psychodynamic conceptualizations, humanistic psychology, cognitive approaches, and behavioral formulations), some of which may align, at least to some extent, with behavior analysis, while others do not.

The typical duties of a psychologist vary depending on the specific field and setting, but generally, their responsibilities include the following:

1. Assessment and diagnosis: Psychologists conduct psychological assessments to diagnose mental, emotional, and behavioral disorders. This involves using tests, interviews, and observation to evaluate a person's psychological state (APA, 2022).
2. Therapeutic intervention: Psychologists provide therapy to individuals, families, or groups to help them cope with various mental health issues such as anxiety, depression, trauma, and relationship problems (National Institutes of Mental Health, n.d.).
3. Research: Many psychologists conduct scientific research to understand cognitive, emotional, and social processes. This research helps develop new treatments and informs best practices in psychology.
4. Development and implementation of treatment plans: Psychologists design and implement treatment plans tailored to a patient's needs. These plans are often based on therapeutic approaches such as cognitive-behavioral therapy (CBT) or psychodynamic therapy (National Institutes of Mental Health, n.d.).
5. Education and consultation: Psychologists often educate clients, students, or other professionals on mental health, stress management, and effective coping mechanisms. They may also provide consultation services to schools, businesses, or healthcare providers.

6. Crisis intervention: In times of mental health crises (e.g., after a trauma event or during a mental health emergency), psychologists provide immediate support and intervention to stabilize clients.

7. Ethical responsibility and confidentiality: Psychologists are expected to follow strict ethical guidelines, particularly regarding confidentiality and appropriately handling sensitive information (APA, 2017).

School Psychology. A school psychologist is a specialized professional in the field of psychology who works within educational settings (typically public schools) to support students' mental health, emotional well-being, and academic success. Their role typically involves assessment and evaluation, consultation, crisis intervention, and special education support.

The typical duties of a school psychologist are specialized to support students' mental health, learning, and behavior within educational settings and may include:

1. Assessment and evaluation: School psychologists conduct assessments to identify students' learning difficulties, emotional issues, or developmental delays. This includes using cognitive, behavioral, and emotional assessment tools to evaluate students (National Association of School Psychologists, 2020; NASP).

2. Consultation and collaboration: School psychologists collaborate with teachers, parents, and administrators to create a supportive educational environment. They also help develop Individualized Education Programs (IEPs) and behavior plans for students with special needs (NASP, n.d.).

3. Intervention and counseling: School psychologists provide direct support to students through counseling, social skills training, and behavioral interventions. They address issues such as bullying, social conflict, anxiety, and trauma to help students succeed academically and emotionally.

4. Prevention programs: School psychologists develop and implement programs to prevent students' academic, emotional, and behavioral problems. This includes promoting positive school climates, implementing social-emotional learning (SEL) programs, and preventing violence or substance abuse (NASP, n.d.).

5. Crisis intervention: In times of crisis, such as natural disasters, student deaths, or school violence, school psychologists provide immediate emotional support and develop strategies to help the school community recover.

6. Research and data analysis: School psychologists conduct research and use data to improve school policies and practices. They analyze student performance data to identify trends and inform decisions about resource allocation, intervention strategies, and program effectiveness (NASP, 2020).

7. Advocacy for students' needs: School psychologists advocate for students' mental health and educational needs by helping schools adopt policies that promote equity, inclusion, and access to mental health resources.
8. Training and education: School psychologists often train teachers, parents, and administrators on topics including mental health awareness, behavior management, and classroom strategies for supporting diverse learners (NASP, n.d.).

Special Education Teachers. Special education teachers are skilled in designing and implementing IEPs for students with diverse learning needs. They may work closely with behavior analysts to ensure educational goals align with behavioral interventions.

The primary duties of the special education teacher focus on meeting the unique educational needs of students with disabilities. These responsibilities may include:

1. IEP development: Special education teachers are responsible for developing, implementing, and monitoring IEPs for students with disabilities. This involves setting specific learning goals tailored to each student's needs and collaborating with parents, administrators, and other professionals (U.S. Department of Education, n.d.).
2. Instructional adaptation: Special education teachers modify the general education curriculum to accommodate the abilities of students with disabilities. This includes using differentiated instruction techniques and specialized teaching methods to ensure students can access the material (National Center for Learning Disabilities, n.d.).
3. Assessment and progress monitoring: Special education teachers conduct formal and informal assessments to measure students' academic and social progress. They use these assessments to track improvements, adjust instruction, and report outcomes to parents and school staff (Council for Exceptional Children, n.d.; CEC).
4. Behavior management and support: Special education teachers develop and implement behavior management plans for students who may have difficulties with self-regulation, attention, or other behavioral challenges. They use positive reinforcement, social skills training, and individualized support to address behavioral concerns (CEC, n.d.).
5. Collaboration with General Education Teachers: Special education teachers work closely with general education teachers to ensure that students with disabilities can participate as much as possible in general education classrooms. This collaboration may involve co-teaching, consultation, or providing accommodations for students in mainstream settings (National Education Association, n.d.; NEA).

6. Parental communication and involvement: Open communication with parents and caregivers is essential. Special education teachers regularly meet with families to discuss students' progress, challenges, and goals, ensuring parents are involved in their child's education (U.S. Department of Education, n.d.).

7. Crisis intervention and emotional support: Special education teachers often help students manage emotional and behavioral crises. They provide support and stability for students with emotional or behavioral disorders, ensuring a safe learning environment (NEA).

8. Professional development and advocacy: Special education teachers engage in ongoing professional development to stay current with best practices, legal requirements, and new strategies for teaching students with disabilities. They also advocate for appropriate resources and accommodations to support their students' success (CEC, n.d.).

Speech-Language Pathology. Speech-language pathologists (SLPs) focus on communication disorders, including language, speech, and social communication challenges. Their work is crucial in supporting individuals with communication deficits, often integrating behavioral strategies to enhance overall communication skills. According to the American Speech-Language Hearing Association (ASHA), and as summarized by LaFrance et al. (2019), speech-language pathology is a profession defined by its overall objective, which is "to optimize individuals' ability to communicate and swallow, thereby improving quality of life" (ASHA, 2007, p. 3) and treating disorders pertaining to the physiological aspects of swallowing and language production, the psychological components of communication, social skills (i.e., pragmatics), and proprioception (i.e., sensory awareness), and the intentionality, joint attention, and reciprocity of communication.

The responsibilities of the SLP include the following:

1. Collaboration: In school-based settings, SLPs collaborate with special education teachers, behavior analysts, occupational therapists, reading specialists, and other SLPs with specialized training.

2. Counseling: Communicating with families and caregivers is critical to meeting their goals for improvement in the home. SLPs counsel families and stakeholders on prognostic indicators when appropriate and make referrals as needed.

3. Research, prevention, and advocacy: ASHA's position statement on prevention requires the SLP to knowledgeably and responsibly share information using common language and consistent terminology, conduct research, and educate colleagues and families.

4. Assessment: In school-based settings, SLPs conduct formal language assessments that include standardized and observational measures. Pragmatic and social skills are observed and summarized. Additional assessments regarding augmentative alternative communication may be conducted if the student is not developing vocal speech. Environmental assessments may also be conducted to investigate the need areas further across daily activities. Goals and recommendations from these assessments are reviewed with the educational team, and treatment plans and IEPs are developed.

5. Treatment and monitoring: SLPs develop treatment and lesson plans targeting the need areas identified during assessment. The SLP also identifies tools and strategies to be used across environments. Teaching methods are recommended and monitored by the SLP and classroom teachers. Service delivery is determined with the team and includes these considerations:

    a. *Setting*: the location of treatment (e.g., home, community-based, school, pull-out, or within the classroom),

    b. *Dosage*: the frequency, intensity, and duration of service,

    c. *Format*: the type of session: one-on-one (i.e., individual), in a group, or via consultation with other school staff and/or family/caregiver,

    d. *Provider*: the person administering the treatment (e.g., SLP, support personnel, trained volunteer, caregiver).

6. Training and maintenance: SLPs may see clients intermittently, but caregivers are with them daily. By equipping caregivers with knowledge and strategies, SLPs ensure that the therapeutic work continues beyond the clinical setting, maximizing the client's progress and generalization of skills in their everyday environments. For example, when working with clients with swallowing disorders, SLPs can help caregivers understand safe feeding techniques, the importance of modified diets, and signs of aspiration or choking. This training reduces the risk of complications like aspiration pneumonia and malnutrition, creating a safer environment for all (ASHA, 2016).

7. Professional development: ASHA emphasizes professional development as essential for SLPs to maintain high standards of service, stay current with research-based practices, and effectively address the diverse needs of clients. ASHA recommends professional development initiatives that will (a) ensure that competency and knowledge remain updated, (b) meet certification and licensure requirements, (c) enhance quality of care and patient outcomes, (d) promote ethical and evidence-based practice, (e) adapt to diverse and emerging needs, and (f) support career advancement and leadership.

ASHA's endorsement of professional development represents its commitment to maintaining skilled, ethical, and adaptive SLPs who can meet the challenges of today's educational and healthcare systems.

SLPs play critical roles in health literacy; screening, diagnosis, and treatment of autism spectrum disorder; and the use of the *International Classification of Functioning, Disability and Health* (ICF; World Health Organization [WHO], n.d.) to develop functional goals and collaborative practice. As technology and science advance, the areas of assessment and intervention related to communication and swallowing disorders grow accordingly.

Occupational Therapy. Occupational therapists (OTs) work on improving individuals' daily living and occupational skills. Their expertise in various life activities, motor skills, and adaptive behaviors is often vital in creating comprehensive care plans that address behavioral and functional needs.

The primary duties of the OT include helping individuals across the lifespan to perform tasks necessary for daily living and working. To that end, these duties may include:

1. Patient assessment and evaluation: OTs assess the physical, cognitive, emotional, and environmental factors affecting a patient's ability to perform daily activities. This includes evaluating patients' motor skills, sensory processing, and cognitive functions to develop an effective treatment plan (American Occupational Therapy Association, n.d.; AOTA).

2. Developing treatment plans: Based on the evaluation, OTs design individualized treatment plans to help patients achieve their personal goals. These plans may include exercises, therapy techniques, or adaptive equipment to improve the patient's ability to complete everyday tasks.

3. Therapeutic interventions: OTs use various interventions to improve a patient's ability to perform daily activities (e.g., dressing, cooking, using the computer). These interventions often focus on improving fine motor skills, balance, coordination, or strengthening muscles for more efficient movement (AOTA, n.d.).

4. Modifying environments and recommending adaptive equipment: OTs assess and modify patients' homes, schools, or work environments to improve their safety and independence. They also recommend and train patients to use adaptive equipment such as grab bars, wheelchairs, or ergonomic tools to enhance functionality.

5. Supporting cognitive and emotional development: Besides physical rehabilitation, OTs work on cognitive and emotional skills such as problem-solving, memory, attention, and coping strategies, which are crucial for independent living and job performance (AOTA, n.d.).

6. Patient and family education: OTs educate patients, caregivers, and family members on supporting rehabilitation and promoting independence at home. This often includes training family members in adaptive equipment, therapy techniques, and home modifications (AOTA, n.d.).

7. Collaboration with healthcare teams: OTs collaborate with physicians, physical therapists, SLPs, social workers, and other healthcare professionals to provide holistic care. They also work with teachers and employers to ensure that environments are conducive to patients' needs (World Federation of Occupational Therapists, n.d.).

8. Documentation and progress monitoring: OTs maintain detailed records of patients' progress and regularly reassess treatment plans to make necessary adjustments. This documentation is essential for tracking improvements, insurance claims, and communicating with other healthcare providers.

Scope of Practice, Scope of Training, and Scope of Competence

The scope of practice refers to the activities of the profession and is determined by external oversight organizations. In contrast, the term scope of competence refers to the activities of a specific individual and is determined by the individual practitioner. When the scope of practice and competence overlap with other professions, responsibility for collaboration and intervention must be clearly outlined.

Scope of Practice and Training

The scopes of practice for each of the six key professions discussed in this chapter were described briefly above. On the other hand, the *scope of training* refers to established requirements for training within a particular profession (e.g., degree requirements, accredited program requirements). However, it should be noted that practice activities for each professional involved in the treatment of autistic individuals are determined, in part, by the general description of each profession (or scope of practice) coupled with the stakeholders' expectations for these professionals and their training program or curricula (scope of training). The training program or curricula may also include supervised practice. Behavior Analysts, for example, as of 2024, must complete up to 2,000 hours of supervised practice before obtaining their certification. Psychologists need to attend to each State's regulations. For example, a psychologist in Massachusetts must complete 3,200 hours of practical supervised experience. During their graduate program, SLPs complete supervised clinical practicums, which involve hands-on practice in assessing and treating clients under the supervision of experienced professionals. These experiences, which occur in various settings such as schools, hospitals, rehabilitation centers, and private practices, help define the SLP's competence in specific practice areas (ASHA, 2020). ASHA's standard V-C states that applicants must complete a minimum of 400 direct client hours of supervised clinical experience in the practice of speech-language pathology.

For more detailed information on scopes of training in behavior analysis, psychology, speech-language pathology, and occupational therapy, the reader is referred to LaFrance et al. (2019).

Scope of Competence

The *scope of competence* extends beyond formal training programs. It includes educational background, supervised experience, population-specific and setting-specific training, intervention-specific experience, ethical training, and continuing education or professional development history. For example, after graduation, SLPs must complete a clinical fellowship (CF) where they practice under a licensed and certified SLP's supervision to obtain certification as a CCC-SLP. The fellowship provides further training and helps to solidify their competence in particular areas, such as speech sound disorders, language intervention, or augmentative alternative communication (ASHA, 2020). Thus, the scope of competence refers to the specific areas of clinical practice where the professional has the necessary education, training, skills, and experience to provide efficacious and ethical services. This scope is distinct from the general scope of practice and the general scope of training, as it varies from one practitioner to another depending on their background, training, and professional experiences. Practitioners within a profession may have a similar scope of practice and training but have varied scopes of competence. Regardless of the scope of competence, professionals in each area must follow ethical codes and certification or licensure laws.

Table 14.1 links each profession's ethical code document across the six distinct professions discussed in this chapter. Although some overlaps exist, some are unique to the profession. A critical aspect of a Behavior Analyst's competence is their adherence to the ethical guidelines set forth by the BACB, which include practicing within their scope of competence, obtaining informed consent, ensuring client dignity, and maintaining confidentiality (BACB, 2020). Ethical competence also involves making appropriate referrals when a client's needs fall outside the Behavior Analyst's expertise. Similarly, SLPs and OTs must adhere to ethical standards set by ASHA and AOTA, which also include practicing within their scope of competence, maintaining client confidentiality, and obtaining informed consent. Ethical competence also involves recognizing when a client's needs exceed their expertise and making appropriate referrals (AOTA, n.d; ASHA, 2016).

Table 14.2 provides links to licensure laws across these six distinct professions. Although some overlaps exist, some are unique to the profession. In the state of Massachusetts, for example, commonalities across behavior analysis, psychology, speech-language pathology, and occupational therapy licensure requirements include (a) educational level (master's degree or higher), (b) supervised experience requirement (though hours vary), (c) certification exams and

Table 14.1 Ethical Codes Across Professions

Profession	National Association and Ethics Document
Behavior Analysis	Behavior Analyst Certification Board (BACB) https://www.bacb.com/ethics/ethics-code/
Psychology	American Psychological Association (APA) https://www.apa.org/ethics/code
School Psychology	National Association of School Psychologists (NASP) https://nasponline.org/standards-and-certification/professional-ethics
Special Education Teacher	Council for Exceptional Children (CEC) https://exceptionalchildren.org/standards/ethical-principles-and-practice-standards
Speech-Language Pathology	American Speech-Language Hearing Association (ASHA) https://www.asha.org/policy/et2016-00342/
Occupational Therapy	American Occupational Therapy Association (AOTA) https://www.aota.org/practice/ethics

Table 14.2 National Scope of Practice Documents Across Professions—Licensure Laws

Profession	Document
Behavior Analysis	https://www.bacb.com/u-s-licensure-of-behavior-analysts/
Psychology	Licensure laws for psychologists in the United States vary by state but generally follow similar standards. Here's an overview of the common requirements
School Psychology	Licensure laws for school psychologists in the United States vary by state but generally follow similar standards. Here's an overview of the common requirements
Special Education Teacher	Licensure laws for Special Education Teachers in the United States are regulated at the state level, but there are common requirements that most states follow
Speech-Language Pathology	Licensure laws for Speech-Language Pathologists (SLPs) in the United States are governed at the state level, and while the requirements can vary, there are several common elements across most states
Occupational Therapy	Licensure laws for Occupational Therapists (OTs) in the United States are regulated at the state level, but there are common elements that most states follow

ongoing CEUs for license renewal, and (d) adherence to professional ethical standards.

The educational background and training requirements for each profession are also unique, building the foundational scope of competence for each profession. Behavior Analysts, for example, must pursue a master's degree to enter the profession; psychologists must pursue a doctorate, and special education teachers may need a bachelor's degree. The development of practical skills is also unique to each profession.

Behavior Analysts develop specific competencies for conducting assessments, designing intervention plans, implementing behavior change programs, and evaluating outcomes during supervised fieldwork or experience. The settings and populations with which professionals work during their supervised experience or training help define their areas of competence (BACB, 2022).

An SLP may work with a specific population during their training to develop competence in working with specific populations, such as children with autism, individuals with intellectual disabilities, or adults with behavioral disorders. Their formal training and practical experience shape their competence in these areas. Most speech pathologists operate within the typical certification process of the Certified Clinically Competent (CCC). However, ASHA has also approved four areas of specialty credentials with educational and experiential requirements, along with an application process. These are (a) Board Certification as a Specialist in Child Language (BCS-CL), (b) Board Certification in Stuttering, Cluttering, and Fluency Disorders (BCS-SCF), (c) Board Certification in Swallowing and Swallowing Disorders (BCS-S), and (d) Board Certification in Intraoperative Monitoring (BCS-IOM; audiology). Oversight occurs from individual boards within ASHA. Additional certifications outside the purview of ASHA can also be held in specific intervention methods, including certification in Picture Exchange Communication System or in Lee Silverman Voice Treatment (LSVT) LOUD for treating voice disorders associated with Parkinson's disease, among others. These certifications further define and expand their scope of competence (ASHA, 2020).

Completing an accredited occupational therapy program establishes an OT's foundational scope of competence. This education provides essential knowledge in areas such as anatomy, physiology, neuroscience, human development, and the theory and application of occupational therapy interventions (American Occupational Therapy Association [AOTA], n.d.). Since 2007, to become an OT, the professional must obtain a master's degree.

Table 14.3 highlights the specific formal training across the six professionals that may be included in an interdisciplinary team working with autistic individuals. While all individuals in a profession will receive the same training based on a standardized curriculum leading up to their degree, professionals start their specialization while obtaining their degrees, as indicated in Table 14.4, in the column labeled "specialized educational training."

These specialized training courses may focus on specific interventions. For example, a Behavior Analyst with extensive experience in early intervention for children with ASD may be highly competent in using interventions like discrete trial training (DTT), natural environment teaching (NET), or verbal behavior therapy. This competence is reinforced by their training and experience with

Table 14.3 General Educational Background

Profession	Requirements
Behavior Analysis	Graduate-level education. Minimum of a master's degree (BACB).
Psychology	Graduate-level education. Typically at the doctoral level (PhD or PsyD) (American Psychological Association [APA]). Specialized coursework during graduate training helps further define areas of competence (e.g., clinical psychology, counseling psychology, school psychology).
School Psychology	Graduate-level education, typically culminates in an Educational Specialist (Ed.S.) degree or a doctoral degree (PhD or PsyD) in school psychology. (National Association of School Psychologists [NASP], 2020).
Special Education Teacher	Bachelor's or master's degree in special education. (Council for Exceptional Children [CEC], n.d.). Their education also covers the legal and ethical aspects of special education, including the Individuals with Disabilities Education Act (IDEA) (U.S. Department of Education, n.d.).
Speech-Language Pathology	Graduate-level education. Typically includes a master's degree in speech-language pathology. This education provides foundational knowledge in speech, language, voice, fluency, swallowing, and cognitive-communication disorders (American Speech-Language-Hearing Association [ASHA], 2020).
Occupational Therapy	The foundational scope of competence for an OT is established through completion of an accredited occupational therapy program. This education provides essential knowledge in areas such as anatomy, physiology, neuroscience, human development, and the theory and application of occupational therapy interventions (American Occupational Therapy Association [AOTA], n.d.).

this population. The same Behavior Analyst may have never worked with an adult who requires vocational training. These differences in competence may exist within each profession and across professions. An SLP with extensive experience working with autistic adults may collaborate more effectively with a Behavior Analyst who has experience with a similar population.

Overlap and disparities in the scope of competence can also be observed in setting-specific competence. A Behavior Analyst who works primarily in educational settings develops competence in areas such as designing and implementing behavior support plans (BSPs) within the context of a school, collaborating with educators, and supporting students with behavioral challenges (Cooper et al., 2020). In comparison, Behavior Analysts who practice in clinics or home settings may develop strong competence in conducting functional behavior

Table 14.4 Specialized Educational Training

Profession	Trainings
Behavior Analysis	Optional specialized coursework in areas such as autism spectrum disorder (ASD), organizational behavior management (OBM), or experimental behavior analysis further defining their competence in these areas
Psychology	Some psychologists pursue specialized training in areas such as neuropsychology, forensic psychology, or health psychology during their doctoral programs. This specialized education contributes to a psychologist's competence in those specific fields (APA).
School Psychology	During their education, school psychologists may focus on specific areas such as behavior management, special education, or early childhood development, further defining their competence in those areas (NASP, 2020).
Special Education Teacher	Within their degree programs, Special Education Teachers may choose to specialize in specific areas, such as autism spectrum disorder (ASD), emotional and behavioral disorders (EBD), or specific learning disabilities (SLD), which further defines their scope of competence in these areas (CEC, n.d.).
Speech-Language Pathology	Some SLPs may choose to focus their studies on specific areas, such as pediatric speech and language disorders, adult neurogenic communication disorders, or voice disorders, which defines their initial scope of competence in those areas (ASHA, 2020).
Occupational Therapy	During their education, some OTs may choose to focus on specific areas of practice, such as pediatrics, geriatrics, mental health, or physical rehabilitation. This specialized training further refines their scope of competence in these areas (AOTA, n.d.).

assessments (FBAs), developing individualized BIPs, and working directly with clients and families to implement interventions (BACB, 2022). For example, the Behavior Analyst in a clinic may not be competent in being part of an IEP team.

Similarly, an SLP may have specialized training in some areas and not in others. SLPs who specialize in working with children develop competence in areas such as developmental language disorders, speech sound disorders, and social communication needs (pediatric practice). SLPs design and implement interventions that promote speech, language, literacy, and social skills in children (Paul & Norbury, 2012). SLPs working with older adults in geriatric practice may focus on issues such as swallowing disorders (dysphagia), cognitive-communication disorders due to dementia, or speech and language rehabilitation following a stroke or other neurological condition. Their competence in this area is shaped by their experience and ongoing training in aging-related issues (Bayles & Tomoeda, 2013). Further, SLPs may also develop competence in assessing and treating adults with neurogenic communication disorders (adult neurogenic disorders), such as aphasia, apraxia, and dysarthria, often resulting from stroke, traumatic brain injury, or neurodegenerative diseases (Duffy, 2013).

The scope of competence goes beyond the populations and settings where the professional works. Professionals may specialize in specific areas and, therefore, have intervention-specific competence. SLPs, for example, may develop a high level of competence in diagnosing and treating articulation and phonological disorders. This includes knowledge of various assessment and intervention strategies such as minimal pairs therapy, phonological process therapy, and motor-based approaches (Bernthal et al., 2016). Consider the SLP who is competent in treating child language disorders yet has a young client who never developed vocal speech or a client with excellent language comprehension but lacks the motor skills to produce intelligible speech. Knowledge in augmentative and alternative communication (AAC) feature matching assessment and system determination becomes critical for this SLP. However, they may not have the additional training and practice to consider themselves competent in this area. Still using the SLP example, some SLPs specialize in voice therapy, treating conditions such as dysphonia, vocal nodules, and resonance disorders. They use techniques like vocal hygiene education, resonance therapy, and voice exercises to improve vocal function (Stemple et al., 2014). Another SLP could specialize in fluency disorders, such as stuttering and cluttering, and develop competence in using interventions like fluency shaping, stuttering modification, and CBT to manage these disorders (Yairi & Seery, 2015). We highlighted that the scope of competence within and across professions can vary. This varied scope of competence within and across professions can sometimes make collaboration complex.

SLPs, for example, use evidence-based approaches to enhance receptive and expressive language skills (Paul & Norbury, 2012). Behavior Analysts have the same objective for clients with language deficits. Collaboration, in this case, would be essential. SLPs rely on service delivery strategies grounded in the principles of evidence-based practice (EBP; ASHA, 2005). EBP involves an approach where current, high-quality research is combined with the clinician's expertise and the preferences and values of the client to guide clinical decisions. This three-pronged approach ensures that services align with the stakeholders' needs, values, and choices of those receiving care. All three areas must be considered. One cannot rely only on the caregiver's opinion, for example. Stakeholders include the client, family, school personnel, and administrative staff or insurance providers. The high-quality research that informs EBP in schools spans subject areas in speech-language pathology, applied behavior analysis, developmental psychology, psycholinguistics, education, literacy, and augmentative and alternative communication. Evidence-based strategies for assessing children's communicative abilities are often grounded in developmental sequences, while instructional methods draw from behavioral frameworks (Hegde & Maul, 2006; Paul & Norbury, 2012).

A different scenario would emerge if the client also engaged in challenging behaviors. Behavior Analysts are trained in a wide range of behavioral interventions, but their depth of competence may vary depending on their experience. For example, a Behavior Analyst with extensive experience in conducting FBAs and designing BIPs may be particularly competent in addressing challenging behavior through positive behavior support (PBS) or functional communication training (FCT; Falligant & Hagopian, 2023; Iwata et al., 1994). It may be the case that the SLP and the Behavior Analyst collaborate on developing a plan that targets challenging behaviors and increases functional communication.

Collaboration across disciplines will include data analysis and decision-making. Competence also includes the ability to collect and analyze data effectively, make data-driven decisions, and adjust interventions based on client progress. Behavior Analysts are expected to be proficient in using single-subject research designs to evaluate the effectiveness of interventions (Cooper et al., 2020). When conversing with other disciplines, the Behavior Analyst needs to translate findings into a common language, which may not be graphs.

While the scope of practice may not change much over time, the scope of competence will be based on experience and training. One way to ensure that professionals stay up-to-date with advances in the profession is to require continuing education and professional development to maintain their certification or license. Behavior Analysts, for example, must engage in continuing education to maintain their certification and stay current with the latest research, techniques, and ethical standards in behavior analysis (BACB, 2022). Some Behavior Analysts pursue advanced certifications or specializations, such as in organizational behavior management or advanced practice in ASD. These additional credentials further define and expand their scope of competence (BACB, 2022).

Similarly, ASHA requires SLPs to participate in professional development activities to maintain their certification and stay current with the latest research, techniques, and ethical standards in speech-language pathology (ASHA, 2020). For SLPs, demonstration of continued professional development is mandated to maintain the CCC. Individuals must accumulate 30 professional development hours (PDHs). Two hours must be in cultural competency, cultural humility, culturally responsive practice, or diversity, equity, and inclusion (DEI), and 1 hour in ethics during each three-year interval to maintain their certification. They must also submit a Certification Maintenance Compliance Form as verification, in addition to paying annual dues or the annual certification fee and abiding by the Code of Ethics. Based on the BCBA Handbook, Behavior Analysts must obtain 32 Continuing Education Units (CEUs) within a two-year cycle. Four of these must be in ethics and three in supervision. Psychologists need to attend to each State's regulations. In Massachusetts, for example, psychologists need 20 hours of continuing education every two years to maintain their certification. There is also an opportunity to attend events that may provide continuing education units to more than one professional group within the same event.

Interdisciplinary Collaboration and Referral

Competence includes collaborating effectively with other professionals (Cooper et al., 2020). A competent Behavior Analyst, for instance, recognizes when a client's needs exceed their expertise and makes appropriate referrals to other professionals, ensuring that clients receive the most appropriate and effective care (BACB, 2020). SLPs are also expected to collaborate effectively with other professionals, such as audiologists, OTs, physical therapists, educators, and medical professionals, to provide comprehensive care for clients (ASHA, 2020). Similar to Behavior Analysts, competent SLPs recognize when a client's needs exceed their expertise and make appropriate referrals to other professionals, ensuring that clients receive the most appropriate and effective care (ASHA, 2016).

Guidance is also available from the World Health Organization and Interprofessional Collaboration Panel (2010). For example, Interprofessional Education (IPE) prepares students for careers in healthcare and education, and Interprofessional Practice (IPP) improves care and outcomes in healthcare settings. All professions mentioned in this chapter incorporate this guidance in their scope of practice with varying degrees of oversight. IPE/IPP uses all team members simultaneously to consider the client's needs and develop alternatives based on the roles of each profession. Negotiation of approaches and other considerations is also incorporated into intervention planning (Johnson, 2016). When professionals work independently of one another, there is often a silo effect that increases redundant interventions and impacts intervention and learning. "Interprofessional education breaks down those professional silos ...enhances collaborative and non-collaborative relationships" (Frenk et al., 2010; p. 1951). Behavior Analysts, SLPs, OTs, psychologists, and educators in IPP may form teams to deliver comprehensive service plans and specific interventions. When career-specific knowledge is shared, IPP teams can collaboratively create solutions that may exceed what each discipline could achieve individually. Teamwork-centered approaches can utilize the strengths of each team member to enhance service delivery and intervention options.

Interdisciplinary Collaboration and Assent

Clients receiving interdisciplinary services will need to have given consent for each of the services, and the professionals in the interdisciplinary team will need to coordinate how they will ensure such consent is obtained for therapy services.

Assent, on the other hand, has many definitions, and various professions have different expectations and rules regarding obtaining it. Informed consent is required in psychology and related fields such as behavior analysis (Flowers & Dawes, 2023). Informed consent is required from the client, participant, or proxy before beginning and at all subsequent steps of change in service provision (BACB, 2020; NASP, n.d.). While the different professional regulatory boards require informed consent, assent is recommended and not necessarily required.

The concept of assent is a legal extension of consent (Breaux & Smith, 2023). Informed consent is described within the law and in ethical and professional codes of conduct in most helping professions. Conversely, assent is a recently emerging legal and ethical concept. Assent is generally described as a legal agreement or contract between someone providing services and someone receiving such services. The person receiving services may be unable to provide informed consent to participate, such as children or people with intellectual and developmental disabilities. Assent can be defined in various ways. Breaux and Smith (2023, p. 113) cited various studies in which assent definitions were included. For example, in their article, they cite that the United States Department of Health and Human Services (2021) defines assent as "assent means a child's affirmative agreement to participate in research. Mere failure to object should not, absent affirmative agreement, be construed as assent" (U.S. Department of Health and Human Services, 2009, 45 CFR 46.402(b)). Breaux and Smith also cite Vitiello (2003, p 89), who writes, "assent is meant to be an explicit, affirmative agreement to participate, not merely absence of objection."

An interdisciplinary team working with a client must first agree on a definition of assent accepted by their professional and ethical codes. However, each professional has to adhere to their professional board requirements related to the use of assent. Flowers and Dawes (2023) highlighted that although guidelines for obtaining informed consent are similar across some professions providing services (e.g., behavioral and psychological therapy), guidelines for obtaining assent differ. Table 1, published in their article, indicated some of these differences. For example, Behavior Analysts are not required to obtain documentation of assent, yet psychologists are. The Behavior Analyst, working with an interdisciplinary team that includes a psychologist, will need to respect the requirements of the APA and work alongside the psychologist to seek and document assent for services.

Establishing Effective Communication and Collaborative Relationships

Promoting language for learners with ASD requires effective communication and professional collaboration. This chapter provides a guide for ABA practitioners working in interdisciplinary teams.

The scopes of practice between professions are different. Each professional receives specialized training in their discipline to promote language for learners with ASD. Understanding the training content received by different professionals increases the likelihood of mutual respect and helps delineate where the practices may overlap and where each provider holds distinct knowledge. For example, an SLP is better trained to work on tongue placement for speech production, while both an SLP and a Behavior Analyst may determine together the best mode of communication for a client.

The scope of competence extends beyond both the scope of practice and training. Conducting experimental functional analysis (FA), for example, is within the scope of practice of Behavior Analysts; however, a recently certified behavior analyst may not have the requisite experience to do so effectively and/or ethically, perhaps because they work with infants and have not had the opportunity to practice conducting an FA. Once again, communication and respect among the various professionals working in an interdisciplinary team will focus on evaluating the scope of practice and competency of each individual on the team.

Earlier, we discussed the emerging practice of assent and how different professions have rules and requirements that are not the same across all professions. Assessing the requirements from each profession and perhaps selecting the most complete or strictest requirements to be implemented should be an exercise conducted by the interdisciplinary team.

Conclusions and Practical Recommendations

Teaching language to autistic individuals is likely the most important goal toward independence, autonomy, and a better quality of life for such individuals and their families and community. Communication difficulties are one of the hallmark characteristics of autistic individuals, as well as being one of the criteria for diagnosis. A team of professionals who can collaborate while focusing on the client using evidence-based practices from each profession will be better positioned to impact progress. We recommend that Behavior Analysts establish open lines of communication with the SLPs, OTs, psychologists, school psychologists, and special education teachers (direct/indirect/consulting from outside agencies) who share their cases. All professionals can benefit from shared information about effective data collection methods, behavior management, and principles of effective teaching. Behavior Analysts, for example, can gain information from SLPs about developmental norms in language and articulation sequences, language sampling procedures, and AAC. Given the potential for overlap between these two professions, it is important to recognize specific areas of practice and competency and to be clear about areas where overlaps exist.

In some cases, collaboration does not result in a favorable outcome. Several challenges can hinder the growth of the fields as integrated and collaborative despite the many opportunities for clinician training. Obstacles include a sense of isolated environments that separate basic research from applied practice and a lack of research that connects these two areas.

Both the fields of speech-language pathology and behavior analysis can benefit from increased collaboration and knowledge sharing (Elcoro et al., 2023). The ASHA practice portal primarily supports research from within the profession, even while promoting cross-disciplinary research. When the behavior analyst and SLP cannot reach a consensus, contacting a third party (if possible) who can provide conflict resolution strategies may help. By developing interventions collaboratively, many barriers resulting from the overlap in scope of competence can be discussed, which can result in socially meaningful communication improvement.

Ideally, a collaborative continuum allows all parties to establish baseline repertoires within each discipline, extending to developing a treatment plan with interconnected goals. Frequent data analysis and sharing of those results using a common language are required to maintain healthy collaborative relationships. Appendix A (available at www.routledge.com/9781032560625) provides an example of a simple table that can be expanded to more professionals and other areas and used during regular meetings with different professionals.

Note

1 There are currently multiple descriptive terms in use across the literature regarding autism. As such, the authors of this chapter will use descriptors such as "individuals with autism," "individuals with ASD," "individuals on the autism spectrum," and "autistic individuals" interchangeably.

References

American Occupational Therapy Association. (AOTA). (n.d.). *Practice.* https://www.aota.org/practice

American Psychological Association. (2010). *Model act for state licensure of psychologists.* American Psychological Association. https://www.apa.org/about/policy/model-act-2010.pdf

American Psychological Association. (2017). *Ethical principles of psychologists and code of conduct.* American Psychological Association. https://www.apa.org/ethics/code/ethics-code-2017.pdf

American Psychological Association. (2022). *Understanding psychological testing and assessment.* https://www.apa.org/topics/testing-assessment-measurement/understanding

American Speech-Language-Hearing Association. (2005). *Evidence-based practice in communication disorders [Position statement].* American Speech-Language-Hearing Association. https://www.asha.org/policy/PS2005-00221/

American Speech-Language-Hearing Association. (2007). *Scope of practice in speech-language pathology.* Retrieved from http://www.asha.org/uploadedFiles/SP2007-00283.pdf

American Speech-Language-Hearing Association. (2016). *Code of ethics [Ethics]*. American Speech-Language-Hearing Association. Retrieved November 16, 2024, from https://www.asha.org/policy/et2016-00342/

American Speech-Language-Hearing Association. (2020). *2020 standards for the certificate of clinical competence in speech-language pathology (CCC-SLP)*. https://www.asha.org/Certification/2020-SLP-Certification-Standards/

Bayles, K. A., & Tomoeda, C. K. (2013). *Cognitive-communication disorders of dementia: Definition, diagnosis, and treatment* (2nd ed.). Plural Publishing.

Behavior Analyst Certification Board. (2020). *Ethics code for behavior analysts*. https://www.bacb.com.

Behavior Analyst Certification Board. (2022). *Applied behavior analysis treatment of autism spectrum disorder: Practice guidelines*. https://www.bacb.com

Bernthal, J. E., Bankson, N. W., & Flipsen, P. Jr. (2016). *Articulation and phonological disorders: Speech sound disorders in children* (8th ed.). Pearson.

Breaux, C. A., & Smith, K. (2023). Assent in applied behaviour analysis and positive behaviour support: Ethical considerations and practical recommendations. *International Journal of Developmental Disabilities*, *69*(1), 111–121. https://doi.org/10.1080/20473869.2022.2144969

Brodhead, M. T. (2015). Maintaining professional relationships in an interdisciplinary setting: Strategies for navigating nonbehavioral treatment recommendations for individuals with autism. *Behavior Analysis in Practice*, *8*(1), 70–78. https://doi.org/10.1007/s40617-015-0042-7

Carr, J. E., & Nosik, M. R. (2017). Professional credentialing of practicing behavior analysts. *Policy Insights from the Behavioral and Brain Sciences*, *4*(1), 3–8. https://doi.org/10.1177/2372732216685861.

Centers for Disease Control and Prevention. (n.d.) *Autism spectrum disorder (ASD): Data & statistics*. Retrieved November 16, 2024, from https://www.cdc.gov/autism/data-research/index.html

Cooper, J. O., Heron, T. E., & Heward, W. L. (2020). *Applied behavior analysis* (3rd ed.). Pearson.

Council for Exceptional Children (CEC). (n.d.). *Professional preparation standards*. https://exceptionalchildren.org/professional-preparation-standards

Duffy, J. R. (2013). *Motor speech disorders: Substrates, differential diagnosis, and management* (3rd ed.). Elsevier.

Elcoro, M., Diller, J. W., & Correa, J. C. (2023). Promoting reciprocal relations across subfields of behavior analysis via collaborations. *Perspectives on Behavior Science*, *46*(3–4), 431–446. https://doi.org/10.1007/s40614-023-00386-x

Falligant, J. M., & Hagopian, L. P. (2023). Application of the evolutionary theory of behavior dynamics to severe challenging behavior. *Journal of Applied Behavior Analysis*, *56*(3), 645–661. https://doi.org/10.1002/jaba.1025

Flowers, J., & Dawes, J. (2023). Dignity and respect: Why therapeutic assent matters. *Behavior Analysis in Practice*, *16*(4), 913–920. https://doi.org/10.1007/s40617-023-00772-6

Frenk, J., Chen, L., Bhutta, Z. A., Cohen, J., Crisp, N., Evans, T., ... Zurayk, H. (2010). Health professionals for a new century: Transforming education to strengthen health systems in an interdependent world. *The Lancet*, *376*(9756), 1923–1958. https://doi.org/10.1016/S0140-6736(10)61854-5

Hegde, M. N., & Maul, C. A. (2006). *Language disorders in children: An evidence-based approach to assessment and treatment*. Pearson.

Iwata, B. A., Dorsey, M. F., Slifer, K. J., Bauman, K. E., & Richman, G. S. (1994). Toward a functional analysis of self-injury. *Journal of Applied Behavior Analysis, 27*(2), 197–209. https://doi.org/10.1901/jaba.1994.27-197

Johnson, A. (2016). *Interprofessional education and interprofessional practice in communication sciences and disorders: An introduction and case-based examples*. Plural Publishing.

Kelly, A. N., & Tincani, M. J. (2013). Collaborative training for paraprofessionals. *Focus on Autism and Other Developmental Disabilities, 18*(1), 11–20. https://doi.org/10 .1177/1088357603018001030301.

Khachadourian, V., Mahjani, B., Sandin, S., Kolevzon, A., Buxbaum, J. D., Reichenberg, A., & Janecka, M. (2023). Comorbidities in autism spectrum disorder and their etiologies. *Translational Psychiatry, 13*(71). https://doi.org/10.1038/s41398-023 -02374-w

LaFrance, D. L., Weiss, M. J., Kazemi, E., Gerenser, J., & Dobres, J. (2019). Multidisciplinary teaming: Enhancing collaboration through increased understanding. *Behavior Analysis in Practice, 12*(3), 709–726. https://doi.org/10.1007/s40617-019 -00331-y

Maski, K., Jeste, S., & Spence, S. J. (2011). Common neurological comorbidities in autism spectrum disorders. *Current Opinion in Pediatrics, 23*(6), 609–615. https://doi .org/10.1097/MOP.0b013e32834c9282

Mitchell, R., Parker, V., Giles, M., & White, N. (2010). Toward realizing the potential of diversity in composition of interdisciplinary health care teams: An examination of multidisciplinary versus interdisciplinary approaches. *International Journal of Nursing Studies, 47*(3), 271–283. https://doi.org/10.1177/1077558709338478

National Association of School Psychologists. (n.d.). *Professional ethics*. https:// nasponline.org/standards-and-certification/professional-ethics

National Association of School Psychologists. (n.d.). *USDOE guidance for the development and implementation of IEPs: FAQ for school psychologists*. Retrieved November 16, 2024, from https://www.nasponline.org/resources-and-publications /resources-and-podcasts/covid-19-resource-center/special-education-resources/ usdoe-guidance-for-the-development-and-implementation-of-ieps-faq-for-school -psychologists

National Association of School Psychologists. (2020). *NASP 2020 professional standards*. National Association of School Psychologists. https://www.nasponline.org/standards -and-certification/nasp-2020-professional-standards-adopted

National Center for Learning Disabilities. (n.d.). *National center for learning disabilities*. https://ncld.org/

National Education Association. (n.d.). *National education association*. https://www.nea .org/

Nebel-Schwalm, M., & Worley, J. (2014). Other disorders frequently comorbid with autism. In T. E. Davis III, S. W. White, & T. H. Ollendick (Eds.), *Handbook of autism and anxiety* (pp. 47–60). Springer International Publishing/Springer Nature. https:// doi.org/10.1007/978-3-319-06796-4_4

Newhouse-Oisten, M. K., Peck, K. M., Conway, A. A., & Frieder, J. E. (2017). Ethical considerations for interdisciplinary collaboration with prescribing professionals. *Behavior Analysis in Practice, 10*(2), 145–153. https://doi.org/10.1007/s40617-017 -0184-x.

Paul, R., & Norbury, C. (2012). *Language disorders from infancy through adolescence: Listening, speaking, reading, writing, and communicating* (4th ed.). Elsevier.

Simonoff, E., Pickles, A., Charman, T., Chandler, S., Loucas, T., & Baird, G. (2008). Psychiatric disorders in children with autism spectrum disorders: Prevalence, comorbidity, and associated factors in a population-derived sample. *Journal of the American Academy of Child & Adolescent Psychiatry, 47*(8), 921–929. https://doi.org /10.1097/CHI.0b013e318179964f

Stemple, J. C., Roy, N., & Klaben, B. K. (2014). *Clinical voice pathology: Theory and management* (4th ed.). Plural Publishing.

The Council of Autism Service Providers. (2024). *Applied behavior analysis practice guidelines for the treatment of autism spectrum disorder – Version 3: Guidance for healthcare funders, regulatory bodies, service providers, and consumers.* The Council of Autism Service Providers. https://casproviders.org

U.S. Department of Education. (n.d.). *Special education laws.* Retrieved November 16, 2024, from https://www.ed.gov/laws-and-policy/individuals-disabilities/special -education-laws

U.S. Department of Health and Human Services. (2009). *Code of federal regulations, title 45 public welfare part 46 protection of human subjects.* https://www.hhs.gov/ ohrp/regulations-and-policy/regulations/45-cfr-46/index.html

Vitiello, B. (2003). Ethical considerations in psychopharmacological research involving children and adolescents. *Psychopharmacology, 171*(1), 86–91.

World Federation of Occupational Therapists. (n.d.). *Homepage.* https://wfot.org/

World Health Organization. (n.d.). *International classification of functioning, disability, and health (ICF).* World Health Organization. Retrieved November 16, 2024, from https://www.who.int/classifications/international-classification-of-functioning -disability-and-health

World Health Organization. (2010). *Framework for action on interprofessional education and collaborative practice.* https://www.who.int/publications/i/item/framework-for -action-on-interprofessional-education-collaborative-practice

Yairi, E., & Seery, C. H. (2015). *Stuttering: Foundations and clinical applications* (2nd ed.). Pearson.

Index

For Product Safety Concerns and Information please contact our EU
representative GPSR@taylorandfrancis.com
Taylor & Francis Verlag GmbH, Kaufingerstraße 24, 80331 München, Germany